Symphony™ Made Easy

Stephen Cobb

Osborne **McGraw-Hill**

Berkeley New York St. Louis San Francisco
Auckland Bogotá Hamburg London Madrid
Mexico City Milan Montreal New Delhi Panama City
Paris São Paulo Singapore Sydney
Tokyo Toronto

Osborne **McGraw-Hill**
2600 Tenth Street
Berkeley, California 94710
U.S.A.

For information on translations and book distributors outside of the U.S.A., please write to Osborne **McGraw-Hill** at the above address.

Symphony™ Made Easy

234567890 DOC 99876543210

ISBN 0-07-881657-2

Acquisitions Editor: Liz Fisher
Technical Reviewer: Michael Katz
Copy Editor: Kay Luthin
Word Processors: Lynda Higham, Carole Latimer, Stefany Otis,
Composition: Bonnie Bozorg
Proofreaders: Julie Anjos, Barbara Conway, Jeff Green
Cover Design: Bay Graphics Design, Inc.
Production Supervisor: Kevin Shafer

CONTENTS AT A GLANCE

TABLE OF CONTENTS

ACKNOWLEDGMENTS

I would like to thank everyone involved in bringing forth this book, in particular: Liz Fisher, who suggested the project in the first place; Jill Pisoni, who patiently guided it through the editing process; and Michael Katz, who reviewed the technical details diligently and with such good humor.

I must also thank those former co-workers back in the Bay Area with whom I first learned how to teach Symphony all those years ago: Mella, Dan, Marty, Greta, Kelly, Bink, Jan, Nancy and Joe. Last, but by no means least, another round of heartfelt thanks to my long-suffering family: Chey, Erin, Dorothy, Michael, Jane, Brea, and Tessier.

INTRODUCTION

This book has been written to help you understand and use Symphony 2.2, the popular integrated software program from Lotus Development Corporation. The word *integrated* means that the program carries out more than one task or applies the computer to more than one type of work. This is certainly true of Symphony, which can compose documents, prepare budgets and projections, sort mailing lists, send information to other computers, and graph statistics, all from within the same program, using a consistent set of commands and menus.

Since the introduction of Symphony Release 1 in 1984, the program has become increasingly popular with users who want one package to handle all of their information. Symphony meets their needs since it provides the five most common applications of personal computer technology: word processing, spreadsheet analysis, database management, computer-to-computer communications, and business graphics. Symphony Release 2.2 builds on this integration of information, providing links between files, as well as direct access to large database files. An extensive range of add-in modules provides specialized features such as text outlining, statistical analysis, improved file management, and spell checking. With the Allways add-in users of Symphony 2.2 have the ability to present information in a variety of fonts and styles, mixing text and graphics on screen as well as on the printed page. By adding desktop publishing features to Symphony's already extensive range of abilities, Lotus has created a powerful and versatile package.

ABOUT THIS BOOK

This book is designed to present the commands and capabilities of Symphony Release 2.2 in an easy-to-learn format that is both clear and concise. Because you are introduced to the commands in the context of practical examples, you will see immediately how to use keystrokes to make things happen as well as learn how the program's capabilities relate to real-life applications.

The exercises within the book are presented in a step-by-step tutorial format that has been tried and tested in the classroom and in one-on-one teaching sessions. Detailed instructions show you how to proceed through the examples. Views of the program screen illustrate important steps. Printed reports are reproduced so that you can compare them with your own results. Exercises build on previous examples so that you will find your mastery of Symphony increasing rapidly as you move from chapter to chapter.

HOW THIS BOOK IS ORGANIZED

This book is divided into 11 chapters. Most chapters contain the information that can be covered in a single session at your computer. Since Symphony's integration is based on the worksheet, the first few chapters concentrate on building your familiarity with this environment and its commands. After you have mastered creating and storing worksheet files, you can pick and choose the other areas of Symphony you want to explore—word processing, database management, business graphics, and communications. If you are already familiar with these various environments but want to practice integrating them effectively, many models in the later chapters are self-contained so that you can work with them without first becoming familiar with the examples in earlier chapters.

In Chapter 1 the features and abilities of Symphony are examined, along with the basic workings of the program. A number of technical terms are introduced and defined along the way. You learn how to enter information into Symphony, as well as how to perform calculations with that information and how to store it in a file on disk.

Chapter 2 reviews more of the basic commands of Symphony's SHEET environment. You learn different methods of entering information and creating formulas. The chapter shows you how to begin building a basic spreadsheet model, which is a set of figures arranged to describe a situation, such as the performance of a company, or the state of your checking account.

Chapter 3 details the process of building a larger spreadsheet model. The use of functions, range names, and other more advanced SHEET features is illustrated. The Symphony commands for viewing information on screen, storing it in files, and printing it on paper are explored.

In Chapter 4 you explore Symphony's word processing capabilities, provided by the DOC environment. Word processing is the activity of preparing printed text using the power of a computer, which provides speed and flexibility to the process of text entry, editing, storage, and retrieval. You learn how to create, edit, and format a typical business document.

In Chapter 5 you read about the database management capabilities of Symphony. You learn how to sort and search information and produce lists of selected data. Programs designed to handle large amounts of information are called database management software. There are three levels of database management in Symphony: SHEET-based, FORM-based, and disk-based. The first two are dealt with in Chapter 5, while the third is dealt with in Chapter 10.

Chapter 6 describes how to create graphs with Symphony. Graphs are visual representations of numeric data and can be an effective means of communicating facts and figures. Symphony has an extensive range of commands to help you design a wide variety of graphs. This chapter presents the basics of graph making with Symphony and touches upon some of the accepted guidelines for effective graph design.

Chapter 7 explores how Symphony's COMM environment enables you to use special hardware to communicate with other computers. In the COMM environment Symphony acts as a communications program, providing a way for you to exchange information between computers, but without leaving the Symphony program. Using the COMM environment you can access files on electronic bulletin boards, obtain news and data from information services, and use electronic mail to communicate with other computer users. This chapter shows you how Symphony lets you control your communications hardware to work with a wide variety of remote computers, from other PCs to large corporate mainframe systems.

In Chapter 8, you learn the more advanced aspects of Symphony files, such as how to link worksheet files together for more practical spreadsheet modelling, and how to access the power of Symphony add-ins. You will learn how to view files from within Symphony without having to retrieve them, how to protect your files with passwords, and how to translate files from other formats. The chapter begins with a review of the basics of operating systems and hard disk management on PCs.

As you become familiar with Symphony and apply it to more and more tasks, you will want to take advantage of macros to reduce repetitive typing and simplify complex command sequences. In Chapter 9 you read how to create, edit, use, and organize macros. Symphony's Learn command makes it is easy to record macros. Using Symphony's macro command language, you can add macro keywords to recorded macros to create sophisticated inter-active sequences that control data entry and even provide customized menus.

Chapter 10 explores some of the more advanced commands for manipulating data in Symphony, including the What-If command for creating result tables and cross-tabulations and the Statistical

Analysis add-in for performing distributions, regression, and matrix arithmetic. There are examples of parsing data from text files into Symphony and exporting data from Symphony by printing to disk. However, the main focus of the chapter is the @BASE add-in which gives you the ability to work with large dBASE-type data files from within Symphony.

Chapter 11 looks at how Symphony's word processing powers are augmented by the Outliner and Spelling Checker add-ins, and how the Allways program brings desktop publishing features to all Symphony documents.

Three appendixes are also provided. The first offers help with the installation of Symphony and Allways and advice on setting up your hard disk efficiently. The second presents all of the Symphony and @BASE functions. The third details the macro keywords introduced in Chapter 9 and provides an example of using macros with @BASE.

CONVENTIONS USED IN THIS BOOK

Throughout this book you will be instructed to make entries in Symphony worksheets, documents, and menus. Each of these entries will be shown in boldface. At times you will be told to press keys that have special names in Symphony, such as MENU. The MENU key is actually the key marked F10 on your keyboard. Whenever such keys are introduced you will be given the actual keyboard equivalent as well.

In some cases two keys need to be pressed. This can either be a keystroke combination, as in ALT-F10 which means press the ALT key and hold it down while you press the F10 key, or a keystroke sequence, as in END HOME which means press the END key, then release it and press HOME. A diagram of the keyboard, showing the location of keys, is provided in Chapter 1.

ADDITIONAL HELP FROM OSBORNE/McGRAW-HILL

Osborne/McGraw-Hill provides top-quality books for computer users at every level of computing experience. To help you build your skills, we suggest that you look for the books in the following Osborne/McGraw-Hill series that best address your needs.

The "Teach Yourself" Series is perfect for beginners who have never used a computer before or who want to gain confidence in using program basics. These books provide a simple, slow-paced introduction to the fundamental usage of popular software packages and programming languages. The "Mastery Learning" format ensures that concepts are learned thoroughly before progressing to new material. Plenty of exercises and examples are used throughout the text, and answers are at the back of the book.

The "Made Easy" Series is also for beginners or users who may need a refresher on the new features of an upgraded product. These in-depth introductions guide users step-by-step from the program basics to intermediate-level usage. Plenty of hands-on exercises and examples are used in every chapter.

The "Using" Series presents fast-paced guides that quickly cover beginning concepts and move on to intermediate-level techniques, and even some advanced topics. These books are written for users who already are familiar with computers and software and who want to get up to speed quickly with a certain product.

The "Advanced" Series assumes that the reader is already an experienced user who has reached at least an intermediate skill level and is ready to learn more sophisticated techniques and refinements.

The "Complete Reference" Series of handy desktop references list every command, feature, and function of popular software and programming languages, along with brief, detailed descriptions of how they are used. Books are fully indexed and often include tear-out command cards. This series is ideal for all users—beginners and pros.

The "Pocket Reference" is a pocket-sized, shorter version of the "Complete Reference" Series and provides only the essential commands, features, and functions of software and programming languages for users who need a quick reminder of the most important commands. This series also is written for all users and every level of computing ability.

The "Secrets, Solutions, Shortcuts" Series is written for beginning users who are already somewhat familiar with the software and for experienced users at intermediate and advanced levels. This series gives clever tips and points out shortcuts for using the software to greater advantage. Traps to avoid are also mentioned.

Osborne/McGraw-Hill also publishes many fine books that are not included in the series described above. If you have questions about which Osborne book is right for you, ask the salesperson at your local book or computer store, or call us toll-free at 1-800-262-4729.

OTHER OSBORNE/MCGRAW-HILL BOOKS OF INTEREST TO YOU

We hope that *Symphony Made Easy* will assist you in mastering this fine product, and will also peak your interest in learning more about other ways to better use your computer.

If you're interested in expanding your skills so you can be even more "computer efficient," be sure to take advantage of Osborne/McGraw-Hill's large selection of top-quality computer books that cover all varieties of popular hardware, software, programming languages, and operating systems. While we cannot list every title here that may relate to Symphony and to your special computing needs, here are just a few related books that complement *Symphony Made Easy*.

DOS Made Easy, by Herbert Schildt, provides a thorough, step-by-step introduction to using both PC-DOS and MS-DOS version 3.3, the popular operating system for the IBM PC and compatible personal computers. If you are a beginning computer user or want to brush up on your DOS skills, this books provides plenty of exercises and examples that enable you to grow from a beginner into an intermediate DOS user. *DOS 4 Made Easy*, also by Herbert Schildt, provides the same format and covers MS-DOS and PC-DOS version 4.0.

If you're looking for an intermediate-level book, see *Using MS-DOS*, by Kris Jamsa, which covers all versions through 3.3. This is a fast-paced, hands-on guide organized into 15-minute sessions that quickly covers basics before discussing intermediate techniques and even some advanced topics. If you have DOS version 4, see *Using DOS 4* by Kris Jamsa.

For all PC-DOS and MS-DOS users (from beginners who are somewhat familiar with the program to veteran users), with any DOS version up to 3.3, see Kris Jamsa's *DOS: The Complete Reference, Second Edition.* This book provides comprehensive coverage of every DOS command and feature. Whether you need an overview of the disk operating system or a reference for advanced programming and disk management techniques, you'll find it here.

WHY THIS BOOK IS FOR YOU

If you are like most personal computer users the time you have to spend learning Symphony's essential features is limited. This book presents the essentials quickly and succinctly, and shows you how they are applied. By following the instructions in this book, you will learn all of the commands that you will need for day-to-day work with Symphony. You will quickly understand the functionality of the program without having to cover every menu and command.

If you are an existing Symphony user who has learned the program on your own, this book provides a concise review of basic techniques as well as valuable shortcuts, tips, and pointers on advanced features. If you do not have the time or money for a formal class, this book allows you to learn on your own and at your own pace. If you are contemplating a class, this book provides a good place to start, plus a handy reference when the class is over.

You may already be using Symphony as a data entry operator, making entries under someone else's guidance and control, but feel it is high time you learned how the program works so that you can create your own Symphony files. The step-by-step approach of this book, with its practical and well-tested examples, will help build the confidence you need.

Whether you are new to Symphony, new to Release 2.2, or even new to personal computers, this book provides direct access to the program's impressive range of features. With this book you can avoid the frustrations that learning a complex computer program can otherwise produce, and focus on increasing your effectiveness, productivity, and creativity.

LEARN MORE ABOUT EXPANDING SYMPHONY

Here is an excellent selection of other Osborne/McGraw-Hill books on products that will help you expand Symphony and build your computer skills.

If you are a beginner with Lotus 1-2-3 Release 2.2, look for *1-2-3 Release 2.2 Made Easy*, by Mary Campbell, a step-by-step, in-depth introduction with plenty of hands-on exercises. If you're just beginning to use another version of Lotus 1-2-3, see *1-2-3 Made Easy*, which covers Releases 1A, 2.0, and 2.01, or *1-2-3 Release 3 Made Easy* covering release 3.0, both by Mary Campbell.

The Shareware Book: Using PC-Write, PC-File+, and PC-Calc+, Second Edition, by Ramon Zamora, Frances Saito, and Bob Albrecht, is an outstanding guide that combines instruction and reference material into one single resource that you'll use again and again. All three of these shareware programs are thoroughly covered from fundamentals to advanced applications.

If you're looking for the best way to get started in telecommunications or to get more out of the on-line services available today, see *Dvorak's Guide to PC Telecommunications*. This book/disk package, written by the internationally recognized computer columnist John C. Dvorak with programming wiz Nick Anis, shows you how to instantly plug into the world of electronic databases, bulletin boards, and on-line services. The package includes an easy-to-read comprehensive guide plus two 5 1/4" diskettes loaded with oustanding free software and is of value to computer users at every skill level.

1

INTRODUCING SYMPHONY

This book has been written to help you understand and use Symphony, one of today's best-selling *integrated software* packages for personal computers. "Software" is a term for programs or instructions which turn inanimate pieces of computer hardware into obedient productivity tools. The word "integrated" means that the software carries out more than one task or applies the computer to more than one type of work. This is certainly true of Symphony, which can prepare budgets and projections, sort mailing lists, compose documents, graph statistics, and send information to other computers.

In this chapter the features and abilities of Symphony will be examined, along with the basic workings of the program. A number of technical terms will be introduced and defined along the way. You will learn how to enter information into Symphony, as well as how to perform calculations with that information and how to store it in a file on disk.

SYMPHONY, THE MULTIPURPOSE SOFTWARE

If you were to conduct a survey of people that use personal computers and ask them what they use their personal computers for, the table of results would probably look like Table 1-1. It shows the five most common applications of personal computer

Rank	Application	Use
1	Word processing	Preparing documents, letters, reports, messages
2	Database management	Collection, sorting, and organizing information or data
3	Electronic spreadsheets	Recording, calculating, and analyzing numerical information
4	Business graphics	Visually representing numerical information in graphs
5	Communications	Exchanging data, messages, or other information between computers

TABLE 1-1 Why People Use Personal Computers

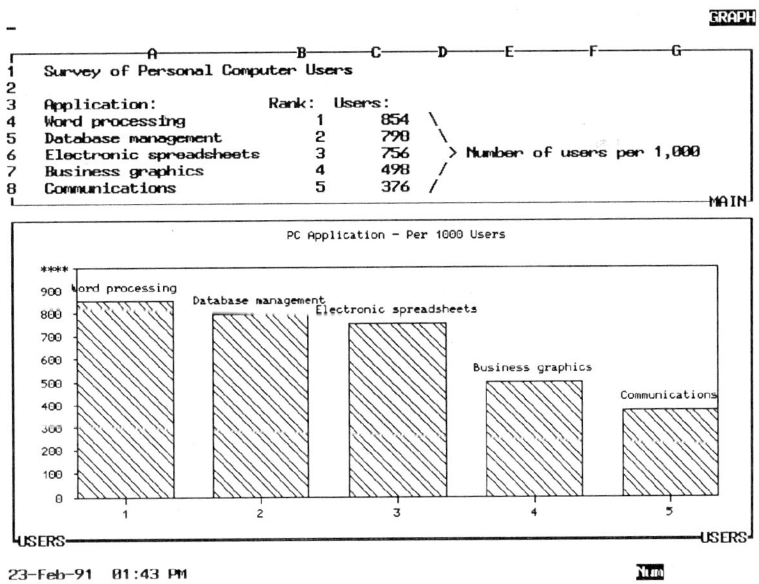

FIGURE 1-1 Survey results

technology. These are the five applications that Lotus Development Corporation has combined in a single program: Symphony.

You can see Symphony at work in the screen shown in Figure 1-1, where the results of a fictitious survey are displayed. The top half of the screen lists the numbers in an electronic spreadsheet. This appears above a graph of the same numbers. This figure shows you Symphony's ability to present "live" graphs of data next to the data itself. If the number of users for word processing had to be changed from 854 to 754, the graph would automatically readjust to reflect the difference.

Note that the term *data* is the plural of *datum,* a given piece of information. Much of the work done with computers falls into the general category of activity known as data processing. While data is, strictly speaking, a plural term, it is often treated as singular, as in "the employee data has been entered into the Symphony database." A collection of data is known as a *database*. Programs that facilitate management of a database are known as *database managers*.

Figure 1-1 also demonstrates Symphony's ability to split the screen into a number of windows, each of which can show a different view of the same information. Although the use of windows, known in computer jargon as *windowing*, is now quite a common program feature, Symphony was one of the first commercially successful programs to use windows.

An Evolving Symphony

First introduced in the mid-'80s, Symphony was the second major product from Lotus. The first was 1-2-3, the immensely popular spreadsheet that also offered business graphics and database management. Using the 1-2-3 electronic spreadsheet, termed a worksheet, as its starting point, Symphony provides the tools to perform all five of the most common personal computer tasks. Each task has its own mode of operation, or module, and in Symphony these are known as environments. They are as follows:

Word processing	DOC
Database management	FORM
Electronic spreadsheet	SHEET
Business graphics	GRAPH
Communication	COMM

Successfully combining all of this computing power in one program has been a major achievement. Since the product was first introduced, the program's abilities have been greatly enhanced. This happened in three stages:

1. A major revision (Symphony, Release 2, in 1987)
2. The creation of add-in programs
3. A semi-major revision (Symphony, Release 2.2, 1990)

The original Symphony was not the first integrated program for personal computers, but many of the earlier integrated packages had either compromised on features in order to fit on existing hardware or made do with separate program modules that were less than seamless in their integration. Each module (or environment) in Symphony is a well-rounded program and easily accessible through a consistent set of commands and menus, collectively known as the *user interface*.

As might be expected, given its lineage, the Symphony spreadsheet was the most powerful of the modules. At first this tended to overshadow the other aspects of the program. However, when Release 2 was introduced, there were significant improvements to the other modules as well as to the program as a whole.

In Release 2, the spreadsheet, or SHEET environment, gained optimal recalculation, an improved method of dealing with new information that prevents the program from slowing down too much when dealing with large collections of information. Release 2 also added global zero suppression, the option to not display or print entries that are zero. In addition, Release 2 offered improvements to the macro feature, which allows you to record and play back your activity with Symphony, bringing a high level of automation to many repetitive or complex tasks. (The term *macro* represents the ability to store many keystrokes under one key, a technique popularized in word processing programs to cut down on repetitive typing).

To expand the range of programs with which Symphony can share information, Release 2 added DCA and SYLK to the categories of data files that the Translate feature can read. All data on your personal computer are stored in files, but the arrangement of information within the files varies. Different programs use different arrangements or formats. The acronyms DCA and SYLK refer to two popular formats, IBM's Document Content Architecture format and Microsoft's Symbolic Linked format, used by DisplayWrite and Multiplan, respectively. These formats joined several others already supported by the Translate feature, including Ashton-Tate's dBASE program (DBF).

A further file management feature added in Release 2 was the Network file add-in. This is an extra program that works with Symphony to provide better control over Symphony files that are shared among users on a network. A network is created when several computers are wired together and controlled by special software that enables them to share resources such as disk storage and printers. If you are connected to a network, you might allow other users to read the Symphony data files you have stored on your hard disk. However, you would want some control over changes to the data in the file. Network software provides some of this control, but it is supplemented by the Symphony Network add-in.

The concept of an *add-in* was developed by Lotus in response to the fact that not all of the users of a particular program, such as Symphony, need all of the same features. Rather than trying to make one single version of Symphony work as all things to all people, Lotus provides some features as separate programs that are then melded, or added in, to Symphony as befits the needs of a particular user. Add-ins provide a way of customizing Symphony for specialized tasks and enhancing the program's performance in certain areas.

The word processor part of Symphony, the DOC environment, was enhanced in Release 2 by the addition of a spelling checker. This allows you to check that the words you have typed are spelled correctly and simplifies the correction of misspellings. An outline feature was also added that allows you to develop documents and ideas as outlines with parts and subparts, and then to flesh them out into full-length works. Other word processing features added in Release 2 were automatic paragraph reform, accelerator keys that provide quicker ways of issuing common commands, improved facilities for pasting text that is being cut or copied from one place to another, and the display of print attributes such as boldface and underline.

Symphony's database management environment, FORM, was improved in Release 2 by enhancements to the data entry and editing commands. Also, the maximum number of fields per record was increased to 256. A *field* is a category of information used in a database. For example, listings in a typical telephone directory are divided into three fields: name, address, and phone number. Each person's listing in the phone book is called a *record,* a collection of related information that can be categorized into fields.

The communications portion of Symphony, the COMM environment, was improved in Release 2 by the addition of something called *VT100 terminal emulation.* A terminal is a piece of equipment used to communicate with a computer. For example, the cash machine at your bank is a terminal that communicates with the bank's central computer. With the right equipment, your personal computer can act as a terminal, communicating with other computers all over the world. You might wonder how this is possible, given the many differences between computers, such as the way the keys on the keyboard are arranged. One way for two different computers to understand each other is to agree on a standard set of keys and commands. One of these standards is called DEC VT100, after the make and model of terminal that first used the standard. Thus, Symphony's "VT100 emulation" allows your personal computer to act like a VT100 terminal when communicating with other computers.

Symphony Today

This book is based on Symphony 2.2, which represents the cumulative effect of the past improvements to Symphony. The most recent enhancements to the program, from version 2.0 to 2.2, added a range of powerful new features, described in the following paragraphs.

ALLWAYS The ability to input and organize data with a program like Symphony can prove frustrating if you cannot output the data in an attractive format. One of the advantages of Symphony when it was first introduced was its combination of word processor and database/spreadsheet, which provided more flexibility in arranging and formatting facts and figures. However, standards for presentation materials have risen rapidly in recent years, with the advent of laser printers and desktop publishing programs that provide a printing quality of near-typeset appearance.

As you can see from Figure 1-2, even a laser-printed report from Symphony 2.0 looked fairly plain. To improve matters, Symphony

Travel Made Easy

Profit:

	Jan-91	Feb-91	Mar-91	Apr-91	May-91	Jun-91	TOTAL
Revenue	9,434	9,248	9,851	10,141	12,547	14,564	65,785
Expenses	8,127	7,895	8,299	8,454	9,651	9,895	52,321
Net Profit	1,307	1,353	1,552	1,687	2,896	4,669	13,464
Profit (%)	13.85%	14.63%	15.75%	16.64%	23.08%	32.06%	Avg:19.34%

Revenue Breakdown:

	Jan-91	Feb-91	Mar-91	Apr-91	May-91	Jun-91	TOTAL
Tours	2,642	2,589	2,758	2,839	3,513	4,078	18,420
Air Fares	5,472	5,364	5,714	5,882	7,277	8,447	38,155
Other	1,321	1,295	1,379	1,420	1,757	2,039	9,210
Total	9,434	9,248	9,851	10,141	12,547	14,564	65,785

FIGURE 1-2 Symphony 2.0 report

Travel Made Easy							
Profit:							
	Jan-91	Feb-91	Mar-91	Apr-91	May-91	Jun-91	TOTAL
Revenue	9,434	9,248	9,851	10,141	12,547	14,564	65,785
Expenses	8,127	7,895	8,299	8,454	9,651	9,895	52,321
Net Profit	1,307	1,353	1,552	1,687	2,896	4,669	13,464
Profit (%)	13.85%	14.63%	15.75%	16.64%	23.08%	32.06%	Avg:19.34%
Revenue Breakdown:							
	Jan-91	Feb-91	Mar-91	Apr-91	May-91	Jun-91	TOTAL
Tours	2,642	2,589	2,758	2,839	3,513	4,078	18,420
Air Fares	5,472	5,364	5,714	5,882	7,277	8,447	38,155
Other	1,321	1,295	1,379	1,420	1,757	2,039	9,210
Total	9,434	9,248	9,851	10,141	12,547	14,564	65,785

FIGURE 1-3 Symphony report improved with Allways

2.2 incorporates an add-in program called Allways, which brings more sophisticated formatting to Symphony reports, as you can see from the example in Figure 1-3. Allways allows you to add different fonts, shading, and lines to reports, and you can combine graphs and text on the same page. If you have the right equipment, you can preview your Allways formatting on the screen in proper WYSIWYG display. The term *WYSIWYG* stands for "what you see is what you get," meaning that the screen display closely matches the printed output.

THE VIEWER This is an add-in program that helps you deal with the many files that quickly accumulate on your disks as you use a program like Symphony. Derived from a separate Lotus product called Magellan, which is a comprehensive hard-disk management utility, the Viewer program provided with Symphony allows you to view the contents of files when you list them. This gets around the problem of looking at a list of filenames and trying

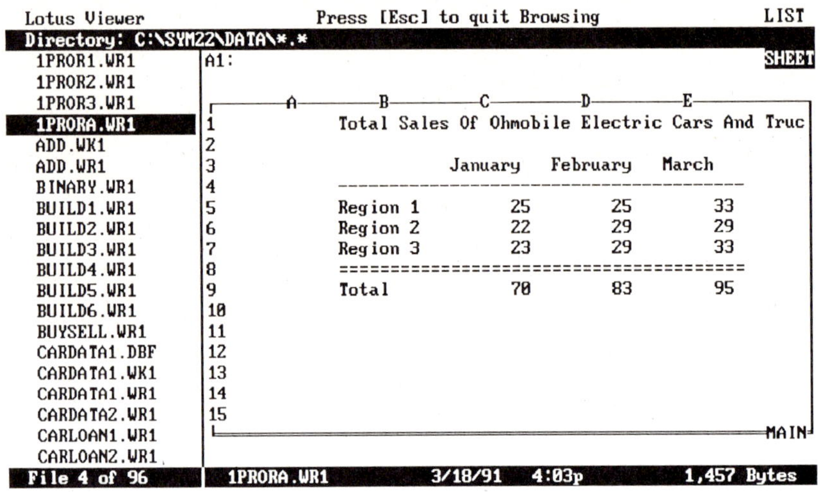

FIGURE 1-4 The Viewer

to determine the contents from just the name. On the right of Figure 1-4 you can see the contents of the file that is highlighted in the list on the left. The Viewer also lets you retrieve a file immediately after you have checked that it is the right one, or even establish a file link, a new Symphony feature described in a moment.

@BASE Users of Symphony 2.2 get another add-in program, called @BASE, which provides "disk-based database functionality." To understand what this means requires a short discussion of the technicalities of personal computer operations. However, this discussion will be useful for understanding several aspects of how Symphony works.

When you are running Symphony on your computer, most of the program is loaded, along with file that you are working on, into your computer's random access memory (RAM). This is an electronic workspace in which information is represented as a series of electrical switches that are either on or off. Information in RAM can be altered very quickly, which is good. However, because RAM depends on the supply of electricity, information in RAM can also be lost very quickly, which is not good. Pull the plug on your PC, and what was in RAM is lost. Furthermore, RAM is quite expensive in terms of the amount of information it can hold compared to magnetic disks—either floppy or hard disks.

Disks are the normal way to retain information on the computer so that it survives a power failure or someone turning off the computer. A disk is like a flat piece of videocassette tape that stores data instead of pictures, and is arranged in circles, rather than as a long strip. Unlike files in RAM, files stored on disk remain there even when the power is off. The "down side" of disk storage is that *reading* information from disk or *writing* it to disk involves a mechanical activity, the moving of the read/write head across the surface of the disk, which is somewhat like the movement of a needle to the right track of a record. This is inevitably slower than the electronic activity in RAM.

Given these factors, you are now in a position to understand the difference between RAM-based and disk-based applications. When you start Symphony, the program files are read into memory from disk storage. When you enter data into a Symphony document, that data is initially held in RAM. This gives you almost instant access to any single piece of information. However, it also means that the size of the document is limited by the amount of RAM you have. When you want to accumulate a lot of records in a database—for example, when you are building a customer mailing list—you may find this limitation quite an obstacle.

Other programs that manage data, such as dBASE or Paradox, approach matters differently. They store each record on a disk as soon as it is entered, thus freeing up memory space for the next record to be entered. They read records from disk into memory only as required for editing and review. Thus, these programs are referred to as *disk-based.* Since the typical personal computer is likely to have at least ten times as much disk storage space as RAM

```
A1: 'Ohmobile                                                     SHEET

     A               B           C       D          E          F          G
1    Ohmobile
2    January Sales               Units Sold - by State
3
4                                State  Units     Revenue
5                                AZ          2    18,390
6                                CA          2    15,990
7                                FL          2    14,690
8                                GA          1     7,395
9                                IL          3    25,185
10                               KY          4    31,280
11                               MD          1     8,195
12                               MN          1     6,795
13                               NC          1     9,195
14                               NV          2    14,690
15                               NY          5    37,475
16                               OH          1     6,795
17                               OK          2    14,190
18                               TX          6    45,370
19                               WA          1     9,195
20                               WI          1     7,395
                                                                        MAIN
18-Mar-91  04:22 PM                                              Num
```

FIGURE 1-5 A cross-tabulation in Symphony, using @BASE

space, this approach greatly increases the total amount of data that the program can manage.

With the @BASE add-in, Symphony users can work with huge collections of data stored in standard database formats. An extensive set of commands is provided to search within, perform math with, and carry out statistical analysis of large databases. In Figure 1-5, you can see a cross-tabulation of a database of sales information showing the number of units sold in each state, summarized by state, as well as the state for each state sorted by revenue. The table appears in a Symphony worksheet, but the data is stored in a dBASE file.

FILE LINKING Symphony 2.2 supports a new feature called file linking. To understand this, you need to have some idea of how electronic spreadsheets have evolved. For many people, electronic spreadsheets were the first personal computer application that

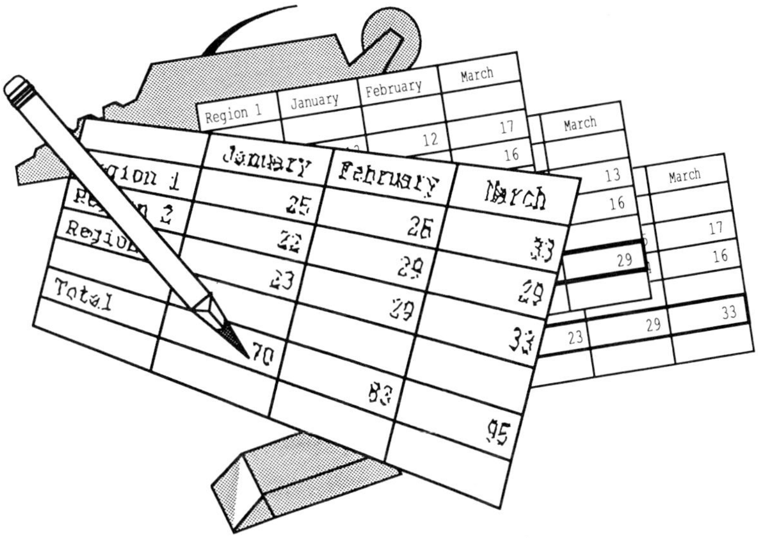

FIGURE 1-6 Projected sales figures on a columnar pad

made it worthwhile to buy a computer. This is because spreadsheets closely mirror the traditional approach to problem solving: the columnar pad, assisted by pencil and calculator. An example of the columnar-pad approach can be seen in Figure 1-6.

From the time of the first commercially successful spreadsheet software, VisiCalc, programmers were faced with a dilemma when attempting to expand the number of columns and rows that the program could handle. This was the same problem facing the accountant with the columnar pad who must deal with a large and growing set of company accounts: either get a larger pad, or divide the work up into pages. Traditionally, the latter approach has proved most practical, and some programmers did create electronic spreadsheets with multiple pages. However, the approach taken by Lotus, when it introduced the 1-2-3 spreadsheet in 1982, was to use a single-page spreadsheet that was very large: 256 columns by

2048 rows. The Symphony spreadsheet increased this size by providing four times as many rows.

The advantage of the large spreadsheet approach was its relative simplicity. Its drawback was that it distorted the traditional paper-and-pencil work pattern. As users added new information, the need to keep all related information on the same sheet resulted in problems of organization. In 1989, Lotus introduced two new versions of 1-2-3 that provided two different solutions to the problem. In 1-2-3 Release 3, you can create multiple sheets within a single spreadsheet file. For example, you can have three regional projections and a consolidated projection within the same file, with the regional sheets stacked behind the consolidation. Unfortunately, this approach only works on more expensive personal computers equipped with large amounts of memory.

In 1-2-3 Release 2.2, Lotus introduced *file linking,* the ability to connect a single spreadsheet in memory with multiple spreadsheets

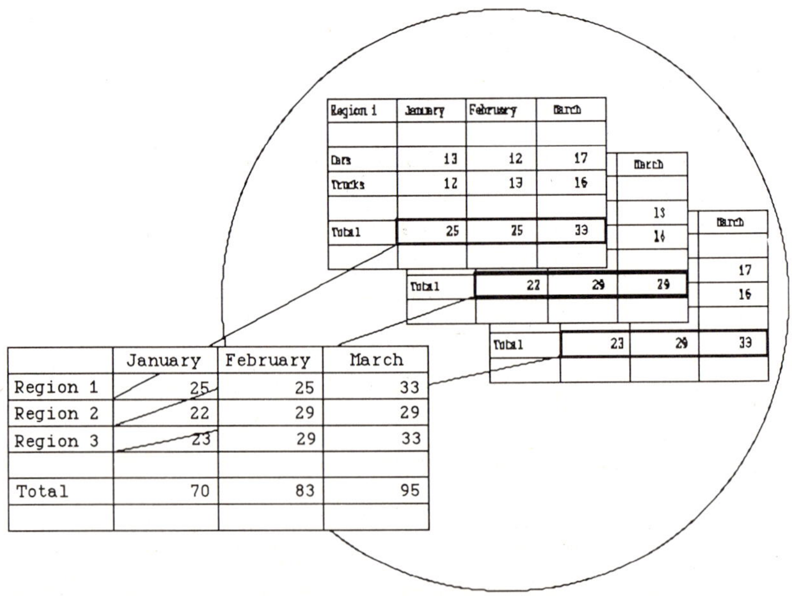

FIGURE 1-7 Diagram of file linking

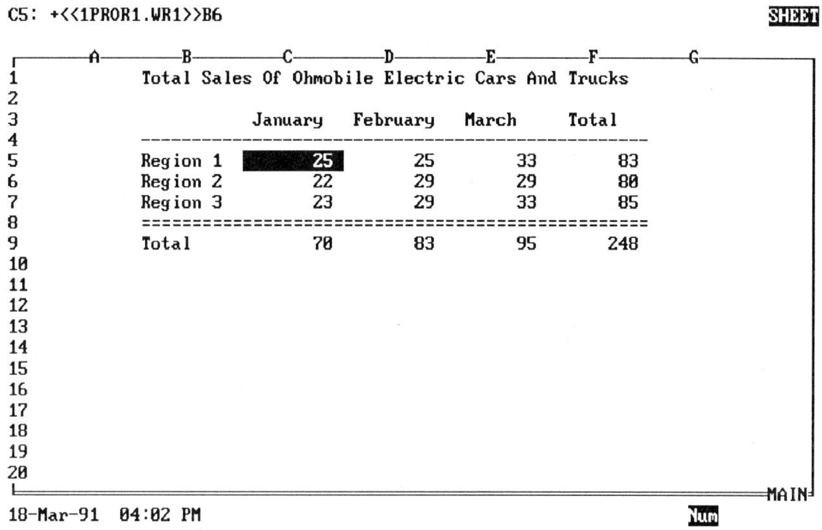

FIGURE 1-8 Consolidated projection, using file linking

on disk. This feature, diagrammed in Figure 1-7, is now provided in Symphony 2.2. As you know from the discussion of disk-based versus memory-based programs, there are advantages to holding information on disk until it is needed. File linking allows you to draw information from one worksheet into another, without trying to fit both worksheets into memory at the same time. With file linking you can create your three regional projections, each in a separate file. Then you can create a fourth file to consolidate the three regions, drawing information from each of the three separate files. An example of this is shown in Figure 1-8.

ENHANCED STEP MODE The ability to create macros with Symphony means that you can record your actions and play back the record to simplify repetitive operations. However, Symphony has a powerful set of commands that can be added to macros to make them more like a programming language, able to carry out complex tasks and build customized menus. When you start to create more complex macros, errors, or *bugs,* are inevitable, and Symphony 2.2 provides an improved feature for debugging macros. A macro can be executed one step at a time, and part of the screen will show the macro instructions as they are carried out in the rest of the screen.

BASIC REQUIREMENTS

You have already learned that memory is the area of the computer that holds information while it is being processed, whereas the disk is where information waits to be read into memory. To run Symphony 2.2, you need a compatible personal computer with a hard-disk drive and minimum amount of memory, described as 512 K. This terminology will be discussed in a moment. In order to see Symphony graphs on screen, as well as the formatting performed by Allways, you need a graphics display system such as Hercules, EGA, or VGA.

The term *compatible* means that your computer must be able to run PC-DOS or MS-DOS. While "DOS" stands for Disk Operating System, "MS" stands for Microsoft, the company that wrote DOS, and "PC" stands for Personal Computer, a term used by IBM, which sells its own version of MS-DOS as PC-DOS. The role of DOS is to allow software such as Symphony to communicate with the hardware—that is, the keyboard, screen, disks, printer, and so on. Although a wide range of different personal computers now uses DOS, Lotus makes no promises about which ones will run Symphony, except for certain models that Lotus tests and certifies as compatible.

Thanks for the Memory

As far as the memory and disk requirements of Symphony are concerned, you need to understand how disks and memory are measured. Both storage and memory space are measured in terms of the amount of information that they can hold. The smallest unit of measurement is a *bit,* which is short for "binary digit," meaning a 1 or a 0. If you put 8 bits together, the possible permutations are 256, enough to represent all the letters of the alphabet (in upper- and lowercase) as well as the numbers 0 through 9 and many common symbols such as plus and minus signs. Taken together, eight bits make up one *byte,* which is essentially the space it takes to store one letter or number. Bytes are used to show the size of files on disk and the size of memory space. Since many files contain several thousand bytes, the term *kilobytes* is used; it is abbreviated as K. There are 1024 bytes in one kilobyte. You might have heard the expression "my personal computer has 640 K of RAM," which means the random access memory of that computer can hold 640 kilobytes of information, or 655,360 bytes (640 times 1024).

For larger measures, *megabytes* are used. There are 1024 kilobytes in a megabyte, or 1,048,576 bytes. The storage capacity of your hard disk is measured in megabytes. You will see several abbreviations for megabytes, as in 10 Meg, 20 MB, and 40 MBytes (this book will use MB as the abbreviation). In the future you will encounter the next stage up in information management, a *gigabyte,* which is 1024 megabytes. At this point in time a typical personal computer might have a 40 MB hard disk and floppy disks that can store anywhere from 360 K to 1.44 MB. The amount of memory might be 640 K, 1 MB, or even more.

For reasons too complex to go into here, there may be several different types of RAM in your computer. On personal computers using DOS, only 640 K of *conventional RAM* can be used directly by DOS. Symphony can run within 512 K of RAM, but to load Allways and other add-ins you really need 640 K. Any further RAM space beyond this must be installed in your personal computer as either *expanded memory,* sometimes referred to as *EMS,* or extended memory. These are described in Chapter 7, together with details of how to use RAM efficiently with Symphony.

Without special software, Symphony cannot use extended memory, but it can use up to 4 MB of expanded memory.

Watch Disk Space

To install Symphony 2.2 and Allways you need quite a lot of hard-disk space: 5 megabytes. The rest of this chapter assumes that you (or someone else) have already installed Symphony on your personal computer. Tips on how to accomplish this are provided in Appendix A. Tips on how to organize your work files on the hard disk and how to deal with shortages of disk space are provided in Chapter 8.

LOADING AND LEAVING

This section gives you the basic commands for entering and leaving Symphony, sometimes referred to as *loading* and *quitting*. If someone has installed Symphony on your computer for you, they may have already set up a procedure or menu to be used for starting Symphony, so you should follow their instructions. Otherwise, you should be able to use the loading directions given here.

Loading Symphony

If you have just installed Symphony according to the instructions in the manual, your screen will probably be displaying the DOS prompt. This will look like one of the following:

C>_	This is the plain prompt. It tells you that drive C is the current drive. The hard disk on most PCs is called C.

C:\>_	This is an improved prompt. It tells you that the current directory is the root directory. *Directories* are areas of the disk used to keep files organized in related groups. The *root* directory is the primary area of the disk.
C:\SYM22\>_	This is the same as the previous prompt, except the current directory is called SYM22, the name recommended by Lotus for the directory used to store the Symphony 2.2 program files.
Wed 1-1-1990 D:\>	This is a prompt that has been modified to display the current date, whatever that happens to be. Note that the drive is called D. Hard disks are usually called C, but can be D, E, or other letters, depending upon the equipment and setup you are using.

To start Symphony from the DOS prompt, you first need to locate the Symphony program files. These are stored in a named area of the disk, called a directory, usually either SYMPHONY or SYM22. To get to this area, you type **CD \SYMPHONY** (or **CD \SYM22**) and press the (ENTER) key. The letters CD stand for Change Directory.

THE ACCESS METHOD You can now enter one of the two different commands that load Symphony. To gain access to all of the parts of Symphony, including the Translate program and the graph printing commands, you type **ACCESS** at the DOS prompt and press (ENTER). You will see a screen like the one shown in Figure 1-9.

```
Start Symphony
Symphony  PrintGraph  Install  File-Translate  Exit

                     Symphony Access System

                   Copyright (C) 1986, 1990
                 Lotus Development Corporation
                      All Rights Reserved
                          Release 2.2

The Access system lets you choose Symphony, PrintGraph, the Install
program, or the Translate utility from the menu at the top of this
screen.  If you're using a diskette system, the Access system may prompt
you to change disks.  Follow the instructions below to start a program.

o  Use [RIGHT] or [LEFT] to move the menu pointer (the highlight bar at
   the top of the screen) to the program you want to use.

o  Press [RETURN] to start the program.

You can also start a program by typing the first letter of the menu
choice.  Press the [HELP] key for more information.
                         Press [NUM LOCK]
```

FIGURE 1-9 The Symphony Access System

At the top of the screen is a list of five actions you can carry out:

Symphony PrintGraph Install File-Translate Exit

The first of these, Symphony, is highlighted. To enter the main Symphony program you simply press **ENTER**. This will take you to a screen that looks like the one in Figure 1-10. This is the main Symphony workspace.

The next three items on the list after Symphony in Figure 1-9 are other parts of the Symphony program that allow you to print Symphony graphs, change the way Symphony has been installed, and translate data to or from Symphony files. The last item, Exit, returns you to DOS. To select one of these other items you type the first letter (for example, type **E** for Exit) or press the **RIGHT ARROW** key until the highlighting moves onto the item you want to select. The arrow keys are located in a special section of

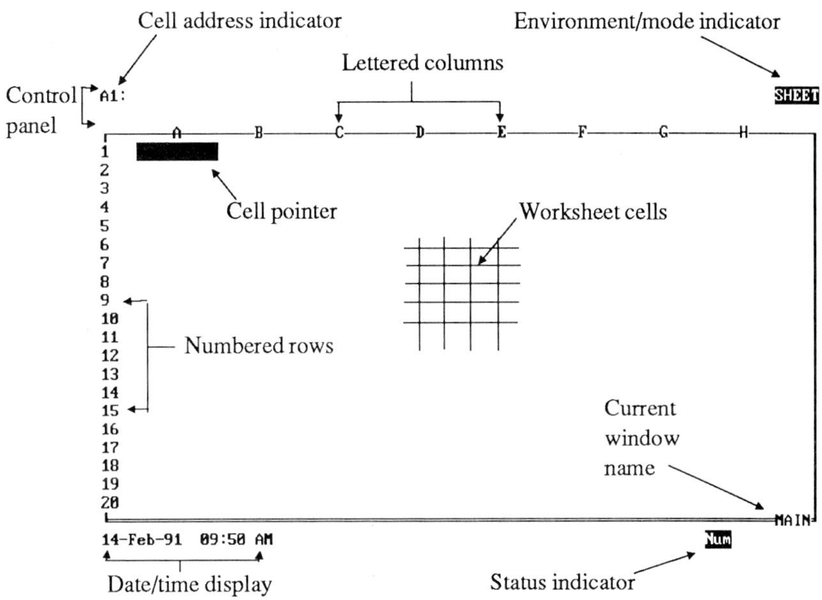

FIGURE 1-10 Annotated workspace

the keyboard, called the *cursor pad,* as shown in Figure 1-11. This method of making choices is typical of the menus used by Symphony to provide you with an easy way of issuing commands.

When you select Symphony from the Access System and then leave the main program, you return to the Access System. You can then choose another part of Symphony from the menu or select Exit to return back to DOS.

THE DIRECT APPROACH An alternative approach to loading Symphony, bypassing the Access System, is to type **SYMPHONY** at the DOS prompt and press (ENTER). When you do this you will soon see a large rectangle on the screen with the word "MAIN" in the bottom right corner and the word "SHEET" in the top right, as shown in Figure 1-10.

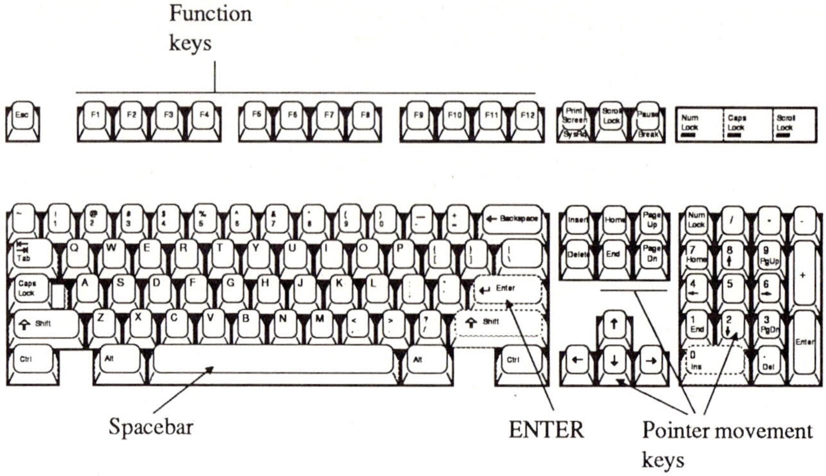

FIGURE 1-11 Keyboard diagram

If you opt for the direct approach, you need to bear in mind that when you exit from Symphony you will return to DOS. This means that if you want to print a graph or translate a file, you will need to enter these parts of the program directly or load the Access System.

Leaving Symphony

When you have entered the Symphony workspace, shown in Figure 1-10, you can begin work. However, before you do any work you should probably know how to leave this area. To quit Symphony you press the (F9) key, known as the SERVICES key. You will get a menu of choices across the top of the screen, beginning with Window and ending with Exit:

Window File Print Configuration Application Settings New Exit

At first, the choice called Window will be highlighted. You can now type **E** to select the Exit command. Alternatively, you can press the RIGHT ARROW key seven times to move the highlighting from Window to Exit, and press ENTER. In fact, pressing the LEFT ARROW just once will work instead of RIGHT ARROW seven times, since the highlighting rotates through the entries.

When you have selected the Exit command, Symphony will ask you the following question:

End Symphony session? (Select "No" if your work isn't saved)

Under the question you will see two choices: No and Yes, with No highlighted. This means that if you immediately press ENTER at this point, No will be selected and the Exit command will be cancelled. To complete the Exit command you must type **Y** for Yes or press the LEFT ARROW or RIGHT ARROW key to move the highlighting to Yes, and then press ENTER.

You may be wondering about the warning that Symphony gives to *save* your work. This means to store your work on disk. The procedures for saving work are dealt with later in the section on saving and filing. The important point to note here is that leaving Symphony is fairly easy but needs to be done with care, because Symphony will not automatically save your work or prevent you from losing it.

THE WORK AREA

When you first load Symphony, you have an empty electronic work space called a *worksheet* in which to place numbers, words, and instructions (formulas and calculations). As shown in the annotated workspace diagram in Figure 1-10, there is a line of letters near the top of the screen and a list of numbers down the side.

The Worksheet Environment

The letters represent a series of columns and the numbers represent a series of rows. The intersection of each column and row forms a rectangle, a box into which you put information. These boxes are called *cells*. One of them is highlighted when you start the program. You can see a flashing line in the cell. This is the *cursor,* which helps you keep track of where you are.

The highlighted cell at the top left of the large rectangle on the screen is called A1 because it is in column A on row 1. Every cell has a name based on its location, or *coordinates,* just like a map. You can move from cell to cell, using the arrow keys, to enter and arrange information. When you first start Symphony, cell A1 is highlighted, and if you enter information at this point, it will be placed in this cell. When A1 is highlighted you are said to be "in cell A1." The cell you are in is called the *current cell.*

A Choice of Environments

This column-and-row work area underlies all of the tasks you perform with Symphony, including word processing and communications. However, when you perform tasks other than spreadsheet calculations, the work area takes on a different appearance. The initial appearance is called SHEET (short for worksheet) as indicated in the top right corner of the screen. In Symphony terminology you are said to be "in the SHEET environment."

There are five different environments for the five different applications that Symphony supports. The five environments are given abbreviated names:

SHEET	The worksheet or spreadsheet environment, for calculations
DOC	The document composition environment, for word processing
GRAPH	The business graphics environment, for designing charts based on data stored in Symphony
FORM	The database management environment, for entering, searching, and reporting data records
COMM	The communications environment, for exchanging data with other computers

You can see these environments listed if you hold down the (ALT) key and press (F10). You will get a list at the top of the screen, in the control panel, as shown in Figure 1-12.

Using Menus

The control panel list in Figure 1-12 is a menu of choices. The second line presents the actual choices: SHEET, DOC, GRAPH, FORM, and COMM. The first line explains the currently highlighted choice. When you first press (ALT-F10), the name "SHEET" is highlighted. This is the default selection, the one chosen by Symphony unless you command otherwise.

The (ALT-F10) key is known in Symphony as the TYPE key, and the screen in Figure 1-12 is displaying the TYPE menu. Note that the text in the top right of the screen has changed from SHEET to MENU. This area of the screen is both the environment indicator and the mode indicator. At this point it is telling you that you are in MENU mode; that is, you are using one of Symphony's menus. Previously it said "SHEET" to let you know you were in the SHEET environment.

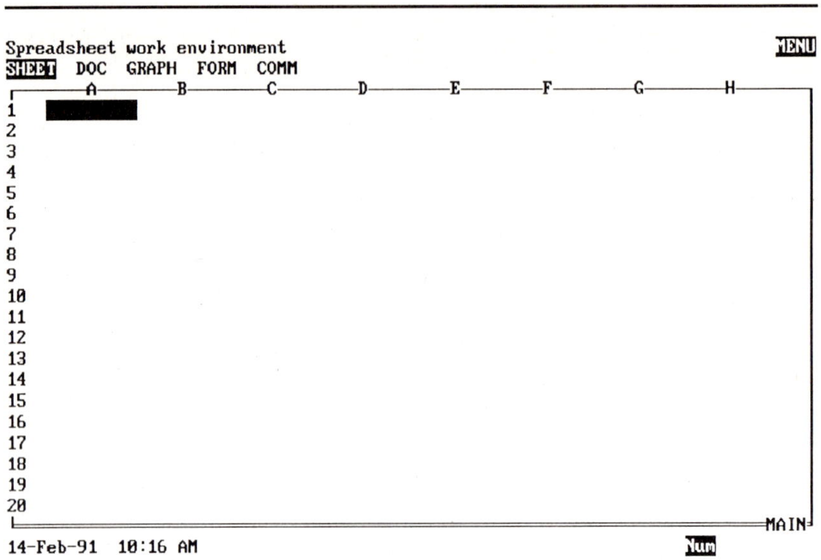

FIGURE 1-12 The environment choices or TYPE menu

To use the menu to choose an environment besides SHEET, you lightly press your **RIGHT ARROW** key. You will see the highlighting move along the control panel from SHEET to DOC.

Note Note the words *lightly press*. Your keyboard has the ability to repeat keystrokes and will do so if you lean on, rather than just tap, a key. Throughout the rest of this book you should take the term *press* to mean tap lightly rather than push and hold down.

To see the keyboard repeat feature in action, you can press the **RIGHT ARROW** key at this point and hold it for two seconds. You will see the highlighting move through the list of names and begin again at the first name. In this situation leaning on the key is not a problem, since you can press **LEFT ARROW** or **RIGHT ARROW** to move the highlighting back to DOC. However, in some situations,

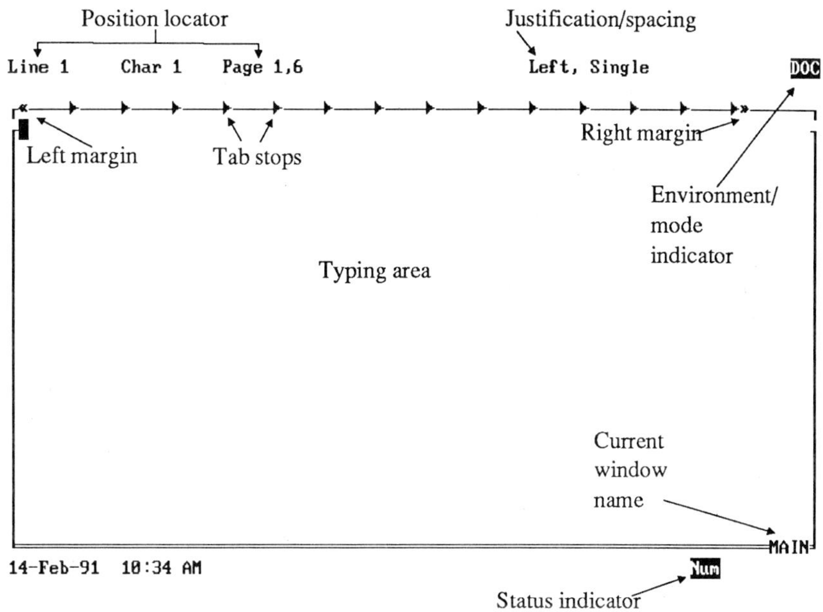

FIGURE 1-13 Annotated diagram of DOC environment

extended pressing of keys can be a problem, so it should be done carefully.

When you have highlighted DOC, note that the text on the first line of the control panel has changed to tell you about the DOC environment. To select this environment you press (ENTER). All of the Symphony menus can be operated in this way: you highlight the item that you want and then press (ENTER).

A Different Environment

When you select the DOC environment, you will see some subtle changes in the work area, as shown in the annotated diagram in Figure 1-13. The DOC environment is designed for writing and represents a sheet of typing paper electronically. Across the screen you have a series of triangular symbols instead of column letters. These indicate tab stops. The double chevrons at each end of the line represent margins. The top line of the screen tells you that you are on line one of page one, and the current position of the cursor is character one. You are also told that the page is left-aligned and single-spaced. The meaning of these settings will be discussed in detail in Chapter 3.

The important observation at this stage is that the underlying electronic area is the same as in the SHEET environment. Changing environments is somewhat like slipping on a pair of colored glasses while looking out of the window: the scenery does not change, but it looks different. To move back to the SHEET environment you can press (ALT-F10) and then (ENTER) to select SHEET which will already be highlighted. An alternative technique is to press (ALT-F9), called the SWITCH key. This key switches you between the current environment and the last one viewed. Because you have just come from the SHEET environment, pressing (ALT-F9) in the DOC environment takes you back to the SHEET environment.

BACK TO THE WORKSHEET

The easiest way to get a feel for how you enter data into Symphony is to begin using the SHEET environment. As you have seen, this is the default environment, the one you enter when you first start Symphony. In computer terminology *default* means what the computer does unless you tell it to do otherwise. When you start Symphony you are, by default, placed in the SHEET environment with cell A1 highlighted. The highlighting that marks the cell you are in, the current cell, is called the *cell pointer*. The cell pointer can be moved from cell to cell with the cursor keys or the arrow keys. When you move the cell pointer, your exact location is recorded by the cell address indicator in the control panel at the top of the screen.

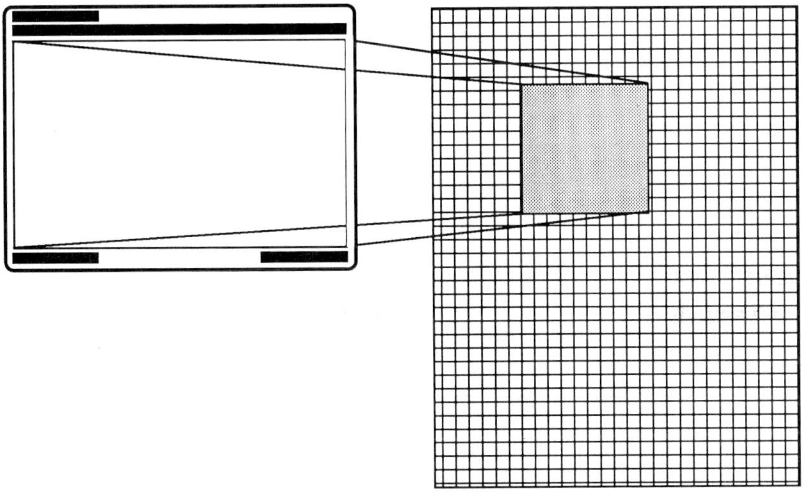

FIGURE 1-14 Symphony screen as cockpit window

Worksheet Size

The Symphony worksheet is very large; the columns continue off the side of the screen through column Z. Further columns are numbered AA through AZ, then BA through BZ, and so on. After repeating the alphabet nine and a half times, you get to the last column, IV, for a total of 256 columns. The rows go beyond 20, down to 8192. Multiplying the columns and rows together gives you a total of over 2 million cells. Obviously, your monitor can show you only a small portion of this huge work area at a time. As you can see from the diagram in Figure 1-14, the screen acts like a cockpit window, showing you different parts of the worksheet as you move the cell pointer around.

Symphony provides important information around the edge of the screen, as shown earlier in Figure 1-10, and also in Figure 1-15. When you are using Symphony, the horizontal and vertical borders, top control panel, and bottom status area work together like

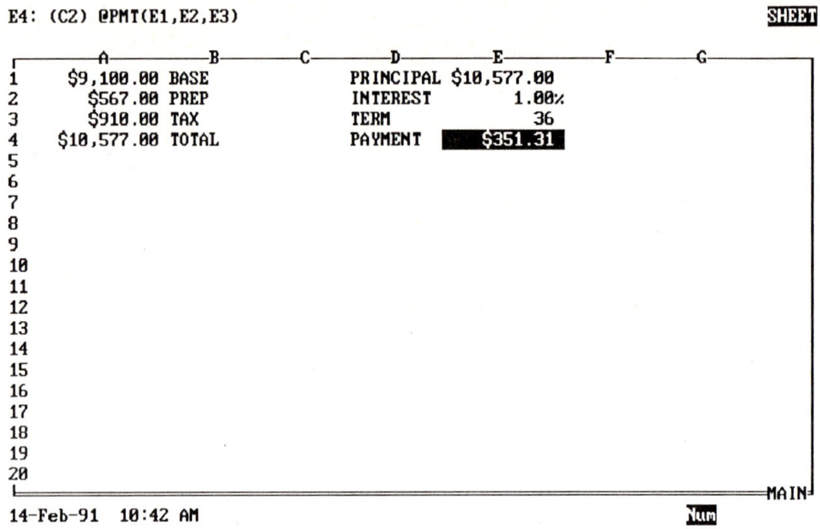

FIGURE 1-15 Detail of SHEET work area

a dashboard, supplying you with important information and mesages. The status of the **CAPS LOCK**, **NUM LOCK**, and **SCROLL LOCK** keys is shown at the bottom of the screen. The environment/mode indicator shows you a variety of messages about the current task. The cell address indicator shows the contents of the current cell and its display format setting. The various parts of this control panel are shown in greater detail in Figure 1-15, which shows data entered into the worksheet.

Movement Keys

To explore the work area, lightly press the **RIGHT ARROW** key once. You will see the highlighting move to the next cell to the right, B1. You are now in cell B1. Lightly press the **DOWN ARROW** key once and you will be in cell B2. Notice that in the top left corner of the screen your current location is being monitored. This indication is very helpful, since eyeballing your location is notably prone to error, particularly after several hours at the screen.

As mentioned before, your keyboard has the ability to repeat keystrokes if you lean on a key. The keyboard repeat feature is helpful when used with the cursor movement keys. For example, press the DOWN ARROW key and hold it for two seconds. You will see the cell indicator move quickly down the screen, and the numbers at the left will scroll rapidly by. You can see that you are dragging the screen with you to view a different area of the spreadsheet. Now press the HOME key. It takes you back to A1. The main cursor movement keys can be seen in Figure 1-16.

The arrow keys move you one cell in each of their respective directions. Used with the CTRL key, the RIGHT ARROW and LEFT ARROW keys move a screen at a time across the worksheet. The PGUP and PGDN keys move you 20 lines at a time up and down the worksheet. The HOME key always places you in A1

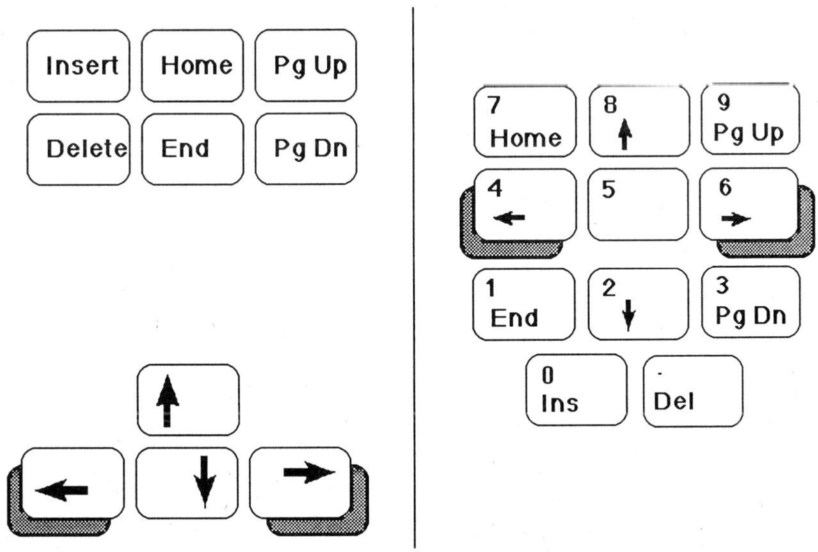

FIGURE 1-16 Cursor movement keys

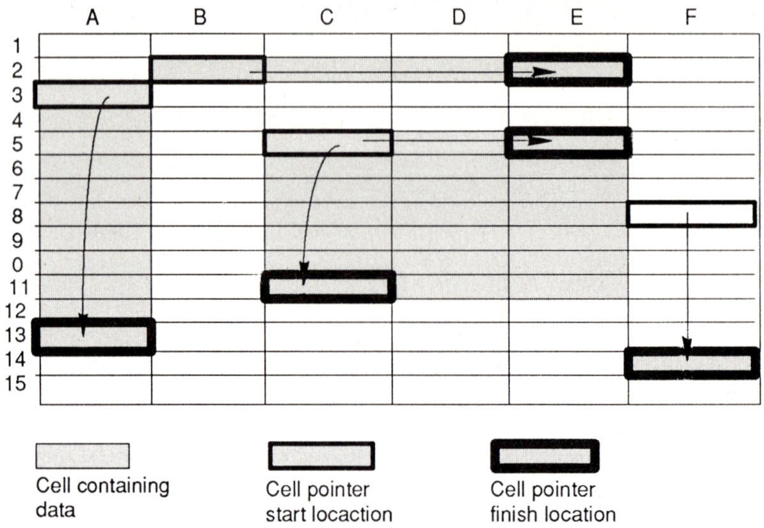

FIGURE 1-17 Diagram of (END) key sequences

(unless you are using locked titles, described in the next chapter). The (END) key followed by an arrow key takes you to the last cell in that direction. The last cell means the last occupied cell in a row or column of contiguous entries, or the first occupied cell if the next cell is empty. This is diagrammed in Figure 1-17.

Note that you do not use the (END) key like the (CTRL) key; you press and release (END) and then the press and release the arrow key. This is called a *keystroke sequence,* while pressing two keys at the same time is called a *keystroke combination.*

The (INS) and (DEL) keys are often grouped with the cursor keys. Pressing (DEL) in SHEET mode does nothing, but you can use it when editing cell entries. Pressing (INS) changes the way that you type in DOC mode, allowing you to add text to the middle of a line without typing over other characters. The DOC mode is described in detail in Chapter 4.

TYPES OF INFORMATION

In the SHEET environment, Symphony categorizes all information into one of two types of data: values or labels. To simplify, *values* are numbers and calculations, and *labels* are words or text. Symphony treats the two categories of data differently. By looking at the first character of each new entry in the worksheet, Symphony determines the appropriate category for that data: value or label.

About Values

To see how you enter information into Symphony and how the program recognizes values, try the following exercise:

1. With the cell indicator in cell A1, type **789** from the row of numbers at the top of the keyboard. Do *not* press (ENTER) or any other key; just observe what has happened. Notice that the number 789 has not yet been placed into the worksheet. Instead, it is on the top line of the control panel, which is now acting as the edit line. The cursor is flashing after the number 9.

2. You can now either continue to type or use the (BACKSPACE) key to erase what you have typed. Also notice that a change has taken place in the bottom status area: the mode indicator now says VALUE. This tells you that Symphony is reading what you have typed as a value.

3. If you did press the (ENTER) key prematurely or otherwise caused the number to leave the top line of the screen, just type **789** again and observe what happens before you press (ENTER).

4. You can now place the number 789 into the worksheet. To do so, press the (ENTER) key and observe that the number disappears from the edit line and is placed into the worksheet in the cell

you are highlighting. The cell address indicator in the top left status area now lists the contents of the cell. Although this might seem like a duplication of effort, you will see in a moment that what Symphony shows you in the cell address is sometimes different from what it displays in the worksheet. The cell address shows the exact content of the cell as Symphony understands it.

5. When you have pressed (ENTER), you will also see that the mode indicator returns to SHEET. The numbers you have entered are placed on the righthand side of the cell, as shown here:

```
A1: 789                                                              SHEET

┌────────A────────B────────C────────D────────E────────F────────G────────H─────┐
1          789                                                                │
2                                                                             │
3                                                                             │
4                                                                             │
5                                                                             │
```

Symphony normally aligns numbers evenly with the right of the column. This is referred to as *flush-right alignment.*

About Labels

Now that you are back in SHEET mode, you can move the cell indicator to another cell. Having seen how Symphony handles values, it is time to see how labels are treated.

1. With the cell indicator still in A1, press the (RIGHT ARROW) key once and you will be in cell B1. Here you will enter a label.

2. Before you type, take a look at your keyboard and locate the (CAPS LOCK) key. This key allows you to type in capital letters without using the (SHIFT) key. Many people find it convenient to type labels all in capitals. Press the (CAPS LOCK) key once, and notice the bottom status area reflects this change with the message "Caps." When you are locked into capitals, the letters

"A" through "Z" are automatically typed as capitals. You still must use the (SHIFT) key to use symbols or commands that are on the upper half of keys.

3. You are going to type the word "BASE" because you will use Symphony to figure out the full price of a car from, among other things, the base price. Type the letter **B** and notice that the mode indicator says LABEL. Also notice that the word is being typed on the edit line so you can change it with the (BACKSPACE) key if you make an error.

4. Type **BASE** and press (ENTER). Observe the cell address at the top of the screen, as shown here:

```
B1: 'BASE                                                    SHEET
┌───────A──────────B──────────C──────────D──────────E──────────F──────────G──────────H──────┐
1          789 BASE
2
3
4
5
```

In front of the word you typed is an apostrophe ('). It was placed there automatically by Symphony as a reminder that this is a label. Although you are not likely to confuse this particular label with a number, you will later encounter instructions that look like labels but are in fact values.

The apostrophe in cell B1 not only tells you that this cell contains a label, but it also signifies that this is a left-aligned label. Labels can either be left-aligned, right-aligned, or centered in the column. Right-aligned labels are preceded by a quotation mark ("). Centered labels begin with a caret (^), which is the shifted 6 on the keyboard. Rather than make you type one of the three label alignment characters (' " ^) before every label, Symphony will assume one of them. This is the *default label alignment* and, as you can see, it is left-aligned.

To enter a label aligned differently from the default, just type the desired alignment before the text of the label. For example, enter **"BASE** if you want the label to be right-aligned. To enter a label that actually begins with one of the alignment characters, you use two of them. Thus, entering **""BASE"** will produce a right-aligned label that reads as "BASE" in the worksheet. Later, you can use menu commands to change the alignment of a group of labels all at once.

Methods of Entering Data

There is a slightly different way of entering data into a cell. You will use this as you enter another label directly below BASE. This will be the word "PREP," for dealer preparation costs.

1. Press (DOWN ARROW) to move to cell B2, and then type **PREP**. It will appear on the edit line like the numbers 789 and BASE did before.

2. Press the (DOWN ARROW) key again. Doing so enters the label and moves you down to the next row. This can be a very useful feature if you want to enter a series of labels or numbers. The direction keys will enter what you are typing and move you in a particular direction with one keystroke. For this reason it is important not to press the cursor keys when you are entering information into an empty cell.

3. Practice this method of entering by typing **TAX** and pressing the (DOWN ARROW) key, and then typing **TOTAL** and pressing the (DOWN ARROW) key. The results will look like this:

```
B5:                                                              SHEET

┌────────A─────────B─────────C─────────D─────────E─────────F─────────G─────────H──────┐
1        789 BASE
2            PREP
3            TAX
4            TOTAL
5
```

Changing Cells

Changing worksheet entries and correcting mistakes is one of the most important procedures you will need to know. In this example, $789 is a ridiculously low price for a car, so you need to change it. Follow these steps to change the price:

1. Press the (HOME) key on the cursor pad. You now will be highlighting cell A1 and the number 789.

2. To change a cell entry completely, you just type a new entry. Type **8000** and press (ENTER). Do *not* put in commas to indicate the thousands when entering numbers in Symphony; they will be put in later. The new number replaces the old one.

3. To modify the contents of the cell rather than completely replacing them—for example, to change 8000 to 8095 to reflect a price increase—you use the EDIT key, (F2). Press (F2) while your cell pointer is in A1. When you do so, the contents of the cell are returned to the edit line:

```
A1: 8000                                                         EDIT
8000
┌────────A─────────B─────────C─────────D─────────E─────────F─────────G─────────H──────┐
1       8000 BASE
2            PREP
3            TAX
4            TOTAL
5
```

4. Press (BACKSPACE) twice to back over the last two zeroes, and type in **95**. Now press (ENTER), and the modified contents are returned to the cell.

5. You now want to add a figure for dealer preparation costs. Press (DOWN ARROW) once. You will be in cell A2.

6. Type the number **567**, and enter it into the cell by pressing the (DOWN ARROW) key. You are now in cell A3.

Now you are ready to do some math with Symphony. However, before doing so you need to think about storing the work that you have done so far so that it will not be lost if the power goes out or if you want to leave Symphony and come back to it later.

SAVING AND FILING

The entries in the Symphony worksheet that you have made so far only exist in your computer's RAM. This is not permanent storage; it will be wiped out if you turn off the power, or if you leave Symphony.

File Saving

To record the information so that it will be there when you return to Symphony, you must place it in a file. This is known as saving the file. All files must have names, and there are some conventions for these names. The names are in two parts, (similar to a first name and a last name) separated by a period. The first name can be up to eight characters long. The last name is limited to three characters. The last name of the file name is known as the *extension*. Symphony files are automatically given the extension WR1. You get to choose the first name. Thus, you could store your current work in a file called

CARPRICE.WR1

To save the current work in a file, follow these steps:

1. Press (F9), which pops up the SERVICES menu.
2. From the SERVICES menu select the second item, File (either type **F** or press (RIGHT ARROW) once to highlight File and then press (ENTER)). This takes you to the File submenu.
3. From this menu select the first item, Save (type **S** or press (ENTER)). This gives you the Save File prompt, which consists of the drive letter of the current disk, together with the default directory area of the disk being used and the characters *.wr1, as shown here:

```
Save file name: C:\SYM22\DATA\*.wr1                                    FILES
ADD.WR1          ANSWER.WR1       BINARY.WR1       CARLOAN1.WR1     CARLOANX.WR1
┌───────A────────B───────C───────D───────E───────F───────G───────H──────┐
1      8095 BASE                                                        │
2       567 PREP                                                        │
3           TAX                                                         │
4           TOTAL                                                       │
```

There is also a list of existing files. Note that the SHEET prompt has changed to FILES. (A complete description of the elements of the Save File prompt can be found in Chapter 8.)

4. You can now type the filename you want to use, as shown here:

```
Save file name: C:\SYM22\DATA\CARPRICE                                  EDIT

┌───────A────────B───────C───────D───────E───────F───────G───────H──────┐
1      8095 BASE                                                        │
2       567 PREP                                                        │
3           TAX                                                         │
4           TOTAL                                                       │
```

Just type the first part, **CARPRICE**, and then press (ENTER). You will see the mode indicator flash the word "WAIT" while the file is stored on disk. You will then be returned to SHEET mode.

Note Note that you do not have to type the name in capitals. DOS does not distinguish between capitals and lowercase. When you enter names in lowercase, DOS converts them to capitals.

When thinking up file names, you need to be descriptive, within the limits of the eight characters you get to choose. In addition to letters, you can use the numbers, 0 through 9, as in PRICE001. You can also use some punctuation characters, but some of these are not allowed, so it is safer to stick to just letters and numbers.

If you now want to leave Symphony you can press (F9) and then type **E** for Exit followed by **Y** for Yes. Your work has been saved, so it is okay to exit and turn off the computer.

Deciding On a Directory

The precise area of the disk used to store a file depends on the current directory setting in Symphony. The first time you use the program, it will suggest storing on the same drive and directory you started the program from, typically C:\SYMPHONY or C:\SYM22. To keep your files well organized, you will want to avoid storing data files among program files. To change the current storage area to another directory on your hard disk, you will first need to have created the directory. However, you can easily change the directory to a floppy-disk drive if you first place a suitable disk in the drive. To change the current data-file storage directory or disk drive,

1. Press (F9) for the SERVICES menu.
2. Select File, followed by Dir.
3. You can now press (ESC) once to remove the existing setting. (If you press (ESC) a second time, it will cancel the operation.)
4. Type the full name of the area you want to use; for example, type **A:** to use a floppy disk in drive A or **C:\SYM22\DATA** to use a subdirectory called DATA that you have created below the SYM22 program directory.
5. Now press (ENTER), and you will return to SHEET mode.

From now on until you restart the program, Symphony will save data files to this drive/directory.

Note You must have a floppy disk in the floppy drive if you want to change the current directory to that drive.

To make a more permanent change to the data storage area, one that persists from one session to the next, you press (F9) and select Configuration followed by File. Again, you can press (ESC) to clear the previous entry and type a new one. When you have typed the name of the storage area, you press (ENTER) (which returns you to the Configuration menu) and type **U** for Update, the command which records your choice for future sessions. Note that if you select a floppy-disk drive as the permanent storage area, you will need to have a floppy disk in that drive whenever the program is loaded.

Making and managing directories is discussed in Chapter 8. Keep in mind that it is actually the disk operating system (DOS) that takes care of writing the file onto the disk. Symphony merely passes on your request to DOS, saying in effect "here is some information—record it on the disk using this name and keep track of where you put it because it will be needed later."

Returning to a File

Suppose that you have saved your file and exited Symphony. Later you reload Symphony and want to get back to work where you left off. What you need the computer to do is read a copy of the file from disk into memory. The Symphony command for this is File Retrieve. To retrieve your file,

1. Press (F9) for the SERVICES menu.
2. Type **F** for File followed by **R** for Retrieve.
3. Now type the name of the file exactly as you did when the file was saved; in this case, type **CARPRICE**.
4. Press (ENTER), and the file will be loaded. The cell pointer will still be where you left it in the worksheet.

An alternative to this procedure is to locate your file in the list of file names that Symphony displays when you issue the File Retrieve command, as shown here:

```
Name of file to retrieve: C:\SYM22\DATA\*.wr?                                       FILES
ADD.WR1          BINARY.WR1       CARLOAN1.WR1     CARLOANX.WR1     CARPRICE.WR1
┌────────A────────B────────C────────D────────E────────F────────G────────H────────
1      8095 BASE
2       567 PREP
3           TAX
4           TOTAL
```

This list shows all of the Symphony files in the current storage area, in alphabetical order. You can press the (RIGHT ARROW) and (LEFT ARROW) keys to move the highlighting through the list. You can press the (HOME) key to return to the first name in the list, or press (END) to get to the last name in the list. When you have highlighted the file you want, press (ENTER), and it is retrieved into the workspace.

Although it is a basic and essential operation, file retrieving is also dangerous. What you read from disk replaces what you already have in memory. For example, suppose you are working on a business file, a departmental budget worksheet. You get a call from the car dealer who has a new deal for you. You want to check the car pricing worksheet. You press (F9) and then select File and Retrieve, type the name of the car price file, and press (ENTER). Presto! You have your loan worksheet in front of you, but you do not have the budget worksheet. Any work you did on that spreadsheet since the last time it was stored on disk is lost. Except when you first load Symphony, always use File Save before using File Retrieve.

Saving a Second Time

Suppose you have saved your file and decide to do more work on the file. When you come to save the file a second time, you will not have to type the name again; it will already be entered for you at the Save File prompt. However, you will have to decide if you want to use the same name again. Doing so means that you will store the new version of the worksheet over the old version. When you press (ENTER) to reuse the same name, Symphony does not automatically accept the command but asks you to confirm that you want to replace the old file with the new one. Answer Yes to complete the command, or No to think again.

Saving new versions over old ones is the usual choice when you are building a worksheet, but later you may want to keep the original version and give a new name to the new version. To do this you press (ESC) when the old name is presented, and then type the new name and press (ENTER). Symphony will immediately accept the command unless that name has already been used, in which case you can try the command again.

A New File

Suppose you have saved your current work and want to go on to a new project. You do not have to exit Symphony and reload to do this; you simply pick the New command from the SERVICES menu. When you do so, Symphony asks you to confirm the command. The reason for this is that all of the current work will be erased from memory to make room for a fresh file. This is fine *if* you have already saved the work or do not want to save it. When you confirm the New command, you get a fresh worksheet, just like the one that appears when you first load Symphony.

Caution You should use the New command with care—after all, you are expunging over 2 million cells. If your worksheet extends beyond the columns and rows on-screen, you should check around to make sure that all the work is saved before erasing. A pre-emptive file save is always a good precaution.

INSTRUCTIONS AND FORMULAS

Returning to the CARPRICE worksheet, you are ready to perform some math with Symphony. In cell A3 you want a figure for the tax that must be paid on the base price of the car, not including the dealer prep. Assume that the tax rate is 10%, or 0.1. The figure you want in cell A3 is 8095 x 0.1. You want Symphony to calculate this for you, so you are going to type an instruction into cell A3 that will tell Symphony to multiply the number in cell A1 by 0.1 and place the answer in cell A3. Note that you are not going to tell Symphony simply to multiply the specific number 8095 by 0.1. Symphony can do that, but that is not the true power of a spreadsheet. What you want to do is establish a relationship between the cells so that even if the number in A1 changes, the relationship will remain and A3 will continue to give you 0.1 times the content of A1.

Doing Math

Like many programs, Symphony uses the asterisk for a multiplication sign. The instruction for calculating the tax in this case will be entered as

.1*A1

Although the instruction contains a letter as well as numbers, Symphony considers the decimal point to be a *value indicator* and so reads what follows it as a value. Type **.1*A1** and press (ENTER). You will immediately see the tax figure calculated:

```
A3: 0.1*A1                                                    SHEET
┌──────A──────────B──────────C──────────D──────────E──────────F──────────G──────────H──────┐
1        8095 BASE
2         567 PREP
3       809.5 TAX
4             TOTAL
5
```

If you look at the cell address indicator in the first line of the screen, you can see that Symphony is not concerned about the actual number in cell A3. It simply records the formula or relationship between the two cells. This will remain the same, whatever number is in cell A1. Suppose that the base price goes up. Press (HOME) to go up to the 8095 in cell A1. Change it by typing **8900**, the new price, and press (ENTER). Symphony instantly updates cell A3. If you move your cell indicator down to cell A3 and look at the cell identifier, you will see that the cell contents have not changed; they are still the same formula you entered before.

Now you want to calculate a total price for the car, including base, prep, and tax. To do this you will need to add several cells together.

1. Place the cell pointer in the cell that is to contain the answer—in this case, cell A4.

2. Now you will type an instruction that tells Symphony that this cell will contain what you get when you add together cells A1, A2, and A3. You might think that you could type A1+A2+A3, and this is almost correct. However, instructions involving only cell references need special treatment; otherwise, Symphony will read the first letter of the entry ("A") as a label. To make sure that Symphony knows that what you are typing is a value, type a plus sign first (+) and then the cell reference. In this case, type **+A1+A2+A3** and press (ENTER).

The results of this exercise are shown here:

```
A4: +A1+A2+A3                                                    SHEET
┌──────A──────B──────C──────D──────E──────F──────G──────H──────┐
1      8900 BASE
2       567 PREP
3       890 TAX
4     10357 TOTAL
5
```

Just as the other formula is updated automatically when you change the base price, so is this new one. Enter **9100** in A1, and you will see the answer change immediately.

Using Functions

If you decided to take out a loan to finance the full price of this car, you might want to calculate how big a monthly payment you would have to make. A loan payment calculation involves three pieces of information: the amount to be borrowed, or principal; the rate of interest to be charged; and the length or term of the loan. Labels for these three items will be typed into column D, starting in D1.

1. Move the cell pointer to D1.

2. Type four labels, using the (DOWN ARROW) key to enter them: **PRINCIPAL**, **INTEREST**, **TERM**, and **PAYMENT**.

3. Now move back up to cell E1, where you will enter the principal amount. Your screen should look like this:

```
D5:                                                                   SHEET
 ┌────────A────────B────────C────────D────────E────────F────────G────────H──────┐
 1       9100 BASE                  PRINCIPAL
 2        567 PREP                  INTEREST
 3        910 TAX                   TERM
 4      10577 TOTAL                 PAYMENT
 5
```

4. The amount that you want to borrow is the total price from cell A4. Instead of typing this number again, simply type **+A4** and press (ENTER). This establishes a relationship between these two cells so that whatever is in cell A4 is also in cell E1.

5. Move the cell pointer to E2. Here you want to enter the rate of interest you will pay. This needs to be expressed as a rate per period of the loan. (Supposing you are going to make monthly payments, you need to enter the amount of interest you will pay in one month, so that if the bank is charging 12% per annum you will enter 0.01, or 1%, per month). To do this, you type **1%** and press (DOWN ARROW) to go to cell E3. Note that Symphony entered 1% as .01.

6. In E3, type the term, the number of months for the loan (say, **36**), and press (DOWN ARROW). In E4, a formula for the payment will be entered.

You do not need to know the details of the actual payment calculation, because Symphony knows exactly how to calculate a loan payment if it is given the principal, interest, and term. Symphony does this with a special function built into the program. In fact, there are dozens of built-in functions covering most common calculations. The name of each of these functions is preceded by the @ sign (shifted number 2 on the keyboard). This is a special code that helps Symphony distinguish functions from other entries.

This gives rise to the term "at-functions" (@functions) for the built-in formulas that use this code.

1. With the cell pointer in E4, type the @ sign followed by **PMT**, the name of the payment function.

2. Now type an opening parenthesis. You need to supply the @PMT function with arguments: the amounts for principal, interest, and term of the loan. This information is presented to the function within parentheses.

3. The amounts you need in this example are in cells E1, E2, and E3, so after the opening parenthesis type **E1,E2,E3)** and press (**ENTER**). This produces the monthly payment, as shown here:

```
E4: @PMT(E1,E2,E3)                                                    SHEET
      A          B          C          D          E          F          G          H
1     9100 BASE                        PRINCIPAL    10577
2      567 PREP                        INTEREST      0.01
3      910 TAX                         TERM            36
4    10577 TOTAL                       PAYMENT   351.3077
5
```

To give you an idea of how flexible a spreadsheet is, you can now try more changes to the assumptions that produce the answer in E4. For example, if you were considering a more expensive model, you could type the new price in A1 and immediately see the new payment in E4. To make payments less expensive each month, type in a longer term, such as 48 months, into E2.

Another aspect to the Symphony spreadsheet's flexibility is the ability to alter the appearance of numbers without affecting the work that they do. This allows you to improve the appearance of your spreadsheet designs. To perform this operation you will use Symphony's menu system.

THE ENVIRONMENT-SPECIFIC MENU SYSTEM

The manipulation of facts and figures in cells is only part of the power of Symphony. As you have begun to discover when saving files and leaving Symphony, there is a whole range of commands, arranged in a series of menus and submenus, that can be accessed by using the menu system that appears at the top of the screen. So far you have explored the TYPE menu and the SERVICES menu. The latter provides basic commands, ones that are the same no matter which Symphony environment you are using. There is another menu that changes according to the environment you are using. For example, the choices when you access this menu from the DOC environment are different than when you access it from the SHEET environment.

The (F10) MENU Key

The environment-specific menu appears when you press (F10), known as the MENU key. There is an alternative MENU key, the slash beneath the question mark on your keyboard (/), for 1-2-3 users accustomed to using this key. Try pressing (F10) now. The choices are as follows:

Copy Move Erase Insert Delete Width Format Range Graph Query Settings

Note that the word "MENU" now appears in the mode indicator in the upper right of the screen to let you know you are using a menu. As you have already seen, Symphony uses the classic two-line menu system, where one line shows the current choices and the other gives an explanation of what each of the items on the first row does. For example, above Copy is the explanation "Copy range of cells."

Using the SHEET Menu

When you want to alter the appearance, or *format,* of numbers within your worksheet, you use a SHEET-specific menu item called Format. For example, you can change the amounts in column A so that they have dollar signs as well as commas for thousands separators.

1. Press (ESC) until you are out of the menu system, and then press (HOME) to move the cell pointer to A1. Now press (F10) to get the SHEET-specific menu.
2. Press (RIGHT ARROW) until Format is highlighted. If you go too far to the right, you can press (LEFT ARROW), or keep pressing (RIGHT ARROW).
3. With Format highlighted, the top line of the screen tells you that this command is used to set the numeric display format for a range of cells.
4. Now press (ENTER). A new set of choices will appear. This "highlight and (ENTER)" method of menu navigation is sometimes called "point and shoot." One benefit of this method is that you can look before you shoot. When you highlight an item on the second line of the screen, you can see an explanation of that item on the first line.
5. Now select the first option on the Format menu, Currency. You can do this by gently pressing (ENTER).
6. Symphony will ask you how many decimal places you want. Type **0** (zero) and press (ENTER).
7. You will now be prompted with "Range to format." This is asking you which group of cells you want the command to

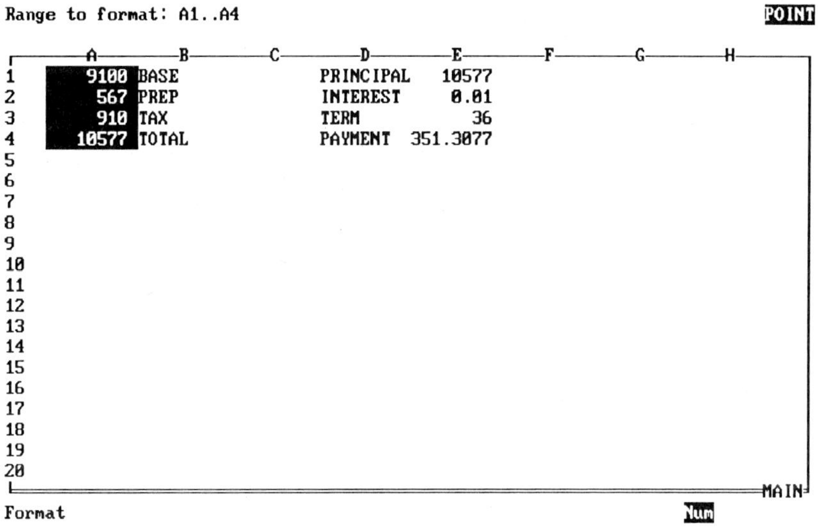

FIGURE 1-18 Formatting cells

affect. If you only wanted to alter cell A1, you would press (ENTER). Cell A1 is referred to as the range A1..A1. To include the other cells in column A, you can press (END) followed by (DOWN ARROW). This will include cells from A1 down to A4, known as the range A1..A4, as shown in Figure 1-18. Note that the cells to be formatted are highlighted, and the bottom left of the screen reminds you which command is in use.

8. With A1 through A4 highlighted, press (ENTER). You will be returned to SHEET mode.

The result of these steps will be numbers that look more like dollar amounts:

```
A1: (C0) 9100                                                    SHEET

 ------A---------B--------C--------D---------E--------F--------G--------H-----
1      $9,100 BASE                PRINCIPAL    10577
2        $567 PREP                INTEREST      0.01
3        $910 TAX                 TERM            36
4     $10,577 TOTAL               PAYMENT   351.3077
5
6
7
8
9
```

However, the numbers themselves have not changed—only their appearance. You can see this if you look in the cell address indicator. The contents of cell A1 are still a simple number. However, there is a notation that lets you know the cell is formatted: (C0). This stands for Currency format, zero decimal places.

Other Menu Strategies

As an alternative to the point-and-shoot approach to using menus, you can type the first letter of the menu item you want. For example, to select Format you type **F**. The advantage of this method is fewer keystrokes for those who know their way around the keyboard. Both methods of menu access have a built-in safety key, (ESC). For example, suppose you select Format and then you change your mind. Just press (ESC) once, and you will be back to the main menu. Press (ESC) again, and you will put away the menu and return to SHEET mode. If you get several levels into the menu system, you can get out by repeatedly pressing (ESC) or by pressing (CTRL-BREAK). The (BREAK) key is sometimes on the (SCROLL LOCK) key. It "breaks you out" of the menu system, returning you to the SHEET mode where you are ready to enter new information.

Two other keys that are handy in the menu system are (HOME) and (END), which take you to the first and last menu items, respectively. Also, the HELP key, (F1), will display helpful information about the menu item you are using.

CONCLUSION

To complete the current session and close this chapter, you will probably want to save the worksheet in its current form. To do this you press (F9) for the SERVICES menu, and then type **F** for File and **S** for Save. You will see the current filename already entered for you. At this point you can press (ENTER), and type **Y** for Yes to store the new version of the file over the old one. Otherwise, you can use a new name and press (ENTER) to keep both the old and new versions of the file.

You are now conversant with Symphony's menu and file storage system, which is used the same way in all environments. You have seen how to enter and manipulate numbers and text in the SHEET environment. In the next chapter you will explore the SHEET environment in greater detail before moving on to the DOC environment.

2

THE SYMPHONY SPREADSHEET

This chapter reviews the basic commands of Symphony's SHEET mode and shows you how to use it for building a typical spreadsheet model. A *model* is any set of figures arranged to describe a situation, such as the performance of a company or the state of your checking account. As you work through this chapter, you may need to save work and come back to it later. Use the commands described in the last chapter to accomplish this. Remember that the environment-specific menu in Symphony is accessed with the MENU key, (F10). The general menu of nonspecific commands is accessed with the SERVICES key, (F9).

DATA ENTRY

In the last chapter you saw that there are two types of data in a Symphony worksheet: values and labels. There are also two methods of entering data into the spreadsheet, whether you are entering values or labels. You can either type your entry and press (ENTER), which puts the data into the cell and leaves that cell highlighted, or you can type your entry and press a cursor movement key, which enters the data and moves you in the direction of the key you pressed. In both cases, you put the cell pointer on the cell, you want to receive the data before you begin typing. Most of the labels and numbers in Figure 2-1 were entered by pointing to the first row of the column, typing the first entry, pressing (DOWN ARROW), typing the next entry, pressing (DOWN ARROW), and so on.

The data in Figure 2-1 will be used as the basis of the examples that follow in this chapter, so you might want to try entering it into a fresh worksheet now as practice. If you have any problems entering the data, see the following sections on editing and altering entries.

1. Make sure that you have saved any previous work by using the SERVICES File Save command, as described in Chapter 1.

2. Create a fresh worksheet with the SERVICES New command, answering Yes to the "Erase all data" prompt.

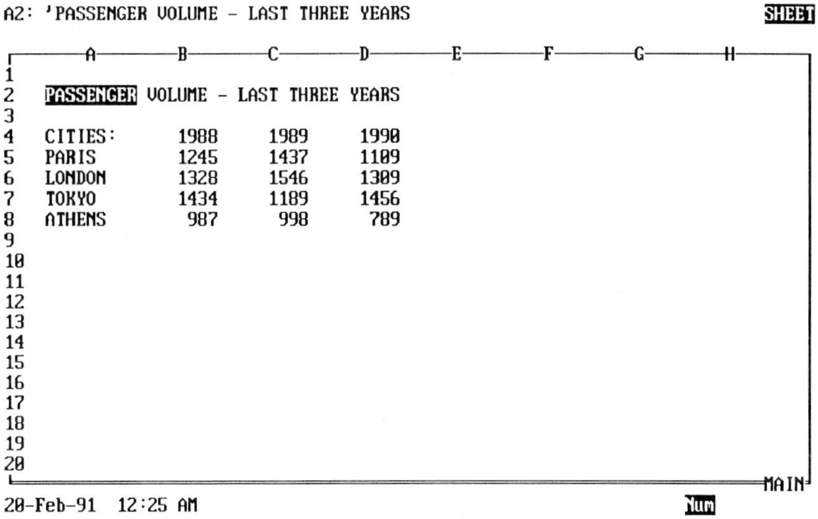

FIGURE 2-1 Sample data

3. Move the cell pointer down to cell A2 and type **PASSENGER VOLUME - LAST THREE YEARS**. Then you press (DOWN ARROW) twice. Note that although the label you have just entered is much longer than the nine-character width of the column, Symphony can display it by borrowing space from the adjoining columns.

4. In cell A4, enter the label **CITIES:** using the (DOWN ARROW) key. Proceed to enter the city names in column A.

5. Now move the cell pointer to B4 and enter the number **1988,** proceeding down the column to enter the rest of the numbers.

6. Finish entering the years and passenger numbers in columns C and D.

7. Use the SERVICES File Save command to store the worksheet on disk as PVF01.WR1.

Changes Before Entering

At times, you will need to change or cancel an entry as you type it. One common situation in which this occurs is when you start typing a piece of new data and realize that your cell pointer is pointing to the wrong cell, perhaps one that already has data in it. The data that you have typed first appears on the input line, the second line of the control panel at the top of the screen. Pressing (ENTER) or an arrow key at this point will place the data from the input line into the wrong cell. If there is already data in the cell, the new data will replace the old, and you will have to re-enter the old data. If the cell is empty but is the wrong cell for the new data, you will have to remove the incorrect entry.

Fortunately, Symphony lets you change your mind before you enter what is on the input line. If you press (ESC), whatever you had begun to type is removed from the input line and you are back in READY mode. Now you can move the cell pointer to the correct location.

If you start typing a new piece of data in the right place but make an error or a spelling mistake, use the (BACKSPACE) key to back the cursor over the data in the input line until you have erased the error, and then resume typing. Remember, you should *not* press the (LEFT ARROW) key to go back and correct mistakes while typing a new entry; doing so will enter the data into the cell. There is one exception to this. If you press (F2), the EDIT key, while entering a new piece of data, you will be placed in EDIT mode and will be able to use the edit keys described in a moment to change what you are typing. When in EDIT mode you use (ENTER) to place the entry into the cell.

Cell Editing

After you have entered data, you can see that it appears in the input line whenever the cell is selected. You can change the contents of a cell in several ways. The method you use will depend on the type of change you need to make. The following paragraphs explain the different ways of editing, using Figure 2-1 as an example.

RE-ENTRY When you re-enter data into a cell, the contents of the cell are changed. The simplest method of re-entry is to type the new data over the old, completely replacing it. For example, if you place the cell pointer on the word "LONDON," type **ROME**, and press (ENTER), the entire word "LONDON" will disappear, not just the first four letters.

THE EDIT KEY If you want to change "LONDON" to "LONDON - HEATHROW," you can avoid retyping the entire entry by using (F2), the EDIT key. When you place the cell pointer on a cell and press (F2), the contents of the cell are returned to the edit line and the mode indicator displays "EDIT." The status line at the top of the screen changes to show you what cell you are editing and what was in the cell before it was entered. With the cell contents back on the input line, you can now add to the cell contents and place the revised entry back in the worksheet by pressing (ENTER).

When you are in EDIT mode, several keys perform differently. Pressing (HOME) moves the cursor to the left side of the entry. Pressing (END) places the cursor back on the right side. You can also move around the contents of the cell with the (LEFT ARROW) and (RIGHT ARROW) keys. Thus, if you have mistakenly entered **LUNDON- EATHROW**, you could press (F2) to edit the cell, press the (LEFT ARROW) key until your cursor is under the erroneous "U," and press the (DEL) key to remove it, as in the following:

```
LUNDON-EATHROW
LNDON - EATHROW
```

You then type the letter **O** to insert it automatically into the text to the left of the cursor.

LONDON - EATHROW

You would then move to the right with the (RIGHT ARROW) key to put the cursor under the "E." There you would type an **H** to complete the editing. As soon as editing is completed you can press (ENTER), regardless of where your cursor is within the data, and the revised text will be placed back into the cell from the input line.

Remember that whenever you are editing a cell in EDIT mode, you are in what is called INSERT mode, in which what you type is inserted into the text instead of replacing what was there before. Table 2-1 lists the keys that can be used in EDIT mode.

CELL DELETE There will be times when you will want to erase the entire contents of a cell. The correct way to clear out a cell is to delete the contents of the cell. Unfortunately there is no "Cell Delete" key. However, you can easily use a MENU command, Erase, to clear a cell. Simply put the cell pointer in the cell you want to erase and press (F10), type **E**, and then press (ENTER). This deletes the contents of the current cell. If you want to erase a whole group of cells, you can extend the range of cells to be affected before pressing (ENTER). Simply use the arrow keys to extend the range, as described later in the chapter.

You may discover another method of erasing a cell. You place the cell pointer on the cell you want to delete and press the (SPACEBAR) and (ENTER). With this method it appears that the cell has been emptied. However, if you look in the cell identifier, you see the apostrophe, which begins a label. You have replaced what was in the cell with a blank label. This method of cell deleting is a bad habit to get into, since the cell is not really emptied. It can also affect some calculations that include those cells. Blank cells are hard to find, since there is nothing to see in them unless you first place the cell pointer on one and observe the cell identifier. Consequently, this method of erasing cells should be avoided.

Key	Action
LEFT ARROW	Moves edit cursor one character left on edit line
RIGHT ARROW	Moves edit cursor one character right on edit line
HOME	Places edit cursor under first character of the entry
END	Moves edit cursor to the right of the last character of the entry
CTRL-RIGHT ARROW	Moves edit cursor five characters to the right
CTRL-LEFT ARROW	Moves edit cursor five characters to the left
DEL	Deletes character at cursor
BACKSPACE	Deletes character to left of cursor
ESC	Cancels editing, returns to READY mode
ENTER	Enters contents
DOWN ARROW	Enters contents and moves cell pointer down one cell
UP ARROW	Enters contents and moves cell pointer up one cell
PGDN	Enters contents and moves cell pointer down one screen
PGUP	Enters contents and moves cell pointer up one screen
Math sign	Adds a math sign to the end of a formula; you can use the cursor movement keys for point method of formula writing
EDIT (F2)	Switches back to VALUE or LABEL mode (use after typing a math sign in the middle of a formula to enable VALUE mode of formula writing)
CALC (F8)	Turns an edited formula into result (press ESC before entering to get the formula back)
CTRL-ESC	Clears entire entry from edit line
CTRL-[	Same as CTRL-ESC

TABLE 2-1 Keys That Can Be Used in the EDIT Mode

EDIT/CALC There may be times when what you want to enter into a cell is the result of a formula. Suppose you are working on a projection of your own revenue and expenses for the year. You know you earn $3655 per month, but you want to enter this as an annual figure. You type **12*3655** and press ENTER. When you enter a formula like this, what you see in the worksheet is the value that results from the formula—in this case, 43860. However, what

Symphony records is the formula itself, and this is displayed in the cell address indicator when you highlight the cell that contains the formula. Normally, the formula remains dynamic. This means that if the formula refers to other cells in the worksheet, the value displayed will change when the values in those other cells change.

At times you will want to "freeze" the results of a formula and convert the formula to the value it created. One way to do this is to edit the cell. When you press (F2) to edit a cell that contains a formula, the formula is placed on the edit line. You press (F8) (the CALC key) to convert the formula to its result. You then press (ENTER) to place the value in the worksheet and replace the formula, or (ESC) to get the formula back. Later in this chapter you will learn how to convert whole ranges of formula cells into values, using the MENU Range Values command.

Automatic Editing

If you type data that Symphony cannot read, pressing (ENTER) to place the data in a cell will cause a beep and automatically place you in EDIT mode. Symphony will try to point out your error. It does this by placing the cursor at the first mistake it reads in what you have tried to enter. For example, Symphony does not accept numbers that contain certain pieces of punctuation. If you type **123 Main Street** and press (ENTER), Symphony rejects the entry with a beep and places you in EDIT mode with the edit cursor under the first space. This is because an entry beginning with 123 appears at first to be a value, but is actually a label. To solve this particular problem, you press (HOME) to move the edit cursor to the front of the entry and type an apostrophe to make the entry a label.

VALUES

You have already seen that Symphony distinguishes between values and labels by means of the first character of a new cell entry.

Anything that begins with one of the following characters is treated as a value:

0 through 9 . + - (@ # $

These items are called *value indicators*. If you do not begin an entry with one of these characters, Symphony will treat the entry as a label. Occasionally, you will need to enter a piece of data that looks like a number but is not. This problem is dealt with later in the section called "Wrong Numbers."

Cell References

Whenever you enter formulas involving both numbers and cells, as in 1.1*A1, the number can be typed first. This lets Symphony know that what follows is a value. When formulas consist of cell references only, as in A3+A4, you obviously cannot do this; you must add a value indicator at the beginning of the entry. In the last chapter you saw that this can be a plus sign, as in +A3+A4. The plus sign does not alter the value of the cell reference it precedes. You can also use a parenthesis or round bracket to begin a value entry, as in (A3+A4).

Parentheses are excellent value indicators when you need to control the order of calculation, as in (A2+A3)*(B2+B3). However, for every opening parenthesis there *must* be a closing parenthesis. You may find it easier to use the single + for simple formulas. (The + on the numeric keypad does not require that you use the SHIFT key).

Big Numbers

You will occasionally need to enter a large number into a Symphony worksheet. Entering the number **123456789** results in "1.2E+08" being displayed in the worksheet unless you have specially formatted the cell or altered the column width. Symphony cannot fit the number into the cell and so converts it to scientific or exponential notation (1.2E+08 stands for 1.2 times 10 to the power of 8). The default column width accommodates nine characters, but only eight digits. This is because a gap, one character wide, is maintained between numbers in adjacent columns in order to stop large numbers from running into each other. The conversion of oversize numbers into scientific notation occurs under the General display format, the one that Symphony uses by default.

If you check the top status area, you can see that the number 123456789 is still stored in the cell by Symphony. Widening the column to 10 characters will restore the number to its normal appearance. If you work with numbers in the millions and billions, you can set Scientific as the default format, as described later in this chapter, and see all of your numbers in the 1.0E+01 style. Instead of converting a number that is too big for a cell into exponential notation, other formats, such as Currency, show a cell full of asterisks, indicating that the cell needs to be widened.

Wrong Numbers

Sometimes you need to work with numbers that are not values. For example, if you were typing a list of phone numbers into the spreadsheet and you typed **555-1212** and pressed (ENTER), you would get -657 in the cell. This occurs because Symphony reads the 5 as meaning a value is coming and performs math on the entry, reading it as 555 minus 1212. To overcome this problem you must precede a wrong number with one of the label indicators described in the next section. For example, the apostrophe is used to indicate a label aligned on the left of the cell. Thus, **'555-1212** will enter the phone number as a left-justified label. Also, preceding a number with a space makes it a label and can be handy.

Another common example of a wrong number is a street address—for example, 123 Main Street. In this case, if you type **123 Main Street** without a label indicator in front of it, Symphony will give you an error message because it expects a value: you began with the value 1. This can also occur when you type a formula or a number incorrectly; for example, if you omit a closing parenthesis or type directly after a number. Remember that in EDIT mode you use **(ENTER)** after you have corrected the data to put it back into the cell. If you want to retype the entire entry, press **(ESC)** to leave EDIT mode and return to READY mode.

LABELS

Although the Symphony worksheet is generally thought of as a number-crunching tool, the role played by labels is very important. Labels tell you and anyone else using the worksheets what the numbers mean. You should never fall into the trap of entering numbers and formulas without first placing appropriate labels to indicate what the numbers represent.

Symphony creates a label whenever a new cell entry begins with one of the following *label indicators:*

A through Z   All punctuation characters except . + - (@ # $

In addition to these characters, a space at the beginning of an entry also tells Symphony that you are typing a label.

Lining Up Labels

You have seen that by default Symphony aligns labels on the left of the column and puts an apostrophe in front of the text to remind you that this is a label. You can tell Symphony to center a label in the column by starting the label with the caret sign (^), the symbol on the 6 key. A label is placed flush-right by preceding it with the double quotation mark ("). This is referred to as *label alignment.* You can see the three possibilities shown here:

```
   ------A--------B--------C--------D--------E--------F--------G--------H-----
1
2         | Paris      | Left-aligned
3         |   Paris    | Center-aligned
4         |     Paris  | Right-aligned (note the one character gap)
5         |            |
```

There are several limitations in Symphony when it comes to aligning a label in a column. The width of the label in relation to the column is important. A nine-character label in a nine-character-wide column will look the same, regardless of alignment. The one-character gap between columns, required to prevent entries from running into each other, means that right-aligned labels are not flush with the right edge of the column. Also, Symphony uses a monospaced font; that is, all of the characters are displayed with the same amount of space for each one. On the screen, the "I" in "PARIS" takes up as much space as the "Y" in "TOKYO." This is different from proportional spacing, which is used in this book, for example. The use of a monospaced font means that Symphony sometimes presents centering that looks uneven.

The label alignment characters can be activated in several ways. You can tell Symphony to make all labels either right-aligned, left-aligned, or centered by default. This is described later in "Worksheet Settings." To vary individual labels from the default label alignment setting, simply type the desired prefix preceding the text of the label. For example, if your default is left alignment, you can create a centered label as an exception by preceding it with the ^ symbol. To right-justify an individual label, type the double quote before the label text.

To make a group of cells vary from the default alignment, you use the MENU Range Label-Alignment command. You can try this by right-aligning the city names in Figure 2-1:

1. Place the cell pointer in A5, the first label in the group you want to alter.

2. Press MENU and choose Range.

```
A5: "PARIS                                                             SHEET

   ------A--------B--------C--------D--------E--------F--------G--------H---
1
2   PASSENGER VOLUME - LAST THREE YEARS
3
4   CITIES:        1988     1989     1990
5       PARIS      1245     1437     1109
6      LONDON      1328     1546     1309
7       TOKYO      1434     1189     1456
8      ATHENS       987      998      789
9
10
```

FIGURE 2-2 Effect of right-aligning labels

3. Select Label-Alignment, and you will see the choices of Left, Center, and Right. Choose Right.
4. You will be prompted to specify the range of labels that you want to affect. Press (DOWN ARROW) three times to include cells A5 through A8.
5. Having selected the cells you want to affect, press (ENTER) to confirm the change.

The results can be seen in Figure 2-2. Note that the apostrophe has now been changed to a quote (") in front of each city name. See the section on ranges later in this chapter for more on how to specify a range of cells.

Long Labels

Symphony labels can contain as many as 240 characters, including the label prefix. You seldom need them this long, but you need to know how Symphony acts on labels wider than one column. In Chapter 3, you will see that the DOC environment wraps text into

```
A4: 'DESTINATION:                                                        SHEET

 ┌──────A────────B─────────C─────────D─────────E─────────F─────────G─────────H─────┐
 1
 2   PASSENGER VOLUME - LAST THREE YEARS
 3
 4   DESTINATI    1988      1989      1990
 5       PARIS    1245      1437      1109
 6     LONDON     1328      1546      1309
 7      TOKYO     1434      1189      1456
 8     ATHENS      987       998       789
 9
10
```

FIGURE 2-3 Effect of a long label

a rectangular area on the spreadsheet to let you compose text for letters, memos, and notations on spreadsheet models. For now, consider the city names in column A of Figure 2-2. They all fit neatly into a column that has the default column width of nine characters. Suppose you decide to change the word "CITIES" to "DESTINATION." You do this by moving the cell pointer to cell A4, typing **DESTINATION:**, and then pressing (ENTER). The result is shown in Figure 2-3.

As a label like this is being entered, Symphony gives no indication that it will exceed the nine-character width of the cell. However, when you press (ENTER) to put this label into the cell, you see that it does exceed the cell width. The label is not completely legible and will not print properly when you print the worksheet. However, looking at the status area at the top of the screen, you can see that the full title is recognized as the contents of cell A4.

When there is nothing in the cells to the right, long labels simply borrow space from the adjacent cells to display their contents, as is the case with the title in A2. As you can see from this illustration, cell B2 contains nothing:

```
B2:                                                              SHEET
┌──────A──────B──────C──────D──────E──────F──────G──────H──────┐
1
2  PASSENGER VOLUME - LAST THREE YEARS
3
```

The contents of cell A2 simply flow over into that display area. The problem arises when you want to enter a long label to the left of an occupied cell, as in Figure 2-3. The solution to this problem is either to abbreviate the label (for example, change it back to CITIES:) or to make the column wider. You will usually choose to widen the column with column commands. In this case,

1. Place the cell pointer in any cell of column A.
2. Press MENU and select Width and then Set. You will be prompted for the column width and told the current setting (9).
3. You can either type the number of desired characters or use the (RIGHT ARROW) key to widen the column. Each time you press (RIGHT ARROW), the column increases one character in width and you can see the effect immediately. (You can use the (LEFT ARROW) key to narrow columns).
4. Continue pressing (RIGHT ARROW) until the whole of the label in A4 is visible.
5. Press (ENTER) to confirm the new setting. The effect can be seen in Figure 2-4.

There may be times when you will choose to shorten the label instead of widening the column, particularly if you are trying to keep the worksheet small or if you want the entries in a column to be more consistent in width. Column-width settings for the entire worksheet are examined later in the chapter.

FORMULAS

Formulas are where much of the power of a spreadsheet lies. When you are simply adding cells together or calculating the internal rate of return on an investment, the ability to establish a relationship between cells gives you tremendous number-crunching ability. Although the word "formula" may remind many people of algebra and science classes, in the context of Symphony the term simply means an instruction written in a form that Symphony understands. As you have seen, the way you give Symphony instructions can be as straightforward as "add cell A1 and cell A2." In fact, even complex instructions follow a consistent arrangement, or syntax. As you learn to manipulate formulas, you will want to use Symphony's built-in formulas, called functions, for more complex calculations. Symphony offers over one hundred functions.

Simple Addition

As a basic example of formulas, consider the row of years required in the table of volume numbers in Figure 2-4. They appear as

1988 1989 1990

```
A4: 'DESTINATION:                                                        SHEET
 ---------A---------B---------C---------D---------E---------F---------G---------H---
1
2   PASSENGER VOLUME - LAST THREE YEARS
3
4   DESTINATION:      1988      1989      1990
5          PARIS      1245      1437      1109
6         LONDON      1328      1546      1309
7          TOKYO      1434      1189      1456
8         ATHENS       987       998       789
9
10
```

FIGURE 2-4 Column A set 12 characters wide

However, these numbers can be created with a simple formula. If 1988 is in cell B4, then C4 can be 1+B4 and cell D4 can be 1+C4. Although the numbers appear as years, the cells contain the following:

```
1988   1+B4   1+C4
```

When the years are entered this way, you only need to type a new year over the 1988 entry, and all the other years will adjust accordingly. For example, changing B4 to **1990** would produce the following:

```
1990   1991   1992
```

At this point you should refrain from altering your sample worksheet to reflect these formulas because later in the chapter, in the section on copying, you will learn how to copy formulas such as the ones used here to quickly create a series of related values.

Entering Formulas

So far, you have created formulas by looking at the worksheet, deciding which cells are involved, and then typing their addresses. For example, you know that the total of the four items in column B of Figure 2-4 is going to be +B5+B6+B7+B8. However, if you are not a good typist, you might want to try the pointing method of entering formulas. This method begins with the plus sign or a value, if there is one in the formula. Then, when Symphony is in VALUE mode, you use the arrow keys to highlight the first number you want in the formula. For example, to build a total figure in cell B9, you would follow these steps:

1. Move the cell pointer to B9.

2. Type + and then press (UP ARROW) four times. You can see that Symphony types the cell address for you (+B5), as shown here:

```
B5: 1245                                                              POINT
+B5
┌──────A──────────B──────────C──────────D──────────E──────────F──────────G──────────H──┐
1
2   PASSENGER VOLUME - LAST THREE YEARS
3
4   DESTINATION:     1988       1989       1990
5          PARIS     1245       1437       1109
```

3. Now type the next math sign, another plus sign, and the cell pointer moves back down to the cell in which you are building the formula (B9).

4. You can now point to the next cell that needs to go into the formula (B6), and it too is added on the input line at the top of the screen as you build the formula. The basic procedure is math sign, point, math sign, point.

5. Type another math sign—plus (+), in this case—and the cell pointer returns to B9. Point to B7, and type + again.

6. Point to B8, and the formula now is +B5+B6+B7+B8, as shown in Figure 2-5.

You can now press (ENTER) to place the formula in the cell. The result is 4994. This method is very useful when you have lots of cells scattered throughout the spreadsheet and you cannot remember where a particular number is. Just remember that you do not press (ENTER) until the formula is complete.

Functions and Ranges

There is another method of adding the four items in cells B5 through B8 one at a time. The alternative is to consider these cells as part of a group, a block or range of cells, and then apply a

```
B9: @SUM(B5..B8)                                                SHEET
   ------A---------B---------C---------D---------E---------F---------G---------H----
1
2   PASSENGER VOLUME - LAST THREE YEARS
3
4   DESTINATION:     1988      1989      1990
5          PARIS     1245      1437      1109
6         LONDON     1328      1546      1309
7          TOKYO     1434      1189      1456
8         ATHENS      987       998       789
9                    4994
10
```

FIGURE 2-7 Completed formula

@SUM(B5..B8), adding an extra period to make it easier to see. You never need to type the second period.

Formula Formats

Simple Symphony formulas combine values, such as numbers or cells containing numbers, with operators, such as the division sign or the plus sign. There are numerous formulas at work in the worksheet shown in Figure 2-8, where calculations relative to a new house are being carried out. You could diagram the formula in cell H7 of Figure 2-8 like this:

```
H7 = H5          *           H6
       \          \           \
       Value      Operator    Value
```

Symphony formulas are algebraic in format. Thus, you can use other formulas within a formula separated, or delimited, by pairs of parentheses, as in the following:

E13 = ((E6*E7)+(E9*E10))*2

```
B6: @IF(0.1*B5>20000,20000,0.1*B5)                                    SHEET

   ------A-----------B------C------D---------E------F------G---------H------
1   Calculation Worksheet - 101 Symphony Street
2
3   Financing:                       Dimensions:          Lot Size:
4
5   Purchase Price      245,500      Room A               Width          100
6   Down Payment         20,000        Wide         20    Length         150
7   Amount to borrow    225,500        Long         33    Area        15,000
8   Interest (A.P.R.)    14.50%      Room B
9   Years for loan           30        Wide         15
10  Payments per year        12        Long         21
11  Payment               2,761
12  Total payments      994,095      Total Floor Space:
13                                   2 Floors     1,950
14                                                        Permit Fees
15                                                        State     County
16                                           Plumbing      56.00     78.00
17                                           Electrical    43.50      5.00
18                                           Construction 203.00    450.00
19
20                                                        Total     835.50
   ----------------------------------------------------------------------MAIN
20-Feb-91  04:50 PM                                                  Num
```

FIGURE 2-8 Sample calculations

This formula, used in E13 of Figure 2-8, means that Symphony should multiply E6 by E7 and add that to the product of E9 multiplied by E10, and then double the answer. The formula calculates the total floor area of a two-story house with two rooms on each floor whose width and length were recorded in cells E6 through E10.

You can use functions to ask Symphony to make decisions about the data to be calculated. When you do this, several formula elements are required, as in this formula:

B6 = @IF(0.1*B5>20000,20000,0.1*B5)

This formula uses the @IF function to tell Symphony that the down payment in B6 should be 10% of the purchase price in B5, unless the product of those two values comes to more than 20,000, in which case B6 should be 20,000. This formula is used to calculate

G17: (P2) @IF(@SUM(B17..F17)=@SUM(G5..G15),@SUM(B17..F17),@ERR) SHEET

	A	B	C	D	E	F	G
1							
2		Monday	Tuesday	Wednesday	Thursday	Friday	Totals
3	------------	------------	------------	------------	------------	------------	------------
4	Meals						
5	B'fast	3.45	0.00	3.89	4.76	5.98	18.08
6	Lunch	5.00	8.95	6.74	5.78	18.96	45.43
7	Dinner	0.00	23.87	5.89	13.45	0.00	43.21
8	Travel						
9	Air	0.00	143.89	0.00	0.00	148.00	291.89
10	Mileage	0.00	0.00	0.00	0.00	3.50	3.50
11	Parking	0.00	0.00	12.00	12.00	12.00	36.00
12	Taxi	0.00	0.00	0.00	0.00	0.00	0.00
13	Miscellaneous						
14	Supplies	34.00	0.00	6.00	0.00	3.00	43.00
15	Other	0.00	0.00	0.00	23.87	0.00	23.87
16	============	============	============	============	============	============	============
17		50.45	176.71	34.52	59.86	191.44	512.98
18							
19			Total =	512.98			
20							

MAIN

20-Feb-91 03:41 PM Num

FIGURE 2-9 Expense report

the down payment, since the buyer has a limit of $20,000 to use for this payment.

An expense report that breaks down expenses for each week by type, like the one in Figure 2-9, might contain the formula

G17 = @IF(@SUM(B17..F17)=
@SUM(G5..G15),
@SUM(B17..F17),@ERR)

This formula says that G17 will have one of two possible answers, depending on a decision made by the @IF function. If the sum of the range of cells B17..E17 is equal to the sum of the range of cells G5..G15, Symphony should insert that sum; otherwise, Symphony should provide an error message, created with the special function @ERR.

You will notice that Symphony capitalizes all cell references and function names that you enter. It does not matter if you enter these as uppercase or lowercase letters; Symphony will store and display them in uppercase. Also, Symphony will add a leading 0 to a decimal value that you enter, so that **.125** entered in a formula is displayed in the cell contents as 0.125.

Acceptable Values

The values in a Symphony formula can be cells containing values, as in +H5*H6. They can be a range of cells containing values, either stated as coordinates, as in +G16..G18+H16..H18, or described by range names, discussed in the next chapter. Values in Symphony formulas can also be results returned by functions like @PMT, which was used in Chapter 1 to calculate a car loan payment. The same function is used in Figure 2-8 to calculate a mortgage payment in cell B11. In that figure you see that you can calculate the total payments to be made on a 30-year loan if you ask Symphony to multiply the payment amount by the number of payments, as in

+B11*B10*B9

Values in Symphony formulas can also be constants. A *constant* is a number, date, or piece of text that you enter directly, such as the 1 in the formula 1+B3. Constants are used in formulas for projections; for example, to figure the projected sales the formula might be B4*1.1, where 1.1 is a constant. A constant is also used in calculations like finding the circumference of a circle. In the formula 2*@PI*Radius, the number 2 is a constant.

Operators and Priorities

There are many different operators that can be used in Symphony formulas. There are the standard arithmetic operators: addition (+),

Operator	Prec	Meaning
^	7	Exponentiation
+	6	Unary plus
–	6	Unary minus
*	5	Multiplication
/	5	Division
+	4	Addition
–	4	Subtraction
<	3	Less than
<=	3	Less than or equal
>=	3	Greater than or equal
>	3	Greater than
=	3	Equal to
< >	3	Not equal to
#NOT#	2	Logical NOT
#OR#	1	Logical inclusive OR
#AND#	1	Logical AND
&	1	String concatenation

Operations in parentheses are performed first. Higher precedence operations take place sooner unless operation is in parentheses. When precedence is equal, operations are performed left to right.

TABLE 2-2 Arithmetic and Logical Operators

subtraction (-), multiplication (*), and division (/). Another operator, the exponent (^), produces powers of a number. In Chapter 5, you will see how you can set search conditions to find data in a database using logical operators, such as the greater than sign in Rank > 5. All of the operators recognized by Symphony are listed in Table 2-2. The order of operations in a formula is also shown in Table 2-2, with 7 as the highest precedence. If all of the operators in a formula are the same, as in

2 * 3 * 4 = 24

the calculation is performed from left to right. You can affect the order of calculation by using parentheses, as in

2 * 3 + 4 = 10
2 * (4 + 3) = 14

When you nest calculations within several parentheses, the innermost calculations are performed first. Earlier, you saw the formula

((E6*E7)+(E9*E10))*2

This arrangement of parentheses means that both the E6*E7 and E9*E10 calculations will occur first, then the two products will be added together, and finally, the sum will be multiplied by *2, which stands outside the parentheses. Actually, the two inner sets of parentheses are not necessary because, as you saw in Table 2-2, * will occur before +, which means that the following is acceptable:

(E6*E7+E9*E10)*2

Common Formula Errors

Note that none of the previous formulas had spaces entered in them when they were entered into Symphony. No spaces is a general rule in all Symphony formulas. If you spell a formula correctly but use improper elements within it, Symphony objects when you press (ENTER). Check the formula to find the error. Symphony attempts to put the cursor near the error, so look at the cursor's location first. You may have neglected to close a pair of parentheses or quotations, or omitted the @ sign before a function name.

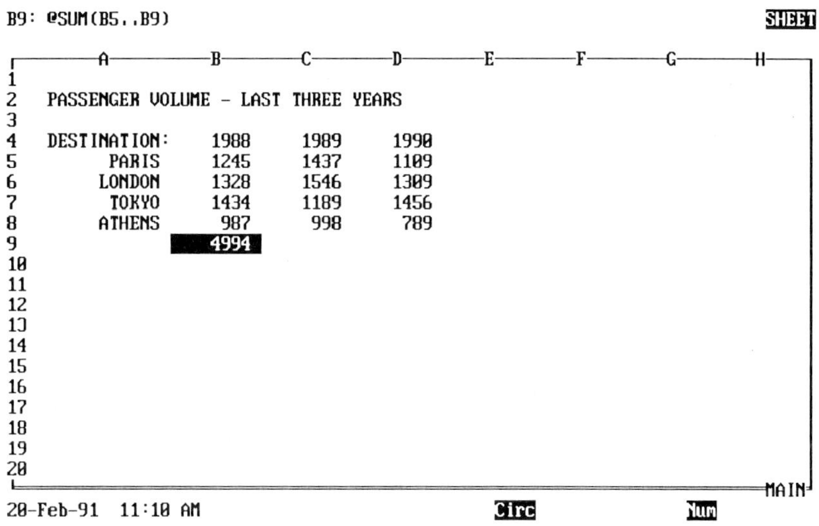

FIGURE 2-10 A circular formula

You may succeed in entering a formula only to see the message "CIRC" appear among the status indicators. This message tells you there is a *circular reference* in the formula, meaning that the formula refers to itself. You cannot ask Symphony to multiply the current cell by 1.1 and to put the answer in the current cell. In Figure 2-10, the SUM formula was entered incorrectly and tries to add the cell that the formula occupies. This kind of problem, which usually becomes apparent as soon as you see what you have asked Symphony to do, is solved by retyping the formula.

If you see the CIRC message and cannot determine which cell is producing it, then you can use the MENU Settings command to find out. In Figure 2-11, you can see the display that the MENU Settings command gives you. In the top left corner of the box is the cell address of the circular formula. You can then select Quit to leave the menu. Back in SHEET mode, you can move to the offending cell and edit it.

```
Set default label alignment (left, right, center)                    MENU
Label-Prefix  Recalculation  Titles  Format  Width  Zero  Auto-Link  Quit

 Circular              B9
 Label-Prefix:         '
                                         Titles
 Recalculation                             Columns: 0
   Method:             Automatic           Rows:    0
   Order:              Optimal           Format:    (G)
   Iterations:         1                 Width:     9
                                         For window: MAIN
 Zero Suppression:  No
 Auto-Link:  Yes
                                                          Sheet Settings

Settings                                        Circ          Num
```

FIGURE 2-11 The MENU Settings display

Function Arguments

Symphony provides you with the basic building blocks of complex formulas in the form of functions. These built-in formulas are specially coded commands that facilitate common calculations. If you use functions, you do not have to enter lengthy instructions.

Some functions simply generate values by themselves. For example, @PI gives the value of PI (3.1415926536), and the date function @NOW tells you what your PC thinks the current date and time is. However, most functions require additional information, called *arguments*. For example, the principal, interest, and term required by the @PMT function are said to be the arguments of @PMT. Some functions require just one argument, like @SUM, which only needs to know what range of cells you want to sum. Others, such as @PMT, require a set number of arguments. Some functions can accept multiple arguments. You can sum several different groups of cells by combining them in a SUM statement.

The multiple arguments are separated by commas, as in the following formula, which adds up all of the volume figures shown in Figure 2-7:

@SUM(B5..B8,C5..C8,D5..D8)

The arguments required by functions can be broken down into three types:

- Numeric: cells containing numbers, as in @PMT(E1,E2,E3)
- Range: a range of cells such as those that are being summed with @SUM(B1..B3), or a named range, such as @SUM(TOTAL_SALES)
- String: a label or piece of text entered into a cell, entered into a function in quotes, or produced by another function

Some functions use more than one type of argument, as is the case with @CHOOSE, which can accept a numeric or range argument and a text argument. Numeric functions can reference a mixture of cell coordinates and range names, as in @PMT(E1,INTEREST,TERM). Range names will be described in the next chapter, along with string formulas.

Function Syntax

There are nearly 100 functions and several ways of classifying them. In addition to the distinction between numeric and string functions, which closely follows that between values and labels, functions can be grouped by the type of work they apply to: financial, date, logical, and so on. However, all Symphony functions are always entered in the same basic format, using a standard arrangement of parts, or *syntax:*

- Functions begin with the leading @ sign.
- Next is the name of the function, typed in upper- or lowercase or a combination of both, and spelled accurately.
- The arguments, when required, follow the function name, enclosed in parentheses.
- When there is more than one argument, you must separate them by commas; the arguments must be in proper order.
- There should be no spaces between the @ sign and the function name.

The function combined with any arguments is referred to as a *function statement.* If you try to enter a function statement that contains an error—for example, an incorrectly spelled function name—Symphony will beep and place the entry on the edit line.

Mastering Functions

You are not likely to memorize all of Symphony's many functions. By using a few simple techniques, however, you can make full use of them. Always assume there is an appropriate function. Chances are that the calculation you want to perform is one that many other spreadsheet users need to perform, so it is probably provided by Symphony. Sometimes you may need to combine several functions in one formula to do the job. Occasionally, you will need to use an intermediate cell to produce part of the answer before completing the calculation in another cell. Later in this chapter you will learn how columns can be hidden from the display and from printed reports so that extra columns used for calculations need not affect the way the worksheet looks.

Save particularly useful function statements. When you come up with a good formula that you are likely to use often, you might consider saving the worksheet under a different name to keep a copy of the formula for reference. In Chapter 7, you will learn how to save portions of a spreadsheet into their own files and combine several files into one. This will allow you to build a library of useful functions. You can also print useful formulas by highlighting the appropriate cell and using the (PRTSC) key. This will copy the information in the whole screen, including the cell identifier, to the printer.

If you follow these guidelines and are prepared to spend some time experimenting with and reading about functions, you will find that they offer tremendous power. A complete examination of each function is beyond the scope of this chapter (with two pages per function, this chapter alone would grow to 200 pages). In Appendix B you will find a series of discussions on different sets of functions grouped according to their practical roles. Examples of how to apply the functions are given in most cases.

RANGE-EDITING COMMANDS

The concept of the *range* is one of the most pervasive in Symphony. It is important to be sure what constitutes a range and how to point one out to Symphony.

Range Rules

The diagram in Figure 2-12 shows what is and is not a range within a worksheet. A range is one or more cells that form a rectangular group. In a regular spreadsheet this means that cell A1 can be considered a range, as can cells A1, B1, A2, and B2. This range would be referred to as A1..B2. Cells A1 through C5 would be the range A1..C5. However, cells A1, B5, and C5 cannot together be termed a range: they do not form a rectangle.

When telling Symphony about ranges, you can type in the cell coordinates, as in **A1.C5**. Note that you do not need to type two periods when entering range information; Symphony adds the

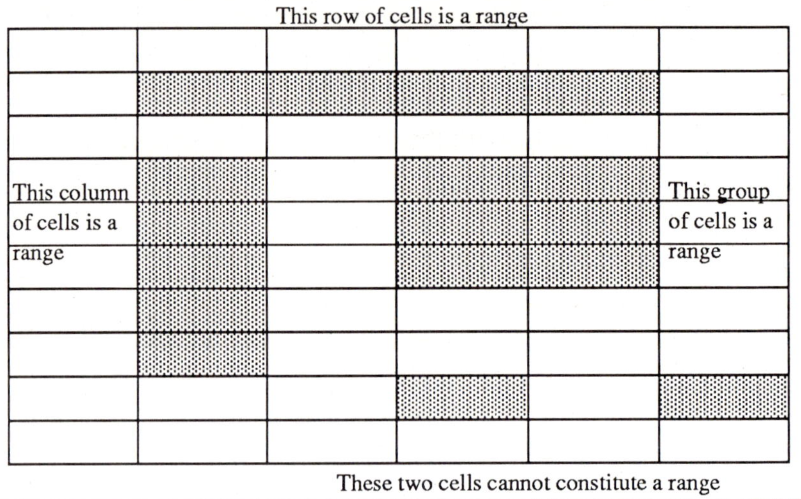

FIGURE 2-12 Range diagram

second period for you. Also, you can tell Symphony about a range by pointing it out. This means placing the cell pointer in one corner of the range and then *anchoring* it there by typing a period. The range of cells may be extended beyond a single cell by moving the cell pointer in any direction while Symphony automatically maintains a rectangular grouping to the cells. You can refer to a range of cells by any two diagonal coordinates.

The cell in which you anchor the beginning point of the range is usually the top cell in a column of cells, or the left cell in a row. If the range includes cells from more than one column or row, you can begin the painting process in the top-left corner of the range, although any corner will do.

When you are defining a range, you can move around it without altering its dimensions by using the (TAB) key. This changes the *active corner* of the range, which is the corner that moves when you press the cursor keys. The active corner is usually the bottom right corner, and you can see the cursor flashing there. However, if you press (TAB) once, the active corner changes to the bottom left cell of the highlighted range. If you keep pressing (TAB), the active corner rotates clockwise around the four corners of the range. This allows you to alter the range in any direction. For example, with the top left corner active, you can alter the top edge of the range or the left edge.

You have seen that the MENU commands include several that affect a group of cells known as a range. For example, the Format command was used in Chapter 1 to alter the appearance of a range of cells, and the Erase command can be used to remove the contents of a range of cells. There are other commands, such as Copy and Move, that can be applied to a range of cells to assist in the designing and layout of a spreadsheet model.

One of the most useful abilities of a computer is its capacity for copying information. This capability is used in Symphony to produce unlimited copies of standard worksheets, such as a weekly expense report model, that have to be used again and again. The MENU Copy command as it applies to a range of cells is particularly useful when you are creating any model in which the same labels, numbers, or formulas are used more than once.

SIMPLE COPY Consider the formulas mentioned earlier for producing a series of years by adding 1 to the previous year, starting with 1988 in cell B4:

	B	C	D
Row 4	1988	1+B4	1+C4

When you create a formula like this in cell C4, which contains 1+B4, you are in effect telling Symphony to add 1 to the cell on the left. The formulas 1+C4 and 1+D4 actually mean the same thing. You can copy the formula from C4 to D4. To try this in your model, you first move to C4, type **1+B4**, and press (ENTER), and then follow these steps:

1. Place your cell pointer in the cell to be copied (C4) and pick Copy from MENU.

2. You are prompted with "Range of cells to copy FROM," which means "which group of cells do you want to copy?" Symphony assumes you want to include the current cell and shows C4..C4. You can then do one of the following:

   Accept this cell reference by pressing (ENTER)
   Reject it with (BACKSPACE) or (ESC)
   Use the cursor keys or mouse to highlight additional cells to be copied
   Type the coordinates of the cell(s) you want to copy

3. In this case, to copy C4, you just press (ENTER) to accept that cell as the range to be copied.

4. A new prompt appears, "Range to copy TO." This prompt asks for the cells you are going to copy into, in this case C4..D4. You can indicate this by typing **C4.D4**, but you might find it easier to type a period (**.**) to anchor the beginning point of the range at C4 and then press (RIGHT ARROW) once to include cell D4. (You could use just D4 as the destination, but it does not matter if you copy the formula over the cell it is in.)

5. Having indicated the destination cells, press (ENTER).

You can see that Symphony copies the formula as instructed and converts each new formula relative to its location. This ability to address cells in a relative manner makes this kind of copying very useful. In the next chapter you will read about the difference between a relative cell address and an absolute one.

In the example in Figure 2-7, you can use the Copy command to copy the formula @SUM(B5..B8) from cell B9 to cells C9 through D9:

1. Move the cell pointer to B9.
2. Press MENU and choose Copy.
3. Press (ENTER) to accept B9..B9 as the range you are copying from.
4. Type a period (.) to anchor B9 as the first cell of the range you are copying to.
5. Press (RIGHT ARROW) twice to expand the range to include D9.
6. Press (ENTER) to complete the copy from B9..B9 to B9..D9.

The results appear in Figure 2-13, where you can see that the formula in D9 has been converted in relation to column D—that is, it now totals column D instead of column C.

LARGER COPIES The Copy command works for groups of cells and for labels as well as values. For example, suppose that you want to use the volume figures in the sample model to produce a revenue estimate for each city and year, as shown in Figure 2-14. To do this, you could copy the entire model and then change the volume figures in the copy to revenue figures.

1. Move the cell pointer to A2, press MENU, and select Copy.
2. When prompted for the range to copy from, press the (DOWN ARROW) and (RIGHT ARROW) keys to extend the highlighted range to D9, as shown in Figure 2-15, and then press (ENTER).

```
D9: @SUM(D5..D8)                                                     SHEET

      A          B          C          D          E          F          G          H
1
2   PASSENGER VOLUME - LAST THREE YEARS
3
4   DESTINATION:    1988       1989       1990
5         PARIS     1245       1437       1109
6        LONDON     1328       1546       1309
7         TOKYO     1434       1109       1456
8        ATHENS      987        998        789
9                   4994       5170       4663
10
```

FIGURE 2-13 Copied @SUM formulas

3. When the Copy command is used to copy more than one cell, you only need to point out the upper-left cell of the TO range. Move the cell pointer to cell A12. The command assumes that

```
A8: \=                                                               SHEET

      A            B            C            D            E            F
1   PASSENGER VOLUME - LAST THREE YEARS
2
3   DESTINATION:       1988         1989         1990
4         PARIS       1,245        1,437        1,109
5        LONDON       1,328        1,546        1,309
6         TOKYO       1,434        1,109        1,456
7        ATHENS         987          998          789
8   ============================================
9   TOTALS            4,994        5,170        4,663
10
11
12  REVENUE - LAST THREE YEARS
13
14  DESTINATION:       1988         1989         1990
15        PARIS    $311,250     $359,250     $277,250
16       LONDON    $332,000     $386,500     $327,250
17        TOKYO    $358,500     $297,250     $364,000
18       ATHENS    $246,750     $249,500     $197,250
19  ============================================
20  TOTALS       $1,240,500   $1,292,500   $1,165,750
                                                                     MAIN
20-Feb-91  02:32 PM                                              Num
```

FIGURE 2-14 Enlarged model

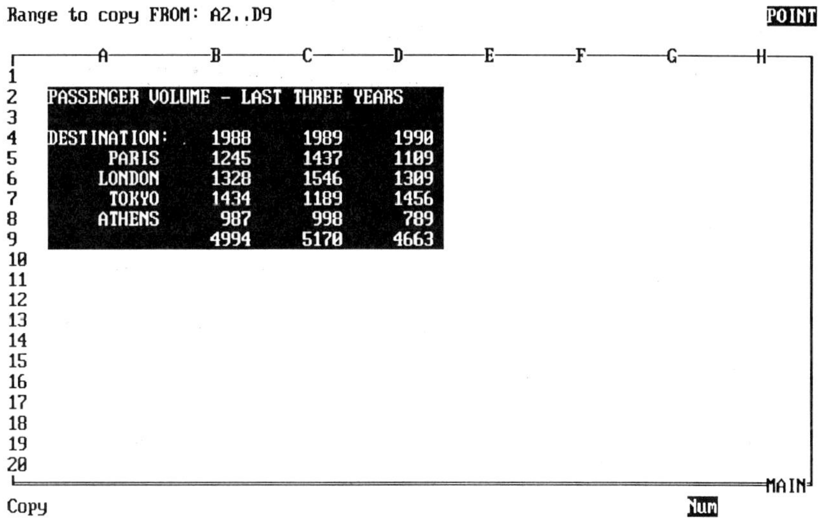

FIGURE 2-15 The FROM range

you have enough free cells below and to the right of this cell to accommodate a range of entries the size of the one you highlighted as the FROM range.

4. With the cell pointer in A12, press (ENTER). The results can be seen in Figure 2-16, where the label in cell A12 has been edited to REVENUE - LAST THREE YEARS.

5. To edit cell A12, you first move the cell pointer there and then press (F2).

6. Press (HOME) to move the edit cursor to the beginning of the line. Now type **REVENUE** and press the (DEL) key a number of times to remove PASSENGER VOLUME. Now press (ENTER) to return the edited contents to the cell.

```
A12: 'REVENUE - LAST THREE YEARS                                        SHEET
 ------A-----------B-----------C-----------D-----------E-----------F-----------G-----------H----
1
2   PASSENGER VOLUME - LAST THREE YEARS
3
4   DESTINATION:     1988        1989        1990
5          PARIS     1245        1437        1109
6         LONDON     1328        1546        1309
7          TOKYO     1434        1189        1456
8         ATHENS      987         998         789
9                    4994        5170        4663
10
11
12  REVENUE - LAST THREE YEARS
13
14  DESTINATION:     1988        1989        1990
15         PARIS     1245        1437        1109
16        LONDON     1328        1546        1309
17         TOKYO     1434        1189        1456
18        ATHENS      987         998         789
19                   4994        5170        4663
20
                                                                                          MAIN
20-Feb-91  12:11 PM                                                                 Num
```

FIGURE 2-16 Completed Copy command

The cells from B15 through D18 can now be filled with calculations that determine revenue. This is done by multiplying the volume figures in the upper half by the average amount for a ticket. A formula is written in B15, multiplying the volume figure in B5 by the amount of 250.

1. With the cell pointer in B15, type the formula **250*B5** and press (ENTER).

2. Issue the Copy command, pressing (ENTER) to select B15..B15 when prompted for the range to copy from.

3. When prompted for the range to copy to, press a period to anchor the range at B15, and then press (RIGHT ARROW) twice and (DOWN ARROW) three times to expand the range to B15..D18.

4. Press (ENTER) to complete the Copy command.

```
B15: 250*B5                                                          SHEET
       A          B          C          D        E        F        G        H
1
2   PASSENGER VOLUME - LAST THREE YEARS
3
4   DESTINATION:     1988       1989       1990
5          PARIS     1245       1437       1109
6         LONDON     1320       1546       1309
7          TOKYO     1434       1109       1456
8         ATHENS      987        998        709
9                    4994       5170       4663
10
11
12  REVENUE - LAST THREE YEARS
13
14  DESTINATION:     1988       1989       1990
15         PARIS   311250     359250     277250
16        LONDON   332000     386500     327250
17         TOKYO   358500     297250     364000
18        ATHENS   246750     249500     197250
19                1248500    1292500    1165750
20                                                                     MAIN
20-Feb-91  12:16 PM                                               Num
```

FIGURE 2-17 Completed formula copy

The results can be seen in Figure 2-17. You can see that the formulas in row 19 automatically sum the new figures.

THE COPY KEYS You will use the Copy command extensively when building spreadsheet models. The rhythm of the command keys will become second nature. To copy one cell to many cells, the pattern is as follows:

1. Use MENU Copy to pick the command.
2. Press (ENTER) to accept the current cell as the one to be copied.
3. Point to move the cell pointer to select the upper-left cell of the destination range.
4. Anchor by typing a period to lock in this cell coordinate.
5. Point to select the rest of the destination range.

6. Press (ENTER) to complete the command.

To copy from many cells to one destination, use these keys:

MENU, Copy, point, (ENTER), point, anchor, point, (ENTER)

Caution Always remember that the Copy command does not check for existing data in the destination cells. You can actually lose data by inadvertently copying over it. Use caution the first few times you use Copy, and always save the worksheet as a precaution before large copy operations.

Erase

You use the MENU Erase command to delete the contents of a single cell or more than one cell. The keystroke sequence MENU E (ENTER) is useful for deleting single cells, but Erase works effectively on large areas that need to be cleared. After selecting the command, highlight the range to be modified and press (ENTER). The contents of all selected cells will be erased. However, the command will not change the formatting or width setting of cells.

Move

You will occasionally need to move a group of cells from one location to another. If you need a few extra columns or rows in a spreadsheet, you can sometimes use the Insert command, described later in this chapter, to accomplish the changes you want. At other times you will be able to use the MENU Erase command to remove extra space, but these commands can be tricky in crowded spreadsheets, and at times you will want to move a group of cells to a new location. The MENU Move command requires that you highlight the cells to be moved and then indicate their destination. Note that any cell entries within the area they are being moved to will be overwritten by the moved cells.

The MENU Move command preserves the integrity of the formulas within the range. Relative cell references are preserved correctly. The following line of cells moved from row 4 to row 6 would be adjusted as shown here. The cell entries on row 4,

	B	C	D
Row 4	1988	1+B4	1+C4

become these when moved to row 6:

Row 6	1988	1+B6	1+C6

Because cells that you move overwrite cells in the area you move to, a good safety precaution is to save your worksheet before a large range move. That way, you can retrieve the unchanged version if the effects of the move are not what you had anticipated. Large range moves will take several moments for the computer to complete. The mode indicator will flash "WAIT" until the operation is over.

Range Values

At times, you may find it necessary to replace the formula in a cell with the value that is the result of that formula. This could be necessary when you have used the @RAND function, one of the built-in functions, which produces random numbers. Many of the examples in this book were created with @RAND to produce values for hypothetical spreadsheets. The @RAND function is constantly recalculated every time a change is made to the spreadsheet; therefore, you may want to replace the formula with the value it created. To do this to one cell, highlight that cell, press

(F2) for the EDIT mode, and press (F8) (the CALC key). This will replace the formula in a single cell with a value.

However, if you needed to perform the same operation on a large number of cells the (F2)/(F8) method would be tedious. For such situations, Symphony provides the Range Values command as a variation of the Copy command, allowing you to copy a group of cells from one location to another while at the same time converting any formulas in the FROM range into values. By choosing the same FROM and TO ranges, you can have the Range Values command convert a range of cells from formulas to values. Any labels or plain values in the range will be unaffected. Among the reasons for doing this is memory conservation, since active formulas take up more memory than plain values.

Range Transpose

Another command that copies cells is Range Transpose. The difference between this command and Copy is that in the TO range—the place that the cells are being copied to—the cells are rearranged. Columns become rows, and rows become columns. For example, if you were to use cells A4..D9 of Figure 2-17 as the FROM range with the Range Transpose command and specify cell A12 as the TO range, the results would appear as in Figure 2-18.

Note that formulas, such as the ones that were on row 9, are not converted to values in column (F.) They are now incorrect. You will usually want to use the Range Values command to convert formulas to values before using the Range Transpose command. However, Symphony does preserve format settings and the alignment of labels in transposed cells. Also note that the Range Transpose command does not erase the original cells but performs a variation of Copy rather than of Move.

```
F13: @SUM(F9..F12)                                                          SHEET
┌─────────A─────────B─────────C─────────D─────────E─────────F─────────G─────────H───┐
1
2   PASSENGER VOLUME - LAST THREE YEARS
3
4   DESTINATION:      1988      1989      1990
5          PARIS      1245      1437      1109
6         LONDON      1328      1546      1309
7          TOKYO      1434      1189      1456
8         ATHENS       987       998       789
9                     4994      5170      4663
10
11
12  DESTINATION:     PARIS    LONDON     TOKYO    ATHENS
13          1988      1245      1328      1434       987         0
14          1989      1437      1546      1189       998         0
15          1990      1109      1309      1456       789         0
16
17
18
19
20
└══════════════════════════════════════════════════════════════════════════MAIN┘
20-Feb-91  01:11 PM                                                      Num
```

FIGURE 2-18 Transposed cells

WORKSHEET SETTINGS

In a program as flexible as Symphony, you can change many aspects of the way the program works. For example, worksheet columns can be from 1 to 240 characters wide, and the width of each column can be set individually with the MENU Width Set command. However, Symphony gives each new worksheet some basic characteristics, known as the *defaults* or *settings*. In computer terms, a default is what the program does, or assumes, unless you tell it differently. Whenever you load Symphony and are in the SHEET environment, you can review the settings for the current worksheet by selecting Settings from the environment-specific menu (press MENU, and then type **S** for Settings). In response to this command, Symphony shows you a Settings screen similar to the one shown earlier in Figure 2-11.

This screen is divided into several areas. You can see that the Label-Prefix setting is an apostrophe for left-aligned. In the box labeled "For window: MAIN," Symphony indicates that the columns are wide enough to accommodate nine characters, and the format for showing numbers is the *General format* (G). This format shows numbers with no commas in the thousands and no decimal places unless they are entered or calculated by a formula. A calculation resulting in many decimal places is shown in the General format with as many decimal places as will fit in the cell. Changing the worksheet to other formats is described in the next section. The other aspects of the Settings command, such as Recalculation and Titles, as well as the meaning of the term "MAIN," will be discussed in the next chapter.

Follow these steps to change the default settings for the sample worksheet to columns that are 11 characters wide:

1. Select Width from the Settings menu. You are shown the worksheet and prompted to enter a default column width. As with the single column Width Set command, you can adjust the width with the (LEFT ARROW) and (RIGHT ARROW) keys or type the desired width as a number (from 1 to 240).

2. Type **11** and press (ENTER) to confirm the new width.

3. You are returned to the Settings menu. The new width setting is indicated (11). Select Quit to return to the worksheet.

You will see that the Settings Width command affects all columns except those, like column A in this example, that are specifically sized with the Width Set command.

To change the default label alignment, you would select Label-Prefix from the Settings menu and pick Left, Center, or Right. Once selected, this format remains in effect for the current worksheet. All new labels will be aligned according to the default setting, but a change to the default setting does not affect labels already entered. The default alignment is in effect for the current worksheet only; new files revert to the program defaults. To leave the Settings menu and return to SHEET mode, you select Quit.

FORMAT COMMANDS

In Chapter 1, you saw that the appearance of numeric values in your worksheet is a function of their format. Formats can be applied to an entire spreadsheet or just to selected cells. The difference between the numbers you see in Figures 2-17 and 2-14 is a result of a change in the format. The format determines how your numbers look. Such things as commas, leading dollar signs, round brackets for negative numbers, and the number of decimal places shown are all functions of the format. In fact, the ability to change the way a number is displayed is a very powerful aspect of Symphony, one that saves you a lot of typing and retyping.

Symphony initially uses the General format. This format only shows decimal places when you enter them or when you enter formulas that result in values with decimal places. Symphony calculates as many as 15 decimal places. When a formula creates a number with decimal places, they are displayed until the complete number is shown or until the cell is filled, whichever comes first. For example, given the following cells, the General format will show cell D4 as 2.5, cell D5 as 3.333333, and cell D6 as 0.333333:

B4:	5	C4:	2	D4:	+B4/C4 = 2.5
B5:	100	C5:	3	D5:	+B5/C5 = 33.33333
B6:	1	C6:	3	D6:	+B6/C6 = 0.333333

Because this format results in the decimal place appearing at a different position in the column, you may want to use a different format for such values as dollars and cents.

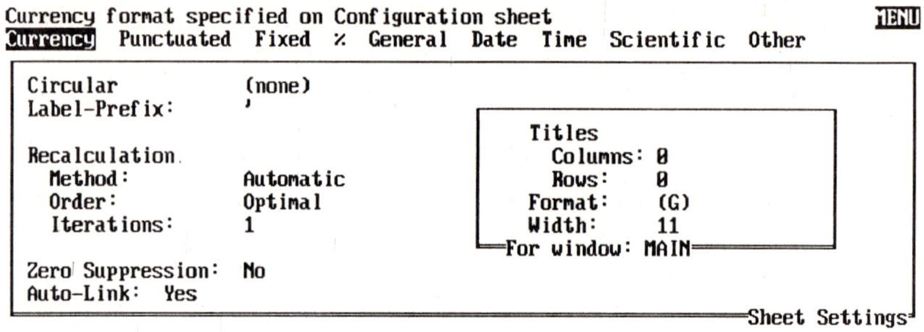

FIGURE 2-19 The Settings Format menu

The Default Format

The format used by Symphony can be changed for a part of the worksheet with the Range Format command, or for all of the cells with the Settings Format command. If all or most of the numbers in a worksheet are dollars, you might want to choose the Currency format as your default format. To do this with the sample model, follow these steps:

1. Press MENU and select Settings, and then Format. You will see a menu like the one in Figure 2-19 that shows all of the format choices. They are listed with examples in Table 2-3.

2. Select Currency. Some of the formats, like Currency, require that you indicate how many decimal places should be used. A prompt automatically appears as follows:

   Number of decimal places (0..15): 2

3. As you can see, the options are from 0 to 15 and the suggested setting is 2. You can type your choice over this. In this case, type **0** before pressing (ENTER) to confirm the format selection.

Format Name	Identifiers and Default Decimal Places
Currency	(C2) Commas placed in 1,000s; negatives in parentheses; user-defined decimal places; currency prefix or suffix: $2,000.99
Punctuated	(P2) Commas placed in 1,000s; negatives in parentheses; user-defined decimal places: 2,000.99
Fixed	(F2) No commas in 1,000s; negatives in parentheses; user-defined decimal places: 2000.99 (2000.99)
%	(%2) Divides contents by 100; uses % sign as suffix
General	(G) As many decimal places as entered or will fit; exponential notation for large numbers
Date	(D1) Various options, described in Chapter 3, to show numbers as dates
Time	(T1) Various options, described in Chapter 3, to show numbers as time
Scientific	(S2) Exponential notation; negatives in parentheses; user-defined decimal places: 2.00E+03 (2.00E+03)
Other	
Bar Graph	(+) Represents positive numbers as plus signs, negatives as minus signs for simple bar charts
Literal	(L) Displays formulas in cells rather than the cells' values
Hidden	(H) Hides cell contents from view; shows contents only on the descriptor line

TABLE 2-3 Format Choices, with Identifiers

4. You are returned to the Settings menu with the new format setting entered (C0 stands for Currency format, 0 decimal places).

5. Select Quit from the Settings menu to view the worksheet. The results will look like those in Figure 2-20.

Note that the default format is in effect for the current worksheet only. New files revert to the program defaults. A change to the

```
B16: 250*B6                                                          SHEET
        A            B            C            D            E            F
1
2   PASSENGER VOLUME - LAST THREE YEARS
3
4   DESTINATION:    $1,988       $1,989       $1,990
5          PARIS    $1,245       $1,437       $1,109
6         LONDON    $1,328       $1,546       $1,309
7          TOKYO    $1,434       $1,189       $1,456
8         ATHENS      $987         $998         $789
9                   $4,994       $5,170       $4,663
10
11
12  REVENUE - LAST THREE YEARS
13
14  DESTINATION:     $1,988       $1,989       $1,990
15         PARIS   $311,250     $359,250     $277,250
16        LONDON   $332,000     $386,500     $327,250
17         TOKYO   $358,500     $297,250     $364,000
18        ATHENS   $246,750     $249,500     $197,250
19               $1,240,500   $1,292,500   $1,165,750
20                                                                    MAIN
20-Feb-91  01:48 PM                                              Num
```

FIGURE 2-20 Default Currency format, 0 decimal places

default format does not affect cells that are already formatted with the Range Format command. However, if you change the default format to Currency and then use the Format Reset command on a cell, it will change to the current default format.

The Regular Format Command

Changing the default format affects the appearance of all values in the active file and the current worksheet, except for those cells formatted with the Range Format command. In Figure 2-20, you can see that using Currency for the default format creates problems: the years, which are actually just numbers, are also changed to Currency format. Symphony needs to be told that there is a range of cells that must be formatted differently. The regular Format command will accomplish this.

1. Move the cell pointer to B4.
2. Press MENU and choose Format, and then Fixed.
3. Type **0** for the decimal places and press (ENTER).
4. Now press (DOWN ARROW) until you have highlighted down to the figure of $1,988 in cell B14.
5. Now press (END) followed by (RIGHT ARROW). This will move the highlighting to the last column on the right of the model, to create the range B4..D14.
6. Press (ENTER) to confirm the command.

The results can be seen in Figure 2-21. Note the message in cell B4. It says (F0) to remind you that this cell is formatted separately from the default format, with the Fixed format, 0 decimal places.

```
B4: (F0) 1988                                                        SHEET

        A            B            C            D          E          F
1
2   PASSENGER VOLUME - LAST THREE YEARS
3
4   DESTINATION:        1988         1989         1990
5          PARIS        1245         1437         1109
6         LONDON        1328         1546         1309
7          TOKYO        1434         1189         1456
8         ATHENS         987          998          789
9                       4994         5170         4663
10
11
12  REVENUE - LAST THREE YEARS
13
14  DESTINATION:        1988         1989         1990
15         PARIS    $311,250     $359,250     $277,250
16        LONDON    $332,000     $386,500     $327,250
17         TOKYO    $358,500     $297,250     $364,000
18        ATHENS    $246,750     $249,500     $197,250
19                $1,248,500   $1,292,500   $1,165,750
20
                                                                      MAIN
20-Feb-91  01:54 PM                                               Num
```

FIGURE 2-21 Fixed format results

Also note that the format commands have not altered the figures in B4, just the way they are displayed.

Format Considerations

When a format change establishes the number of decimal places that can be displayed, Symphony rounds the number for display purposes only. Symphony remembers the number to 15 decimal places, even if the format says 0 decimal places are to be displayed. In Appendix B, you will learn more about the @ROUND function, which causes Symphony to round numbers permanently.

Do not use a global format with 0 decimal places if you will have many cells whose values are less than 0. The problem with a 0 decimal-place setting is that a value of less than 0 will just look like 0 and may be accidentally deleted. For example, 0.12 looks like 0 when displayed with Fixed format, 0 decimal places. This 0.12, which corresponds to 12%, could be a valuable number in a calculation. Of course, you can format 0.12 with the Percent format (%) so that it appears as 12%, or 12.00% if you use two decimal places.

Use formats to avoid worrying about the appearance of your numbers. In this way you can concentrate on building your spreadsheets and writing formulas. By setting the correct default format, you save a lot of time changing the appearance of separate groups of cells. When you do need to distinguish a group of cells from the whole, use the Format approach.

If a change in format results in one or more cells filling up with asterisks, you will need to reduce the number of decimal places in the format or widen the column. The normal width of Symphony columns is nine characters, and because Symphony needs to distinguish the numbers in adjacent cells and prevent them from appearing to run together, there is always a single character space to the right of a value entry. This means a nine-character column can only accept eight digits. When you apply a format other than General or Scientific, it produces numbers longer than will fit into the nine-character columns, so Symphony uses asterisks to point out the problem. The number itself is not lost. For example, if you use the Currency format to turn 1245 into $1,245.00 in a nine-wide column, the cell shows *********, which will change to $1,245.00 if you widen the column to 10 characters.

COMMANDING COLUMNS AND ROWS

There are several useful commands that you can apply to the columns from which the worksheet is built. In addition to setting widths, you can add new columns, delete columns, and even hide columns.

Inserting and Deleting Columns

At times, you will have entered data only to find you need an extra column. A new column is easy to create. Just select Insert from the Worksheet menu, and you will be asked if you want to insert a column, row, or global. The Global option applies to worksheets with restricted ranges, as discussed in the next chapter. Normally, you will select Column. You are then asked to indicate the number of columns you want inserted. Columns are added to the left of the current column. Press (ENTER) to insert one column. Press the (RIGHT ARROW) key once for each additional column you want to add, and then press (ENTER). The new columns are added down all 8192 rows of the worksheet, so you should consider if there is any unseen data that will be affected at the time of the insert. You can press (END) plus (DOWN ARROW) and (END) plus (UP ARROW) while inserting a column in order to view lower and upper areas of the worksheet before you press (ENTER) to confirm the insertion.

Deleting columns works the same way: you select Delete from the Worksheet menu, then Column. Highlight the columns you want to delete. Deleting removes all the data in those columns, so it should be used with care. Check areas above and below the current screen for valuable data that might be deleted with the column.

Working with Rows

You can use the Insert and Delete commands to manipulate spreadsheet rows. There will be times when you have entered data only to find you need an extra row. Just select Insert from the Worksheet menu, and then select Rows. You will be asked to indicate the number of rows you want inserted. New rows are added above the current row. Press (ENTER) to insert one row. Press the (DOWN ARROW) key once for each additional row you want to add, and then press (ENTER). New rows are added across all 256 columns of the worksheet, so you must consider if there is any unseen data that will be affected at the time of the insert. You can press (END) plus (LEFT ARROW) and (END) plus (RIGHT ARROW) while inserting a row in order to view other areas of the worksheet before you press (ENTER) to confirm the insertion.

Suppose that you would like to add a row to the model in Figure 2-22, to separate the row of @SUM totals from the numbers.

1. Move the cell pointer to row 9 and press MENU.
2. Select Insert and then choose Rows.
3. Press (ENTER), and one row will be inserted.

Note that the @SUM formulas are still correct.

The Delete command works the same way: you select Delete from the Worksheet menu, followed by Rows. You then highlight the rows you want to remove. The Delete Rows command removes all the data in those rows across all 256 columns, so it should be used with care. Check the areas to the left and right of the current screen for valuable data that might be deleted with the rows.

```
B5: (P0) 1245                                                          SHEET

┌─────────A──────────B──────────C──────────D──────────E──────────F─────────┐
1
2   PASSENGER VOLUME - LAST THREE YEARS
3
4   DESTINATION:      1988       1989       1990
5         PARIS      1,245      1,437      1,109
6        LONDON      1,328      1,546      1,309
7         TOKYO      1,434      1,189      1,456
8        ATHENS        987        998        789
9                    4,994      5,170      4,663
10
11
12  REVENUE - LAST THREE YEARS
13
14  DESTINATION:      1988       1989       1990
15        PARIS   $311,250   $359,250   $277,250
16       LONDON   $332,000   $386,500   $327,250
17        TOKYO   $358,500   $297,250   $364,000
18       ATHENS   $246,750   $249,500   $197,250
19              $1,248,500 $1,292,500 $1,165,750
20
└──────────────────────────────────────────────────────────────────────MAIN┘
20-Feb-91  02:12 PM                                                   Num
```

FIGURE 2-22 Punctuated format in effect

To delete row 1 of the model worksheet, follow these steps:

1. Press (HOME), and then MENU.
2. Select Delete, and then Rows.
3. Press (ENTER) to confirm the command.

Again, the rows are reshuffled and the formulas stay correct. You can now insert a row at row 19 to produce the result seen in Figure 2-23.

Inserting, Deleting, and Formulas

Note that Symphony tries to preserve the integrity of formulas in a worksheet whenever you insert or delete columns or rows. If you

```
A19:                                                              SHEET

     A            B           C           D           E          F
1   PASSENGER VOLUME - LAST THREE YEARS
2
3   DESTINATION:       1988        1989        1990
4          PARIS      1,245       1,437       1,109
5         LONDON      1,328       1,546       1,309
6          TOKYO      1,434       1,189       1,456
7         ATHENS        987         998         789
8
9                     4,994       5,170       4,663
10
11
12  REVENUE - LAST THREE YEARS
13
14  DESTINATION:       1988        1989        1990
15         PARIS   $311,250    $359,250    $277,250
16        LONDON   $332,000    $386,500    $327,250
17         TOKYO   $358,500    $297,250    $364,000
18        ATHENS   $246,750    $249,500    $197,250
19
20              $1,248,500  $1,292,500  $1,165,750
                                                                  MAIN
20-Feb-91  02:24 PM                                           Num
```

FIGURE 2-23 Rows inserted and deleted

insert a new row into a range of cells that are being summed, the total will remain correct. For example, suppose you want to add the volume figures for two new cities. You decide to insert the additions between LONDON and TOKYO. You place the cell pointer on the TOKYO row and issue the Insert Rows command. The prompt for the row insert range appears, and you press the (DOWN ARROW) key once to expand the insert range to two rows.

When you press (ENTER), the insert is completed and two new rows are available for the new figures. The total figures remain unchanged. However, the total formulas will have been altered to include the new rows. When you add the new data, it is included in the total.

You could add columns anywhere in this model without producing an error, or you could delete any of the columns or rows. The references in formulas would be adjusted. The only exception is if you deleted any of the rows that begin or end the range referred to in the @SUM formula. When you delete either a beginning or ending cell of a range, or the entire argument used by a formula, then Symphony does not know what to make of things and returns ERR. You will have to correct the formula by editing it.

SPECIAL LABELS AND VALUES

There are a couple of categories of labels and values that deserve separate discussion. You can use labels to create lines within a spreadsheet model, and you can enter dates that look like labels but are in fact values.

Repeating Labels

Symphony alone cannot underline labels. If you want to create the impression of a line beneath a label or across a spreadsheet as a visual divider, you can enter a line or lines into a separate row. In Figure 2-14, you saw equal signs used for a dividing line. To create this line you want to fill up each cell with a single character, such as the equal sign or the hyphen. Instead of typing enough characters to fill the column, you use the backward slash, which is the "cell fill" command. The \ is followed by the character you want to repeat. Thus, \= produces =========, * produces *********, and \+= produces +=+=+=+=+.

This technique is a lot faster than manually entering a series of symbols. The cell fill command has the added advantage that when columns are altered in width, the command keeps the correct number of characters in the cell.

To complete the model in Figure 2-23 so that it appears like the one in Figure 2-14, try following these steps:

1. In cell A8, type \= and press (ENTER).

2. Copy this cell to B8..D8.

3. Copy A8..D8 to A19.
4. Enter the label **TOTALS** in cell A9, and copy it to cell A20.

You should now use the SERVICES File Save command to store this file, since it will be used in the next chapter.

Number Series

Symphony provides several methods for entering a series of numbers like 101, 102, 103, and so on. Such series are often needed to number consecutive columns and rows, as in the numbering of inventory items and their locations shown in Figure 2-24.

With the MENU Range Fill command, Symphony lets you automatically fill a group of cells with consecutive numbers. You choose the starting number, the step or interval between numbers, and the ending number; for example, starting at 101, incrementing

A4: 101 SHEET

	A	B	C	D	E	F	G	H
1	Inventory Distribution							
2		Warehouse						
3	Product	1	2	3	4	5	6	
4	101	257	79	270	224	149	96	
5	102	150	277	288	42	44	7	
6	103	194	203	166	17	235	20	
7	104	180	259	13	51	155	227	
8	105	68	219	77	152	124	166	
9	106	118	10	29	156	186	53	
10	107	162	179	93	239	101	270	
11	108	142	98	105	140	117	277	
12	109	10	48	20	51	224	255	
13	110	212	256	4	281	83	2	
14	111	64	151	77	197	286	8	
15	112	25	217	169	91	278	272	
16								
17								
18								
19								
20								

MAIN

20-Feb-91 03:52 PM Num

FIGURE 2-24 Series of numbers

by 1, and ending at 105. In the example in Figure 2-24, the consecutive product numbers in column A were created by the Range Fill command, as were the horizontal warehouse numbers.

The Range Fill command needs four pieces of information:

Fill range	The cells that the number series will occupy
Start value	The first number in the sequence
Step value	The interval between numbers
Stop value	The last number in the series

The default settings for Start, Step, and Stop are 0, 1, and 8191, which can be used to number every row in a worksheet from 0 to 8191. You can type your values over these. If you do not know the last number, you can enter a number larger than the last number you want and Symphony will fill the range you have specified, stopping at the last cell in the range rather than the last number.

Once you have made the settings and pressed (ENTER), the range is filled with numbers. These overwrite any previous contents of cells in the range. The numbers are simply numeric entries, not formulas. The numbers do not change interactively, so to alter a series you must re-enter it.

Once you have used the Range Fill command in a file, the settings remain for that file. This makes for fast repetition of the command but can be a nuisance when you need to fill a different area. When you are prompted for the fill range and need to specify a different range, press (BACKSPACE) to remove the old setting and return the cell pointer to the current cell. You can press (ESC) at the fill-range prompt to simply unlock the coordinates of the range.

WORKSHEET NAVIGATION

Once you have built a worksheet, there are some tricks to navigating it. Practicing these will speed up your work with the Symphony worksheet.

The SHEET Position

When Symphony's mode indicator says "SHEET," Symphony is waiting for you to enter data or issue a command. This is the mode in which you are free to move around the spreadsheet to view it and position your cell pointer in preparation for entering and editing information or executing a command. The following techniques are designed to make the process of moving as fast and convenient as possible.

The Big Keys

(CTRL-LEFT ARROW) and (CTRL-RIGHT ARROW) move your cell pointer a screen to the left or to the right, respectively. These options are sometimes referred to as *Big-Right* and *Big-Left,* and they are keystroke combinations as opposed to keystroke sequences. A screen normally means eight columns. If you are using one of Sym-phony's high-resolution display modes, you may be able to see more than eight columns at once.

The (END) Key

One key that plays a special role in cell-pointer movement is the (END) key. This key lets you move around the worksheet quickly, particularly when you have built a sizable model. The (END) key followed by an arrow key takes you to the most distant active cell in the direction you point. This is the last occupied cell in a row or column of contiguously occupied cells, or the last blank cell if all of the cells in the direction you point are blank. You are taken to the next occupied cell if you are on a blank cell and use (END) followed by an arrow pointing in the direction of additional data.

Thus, to get to the bottom of a column of numbers you can simply press (END) and then (DOWN ARROW), as long as there are no gaps in the numbers. To get to the cell below the last number in the column, as you might want to do when summing a column, you would press (DOWN ARROW) one more time. If you happen to press (END) and then (DOWN ARROW) with the cell pointer in an empty column, you will find you are suddenly on row 8192. Similarly, if you press (END) and then (RIGHT ARROW) with the cell pointer in an empty row, you will find you are in column IV, the 265th column.

One situation in which (END) can be used even if you do *not* have contiguous entries is the "hitchhiker" technique. This simply means placing your cursor in a cell that is part of a contiguous group in the direction you are headed, and then using (END) and an arrow key to get closer to your target.

The GOTO Key

You can go to any cell in the worksheet by pressing GOTO ((F5)) and then typing the cell address. If you use range names, described in the next chapter, you can enter a range name at the GOTO prompt, and Symphony will place the cell pointer in the top left corner of the range.

If you have a large model that does not occupy contiguous columns and rows, you can use the (F5) key to go to a distant location (such as IV8192) and then use (END) (UP ARROW) and (END) (LEFT ARROW) to get to the edge of the model.

The (HOME) Question

As well as using the (END) key with one of the arrow keys, you can also use it with the (HOME) key. The (END) (HOME) sequence moves the cell pointer to the furthest corner of the spreadsheet from A1, the last row and column that have been used. In other words, if the last column containing entries is column X and the last row is 40, pressing (END) followed by (HOME) places the cell pointer in X40.

This happens even if the intermediate area between A1 and X40 is not filled with contiguous entries.

This keystroke sequence is useful for locating the bounds of the current worksheet entries. For example, if you want to delete all of the rows from the current one to the bottom of the spreadsheet, then (END) (HOME) is a more reliable key than (END) (DOWN ARROW), since it does not depend on contiguous entries.

The use of (END) (HOME) reveals a minor glitch in Symphony's logic. Suppose that most of your data is in cells A1 through T30 of a Release 2 worksheet, but you have entered data in cell X40. You then erase that data from X40. Using (END) (HOME) shows that the program still thinks of X40 as the last cell. When you save the file and then retrieve it, this "phantom cell" is removed.

Keys for Editing

As you know, Symphony changes the actions of the cursor keys when you are in EDIT mode. The (HOME) key moves the edit-line cursor to the first character and the (END) key moves it to the end of the entry. The (LEFT ARROW) and (RIGHT ARROW) keys move the cursor a character at a time. In EDIT mode, the (CTRL-RIGHT ARROW) key moves the edit cursor five positions to the right in the entry, and the (CTRL-LEFT ARROW) combination moves it five to the left.

When changing a formula's cell references in EDIT mode, you can use the (F2) (EDIT) key to toggle back into VALUE mode and point to the appropriate cell. You can use the pointing method in EDIT mode without toggling to VALUE mode if you are adding cells to the formula after typing a new math operator.

Mouse Keys

Being able to select menu items, highlight ranges, and enter common formulas with a flick of the wrist and a click of a button turns the already fast Symphony into a very dynamic program. No,

Symphony does not come with built-in support for a mouse, the small pointing devices that are increasing in popularity as a computer input device. However, you can easily use a mouse with Symphony if you have a "Symphony mouse driver." This is a small program that relates the movement of your mouse and the clicking of its buttons to the keys that Symphony uses. Many mouse suppliers include a Symphony driver with their mouse software.

Multiple Copies

When you become familiar with the Copy command, you will find that copying one cell to many is easy, as is making a single copy of many cells. However, you may also want to make multiple copies of multiple cells. For example, suppose that you are creating a spreadsheet to analyze expenses for four buildings. You want to copy the labels in cells A2..A6 in Figure 2-25 three times over because you have four properties.

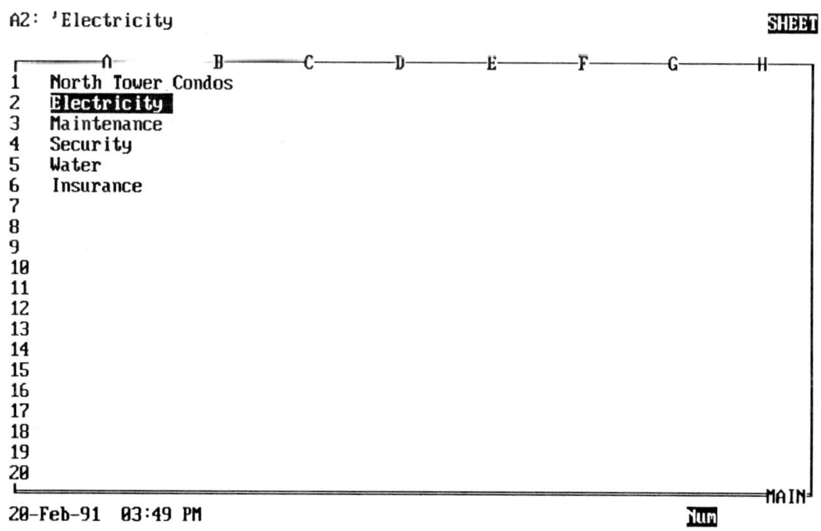

FIGURE 2-25 Expense categories

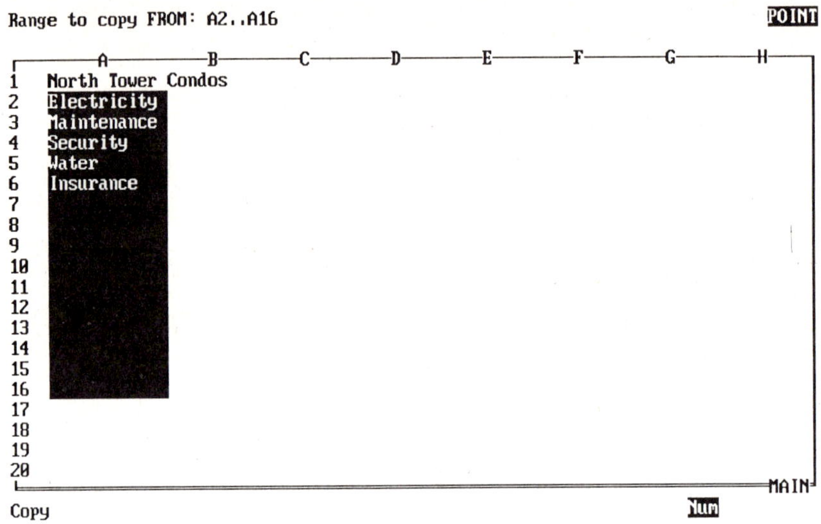

FIGURE 2-26 Extended Copy FROM range

If you use the Copy command and identify A2..A6 as the FROM range and A7 as the TO range, you will create one copy of the labels. However, if you specify A2..A16 as the FROM range, as seen in Figure 2-26, and then point to A7 as the TO range, you will create three new copies of the labels in cells A7 through A21.

The reason for this response is that you included in the copy FROM range 15 rows of cells. The TO range is then forced to be 15 cells. Since there is no data in 10 of the 15 cells of the FROM range, Symphony repeats the data in the first 5 to fill up the TO range. The rule of this method of copying is that the total number of cells in the FROM range must be an exact multiple of the number of occupied cells. To make three copies of three cells, the FROM range will be nine cells in size, with the first three occupied.

You can actually include blank cells in a multiple copy to produce a result that has spaces in it. A FROM range of A2..A19 with A8 as the TO range in the previous example will produce four copies of the labels in A2..A6, with a blank cell between each set of labels.

Unlocking Coordinates

Many Symphony commands use *locked* cell coordinates for range settings. For example, when you begin the Copy command, the current cell is suggested as the FROM range with the cell coordinates locked, as in A1..A1. When you press (ESC) at a locked range prompt, the range is unlocked: A1..A1 turns to A1. This means that you can move the cell pointer without increasing the size of the range.

There are times when you will want to use (BACKSPACE) instead of (ESC) to unlock range prompts. An example of this arises when dealing with "sticky" range settings, those that Symphony remembers, such as the Range Fill range described earlier. If you unlock the range with (BACKSPACE), it immediately places the cell pointer back in the cell it occupied before entering the menu system. This is because the (BACKSPACE) key unlocks *and* rejects range settings, while the (ESC) key merely unlocks them.

SUMMARY

You have now seen Symphony's SHEET environment in action and practiced many of the commands you need to create your own spreadsheet models. By using the Copy command, you can create large models from a small amount of input. Because Symphony keeps track of formulas when you rearrange the spreadsheet, you can adjust designs to meet your needs and improve appearances.

In the next chapter more advanced SHEET commands will be examined, along with the procedures to print your work from the SHEET environment. The window commands will also be examined to provide you with a new perspective on your work with Symphony.

3

FURTHER SPREADSHEET COMMANDS

Building a Typical Worksheet
Getting a Date
Model Values
Saving Your Work: Part One
Further Refinements
Using Range Names
Windows
Updating the Model
Saving Your Work: Part Two
Printing
Calculating
Protection
Relating to Other Environments
Summary

In previous chapters you saw several methods of entering information into Symphony. You have seen how formulas are created and copied to produce extensive spreadsheets from a few simple entries. You have also seen how data is organized in the worksheet so that the worksheet can be treated like a database. This chapter reviews the process of building a spreadsheet model and explains the commands for viewing information on the screen and for printing it on paper.

BUILDING A TYPICAL WORKSHEET

Using the step-by-step instructions provided in this chapter, you will learn about the techniques used to build a typical spreadsheet model. You will learn how to organize the worksheet with titles and windows and how to print it out. You can perform these steps yourself as a practical exercise, or simply use them as a reference when building your own models.

The suggestions made here offer you approaches that you can take when using Symphony's features. These are effective methods, but they are not hard-and-fast rules; as you become more experienced with Symphony, you may develop other techniques that are more suited to the particular demands of your work.

Basic Design

The sample worksheet presented here is a 12-month expense projection for a new automobile company, Ohmobile, that is selling electric cars across the country through four regional offices. Part of the completed model can be seen in Figure 3-1. The January figures are multiplied by a growth factor of one percent to produce the February figures. In each successive month, the expenses increase by the same factor. The growth factor ensures that the company budgets sufficient funds to cover rising expenses.

A1: 'Ohmobile: Projected Operating Expenses SHEET

	A	B	C	D	E	F	G	H
1	Ohmobile: Projected Operating Expenses							
2								
3		Jan-91	Feb-91	Mar-91	Apr-91	May-91	Jun-91	Jul-91
4	REGION 1							
5	Personnel	6,500	6,565	6,631	6,697	6,764	6,832	6,900
6	Lease	2,500	2,525	2,550	2,576	2,602	2,628	2,654
7	Utilities	500	505	510	515	520	526	531
8	Phone	300	303	306	309	312	315	318
9	Advertising	1,250	1,263	1,275	1,288	1,301	1,314	1,327
10	REGION 2							
11	Personnel	4,500	4,545	4,590	4,636	4,683	4,730	4,777
12	Lease	2,100	2,121	2,142	2,164	2,185	2,207	2,229
13	Utilities	450	455	459	464	468	473	478
14	Phone	250	253	255	258	260	263	265
15	Advertising	1,250	1,263	1,275	1,288	1,301	1,314	1,327
16	REGION 3							
17	Personnel	6,250	6,313	6,376	6,439	6,504	6,569	6,635
18	Lease	2,500	2,525	2,550	2,576	2,602	2,628	2,654
19	Utilities	500	505	510	515	520	526	531
20	Phone	300	303	306	309	312	315	318

MAIN

27-Feb-91 02:37 PM Num

FIGURE 3-1 Completed Ohmobile model

In general, the best approach to building spreadsheets is to enter data in the following order:

1. You use **labels** to identify the contents and arrangement of the model. Do not worry about the exact titles for columns and rows, since you can change them later. The width of columns can also be adjusted later. Do add any special alignment to labels if they are going to be copied, because the Copy command will reproduce the alignment.

2. **Numbers** make up the basic data in a worksheet. As you enter the numbers, you will get a general idea of the dimensions of the model.

3. Enter the first few **formulas** and make sure they work before copying them. Don't worry about the format of the results.

4. When you know what kind of numbers you are using, make any necessary **format** changes. Use the MENU Settings Format command for the most common format, and the MENU Format command for exceptions. Cells that will be copied can be formatted before copying, which reproduces the format.

5. Adjust column **widths** as needed. Use a global setting (MENU Settings Width) for the most common width, and adjust other columns individually (MENU Width Set).

Working in this order, you will proceed more quickly than if you spend a lot of time adjusting formats and column widths before most of the data is entered. You can always expect to have to adjust some widths, formats, and alignments after the model is completed. The decision to build the model column by column or row by row depends on the kind of data you are working with. The sample model will be built column by column; that is, the column of labels will be followed by the starting values and then by the first column of formulas, and the first formula column will then be copied to the rest of the columns. This approach follows the natural progression of the data and will require the least number of keystrokes.

Entering and Reusing Labels

Whenever possible, you should use the Copy command to reuse labels that you have already entered in the worksheet. Doing this saves time and also avoids inconsistent spelling and typos. Make sure you check your data before copying it. If the labels are to be specially aligned, apply the alignment command before copying

```
A9: 'Advertising                                                    SHEET

     A         B         C         D         E         F         G         H
1    Ohmobile: Projected Operating Expenses
2
3
4    REGION 1
5    Personnel
6    Lease
7    Utilities
8    Phone
9    Advertising
10
```

FIGURE 3-2 Beginning the model

to reduce the need for later adjustments. For example, to copy the labels for the sample worksheet, follow these steps:

1. Type in the labels in column A as they appear in Figure 3-2. The label in capital letters is the name of the office, which is followed by five categories of expenses incurred by that office. All six lines are initially entered as left-aligned labels. Note that the last label, Advertising, exceeds the default width of nine characters. This will be dealt with in a moment.

2. To offset the expense categories from the office name, right-align the expenses. With your cell selector in A5, press MENU ((F10)) and select Range. Then select Label-Alignment, followed by Right.

3. When prompted for the range of labels, you can use the (END) and arrow keys shortcut: Press (END) and then press (DOWN ARROW). This will highlight all of the labels from A5 through A9 in one step.

4. Press (ENTER) to confirm A5..A9 as the range to be right-aligned. Note that the results do not look too impressive. This is because of the width of the column and the "spare" character maintained by Symphony between columns.

5. To correct this, press MENU, choose Width, and choose Set. Type **12** and press (ENTER). This will widen the column to 12 characters and display the labels better.

Note that the Label-Alignment command has deleted the apostrophe label prefix and replaced it with the one you specified—quotes—for right alignment.

Multiple Copies

After aligning the labels through row 9 of column A, you can reuse the office name and expense category labels from cells A4 through A9. In the following steps you will create four copies of the labels to make the headings for the four offices:

1. Move the cell selector up to A4 and select MENU Copy. Symphony assumes that the FROM Range begins at A4, where your cell selector was located when you issued the command. This coordinate is already anchored as the beginning point of the range; it is indicated by the double dots A4..A4.

2. Highlight the other labels with the (DOWN ARROW) key.

3. To make headings for the four offices, you need four copies of the existing labels. Highlighting the six rows in A4..A9 prepares you for one copy. Adding six blank rows to the FROM range will make two copies. Adding another twelve rows to the FROM range will allow you to create the four copies you need, so the highlighting of the FROM range should be extended to

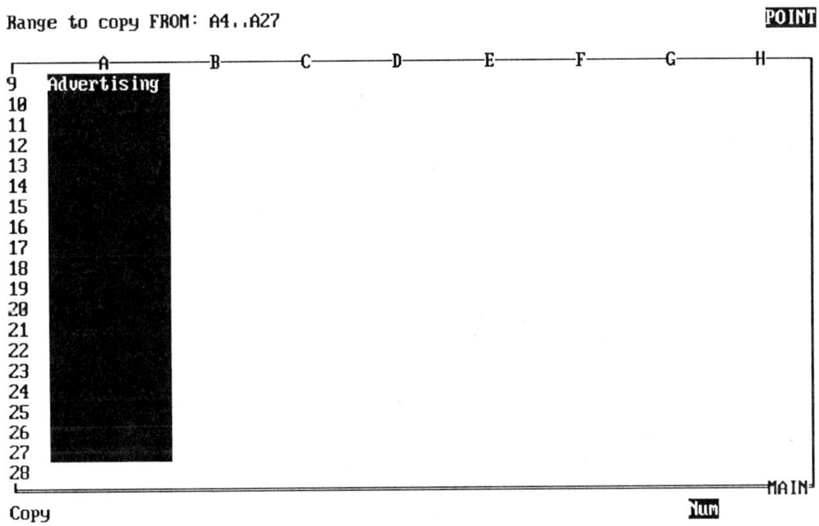

FIGURE 3-3 Extended copy FROM range

row 27 (9 plus 6 plus 12 = 27). Use the DOWN ARROW key to make the FROM range A4..A27, as shown in Figure 3-3.

4. Press ENTER to confirm A4..A27 as the FROM Range.

5. To indicate the correct TO range, press DOWN ARROW to move the cell selector to A10. Now press ENTER to confirm the destination. The labels, complete with right-alignment indicators, will be copied into position for the other offices. Your cell selector will be left in A4.

6. Now you need to move the cell pointer to A10 and edit the office name so that it becomes REGION 2.

7. Press F2 and then press the BACKSPACE key. Type **2** and press DOWN ARROW. Edit the other office names in A16 and A22 to REGION 3 and REGION 4, respectively.

```
A1: 'Ohmobile: Projected Operating Expenses                              SHEET

      A        B        C        D        E        F        G        H
1   Ohmobile: Projected Operating Expenses
2
3
4   REGION 1
5     Personnel
6         Lease
7     Utilities
8         Phone
9   Advertising
10  REGION 2
11    Personnel
12        Lease
13    Utilities
14        Phone
15  Advertising
16  REGION 3
17    Personnel
18        Lease
19    Utilities
20        Phone
21  Advertising
22  REGION 4
23    Personnel
24        Lease
25    Utilities
26        Phone
27  Advertising
28
29
                                                                      MAIN
25-Feb-91  03:12 PM                                                Num
```

FIGURE 3-4 Completed copy and edit of labels

Figure 3-4 shows the results of this operation. Note that this view of the screen shows 29 rows, as opposed to 20 in other figures. A different display was used for this figure—one that offers a larger view of the work area. This alternative view will be used in figures that need to show a larger section of work. You can read about installing different display systems in Appendix A.

GETTING A DATE

Now that you have entered the headings for the rows of the model, you need to think about the column headings. Since this worksheet is a one-year projection divided into months, you need to enter the names of the months across the worksheet. To do this you could use simple labels like Jan, Feb, and so on. You would place the cell selector on row 3 and, starting in column B, type **Jan** and then press (RIGHT ARROW). You would then type **Feb** and press (RIGHT ARROW), and so on, through to **Dec**. After Dec, you would move to cell N3 and enter **TOTALS** for the year-end totals that will eventually be created.

When entering a series of labels like this, you will appreciate the usefulness of the arrow method for entering data. However, an alternative method of entering months is available, thanks to the date-math capabilities of Symphony. This method will be described after you look at how Symphony handles dates.

Date Math

Symphony can treat dates mathematically, allowing you to quantify time-related information and manipulate it for spreadsheet and database applications. For a computer program to read a date (such as April 1, 1991) as something that has value, the date must be converted to a number. Symphony performs this conversion by calculating the number of days between the date involved and the end of the last century. This is the date's *serial number*. Thus, January 1, 1900, is date number 1. Move ahead 1000 days and you have September 27, 1902. Day number 33,333 is otherwise known as April 5, 1991.

The @DATE function is used to convert dates to numbers. The function takes the form

@DATE(YY,MM,DD)

where YY is the year, MM is the month, and DD is the day of the month. Thus April 5, 1991 is entered as

```
@DATE(91,4,5)
```

Note that months and days less than 10 do not need to be entered with leading zeros. The year 2000 is entered 100, so 2001 is 101. The first day of the year 2001 is thus

@DATE(101,1,1)

Any illegal dates—for example, @DATE(87,2,29)—return ERR as their value. This date corresponds to February 29, 1987, which is invalid because 1987 was not a leap year.

Converting dates to numbers allows you to compare dates and calculate differences. You can see the power of this feature if you use Symphony to answer this simple question: How many days have you been alive? In an unused part of the current worksheet, you can answer this by following these steps:

1. In F1, type your birthday in the form of an @DATE function, as in @DATE(53,11,23) for someone born on the 23rd of November, 1953.

2. Press (DOWN ARROW) to enter this date and move down to the next cell.

3. In F2, type **@NOW**, which is a special function that reads the date from the operating system. Press (DOWN ARROW) to enter this function and move down to the next cell.

4. In F3, type **+F2-F1** and press (ENTER). This is the number of days from your birthday to today. The number in (F2) is the number of days from the turn of the century to the current date.

You can see the results in Figure 3-5. Note that the number in (F2) has a decimal portion. This is a fraction of a day, representing the time. The @NOW function used in (F2) tells you what the date and time are, according to the operating system. This same information is used in the Symphony calendar/clock in the lower left of

```
F3: +F2-F1                                                              SHEET
      A          B          C          D         E          F          G          H
1  Ohmobile: Projected Operating Expenses                  19686
2                                                        33295.41
3                                                        13609.41
4  REGION 1
```

FIGURE 3-5 Date-math example

the screen. In the worksheet it is presented by @NOW in the form of a serial date and decimal time. If you have not set the date and time correctly in your system, this calculation will not work properly. As a rough guide, the number in F2 should be greater than 33000 (see Appendix A for more on setting the date and time in your system).

More typical applications for this date-math capability are scheduling projects, dating and sorting records, and calculating loans. Date math is also useful in producing a series of dates, such as a row with the names of the months or a column of payment-due dates.

Date Formats

At this point the two dates in Figure 3-5 do not look like dates—they just look like large numbers. To make a serial number look like a date, you must format the number. With the cell pointer in F1, use MENU Format Date and select option 4. Press DOWN ARROW to select F1..F2 as the range to format, and press ENTER. The results should be similar to Figure 3-6. Note the format indicator (D4) at the top left of the screen, showing which format is applied to this cell. Bear in mind that the number in F3 is not a date, it is a number of days.

Before getting back to the sample model, take another look at the date format options, shown in Figure 3-7. You can see that the

```
F1: (D4) @DATE(53,11,23)                                                   SHEET

┌─────────A──────────B──────────C──────────D──────────E──────────F──────────G──────────H──┐
1   Ohmobile: Projected Operating Expenses                    11/23/53
2                                                             02/26/91
3                                                             13609.42
4   REGION 1
```

FIGURE 3-6 Formatted dates

fourth format is called Full Intn'l, or Full International. This usually gives the appearance shown in Figure 3-6; that is, a two-digit representation of month/day/year with slashes between the date parts, as in 02/26/91. This way of showing dates is common in America but not in Europe. Fortunately, Symphony allows you to change the display of dates and numbers to match other conventions. This is done with the SERVICES Configuration Other International command, which produces this screen:

```
Specify numeric punctuation                                                MENU
Punctuation  Currency  Date  Time  Negative  Quit

Punctuation:   A                              Date format D4:  A (MM/DD/YY)
        Point Dot
     Argument Comma                           Time format T3:  A (HH:MM:SS)
    Thousands Comma

Currency sign: $                  (Prefix)    Negative:          Parentheses
═══════════════════════════════════════════════════════International Settings
```

The options in this menu are described in detail in Appendix A.

The first date format is called the Lotus standard long form. When you apply this format to the dates in the example, the results

```
Lotus standard long form                                                    MENU
1 (DD-MMM-YY)  2 (DD-MMM)  3 (MMM-YY)  4 (Full Intn'l)  5 (Partial Intn'l)
┌─────────A──────────B──────────C──────────D──────────E──────────F──────────G──────────H──┐
1   Ohmobile: Projected Operating Expenses                    *********
2                                                             *********
3                                                             13609.42
4   REGION 1
```

FIGURE 3-7 Date format options

Identifier	Format	Display for April 1, 1991
D1	DD-MMM-YY	01-Apr-91
D2	DD-MMM	01-Apr
D3	MMM-YY	Apr-91
D4	Full International	04/01/91
D5	Partial International	04/01

TABLE 3-1 Date Formats

are as shown in Figure 3-7. In cell F2, Symphony is attempting to display "23-Nov-91," which is nine characters. Since the date is a value and only eight digits of a value can be displayed in a nine-character column, the result is the series of asterisks that tell you to change the format or column width. You only need to enlarge the column by one character to see the full date. If much of your work includes dates, you can change the default column width to 10 with the MENU Settings Width command.

The full range of date formats are shown in Table 3-1. Note that format D3 shows the month and year of a date. This will be used to create the month headings for the model. Before that, however, you will want to erase the date experiment from cells F1..F3. Simply move the cell pointer to F1, press MENU, select Erase, and press (DOWN ARROW) twice. Then press (ENTER) to confirm the command.

The Month Headings

At the beginning of this section it was suggested that month names could be typed into the worksheet. However, the same data can be created more quickly with date values. As values, the dates can easily be updated for next year's figures.

To create a series of the names of the months with date values, you enter the date as the first day of the first month of the series. Then you format the date with the MMM-YY format. Entering **1/1/91** and changing the format to MMM-YY produces Jan-91. You can then add 31 days to this date to produce the first of the next month, Feb-91, and so on. To do this in the model, follow these steps:

1. To begin the series, move the cell pointer to B3, type **@DATE(91,1,1)**, and press (ENTER).

2. To format the date, press MENU and select Format, followed by Date. Choose format 3, and when you are prompted for the range, press (RIGHT ARROW) once to include C3. This will save formatting the cell later.

3. Now move the cell pointer to C3 and enter this formula:

   ```
   31+B3
   ```

   The result will appear as "Feb-91."

4. Now you need to copy this cell as far as column M. With the cell pointer still in C3, press MENU, select Copy, and press (ENTER) to accept C3..C3 as the FROM range.

5. Type a period (**.**) to anchor C3 as the beginning of the TO range and then press (RIGHT ARROW) until the range extends to column M. Press (ENTER) to confirm C3..M3 as the TO range.

The result, shown here, is a series of month headings for the model:

```
C3: (D3) 31+B3                                                    SHEET

     A         B         C         D         E         F         G         H
1  Ohmobile: Projected Operating Expenses
2
3              Jan-91    Feb-91    Mar-91    Apr-91    May-91    Jun-91    Jul-91
4  REGION 1
5    Personnel
6        Lease
7    Utilities
8        Phone
9  Advertising
10 REGION 2
```

The actual dates created by repeatedly adding 31 to the first of January are not the first of every month, but in this case the variation is not important. The D3 format ignores the day of the month to give the date series just created an acceptable appearance.

The major advantage of entering dates in this manner is the ease with which you can update them for next year's budget. By highlighting the starting date of the series in cell B3, pressing (F2) to edit it, and changing @DATE(91,1,1) to @DATE(92,1,1), you could update the entire series to the months of 1992. (If you try this, change 92 back to 91 before continuing.) The technique of repeatedly adding 31 days to a beginning date of January 1 will produce acceptable consecutive MMM-YY dates for at least 48 months.

Date Filling

An alternative method of creating a regular series of dates is to use the Range Fill command. To create the month headings in this example by this method, you would select Fill from the Range menu and select the cells into which you wanted the dates placed, B3..M3, as the fill range. For the start value you would enter **@DATE(91,1,1)**. For the step value you would enter 31. For the stop value you must enter a number larger than the default of 8191, and at least as large as the highest date serial number in the series (111111 would work and is easy to type). When you enter the stop value, the range will be filled with the series of numbers and you can format them as dates. However, a date series created with the Range Fill command is not interactive and will not be updated when the first date in the series is changed.

Dates and Functions

A further approach to producing month names is to use a combination of several functions, including the @MONTH function, which has the syntax @MONTH(*DateNumber*). This function returns the number (1 through 12) corresponding to the month of the year represented by *DateNumber*. Thus, @MONTH(A1) returns 12, if the number in A1 is 33232 or if A1 contains @DATE(90,12,25). This is one of a number of "date-part" functions. The date-part functions can be used with cell references or in combination with other date functions. Thus, the formula @MONTH(@DATE(90,12,25)) returns the answer 12.

You can combine date functions with other functions for some useful formulas, such as this one, which could be used in C3:

```
@CHOOSE(@MONTH(B3+31)-1,"January","February","March","April",
"May","June","July","August","September","October","November",
"December",@ERR)
```

This formula lets you create the full name of the month represented by whatever date serial number is the argument for the @MONTH function. None of the built-in date formats produce the full name of the month. The @MONTH(B3+31)-1 calculation returns a number from 0 through 11 for the case number, which the @CHOOSE function then reads into the cell. The formula uses the @CHOOSE function to pick a name from the list of names that are typed as labels in the formula. The syntax of the @CHOOSE function is

@CHOOSE(*X*,*Case0*,*Case1*,*Case2*,*Casen*)

where *X* is the index, the number of the case to be selected from the list of cases, and *Case0, Case1,* and so on are either numbers or labels. The month-name formula has the 12 months entered as the cases. Because they are labels, they are entered in quotes. The @ERR function is used in case the month number is incorrect; it will produce the message ERR in the cell if there is a problem.

MODEL VALUES

Returning to the model, it is time to enter the first figures. All projections must have a starting point. In the case of the expense projection example you are building, the January figures could be based on the actual figures for the last month of the previous year. In the case of a new company such as Ohmobile, the numbers are just estimates. They are entered in column B, as shown in Figure 3-8. Again, you can make use of the arrow method as you enter the list of numbers.

Total Calculation

At the bottom of column B, you want to enter a formula that will sum the January expenses for all four offices.

1. First enter the right-aligned label **"TOTALS** in A29.
2. Now move to B29 to create the formula, which will use the @SUM function.
3. Type **@SUM(** to begin the formula. You are now ready to use the pointing method to indicate the range of cells to be summed.

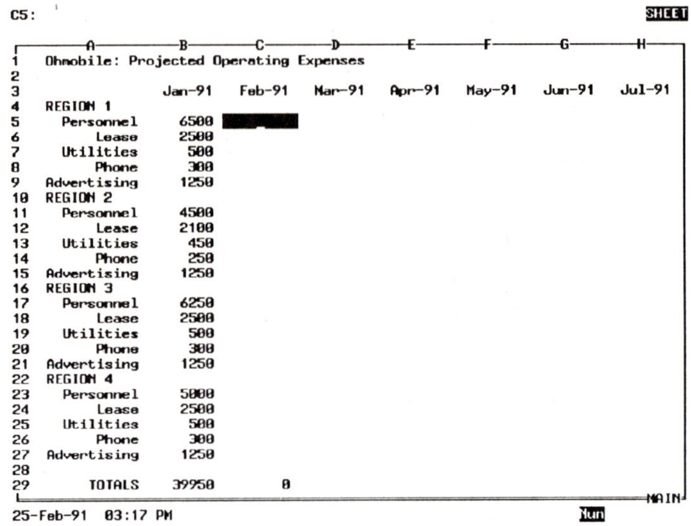

FIGURE 3-8 Figures for January

4. Use (PGUP) and (DOWN ARROW) to get to B5. Anchor the beginning point of the range by typing a period.

5. You now need to move the highlighting down the column. There is a quick way to do this. Press (LEFT ARROW), and your cell selector will be in a column that contains consecutive rows of data (A).

6. Now press (END) and (DOWN ARROW). This takes the cell pointer directly to row 27, as shown in Figure 3-9. Do *not* press (ENTER).

7. In essence you have "hitched a ride" on a range of occupied cells that is continuous in the desired direction (down). Now press (RIGHT ARROW) to move back into the original column. The highlighting will appear in B5..B27.

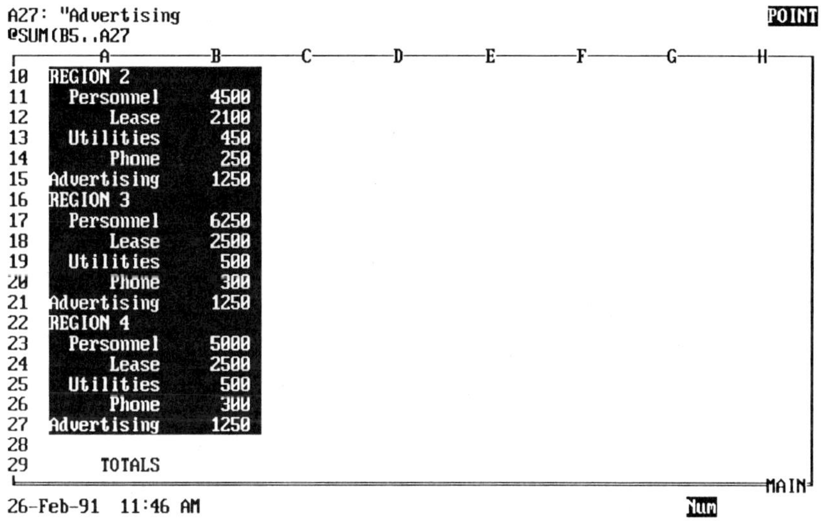

FIGURE 3-9 Moving the cell pointer down the model

8. Complete the formula with the closing parenthesis and then press (ENTER). The formula should read @SUM(B5..B27), and the answer is 39950.

The technique of using an adjacent column or row to move the cell pointer is very useful when you are building a model, since often you need to move the cell selector to the end of the model in a row or column that is not yet completely filled. However, you must always remember to come back to the original column or row before completing the maneuver.

Before moving on, while your cell selector is still in B29, you can save some time by copying the total formula to C29. Press MENU, select Copy, and press (ENTER). Now press (RIGHT ARROW), and press (ENTER) to finish copying the formula to C29. Note that the formula returns 0 because the cells it sums are empty. This will change when you fill column C with formulas in the next stage.

Copying Formulas

The figures that occupy column C of the completed model are actually formulas that multiply the expenses in column B by a factor that increases them. These formulas are repeated across the model so that a steady month-to-month increase in expenses is built into the budget. (Although in practice lease payments rarely increase on a gradual monthly basis, the overall effect will be to allocate sufficient funding for probable long-term lease cost increases).

The formula in C5 is 1.01 times the value in the cell one column to the left, or 1.01*B5. You need to enter this formula in C5 and leave your cell selector there, since this formula will be copied down the column, making each cell in column C 1.01 times the value in the cell to the left. To perform the copy,

1. Select MENU Copy. The FROM range will be C5..C5, which Symphony is already suggesting. Press (ENTER) to confirm this.

2. The quickest way to point out the destination for the copy is to type a period while the cell selector is still in C5. This anchors the beginning point of the range in C5, and you can use (PGDN) and (DOWN ARROW) to highlight down to C27.

3. Press (ENTER) to confirm C5..C27 as the TO range. This will complete the copy process, with results like those shown in Figure 3-10.

Including the source cell C5 in the TO range copies that cell over itself, but this causes no problems. Each cell in column C from row 5 to 27 is now 1.01 times the value of the corresponding cell in column B. One small problem is that the rows without expenses in column B are also multiplied in column C, producing zeros. These rows are easily removed by erasing the contents of cells C10,

```
C5: 1.01*B5                                                        SHEET

   A              B          C          D          E          F          G          H
1  Ohmobile: Projected Operating Expenses
2
3                 Jan-91     Feb-91     Mar-91     Apr-91     May-91     Jun-91     Jul-91
4  REGION 1
5    Personnel      6500       6565
6        Lease      2500       2525
7    Utilities       500        505
8        Phone       300        303
9  Advertising      1250     1262.5
10 REGION 2                       0
11   Personnel      4500       4545
12       Lease      2100       2121
13   Utilities       450      454.5
14       Phone       250      252.5
15 Advertising      1250     1262.5
16 REGION 3                       0
17   Personnel      6250     6312.5
18       Lease      2500       2525
19   Utilities       500        505
20       Phone       300        303
                                                                   MAIN
26-Feb-91  11:53 AM                                           Num
```

FIGURE 3-10 The completed copying of C5

C16, and C22. Go ahead and highlight each one in turn, typing /E and pressing (ENTER) to remove its contents.

Copying Columns

Since you have already copied the sum formula from the bottom of column B to the bottom of column C (from B29 to C29), you can copy the whole of column C, from rows 5 through 29, to columns D through M to complete the projection for twelve months. Follow these steps to perform the copy for the column:

1. With your cell pointer in C5, select MENU Copy. The FROM range needs to be expanded downward. Press (PGDN) and you will move the highlighting to C25. Press (DOWN ARROW) four times to include C29. Press (ENTER) to confirm C5..C29 as the FROM range.

2. Move the cell pointer to D5 and anchor it with a period. Press (UP ARROW) twice, and you will be able to "hitch" to the end of the model using the line of months in row 2.

3. Press (END) and then (RIGHT ARROW), and the highlighting will move to column M. Then press (DOWN ARROW) twice so that the highlighted TO range is D5..M5.

4. Symphony will assume that row 5 and the area below it, down as far as row 29, are available for copying into. If you want to be sure, move the highlighting down to line 29 to correspond with the FROM range and to view the full range of destination cells. However, this is not essential; you are working on a new worksheet and therefore know that nothing has been entered in this area. Press (ENTER) to confirm the destination of the copy.

C5: 1.01*B5 SHEET

	A	B	C	D	E	F	G	H
1	Ohmobile: Projected Operating Expenses							
2								
3		Jan-91	Feb-91	Mar-91	Apr-91	May-91	Jun-91	Jul-91
4	REGION 1							
5	Personnel	6500	6565	6630.65	6696.956	6763.926	6831.565	6899.880
6	Lease	2500	2525	2550.25	2575.752	2601.510	2627.525	2653.800
7	Utilities	500	505	510.05	515.1505	520.3020	525.5050	530.7600
8	Phone	300	303	306.03	309.0903	312.1812	315.3030	318.4560
9	Advertising	1250	1262.5	1275.125	1287.876	1300.755	1313.762	1326.900
10	REGION 2							
11	Personnel	4500	4545	4590.45	4636.354	4682.718	4729.545	4776.840
12	Lease	2100	2121	2142.21	2163.632	2185.268	2207.121	2229.192
13	Utilities	450	454.5	459.045	463.6354	468.2718	472.9545	477.6840
14	Phone	250	252.5	255.025	257.5752	260.1510	262.7525	265.3800
15	Advertising	1250	1262.5	1275.125	1287.876	1300.755	1313.762	1326.900
16	REGION 3							
17	Personnel	6250	6312.5	6375.625	6439.381	6503.775	6568.812	6634.500
18	Lease	2500	2525	2550.25	2575.752	2601.510	2627.525	2653.800
19	Utilities	500	505	510.05	515.1505	520.3020	525.5050	530.7600
20	Phone	300	303	306.03	309.0903	312.1812	315.3030	318.4560

MAIN

26-Feb-91 12:00 PM Num

FIGURE 3-11 Completed column copy

The impressive results of this copy appear in Figure 3-11. You can see the speed with which Symphony reproduces a set of formulas. Since much of the work you do with numbers requires repetition of the same calculations, you will probably use the Copy command a great deal in your own spreadsheets.

SAVING YOUR WORK: PART ONE

At this point you might want to issue the SERVICES File Save command to give the worksheet a name and store the work you have done so far. When you issue the File Save command for a worksheet that has not yet been saved, you are provided with a list of files in the current directory, as shown here:

```
Save file name: C:\SYM22\DATA\*.wr1                                                 FILES
ADD.WR1           BINARY.WR1        BUILD1.WR1        CARDATA1.WR1      CARLOAN1.WR1
         A               B        C         D          E         F         G         H
1   Ohmobile: Projected Operating Expenses
2
3                    Jan-91    Feb-91    Mar-91    Apr-91    May-91    Jun-91    Jul-91
4   REGION 1
5     Personnel        6500      6565   6630.65  6696.956  6763.926  6831.565  6899.880
```

You can move the highlighting along this list to use an existing filename for the current model. Of course, this will replace the existing contents of the disk file with the current worksheet.

Most likely, you will want to use a new name for this worksheet. To do this you simply type an appropriate name, such as **OHMEXP91**. The name appears at the prompt. There is no need to type the extension, because WR1 is added automatically at the end of the file name. Press (ENTER) to confirm the name, and your work so far will be stored in a file on disk. As you continue to develop the worksheet, further changes can quickly be saved to the same file.

FURTHER REFINEMENTS

After a large copy operation, you will probably want to fine-tune some of the results. As you can see in the example, the appearance of many of the numbers leaves something to be desired. This is because they are displayed in the General format, which shows as many decimal places as it takes to complete the calculation or fill the cell. When the growth factor produces lengthy fractions, the cell fills with many decimal figures.

Adjusting the Format

To correct this and format the numbers consistently, you can use the Format command and use the Punctuated format with the value cells of the model. This places a comma in the thousands and lets you limit the number of decimal places displayed. In this case you can use zero decimal places.

1. Place your cell selector in B5, the top left of the range of cells that need to be formatted. Select MENU Format.
2. Select the Punctuated format. This format assumes that you want two decimal places, but you can easily change that to zero by typing **0** and pressing (ENTER).
3. You will be prompted for the range of cells to be formatted. This includes all of the cells from B5 to the end of the model, so you can press (END) and then (HOME) to include a range of cells that extends all the way to the last column and row used in the current worksheet (which should be B5..M29). Press (ENTER) to confirm the range.

The very tidy results can be seen back in Figure 3-1. Notice that the decimal places are rounded by the format, not truncated. If you later change the format to display several decimal places, Symphony will reveal the decimal digits that the zero decimal format removed from view. Now try placing your cell selector in one of the cells that did have a lot of decimal places, such as E5. You will see from the top status area that the real contents of the cell is the formula, 1.01*D5, together with the format notation (P0) for Punctuated format, zero decimal places.

Summing the Rows

Now you are ready to perform the last calculation needed to complete the model. In column N, you calculate the totals for each row over the 12-month period. These totals will be a series of @SUM formulas, the first of which is entered in N5. First, however, you will want to put a label in N3.

1. In cell N3, type **^TOTALS** and press (ENTER).
2. In cell N5, type **@SUM(** and then press (LEFT ARROW) followed by (END) and then (LEFT ARROW) again. This moves the cell pointer to the extreme left of the model. Now press (RIGHT ARROW) once so that you are in cell B5.
3. Type a period to anchor the beginning point of the range in B5.
4. Press (END) and (RIGHT ARROW) to include all the cells B5..M5. Type the closing parenthesis to complete the formula, and press (ENTER) to place the formula in N5, as shown here:

N5: @SUM(B5..M5) SHEET

	H	I	J	K	L	M	N	O
1								
2								
3	Jul-91	Aug-91	Sep-91	Oct-91	Nov-91	Dec-91	TOTALS	
4								
5	6,900	6,969	7,039	7,109	7,180	7,252	82436.26	
6	2,654	2,680	2,707	2,734	2,762	2,789		
7	531	536	541	547	552	558		
8	318	322	325	328	331	335		
9	1,327	1,340	1,354	1,367	1,381	1,395		

5. Before copying this formula, you will format it. Press MENU, select Format, and then select Punctuated. Type **0** for the decimal places and press (ENTER). Press (ENTER) again to confirm the format range as N5..N5.

6. To sum all the rows in the model, select MENU Copy with the cell selector still in N5. Press (ENTER) to accept N5..N5 as the FROM range.

7. Type a period to anchor N5 as the start of the TO range, and press the (PGDN) key. Press (DOWN ARROW) several more times to include the last row of the model, 29. Press (ENTER) to confirm the copy.

The formula in cell N29 is actually the grand total of all the expenses, since it sums the row of column totals. You will find several cells in column N containing zeros, because the formula copied into them is inappropriate. Simply delete these with the MENU Erase command.

Using the Model

Having built the model, you are almost ready to use it. However, before going any further you should make sure that the latest changes are stored. Assuming that you have already used the File Save command to give the worksheet an appropriate file name, issue the File Save command to update the file. When asked by Symphony if you want to replace the existing file, answer Yes.

From a practical point of view, the model has several uses. The basic use is to determine the total expenses for the year based on the assumed beginning values and growth factor. For example, if you change the Lease amount for Region 1 to 7,000, the change affects the figures across the model. This results in a new grand total in N29, but you will need to move the cell pointer there to look at this figure. Symphony has a number of commands that enable you to move around the spreadsheet and view it more easily.

Navigation

You have already seen that the (END) key can be of great help during copy operations. Now that the model is built, (END) and (RIGHT ARROW) move you to the right side of the model. Be sure to have your cell selector on a completed row of data before using this combination. Asking Symphony to go to the end on the right on a blank line means you end up in column IV. Simply press (HOME), or (END) and (LEFT ARROW), to return to the worksheet area. Using (END) and (HOME) will take you to the last cell of the worksheet that has been used.

You may have noticed that the arrow keys are not always the most efficient way to move to a specific location, particularly if that location is some distance from your current position. For this reason, you will often want to use the GOTO key, (F5). When you press (F5), you are prompted for the location to which you want the cell pointer moved. Simply type in the coordinates of your destination and press (ENTER). Your selector will be placed in the new cell.

Normally when you use (F5), your screen will scroll to show the destination cell in the top left of your screen. Unless the destination cell is very close to A1, this move may disorient you at first—for example, when you are using GOTO to move to the bottom right corner of the model. If you use GOTO to get to N29, Symphony shows just one cell, N29, on the screen. You could use J13 as the cell to go to, which would give you a view of the bottom corner of the worksheet, but this is a difficult coordinate to remember. To avoid having to remember cell coordinates and to further streamline spreadsheet work, you can use range names.

USING RANGE NAMES

In larger models, remembering cell coordinates becomes increasingly difficult. Range names can be a great help. A *range name* is a name attached to a cell or group of cells, enabling commands and formulas to refer to the cells by name, rather than coordinates.

Why You Should Use Range Names

Many Symphony commands require that you supply the location of certain pieces of information. These locations can be a single cell or a group of cells. Entering coordinates can be tricky and is an error-prone process. A better approach is to assign names to the groups of cells you want to indicate. For example, to view the bottom corner of the model you have built you can attach a name to some of the cells in that area of the worksheet:

1. First press (HOME), and then press (F5), type **J13**, and press (ENTER). The cell pointer will move to J13.

2. Press MENU and select Range, followed by Name, as shown in Figure 3-12. Here you can see the Range Name menu, which is used to create and delete range names, as well as to list them in the worksheet (Table), erase all of the names in a worksheet (Reset), or create range names from labels, as described in a moment.

3. Select Create. You will be prompted to enter a name. If there are already range names in the worksheet, they will be listed below the prompt.

4. Type **end** and press (ENTER). You can type this in uppercase or lowercase. You will be asked to specify which cells you want to call END, as shown in Figure 3-13. Note that the beginning point of the range is not anchored.

```
Add or revise entry in range name list                                   MENU
Create  Delete  Labels  Reset  Table
     A            B         C         D         E         F         G         H
1   Ohmobile: Projected Operating Expenses
2
3                Jan-91    Feb-91    Mar-91    Apr-91    May-91    Jun-91    Jul-91
4   REGION 1
5     Personnel   6,500     6,565     6,631     6,697     6,764     6,832     6,900
6         Lease   2,500     2,525     2,550     2,576     2,602     2,628     2,654
7     Utilities     500       505       510       515       520       526       531
8         Phone     300       303       306       309       312       315       318
9   Advertising   1,250     1,263     1,275     1,288     1,301     1,314     1,327
10  REGION 2
11    Personnel   4,500     4,545     4,590     4,636     4,683     4,730     4,777
12        Lease   2,100     2,121     2,142     2,164     2,185     2,207     2,229
13    Utilities     450       455       459       464       468       473       478
14        Phone     250       253       255       258       260       263       265
15  Advertising   1,250     1,263     1,275     1,288     1,301     1,314     1,327
16  REGION 3
17    Personnel   6,250     6,313     6,376     6,439     6,504     6,569     6,635
18        Lease   2,500     2,525     2,550     2,576     2,602     2,628     2,654
19    Utilities     500       505       510       515       520       526       531
20        Phone     300       303       306       309       312       315       318
                                                                             MAIN
Range Name                                                          Num
```

FIGURE 3-12 The Range Name menu

```
Range name: end                            Specify range: J13               POINT

         J         K         L         M         N         O         P         Q
13      487       492       497       502     5,707
14      271       273       276       279     3,171
15    1,354     1,367     1,381     1,395    15,853
16
17    6,768     6,836     6,904     6,973    79,266
18    2,707     2,734     2,762     2,789    31,706
19      541       547       552       558     6,341
20      325       328       331       335     3,805
21    1,354     1,367     1,381     1,395    15,853
22
23    5,414     5,468     5,523     5,578    63,413
24    2,707     2,734     2,762     2,789    31,706
25      541       547       552       558     6,341
26      325       328       331       335     3,805
27    1,354     1,367     1,381     1,395    15,853
28
29   43,260    43,693    44,130    44,571   506,666
30
31
32
                                                                             MAIN
Range Name Create                                                   Num
```

FIGURE 3-13 Creating the END range

5. Type a period (.) to anchor J13 as the beginning point of the range, and use (RIGHT ARROW) and (DOWN ARROW) to expand the range to N29.

6. Press (ENTER) to confirm the range, and you will be back in SHEET mode.

To use this range name, you can press (HOME), then (F5), and then type **end** and press (ENTER). Your screen will be arranged so that you can see the bottom corner of the model.

Note Note that when you move to a range with GOTO, your cell pointer is placed in the top left cell of the range.

An even simpler method of moving, which is particularly useful when you have larger worksheet models, is to use the (F10) key to list all existing range names. Thus, you can press (F5) followed by (F10) to list the range names, and then select whichever one you want to move to by using the highlight and (ENTER) method.

Uses for Range Names

In addition to making it easier to move to a specific location in your worksheet, range names make it easier to switch between different range settings, such as those for printing, which is discussed later in the chapter. Range names also provide a form of documentation for a worksheet. For example, range names can be used in formulas, making the formulas much more readable than when you use cell addresses.

The expenses in your model can be summed with the formula @SUM(EXPENSES) if the range name EXPENSES is assigned to cells B5..M27. Use MENU Range Name Create to do this, and you will see the END range listed as an existing range, as shown here:

```
Range name:                                                              NAMES
END
       A            B         C         D         E         F         G         H
1  Ohmobile: Projected Operating Expenses
2
3                 Jan-91    Feb-91    Mar-91    Apr-91    May-91    Jun-91    Jul-91
```

Type **expenses** and press (ENTER). Select B5..M27 as the range. To use this name, move the cell pointer to G1, type **@SUM(EXPENSES)**, and press (ENTER). The result will be essentially the same number as in N29. To confirm that this is true, press (F5) followed by (F10). You will see the range names listed horizontally, in alphabetical order, as in Figure 3-14. Notice that the range names are stored in uppercase by Symphony.

If you press (F10) again at this point, you will see a variation on the range-name list, used when there are a lot of range names. This list fills the screen:

```
Address to go to:                                          NAMES

  BASE PRICE   INTEREST     PAYMENT      PREP COSTS   PRINCIPAL
  SALES TAX    TERM         TOTAL        TOTAL PRICE
```

You can navigate the list with the arrow keys to highlight the name you want, and press (ENTER) to select it.

You can see from Figure 3-14 that in the model, the END range is the first in the list, so you can simply press (ENTER) to move to that range. This will show you cell N29, which is a rounded version of the result in G1. To keep the model looking professional, you should now return to G1 and erase the formula there.

An advantage of using range names is that you are less prone to error when writing formulas. It is easier to type EXPENSES than to type B5..M27. If you typed B6..M27 by mistake, Symphony would not know you missed a row of numbers, but if you typed SXPENSES by mistake, Symphony would beep and tell you that the name had not been found. Also, range names stay with the cells to which they are attached during insert operations. Names also

```
Address to go to:                                                    NAMES
END                 EXPENSES
        A          B          C          D          E          F          G          H
1  Ohmobile: Projected Operating Expenses                             506665.9
2
3                 Jan-91     Feb-91     Mar-91     Apr-91     May-91     Jun-91     Jul-91
```

FIGURE 3-14 Range names listed by (F10)

stay with ranges during MENU Move commands that include the entire named range. Range names are not duplicated by the Copy command.

Tips for Creating Range Names

There are three rules concerning Symphony range names:

- They cannot exceed 15 characters.
- They must be unique within the worksheet.
- They should not be the same as cell names.

The last rule simply refers to the fact that naming a range P88 would be confusing since there is also a cell called P88. However, 88P would be okay, as would "P88" with quotes as part of the name. Any characters are acceptable in range names, including spaces. However, spaces are not advisable; as an example, the name SALES FORCE might be confused with the two ranges SALES and FORCE. Similarly, you will want to avoid names that use math characters, like SALES/FORCE, which could be confused with the command to divide the range SALES by the range FORCE. To connect words in a range name, use the underline symbol, as in SALES_FORCE.

Symphony will not differentiate between uppercase and lowercase letters in a name. Thus, SALES, Sales, and sales will all be recorded as the same name and listed as SALES. One cell can be in several different named ranges, and you can assign more than one name to an identical range of cells. These other names are thought of as synonyms for the original name.

Tracking Range Names

As you begin to use more range names in a worksheet, it becomes more difficult to remember what range names you have used and what cells they have been assigned to. Symphony shows you existing range names when you use the Range Name Create command.

For a more permanent record of range names, you can ask Symphony to place a list of the range names and their coordinates into the spreadsheet with the Range Name Table command. When you issue this command, you simply need to indicate the upper-left cell of the area on the spreadsheet into which you want Symphony to place the information. The data takes up two columns and one row for each name. Be aware that this data is destructive; that is, it will overwrite data in unprotected cells if it needs the room to list all the names.

An example of a range-name table is shown in Figure 3-15. Note that the first column of the table range will need to be widened if you have used long range names. Also note that this table is not dynamic: it is not updated automatically. You must use the Range Name Table command each time you want a current listing of range names.

If you lose track of range names or have some other reason for starting fresh, you can use the Range Name Reset command to clear all existing range names. Symphony will prompt you to confirm the action. A less drastic alternative is the Range Name

```
A8: 'BASE PRICE                                                        SHEET

   ------A--------------B-----------C----------D-----------------E-----------F--------
1  Principal     $10,577.00              Base Price          $9,100.00
2  Interest           1.00%              Prep Costs            $567.00
3  Term                  36              Sales Tax             $910.00
4  Payment          $351.31              Total Price        $10,577.00
5  Total         $12,647.08
6
7
8  BASE PRICE  E1
9  INTEREST    B2
10 PAYMENT     B4
11 PREP COSTS  E2
12 PRINCIPAL   B1
13 SALES TAX   E3
14 TERM        B3
15 TOTAL       B5
16 TOTAL PRICE E4
17
18
19
20
   ------------------------------------------------------------------------------MAIN-
27-Feb-91  03:11 PM                                                       Num
```

FIGURE 3-15 Range-name table in worksheet

Delete command, which lets you delete one name at a time from the name list.

Range Names from Labels

A very convenient command in the Range Name menu is Labels, which allows you to assign names to ranges from labels in the spreadsheet that are adjacent to the named cells. Consider this example:

```
B4: (C2) @PMT(PRINCIPAL,INTEREST,TERM)                                          SHEET

   A              B              C          D                E              F
1  Principal      $10,577.00                Base Price       $9,100.00
2  Interest            1.00%                Prep Costs         $567.00
3  Term                   36                Sales Tax          $910.00
4  Payment           $351.31                Total Price     $10,577.00
5  Total          $12,647.08
6
7
```

Here, you could assign the names of the labels in column A to the values in column B, allowing you to enter the arguments for the @PMT function as names.

To name the cells in column B with the labels in column A, you first place the cell pointer in A1 and then issue the Range Name Labels Right command, because you are naming the cells on the right of the labels. Symphony then prompts you for a range of labels to use, and you select A1..A5. When you press (ENTER) to confirm the command, the names are assigned. Cell B1 is now called PRINCIPAL, B2 is INTEREST, and so on. Blank cells in the range of labels have no effect, so you can use ranges that contain empty cells. You can also name cells that are above or below the range of labels or that are to the left of the labels.

One limitation of this command is that it only names single cell ranges. You cannot name cells B5..M9 in Figure 3-1 as REGION 1 by using this command. However, you could use it to attach the name to B4 and then expand the range with the Range Name Create command, highlighting REGION 1 from the range-name list and pressing (ENTER) to redefine it. Note that the Range Name Labels command does not object to spaces in range names—they are not illegal—but it is not advisable to use them.

WINDOWS

You have seen that creating a model that flows across several screens presents problems when you want to compare separate parts of the model. For example, you have already found that you cannot see the yearly total column when you are viewing the January column. Symphony provides a feature called Windows that allows you to see several parts of the same spreadsheet at the same time.

Basic Windows

Using the window commands, found on the SERVICES menu, you can evenly divide the screen horizontally and vertically into parts called *window panes*. You can also create free-form windows in whatever size and shape you choose. In each window you can view a different part of the worksheet, or you can view the same area in several windows by using different formats. You can also use different environments in different windows.

All Symphony windows have names. The name is placed in the bottom right of the window frame. In fact, the word MAIN in the lower right of your screen is the name of the current window. This is the default name of the first window that Symphony makes when a new worksheet is created. You always have at least one window in operation when you are working with Symphony. By using a system of named windows, you can store a variety of windows and recall each one at will.

To explore the window commands, press SERVICES (F9) and select Windows. You will see the following commands:

Use Create Delete Layout Hide Isolate Expose Pane Settings Quit

Select Use, and you will see a list with one item in it: MAIN. This shows how the current window is named. This list is somewhat like the one used for range names. It will be alphabetical when it grows, and you can use the (F10) key at this point for a full-screen list when you have a lot of window names. You can press (ESC) twice to move back to the Window menu. To begin using windows with the example, follow these steps:

1. From the Window menu, select Create. You will be prompted for a name. Type **YEAR_TOTAL** and press (ENTER).

2. You will be asked what kind of environment this should be. Press (ENTER) to select SHEET. The entire screen will be highlighted, and you will be asked to identify the window area.

3. Notice the cursor flashing in the lower right of the screen. Press (TAB), and this will move to the lower-left corner. Press (TAB) again, and the cursor will move to the top left corner. This is the corner you want to alter.

4. Press (RIGHT ARROW) and (DOWN ARROW) to drag the edge of the highlighting across and down the model, to approximately the position shown in Figure 3-16.

5. Now press (ENTER). This confirms the size of the window and takes you to a settings screen like the one shown here:

```
Change window name                                              MENU
Name  Type  Restrict  Borders  Auto-Display  Quit

 Name:          YEAR_TOTAL
 Type:          SHEET
 Restrict:      A1..IV8192
 Borders:       Standard
 Auto-Display:  Yes
                                                     Window Settings
```

   This lists the name and type of the window and three other factors, Restrict, Borders, and Auto-Display, that will be dealt with in a moment.

6. Press (ESC) and you will be back in SHEET mode. You will also be "in" the YEAR_TOTAL window. You can tell this

Identify window area POINT

	A	B	C	D	E	F	G	H
1	Ohmobile: Projected Operating Expenses							
2								
3		Jan-91	Feb-91	Mar-91	Apr-91	May-91	Jun-91	Jul-91
4	REGION 1							
5	Personnel	6,500	6,565	6,631	6,697	6,764	6,832	6,900
6	Lease	2,500	2,525	2,550	2,576	2,602	2,628	2,654
7	Utilities	500	505	510	515	520	526	531
8	Phone	300	303	306	309	312	315	318
9	Advertising	1,250	1,263	1,275	1,288	1,301	1,314	1,327
10	REGION 2							
11	Personnel	4,500	4,545	4,590	4,636	4,683	4,730	4,777
12	Lease	2,100	2,121	2,142	2,164	2,185	2,207	2,229
13	Utilities	450	455	459	464	468	473	478
14	Phone	250	253	255	258	260	263	265
15	Advertising	1,250	1,263	1,275	1,288	1,301	1,314	1,327
16	REGION 3							
17	Personnel	6,250	6,313	6,376	6,439	6,504	6,569	6,635
18	Lease	2,500	2,525	2,550	2,576	2,602	2,628	2,654
19	Utilities	500	505	510	515	520	526	531
20	Phone	300	303	306	309	312	315	318

MAIN

Window Create

FIGURE 3-16 Identifying the window area

because the cell pointer is there, and the window has a double line at the bottom, as shown in Figure 3-17.

Whenever you create a new window, it automatically becomes the current window. To change the current window, press (F6), the WINDOW key. This moves you back to the MAIN window. Press (F6) again, and the YEAR_TOTAL window reappears and is again the current window. You can also select a window by using the SERVICES Window menu and selecting Use. This will list all of the worksheet's windows. Highlight the one you want to make current, and press (ENTER) to select it.

If you move to a window that occupies less than the entire screen, you can temporarily expand the window to the border of the display. To do this you press (ALT-F6), the ZOOM key. To remind you that you are zooming a window, Symphony places the

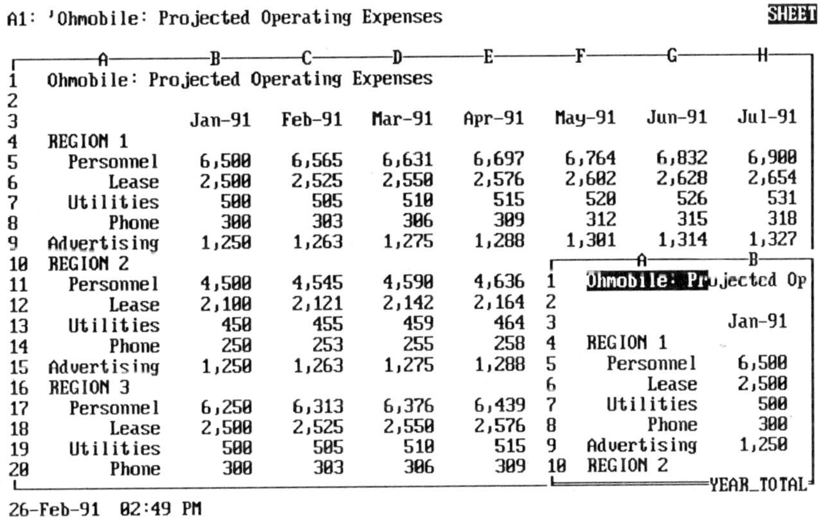

FIGURE 3-17 The YEAR_TOTAL window

message "Zoom" in the status area at the bottom of the screen. To return a zoomed window to its normal size, press (ALT-F6) again.

Changing the View

At this point both windows are showing much the same view, albeit a smaller portion in YEAR_TOTAL. To alter the view in the new window, make sure it is active (has a double line at the bottom of the frame) and press (END) followed by (HOME). As you can see from Figure 3-18, this will move you to the bottom of the model with cell N29 highlighted. (You may need to move the cell pointer to get it right on N29.)

Note that altering the view in YEAR_TOTAL did not affect the view in MAIN. You can now press (F6) to move to the MAIN window. Move the cell pointer to B5 and enter **7500**. Now press (F6), and you can see the updated total in N29.

```
N29: (P0) @SUM(B29..M29)                                                    SHEET

     A           B        C        D        E        F        G        H
1  Ohmobile: Projected Operating Expenses
2
3              Jan-91   Feb-91   Mar-91   Apr-91   May-91   Jun-91   Jul-91
4  REGION 1
5    Personnel  6,500    6,565    6,631    6,697    6,764    6,832    6,900
6        Lease  2,500    2,525    2,550    2,576    2,602    2,628    2,654
7    Utilities    500      505      510      515      520      526      531
8        Phone    300      303      306      309      312      315      318
9  Advertising  1,250    1,263    1,275    1,288    1,301    1,314    1,327
10 REGION 2                                            M         N
11   Personnel  4,500    4,545    4,590    4,636 20      335     3,805
12       Lease  2,100    2,121    2,142    2,164 21    1,395    15,853
13   Utilities    450      455      459      464 22
14       Phone    250      253      255      258 23    5,578    63,413
15 Advertising  1,250    1,263    1,275    1,288 24    2,789    31,706
16 REGION 3                                      25      558     6,341
17   Personnel  6,250    6,313    6,376    6,439 26      335     3,805
18       Lease  2,500    2,525    2,550    2,576 27    1,395    15,853
19   Utilities    500      505      510      515 28
20       Phone    300      303      306      309 29   44,571   506,666
                                                              YEAR_TOTAL
26-Feb-91  02:56 PM
```

FIGURE 3-18 Viewing the total in YEAR_TOTAL

Of course, this arrangement still does not allow you to see both ends of the worksheet at once. To do this you need to adjust the MAIN window. In fact, the following steps will show you how to adjust both windows:

1. Make MAIN the active window.
2. From the SERVICE menu, select Window Layout, and use the (LEFT ARROW) key to move the right edge of the frame to the position shown in Figure 3-19.
3. Press (ENTER) to fix the window at this point. Notice that you are not taken to the settings menu or returned to SHEET mode.

Note The settings menu is only presented when you create a window or if you use the Settings command from the Window menu.

Identify window area **POINT**

	A	B	C	D	E	F	G	H
1	Ohmobile: Projected Operating Expenses							
2								
3		Jan-91	Feb-91	Mar-91	Apr-91	May-91	Jun-91	Jul-91
4	REGION 1							
5	Personnel	7,500	7,575	7,651	7,727	7,805	7,883	7,961
6	Lease	2,500	2,525	2,550	2,576	2,602	2,628	2,654
7	Utilities	500	505	510	515	520	526	531
8	Phone	300	303	306	309	312	315	318
9	Advertising	1,250	1,263	1,275	1,288	1,301	1,314	1,327
10	REGION 2							
11	Personnel	4,500	4,545	4,590	4,636	4,683	4,730	4,777
12	Lease	2,100	2,121	2,142	2,164	2,185	2,207	2,229
13	Utilities	450	455	459	464	468	473	478
14	Phone	250	253	255	258	260	263	265
15	Advertising	1,250	1,263	1,275	1,288	1,301	1,314	1,327
16	REGION 3							
17	Personnel	6,250	6,313	6,376	6,439	6,504	6,569	6,635
18	Lease	2,500	2,525	2,550	2,576	2,602	2,628	2,654
19	Utilities	500	505	510	515	520	526	531
20	Phone	300	303	306	309	312	315	318

MAIN

Window Layout

FIGURE 3-19 Changing the layout of MAIN

4. Press (F6) to change windows while still at the Windows menu. You will activate YEAR_TOTAL.

5. Select Layout, and press (TAB) twice to alter the active corner of the window. Press (UP ARROW) until Symphony beeps to tell you the window will not grow any further in that direction.

6. Press (LEFT ARROW) until the left edge of the current window frame almost touches the right edge of the MAIN window. Press (ENTER) to confirm the window layout, and select Quit from the Window menu.

Back in SHEET mode you can see the effects of this rearrangement, which should look something like Figure 3-20. Using the MAIN window, you can make entries in column B of the worksheet, and the effects will be visible immediately in the YEAR_TOTAL window.

```
N29: (P0) @SUM(B29..M29)                                                     SHEET

   A              B        C        D           L          M          N
1  Ohmobile: Projected Operating Expenses   10
2                                           11   4,971      5,021     57,071
3                 Jan-91   Feb-91   Mar-91  12   2,320      2,343     26,633
4  REGION 1                                 13     497        502      5,707
5    Personnel    7,500    7,575    7,651   14     276        279      3,171
6        Lease    2,500    2,525    2,550   15   1,381      1,395     15,853
7    Utilities      500      505      510   16
8        Phone      300      303      306   17   6,904      6,973     79,266
9  Advertising    1,250    1,263    1,275   18   2,762      2,789     31,706
10 REGION 2                                 19     552        558      6,341
11   Personnel    4,500    4,545    4,590   20     331        335      3,805
12       Lease    2,100    2,121    2,142   21   1,381      1,395     15,853
13   Utilities      450      455      459   22
14       Phone      250      253      255   23   5,523      5,578     63,413
15 Advertising    1,250    1,263    1,275   24   2,762      2,789     31,706
16 REGION 3                                 25     552        558      6,341
17   Personnel    6,250    6,313    6,376   26     331        335      3,805
18       Lease    2,500    2,525    2,550   27   1,381      1,395     15,853
19   Utilities      500      505      510   28
20       Phone      300      303      306   29  45,234     45,687    519,348
                                      MAIN                        YEAR_TOTAL
26-Feb-91  03:14 PM
```

FIGURE 3-20 The completed arrangement

Using Titles

You can see from Figure 3-20 that when you are using windows, the column headings disappear if the right side of the worksheet is moved down. In fact, you may have found this to be a problem even when you were working without windows. As you move to the lower areas of the worksheet and the month labels disappear, it becomes difficult to know which months you are viewing. Knowing where you are is particularly important when you have to update cells in the middle of a large spreadsheet.

The Symphony solution is to freeze certain rows and columns to act as titles that do not disappear when you move the cell pointer. To freeze titles in the example, you would place the cell pointer in cell B4. You could then freeze the rows above this and the columns to the left of it as titles. The Titles command is on the MENU Settings menu. Try setting titles in the YEAR_TOTAL window of the example by following these steps:

1. Make YEAR_TOTAL the active window and press (HOME). Place the cell selector in the top left cell of the worksheet area that you still want to move—in this case, B4.

2. Issue the MENU Settings Titles command. This leads to the menu shown in Figure 3-21. The Horizontal option freezes the area above the cell selector. The Vertical option freezes the area to the left of the cell selector. You want to pick Both, which locks areas above and to the left of the cell selector, so that both the months and the expense categories stay on the screen while you scan the model.

3. When you pick Both, you are returned to the settings sheet. Note that the small inner box now shows the title setting as Columns 1, Rows 3, meaning one column from the left edge of the worksheet and three rows from the top.

4. Select Quit to return to SHEET mode. Press (END) and then (HOME) to get to the end of the worksheet. Notice that the column and row headings remain on the screen, as shown in Figure 3-22. Column M is now adjacent to column A.

```
Set both horizontal and vertical titles                                MENU
Both  Horizontal  Vertical  Clear

Circular             (none)
Label-Prefix:        '
                                          Titles
Recalculation                               Columns: 0
  Method:            Automatic              Rows:    0
  Order:             Optimal              Format:    (G)
  Iterations:        1                    Width:     9
                                        For window: YEAR_TOTAL

Zero Suppression:    No
Auto-Link:  Yes
                                                          Sheet Settings
```

FIGURE 3-21 The Settings Titles menu

```
N29: (P0) @SUM(B29..M29)                                                          SHEET

 ----A----------B---------C---------D----   ----A-----------M--------N----
1  Ohmobile: Projected Operating Expenses  1  Ohmobile: Pr
2                                          2
3               Jan-91    Feb-91    Mar-91 3                 Dec-91  TOTALS
4  REGION 1                                13   Utilities       502   5,707
5    Personnel  7,500     7,575     7,651  14       Phone       279   3,171
6        Lease  2,500     2,525     2,550  15 Advertising     1,395  15,853
7    Utilities    500       505       510  16 REGION 3
8        Phone    300       303       306  17   Personnel     6,973  79,266
9  Advertising  1,250     1,263     1,275  18       Lease     2,789  31,706
10 REGION 2                                19   Utilities       558   6,341
11   Personnel  4,500     4,545     4,590  20       Phone       335   3,805
12       Lease  2,100     2,121     2,142  21 Advertising     1,395  15,853
13   Utilities    450       455       459  22 REGION 4
14       Phone    250       253       255  23   Personnel     5,578  63,413
15 Advertising  1,250     1,263     1,275  24       Lease     2,789  31,706
16 REGION 3                                25   Utilities       558   6,341
17   Personnel  6,250     6,313     6,376  26       Phone       335   3,805
18       Lease  2,500     2,525     2,550  27 Advertising     1,395  15,853
19   Utilities    500       505       510  28
20       Phone    300       303       306  29      TOTALS    45,687 519,348
 --------------------------------------MAIN  ----------------------YEAR_TOTAL
26-Feb-91  04:45 PM
```

FIGURE 3-22 The effect of using titles

The frozen titles work very well when a model has been built and only the data is being updated. They allow you to browse without losing track of where you are. However, you may need to unlock the titles when making major changes to the spreadsheet. To clear the titles, select MENU Settings Titles Clear.

To experiment with titles in place, try pressing (HOME) while remaining in the YEAR_TOTAL window. Instead of moving the cell pointer to A1, this key will now take you to the cell from which you locked the titles. You may wonder how you can change headings if you are locked out of those cells. After all, you cannot use the regular cursor movement keys to get to the headings. One way is to use the (F5) key, which will allow you to enter the address of a cell that is within the title area so that you can edit it. Another approach is to use the other window, in which the titles are not locked. Titles are one of the three settings that are specific to the window in which they are made. The other two are format and width.

Window-Specific Formats and Widths

The settings sheet in Figure 3-21 shows you that the current window has the General format and a column width of 9 as its default settings. If you wanted to, you could change the settings for the YEAR_TOTAL window so that it showed the figures in Currency format with 12-wide columns, while the MAIN window still used General format with 9-wide columns.

There is no need to carry out this experiment yourself, since it involves several changes. First you would use the MENU Format Reset command, issued from either window, to change all of cells B4 through N29 back to the default format. The MENU Format command affects cells in all windows. Next, you would make the MAIN window active, select MENU Settings Format, and select Punctuated, with 0 decimal places. This would only affect the appearance of cells seen through the MAIN window. Then you would make YEAR_TOTAL the active window, select MENU Settings Format, and select Currency with two decimal places. This would only alter the appearance of cells seen through the YEAR_TOTAL window. Before leaving the Settings menu, you would select Width and type **12**. When you left the Settings menu, the effect would be quite dramatic, as shown in Figure 3-23. The YEAR_TOTAL window would show the same worksheet, but with completely different width and format settings from the MAIN window.

UPDATING THE MODEL

Having built the model and explored several ways of making it easier to view, you may want to update it to reflect a revised estimate of how much costs will rise. As you will recall, all of the expenses in columns C through M are based on a factor of 1.01. This was done by copying the formula 1.01*B5 from C5 to all the other cells. To change the growth basis of the spreadsheet to 1.015,

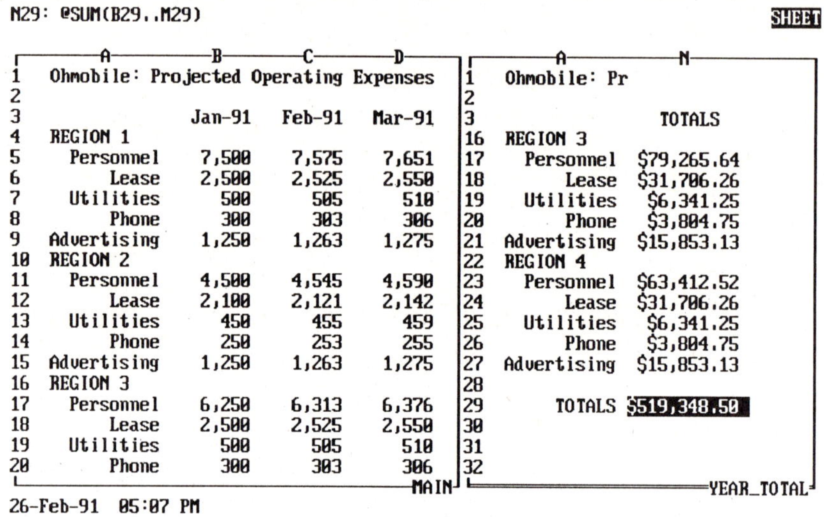

```
N29: @SUM(B29..M29)                                                         SHEET

   ----A--------------B----------C----------D----    ----A-----------N----
1  Ohmobile: Projected Operating Expenses          1  Ohmobile: Pr
2                                                  2
3                   Jan-91     Feb-91     Mar-91   3                TOTALS
4  REGION 1                                        16 REGION 3
5     Personnel     7,500      7,575      7,651    17   Personnel  $79,265.64
6         Lease     2,500      2,525      2,550    18       Lease  $31,706.26
7     Utilities       500        505        510    19   Utilities   $6,341.25
8         Phone       300        303        306    20       Phone   $3,804.75
9  Advertising      1,250      1,263      1,275    21 Advertising  $15,853.13
10 REGION 2                                        22 REGION 4
11    Personnel     4,500      4,545      4,590    23   Personnel  $63,412.52
12        Lease     2,100      2,121      2,142    24       Lease  $31,706.26
13    Utilities       450        455        459    25   Utilities   $6,341.25
14        Phone       250        253        255    26       Phone   $3,804.75
15 Advertising      1,250      1,263      1,275    27 Advertising  $15,853.13
16 REGION 3                                        28
17    Personnel     6,250      6,313      6,376    29      TOTALS $519,348.50
18        Lease     2,500      2,525      2,550    30
19    Utilities       500        505        510    31
20        Phone       300        303        306    32
                                             MAIN                 YEAR_TOTAL
26-Feb-91  05:07 PM
```

FIGURE 3-23 The effect of window-specific settings

you could write a new formula, 1.015*B5, in C5 and then copy it to all the other cells. That would involve several steps, however, and those steps would all have to be repeated every time you wanted to see the effect of a different factor. As you will see, this is not necessary with Symphony.

Relative and Absolute References

Your goal is take the growth factor out of the model so that it can be changed without rewriting formulas. To start this, make the MAIN window active and use the ZOOM key, (ALT-F6), to expand the frame of the window. Move the cell pointer to F1, and enter **Growth factor of:** as a regular label. Now move to cell H1 and enter **1.015**.

Now that the growth rate is stated in H1, you might be tempted to write a new formula (such as +H1*B5) in C5. You would then copy this to all the other cells. That way, you could simply change the factor in H1 and it would be reflected throughout the budget. Unfortunately, such an approach runs into problems because of Symphony's *relative addressing* of cell references in formulas.

Remember that entering a formula like 1.01*B5 in C5 means that B5, the cell one to the left of C5, is multiplied by 1.01. When you copy this formula to D5, the cell addresses change, *relative* to the new location. The formula becomes 1.01*C5, or 1.01 times the cell one to the left of D5. The formula +H1*B5, entered in C5, means "Multiply the cell that is up four rows and over five by the cell one to the left." If you copy this formula from C5 to D5, you get +I1*C5, which says to take the cell that is up four rows and over five columns, and multiply it by the cell to the left. Since I1 is empty, the answer is 0. The same would apply to all other cells in the row if you copied the formula across the row.

Absolute Solutions

The solution to the relative problem is to make any references to fixed cells *absolute*. Thus, you can say that C5 is absolutely H1 times B5. You indicate this in the formula by placing a dollar sign in front of the coordinates. Thus, $H$1*B5 can be copied anywhere, and the result will always be H1 times the cell to the left.

There are two ways to make a cell reference absolute: You can type in the dollar signs yourself, or, with the cursor next to the cell reference on the edit line, you can press the Absolute, or ABS, key, (F3), and Symphony will add dollar signs for you. In fact, if you keep pressing (F3), Symphony will show you the four possible cell references:

$H$1	Absolutely column H row 1
$H1	Absolutely column H, but any row
H$1	Any column, but absolutely row 1
H1	Completely relative

For the sample model, follow these steps to create the correct formula to reference the growth rate in H1 and copy it throughout the model:

1. With the MAIN window active and zoomed, place the cell pointer in C5. Type the formula **+$H$1*B5** and press (ENTER).
2. Press MENU and select Copy. Press (ENTER) to use C5 as the FROM range. The following steps will perform the copy without creating any extra entries that require deleting.
3. Select cells C5..M9 as the TO range. This will update the formulas for REGION 1 (taking care not to copy over the very last column in the model, which contains the sum formulas).
4. Still in C5, select Copy again. This time select C5..M21 as the FROM range. Select C11 as the TO range, and the new formula will be copied throughout the worksheet.

You can now update the rate in H1 and see all of the growth cells in the model change. An example is shown in Figure 3-24.

SAVING YOUR WORK: PART TWO

You have improved and expanded the model, and it is almost ready to be printed. However, before going any further you should make sure that the latest changes are stored. Assuming that you have already used the File Save command to give the worksheet an appropriate file name, you can simply issue the File Save command to update the file and answer Yes when asked if you want to replace the existing file. However, at this point you might want to keep the earlier version, in which case you can give the improved worksheet a new name. To replace the old name with the new one you only need to type the new name at the File Save prompt, and the old name will be replaced. As an alternative, when you are presented

C5: +$H$1*B5 SHEET

	A	B	C	D	E	F	G	H
1	Ohmobile: Projected Operating Expenses					Growth factor of:		1.015
2								
3		Jan-91	Feb-91	Mar-91	Apr-91	May-91	Jun-91	Jul-91
4	REGION 1							
5	Personnel	7,500	7,613	7,727	7,843	7,960	8,080	8,201
6	Lease	2,500	2,530	2,576	2,614	2,653	2,693	2,734
7	Utilities	500	508	515	523	531	539	547
8	Phone	300	305	309	314	318	323	328
9	Advertising	1,250	1,269	1,288	1,307	1,327	1,347	1,367
10	REGION 2							
11	Personnel	4,500	4,568	4,636	4,706	4,776	4,848	4,920
12	Lease	2,100	2,132	2,163	2,196	2,229	2,262	2,296
13	Utilities	450	457	464	471	478	485	492
14	Phone	250	254	258	261	265	269	273
15	Advertising	1,250	1,269	1,288	1,307	1,327	1,347	1,367
16	REGION 3							
17	Personnel	6,250	6,344	6,439	6,535	6,634	6,733	6,834
18	Lease	2,500	2,538	2,576	2,614	2,653	2,693	2,734
19	Utilities	500	508	515	523	531	539	547
20	Phone	300	305	309	314	318	323	328

MAIN

26-Feb-91 05:41 PM Zoom

FIGURE 3-24 The completed growth factor formula

with the old filename you can press (BACKSPACE) to delete part of the name and change it to a new name, pressing (ENTER) to confirm the name and store the file. If you have not yet used the File Save command to store the worksheet you have been building, see the earlier section on saving your work.

Suppose that you have saved your work, quit Symphony, and are returning to the program. At first you will see a blank sheet. You issue the SERVICES File Retrieve command and see the alphabetical list of files across the screen. You know you only have to highlight the name you want and press (ENTER) to retrieve it, but you cannot remember the name of the file. One way to refresh your memory is to press (F10) while viewing the single-line file list. This gives you a full-screen file list, like the one shown in Figure 3-25. Any file you highlight in this list will appear at the top of the screen, with the date and time of storage and the file size. If you know when the file was last saved, this information will help you remember which file you want to retrieve. Several other options

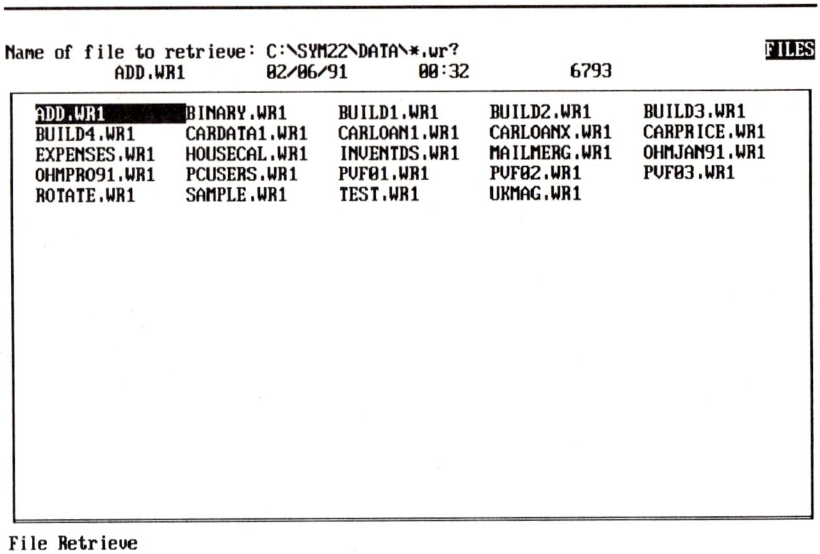

FIGURE 3-25 The expanded file list

on the File menu can be helpful for managing files; these are discussed in Chapter 8, where you will also learn about the View feature, which lets you further explore files before retrieving them.

PRINTING

Now that you have explored various methods for viewing and updating the spreadsheet, it is time to look at how you produce a printed copy. Symphony can produce anything from a simple one-page printout to a carefully formatted multi-page report with headers, footers, and other enhancements. All printing, simple or complex, begins with the Print menu, which you select from the SERVICES menu. It is shown in Figure 3-26.

```
Start printing using current settings                                    MENU
Go  Line-Advance  Page-Advance  Align  Settings  Quit

 Page                    Source:
   Length:     66        Destination: Printer
   Spacing:    1         Init-String:
   Number                Margins               Other
     Print-Number: 1       Left:   4             Space Compression: No
     Start-Page:   1       Right:  76            Attributes:        Yes
     End-Page:     999     Top:    2             Format: As-Displayed
   Breaks:     Yes         Bottom: 2             Top-Labels:
   Wait:       No                                Left-Labels:
   Header:
   Footer:
                                                    Print Settings: MAIN
```

FIGURE 3-26 The Print menu

A Basic Print

The first print command to use is Settings, which presents the following options:

Page Source Destination Init-String Margins Other Name Quit

The most important of these settings is Source, which you use to tell Symphony which cells are to be printed. There are two possible choices for Source: Range and Database. The latter is used when you are printing from FORM mode, described in Chapter 5. The Range option is used for printing from SHEET mode.

You specify what part of the worksheet you want printed by indicating a range of cells. You can give the coordinates for the cells to be printed either by typing them or by pointing out the cells. You can also define the range by entering a range name.

Suppose that you want to print the expenses for the first three months of the model projection.

1. You can define the source range from any point in the spreadsheet. Press SERVICES, and then select Print, followed by Settings.

2. Select Source and then Range, and type or highlight the range **A1..D29**. Press (ENTER) to confirm the range, and you are returned to the settings menu.

3. After you define the source range, it is listed in the Print Settings box. To actually print the range you must first move from the settings menu back to the first Print menu, shown in Figure 3-26. This can be done by selecting Quit or pressing (ESC).

4. Make sure your printer is connected, turned on, and loaded with paper. Unless you have a printer with a sheet feeder, you will need to make sure that the print head is at the top of the page that is in the printer.

5. From the Print menu, select Align. This makes sure that Symphony and the printer both agree that the print head is at the top of the page.

6. Select Go. This sends the information in the range you have selected to the printer. Remember, the printer must be powered up and loaded with paper before printing. Otherwise, the program may delay a long time before allowing you to correct the problem and continue.

7. When you select Go, the mode indicator will flash the word "WAIT" for a moment and then the completed print job will emerge from the printer.

The results will probably look something like the printout you see in Figure 3-27. All of the information you requested fits on a single page. When you define a range and tell Symphony to print it, your printed output is based on the size of the source range you specified and the other menu settings. These include the size of the

Ohmobile: Projected Operating Expenses

	Jan-91	Feb-91	Mar-91
REGION 1			
Personnel	7,500	7,613	7,727
Lease	2,500	2,538	2,576
Utilities	500	508	515
Phone	300	305	309
Advertising	1,250	1,269	1,288
REGION 2			
Personnel	4,500	4,568	4,636
Lease	2,100	2,132	2,163
Utilities	450	457	464
Phone	250	254	258
Advertising	1,250	1,269	1,288
REGION 3			
Personnel	6,250	6,344	6,439
Lease	2,500	2,538	2,576
Utilities	500	508	515
Phone	300	305	309
Advertising	1,250	1,269	1,288
REGION 4			
Personnel	5,000	5,075	5,151
Lease	2,500	2,538	2,576
Utilities	500	508	515
Phone	300	305	309
Advertising	1,250	1,269	1,288
TOTALS	40,950	41,564	42,188

FIGURE 3-27 First printed report

page and the margins that define the printing area on the page. In other words, they are the parameters by which Symphony relates to a piece of paper. The defaults for these settings are shown in Figure 3-28. Margins and page length can be changed to accommodate different sizes of paper and type styles.

```
Overall page settings                                                    MENU
Page  Source  Destination  Init-String  Margins  Other  Name  Quit

 Page                    Source:      Range A1..D29
   Length:      60       Destination: Printer
   Spacing:     1        Init-String:
   Number                Margins               Other
     Print-Number: 1       Left:   5             Space Compression: No
     Start-Page:   1       Right:  80            Attributes:        Yes
     End-Page:     999     Top:    2             Format: As-Displayed
   Breaks:      Yes        Bottom: 2             Top-Labels:
   Wait:        No                               Left-Labels:
   Header:
   Footer:
                                                    Print Settings: MAIN
```

FIGURE 3-28 Default print settings

Adjusting the Settings

You may already be saying that your printed results do not look like those in Figure 3-27. Unfortunately, printing is one of the most difficult areas of Symphony to describe in universal terms. There are so many different printers in use today that it is very difficult to describe exactly what you should do to get acceptable results on your printer. The example in Figure 3-27 comes from a Hewlett-Packard LaserJet, a popular printer (but certainly not universal). In addition to the differences between printers, the task of laying down rules about printing is complicated by the aesthetic factor: A report that looks good to one person may not be acceptable to another. The following sections will attempt to describe the various parameters that control the results of printing and suggest ways of achieving commonly accepted levels of appearance.

If you define the entire sample spreadsheet as the source range, from A1..N29, Symphony's default print settings produce results similar to the two pages shown in Figure 3-29. However, these results have several problems. The information flows over two pages, and the second page lacks headings to explain the data. The solutions to these problems are numerous. You can increase the size of the paper, reduce the size of the type, add headers and

Ohmobile: Projected Operating Expenses Growth factor of:

	Jan-91	Feb-91	Mar-91	Apr-91	May-91	Jun-91
REGION 1						
Personnel	7,500	7,613	7,727	7,843	7,960	8,080
Lease	2,500	2,538	2,576	2,614	2,653	2,693
Utilities	500	508	515	523	531	539
Phone	300	305	309	314	318	323
Advertising	1,250	1,269	1,288	1,307	1,327	1,347
REGION 2						
Personnel	4,500	4,545	4,590	4,636	4,683	4,730
Lease	2,100	2,121	2,142	2,164	2,185	2,207
Utilities	450	455	459	464	468	473
Phone	250	253	255	258	260	263
Advertising	1,250	1,263	1,275	1,288	1,301	1,314
REGION 3						
Personnel	6,250	6,313	6,376	6,439	6,504	6,569
Lease	2,500	2,525	2,550	2,576	2,602	2,628
Utilities	500	505	510	515	520	526
Phone	300	303	306	309	312	315
Advertising	1,250	1,263	1,275	1,288	1,301	1,314
REGION 4						
Personnel	5,000	5,050	5,101	5,152	5,203	5,255
Lease	2,500	2,525	2,550	2,576	2,602	2,628
Utilities	500	505	510	515	520	526
Phone	300	303	306	309	312	315
Advertising	1,250	1,263	1,275	1,288	1,301	1,314
TOTALS	40,950	41,420	41,895	42,376	42,863	43,355

1.015

Jul-91	Aug-91	Sep-91	Oct-91	Nov-91	Dec-91	TOTALS
8,201	8,324	8,449	8,575	8,704	8,835	97,809
2,734	2,775	2,816	2,858	2,901	2,945	32,603
547	555	563	572	580	589	6,521
328	333	338	343	348	353	3,912
1,367	1,387	1,408	1,429	1,451	1,472	16,302
4,777	4,825	4,873	4,922	4,971	5,021	57,071
2,229	2,251	2,274	2,297	2,320	2,343	26,633
478	482	487	493	497	502	5,707
265	268	271	273	276	279	3,171
1,327	1,340	1,354	1,367	1,381	1,395	15,853
6,635	6,701	6,768	6,836	6,904	6,973	79,266
2,654	2,680	2,707	2,734	2,762	2,789	31,706
531	536	541	547	552	558	6,341
318	322	325	328	331	335	3,805
1,327	1,340	1,354	1,367	1,381	1,395	15,853
5,308	5,361	5,414	5,468	5,523	5,578	63,413
2,654	2,680	2,707	2,734	2,762	2,789	31,706
531	536	541	547	552	558	6,341
318	322	325	328	331	335	3,805
1,327	1,340	1,354	1,367	1,381	1,395	15,853
43,854	44,358	44,869	45,385	45,908	46,437	523,671

FIGURE 3-29 The entire model printed

footers to identify the report, and repeat some label headings on successive pages.

Setting Headings

You can add missing column and row headings to a printout that will not fit on one page. The information on the second and successive pages will then be much easier to understand. This works much the same way as using titles when you are viewing a spreadsheet on screen. You identify the columns and rows containing the heading labels above and to the left of the main data area. These labels are then repeated on each page as borders. The source range is redefined to exclude the areas that are included in the borders, so that those cells will not be printed twice.

The command to create these print borders is on the Other menu, selected from the Print Settings menu. You select Top-Labels to define cells that are repeated over the top of each new page of data. In the sample model you could define cells A1..N3 as top labels. The Left-Labels command is used to define an area that is repeated at the side of each new page of data. In the sample model this could be cells A4..A29. If you set border labels, you *must* define the source range to exclude these areas. In this case, the source range should be redefined as B4..N29. The results of printing with these settings can be seen in Figure 3-30. You can remove top and left labels by using the No-Labels command.

Your report has now been improved so that the border labels work for the expense categories and months. Unfortunately, Symphony has difficulty repeating the labels from row 1. This could be solved by leaving row 1 out of the Top-Labels range and using a header (described in a moment) to supply the title for the report. Also, you can see that adding borders forced the results onto three pages, rather than two. This could be avoided by increasing the margins, decreasing the size of the print, or narrowing the columns.

Changing Margins

You saw in Figure 3-28 that the margins are a critical factor when you are adjusting print settings. The command to change margins

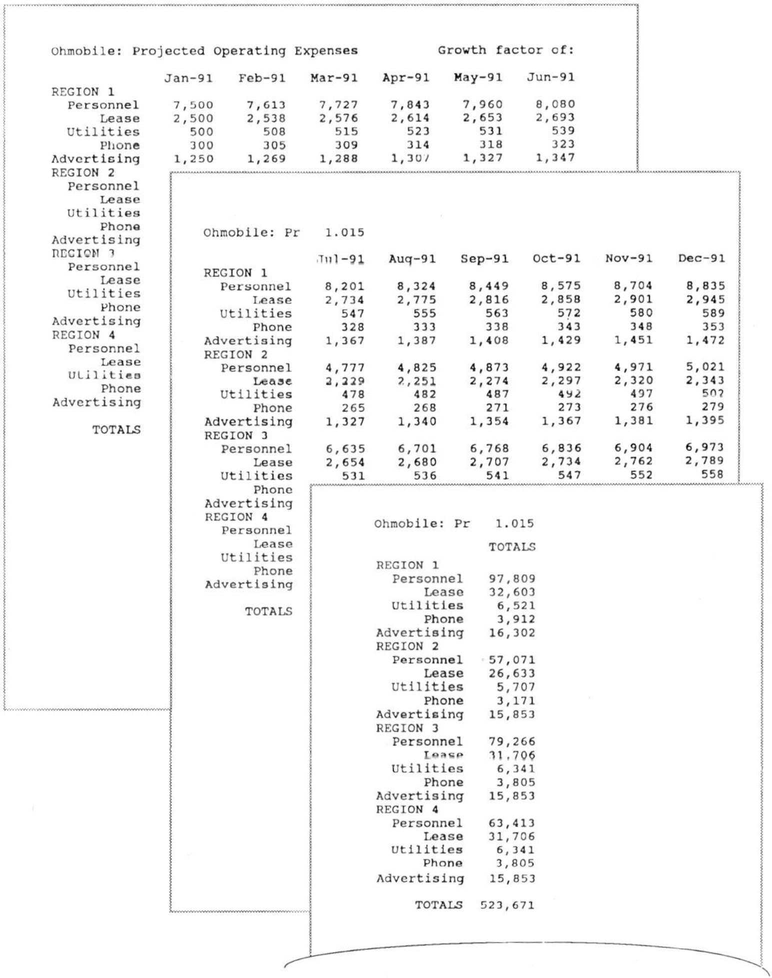

Ohmobile: Projected Operating Expenses   Growth factor of:

	Jan-91	Feb-91	Mar-91	Apr-91	May-91	Jun-91
REGION 1						
Personnel	7,500	7,613	7,727	7,843	7,960	8,080
Lease	2,500	2,538	2,576	2,614	2,653	2,693
Utilities	500	508	515	523	531	539
Phone	300	305	309	314	318	323
Advertising	1,250	1,269	1,288	1,307	1,327	1,347
REGION 2						
Personnel						
Lease						
Utilities						
Phone						
Advertising						
REGION 3						
Personnel						
Lease						
Utilities						
Phone						
Advertising						
REGION 4						
Personnel						
Lease						
Utilities						
Phone						
Advertising						
TOTALS						

Ohmobile: Pr   1.015

	Jul-91	Aug-91	Sep-91	Oct-91	Nov-91	Dec-91
REGION 1						
Personnel	8,201	8,324	8,449	8,575	8,704	8,835
Lease	2,734	2,775	2,816	2,858	2,901	2,945
Utilities	547	555	563	572	580	589
Phone	328	333	338	343	348	353
Advertising	1,367	1,387	1,408	1,429	1,451	1,472
REGION 2						
Personnel	4,777	4,825	4,873	4,922	4,971	5,021
Lease	2,229	2,251	2,274	2,297	2,320	2,343
Utilities	478	482	487	492	497	502
Phone	265	268	271	273	276	279
Advertising	1,327	1,340	1,354	1,367	1,381	1,395
REGION 3						
Personnel	6,635	6,701	6,768	6,836	6,904	6,973
Lease	2,654	2,680	2,707	2,734	2,762	2,789
Utilities	531	536	541	547	552	558
Phone						
Advertising						
REGION 4						
Personnel						
Lease						
Utilities						
Phone						
Advertising						
TOTALS						

Ohmobile: Pr   1.015

	TOTALS
REGION 1	
Personnel	97,809
Lease	32,603
Utilities	6,521
Phone	3,912
Advertising	16,302
REGION 2	
Personnel	57,071
Lease	26,633
Utilities	5,707
Phone	3,171
Advertising	15,853
REGION 3	
Personnel	79,266
Lease	31,706
Utilities	6,341
Phone	3,805
Advertising	15,853
REGION 4	
Personnel	63,413
Lease	31,706
Utilities	6,341
Phone	3,805
Advertising	15,853
TOTALS	523,671

FIGURE 3-30 Three-page layout

is Print Settings Margins. The default settings for left and right margins, which determine how wide your printout will be, are a left margin of 4 characters from the left of the page and a right margin of 76 characters from the left edge of the page. This works for most personal computer printers that use 10 pitch (10 characters per inch). On a Hewlett-Packard LaserJet, you should change the settings to left:5 and right:80 for normal printing. This matches the actual print area used by the printer.

If you use wider paper, you must use the Print Settings Margins command to increase the right margin. The 15-inch-wide paper used in many wide-carriage printers calls for a right margin of 140. A sheet of 8 1/2-inch by 14-inch legal paper turned on its side—so that the width is 14 inches—can use a 132-character right margin. If you reduce printer pitch, using smaller characters, you must increase the margins. The condensed pitch of 17 characters per inch used on many dot-matrix and laser printers allows a right margin of 140 on 8 1/2-inch-wide paper and 250 on 15-inch-wide paper.

Note

Bear in mind that Symphony has no way of knowing when you alter the paper in your printer or manually adjust the pitch of the print; you must set the margin yourself when you change paper size or print pitch.

Altering Page Size

In the rapidly changing field of personal computers, users are grateful for any standards that can be relied upon. Such a standard is the six lines per inch used by every popular printer. This makes an 11-inch page 66 lines long. As you can see in Figure 3-28, Symphony leaves a top and bottom margin. If you are working with paper that is longer or shorter than 11 inches, you must tell Symphony the length measured in lines. Thus, an 8 1/2-inch by 11-inch piece of paper printed on its side is 53 lines long. You can actually tell Symphony you have a 33-line sheet of paper, and it will treat a regular sheet of paper as though it were two sheets. This can be useful if you print a model that has less than 18 rows.

If you are using a Hewlett-Packard LaserJet, you should set the page length to 60 when using regular letter-size paper. This is because the LaserJet cannot print on all of the page. Using 60 lines instead of 66 will mean that the page breaks are properly spaced.

Setting Setups

Many printers can be told to change their print style, print pitch, and other aspects by codes transmitted as part of the print data sent from the program. Symphony accommodates these *printer control sequences* with the Init-String command. It allows you to enter the codes for your printer, which are then sent ahead of the data transmitted to the printer. The codes for your printer model can be found in the printer manual. As an example, most IBM and Epson dot-matrix printers respond to the characters \015 as specifying condensed print.

Writing Headers and Footers

In addition to setting parts of the spreadsheet as border headings, you can repeat other information from page to page in a multi-page Symphony printout by using the Header and Footer commands. These commands, found on the Print Settings Page menu, provide a line of space that is placed at the top (a Header) or bottom (a Footer) of each page. When you select Header or Footer, you type the text to be printed. For example, in the sample model you could select Header and enter

Ohmobile: Projected Operating Expenses

This would appear on the left at the top of each page. You can also enter formatting codes in headers and footers that tell Symphony how to align the text. The # sign tells Symphony to enter the page number in a header or footer. You could enter

Page #

in a footer to have the page number printed, along with the word "Page," at the bottom of every page. The @ sign prints the current date, according to your PC's clock.

To arrange header and footer text between the margins, the straight line symbol | is used like a tab stop. Typing the header text with no | symbol causes Symphony to left-align everything. Preceding text with one | symbol results in centering. Using two || symbols places the text on the right. Consider this header:

```
|Ohmobile: Projected Operating Expenses
```

It will produce this result:

Ohmobile: Projected Operating Expenses

Entering

```
Ohmobile: Projected Operating Expenses||Page #.
```

will produce this:

Ohmobile: Projected Operating Expenses   Page 1.

By creative use of these codes, you can accommodate most information that you will need in headers and footers. Figure 3-31 shows headers and footers used with the sample model.

Making Page Breaks

Symphony automatically inserts page breaks specified by the Page Length setting. These settings are referred to as *soft page breaks,* since they change position according to the size of the print range. However, you can specify *hard page breaks* to force breaks at chosen points in the printout. Hard page breaks are indicated by the | character and two colons inserted manually into the

Ohmobile: Projected Operating Expense

	Jan-91	Feb-91	Mar-91	Apr-91	May-91	Jun-91	Jul-91
REGION 1							
Personnel	7,500	7,613	7,727	7,843	7,960	8,080	8,201
Lease	2,500	2,538	2,576	2,614	2,653	2,693	2,734
Utilities	500	508	515	523	531	539	547
Phone	300	305	309	314	318	323	328
Advertising	1,250	1,269	1,288	1,307	1,327	1,347	1,367
REGION 2							
Personnel							
Lease							
Utilities							
Phone							
Advertising							
REGION 3							
Personnel							
Lease							
Utilities							
Phone							
Advertising							
REGION 4							
Personnel							
Lease							
Utilities							
Phone							
Advertising							
TOTALS							

02/27/91

Ohmobile: Projected Operating Expense

	Aug-91	Sep-91	Oct-91	Nov-91	Dec-91	TOTALS
REGION 1						
Personnel	8,324	8,449	8,575	8,704	8,835	97,809
Lease	2,775	2,816	2,858	2,901	2,945	32,603
Utilities	555	563	572	580	589	6,521
Phone	333	338	343	348	353	3,912
Advertising	1,387	1,408	1,429	1,451	1,472	16,302
REGION 2						
Personnel	4,825	4,873	4,922	4,971	5,021	57,071
Lease	2,251	2,274	2,297	2,320	2,343	26,633
Utilities	482	487	492	497	502	5,707
Phone	268	271	273	276	279	3,171
Advertising	1,340	1,354	1,367	1,381	1,395	15,853
REGION 3						
Personnel	6,701	6,768	6,836	6,904	6,973	79,266
Lease	2,680	2,707	2,734	2,762	2,789	31,706
Utilities	536	541	547	552	558	6,341
Phone	322	325	328	331	335	3,805
Advertising	1,340	1,354	1,367	1,381	1,395	15,853
REGION 4						
Personnel	5,361	5,414	5,468	5,523	5,578	63,413
Lease	2,680	2,707	2,734	2,762	2,789	31,706
Utilities	536	541	547	552	558	6,341
Phone	322	325	328	331	335	3,805
Advertising	1,340	1,354	1,367	1,381	1,395	15,853
TOTALS	44,358	44,869	45,385	45,908	46,437	523,671

02/27/91 Page 2.

FIGURE 3-31 Improved report

spreadsheet on a blank row (|::). These characters are stored as part of the spreadsheet and are not removed until they are deleted individually from the spreadsheet.

To create hard page breaks, you should find or insert a blank row at the point where you would like the break to occur. Any other data on a page-break row will not be printed. Enter the page-break characters |:: in the cell on the blank row that is furthest to left of the print range. When Symphony comes to that cell, it will end the page and go on to a new sheet. Page breaks should be inserted in the source range, not in border ranges.

Resetting Options and Storing Defaults

When you save a worksheet, the print settings in effect at the time you perform the save are stored together with the spreadsheet data. This means that when you retrieve the file, the print settings will be intact. Symphony refers to a particular combination of print settings as a *settings sheet.* Symphony can store several settings sheets. For example, you may want to try a different combination of settings without losing the original settings, or keep several different settings for different reports from the same worksheet.

The Print Settings Name command is used to manage your settings sheets. When you select Name, you have the following options:

Use   Create   Delete   Previous   Next   Initial-Settings   Reset   Quit

These commands work similarly to those for range names. The Create option is used to give a name to whatever the current settings are. Symphony assigns the default name of MAIN to the current settings unless you provide your own name. The Use command lists previously named settings in alphabetical order. By selecting a name, you display that sheet, and its settings will be in effect until a different sheet is chosen. The Delete command removes a named settings sheet, whereas the Reset command removes all named settings at once and returns the settings to their initial values. The Previous and Next commands can be used to recall the settings sheet before or after the current one within the alphabetical list or catalog that Symphony maintains.

If you need to change the print settings completely—perhaps to print out a different section of the same worksheet—you can use Initial-Settings to clear the source, borders, margins, and so on. This will return the settings to those stored in the program's configuration. For more on printer configuration, see the section later in this chapter.

Adjusting the Printer

When working with printouts, you may want to advance the paper in the printer. You use the main Print menu to move the paper forward a line at a time (Line-Advance). You can use the Align option to let Symphony know that the current position of the paper in the printer is correct (the print head is at the top of the form). You can use the Page-Advance command to eject the current sheet of paper. This is particularly useful if you have a printer with a sheet feeder and find that the last page of the printout is not ejected automatically. Note that ejecting paper with the Page-Advance command ensures that Symphony prints the page number on the last page of a report.

Unformatted Printing

Normally, Symphony recognizes hard page breaks and inserts soft page breaks as needed, incorporating room for headers and footers.

If a continuous stream of printed output is desired—for example, to print mailing labels—you can use the Print Settings Page Breaks command and select No. Symphony will still respond to hard page breaks you have placed in the worksheet, but soft page breaks and headers/footers will not be printed.

Cell Listings

What you want to print from Symphony is not always a neatly arranged set of numbers; you may sometimes want a quick snapshot of what is on the screen. Perhaps you also wish to include a complex formula in the cell pointer to show someone how an aspect of a model works. This can be done with the (PRTSC) (PRINT SCREEN) key. Combined with (SHIFT) on some keyboards, the (PRTSC) key sends a literal picture of the cell and row numbers on the screen to your printer. Sometimes called a *screen shot* or *screen dump,* such a printout can be very useful as a reference.

If (PRTSC) does not work on your system, you may need a special graphics program to capture your Symphony screens. You can use Grafplus, from Jewell Technologies, or INSET, from INSET Systems. The latter includes commands for storing screens in files and even allows you to combine screens with printed reports. INSET was used for most of the illustrations in this book.

If what you want is not a screen shot but a list of what is in every cell in a worksheet, including the cell format if it differs from the global setting, select the Cell-Formulas option from the Print Settings Other Format menu. The resulting printout shows the full contents of all of the cells that are in the source range, listed down the side of the page. This is useful for reference or for communicating with other users. An example is shown in Figure 3-32. You can see that the cell contents are printed as they appear in the status

```
A1: 'Ohmobile: Projected Operating Expenses
B3: (D3) @DATE(91,1,1)
C3: (D3) 31+B3
D3: (D3) 31+C3
A4: 'REGION 1
A5: "Personnel
B5: (P0) 6500
C5: (P0) 1.01*B5
D5: (P0) 1.01*C5
A6: "Lease
B6: (P0) 2500
C6: (P0) 1.01*B6
D6: (P0) 1.01*C6
A7: "Utilities
B7: (P0) 500
C7: (P0) 1.01*B7
D7: (P0) 1.01*C7
A8: "Phone
B8: (P0) 300
C8: (P0) 1.01*B8
D8: (P0) 1.01*C8
A9: "Advertising
B9: (P0) 1250
C9: (P0) 1.01*B9
D9: (P0) 1.01*C9
A10: 'REGION 2
A11: "Personnel
B11: (P0) 4500
C11: (P0) 1.01*B11
D11: (P0) 1.01*C11
A12: "Lease
B12: (P0) 2100
C12: (P0) 1.01*B12
D12: (P0) 1.01*C12
A13: "Utilities
B13: (P0) 450
C13: (P0) 1.01*B13
D13: (P0) 1.01*C13
A14: "Phone
B14: (P0) 250
C14: (P0) 1.01*B14
D14: (P0) 1.01*C14
A15: "Advertising
B15: (P0) 1250
C15: (P0) 1.01*B15
D15: (P0) 1.01*C15
A16: 'REGION 3
A17: "Personnel
B17: (P0) 6250
C17: (P0) 1.01*B17
```

FIGURE 3-32 Cell-Formulas printout

area. Another user could recreate a spreadsheet design from a listing like this.

Print Destinations

When you select the Destination option on the Print Settings menu, you can see that there are several different places that Symphony can send what you "print."

Printer File Range Erase Cancel

The printer is the default destination. Symphony can also perform something called a *print to disk,* represented by the File option. This operation is used to create a file of the printed information, allowing you to export data from Symphony to other programs such as word processors. When you select this option, you must provide a name for the file in which the data will be stored. These files usually have the extension PRN instead of WR1, and they are referred to as *print files*.

With the Range option, Symphony can print from one area of a worksheet to another. This lets you examine your printed output without using paper. You specify an unused range of cells in the worksheet to take the place of the printer. The range must be large enough to receive the printed report and must not contain any other data. In the sample worksheet, you could use the area Q1..AA200. With Destination set to Range, you select Align and Go from the main Print menu to get the printed report sent to the worksheet. You can then select Quit to examine the print area. As you can see from Figure 3-33, the information is printed in the worksheet as a series of long labels in the first column of the specified range. The header information, borders, and footers are included in the results.

You might want to name a large section of the worksheet with the range name OUTPUT so that you can use it for this purpose. You might also want to save a named settings sheet that includes Range as the Destination. Use the Erase command to clear the

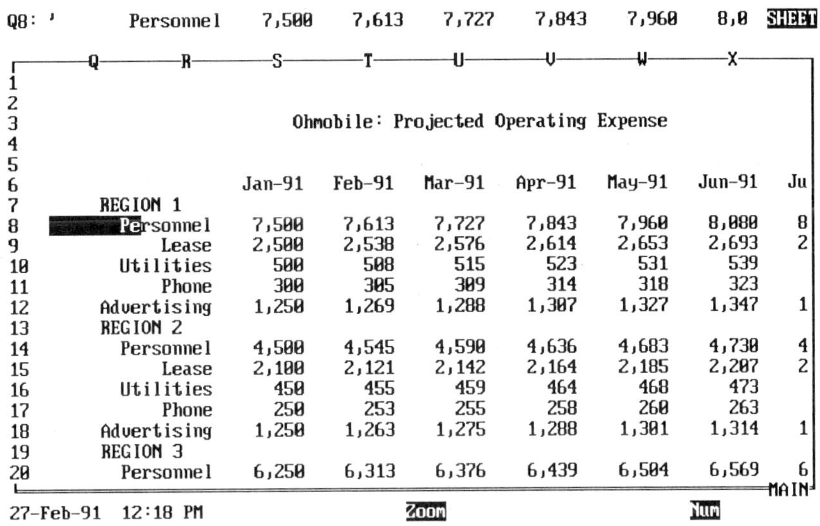

Q8: ' Personnel 7,500 7,613 7,727 7,843 7,960 8,0 SHEET

	Q R	S	T	U	V	W	X	
1								
2								
3		Ohmobile: Projected Operating Expense						
4								
5								
6		Jan-91	Feb-91	Mar-91	Apr-91	May-91	Jun-91	Ju
7	REGION 1							
8	Personnel	7,500	7,613	7,727	7,843	7,960	8,000	8
9	Lease	2,500	2,538	2,576	2,614	2,653	2,693	2
10	Utilities	500	508	515	523	531	539	
11	Phone	300	305	309	314	318	323	
12	Advertising	1,250	1,269	1,288	1,307	1,327	1,347	1
13	REGION 2							
14	Personnel	4,500	4,545	4,590	4,636	4,683	4,730	4
15	Lease	2,100	2,121	2,142	2,164	2,185	2,207	2
16	Utilities	450	455	459	464	468	473	
17	Phone	250	253	255	258	260	263	
18	Advertising	1,250	1,263	1,275	1,288	1,301	1,314	1
19	REGION 3							
20	Personnel	6,250	6,313	6,376	6,439	6,504	6,569	6

MAIN

27-Feb-91 12:18 PM Zoom Num

FIGURE 3-33 The printout in the worksheet

contents of a disk file that you are using as the print destination, or use it to clear the worksheet range that you specified as the destination. You will find this useful between successive test print operations.

Print Configuration

When you have explored the various print options available in Symphony and have experimented with them on your printer, you can apply the ones you need to a final report of the model. In Figure 3-31, you can see a report that has been much improved. The settings for this report are shown in Figure 3-34. Note that the settings have been given a name: FINAL.

Note Bear in mind that the print settings, even if they are named, are not stored until the whole file itself is stored. If you do not store your file, you will lose the print settings.

```
Start printing using current settings                                    MENU
Go  Line-Advance  Page-Advance  Align  Settings  Quit

Page                    Source:      Range B4..M29
  Length:      60       Destination: Range Q1..EX621
  Spacing:     1        Init-String:
  Number                Margins                 Other
    Print-Number: 1       Left:    5              Space Compression: No
    Start-Page:   1       Right:   80             Attributes:          Yes
    End-Page:     999     Top:     2              Format: As-Displayed
  Breaks:      Yes        Bottom:  2              Top-Labels:  B3..M3
  Wait:        No                                 Left-Labels: A4..A29
  Header: !Ohmobile: Projected Operating Expense
  Footer: @!!Page #.
                                                   Print Settings: FINAL
```

FIGURE 3-34 The FINAL print settings sheet

Finally, you need to remember that there is always an underlying set of print settings in Symphony: the ones that are attached to each new worksheet and put in place by the Name Initial-Settings and Name Reset commands. These settings are accessed through the SERVICES Configuration menu, shown in Figure 3-35. The other configuration options are discussed in Chapter 8, but the print options can be addressed now. When you select Print from the Configuration menu, you have these choices:

Type Auto-LF Wait Margins Page-Length Init-String Name Quit

When you change these settings and then pick Update from the Configuration menu, you will store changed settings permanently so that they are there from session to session. This saves you from having to make the same basic changes for every print job.

The Type option refers to how the printer is connected. This is usually Type 1, meaning that the printer is attached to the parallel port on your personal computer. If you have a serial printer, then you will probably select Type 2, which also requires that you select a *baud rate*. The baud rate is the speed at which data is sent to the printer; it should be specified in your printer manual. If you have

```
Directory to become current at start of session                             MENU
File  Printer  Communications  Document  Window  Help  Auto  Other  Update  Quit

File: C:\SYM22\DATA                 Document                 Window
Printer                               Tab interval:    5        Type: SHEET
  Type:       Parallel 1              Justification:   1        Name:
  Auto-LF:    No                      Spacing:         1          MAIN
  Wait:       No                      Left margin:     1       Help: Removable
  Margins                             Right margin:            Auto-Worksheet:
    Left:  4       Top:      2        Blanks visible: No
    Right: 76      Bottom:   2        CRs visible:     Yes     Clock on Screen:
  Page-Length: 66                     Auto-Justify:    Yes       Standard
  Init-String:                        Hard-Tabs:       Yes     File-Translation:
  Name: HP 2686 LaserJet Series                              IBM PC or Compatible
Communications name:                                              AEM: Yes
                                                          Configuration Settings
```

FIGURE 3-35 The Configuration menu

more than one parallel or serial port, you might need to use one of the other Type settings.

The Auto-LF setting is rarely used and should only be changed if your reports are coming out unexpectedly double-spaced. The Wait option is for printers that have their pages loaded by hand. Select this if you are using a manually fed printer, and Symphony will wait between pages while you load paper.

The Margins, Page-Length, and Init-String settings correspond directly with those on the Print Settings menu. Use them to set default values for these parameters. The Name option is used to select which printer model you want to use if you defined more than one printer through the Install program. Remember to use the Update option on the Configuration menu if you want to store the new settings as the defaults for the next session.

CALCULATING

Symphony is designed to update the answers to all formulas quickly. Whenever you enter new information, Symphony checks to see if the new data affects any other cells. Cells containing formulas that depend on the new data are automatically updated.

There may be times when you will need to alter the way information is calculated, either for the whole worksheet or for only a few cells. There are some situations in which the normal method of calculation used by Symphony will not be suitable. For example, old spreadsheet programs like VisiCalc could only calculate one row or column at a time. This meant that users would design models to work with column-wise or row-wise calculation, arranging formulas so that when calculation occurred, moving down the spreadsheet row-by-row or across it column-by-column, the results would come out right. Sometimes designs had formulas in upper rows depending on answers in lower rows, thus requiring a second calculation of the spreadsheet to be accurate.

The number of times a sheet is calculated is called *iteration*. The default method of calculation in Symphony uses just one iteration, because Symphony dispenses with column- or row-wise calculation in favor of the *Natural* method, in which least-dependent formulas are calculated before more-dependent ones, regardless of worksheet location. In fact, Symphony 2.2 has a refined version of the Normal method of recalculation, called Optimal, in which only the formulas that have changed are recalculated. This makes for faster data entry because less of the worksheet is reviewed between changes.

If you are using an old worksheet design, you may need to change the MENU Settings Recalc Order command to select Column-by-Column or Row-by-Row and increase the number of iterations. However, such situations are rare, and you can usually leave these settings unchanged.

Recalculation

Normally, Symphony automatically calculates the result of a formula when the formula is entered. When data is entered, any formulas affected by that data are updated. The program does this "in the background," meaning that the calculation proceeds while you are working on the worksheet. However, Symphony can be changed from this mode of calculation, called Automatic mode, to Manual mode.

If you select Manual from the choices offered by the MENU Recalc Method command, you can stop Symphony from doing any calculation until you have finished a series of entries. If you change to Manual mode and make a change to the worksheet, you will see the message "Calc" in the status line. This reminds you that the worksheet is not up-to-date. You can then press (F8), the CALC key, to recalculate formulas all at once. An alternative is to return to Automatic recalculation, which causes Symphony to make the worksheet current as soon as you select another cell or make another entry.

Manual recalculation tells Symphony to recalculate formulas only in the following situations:

- When the formulas are entered or edited
- When you press (F8) (the CALC key)
- When you turn Automatic recalculation back on

Manual recalculation is sometimes useful when you are entering a lot of data and do not want to see the results until all the data is entered. If enough calculated cells are affected, the data entry will be faster with recalculation set to Manual, so that recalculation occurs only after all the data is entered. However, given the improved technique of calculation in Symphony, the default Automatic mode of calculation will generally allow you to keep entering data and get up-to-date results in your spreadsheet without noticeable performance degradation or the risks of assuming an uncalculated worksheet to be correct.

PROTECTION

You probably will expend a great deal of time and effort getting information into your worksheet. Thus, it is a good idea to take steps to protect your worksheets. The following sections describe the forms of protection offered by Symphony.

Global Protection

If you work in an office with several other people or share a computer with several people, there is always the chance that one of them will retrieve a spreadsheet you have been working on and unwittingly damage it by entering new data over the top of complex formulas. To prevent this, you can protect all or part of a worksheet to prevent new data from being entered.

To protect the entire worksheet, you select Global-Protection, followed by Yes, from the SERVICES Settings menu. This is effective immediately. You can still move around the spreadsheet, but if you try to change the contents of a protected cell Symphony responds with a beep and the error message "Protected cell." You will need to press (ENTER) or (ESC) to remove the message. You will not be allowed to enter data into any cell unless it has been specifically unprotected (as described in a moment). If you save the worksheet with Global-Protection enabled, anyone who retrieves the worksheet will be prevented from changing any data until protection is turned off through the same menu.

Partial Protection

As you develop spreadsheet models that perform useful functions in your business, you may want to have some of the data entry work done by other people. Suppose you are maintaining inventory records. Each week, you have to update the inventory levels for 100 items. Instead of typing in the numbers yourself, you want the inventory clerk to do it for you. This clerk is a good typist, but not an experienced Symphony user. You are worried, for example, that numbers will be entered over the labels.

In such a case you can apply protection to the entire worksheet and then remove protection from the column where the numbers will be entered. You can protect the entire worksheet with the SERVICES Settings Global-Protection command, and then unprotect certain cells. You use the MENU Range Protect command to do this. When you select Protect from the Range menu, you are asked whether you want to allow changes or prevent changes. Choose Allow-Changes, and you will be prompted for a group of cells to change. When you select the cells and press (ENTER) to confirm the command, those cells will be marked "A" in the cell status area. You are free to change these cells. If you later decide that you want to protect these unprotected cells, you can use the Range Protection Prevent-Changes command.

RELATING TO OTHER ENVIRONMENTS

Having learned how to create and print a full-size model, you may be wondering how SHEET mode relates to Symphony's other environments. For example, you might want to add notes to a model, explaining assumptions and methodology. Versatile as Symphony's worksheet is, it is not a good place to do word processing. In the next chapter the DOC environment is explored; it is the environment to use for word processing with Symphony. However, the DOC environment is not completely separate from the worksheet.

To see how the DOC environment looks at a worksheet, you can use it to add some notes to this model. This will be done in a new window.

```
A32:                                                                   SHEET
┌────A─────────B─────────C─────────D────┐┌────A──────────N──────────────┐
21 Advertising  1,250     1,263     1,275 │1  Ohmobile: Pr
22 REGION 4                               │2
23   Personnel  5,000     5,050     5,101 │3              TOTALS
24       Lease  2,500     2,525     2,550 │16 REGION 3
25   Utilities    500       505       510 │17   Personnel $79,265.64
26       Phone    300       303       306 │18       Lease $31,706.26
27 Advertising  1,250     1,263     1,275 │19   Utilities  $6,341.25
28                                        │20       Phone  $3,804.75
29      TOTALS 40,950    41,420    41,895 │21 Advertising $15,853.13
30                                        │22 REGION 4
31                                        │23   Personnel $63,412.52
32                                        │24       Lease $31,706.26
33                                        │25   Utilities  $6,341.25
34                                        │26       Phone  $3,804.75
35                                        │27 Advertising $15,853.13
36                                        │28
37                                        │29      TOTALS $523,670.93
38                                        │30
39                                        │31
40                                        │32
└══════════════════════════════════MAIN┘└──────────────────YEAR_TOTAL┘
27-Feb-91  01:35 PM                                           Num
```

FIGURE 3-36 Preparing for a new window

1. Begin with the screen as shown in Figure 3-36, placing the cell pointer in A32.

2. Issue the SERVICES Window Create command, and use the name **NOTES**. Select DOC as the window type.

3. Size the window as shown in Figure 3-37 by first pressing (TAB) twice and then moving the top of the frame down.

4. Press (ENTER) to confirm the window size, and select Quit to return to the work area. You can see the results in Figure 3-38, where the first of the notes is being typed.

Note that the top border of the window shows the margins (« and ») as well as tab stops (▶) that are associated with word processing. The first difference that you notice when typing is that a number 1 does not create a value entry. All entries in the DOC

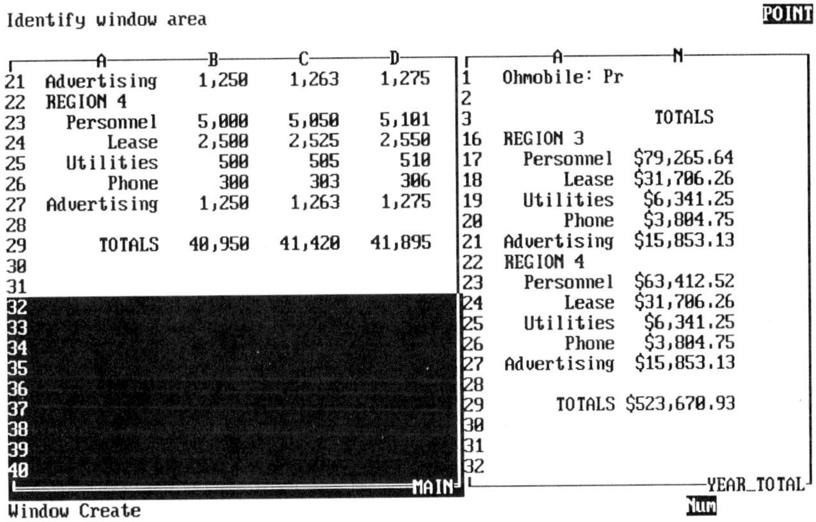

FIGURE 3-37 Sizing the new DOC window called NOTES

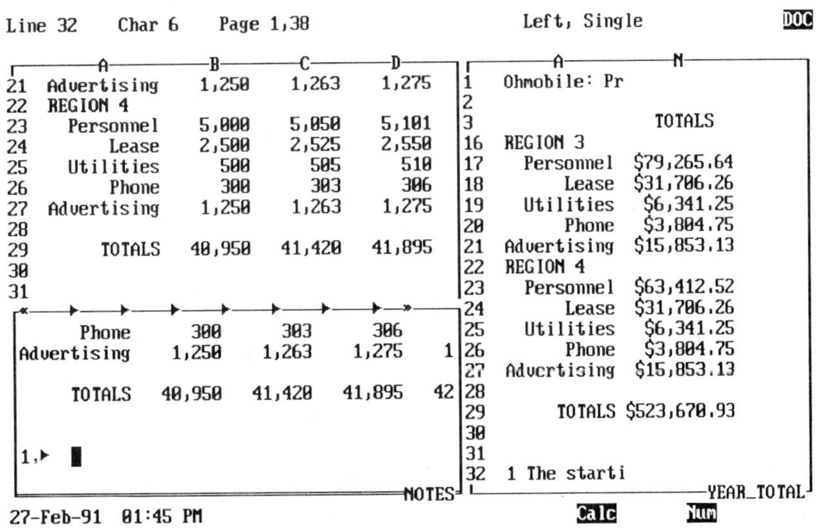

FIGURE 3-38 The new window being used

```
Line 36    Char 28    Page 1,42                    Left, Single              DOC

┌──────A──────────B─────────C─────────D──────┐┌──────A──────────N──────────────┐
21  Advertising   1,250     1,263     1,275   │1   Ohmobile: Pr                 │
22  REGION 4                                  │2                                │
23    Personnel   5,000     5,050     5,101   │3                  TOTALS        │
24        Lease   2,500     2,525     2,550   │16  REGION 3                     │
25    Utilities     500       505       510   │17    Personnel  $79,265.64      │
26        Phone     300       303       306   │18        Lease  $31,706.26      │
27  Advertising   1,250     1,263     1,275   │19    Utilities   $6,341.25      │
28                                            │20        Phone   $3,804.75      │
29       TOTALS  40,950    41,420    41,895   │21  Advertising  $15,853.13      │
30                                            │22  REGION 4                     │
31                                            │23    Personnel  $63,412.52      │
┌«────▸────▸────▸────▸────▸────▸────▸──»─────┐24        Lease  $31,706.26      │
│                                            │25    Utilities   $6,341.25      │
│1.▸ The January figures are based on        │26        Phone   $3,804.75      │
│recent industry trends.◂                    │27  Advertising  $15,853.13      │
│                                            │28                               │
│2.▸ The final figure of $523,671 is         │29       TOTALS $523,670.93      │
│quite within our resources.█                │30                               │
│                                            │31                               │
│                                            │32  1 The starti                 │
└══════════════════════════════════════NOTES═┘└─────────────────────YEAR_TOTAL─┘
27-Feb-91  01:47 PM                                  Calc        Num
```

FIGURE 3-39 The completed notes

environment are considered to be labels. After typing **1.**, the user pressed the (TAB) key to move the cursor to the first tab stop. You can see the notes entered in Figure 3-39.

As you type this text, the lines are "wrapped" when they cross the margin. The (ENTER) key is used to provide "carriage returns" down to new lines. The (BACKSPACE) key will erase characters to the left of the cursor and reverse-wrap up to the previous line. The cursor keys are used to move the cursor through the text, and the (DEL) key will erase characters at the cursor and draw them in from the right.

To see how the different Symphony windows work together, you can now press (F6) and see that each window in turn becomes active. You can even zoom the DOC window with (ALT-F6) to see all of the model as a document, or zoom the MAIN window to see the notes as part of the worksheet.

SUMMARY

You are now well-versed in Symphony's worksheet commands and many of the general commands that will be used in the other environments. You have also seen how windows can be used to give different views of your data—even different environments that can be used for specialized work. In the next chapter the full range of DOC commands will be explored for full-featured word processing.

4

WORD PROCESSING

This chapter explores Symphony's word processing capabilities, which are provided by the DOC environment. Word processing is the activity of preparing printed text, using the power of a computer to provide speed and flexibility to the process of text entry, editing, storage, and retrieval. With a word processor you can create better-looking documents, produce more documents per day, and maintain tighter control of your documents. With a word processor you can get more work done in a shorter amount of time.

GETTING INTO WORD PROCESSING

Suppose that you want to use Symphony to create a letter to a prospective client. You have experienced the powers of Symphony's electronic spreadsheet, so you probably wonder if there is any way to apply what you have already learned to the task of word processing. The answer is yes. As you saw at the end of the last chapter, word processing in Symphony is really just another way of looking at a worksheet.

The DOC Environment

Using a DOC window, rather than a SHEET window, you can arrange text in a Symphony worksheet and use such benefits of word processing as word wrap, paragraph justification, and search and replace. At the same time, you can store and print your text with the commands you already learned when working with worksheets. You can even combine the formula capability of a spreadsheet with the text-formatting ability of a word processor.

At the end of the last chapter, you learned to create a DOC window to view part of a worksheet. You will probably find it easier to explore the full range of DOC environment commands if you start with a new file. Before you do this, you should save your current work. Unfortunately, Symphony does not know whether or not you have saved your work, so when you issue the New or

Exit command, Symphony cannot tell you that you have not yet saved work or that it is okay to proceed with the commands. You have to manage this aspect of the filing system yourself.

Once your current work is saved, press SERVICES (F9) and choose the New command. This will give you a blank worksheet with a single SHEET window, called MAIN, that occupies the whole screen and uses the default settings. To do word processing you want to change the window type to DOC, so you press TYPE (ALT-F10) and select DOC. You now have a full-screen word processing window called MAIN, as shown in Figure 4-1. The various parts of the screen in the DOC environment are pointed out in Figure 4-1 and are described in the next section.

The DOC Window

In a DOC window, the top line of the control panel provides several important facts. First of all, you are informed of the position of the cursor according to the current line, character, and page. Your first line for typing is line 1. The Line indicator shows vertical position, and the Char indicator shows horizontal position across the page, measured in characters, starting at Char 1, which is at the left margin.

The Page indicator tells you which page you are on. You begin on page 1. The second number of this indicator (6) is the printed line number, meaning the line of the printed page on which the current line will appear on. Given the default print settings of 2 lines of top margin, one line for a header, and two lines between the header and the body of the report, the printed line number will be 6 for typing line 1. Unless you change the settings, the text you type on line 1 of the DOC window will appear on line 6 of the printed page.

The current justification setting of the document is shown as Left, meaning that all text will be flush with the left margin and extend as far as possible toward the right margin without going beyond it or splitting words (referred to as a *left-justified,* or a

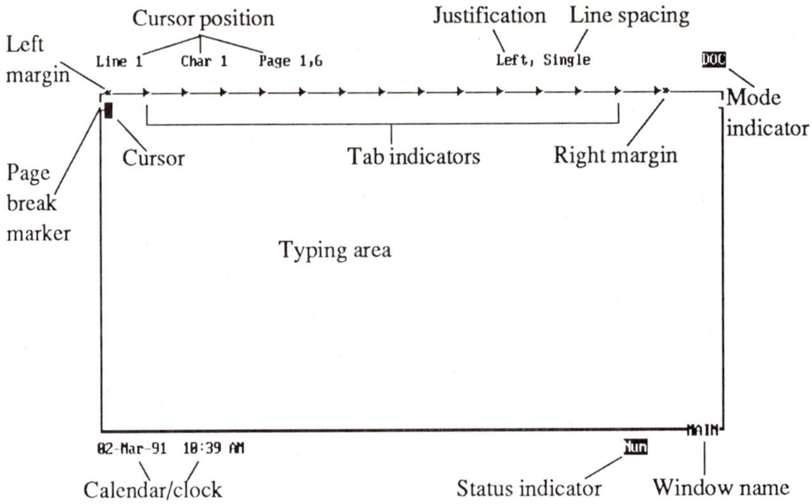

FIGURE 4-1 Annotated DOC screen

ragged right, margin). You can change this setting later if you wish. The current spacing is shown as Single, meaning that text will appear on every line unless you insert blank lines. The area to the right of the line-spacing indicator will show the current print attribute, such as bold or underlined, if the cursor is positioned over text that has been enhanced in this way. On the far right of the first line of the screen is the trusty mode indicator, letting you know that you are in the DOC environment.

The second line of the screen in the DOC environment is used for issuing commands, such as assigning print attributes or moving to a specific line. The third line is a format line, which shows where the margins and tab stops are located. The left and right margins are shown as chevron symbols (« and »), and the tab stops, shown as triangles (▶), are set every five characters to begin with. You can change margins and tab settings any time. The first line of the actual typing area displays the rectangular cursor, and also, in a normal DOC window with borders, page break markers that indicate where each print page starts and ends.

Note that as you begin to enter text in the DOC environment, you may see the "Calc" message at the bottom of the screen. This simply indicates that you have entered new information, and you can ignore it unless you are using formulas in your document, as described at the end of the chapter.

THE KEYS TO EDITING

You can now begin to familiarize yourself with the basic editing keys, the ones that Symphony uses to let you correct your typing or change your mind about your text. If you are coming to Symphony from another word processor, the editing keys will be somewhat similar to those you have used before, but with some important differences that may take some practice to get used to. Resist the temptation to compare your old word processor with Symphony until you have had a chance to really get to know the Symphony DOC environment.

The BACKSPACE Key

Suppose you are the sales manager for Connie's Comestibles, an innovative food service company specializing in the delivery of snacks to office workers in isolated office buildings. You want to write a letter to a prospective client in a new office park. You decide to begin the letter the way many word processing users do when seized by inspiration—that is, by typing the important stuff first before worrying about the address and other details.

1. Without pressing the ENTER key, type the following:

   Welcome to your office in Enterprise Office Estate

2. Notice that the cursor moves ahead of your text as you type it. As in the editing of worksheet cell entries, the (BACKSPACE) key works nicely at this point to back over any mistakes.

3. No sooner have you typed the word "Estate" than you remember it should be "Park." Your cursor is just past the "e" in "Estate." Simply press the (BACKSPACE) key a few times to get rid of "Estate," as shown here:

```
Line 1     Char 45    Page 1,6                     Left, Single           DOC
Welcome to your office in Enterprise Office █
```

4. Now you can type **Park** and the period at the end of the sentence.

Arrow Keys

Before proceeding with the rest of the letter, you should try some other ways of changing what you have typed so far. For example, the clumsy repetition of the word "office" needs to be changed. The second occurrence is part of a proper name, so you have to keep it, but you can remove the first occurrence. However, you do not want to (BACKSPACE) all the way back there. You would lose most of your sentence. This is where the cursor movement keys (or arrow keys) come in very handy.

1. Press (LEFT ARROW) a few times, and you will see that it moves through your text without damaging it, highlighting each letter or space as it goes.

2. Like most of the keys on the keyboard, this one repeats if you hold it down. Thus, pressing (LEFT ARROW) and leaning on it a

little will quickly move the cursor into the general vicinity of the word "office"—in fact, onto the "o" would be great.

3. If you go too far, just press (RIGHT ARROW) to come back to the position shown here:

```
Line 1     Char 17   Page 1,6                         Left, Single          DOC

Welcome to your office in Enterprise Office Park.
```

Insert Mode

The normal method of typing in the Symphony typing area is called the *Insert* mode. This means that when you type new text in the middle of old text, what you type is inserted into the text instead of replacing what is already there. You decide to refer to your prospective client's new office as "home," so follow these steps:

1. Type **home**, and notice that you end up with "homeoffice":

```
Line 1     Char 21   Page 1,6                         Left, Single          DOC

Welcome to your homeoffice in Enterprise Office Park
```

2. Note that the new text did not overwrite the old. The sentence expanded to make room for it. You have both words on the screen at the same time. This is very handy, since you decide you do not like the possible ambiguity of the word "home."

3. With your cursor still on the "o" in "office," use (BACKSPACE) to back over the word "home." The sentence is drawn back together by the (BACKSPACE) key. In a moment, you try another alternative to "office."

If you are coming to Symphony from a program like Multimate or the Wang word processing system, Insert mode may take some getting used to. That is because those systems are normally in what Symphony refers to as Overstrike mode, and you have to specially request to insert text. However, with a little practice, you will find that you will be very comfortable with Symphony's Insert mode.

Overstrike Mode

The alternative to Insert mode is called *Overstrike* mode, which you can explore in a moment. Symphony always puts you into Insert mode when you enter the typing area. Insert is the *default* mode and is generally a more forgiving way of operating, since it does not require you to give any warning when you want to add new text. Overstrike mode has value when you are updating text that is a constant length. If you had to type a new phone number over an old one, Overstrike mode would be useful. Similarly, the conversion of a word from lowercase to uppercase could be done by typing over the old characters with the new.

To test this, you will type a new word over the word "office." For this to work properly, your cursor should be on the "o" in "office."

1. Press (INS) so that the bottom status area shows "Ovr."

2. Carefully type **suites**, which will exactly replace "office." This example was a little contrived, since the replacement word was exactly the same length as the old word. The results are as follows:

```
Line 1     Char 23   Page 1,6                    Left, Single          DOC

Welcome to your suites in Enterprise Office Park.
```

Overstrike mode is not smart: It did not know you were replacing one word with another.

3. To see the negative effects of overstrike typing, stay in Overstrike mode and press the (SPACEBAR) twice. You lose the "i" in "in."

4. To fix this, press (INS) again to get back to Insert mode. Now type the missing **i**, and it will be inserted in the text.

5. Remember that characters are inserted to the left of the cursor. Everything now looks fine, except there is an extra space between "Suites" and "in." Just press (LEFT ARROW) once to highlight the letter "i" and press (BACKSPACE) once. Notice that when (BACKSPACE) removes a character, it pulls your text back together, just as typing in Insert mode pushes the text apart to add the new characters.

6. You decide to change the tone of the sentence a little by adding the word "here" before the word "in." If your cursor is on the "i" of "in," and you are in Insert Mode, just type **here** and press the (SPACEBAR), and it will fit nicely into the text:

```
Line 1     Char 29    Page 1,6                        Left, Single        DOC

Welcome to your suites here in Enterprise Office Park.
```

Deleting Text

Getting rid of text is just as easy as adding it. Suppose you decided to get rid of the word "in," and your cursor is on the letter "i" of that word as it was in the last illustration. The quickest way to do this is to press the (DEL) key (located next to the (INS) key on most keyboards). The (DEL) key takes out the character the cursor is on and pulls in the text from the right. To change the word "in" to "at" in the example,

1. Press (DEL) twice, and you will remove the word "in."
2. Check that you are still in Insert mode, and type the new word. Your text now reads

   Welcome to your suites here at Enterprise Office Park.

The (DEL) key is great for removing unwanted characters. Like the other keys, it repeats; do not lean on it unless you want to get rid of a lot of characters. You can use it in many situations where (BACKSPACE) might also work, and you will find yourself developing a feel for the best method to use in any given situation. In the example, you can use (DEL) to change your mind, again, about what to call the offices:

1. Move your cursor under the first letter of the word "suites."
2. Press (DEL) enough times to remove the word. Now type **new place**, and it will be inserted into the text.
3. Move to the first letter of the word "here," and press (DEL) enough times to remove "here" and the extra space. The text now reads

   Welcome to your new place at Enterprise Office Park.

Editing Technique

People seem to use the editing keys in two different styles. You can correct mistakes as you type, or you can come back to them when you have completed a section of typing. As you develop your own style, you will also get a feel for making changes in either Insert or Overstrike mode. After a while, the use of the (BACKSPACE) and (DEL) keys becomes natural. Later in the chapter you will explore methods of changing large amounts of text at once.

MENUS, COMMANDS, AND KEYS

Before going any further, you may want to save your work so far. To do this you use the same SERVICES menu that you used in the SHEET environment. Press (F9) and select File followed by Save. You can now give a name to the file that will store your work so far. This file will be a worksheet file with the regular extension, WR1. However, since you are saving the file while you are in the DOC environment, it will reappear in the DOC environment when you retrieve it. Type a name like **LETTER01** and press (ENTER). The file will be stored on disk.

In addition to the general (F9) SERVICES commands, the DOC environment has its own set of environment-specific (F10) MENU commands, described in a moment. Whereas the SHEET environment allows you to use the / key to access the (F10) menu, the DOC environment does not. There are several function keys that will be used extensively in the DOC environment. These are listed, along with some other special keys, in Table 4-1.

Word Processing Menus

While the (F9) SERVICES menu is the same in both DOC and SHEET environments, the (F10) MENU contains commands specifically for word processing. Press (F10) while in the DOC environment, and you will see the following commands:

Copy Move Erase Search Replace Justify Format Page Line-Marker Quit

These commands allow you to copy, move, and erase blocks of text; search for pieces of text and replace them with others; align text and alter its format; insert page breaks; and attach names to

Key	Name	Action
F2	JUSTIFY	Justifies current paragraph
ALT-F2	WHERE	Displays the current page number and what the line number of current line will be if you print the document
F3	INDENT	Indents text in current paragraph
ALT-F3	SPLIT	Pushes text following cursor to next line
F4	ERASE	Erases specified block of text
ALT-F4	CENTER	Centers a line between the margins
F5	GOTO	Moves cursor to specified line
F9	SERVICES	Accesses general Symphony commands
F10	MENU	Accesses DOC-specific commands
ENTER		Inserts a hard carriage return to end short lines and paragraphs; adds blank lines
BACKSPACE		Deletes preceding character
DEL		Deletes character at cursor
INS		Switches between insert and overstrike modes
TAB		In Insert mode, moves cursor and inserts spaces up to next tab stop; in Overstrike mode, moves cursor to next tab stop; when specifying blocks of text, anchors the beginning point of the highlighting

TABLE 4-1 Important Keys for the DOC Environment

places in the text. All of these commands will be explored in the course of this chapter. Some of them can be selected without using the menu. By using what are referred to as *accelerator keys,* Symphony allows you to select commonly used commands with a single keystroke consisting of CTRL and another key. The accelerator keys are listed in Table 4-2.

Name	Key Combination
AUTO (justify)	CTRL-J
BEGIN (text attribute)	CTRL-B
CASE (change)	CTRL-X
COPY (text)	CTRL-C
DELETE WORD	CTRL-BACKSPACE
DELETE LINE	CTRL-D
DELETE RIGHT	CTRL-Y
DELETE LEFT	CTRL-T
FORMAT (line create)	CTRL-F
MERGE (character)	CTRL-O
MOVE (text)	CTRL-M
NEXT PAGE	CTRL-PGDN
PAGE (break)	CTRL-N
PASTE (text)	CTRL-P
REPLACE (text)	CTRL-R
SEARCH (for text)	CTRL-S
STOP (text attribute)	CTRL-E
TOP PAGE	CTRL-PGUP

TABLE 4-2 The Accelerator Keys in the DOC Environment

Basic Location Keys

In a moment, you will continue with the letter. Before proceeding, however, you need to think about where your cursor is. The cursor is the point at which your new characters appear. Obviously, continuing the letter requires the cursor to be at the end of the text you have already typed, and in this example, where there is only one line of text, that means at the end of the line.

Key	Alone	With SCROLL on	Preceded by (END)
(UP ARROW)	Line up	Window up 1 row	Start of paragraph
(DOWN ARROW)	Line down	Window down 1 row	End of paragraph
(LEFT ARROW)	1 character left	Window 25% left	Left edge of text
(RIGHT ARROW)	1 character right	Window 25% right	Right edge of text
(PGUP)	Windowful up		
(PGDN)	Windowful down		
Big-Left	Word left		
Big-Right	Word right		
(HOME)	Upper left of document		End of document
(CTRL-PGUP)	To top of current page or next page up		
(CTRL-PGDN)	To top of current/next page		
(CTRL-HOME)	To start of line		
(CTRL-END)	To end of line		
(END) *X*			To the next *X* (can be any character)
(END) JUSTIFY			To next format line
(END) WHERE			To the previous format line

TABLE 4-3 Cursor Movement Keys in DOC Window

There are several ways to move the cursor to this location. You can press the (END) key followed by the (RIGHT ARROW) key, or you can press (CTRL-END). You can see all of Symphony's cursor movement keys for the DOC environment in Table 4-3. After you have typed more of the letter, you can experiment with more of the keystrokes that change the location of the cursor.

WORD WRAP AND JUSTIFICATION

The next word processing feature you are going to see is *word wrap*. This will be demonstrated by typing more of the letter. Go ahead and type the text shown here:

```
Line 1     Char 1    Page 1,6                       Left, Single          DOC

Welcome to your new place at Enterprise Office Park.  We hope you are
settling in nicely in this terrific new facility.  One problem
encountered by pioneering companies such as yours arises from the
simple, but almost universal need for something to munch on during the
morning coffee break.
```

Do not worry about where the lines are supposed to end; just keep typing, and the program will take text down to a fresh line automatically.

Word Wrap

In word processing (as opposed to the very interesting form of popular music that bears a similar name) "wrap" means never having to worry about where the line ends. It is a very basic ingredient of word processing, one that experienced users often take for granted. The first time you see it in action, it is not hard to understand what a tremendous advantage it offers over the old method of typing. Wordwrap beats waiting for the "end-of-the-line" bell and having to decide exactly when to perform a carriage return. Symphony inserts carriage returns for you.

The right margin marker on the ruler or scale line at the top of the page determines where on the line Symphony places the carriage return. This marker looks like a pair of greater-than signs: ». If you imagine a line drawn straight down the screen below the right margin symbol, you can see that none of the text you have typed goes past this imaginary line. Later, you will see how this can be moved in order to lengthen or shorten the lines.

The (ENTER) Key

Although Symphony can automatically end lines for you, it does not automatically know where you want to end a paragraph, or if you want to end a line short of the right margin. To let Symphony know when you have finished typing a paragraph and want to go

```
Line 15    Char 20   Page 1,20                  Left, Single            DOC

Welcome to your new place at Enterprise Office Park.  We hope you are
settling in nicely in this terrific new facility.  One problem
encountered by pioneering companies such as yours arises from the
simple, but almost universal need for something to munch on during the
morning coffee break.◄

So, can we add your office to the growing list of satisfied customers
who receive a daily visit from our employees, who deliver fresh
comestibles every morning, right to your office?◄

Yours truly,◄


Your Name◄
New Account Manager
                                                                    MAIN
03-Mar-91  01:31 PM                                              Num
```

FIGURE 4-2 The close of the letter

on to the next one, you press the (ENTER) key. This acts as a carrier return, taking your cursor down one line and over to the left margin.

To continue the example, go ahead and press (ENTER) now. You probably want one blank line between paragraphs, so press (ENTER) again. Now type the closing of the letter from Figure 4-2, using your name instead of "Your Name." Remember to press the (ENTER) key twice after the paragraph. Also use it to end the short lines. When you are finished you are on line 15, as shown by the cursor position indicator in the top status area.

You can see that when you end a line of text with (ENTER), Symphony places a triangular symbol at the end of the line (◄). This symbol does not appear on lines where there is no text at all. The symbol indicates the type of line ending that you have created. There is an important difference between the carriage returns that Symphony automatically gives you with word wrap and the ones that you put in with the (ENTER) key.

The carriage returns you place with (ENTER) are called *hard returns,* whereas the ones Symphony inserts with word wrap are called *soft returns*. The location of soft returns will change in direct relation to the words you type. When you add words to a line, the extra text will force words to wrap to the next line, altering the position of the soft return in relation to the words. The hard returns are firmly located and will not change position in relation to the words. Of course, you can remove hard returns with the (DEL) or (BACKSPACE) key.

To test this, and to see how Symphony automatically justifies paragraphs to keep the text within the margins, try these steps with the example:

1. Press (UP ARROW) seven times, to place the cursor between the words "daily" and "visit" on line 8, character position 20 (as shown by the cursor indicator in the top status area).

2. Press (CTRL-RIGHT ARROW). This will move the cursor to the first character of the next word—in this case, the "v" in "visit." Press (CTRL-RIGHT ARROW) four more times to place the cursor on the first character of the second occurrence on this line of the word "who." (You can use (CTRL-LEFT ARROW) to move one word at a time to the left).

3. Note that this line ends in the word "fresh" and there is a hard return after "office?". Now press (ENTER).

4. The cursor is taken back to the left margin on line 9. As you can see from Figure 4-3, the line is broken by a hard return where your cursor was located. The soft return that was located after "fresh" has disappeared, but the hard return after "office" is still there, even though the word has moved further along the line.

5. Even if you were to change the amount of text on line 9, the hard return would not be detached from "office." Press (DEL) three times to remove the word "who." Now type **cheerfully**.

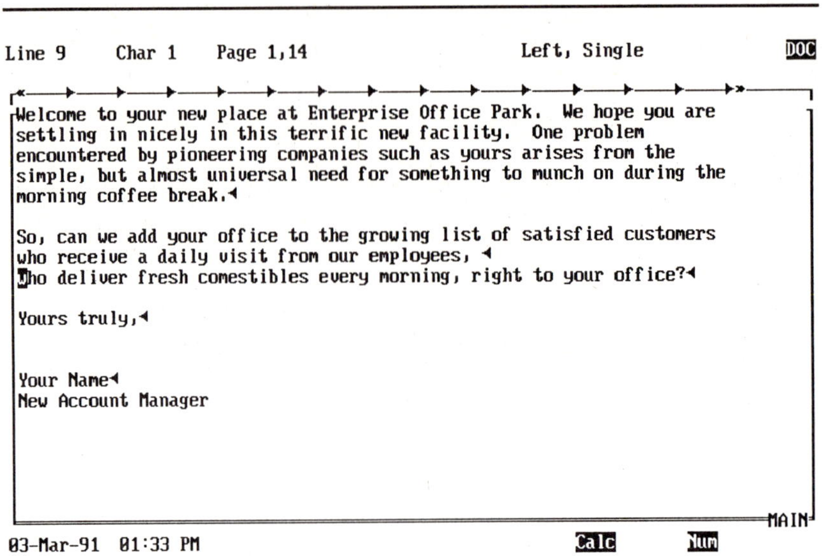

FIGURE 4-3 Inserting a hard return

6. You will see the text on line 9 wrap around, as Symphony inserts a soft return after "your." But the hard return stays attached to "office."

7. To remove the hard return you inserted on line 8, press (UP ARROW) once and then press (END), followed immediately by (RIGHT ARROW). You are highlighting the hard return symbol.

8. Press (DEL) once, and note how the paragraph reforms itself within the margins.

9. Move the cursor to the space between "deliver" and "fresh," and type **ing**. Again, the paragraph is justified automatically. The results are shown in Figure 4-4.

```
Line 8     Char 68   Page 1,13                      Left, Single              DOC

Welcome to your new place at Enterprise Office Park.  We hope you are
settling in nicely in this terrific new facility.  One problem
encountered by pioneering companies such as yours arises from the
simple, but almost universal need for something to munch on during the
morning coffee break.◄

So, can we add your office to the growing list of satisfied customers
who receive a daily visit from our employees, cheerfully delivering█
fresh comestibles every morning, right to your office?◄

Yours truly,◄


Your Name◄
New Account Manager

                                                                          MAIN
03-Mar-91  01:35 PM                                          Calc      Num
```

FIGURE 4-4 Adding text and resulting rejustification

The Justify Command

Keeping text within the margins is referred to in Symphony as *justifying* the text. The automatic rejustification of paragraphs is a very useful feature; normally, it is done after every keystroke in order to keep text looking as close as possible to its final appearance. However, you may want to disable this feature. It does take up more and more time as documents grow longer, and some people are more comfortable having the text rejustified on command rather than automatically.

If you do not want your text to be justified automatically, you can use the accelerator key called AUTO (CTRL-J) to turn it off. Simply select No from the menu that appears when you use this keystroke. As an alternative to this keystroke, you can use the MENU Format Settings Auto-Justify command. To change the justification setting permanently, use the SERVICES Configuration Document Auto-Justify command.

When you set Auto-Justify to No, you will need to use the justification commands to tell Symphony to reform paragraphs after editing. When you select MENU Justify, you have a choice between Paragraph, which justifies the paragraph containing the cursor according to current format line, and All-Remaining, which justifies all of the document from the cursor forward, with each section being justified according to the format line preceding it. For more on format lines, see the section later in this chapter. You can also justify the current paragraph by pressing the JUSTIFY key (this is the (F2) key, used as the EDIT key in the SHEET environment).

FURTHER MOVEMENT AND EDITING

So far, you have seen several ways of moving the edit cursor. Use (LEFT ARROW) and (RIGHT ARROW) to move one character at a time along rows and around soft returns. The (END) and (LEFT ARROW) sequence takes the cursor to the left end of the current line. The (END) and (RIGHT ARROW) sequence takes the cursor to the right end of the current line. You can also use (CTRL-HOME) and (CTRL-END) to take the cursor to the left and right ends of the line, respectively.

The Big-Right combination, (CTRL-RIGHT ARROW), places the cursor on the first character of the next word to the right, allowing you to move through your text from word to word. This keystroke also places the cursor on any invisible hard returns that are at the left margin. The Big-Left keystroke, (CTRL-LEFT ARROW), moves the cursor in the same way in the opposite direction, stopping on all hard returns.

The (HOME) Key

Suppose you want to add text to the beginning of the letter. Since you are in Insert mode, new text will be inserted wherever your cursor happens to be. To add new text to the beginning of the document, you need to get your cursor back to that point. As in the SHEET environment, the (HOME) key gets you to the beginning of your document.

1. Press the (HOME) key now, and you will see that in Symphony this puts your cursor on line 1, character 1 at the left margin. The pair of less-than signs («) on the scale line at the top of the screen indicate the left margin.

2. Although it looks as though there is no room for your new text at the beginning of the letter, just type **Dear Office Manager:**. You will see that words are being pushed off the end of the first line of the text, automatically wrapped around to the second line. The paragraph is rearranged to keep within the margins.

3. Now press (ENTER) twice to move the text down and insert two blank lines. Again, the paragraph is reformed.

The (TAB) Key

Suppose that you want to indent the first line of the first paragraph of your letter. Indenting is done with the (TAB) key.

1. With the cursor on the "W" in "Welcome," press the (TAB) key once. The text is indented, moved to the right in line with the first tab-stop symbol on the format line. A tab symbol (▶) is placed in the text.

2. Press the (TAB) key again. The text is moved to the second tab position, and a second tab code is placed in the text.

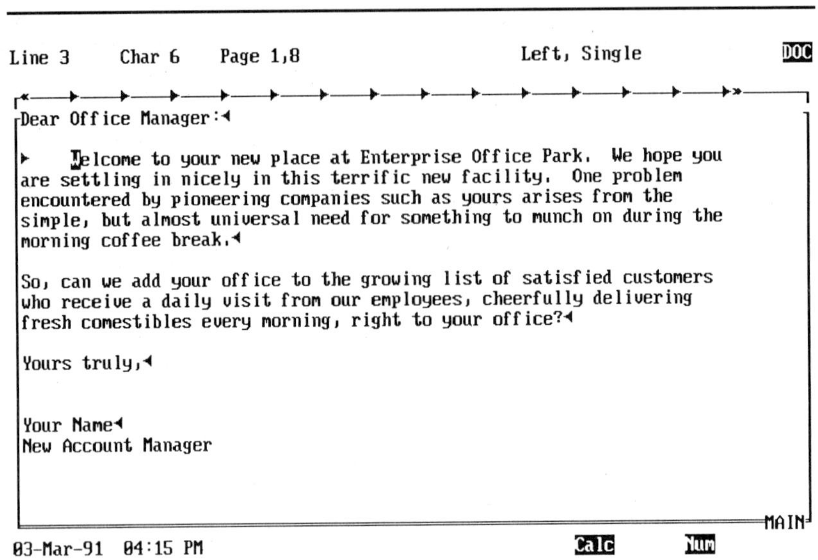

FIGURE 4-5 Indented paragraph

3. You decide that one tab is enough, so you press (BACKSPACE), which erases the second tab stop and moves the text back to the first tab stop. The results can be seen in Figure 4-5.

Further Movement

Suppose that you wanted to add more text to the end of your letter. To get there you press (END) and then (HOME). This places the cursor just to the right of the last character you have typed.

A further use of the (END) key is to locate the next occurrence of a particular character. For example, press (HOME) to move the cursor to the top of the document. Now press (END) and type **w**. Your cursor will be placed on the "W" in "Welcome." If you now press (END) and type **S**, the cursor will be placed on the "S" at the beginning of the second paragraph. If you do type a lowercase letter for this (END) command to locate, the next upper- or lowercase character will be located. If you type a capital, the next occurrence of that capital will be located.

The various keystrokes for moving the cursor around a piece of text in the DOC environment are summarized in Table 4-3. In addition to these keystrokes, there are three techniques for locating the cursor that have not yet been discussed: using line numbers, marking text, and searching.

Line Numbers

There may be times when you want to move the cursor to the beginning of a specific line of the document. You can do this with the GOTO key, (F5). Press (F5), type **9**, and press (ENTER). The cursor will be placed at the beginning of line 9. If you have several pages, you can move to another page by entering a page number followed by a comma and a printed line number. For example, to move to page 3, printed line 6 (typing line 1), you would enter **3,6**.

You can also move from page to page with the (CTRL-PGDN) and (CTRL-PGUP) keys, which respectively move you a page down and a page up in the document. You can also go to a specific place anywhere in a document if you mark the text.

Marking Text

Since line numbers get hard to deal with in long documents, you can assign names to particular points in the text. These names are called *line markers*. For example, you can attach the name CLOSE to the first line of the last paragraph of the letter. To do this, you place the cursor on the "S" in "So" and press MENU. Select Line-Marker and then select Assign. As with the Range Name Create command in the SHEET environment, you are shown a list of existing names, and are asked to enter a name. Type **CLOSE** and press (ENTER). Now press (HOME), and you can test this feature. Press GOTO and then MENU, and you will see the name CLOSE listed and highlighted. Press (ENTER) to select it, and the cursor will be placed on the "S" in "So."

As you create additional line markers, they will be listed when you use the Assign command and when you press (F10) at the GOTO prompt. You can remove a line marker at any time by selecting Remove instead of Assign and selecting the name you want deleted.

Searching

The ability to search for and locate a specific piece of text within a document is one of the most powerful features of a good word processing program. To experiment with Symphony's Search command in the sample document, first press (HOME) to move to the top of the letter. You can access the Search command either by pressing MENU and selecting Search or by using the accelerator key (CTRL-S). When you use either method, you are presented with the prompt "Search for what?" Type the word **munch**. This is what Symphony refers to as the *search string*. Now press (ENTER). You will then have to choose one of three options: Forward, Backward, or Quit. The first option tells Symphony to look for the characters you have typed from the current position of the cursor forward through the document, whereas the second option tells Symphony to look backwards. The third option, Quit, tells Symphony to stop searching. In this case you can just press (ENTER) to select Forward, and Symphony will highlight the word "munch."

Note that the previous menu reappears. This is in case you want to repeat the command. For now, select Forward, and you will get the message "String not found," indicating that Symphony can find no further instances of this set of characters. Select Quit, and the search process is abandoned.

To try searching with the Backwards option, press (END) and (HOME) to move to the end of the document. Press (CTRL-S), and you will see that Symphony remembers what you looked for last time. You can press (ESC) to clear this entry and type another, or you can press (ENTER) to reuse the existing string (you can also edit the search string if you first press (F2)). Try pressing (ENTER) to accept "munch" as the search string, and again, the string will be highlighted.

Note that the Search command in Symphony is partially case-sensitive, meaning that if you enter **MUNCH**, Symphony will only look for "MUNCH." If you enter **Munch**, Symphony will only look for "Munch." However, if you enter **munch**, Symphony will look for "MUNCH," "Munch," and "munch." Bear in mind that if you only need to locate a single character, you can use (END) followed by the character.

Sometimes you will want to search for an approximate string of characters, where part of what you are searching for is constant, but the rest is variable. For example, you might want to find each use of the root word "munch," including "munchies" and "munching," as well as "munch." Symphony does this automatically, since it looks for the search string "within" words. If you look for "unc," then Symphony will find those characters in "munch" and highlight them.

There may be times when you want to search for a word but are not sure of the spelling—for example, to find "receivable" when you cannot remember if the "i" comes before the "e." To do this you use a *wildcard* character in your search string. These are special characters that Symphony recognizes. The wildcard for "any character" is the question mark. Wildcards are entered in search strings bracketed by the backward slash (\); for this example, **rec\?\\?\vable** will find "receivable."

You can also use wildcard characters to find any letters or numbers, any uppercase letters, carriage returns, tabs, and page breaks. The wildcard characters are listed in Table 4-4. If you are using the Search command to locate text that you would like to alter, you can use the Replace command to automatically change instances of one string into another. This command is described later in the chapter.

Wildcard String	Symphony Finds
\?\	Any character
\&\	Any letter or number
\a\	Any letter
\A\	Any uppercase letter
\#\	Any number
\~\	Carriage return character
\^\	Tab character
\:\	Page break character
\-\	Space, tab, or hard space
\\	Backslash character

TABLE 4-4 DOC Environment Wildcards

DOCUMENT PRINTING

The letter is almost finished at this point, requiring just one more paragraph. Go ahead and add the paragraph shown in Figure 4-6 into your text. To do this, first put your cursor on the line after the paragraph ending in "coffee break," line 8, and then press (ENTER). Then type the text and press (ENTER) once more to put a blank line between paragraphs.

The letter is looking pretty good, and you would like to print out a copy in order to show it to someone else. However, just like entering data in the worksheet, typing in the DOC environment is at risk until it is stored on disk. Symphony does not do this automatically, so you must issue the SERVICES File Save command to store the document.

Basic Printing

Suppose you decide to print the letter you just created. You select Print from the SERVICES menu. The Print menu appears, as shown in Figure 4-7. This is the same menu you used to print your

```
Line 16    Char 1    Page 1,21                    Left, Single          DOC

Dear Office Manager:◄

►    Welcome to your new place at Enterprise Office Park.  We hope you
are settling in nicely in this terrific new facility.  One problem
encountered by pioneering companies such as yours arises from the
simple, but almost universal need for something to munch on during the
morning coffee break.◄

The nearest food store is miles away, but Connie's Comestibles have the
nutritious and delicious snacks that your employees want, and we
deliver!  Time consuming donut runs and employees going missing in the
middle of the morning can become a thing of the past.  With your
permission, one of our trained representatives will add your office to
their delivery route and personally present the daily selections to your
employees.◄

So, can we add your office to the growing list of satisfied customers
who receive a daily visit from our employees, cheerfully delivering
fresh comestibles every morning, right to your office?◄
                                                                    MAIN
03-Mar-91  04:51 PM                                  Calc        Num
```

FIGURE 4-6 Added paragraph

worksheet in the SHEET environment. However, when printing from a DOC window you do not need to enter a Source setting: Symphony assumes that you want to print the contents of the DOC window. After making sure that your printer is turned on and has

```
Start printing using current settings                                 MENU
Go  Line-Advance  Page-Advance  Align  Settings  Quit

 Page                       Source:
   Length:      66          Destination: Printer
   Spacing:     1           Init-String:
   Number                   Margins              Other
     Print-Number: 1          Left:    4           Space Compression: No
     Start-Page:   1          Right:   76          Attributes:        Yes
     End-Page:     999        Top:     2           Format: As-Displayed
   Breaks:      Yes           Bottom:  2           Top-Labels:
   Wait:        No                                 Left-Labels:
   Header:
   Footer:
                                                    Print Settings: MAIN
```

FIGURE 4-7 The Print menu

Dear Office Manager:

Welcome to your new place at Enterprise Office Park. We hope you are settling in nicely in this terrific new facility. One problem encountered by pioneering companies such as yours arises from the simple, but almost universal need for something to munch on during the morning coffee break.

The nearest food store is miles away, but Connie's Comestibles have the nutritious and delicious snacks that your employees want, and we deliver! Time consuming donut runs and employees going missing in the middle of the morning can become a thing of the past. With your permission, one of our trained representatives will add your office to their delivery route and personally present the daily selections to your employees.

So, can we add your office to the growing list of satisfied customers who receive a daily visit from our employees, cheerfully delivering fresh comestibles every morning, right to your office?

Yours truly,

Your Name
New Account Manager

FIGURE 4-8 The first report

paper loaded, simply select Align, followed by Go, and Symphony will send the sample document to the printer. The results are shown in Figure 4-8.

Symphony uses the same print settings for the DOC window as it does for the SHEET window. Based on a horizontal spacing of 10 characters per inch, the normal 8 1/2-inch-wide piece of paper is regarded as 85 characters wide. There is a default 4-character left margin so that the document text starts printing at the fifth character across the page, leaving just less than a half-inch space between the edge of the page and the beginning of the text. The default right margin is 76 characters from the left edge of the page, leaving just under an inch between the right edge of the text and the right edge of the page. The difference between the margins of 4 and 76 leaves you room for 72 characters of typing per line. Note that these are the print margins and not the document margins, which are set within the print margins.

Based on a vertical spacing of 6 lines per inch, there is a default top margin of 2 lines from the top of the page to the header line. There is a fixed space of two lines below the header and above the first line of printing, so the first line of text prints on the sixth line of the page, creating just less than an inch space between the top of the page and the first line of text.

You might want to alter some aspects of the results, for example, to leave more space at the top of the page and create wider margins. When working with documents, it is better to do this with the format commands, described in the next section, than with the Print Settings commands. You might also want to emphasize parts of the text, having them boldface or underlined. You can do this with the print attributes, described later in the chapter.

Document Headers and Footers

As with worksheet reports, documents printed from the DOC window can use headers and footers. The commands for these, found on the Print Settings Page menu, provide a line of space that is placed at the top (Header) or bottom (Footer) of each page. When you select Header or Footer, you type the text to be printed. In addition to text, you can also enter formatting codes in headers and footers that tell Symphony how to align the text. As in the SHEET environment, the # sign tells Symphony to enter the page number in a header or footer. Thus, you could enter **Page #** in a header to have the page number, along with the word "Page," printed at the top of every page. The @ sign causes the current date, (according to your PC's clock) to be printed.

To arrange header and footer text between the margins, the straight line symbol | is used like a tab stop. Typing the header text with no | symbol causes Symphony to left-align everything. Preceding text with one | results in centering. Using two || symbols places the text on the right. By creative use of these codes, you can accommodate most information that you will need in headers and footers. In a one-page business letter it is unlikely that you will need headers or footers.

Note Unfortunately, if you enter a header or footer for a document, there is no command to tell Symphony not to print it on the first page of the document.

Page Breaks

When you create documents that will not fit into one page, you will encounter page breaks. The default print settings are a two-line bottom margin between the bottom of the page and the footer line, plus a fixed space of two lines between the last line of text and the footer line. This amounts to a gap of five lines, or nearly one inch, between the last line of text and the bottom of the sheet of paper. If you subtract the top and bottom margins of 5 lines each from the total page length of 66 lines, you are left with room for 56 lines of text on each page.

Normally, the need for page breaks arises in one of two situations. First, you can start a document and just keep typing, in which case the text will flow onto the next page and Symphony will automatically insert a page break. Second, you can decide that part of the text needs to be placed on a new page, in which case you can insert a page break. These two types of page breaks are like the two types of carriage returns. The breaks that Symphony inserts for you are *soft page breaks,* and they may change position or even disappear as you add or remove text. The breaks that you insert manually are *hard page breaks* and always remain in the text.

Suppose that you want your letter to be accompanied by a list of products on a separate sheet. This can be done by inserting a hard (forced) page break. With the cursor positioned after the last line of the text of the letter, you would press MENU and select Page. A blank line would be inserted in the document with the double colon symbol (::). You cannot type text on this line. When the cursor is moved below this line, the page counter changes to 2—text typed below this line will appear on page 2. The DOC window border will also indicate the presence of a page break.

You remove hard page breaks with the Erase command described later in this chapter. The accelerator key for inserting hard page breaks is (CTRL) and the letter "N" for new page ((CTRL-N)). An alternative to inserting a hard page break is to keep pressing (ENTER) to add blank lines until you reach a new page and Symphony inserts an automatic page break.

FORMATTING

To change the way your Symphony word processing documents are presented on the page, you use the format commands. Each document has an overall format for tab intervals, justification, spacing, and margin settings. Something called a *format line* defines these settings for a section of the document and can be inserted at any point in the document, overriding the overall format. A format line affects the text below it as far as the next format line or the end of the document.

The Format Command

To alter the overall margins of the sample document, press (HOME) to move the cursor to the top of the document and then press MENU, followed by Format. Your choices are

Create Edit Use-Named Settings

The Create command defines a new format line. Edit is used to make changes to an existing format line. The Settings command alters the default format for the whole document.

Select Create, and Symphony will ask you where the format line should be inserted. You can use (UP ARROW) and (DOWN ARROW) to indicate a line other than the one your cursor was on when you issued the command. Press (ENTER) when you have selected the correct line. In this case you want line 1, since the format is to affect all of the text. Note that you can issue the Format Create command with the accelerator key (CTRL-F).

After indicating where the format line should be placed, Symphony inserts some characters into the DOC window and presents a menu of format options, as shown here:

```
Change margins and tabs: (L)eft margin, (R)ight margin, (T)ab stop              MENU
Margins/Tabs  Justification  Spacing  Line-Marker  Use-Named  Reset  Quit
L   T   T   T   T   T   T   T   T   T   T   T   T   T   TR11
Dear Office Manager:

     Welcome to your new place at Enterprise Office Park.  We hope you
```

The line that Symphony inserts represents the current margins and tab stops with letter markers: L for left margin, T for tab, and R for right margin. Unless you choose the Use-Named or Reset options, described in a moment, the format line you create starts out with the settings of the format line above it.

You can edit this line if you select the first menu item, Margins/Tabs. Symphony places the cursor on the L marker, and you can rearrange the line by inserting and deleting spaces. To move the left margin five characters to the right and reduce the right margin by five characters, you would follow these steps:

1. With the cursor on the L marker, press the spacebar five times. This moves the line to the right.

2. Press (CTRL-RIGHT ARROW) until you are highlighting the last T marker.

3. Press (BACKSPACE) five times. This moves the right margin toward the left.

4. Press (DEL), and the last tab stop is removed, bringing the right margin one character closer to the left. The effect can be seen here:

```
Line 1      Char 66    Page 1,6                    Left, Single             DOC

     L    T    T    T    T    T    T    T    T    T    T    T    R
Dear Office Manager:
     Welcome to your new place at Enterprise Office Park.  We hope you
```

5. Press (ENTER) to confirm the settings.

You have now established margins and tabs that will be used in the text that follows the format line. Symphony will readjust text within these settings after you finish defining the format line.

Before you leave the Format Create menu, it is worthwhile to consider the other options. The second option, Justification, has four settings: None, Left, Even, and Center. The None option allows you to turn off word wrap. The default option is Left, which gives you word wrap with a ragged-right margin. You can choose Even to align the text smoothly between the margins. You can also choose Center to align the text around the midpoint of the format line, as in centering titles.

The Format Spacing option sets the line spacing for printing. The choices are single space (1), meaning no blank lines between lines of text, double space (2), which inserts one blank line between each line of text, and triple space (3), which inserts two blank lines.

The Line-Marker option allows you to assign a name to this format line. Earlier, you learned how to assign a name to a point in the text. You can also assign names to format lines, allowing them to be duplicated very easily. For this example, select Line-Marker and Assign, type **BODY**, and press (ENTER). The new format line you are creating will now be called BODY.

The Use-Named command inserts a copy of an existing named format line. This can be used to repeat a format line. The Reset command restores overall document settings to the format line you are creating.

Having edited and named your new format line, you can select Quit, which completes the changes to the format line and prompts Symphony to justify the text below the format line according to the new margins and tabs. You can see the effect in Figure 4-9.

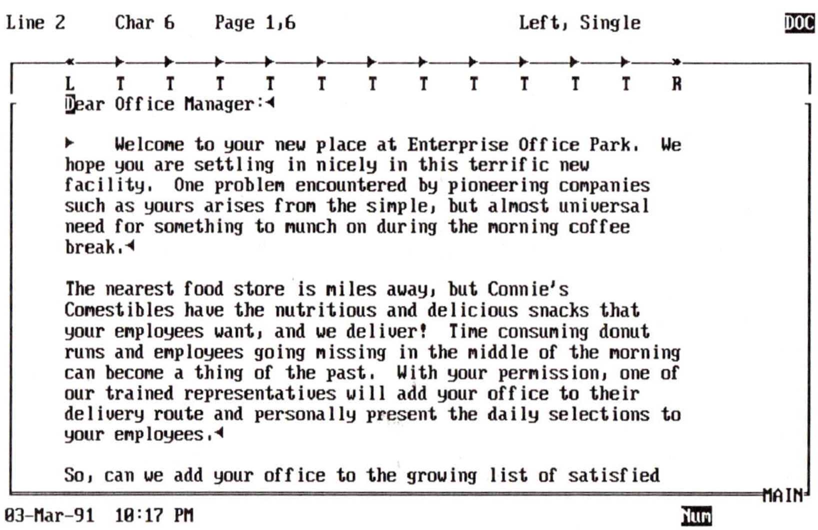
```
Line 2     Char 6     Page 1,6                    Left, Single          DOC

     L    T    T    T    T    T    T    T    T    T    T    T    R
     Dear Office Manager:

          Welcome to your new place at Enterprise Office Park.  We
     hope you are settling in nicely in this terrific new
     facility.  One problem encountered by pioneering companies
     such as yours arises from the simple, but almost universal
     need for something to munch on during the morning coffee
     break.

     The nearest food store is miles away, but Connie's
     Comestibles have the nutritious and delicious snacks that
     your employees want, and we deliver!  Time consuming donut
     runs and employees going missing in the middle of the morning
     can become a thing of the past.  With your permission, one of
     our trained representatives will add your office to their
     delivery route and personally present the daily selections to
     your employees.

     So, can we add your office to the growing list of satisfied
                                                                  MAIN
03-Mar-91   10:17 PM                                       Num
```

FIGURE 4-9 The new format line in place

You can move your cursor into the area of the screen occupied by the format line characters, but you cannot type there. This is indicated by the asterisk that appears in the top line of the screen. You can remove the format line by using the Erase command, which is described in a moment. When you erase a format line, the format of the document reverts to that of the next format line above. In our example, this would mean reverting to the default format.

Indenting Paragraphs

Earlier, you saw that the (TAB) key will indent the first line of a paragraph from the left margin. You have now seen that changing a format line can move the left margin of a document to the right. You may wonder how you indent a single paragraph, perhaps for emphasis, as shown in Figure 4-10. To do this you use the INDENT key, (F3).

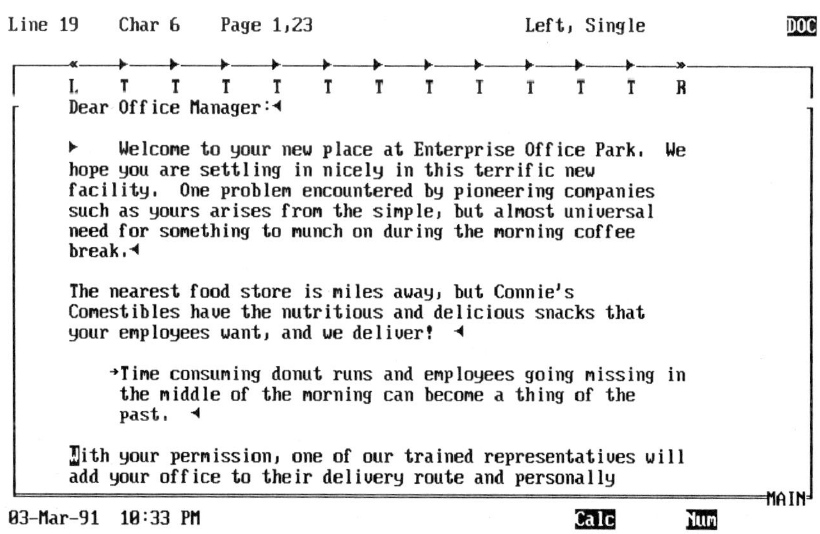

FIGURE 4-10 Indented paragraph

1. Place the cursor on the first character of "Time" on line 12.

2. Press (ENTER) twice, and then press the spacebar four times.

3. Press (F3). This inserts an indent character (→) and lines the text up at that point. The rest of the paragraph is flush with this symbol.

4. Press (END) and type **w**, and the cursor will move to the beginning of the next sentence.

5. Press (ENTER) twice, and the text will look as it does in Figure 4-10.

The indent command can be issued at any point across the page to line up text; you do not have to use a tab stop. You can delete an indent character with any of the delete keystrokes.

Using a Named Format Line

Suppose that you want to offset part of your document from both margins, as shown in Figure 4-11. The indent command only works on the left margin of your text. To indent from both margins, you need to set a format line immediately above the paragraph to be indented that narrows the margins, and then expand the margins below the indented paragraph. To do this in the sample document,

1. Move the cursor to line 15, and use (BACKSPACE) or (DEL) to remove the indent symbol and move the text back to the left margin.

2. Press the accelerator key for Format Create, (CTRL-F).

3. Press (ENTER) to confirm that this is the line on which you want to create the new format line.

```
Line 21    Char 6    Page 1,23                    Left, Single          DOC

        The nearest food store is miles away, but Connie's
        Comestibles have the nutritious and delicious snacks that
        your employees want, and we deliver! ◄

            L   T   T   T   T   T   T   T   T   R11
            Time consuming donut runs and employees going
            missing in the middle of the morning can
            become a thing of the past.◄
@BODY
        With your permission, one of our trained representatives will
        add your office to their delivery route and personally
        present the daily selections to your employees.◄

        So, can we add your office to the growing list of satisfied
        customers who receive a daily visit from our employees,
        cheerfully delivering fresh comestibles every morning, right
        to your office?◄

        Yours truly,◄
                                                                      MAIN
03-Mar-91  10:41 PM                                              Num
```

FIGURE 4-11 Paragraph indented from both margins

4. Select Margins/Tabs from the menu. Press the spacebar five times to move the left margin to the right, as shown in Figure 4-12.

5. Press (CTRL-RIGHT ARROW) twice so that you are highlighting one of the T tab-stop markers. Press (DEL) three times to remove three tab stops and move the right margin to the left. Press (ENTER) to confirm the line and return to the menu.

6. Select Line-Marker from the menu, and press (ENTER) to select Assign. Type **NARROW** as the name of this format line, and press (ENTER). Select Quit from the menu to return to the document. The results will look like Figure 4-13.

Notice that *all* of the text below the format line is arranged into the narrower margins. The right of the new format line has the

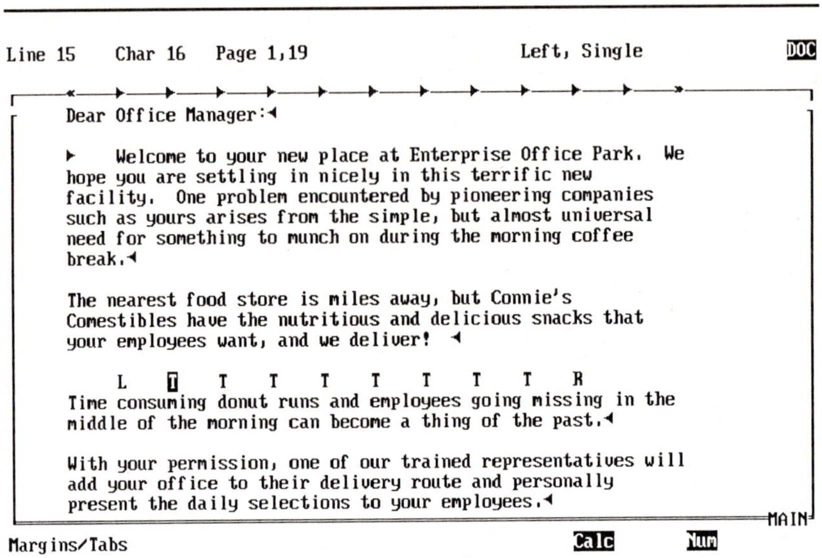

FIGURE 4-12 Effect of the NARROW format line

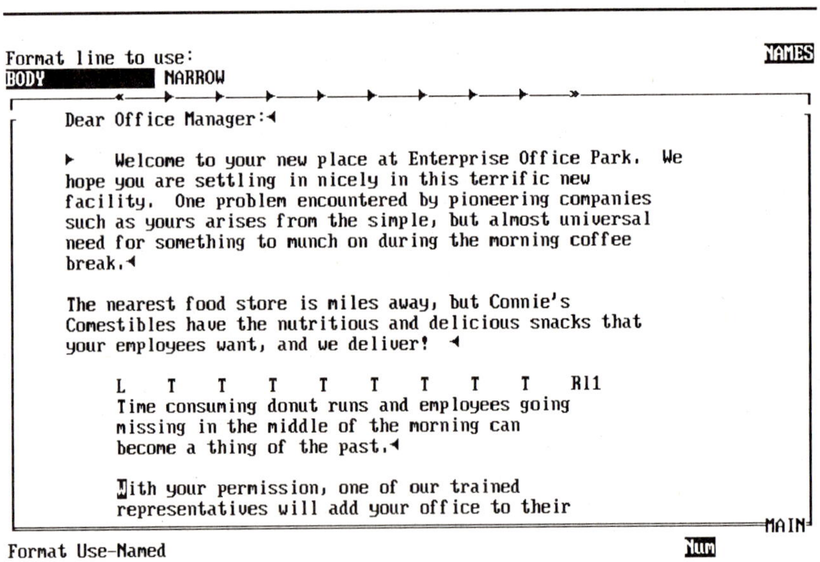

FIGURE 4-13 Named format line

characters 11, which stand for left-justified, single-spaced. Symphony includes this coding on format lines that are not at the top of the document. Also notice that when your cursor moves below the new format line, the margin and tab indicators in the frame of the typing window change to reflect the settings that are in effect in that portion of the document.

Now you want to expand the margins below the first indented paragraph. This will give you a chance to reuse the named format line, BODY, that you created at the top of the document.

1. Move the cursor down to line 19. Press MENU and choose Format and then Use-Named. The existing named format lines will appear, as shown in Figure 4-13.

2. Press (ENTER) to select BODY, the format line used at the top of the document.

3. Press (ENTER) to confirm that you want this format line inserted at line 19. The results will appear as in Figure 4-11.

Instead of displaying a format line on the line where you inserted BODY, Symphony displays @, followed by the name of the format line being used. Being able to reuse named format lines makes switching formats very easy. You could indent another section with NARROW, and then switch back to BODY.

Although the format lines take up a line's worth of space on screen, they do not take up any space in the printed page. You can check this by observing the line and page counters at the top of the screen as you move your cursor down the page. The Line indicator will go from 19 to 20, and then to 21 as you move past the @BODY marker, but the Page indicator, which also shows the printed line occupied by the text, will go from 1,21 to 1,22, and then to 1,22 again, indicating that the line does not print.

BLOCK EDITING

One of the very useful features of word processing is that it allows you to rearrange text after you have typed it. Symphony has a range of editing commands that allow you to move, copy, and erase whole blocks of text at a time. In a DOC window, a *block* of text is defined as a series of consecutive characters that you want to treat as a group. This can be anything from a single character or a part of a sentence to several sentences or paragraphs.

To specify a block of text, you use the cursor movement keys to highlight the area making up the block. To "anchor" the highlight so that you can extend it, you press (TAB). To "unanchor" the highlighting in order to specify a different block elsewhere, you press (ESC) or (BACKSPACE). When highlighting blocks of text, you can perform a "speed search" by typing any character. Symphony will immediately extend the highlighting to the next instance of the character in the text. To complete the definition of a block of text, you press (ENTER).

Erase

Suppose that you decide the indenting of the paragraph is not suitable for your letter. You want to erase the format lines you have added, but the (DEL) and (BACKSPACE) keys cannot do this. To erase a format line you place the cursor on the line, press MENU, and select Erase. Immediately, Symphony will highlight the format line, as shown in Figure 4-14. Press (ENTER) to confirm the action, and the format line will be removed.

You can now use the (BACKSPACE) or (DEL) key to edit the sentence back into the previous paragraph. The format line BODY is now redundant, so move to line 17 and repeat the Erase command. Instead of using the Erase command from the menu, you can press the ERASE key, (F4). Note that when you erase text, Symphony rejustifies the remaining text as long as you are in

```
Line 15    Char 10   Page 1,19          *         Left, Single              POINT
Erase what block? 15,10..15,10
    L    T    T    T    T    T    T    T    T    T    T    T    R
    Dear Office Manager:◄

    ►Welcome to your new place at Enterprise Office Park.  We
    hope you are settling in nicely in this terrific new
    facility.  One problem encountered by pioneering companies
    such as yours arises from the simple, but almost universal
    need for something to munch on during the morning coffee
    break.◄

    The nearest food store is miles away, but Connie's
    Comestibles have the nutritious and delicious snacks that
    your employees want, and we deliver!◄

         L    T    T    T    T    T    T    T    T   R11
         Time consuming donut runs and employees going
         missing in the middle of the morning can
         become a thing of the past.◄

@BODY
                                                                        MAIN
Erase                                                   Calc       Num
```

FIGURE 4-14 Erasing the format line

Auto-Justify mode. Otherwise, the text is left unjustified and you can manually justify it with (F2).

Apart from removing format lines, Erase is useful for regular editing of text. Suppose your boss reviews the sample letter and tells you to remove the second sentence of the second paragraph. To do this,

1. Move the cursor to the "T" in "Time" on what should now be Line 12, and press (F4).

2. Notice how the beginning point of the block is indicated: 12,23. This means line 12, character position 23. You can extend the highlighting to the end of sentence by typing a period (.).

3. The highlighting will now extend to 14,10, as shown here:

```
Line 15    Char 36   Page 1,19                      Left, Single             POINT
Erase what block? 13,44..15,36

      The nearest food store is miles away, but Connie's
      Comestibles have the nutritious and delicious snacks that
      your employees want, and we deliver! Time·consuming·donut
 ·····runs·and·employees·going·missing·in·the·middle·of·the·morning
 ·····can·become·a·thing·of·the·past.

      With your permission, one of our trained representatives will
      add your office to their delivery route and personally
```

The complete block is denoted as 12,23..14,10, which is a lot like the way Symphony indicates ranges in the SHEET environment.

4. Press (ENTER) to complete the erase operation, and the text will reform to fill in the gap.

What if, after further consideration, the boss says that the sentence should stay but be placed in front of the preceding sentence? Fortunately, Symphony retains the last block of text you erased in an area of memory called the *clipboard*. You can recall the erased sentence with a paste command, but first you need to place the cursor in the correct location—that is, highlighting the "T" in "The nearest." The paste command is one that does not appear on the menu. You use the (CTRL-P) accelerator key to paste erased text where the cursor is located. Press (CTRL-P) now, and the sentence will be restored in its new location, as shown here:

```
Line 11    Char 6    Page 1,15                      Left, Single             DOC

      Time consuming donut runs and employees going missing in the
      middle of the morning can become a thing of the past.  The
      nearest food store is miles away, but Connie's Comestibles
      have the nutritious and delicious snacks that your employees
      want, and we deliver!
```

The clipboard area retains the last piece of text that you highlighted with any of the block-editing commands, Erase, Copy, or Move. This allows you to repeatedly paste the same piece of text at different locations within a document.

In addition to using the ERASE key or the Erase command on the menu, you can delete sections of text with the following keys:

CTRL-T	Erases text from the cursor to the left margin
CTRL-Y	Erases text from the cursor to the right margin
CTRL-D	Erases the entire line of text occupied by the cursor
CTRL-BACKSPACE	Erases the word or fragment of a word to the left of the cursor

Text erased by any of these commands can be restored with CTRL-P. Note that CTRL-BACKSPACE is not strictly a "word delete" as it is listed in the Symphony documentation. The command deletes characters to the left of the cursor as far as the next space, so that pressing CTRL-BACKSPACE while highlighting the "n" in "munch" leaves you with "nch." If you are highlighting the first character of a word, CTRL-BACKSPACE actually deletes the preceding word to the left.

Copy

Whereas the Erase command removes a block of text, the Copy command takes a copy of a block of text and allows you to insert it anywhere in the document. For example, say you want to copy part of what is now the second paragraph and place it at the top of the document:

1. Place the cursor on the "C" in "Connie's," the beginning point of the text you want to copy.

2. Now you can either press MENU and then select Copy, or press the Copy accelerator key: CTRL-C. Note that the prompt at the

top of the screen is similar to the one you get with the Copy command in the SHEET environment.

3. Type an exclamation mark (!) to move the highlighting of the copy FROM block to the end of the sentence, and press **ENTER**.

4. The prompt at the top of the screen now says "Copy TO where?" Move the cursor to the "D" in "Dear." Do not use the **HOME** key alone for this, as it will place your cursor above the format line.

5. Press **ENTER** to confirm the copy. Then press **HOME**, followed by **CTRL-RIGHT ARROW**. Press **ENTER** twice more to separate the copied text from the opening of the letter. The text will look like this:

```
Line 5     Char 6     Page 1,9                    Left, Single             DOC

   L  T   T   T   T   T   T   T   T   T   T   T   R
   Connie's Comestibles have the nutritious and delicious snacks
   that your employees want, and we deliver!

   Dear Office Manager:

   ▸    Welcome to your new place at Enterprise Office Park.  We
   hope you are settling in nicely in this terrific new
```

Now you can edit this text, which will be used as a title for the letter, so that it looks like this:

```
Line 2     Char 40    Page 1,6                    Left, Single             DOC

   L  T   T   T   T   T   T   T   T   T   T   T   R
   Connie's Comestibles - We deliver!

   Dear Office Manager:

   ▸    Welcome to your new place at Enterprise Office Park.  We
```

In a moment, you will learn how to center this text and underline it as a title for the letter.

You cannot copy text onto itself. The TO location must be outside the FROM location. However, the Copy command, like

Erase and Move, leaves a copy of the text you highlighted in the clipboard, so you can use the paste command to insert multiple copies of the text.

Move

When you want to move a piece of text from one location to another, you can either use the Erase command followed by the paste command, or you can use the Move command, which uses (CTRL-M) as its accelerator key. When you select Move, you highlight the text to be moved just as you do text to be copied. When you have pressed (ENTER) to confirm the highlighted area as the text you are going to move, you are immediately prompted for the new location. When you point this out and press (ENTER), the highlighted text is moved to the new location.

When you move text into existing text, Symphony opens up a space for it. If you are in Auto-Justify mode, Symphony rejustifies the text affected by the move.

Editing Tips

Each time you select a block of text to move, Symphony stores the text in the clipboard, just as it does with the Erase and Copy commands. You can use the paste command to insert the text elsewhere in the document at a later time.

Note: Note that the difference between Erase/paste and Move is that the Move command requires you to identify the new location immediately, whereas Erase/paste allows you continue editing before pasting the text to the new location.

Bear in mind that the same clipboard is used by the Erase, Copy, and Move commands. You must paste erased text that you want to keep before using one of these three commands. Also bear in

B	Bold	0	Bold italic	6	Bold subscript
I	Italic	1	Bold underlined	7	Italic subscript
U	Underlined	2	Bold italic underlined	8	Bold italic subscript
+	Superscript	3	Italic underlined	9	Bold italic superscript
–	Subscript	4	Bold superscript	S	Attribute spaces
X	Struck-through	5	Italic superscript	Q	Do not attribute spaces

TABLE 4-5 Print Attributes in the DOC Environment

mind that when you have several documents in one file, as described towards the end of the chapter, you can erase/copy/move and paste between documents, using the (F6) key to change from one window to another.

PRINT ATTRIBUTES

When you want to emphasize or otherwise distinguish parts of your text in Symphony, you use the print attributes. These include such features as bold, underlined, and italic, although which features you can actually print will depend on your printer. To assign attributes, you tell Symphony where in the text to begin the attribute, select a code for the attribute, and then move the cursor to the end of the text that will be assigned the attribute and press (ENTER). The print attribute codes are listed in Table 4-5.

Assigning Attributes

Suppose that you want the words "nutritious and delicious" to be emphasized. You will assign the bold attribute to accomplish this.

1. Move the cursor to the first character you want to be boldface, and press (CTRL-B) (for Begin) to commence application of the attribute.

2. Select an attribute from the menu:

```
Bold                                                            MENU
B I U + - X 0 1 2 3 4 5 6 7 8 9 S Q

  Time consuming donut runs and employees going missing in the
  middle of the morning can become a thing of the past.  The
  nearest food store is miles away, but Connie's Comestibles
  have the nutritious and delicious snacks that your employees
  want, and we deliver!◂
```

Although each item on the menu is only one character, the item is described on the top line of the screen to make the menu easier to use.

3. Select B for Bold. You should notice a change in your text from the character the cursor is on until the end of the document. This is because you have begun an attribute and not ended it.

4. To end an attribute you move the cursor one character past the last character you want to possess the attribute—in this case, to the space past "delicious"—and press (CTRL-E) (for End).

You will see that the attribute remains in the area of text between your (CTRL-B) and (CTRL-E) kcypresses.

The way that each attribute is shown on screen varies between display systems. You may find the attribute difficult to see on your monitor without adjusting the contrast and brightness controls. However, you can always tell which attribute is applied to a particular piece of text, because whenever the cursor is highlighting text that has a print attribute, the code letter is displayed on the top line of the screen.

Underlining

Now you want to underline the text you have placed at the top of the document for the title.

1. Move the cursor to the top of the document, highlighting the "C" in "Connie's."
2. Press (CTRL-B) and select U for Underlined. Notice that the appearance of the text changes all the way through the document until the point at which you entered (CTRL-E) in the previous exercise.
3. Now move the cursor to the end of the line, and press (CTRL-E). This will leave all the words on the line underlined.

You may notice on your screen—and will definitely notice when printing—that there are no underlines for the spaces between the words in the section you just underlined. This is Symphony's default mode of assigning print attributes: Attributes are not assigned to spaces. However, you can change this by using the S attribute, which defines an area in which the attributes *are* assigned to spaces.

1. Move the cursor to highlight the "C" in "Connie's."
2. Press (CTRL-B) and select S for Spaces.
3. Since you already have a (CTRL-E) at the end of the line, this special attribute will be ended at the end of the line. The text will be printed with the spaces between the words underlined.

Changing Attributes

Suppose you decide that the boldfacing you assigned is not really appropriate. To remove a print attribute, you use the ERASE key ((F4)). Move the cursor to the first character that displays the attribute (remembering to check the top status line for the print attribute code). Press (F4), and you will see something of a change

```
Line 16    Char 16    Page 1,20          B          Left, Single                POINT
Erase what block? 16,15..16,16

      L   T   T   T   T   T   T   T   T   T   T   T   R
      ▲U▲SConnie's Comestibles - We deliver!▼◄

      Dear Office Manager:◄

      ►Welcome to your new place at Enterprise Office Park.  We
      hope you are settling in nicely in this terrific new
      facility.  One problem encountered by pioneering companies
      such as yours arises from the simple, but almost universal
      need for something to munch on during the morning coffee
      break.◄

      Time consuming donut runs and employees going missing in the
      middle of the morning can become a thing of the past.  The
      nearest food store is miles away, but Connie's Comestibles
      have the ▲Bnutritious and delicious▼ snacks that your
      employees want, and we deliver!◄

      With your permission, one of our trained representatives will
      add your office to their delivery route and personally
                                                                           MAIN
04-Mar-91  07:38 PM                                         Calc      Num
```

FIGURE 4-15 Erasing print attributes

in your text, as shown in Figure 4-15. When you assign print attributes, Symphony places codes in the text that tell the printer how to treat the text that follows the code. These codes are not normally visible, but the Erase command reveals them. Simply highlight the code that you want removed (in this case, B) but *not* the actual text, and then press (ENTER). This removes the beginning of the highlighting.

You can probably leave the end attribute code (◄) in place unless you are using a lot of attributes throughout the document. Finding end codes is rather tricky when there is no begin code nearby. To remove an end code, you can press (F4) to view the document with the codes revealed and then press (ESC) to unlock the text coordinates. Using the cursor, you can move through the document until you highlight the code, and then press (ENTER) to delete it.

Centering Lines

One method of altering the appearance of text that does not use print attributes or format lines is centering lines of text. Each line to be centered should end in a hard return. Centering is done by pressing the CENTER key, (ALT-F4), with the cursor anywhere within the line to be centered. For example, to center the title of the letter, you would simply place the cursor somewhere within the line and press (ALT-F4). The results would be as follows:

```
Line 2     Char 19   Page 1,6          U         Left, Single              DOC

   L    T    T    T    T    T    T    T    T    T    T    T    R
                   Connie's Comestibles - We deliver!◄

   Dear Office Manager:◄

   ►    Welcome to your new place at Enterprise Office Park.  We
```

To remove the centering, you simply place the cursor on the first character of the line and press (BACKSPACE) until the text is again flush with the left margin. You can also press (CTRL-BACKSPACE) followed by (F2) to rejustify the text. If you want to center a large section of text, you can insert a format line that uses Center as the justification setting.

USING THE REPLACE COMMAND

Few word processing operations are as satisfying as that known as *search and replace*. You can change all or some instances of one word or string of words into another. For example, you can change all instances of "Connie's Comestibles" into "Fred's Snacks," or all cases of "employees" into "staff." To see this command in action in the sample document, press (HOME) to get to the top of the document. This will ensure that all instances of the text string you want to replace are found. (Unlike the Search command, Replace can only look forward.)

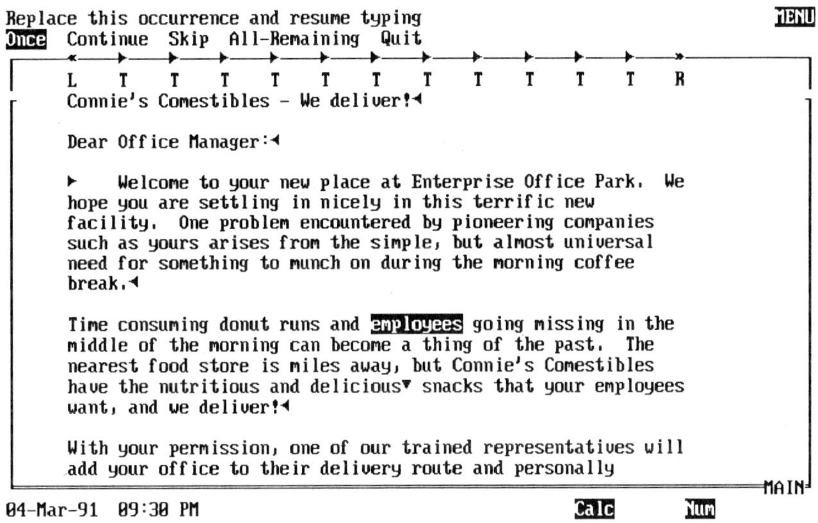

FIGURE 4-16 The Replace menu

1. Press the Replace accelerator key, (CTRL-R).
2. Respond to the "Replace what?" prompt by typing **employees** and pressing (ENTER).
3. Respond to the "Replace it with what?" prompt by typing **staff** and pressing (ENTER).
4. Symphony will highlight the first instance of the text you want to replace and present a menu like the one shown in Figure 4-16. You have five options at this point:

Once	Replace this instance, then return to typing mode
Continue	Replace this instance and find the next
Skip	Leave this instance unchanged and find the next
All-Remaining	Replace this instance and all others

Quit	Return to typing mode without changing this instance or any others

5. Choose Continue and you will see the first highlighted instance change and the second instance selected. You decide to leave this one as is, so you select Skip.

6. A third instance is highlighted. Select Skip to leave this one intact, and Symphony will respond by telling you at the bottom of the screen that there are no more occurrences of the string you want to change.

7. Select Quit. You will return to the typing area, with your cursor in the position it occupied before you issued the command.

Note that if the search string is entered in uppercase (as in **MUNCH**) Symphony only looks for it in uppercase. If the string is entered in lowercase (as in **munch**), Symphony recognizes all instances of the string (such as "munch," "MUNCH," and "Munch"). If the string you are looking for includes a space, as in entering **to munch**, Symphony recognizes the string even if it has several spaces in it (as in "to   munch").

The string you enter as the replacement is always used literally. While searching for "munch" and replacing with "eat," Symphony will find "Munch" but will replace it with "eat," not "Eat." To search and replace text that might be capitalized, you will need to perform two passes on the text.

Despite these limitations, the Replace command is a powerful one, and quite long text strings can be used (up to 50 characters). This allows you to make a lot of shortcuts when typing. Instead of always typing "Connie's Comestibles" you can type **CC** and then later perform a search for it, replacing "CC" with "Connie's Comestibles." In technical documents this is particularly effective. A pharmacist could type **DPX** instead of "Depronalpropoxyphene" and perform a search/replace when the document is almost completed. If you keep track of the abbreviations you use and are consistent, this can be a great time-saver.

The one danger of a search and replace is the All-Remaining option. Do not select this unless you are sure of the results. In the case of the CC abbreviation, you could end up turning "OCCIDENTAL" into "OConnie's ComesitblesIDENTAL."

SPREADSHEETS, FORMULAS, AND DOCUMENTS

So far, you have seen that Symphony's DOC environment is quite capable of tackling word processing, but you may be wondering how it relates to the SHEET environment. At the end of the last chapter you saw how a DOC window could be created to write notes for a worksheet. In this section you will see how the SHEET environment can be used to provide a table and calculations for the DOC environment.

Before you take a look at how the SHEET environment regards your letter, you may want to embellish the beginning in keeping with normal office practice. Basically, this means adding the date and address at the top of the document, as shown in Figure 4-17, along with some extra lines to move the date down further from the top of the page in order to make room for the company letterhead.

Now use the (END) and (HOME) keys to move to the bottom of the letter. Here, you will insert enough blank lines to extend the typing area to a second page. This will demonstrate how Symphony inserts page breaks when text extends beyond the set page length. Once you are on page 2, as shown in Figure 4-18, you can type the line of text you see in the figure to prepare you for the next exercise, creating a table in the SHEET environment.

```
Line 11    Char 6    Page 1,15                    Left, Single          DOC

    L    T    T    T    T    T    T    T    T    T    T    T    R



     March 31, 1991◄

     Strafer & Hitch◄
     Suite 1103 1001 Enterprise Drive◄
     Santa Clarissa, CA 93104◄
     █

                  Connie's Comestibles - We deliver!◄

     Dear Office Manager:◄

     ►  Welcome to your new place at Enterprise Office Park.  We
     hope you are settling in nicely in this terrific new
     facility.  One problem encountered by pioneering companies
     such as yours arises from the simple, but almost universal
                                                                      MAIN
04-Mar-91  10:15 PM                                  Calc        Num
```

FIGURE 4-17 Completed opening

```
Line 58    Char 46    Page 2,6                    Left, Single          DOC

     Your Name◄
     New Account Manager



     Here is a list of our current offerings:█

                                                                      MAIN
04-Mar-91  10:16 PM                                  Calc        Num
```

FIGURE 4-18 A second page

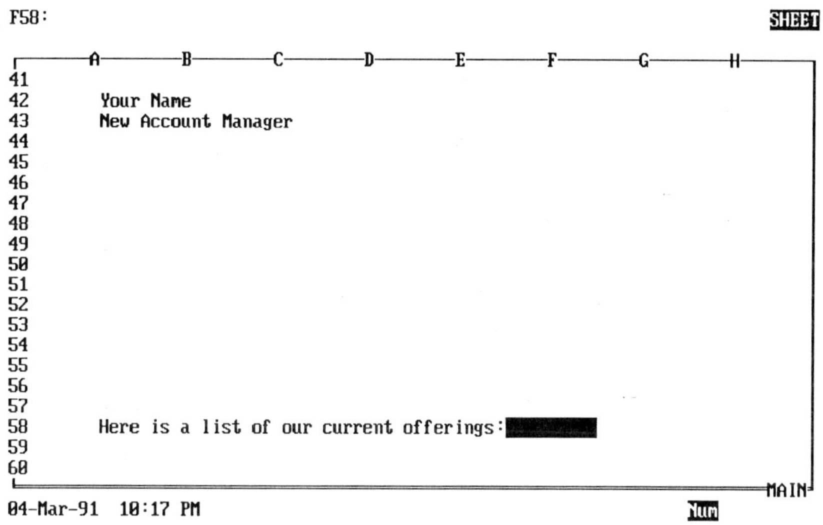

FIGURE 4-19 The document in the SHEET environment

To get to the SHEET environment, press (ALT-F9), the SWITCH key. This switches you between SHEET and any other environments you have used. As you can see from Figure 4-19, the document text appears in the SHEET environment. If you highlight any of the text, you can see that it consists of labels in column A of the worksheet. To create the table of products and prices shown in Figure 4-20, follow these steps:

1. Move the cell pointer to B60. Type **Item** and press (ENTER).
2. Press (DOWN ARROW) to move the cell pointer to B61, and type \= to fill the cell with equal signs as a form of underlining. The backslash character (\) repeats whatever you type after it enough times to fill the cell, no matter how wide you make the cell.

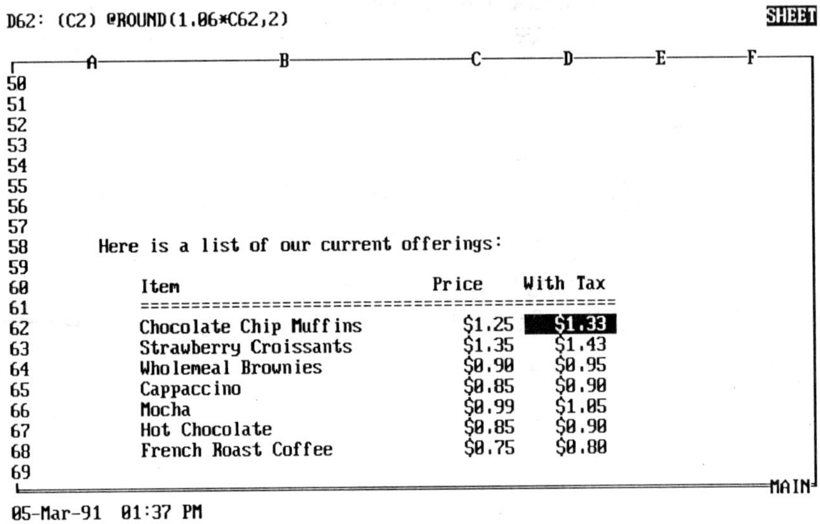

FIGURE 4-20 The completed table

3. Press MENU, select Width, and then Set. Type **15** and press (ENTER).

4. Press MENU, select Copy, press (ENTER), and type a period (.). Press (RIGHT ARROW) twice and then (ENTER) to copy the underlining label to cells C61 and D61.

5. Enter the labels in C60 and D60, as well as B62 through B68.

6. Enter the prices in C62 through C68. Then use the Format command to assign the Currency format (2 decimal places) to the range C62..D68.

7. Delivered food is subject to 6% sales tax in this area. Enter the sales tax formula in D62: **@ROUND(1.06*C62,2)**.

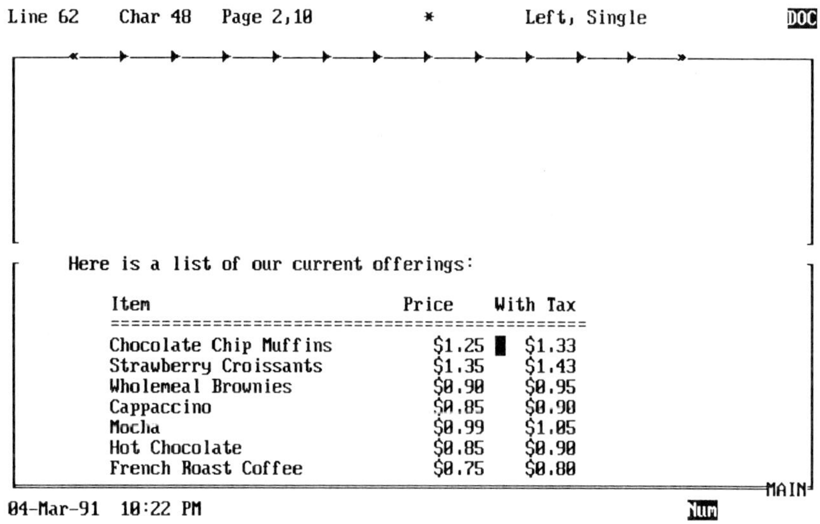

FIGURE 4-21 Table viewed in the DOC environment

8. Press MENU, select Copy, press (ENTER), and type a period (.). Press (DOWN ARROW) six times and then (ENTER) to copy thc formula to cells D63 through D68.

Now that the table has been built in the SHEET environment, you can press (ALT-F9) to switch back to the DOC environment and see how it looks there. As you can see from Figure 4-21, the area occupied by the worksheet cells cannot be altered in the DOC environment. The asterisk in the top status line reminds you of this. You can add document text on either side of the table if there is room, and you can add any amount of text below the table.

Unfortunately, the table will not automatically print with the rest of the document. When you want to combine SHEET and DOC information in the same document, you will need to tell Symphony the exact print source. You can do this from the DOC window. First press (HOME) to move the cursor to the top of the document, and then select Print from the SERVICES menu. Choose Settings, then Source, and then Range. Initially the range will be 1..1, so press (PGDN) to extend this to 1..68 so that you include the last line of the table. Now press (ENTER). With the source identified like this, the table and letter will print together, as you can see in Figure 4-22, where the document is printed on company letterhead.

Connie's Comestibles
2301 Lanark Ave
San Gino, CA 94513

Call 555-3423 for deliveries

March 31, 1991

Strafer & Hitch
Suite 1103 1001 Enterprise Drive
Santa Clarissa, CA 93104

Connie's Comestibles - We deliver!

Dear Office Manager:

Welcome to your new place at Enterprise Office Park. We hope you are settling in nicely in this terrific new facility. One problem encountered by pioneering companies such as yours arises from the simple, but almost universal need for something to munch on during the morning coffee break.

Time cons
middle of
nearest f
have the
want, and

With your
add your
present t

So, can w
customers
cheerfull
to your o

Yours tru

Your Name
New Accou

Here is a list of our current offerings:

Item	Price	With Tax
Chocolate Chip Muffins	$1.25	$1.33
Strawberry Croissants	$1.35	$1.43
Wholemeal Brownies	$0.90	$0.95
Cappaccino	$0.85	$0.90
Mocha	$0.99	$1.05
Hot Chocolate	$0.85	$0.90
French Roast Coffee	$0.75	$0.80

FIGURE 4-22 Printout of completed document

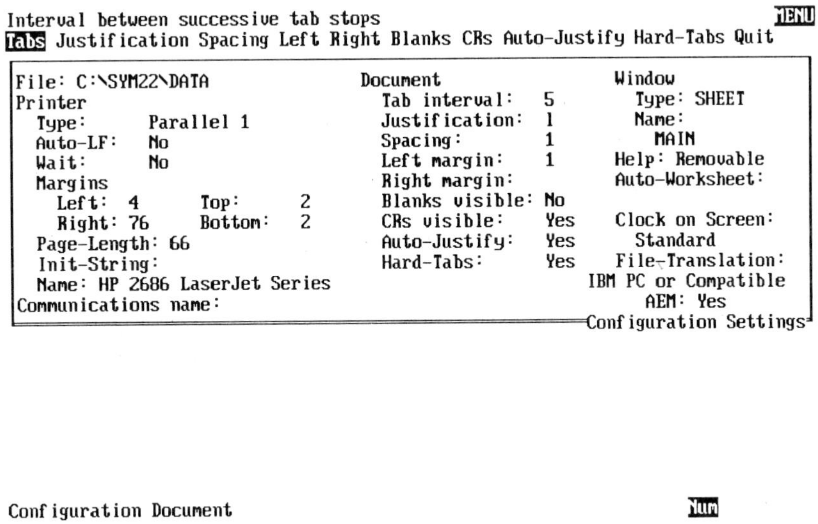

```
Interval between successive tab stops                                    MENU
Tabs Justification Spacing Left Right Blanks CRs Auto-Justify Hard-Tabs Quit

File: C:\SYM22\DATA                  Document                   Window
Printer                                Tab interval:    5         Type: SHEET
  Type:       Parallel 1               Justification:   1         Name:
  Auto-LF:    No                       Spacing:         1           MAIN
  Wait:       No                       Left margin:     1       Help: Removable
  Margins                              Right margin:            Auto-Worksheet:
    Left:  4      Top:     2           Blanks visible:  No
    Right: 76     Bottom:  2           CRs visible:     Yes     Clock on Screen:
  Page-Length: 66                      Auto-Justify:    Yes       Standard
  Init-String:                         Hard-Tabs:       Yes     File-Translation:
  Name: HP 2686 LaserJet Series                                IBM PC or Compatible
Communications name:                                              AEM: Yes
                                                         Configuration Settings

Configuration Document                                                  Num
```

FIGURE 4-23 The configuration settings sheet

Remember that the table is in the SHEET environment, so you can alter the calculations and numbers there in true spreadsheet style simply by switching to the SHEET environment.

DOCUMENT SETTINGS

Symphony sets formats and parameters for documents at several different levels. Each time you open a document window, Symphony assigns to it standard format and procedure settings taken from the SERVICES Configuration sheet, shown in Figure 4-23. By adjusting these settings with the SERVICE Configuration Document command, you can have all of your documents start off with your preferred settings, rather than the Symphony defaults.

Once you have created a document window, you can override the SERVICES Configuration format settings by using the MENU Format Settings command. Within any document window, you can further vary the format from both the SERVICE Configuration Document and MENU Format settings by using format lines. The following sections review the options at the basic SERVICES Configuration Document level to help you establish a standard format for your documents.

Tabs and Margins

You can define initial tabs and settings on the Configuration settings sheet. You can override them on a window's Document settings sheet. You can also reposition them manually for specific parts of a document by using a format line. The Tabs command on the Configuration Document menu sets the number of characters or interval between tab stops, from 1 to 240 characters.

The Left command sets the starting column for text. This is from 1 to 240 characters from the edge of the printed area, based on the settings under "Printer." For example, if the left margin under "Printer" is 4 characters, and the left margin under "Document" is 1 character, Symphony will begin printing the text of the document 5 characters from the left edge of the page.

The Right command sets the ending column for text. The command has two options. The Set option is used to place the margin in a specific column (1 to 240 characters from the left edge of the page). The Reset option causes Symphony to determine the right margin automatically, according to the width of the DOC window. This is the default setting, and much easier to work with. When the Reset option is in effect, the settings sheet shows no entry for "Right margin" in the Document column, as you can see from Figure 4-23.

Justifying and Justification

By default, Symphony rejustifies text automatically whenever you make changes. However, if you do not want Symphony to rejustify automatically, you can change the Auto-Justify setting (SERVICES Configuration Document Auto-Justify) to No. This leaves the text unjustified until you explicitly justify it by pressing JUSTIFY or selecting Justify from the DOC menu. The AUTO accelerator key (CTRL-J) also turns Auto-Justify on and off.

The Justification option allows you to set the default alignment of text between the margins to Left, Right, or Center. The None option means that text is not justified at all until you press the JUSTIFY key.

Symbols

Symphony can display special symbols to represent blank spaces and carriage returns in documents. Select the Blanks option and choose Yes to display dots in place of blanks within documents. Choose No to display spaces as blanks. Select CRs, short for "carriage returns," and choose Yes to have Symphony represent hard carriage returns as ◀, or choose No to suppress the display of hard returns.

The Hard-Tabs option is used to control how Symphony stores the tabs you insert with the TAB key. If you select the No option, then tabs are stored as spaces, which is the way that some other word processing programs store tabs. The Yes option, which is the default, tells Symphony to store tabs as proper tab characters within the disk file.

Note Remember to use the Update command on the Configuration menu in order to record changes to the settings for future sessions.

WINDOW SETTINGS

Having created and stored the letter and table shown in Figure 4-22, you may want to create another document. You can approach this in several ways. You can start a new file, change the MAIN window to the DOC environment, and begin typing, or you can create a second document in the same file as the first, using a second DOC window. To take the latter approach, you would follow these steps:

1. Press SERVICES, select Window, and select Create. Type a name for the window such as **NOTES.**
2. Select DOC from the Type list, and you will be asked to identify the window area. You want the window to occupy the whole screen, which is the default setting, so you press (ENTER) to accept this. Don't worry about the existing document appearing in the new window at this point.
3. You will be shown the Window Settings screen. This will look like the one in Figure 4-24, except for the Restrict setting, which has been changed. In order to make sure that typing in the new document window does not interfere with the existing document, select Restrict from the Window Settings menu. Now choose Range.
4. The default setting for Restrict Range in a new window is the entire worksheet, defined as cells A1..IV8192. Press (ESC) to unlock these coordinates and move the cell pointer to G1, which is to the right of the area occupied by the first document.

```
Change window name                                              MENU
Name  Type  Restrict  Borders  Auto-Display  Quit
 Name:          NOTES
 Type:          DOC
 Restrict:      G1..IV8192
 Borders:       Standard
 Auto-Display:  Yes
                                                     Window Settings
```

FIGURE 4-24 Settings for new DOC window

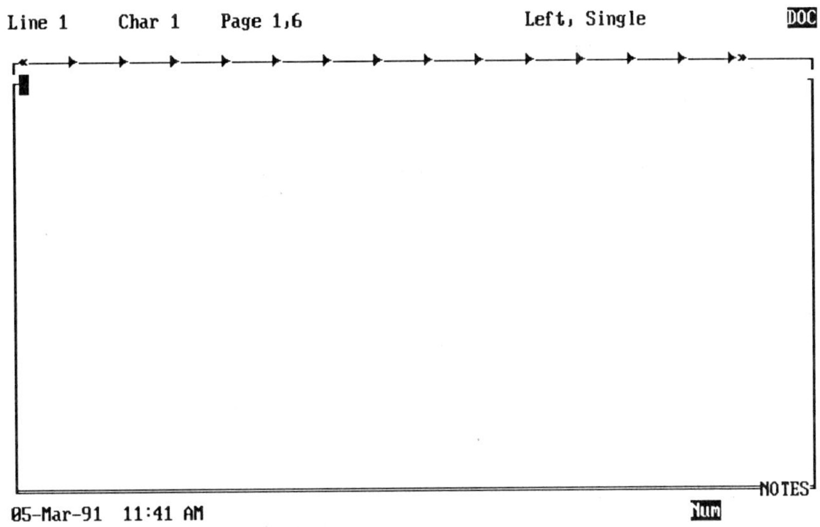

FIGURE 4-25 New document window

5. Type a period (.) to anchor the range at this point, and then press END, RIGHT ARROW, END, and DOWN ARROW to take the highlighting to the far corner of the worksheet. The range will now be G1..IV8192. Press ENTER, and the settings sheet will appear exactly like the one in Figure 4-24.

6. Select Quit, and you will be looking at a new window, like the one shown in Figure 4-25.

As you can see, the new window has the default tab and margin settings and is ready for typing into. When you use the File Save command, both documents will be stored in the same file. You can switch between documents with the F6 key. You can even copy text from one window/document to another if you use the F6 key. Numerous DOC windows can be created within one file in this manner, using successive areas of the worksheet for columns of text. When you want to print one of the documents, you move to that document, select Print from the SERVICES menu, and choose Go. Symphony will print whichever document is current at that time.

FURTHER POWERS

You can see that Symphony's word processing abilities are extensive. The DOC environment includes most of the features found in programs that only do word processing, but several aspects of document preparation are missing from the main Symphony program. However, such features as spell-checking and outlining are provided by means of additional programs, called add-ins. Since these programs impose additional demands on memory, the loading of add-ins is discussed in Chapter 8; Symphony's spelling checker and outliner commands are described in Chapter 11, which also reviews using the Allways add-in to enhance Symphony's printing capabilities.

SUMMARY

Now that you have used Symphony's word processing commands you can use Symphony to prepare letters, memos, reports, and other documents. You can create these documents in files that are just for word processing, or you can combine word processing with spreadsheet work. In the next chapter, you will see how Symphony handles collections of information known as databases, and how it allows you to combine information from a database with documents such as form letters.

5

DATABASES

In this chapter you will learn about the database management capabilities of Symphony. A *database* is any collection of information arranged in a meaningful way. This could be a phone book or an inventory list, a file of business cards, or a collection of

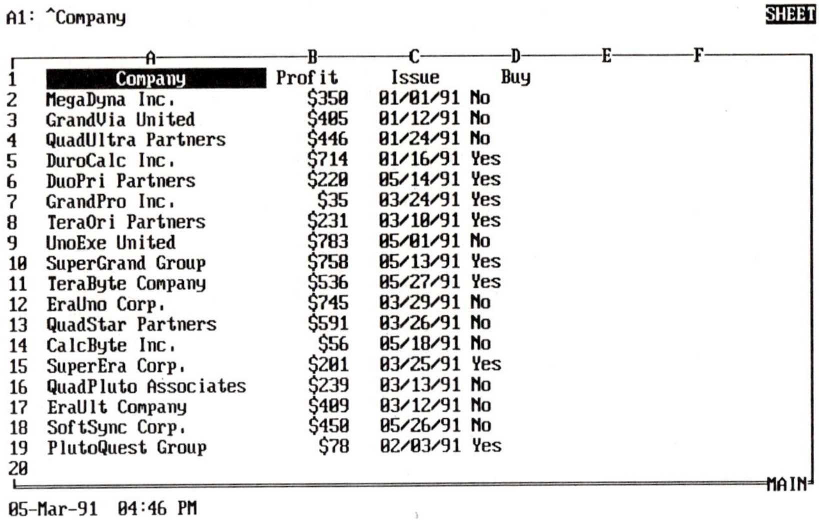

A1: ^Company SHEET

	A	B	C	D	E	F
1	Company	Profit	Issue	Buy		
2	MegaDyna Inc.	$350	01/01/91	No		
3	GrandVia United	$405	01/12/91	No		
4	QuadUltra Partners	$446	01/24/91	No		
5	DuroCalc Inc.	$714	01/16/91	Yes		
6	DuoPri Partners	$220	05/14/91	Yes		
7	GrandPro Inc.	$35	03/24/91	Yes		
8	TeraOri Partners	$231	03/10/91	Yes		
9	UnoExe United	$783	05/01/91	No		
10	SuperGrand Group	$758	05/13/91	Yes		
11	TeraByte Company	$536	05/27/91	Yes		
12	EraUno Corp.	$745	03/29/91	No		
13	QuadStar Partners	$591	03/26/91	No		
14	CalcByte Inc.	$56	05/18/91	No		
15	SuperEra Corp.	$201	03/25/91	Yes		
16	QuadPluto Associates	$239	03/13/91	No		
17	EraUlt Company	$409	03/12/91	No		
18	SoftSync Corp.	$450	05/26/91	No		
19	PlutoQuest Group	$78	02/03/91	Yes		
20						

MAIN

05-Mar-91 04:46 PM

FIGURE 5-1 Sample database

medical records. Programs designed to handle large amounts of information are called *database management software*.

There are three levels of database management in Symphony: SHEET-based, FORM-based, and disk-based management. The first two will be dealt with in this chapter, and the third is the subject of Chapter 10. You will begin this chapter by working with a sample collection of information, shown in the worksheet in Figure 5-1. The arrangement of information in Figure 5-1, with headed columns of data, is what Symphony refers to as a "database." You will learn how to sort and search this information and produce lists of selected data.

SYMPHONY AS A DATABASE

Many different software packages offer some level of database management abilities. These programs can be divided into two groups: relational and simple. *Simple database managers* are the personal-computer equivalent of card files, designed to make creating, sorting, and searching of records as easy as possible. Sometimes called "flat-file" databases, many of these simple programs lack the graphics and math capabilities found in Symphony. For this reason, Symphony offers considerable advantages as an alternative to a simple database manager. If you are learning to use Symphony for spreadsheet work anyway, you will also want to use it for simple database management tasks. In this way, you can easily add database management capabilities to your repertoire of computer skills without learning another program.

Relational database managers can relate the data in several different files based on common elements. These programs can handle large amounts of data. Many of them also have a command language that can be used to compose complex sets of instructions in order to present users with complete menu-driven applications. Such programs are referred to as *programmable* relational databases. Examples of these kinds of databases are Ashton-Tate's dBASE series and Borland International's Paradox.

Another term used to describe such programs as dBASE is "disk-based." This contrasts with Symphony which, as you have seen, is memory-based. All of the information in a Symphony worksheet is in memory at once, whereas a disk-based program like dBASE leave most of the information in a file on disk until it is needed, for example, for editing. This gives disk-based programs a big advantage in terms of file size, since files are limited by disk space, not memory space.

Symphony uses the @BASE add-in program to provide features similar to those of a disk-based relational database. This allows Symphony to offer the best of both worlds. When dealing with smaller databases that will fit in memory, Symphony performs operations like sorting and finding data very quickly. If a database grows too large for memory-based operation, then @BASE can be invoked to provide disk-based database management.

When you are working with databases in Symphony, you have all the power of Symphony's built-in functions and graphics on hand to help analyze your data. In addition, Symphony's macro command language allows you to make customized, menu-driven database management applications.

DATABASE TERMS

Symphony performs three main tasks as a database manager: sorting, finding, and reporting data. The sort capability lets you order information according to your specifications. The ability to query a collection of data with the Find command means that you can ask Symphony to locate selected data. For example, Symphony can search the database of companies in Figure 5-1 for all those with a profit figure greater than 300 that also have a Yes in the Buy column. Symphony also lets you extract fresh collections of information such as a list of all companies with a profit figure of less than 300.

Symphony's fast and flexible spreadsheets make it an excellent place to put together lists of information. There are just a few rules to follow in order for your lists to work with the Symphony database commands. These rules concern the fields and records by which the database is organized.

Fields

All information in a database is categorized by fields. The *fields* are the categories into which each set of facts, called a record, is broken down. In Symphony, each field is a separate column, and each field has a name, which is placed at the top of the column. For example, in Figure 5-1 the fields are columns A through D, headed Company, Profit, Issue, and Buy. A Symphony database is composed of a series of consecutive columns. Each column contains consistent types of data; for example, each column should contain either all values, all labels, or all dates. Each column should have a unique title.

Records

Each set of facts about one item in a database table is a *record.* Records correspond to each line on a list or to each card in a card file. In a Symphony database table, each complete set of facts occupies one row. The rows of records are placed one after another with no empty rows between them. There should not be a blank row between the field name and the first record.

Database Limits

Because a Symphony database table is essentially a range of consecutive rows and named columns, some limits apply to the database's dimensions. The maximum number of fields is 256, the total number of columns in Symphony. The maximum number of records is the total number of rows minus one row for the field names: 8191. The maximum field size is 239 characters, which is the maximum column width minus 1 for the label identifier that the field name will require.

DATABASE CREATION

A Symphony database does not need to be a special area of the program. As far as Symphony is concerned, any data entered into a worksheet and falling within the definition of consecutive rows and named columns can be considered a database. You may already have created a database table while working on a spreadsheet.

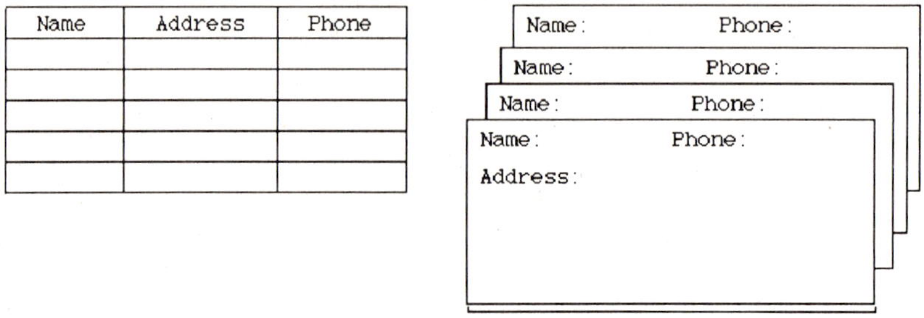

FIGURE 5-2 Two types of database arrangements

Database Designs

Any collection of information can be arranged in two different ways. A business card file organizes names, addresses, and phone numbers in a form-oriented database. Each form, or card, represents a different person, a separate record. A phone book presents similar data in a tabular format. A series of columns lists names, addresses, and phone numbers. Each row in the table is a different record.

You can see the two types of database formats in Figure 5-2. Any data that is arranged card-file style—that is, as a collection of forms—can be rearranged into a table, and vice versa. Symphony offers the best of both approaches. In this chapter you will begin by assembling data in a worksheet. Toward the end of the chapter, you will learn how to design data forms in the FORM environment to create a card-file type database.

The Sample Database

To create the database in Figure 5-1 for use in the examples in the first part of this chapter, you need to start with a new worksheet. Enter the field on row 1 as centered labels with the center-label prefix (^). The fields represent the names of companies involved in recent stock issues. The Profit column lists the profit that each company made in the last fiscal year; the Profit figure is actually thousands of dollars. The Issue column is the date on which the issue will start trading. The Buy column shows whether the stock currently has a buy recommendation. Each column constitutes a field, and each row makes a complete record.

After creating the field names, you can enter the company names and then the profit figures. When the profit figures are in place, use the MENU Format command to assign the Currency format, zero decimal places, to the numbers in B2..B19. Enter the dates with the @DATE function. Thus, the date in cell C2 is entered as **@DATE(91,1,1)** and the date in C3 is **@DATE(91,1,12)**. When you have entered the date values, you can format the range C2..C19 with the date format number 4: Full International. Finally, enter the Yes/No labels in column D.

When you have created the database, save the file with SERVICES File Save and the name **COMPANY1**. As you make changes to this worksheet, do not save changes to the same file; the original version will be needed later in the chapter. Bear in mind that Symphony databases are by no means confined to one screen of data. However, as you can tell, databases require a lot of typing to create, so it is easier to practice on a small example.

Types of Data

Your entries in a database table may be labels, numbers, dates, times, or formulas. The labels can be left-, right-, or center- aligned because their alignment will not affect the operation of the database commands. In Figure 5-1, the field names are centered but all of the labels in the records are left-aligned.

Symphony's numeric dates are particularly important in databases, since many collections of information include dates. In many cases, records may need to be sorted or selected according

```
A2: 'MegaDyna Inc.                                              SHEET
```

	A	B	C	D	E	F
1	Company	Profit	Issue	Buy		
2	MegaDyna Inc.	$350	01/01/91	No		
3	GrandVia United	$405	01/12/91	No		
4	DuroCalc Inc.	$714	01/16/91	Yes		
5	QuadUltra Partners	$446	01/24/91	No		
6	PlutoQuest Group	$78	02/03/91	Yes		
7	TeraOri Partners	$231	03/10/91	Yes		
8	EraUlt Company	$409	03/12/91	No		
9	QuadPluto Associates	$239	03/13/91	No		
10	GrandPro Inc.	$35	03/24/91	Yes		
11	SuperEra Corp.	$201	03/25/91	Yes		
12	QuadStar Partners	$591	03/26/91	No		
13	EraUno Corp.	$745	03/29/91	No		
14	UnoExe United	$783	05/01/91	No		
15	SuperGrand Group	$758	05/13/91	Yes		
16	DuoPri Partners	$220	05/14/91	Yes		
17	CalcByte Inc.	$56	05/18/91	No		
18	SoftSync Corp.	$450	05/26/91	No		
19	TeraByte Company	$536	05/27/91	Yes		
20						

```
                                                                MAIN
19-Mar-91  06:10 PM                                          Num
```

FIGURE 5-3 Sample data sorted by date

to dates. In Figure 5-1, the date that issues go on sale is an important part of the database. The same information is sorted by date in Figure 5-3.

Problem Data

Many database tables contain non-numeric numbers—that is, numbers that are entered as labels. A typical example would be ZIP codes in addresses. If you enter **01234** as a number, it will appear as "1234" in the cell, because a leading 0 in a number does not register. In the SHEET environment you get around this problem and the ones created by nine-digit ZIP codes, telephone numbers, and part numbers containing letters as well as digits by entering these figures as numbers preceded by label prefixes. (If you do not do so, the ZIP code "94109-4109" entered as a number would result in "9000," because Symphony will read the dash as a minus sign).

Note that when you enter telephone numbers with area codes, beginning the entry with a square bracket will make it a label, as in **[415] 555-1212**. Symphony can sort numbers correctly and search through them even if they are entered as labels.

The distinction between values and labels gives rise to another data entry problem, one that is immediately apparent when you try to enter a typical street address such as 10 Downing Street. Symphony takes its cue from the first character of the entry, in this case, the number 1. This is a value, and it leads Symphony to assume that what follows is also a value, an assumption that proves erroneous when you type the rest of the address and attempt to enter it. As with numbers such as ZIP codes, the answer is to place a label prefix at the beginning of an alphanumeric entry that is not a formula. Note that by assigning data types to fields, Symphony's FORM environment provides a way around problem data.

Column Widths

Since the requirements of a database table allow only one row for each record, fields containing lengthy information may require extensive widening of the column. Notice that the Company field in Figure 5-1 had to be made wider than the others. In order to compensate for widening, you can narrow the columns containing short data, such as the Buy field.

Keep in mind that you do not have to make each column wide enough to show all the data that it contains in order for Symphony to store long entries. However, if you want all of the data to print, you will need to expand the columns prior to printing.

The Column Hide command will let you temporarily remove selected columns from view if necessary. In Figure 5-4, column D is missing. This is because it contains the buy/sell recommendations and is hidden to avoid disclosing that information.

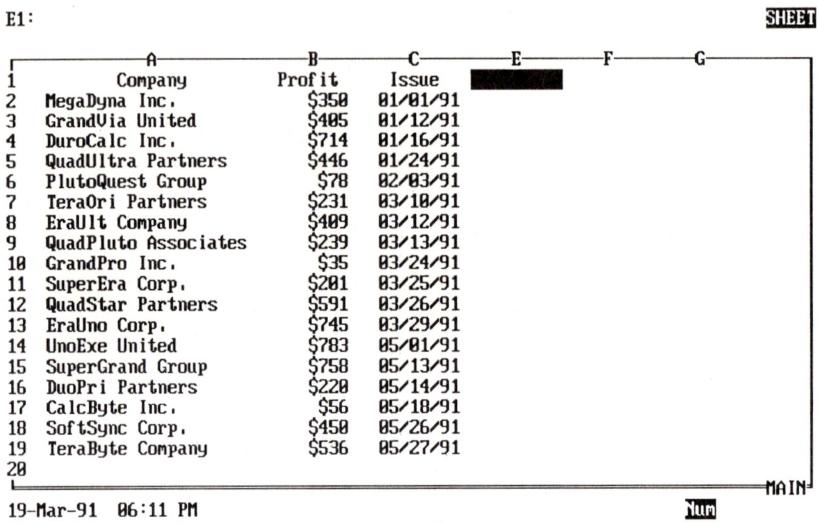

E1:

SHEET

	A	B	C	E	F	G
1	Company	Profit	Issue			
2	MegaDyna Inc.	$350	01/01/91			
3	GrandVia United	$405	01/12/91			
4	DuroCalc Inc.	$714	01/16/91			
5	QuadUltra Partners	$446	01/24/91			
6	PlutoQuest Group	$78	02/03/91			
7	TeraOri Partners	$231	03/10/91			
8	EraUlt Company	$409	03/12/91			
9	QuadPluto Associates	$239	03/13/91			
10	GrandPro Inc.	$35	03/24/91			
11	SuperEra Corp.	$201	03/25/91			
12	QuadStar Partners	$591	03/26/91			
13	EraUno Corp.	$745	03/29/91			
14	UnoExe United	$783	05/01/91			
15	SuperGrand Group	$758	05/13/91			
16	DuoPri Partners	$220	05/14/91			
17	CalcByte Inc.	$56	05/18/91			
18	SoftSync Corp.	$450	05/26/91			
19	TeraByte Company	$536	05/27/91			
20						

MAIN

19-Mar-91 06:11 PM Num

FIGURE 5-4 Hiding a column

Symphony lets you place selected columns in the background and closes up the ones in the foreground, as Figure 5-5 illustrates. Thus, Symphony allows you to pick and choose which columns to view. The Width Hide command is also useful when you are dealing with confidential data or arranging a worksheet before printing. The hidden data is not lost, and hidden formulas continue to be active.

To hide the Profit column in the sample database, column B, you would place your cell pointer on any row in column B and then select Width Hide. You then anchor the beginning column by typing a period, and then press (RIGHT ARROW) to move the highlighting through as many columns as you want to hide. In this case, it is just column B, so you can just press (ENTER). The columns disappear from view and cannot be accessed. To return the col-

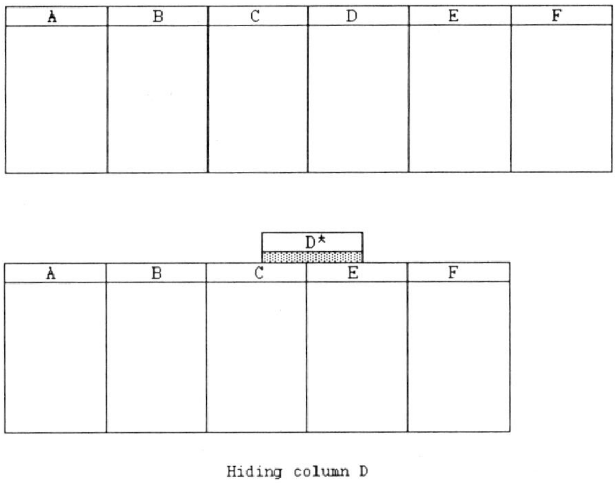

FIGURE 5-5 Hiding columns

umns to view, simply select Width Display. All of the columns will be shown, with asterisks next to the column letters of columns that are currently hidden, as shown in Figure 5-6. To return hidden columns to display, simply highlight them and press (ENTER). If you press (ESC) and do not select any columns, the marked columns remain hidden.

The column width and format remain unaffected by the hide-and-display process. When you carry out any command using POINT mode to indicate cell references, Symphony temporarily reveals hidden columns, marked by asterisks, so that they can be considered in the command. For example, if you use the Move or Copy command or formulas built with the point method, the columns will be temporarily revealed so you can correctly complete the operation.

```
Columns to Display: E1..E1                                            POINT

          A                    B          C          D*       E        F
1      Company              Profit     Issue       Buy
2   MegaDyna Inc.             $350   01/01/91 No
3   GrandVia United           $405   01/12/91 No
4   DuroCalc Inc.             $714   01/16/91 Yes
5   QuadUltra Partners        $446   01/24/91 No
6   PlutoQuest Group           $78   02/03/91 Yes
7   TeraOri Partners          $231   03/10/91 Yes
8   EraUlt Company            $409   03/12/91 No
9   QuadPluto Associates      $239   03/13/91 No
10  GrandPro Inc.              $35   03/24/91 Yes
11  SuperEra Corp.            $201   03/25/91 Yes
12  QuadStar Partners         $591   03/26/91 No
13  EraUno Corp.              $745   03/29/91 No
14  UnoExe United             $783   05/01/91 No
15  SuperGrand Group          $750   05/13/91 Yes
16  DuoPri Partners           $220   05/14/91 Yes
17  CalcByte Inc.              $56   05/18/91 No
18  SoftSync Corp.            $450   05/26/91 No
19  TeraByte Company          $536   05/27/91 Yes
20
                                                                      MAIN
Width Display                                                    Num
```

FIGURE 5-6 Displaying hidden columns

SORTING DATA

Sorting is the process of rearranging rows of information according to alphabetical or numerical order. It is usually used to place the records in a database in a new order. In the case of the sample model, the records could be placed in alphabetical order by company name, or they could be listed from highest profit to lowest. You could also create a chronological list of issue dates.

A Basic Sort

To perform a sort, you must tell Symphony which cells the database occupies, which column(s) will be the basis of the sort, and whether you want Ascending or Descending order. For example, to sort according to profits, column B would be the basis of the sort, referred to by Symphony as a *sort key*. To sort from highest to lowest, the sort order would be Descending. To sort the sample database alphabetically according to company name, follow these steps:

1. Press (HOME) to move the cell pointer to A1, the top left cell of the database. Now press MENU and select Query. The resulting menu is shown here:

```
Database definitions                                                    MENU
Settings  Find  Extract  Unique  Delete  Record-Sort  Parse  Quit
┌──────────────A───────────────B──────────C──────────D──────────E──────────F──────┐
1      Company             Profit     Issue      Buy
2   MegaDyna Inc.             $350   01/01/91 No
3   GrandVia United           $405   01/12/91 No
4   QuadUltra Partners        $446   01/24/91 No
5   DuroCalc Inc.             $714   01/16/91 Yes
```

2. The first item, Settings, is used to tell Symphony where the data to be sorted is located, and the basis of the sort. Select Settings, and you will see a screen like the one in Figure 5-7.

3. The first item on the Settings menu is Basic. You will need to select this now in order to tell Symphony which cells the database occupies.

```
Database, Criterion, Output ranges                                          MENU
Basic  Form  Underscores  Sort-Keys  Report  One-Record  Name  Cancel  Quit
┌─────────────────────────────────────────────────────────────────────────────┐
Basic Ranges                              Report Ranges
  Database:                                 Main:
  Criterion:                                Above:
  Output:                                   Below:
Form Ranges                                 Type              Single
  Entry:                                      Entry list:
  Definition:                                 Input cell:
Underscores:      Yes                       One-Record:       No
Sort-Keys
  1st-Key:                 2nd-Key:                     3rd-Key:
    Order:                   Order:                       Order:
══════════════════════════════════════════════════Database Settings: MAIN═
```

FIGURE 5-7 Initial settings sheet

4. When you select Basic, there are three main options: Database, Criterion, Output. For record sorting, you only need to select Database.

5. When you select Database, Symphony presents the worksheet and asks you to point out the database cells. This is the range that stretches from the first field name to the last column of the last record. In the sample model, the database is A1..D19. You can type the coordinates or point them out. To point out the coordinates, type a period to anchor the top left corner of the range at A1. Now press (END) and then (RIGHT ARROW) followed by (END) and then (DOWN ARROW). This will include all of the cells of the database.

Note: Instead of typing a period to anchor the coordinates of a range, you can press (TAB).

6. Press (ENTER) to confirm the database range, and you will be returned to the Settings sheet. Select Quit to return to the main Settings menu, and select Sort-Keys.

7. You can use up to three keys, but you only need one to sort by company name, so select 1st-Key.

8. You must indicate the column that will be the basis of the sort by moving the cell pointer to a cell in that column and pressing (ENTER). In this case the cell pointer is already in the correct column (A), so press (ENTER).

9. You are returned to the settings sheet, where Symphony asks if you want Ascending or Descending order. Type **A** for Ascending and press (ENTER). The settings sheet should now look like Figure 5-8.

```
1st, 2nd, 3rd                                                          MENU
Basic  Form  Underscores  Sort-Keys  Report  One-Record  Name  Cancel  Quit

Basic Ranges                              Report Ranges
  Database:        A1..D19                  Main:
  Criterion:                                Above:
  Output:                                   Below:
Form Ranges                                 Type            Single
  Entry:                                      Entry list:
  Definition:                                 Input cell:
Underscores:       Yes                    One-Record:       No
Sort-Keys
  1st-Key: A1..A1          2nd-Key:                 3rd-Key:
    Order: Ascending         Order:                   Order:
                                              Database Settings: MAIN
```

FIGURE 5-8 Settings sheet with sort information

10. All you need to do now is select Quit or press (ESC) to return to the first Query menu and select Record-Sort, the command that tells Symphony to sort the records according to the current sort settings. The Record-Sort command needs one more piece of information: do you want Unique or All? In most situations you are safe choosing Unique, which is the default choice. Press (ENTER) to select Unique, and the database is re-ordered.

The sorted database appears in Figure 5-9. After the Record-Sort command is executed, you are returned to the Query menu. From this you can select Quit to return to SHEET mode.

Note Ascending order means from A to Z alphabetically and from 1 to 26 when sorting numbers.

Note Because a database occupies consecutive columns and rows, the (END) key works well to select the database range because it automatically encompasses the entire range of data.

```
Sort data records                                                        MENU
Settings  Find  Extract  Unique  Delete  Record-Sort  Parse  Quit
             A                        B          C         D         E         F
1          Company                Profit      Issue      Buy
2   CalcByte Inc.                    $56   05/18/91 No
3   DuoPri Partners                 $220   05/14/91 Yes
4   DuroCalc Inc.                   $714   01/16/91 Yes
5   EraUlt Company                  $409   03/12/91 No
6   EraUno Corp.                    $745   03/29/91 No
7   GrandPro Inc.                    $35   03/24/91 Yes
8   GrandVia United                 $405   01/12/91 No
9   MegaDyna Inc.                   $350   01/01/91 No
10  PlutoQuest Group                 $78   02/03/91 Yes
11  QuadPluto Associates            $239   03/13/91 No
12  QuadStar Partners               $591   03/26/91 No
13  QuadUltra Partners              $446   01/24/91 No
14  SoftSync Corp.                  $450   05/26/91 No
15  SuperEra Corp.                  $201   03/25/91 Yes
16  SuperGrand Group                $758   05/13/91 Yes
17  TeraByte Company                $536   05/27/91 Yes
18  TeraOri Partners                $231   03/10/91 Yes
19  UnoExe United                   $783   05/01/91 No
20
                                                                       MAIN
Query                                                             Num
```

FIGURE 5-9 Database sorted by company name

Sort Tips

When setting the database range, you should avoid defining the data to be sorted as just one or two columns out of a block of related data. In other words, do not think "I am going to sort company names," but rather think of the entire data as one entity and think of it as "I am going to sort the data according to company names."

You saw that Symphony can accommodate three sort keys, so if you wanted to sort a list of employee names alphabetically you would select the Last Name column as the first key. If you wanted a complete sort by name so that the several Smiths were sorted by their first names as well, you would select a second key, the First Name column. When two or more items have identical entries in the field chosen for the first key, the second key acts as a tie-breaker. A third key will sort items that match in the first and second key columns. A Middle Initial field could be used to ensure a complete alphabetical sort of employees based on their full names.

The Record-Sort option Unique/All allows you to perform some database housekeeping. One problem with larger databases and lists that are maintained by several people is the duplication of records. Sorting a list is one way to find duplicates, because they will be next to each other in the list. The Unique option automatically removes any duplicate records from the list. The All option simply sorts the list without doing anything to duplicate records.

Caution When the sort operation is performed, a large amount of information is moved. Unless you are very sure of the effects of the sort, you should always save a worksheet before sorting, particularly as most databases represent many hours of work.

Further Sorts

If you are performing a series of sorts—for example, if you are editing names and you want to check that the alphabetical order is correct—you do not need to redefine the database range or the sort keys already set. Symphony remembers the location of these items. If you select Database and find that the correct range of cells is already defined, simply press (ENTER) to reconfirm it. Do not press (ESC), which would unlock the range coordinates. For an example, edit "UnoExe United" to read "AnoExe United" and repeat the Record-Sort command. The edited name goes to the top of the list. Edit the name back to "UnoExe United" and sort again; the name returns to the bottom of the list.

Suppose that you now decide to sort the list of companies according to the Buy column. This will group the records into those that have No in column D and those that have Yes. Within these two groups, you want the companies to be sorted according to the date in the Issue column, with oldest dates ahead of more recent dates. The database range is already set, so you simply need to change the 1st-Key definition and add a 2nd-Key definition.

1. Press (HOME) and then press MENU. Select Query, followed by Settings and then Sort-Keys.

2. Select 1st-Key and press (ESC) to unlock the range coordinates.

3. Move the cell pointer to column D and press (ENTER). Then type **D** for Descending, which will put the Yes records above the No records, and press (ENTER).

Note: You only need to type the order letter (A or D) if you are changing the order. The default for all three keys is A, but when you change a key to D it stays that way until you cancel the sort key or change it again.

```
Database, Criterion, Output ranges                                         MENU
Basic  Form  Underscores  Sort-Keys  Report  One-Record  Name  Cancel  Quit

Basic Ranges                               Report Ranges
  Database:        A1..D19                   Main:
  Criterion:                                 Above:
  Output:                                    Below:
Form Ranges                                  Type          Single
  Entry:                                       Entry list:
  Definition:                                  Input cell:
Underscores:       Yes                     One-Record:     No
Sort-Keys
  1st-Key: D1..D1           2nd-Key: C1..C1           3rd-Key:
    Order: Descending         Order: Ascending          Order:
                                                 Database Settings: MAIN

Query Settings                                                   Num
```

FIGURE 5-10 Altered settings sheet

```
Sort data records                                                          MENU
Settings  Find  Extract  Unique  Delete  Record-Sort  Parse  Quit
         A                     B          C          D         E        F
1       Company               Profit     Issue      Buy
2    DuroCalc Inc.             $714   01/16/91 Yes
3    PlutoQuest Group           $78   02/03/91 Yes
4    TeraOri Partners          $231   03/10/91 Yes
5    GrandPro Inc.              $35   03/24/91 Yes
6    SuperEra Corp.            $201   03/25/91 Yes
7    SuperGrand Group          $758   05/13/91 Yes
8    DuoPri Partners           $220   05/14/91 Yes
9    TeraByte Company          $536   05/27/91 Yes
10   MegaDyna Inc.             $350   01/01/91 No
11   GrandVia United           $405   01/12/91 No
12   QuadUltra Partners        $446   01/24/91 No
13   EraUlt Company            $409   03/12/91 No
14   QuadPluto Associates      $239   03/13/91 No
15   QuadStar Partners         $591   03/26/91 No
16   EraUno Corp.              $745   03/29/91 No
17   UnoExe United             $783   05/01/91 No
18   CalcByte Inc.              $56   05/18/91 No
19   SoftSync Corp.            $450   05/26/91 No
20
                                                                         MAIN
Query                                                            Num
```

FIGURE 5-11 Records sorted by columns D and C

4. Select Sort-Keys again and then choose 2nd-Key. Move the cell pointer to column C and press (ENTER). Type **A** for Ascending, and press (ENTER). The settings sheet will now look as it does in Figure 5-10.

5. Select Quit, then Record-Sort, and then Unique.

The results are shown in Figure 5-11. You can see that the records with Yes in column D come before those with No. Within the Yes group, records are listed by the date in column C.

Note: When you sort by dates, Ascending orders dates from oldest to youngest—in other words, from 1/1/80 to 1/2/80, and so on—based on the date serial number, which is smaller for dates closer to 1900.

USING NAMED QUERY SETTINGS

It takes very little effort to alter the sort keys, but you might want to name each different sort so that you can repeat it later. You can see that on the right of Figure 5-10, the database settings are called MAIN. Symphony allows you to create, use, and manage named database settings with a system similar to that used for range names in the SHEET environment or format lines in the DOC environment. To give a name to the current sort order, select Settings from the Query menu. You should be viewing the settings shown in Figure 5-10.

1. Select Name, and you will see a menu of naming commands just like those used in the Print Settings Name command. Highlight Create. This command creates a copy of the sheet you are viewing, under a new name.

2. Press (ENTER) to select Create. Type the name you want for the copy of the current settings (for example, **YES_KEYS**) and then press (ENTER). This name replaces MAIN. You have stored the current settings under the new name, and any changes you make to the settings at this point will remain attached to the name that is displayed in the lower right of the settings box.

3. Now select Name Create again, and you will see the named settings you just created, as well as the MAIN settings name, as shown in Figure 5-12. Type **ALPHA**, which is the name you want to use for the alphabetical sort setting, and press (ENTER). The name of the current settings is now ALPHA, and you will change the sort keys so that they perform an alphabetical sort by company name.

4. You need to change 1st-Key to A1 and remove the second key. There is only one way to remove a sort-key setting: Move back to the Query Settings menu and select Cancel. Choose Sort-Keys, which will wipe out the sort-key settings.

```
Name for new Database settings sheet:                                  NAMES
MAIN            YES_KEYS

Basic Ranges                              Report Ranges
  Database:       A1..D19                   Main:
  Criterion:                                Above:
  Output:                                   Below:
Form Ranges                                 Type          Single
  Entry:                                      Entry list:
  Definition:                                 Input cell:
Underscores:      Yes                     One-Record:     No
Sort-Keys
  1st-Key: D1..D1          2nd-Key: C1..C1          3rd-Key:
    Order: Descending        Order: Ascending         Order:
                                        Database Settings: YES_KEYS
```

FIGURE 5-12 Creating a named database settings sheet

5. Select Sort-Keys followed by 1st-Key. Then select cell A1 and press (ENTER). Type **A** for Ascending, and press (ENTER). As you can see from the settings sheet, the settings that are now in place are called ALPHA.

To test the two names you have created, move back to the main Query menu and select Record-Sort followed by Unique. The list will be ordered by company name. Then choose Settings, select Name, and then Use. Select YES_LIST from the names that are presented. Choose Quit or press (ESC) to move back to the main Query menu, and select Record-Sort followed by Unique. The list is now back the way it was in Figure 5-11. Remember that names of settings are not stored with the worksheet until the worksheet is saved. You should now save the current version of the file under a new name, COMPANY2, using the SERVICES File Save menu.

Later in this chapter you will learn how to use the naming system for more complex settings, such as those used to search for information in the database. Bear in mind that when you choose the Use command and select a name, Symphony recalls whatever settings were in place when that name was last on-screen. A new settings sheet is created by copying an existing sheet to a new name and then altering the settings to match the name.

Database Expansion

When you add data to the bottom of a database, Symphony does not automatically include the added data in the database range or place the data in the correct order. Suppose you are adding a company to the bottom of the list in Figure 5-9, using the empty cells on row 20. After adding the new company, you need to redefine the database range and issue a command to sort the new records into the database. Symphony will not automatically extend the database range to cover new additions unless you add a fresh row before the end of the database, as shown in Figure 5-13.

Rows inserted into the worksheet within any named or recorded range of cells become part of that range. The coordinates of the

Row insert range: A19..A19 POINT

	A	B	C	D	E	F
1	Company	Profit	Issue	Buy		
2	CalcByte Inc.	$56	05/18/91	No		
3	DuoPri Partners	$220	05/14/91	Yes		
4	DuroCalc Inc.	$714	01/16/91	Yes		
5	EraUlt Company	$409	03/12/91	No		
6	EraUno Corp.	$745	03/29/91	No		
7	GrandPro Inc.	$35	03/24/91	Yes		
8	GrandVia United	$405	01/12/91	No		
9	MegaDyna Inc.	$350	01/01/91	No		
10	PlutoQuest Group	$78	02/03/91	Yes		
11	QuadPluto Associates	$239	03/13/91	No		
12	QuadStar Partners	$591	03/26/91	No		
13	QuadUltra Partners	$446	01/24/91	No		
14	SoftSync Corp.	$450	05/26/91	No		
15	SuperEra Corp.	$201	03/25/91	Yes		
16	SuperGrand Group	$758	05/13/91	Yes		
17	TeraByte Company	$536	05/27/91	Yes		
18	TeraOri Partners	$231	03/10/91	Yes		
19	UnoExe United	$783	05/01/91	No		
20						

MAIN

Insert Rows Num

FIGURE 5-13 Using Insert Rows to add a row for a new company

range expand to accommodate the new cells. A quick check of Query Settings after completing the Insert Rows command in Figure 5-13 would show that the database range is now A1..D20. A new company entered on an inserted row is thus included in the database range and sorted in the list the next time the Record-Sort command is issued.

Inserted rows are added to the database range if you use Insert Rows with your cell pointer on any row in the database except the first one. Thus, if you want to add names in their correct alphabetical location, you can normally do so with Insert Rows. In this way you will be sure that they will be included in the database range.

Note If you delete the lowest record in the database with the Delete Rows command, the database range setting will be erased. To delete records, see the section later in this chapter.

SORT ORDER AND APPLICATION

You may wonder how Symphony decides exactly what order to place the rows in when the Record-Sort command is issued. The program looks at the column that is designated the 1st-Key, sorts it, and the rest of the cells are moved along with their entries in the key column. If 2nd-Key is defined, it will determine the order of records that have identical entries in the 1st-Key column.

Collating Sequence

A column usually consists of all labels or all values, in which case the order is fairly easy to predict. If you have chosen Ascending order, numbers go from lowest to highest and words go from those beginning with "A" to those beginning with "Z." Dates are sorted according to how close they are to 1900: The closer they are, the higher in the list they are placed in Ascending order.

There are special rules that Symphony uses to determine the exact details of alphabetical sort order. Symphony refers to the sorting rules as the *collating sequence*. When a key column contains labels that begin with numbers, they are normally placed above ordinary labels, as in the following sequence:

101 Washington Street
102 Washington Street
Washington Plaza
Washington Square

The default collating sequence used by Symphony performs an Ascending sort, as shown in Table 5-1. Symphony normally places equal value on uppercase and lowercase letters when sorting label data. This program setting can be changed, as can the "numbers first" rule, but you must use the Install program to change the collating sequence. This should not be necessary for most applications, but if you want to explore this subject, see Appendix A.

Reordering with Edit Fill

Although records in a database may not be in numeric or alphabetic order, the order in which they are entered may be significant. If the original order of records is important, you can preserve it by numbering each record before sorting. The Range Fill command lets you insert a column to the left of the database and fill it with a series of numbers that correspond to each of the records.

1. After saving the sorted worksheet under the name COMPANY2, use SERVICES File Retrieve to bring back the original version of the database file, which you saved as COMPANY1. This is the database as it is shown in Figure 5-1.

Uppercase and lowercase letters are equal.

Foreign characters are appropriately ranked within the normal alphabet.

In Ascending order, among mixed entries:
Empty cells come first.
Label cells come next.
Numeric cells come last, in numeric order.

In Ascending order, among labels:
Labels starting with spaces are first, ranked by the first non-space.
Labels beginning with numbers come next, in numeric order.
Labels beginning with special characters are ranked thus:
! " # $ % & ' ( ) * + . / : ? @ [\ ^ _ { } ~
Labels beginning with letters of the alphabet are ranked "A" to "Z."

In Ascending order, among numbers:
Values are ranked from lowest to highest.
Dates are ranked by serial number.
Dates closer to 1900 have smaller serial numbers.
Sort order is not affected by cell formatting.

TABLE 5-1 Default Sort Sequence

2. Press (HOME) to make sure that the cell pointer is in cell A1. Then press MENU. Select Insert and then Columns, and then press (ENTER). A fresh column A will appear.

3. Enter a field name such as **Record#** in cell A1, and then move the cell pointer to A2.

4. Press MENU and select Range Fill. You will be asked to define a range of cells to fill. Anchor this range in A2 by pressing (TAB). Extend the highlighting down the worksheet to include the row of the last record. To do this quickly, press (RIGHT ARROW), then (END), (DOWN ARROW), and (LEFT ARROW). This action takes the

```
Fill range: A2..A19                                                    POINT

   A          B                      C          D          E        F
1  Record#         Company           Profit     Issue      Buy
2            MegaDyna Inc.           $350      01/01/91 No
3            GrandVia United         $405      01/12/91 No
4            QuadUltra Partners      $446      01/24/91 No
5            DuroCalc Inc.           $714      01/16/91 Yes
6            DuoPri Partners         $220      05/14/91 Yes
7            GrandPro Inc.            $35      03/24/91 Yes
8            TeraOri Partners        $231      03/10/91 Yes
9            UnoExe United           $783      05/01/91 No
10           SuperGrand Group        $758      05/13/91 Yes
11           TeraByte Company        $536      05/27/91 Yes
12           EraUno Corp.            $745      03/29/91 No
13           QuadStar Partners       $591      03/26/91 No
14           CalcByte Inc.            $56      05/10/91 No
15           SuperEra Corp.          $201      03/25/91 Yes
16           QuadPluto Associates    $239      03/13/91 No
17           EraUlt Company          $409      03/12/91 No
18           SoftSync Corp.          $450      05/26/91 No
19           PlutoQuest Group         $78      02/03/91 Yes
20
                                                                        MAIN
Range Fill                                                     Num
```

FIGURE 5-14 Fill range defined in new column A

highlighting into the first column currently occupied by data in the database, down to the last row of data, and then back into the original column you want to fill, as shown in Figure 5-14.

5. When you press (ENTER) to confirm the fill range, Symphony prompts you for a start value. You can use the suggested default of 0, or any other number, such as 1001. Then press (ENTER), and you will be prompted for the step value. You will usually select 1, although you can use decimals or units larger than 1, or even negative numbers for a descending sequence.

6. After entering the step value, you must specify the stop value. Unless you have used a negative step value, simply type in a number that is larger than the last number in the sequence you are creating. Press (ENTER), and Symphony will fill numbers into the range as shown in Figure 5-15.

A2: 1001 SHEET

	A	B	C	D	E	F
1	Record#	Company	Profit	Issue	Buy	
2	1001	MegaDyna Inc.	$350	01/01/91	No	
3	1002	GrandVia United	$405	01/12/91	No	
4	1003	QuadUltra Partners	$446	01/24/91	No	
5	1004	DuroCalc Inc.	$714	01/16/91	Yes	
6	1005	DuoPri Partners	$220	05/14/91	Yes	
7	1006	GrandPro Inc.	$35	03/24/91	Yes	
8	1007	TeraOri Partners	$231	03/10/91	Yes	
9	1008	UnoExe United	$783	05/01/91	No	
10	1009	SuperGrand Group	$758	05/13/91	Yes	
11	1010	TeraByte Company	$536	05/27/91	Yes	
12	1011	EraUno Corp.	$745	03/29/91	No	
13	1012	QuadStar Partners	$591	03/26/91	No	
14	1013	CalcByte Inc.	$56	05/18/91	No	
15	1014	SuperEra Corp.	$201	03/25/91	Yes	
16	1015	QuadPluto Associates	$239	03/13/91	No	
17	1016	EraUlt Company	$409	03/12/91	No	
18	1017	SoftSync Corp.	$450	05/26/91	No	
19	1018	PlutoQuest Group	$70	02/03/91	Yes	
20						

MAIN

12-Mar-91 01:17 PM Num

FIGURE 5-15 Range of numbers filled

Note: If you know the stop value you need, you can type that in. The stop value must be smaller than the start value if you are creating a declining sequence.

Note: Range Fill can also produce a horizontal series of numbers if you define a row as the fill range. You can even fill a rectangle with a series of values if you select a rectangular fill range.

To use this new column of numbers as the basis for a sort you must include it in the database range. Since you are working with the original version of the file, there are no Query settings in place. To name settings for an alphabetical sort,

1. Press (HOME) and MENU, and select Query Settings Name Create. Type **ALPHA** and press (ENTER).

2. Now select Basic, followed by Database, and define the database as A1..E19. Select Quit to move back to the Query Settings menu.

3. Select Sort-Keys and then 1st-Key. Choose B1 as the key to sort the list alphabetically, and A for the order.

4. Quit the Query Settings menu and select Record-Sort Unique. The order changes to alphabetical, and the record numbers are mixed up.

5. To return the list to record-number order and name the sort setting, choose Settings Name Create and enter **RECORD**. Select Sort-Keys, 1st-Key, and A1. Confirm Ascending as the order and quit this menu. Choose Record-Sort Unique, and you will see the records put back in numerical order.

You have now created two named sort settings that can be used with this expanded version of the database. Save the new version in a file called **COMPANY3** using the SERVICES File Save command.

MAKING INQUIRIES

Symphony not only sorts collections of data in a worksheet, but it also locates specific records or groups of records through the Query Find feature. After it has located the records, it allows you to browse through them. You can even copy matching records to a separate list.

Lines of Questioning

As an example of the Query Find feature, you can use the sample database with the column of record numbers added. You will also want to imagine that this is a much larger database than it really is. Suppose you want to browse through the list of companies, looking at only those that have a Yes recommendation in the Buy column. As you have seen, you could sort the database according to the Buy column, but you may not want to sort the database at this point. The Find command can highlight the records you want to look at without altering the sort order in the database.

You can phrase your request as a query: "Find companies that have Yes as their buy recommendation." The condition you place on a request to find specific data in Symphony is called a *criterion*. Symphony can handle several conditions at once, in which case they are *criteria*. In this example, the criterion can be rephrased as "Find companies that have the entry Yes in the Buy field." When given this command in the appropriate manner, Symphony will respond either by highlighting records that match the criteria or, if there are no matches, by beeping to let you know.

In order to find data that match your criteria, Symphony needs to know two things:

Where the data is	The database range; that is, the entire database table including the field names
Which data to find	The criterion range is used to specify the criteria of your search; that is, what data to match

After you have given Symphony these two pieces of information, it locates matching records by highlighting them. If you provide a third piece of information, called an *output range,* Symphony extracts a list of items into that area of the worksheet.

Where the Data Is

To undertake any query operation, you first need to tell Symphony about the database range. If you have just sorted the database, you have already defined the database range and answered the question "Where is the data?"

Note You do not have to include the entire database table in the range to be searched. You can leave some records off the bottom of the block. However, the range must include the row containing field names for the columns you are searching.

Note With large database tables, it is a good idea to use the Settings Titles command to set the field names as titles. This will allow you to see the field names as you examine records that are located by the Find command.

Which Data to Find

To tell Symphony which data you are looking for, you establish a criterion range. In its simplest form a criterion range consists of a field name entered into one cell with the data to be matched in the cell below it. In this example the criterion range will be

Buy	The name of the field to look in
Yes	The data to match in that field

After you enter this information into the cells of your worksheet, you tell Symphony the location of the criterion and ask the program to locate the records. Symphony does this by trying to match what you have specified in the criterion to each row of the appropriate column in the database range. In this example, Symphony looks in the field/column that is named "Buy." The program checks for the text "Yes." When a match for this text is found, the entire record that contains the matching text is highlighted.

The data that you ask Symphony to match can consist of formulas as well as simple text or value entries. Also, as you will see in a moment, multiple criteria can be used, with up to 32 fields being checked at once.

Creating a Criterion Range

To build a criterion range, you type the field names of the columns you want to match data in, followed by the data you want to match, in a separate area of the worksheet.

1. Move the cell pointer to F5 and enter the label **Buy**. This does not have to be centered in the column.
2. Move the cell pointer to F6 and enter the target data **Yes**.
3. Define the criterion range to Symphony by selecting Query Settings Basic Criterion. Highlight the appropriate block of cells, F5..F6, as shown in Figure 5-16, and press (ENTER).

```
Criterion range: F5..F6                                                 POINT

      A               B                   C          D          E         F
1  Record#         Company             Profit     Issue       Buy
2     1001 MegaDyna Inc.                 $350  01/01/91 No
3     1002 GrandVia United               $405  01/12/91 No
4     1003 QuadUltra Partners            $446  01/24/91 No
5     1004 DuroCalc Inc.                 $714  01/16/91 Yes       Buy
6     1005 DuoPri Partners               $220  05/14/91 Yes       Yes
7     1006 GrandPro Inc.                  $35  03/24/91 Yes
8     1007 TeraOri Partners              $231  03/10/91 Yes
9     1008 UnoExe United                 $783  05/01/91 No
10    1009 SuperGrand Group              $750  05/13/91 Yes
11    1010 TeraByte Company              $536  05/27/91 Yes
12    1011 EraUno Corp.                  $745  03/29/91 No
13    1012 QuadStar Partners             $591  03/26/91 No
14    1013 CalcByte Inc.                  $56  05/10/91 No
15    1014 SuperEra Corp.                $201  03/25/91 Yes
16    1015 QuadPluto Associates          $239  03/13/91 No
17    1016 EraUlt Company                $409  03/12/91 No
18    1017 SoftSync Corp.                $450  05/26/91 No
19    1018 PlutoQuest Group               $70  02/03/91 Yes
20
                                                                      MAIN
Query Settings Basic Criterion                                 Num
```

FIGURE 5-16 Defining the criterion range

FIND

	A	B	C	D	E	F
1	Record#	Company	Profit	Issue	Buy	
2	1001	MegaDyna Inc.	$350	01/01/91	No	
3	1002	GrandVia United	$405	01/12/91	No	
4	1003	QuadUltra Partners	$446	01/24/91	No	
5	1004	DuroCalc Inc.	$714	01/16/91	Yes	Buy
6	1005	DuoPri Partners	$220	05/14/91	Yes	Yes
7	1006	GrandPro Inc.	$35	03/24/91	Yes	
8	1007	TeraOri Partners	$231	03/10/91	Yes	
9	1008	UnoExe United	$783	05/01/91	No	
10	1009	SuperGrand Group	$758	05/13/91	Yes	
11	1010	TeraByte Company	$536	05/27/91	Yes	
12	1011	EraUno Corp.	$745	03/29/91	No	
13	1012	QuadStar Partners	$591	03/26/91	No	
14	1013	CalcByte Inc.	$56	05/18/91	No	
15	1014	SuperEra Corp.	$201	03/25/91	Yes	
16	1015	QuadPluto Associates	$239	03/13/91	No	
17	1016	EraUlt Company	$409	03/12/91	No	
18	1017	SoftSync Corp.	$450	05/26/91	No	
19	1018	PlutoQuest Group	$78	02/03/91	Yes	
20						

MAIN

Query Find Num

FIGURE 5-17 The Find command

Caution Be careful not to include any blank lines in the criterion range, since this will cause Symphony to find everything in the database table.

4. When you have defined the criterion range, you are returned to the Query Settings Basic menu. Note that the database range is already defined because you used it when sorting the database.

5. Select Quit twice to move back to the main Query menu. To find the records meeting your criteria, select the Find command. This causes Symphony to highlight the first item meeting your criteria, as shown in Figure 5-17.

The mode indicator shows the word "FIND" to let you know you are in a special mode. As you can see from Figure 5-17, the special highlight bar runs the full length of the record. A cursor is flashing in column A of the highlight bar. If the database is wider than one screen, this cursor can be moved to the right with (RIGHT ARROW) to bring the rest of the database into view.

If there are no records meeting your criteria, Symphony will beep in response to the Find command and return to the Query menu. If you are sure that there are matching records, this is an opportunity to check that you have specified the criterion correctly.

Note: If you do not find any records, check the spelling of the entries E1, F5 and F6. Sometimes an entry has a trailing space, and that is enough to confuse Symphony.

You can move to further records that meet the criterion by pressing (DOWN ARROW). The highlight bar skips records that do not meet the criterion. When you get to the last matching record and try to go farther, Symphony will beep. You can move back up a record with (UP ARROW) and continue to browse through the matching items by using (UP ARROW) or (DOWN ARROW). The (END) key takes you to the last matching record, whereas (HOME) takes you to the first.

Note: If you find all of the records—that is, if the highlight bar does not skip any entries—make sure you have defined the criterion range correctly.

Find Tips

After you have used Find, you can leave the FIND mode by pressing (ESC), which takes you back to the Query menu, where you can make changes to settings. Alternatively, you can move out of FIND with the key that takes you out of any menu back to the SHEET mode: (CTRL-BREAK).

You can create many different criterion ranges and define them by using named settings sheets, just as you used named settings sheets for different sorts. That way you can switch from one set of criteria to another by means of the Settings Name Use command.

Note that a criterion is matched in the database on the basis of its value and not the formula that produced the value. When you search for Yes in column E, you are looking for a cell that contains the label Yes or a formula that results in Yes. If you are looking for a specific figure in the profit column, it would not matter if the figure was a straight value or a value produced by a formula.

The Find feature is very useful for quick searches when you do not want to print out a separate list—to perform a quick check of a specific item in stock, a specific employee record, and so on. If you want to copy the records that have been located to another part of the worksheet or to another worksheet, then you need the Extract command. This will be covered in a moment, after criteria have been examined in greater depth. The real strength of Query Find comes when you use criteria that are more complex.

The actual positioning of the criterion range on the spreadsheet is not critical to the performance of the Find operation, but the criterion range should be set apart from the database table in an unused portion of the worksheet. Do not place it directly to the right or left of the database table if you expect to be deleting records or rows from the database table with the Edit Delete Row command. Also, do not move the criterion range too far from the database table, or you will be consuming memory needlessly.

ENHANCED CRITERIA

So far, you have seen that a criterion range offers a simple but effective way of indicating the parameters of your search for data. You can take the criterion range even further by using multiple criteria and formulas to create detailed search specifications.

Formulas for Criteria

Suppose that you want to find all companies with a profit figure greater than 450. This requires a criterion range with the heading Profit, and below it a formula. Formulas in criteria use what are called *logical* operators. Thus, you could use **>450** to find companies with a profit greater than 450. The logical operators you can use are as follows:

>	Greater than: >300 means 301, 302, and so on
<	Less than: <300 means 299, 298, and so on
>=	Greater than or equal to: >=300 means 300, 301, and so on
<=	Less than or equal to: <=300 means 300, 299, and so on
<>	Not equal to: <>300 means anything other than 300
=	Equal to: =300 means only 300

You cannot simply enter <300 or >450 as a criterion, which would tell Symphony to look for a piece of text. You have to create a formula using the logical operators *plus* a reference to the location of the field in the database. The reference can either be a range name or a cell coordinate. You use the first cell in the column that is being referenced. Thus, you can use +C2>450 to find values in column C that are greater than 450.

The formula +C2>450 asks the question "Is the value in cell C2 greater than 450?" and returns 1 if the answer is Yes or 0 if the answer is No. The value 1 can be taken to mean either Yes or True, and 0 stands for False or No. With a formula like this in a criterion, Symphony compares each cell from C2 on down the column and "finds" every record in which the formula is true. To see how this works, follow these steps:

1. With the cell pointer in F5, change the Buy label to **Profit** and then move the cell pointer to F6.

2. Type **+C2>450** and press (ENTER). The response will be either 1 or 0, depending on whether or not the value in C2 at this point is greater than 450.

3. To show this formula in more readable form, you can format it. Use MENU Format Other Literal and press (ENTER) to format F6. The result will be the text of the formula rather than its result.

4. Since the location of the database and criterion ranges has not changed, you can issue the MENU Query Find command at this point and Symphony will locate the first record in the list with a profit greater than 450, as shown in Figure 5-18.

If you move the highlight bar down, you will notice that Symphony does not find the record that has a profit of exactly 450,

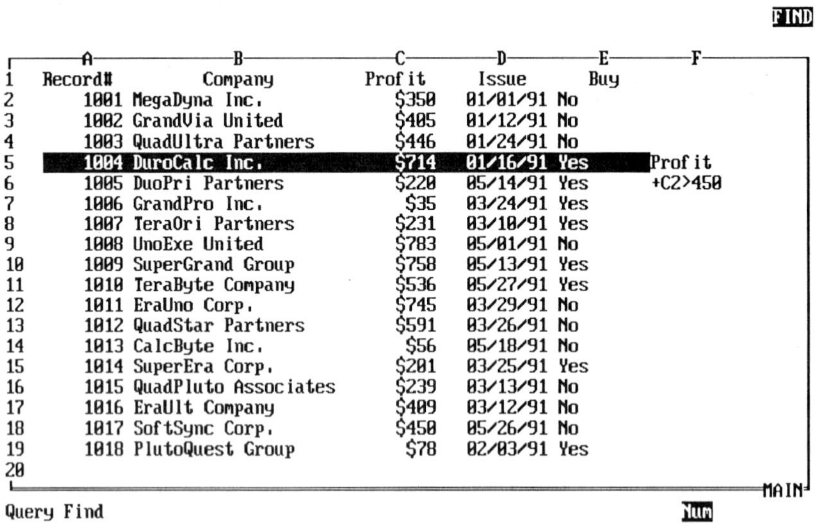

FIND

	A	B	C	D	E	F
1	Record#	Company	Profit	Issue	Buy	
2	1001	MegaDyna Inc.	$350	01/01/91	No	
3	1002	GrandVia United	$405	01/12/91	No	
4	1003	QuadUltra Partners	$446	01/24/91	No	
5	1004	DuroCalc Inc.	$714	01/16/91	Yes	Profit
6	1005	DuoPri Partners	$220	05/14/91	Yes	+C2>450
7	1006	GrandPro Inc.	$35	03/24/91	Yes	
8	1007	TeraOri Partners	$231	03/10/91	Yes	
9	1008	UnoExe United	$783	05/01/91	No	
10	1009	SuperGrand Group	$758	05/13/91	Yes	
11	1010	TeraByte Company	$536	05/27/91	Yes	
12	1011	EraUno Corp.	$745	03/29/91	No	
13	1012	QuadStar Partners	$591	03/26/91	No	
14	1013	CalcByte Inc.	$56	05/18/91	No	
15	1014	SuperEra Corp.	$201	03/25/91	Yes	
16	1015	QuadPluto Associates	$239	03/13/91	No	
17	1016	EraUlt Company	$409	03/12/91	No	
18	1017	SoftSync Corp.	$450	05/26/91	No	
19	1018	PlutoQuest Group	$78	02/03/91	Yes	
20						

MAIN

Query Find NUM

FIGURE 5-18 The completed find operation

since the > symbol means "greater than." To leave FIND mode and return to SHEET mode, press (CTRL-BREAK).

To make the use of formulas like this a little easier, Symphony allows you to use range names instead of the cell coordinates of the first piece of data in each database field. In fact, there is a quick way of assigning range names to each of the cells on row 2 from A2 through E2, using the labels in row 1:

1. With the cell pointer in A1, select MENU Range Name Labels and then select Down. With this command each label in row 1 will name the cell below.

2. Press (END) and (RIGHT ARROW) to extend the highlighting from A1 through E1. Press (ENTER) to confirm.

3. You will immediately see the formula in F6 change: The reference to cell C2 changes to PROFIT. To see this more clearly, move the cell pointer to column F and use MENU Width Set to enter a new column width of **12**. The full formula will now be visible.

The Question of Dates

When you are using dates in a database and want to locate specific dates or a range of date values, you need to be careful. If you enter dates using the @DATE function, as in @DATE(91,1,1), used in the sample database, you cannot locate a specific date simply by using the date value. For example, to find any companies issuing shares on a particular date, as in March 12, 1991, you might try using the field name Issue in F5 and the formula @DATE(91,3,12) in F6. Unfortunately, this will locate all of the records, not just the one you want to find.

You can get around this problem in several ways. You can change the date in the criterion in F6 from a date function to a date serial number. To do this you highlight the cell, press (F2) followed by (F8), and then press (ENTER). The Find command will then be able to locate the correct record.

As an alternative, you could convert all of the values in the date field to serial numbers with the Range Values command. In the example, this would mean selecting D2..D19 as the FROM range and also as the TO range. The appearance of the dates would not change, but the actual contents of the cells would. Cell D1 would change from @DATE(91,1,1) to 33239. You could then use the date in the criterion as before, entering @DATE(91,3,12) and then converting it to a serial number.

A further alternative is to leave the dates entered as @DATE functions and use a logical formula as the criterion. The formula would be +D2=@DATE(91,3,12). If D2 is named ISSUE, then the formula would appear as +ISSUE=@DATE(91,3,12) and could be entered that way. When querying dates, always check the form that the dates take in the database and check the results of the Find command.

Multiple Fields

So far, you have seen a single criterion in action. You can create multiple criteria to narrow down a search. One way to do this is to create a criterion range that includes all of the field names, since you can include more fields in a criterion range than you actually use in any one query. For this reason, and in order to keep field names straight, one common method for creating a criteria table is to copy the entire row of field names from the database table to a separate part of the worksheet. You can see that this has been done here and that the criterion range is being redefined:

```
Criterion range: A21..E22                                              POINT

       A          B          C         D        E         F         G         H
17       1016 EraUlt Co   $409 03/12/91 No
18       1017 SoftSync    $450 05/26/91 No
19       1018 PlutoQues     $78 02/03/91 Yes
20
21   Record#    Company  Profit    Issue      Buy
22
23
24
```

To create a multiple criteria range like this, follow these instructions, which include a trick called "reverse copy":

1. Place the cell pointer below the database in A21. An easy way to do this is to press (HOME) and then (PGDN).

2. Now issue the MENU Copy command, and press (ESC) when prompted with A21..A21 as the range to copy from.

3. Press (HOME) to move the cell selector back to A1. Press (TAB) to anchor the copy FROM range at A1, and then press (END) and (RIGHT ARROW) to move the cell pointer to E1, creating a FROM range of A1..E1. Press (ENTER) to confirm this.

4. The cell pointer now returns to A21, the top left cell of the range to which you want to copy A1..E1, so press (ENTER) to complete the copy. This method of copying, starting with the TO range, has the advantage of leaving the cell pointer in the starting cell when the command is completed.

5. With a copy of the field names now on row 21 and the cell pointer in A21, you can define A21..E22 as the new criterion range. Select MENU Query Settings Basic Criterion, and the existing range will be highlighted. Press (BACKSPACE) and the range will be unlocked, with the cell pointer back in A21.

6. Press (TAB) to anchor the beginning point of the range, and then you press (END) followed by (RIGHT ARROW). Now you press (DOWN ARROW) once and press (ENTER) to confirm the new setting of A21..E22.

Notice that row 22 is being included in the criterion range. If nothing is entered in this row, the next Find command will locate every record. To find all records with a Yes recommendation that have issue dates after 3/15/91, do the following:

1. At cell D22, type **+ISSUE>=@DATE(91,3,15)** and then press (ENTER).

2. At cell E22, type **Yes** and press (ENTER). The completed criteria will appear as in Figure 5-19 if you format cell D22 with the Format Other Literal command.

3. Select MENU Query Find. There should be five records that meet these combined criteria.

The AND/OR Question

If the entries beneath the field names in a multiple criteria range are all on the same line, as they are in Figure 5-19, then the relationship between them is AND. This means that a record must

```
D22: (L) +ISSUE>=@DATE(91,3,15)                                    SHEET
 ---------A-----------B-------------C-----------D---------E---------F---
21  Record#          Company        Profit      Issue      Buy
22                                          +ISSUE>=@D Yes
23
24
```

FIGURE 5-19 Multiple criteria entered

meet both criteria to be included in the locate operation. If the entries are on separate lines, the relationship is OR, meaning that Symphony locates records that match any one of the criteria. For example, if you move the entry in cell E22 to cell E23 using the Move command and then execute a Find, you will come up with many more records. That is because all records with Yes are included, regardless of issue date, as well as all records with issue dates of 3/15/91 or later, regardless of the buy recommendation.

Note When you use the Move command to relocate the Yes from E22 to E23, Symphony automatically extends the criterion range to include E23. However, it is wise to check the criterion range whenever you alter the criteria, just to make sure that Symphony is keeping track of the coordinates accurately.

Complex Formulated Criteria

To place additional qualifications on the criteria you use for querying items, you can use the following logical operators: AND, OR, and NOT. These are entered between # signs:

AND, as in +PROFIT>450#AND#BUY="Yes"
OR, as in +PROFIT>450#OR#BUY="Yes"
NOT, as in +PROFIT>450#NOT#ISSUE>@DATE(91,5,15)

Note that the formula must be preceded with a plus sign, and text that is being matched must be entered within double quotes. The AND, OR, and NOT operators must be placed in the formula within # signs or Symphony will get confused.

You can create multiple conditions with the logical operators to make your search more specific without using multiple criteria. To increase your options even further, Symphony allows you to supply parts of the formula from other cells. Thus, you could supply the parameters for a search from cell entries, as in a statement like

+PROFIT>450#AND#ISSUE>G7

where G7 contains a date value. You can also supply parameters for a search using functions, as in a statement like

+PROFIT>450#AND#ISSUE>@NOW

This will tell you if there are any companies with profits over 450 that have an issue date after whatever your computer thinks the current date is.

Alternative Criteria

Formulas are not the only way to increase flexibility in criteria. For example, you saw earlier that supplying two criteria on the same line meant that the relationship between them was AND, whereas placing them on separate lines implied an OR relationship. You can also use the same field name more than once in a criteria table, which can be to your advantage. For example, the following table will find all companies with profits between 300 and 400:

Profit	**Profit**
+C2>300	+C2<400

You can locate multiple groups by using the OR relationship, as in the following criteria table, which locates all records with less than 200 plus all those with 300 to 400:

Profit	**Profit**	**Profit**
+C2>300	+C2<400	
		+C2<200

Matching Text

To add scope to your searches for a text match, you can use wildcards. These are the question mark (?), the asterisk (*), and the tilde (~). The question mark stands for any character in that position in a string, as in **V?LE**, which would find VALE, VOLE, VILE, and so on. The asterisk means anything from this character to the end of the label, as in **VERN***, which would find anything beginning with VERN, like VERNAL, VERNON, and so on. The tilde means "not," as in **~TEXAS**, which means "anywhere but TEXAS."

If what you want to match is a piece of text in a criterion—that is, something that had been entered as a label or results in a label—and you want to incorporate it in a formula you must place it in double quotes, as in **"paris"**, which will find PARIS, Paris, and paris. When you use the comparison operators with labels, Symphony interprets > as meaning higher in the alphabet. This means you can use these operators with non-numeric fields like ZIP codes to specify codes equal to or greater than a certain number. For example, to locate all records with ZIP codes greater than 94100, you could use **+ZIP>="94100"**.

THE QUERY EXTRACT

So far, you have seen that Symphony is adept at locating records in a database table. At some point you will probably want Symphony to provide you with a list of items matching your criteria. You do this once you have established the database table and the criteria. The list can then be placed anywhere in the current worksheet.

What a Query Requires

You create a subset of data from a Symphony database by using the Extract command. The data meeting your criteria is copied into a separate area of the spreadsheet. The Extract command needs four pieces of information:

Where the data is	The database range
What to extract	The criterion range
Where to output	The output range: cells in which to place the extracted data
What data to output	The names of fields to be included in the output

If you have already used the Find feature, you will have used the first two items. The last two involve moving to an empty part of the worksheet and typing in the names of the fields you want reported.

The Output Range

Suppose you are planning to buy shares issued by companies with a Yes recommendation in sales on or after 3/15/91. To create a list of all such companies that includes name, issue date, and profit, you would

1. Check that the criterion range is set to A21..E22 and the entries match Figure 5-19.

2. Move the cell pointer to B25 and enter **Company**, enter **Profit** in cell C25, and enter **Issue** in cell D25.

3. When you have entered the names of the fields you want reported, you must next record the output range. Place your cursor on the leftmost field name, cell B25, and select Output

```
Copy all records matching criteria to Output range                        MENU
Settings  Find  Extract  Unique  Delete  Record-Sort  Parse  Quit
------A-----------------B---------------C----------D---------E---------F--------
21  Record#          Company          Profit      Issue      Buy
22                                              +ISSUE>=@D Yes
23
24
25          Company                 Issue     Profit
26          DuoPri Partners         05/14/91        $220
27          GrandPro Inc.           03/24/91         $35
28          SuperGrand Group        05/13/91        $758
29          TeraByte Company        05/27/91        $536
30          SuperEra Corp.          03/25/91        $201
31
32
33
34
35
36
37
38
39
40
--------------------------------------------------------------------------MAIN-
Query                                                  Calc       Num
```

FIGURE 5-20 Completed output

from the Query Settings Basic menu. Anchor the cell you are in, and press (END) and (RIGHT ARROW) to include all of the field names. The output range is defined as B25..D25.

4. With the output range defined, quit back to the Query menu and select Extract to tell Symphony to place copies of the records identified by your criteria into the output cells. Symphony uses the last criteria you defined to select the items. The results can be seen in Figure 5-20.

When you have performed the extract, the data can be printed, copied, or further manipulated. If you change the criteria or change the data in the database, a repeat of the Extract command will supply new data to this area of the worksheet, removing the current entries and replacing them with new ones. Numerous output ranges can be defined in one file by using named settings sheets.

Extract Tips

Extracted data is automatically formatted; that is, it retains the format it had within the database. You may want to format numbers in your output range differently before printing them. Extracted labels do retain their alignment.

When Symphony extracts numbers from the database to an output range, they are only numbers. Formulas in the database table are converted to their numeric value upon extraction.

In step 3 of the previous exercise, you defined the output range as a single line, the one that contained the field names for the list. You can extend the output range if you want to. If you do not move the highlighting down from the field names, you are telling Symphony that it can use any number of rows below the field names for the output. If you press (PGDN) once, you are saying that there are 20 lines available, and Symphony will highlight this area.

As your worksheets get crowded, it is a good idea to limit the output range like this so that Symphony is prevented from outputting over occupied cells. The problem with limiting the range is that large extracts might overflow the space you have allowed and result in the error message: "Too many records for Output range." If you are not cramped for space or if you place the output range on the last active row of the worksheet, you can just select the field names as the output range.

There is no limit to the number of fields you can include in the output range. The output range does not need to include fields that were part of the criteria. Of course, you can include all fields in the output if you want to. The order of fields in the output range can be different from the order in the database table, as you saw in the example.

Deleting Records

When you are cleaning up or maintaining a database table, you may need to get rid of records. One way of doing this is to find the record and then delete it with the Delete Row command. However, this has the possibly negative side effect of removing any data that is on the same row as the deleted record, all the way across the worksheet.

Symphony has an automated alternative, called Query Delete, that does not interfere with cells outside the database table. To use this command you set the criteria for the records you want deleted and then select Delete instead of Find or Extract. You will be prompted to confirm this action; because it means removing cells from the worksheet, it can be dangerous. Be certain that your criteria are correct before using this command and perform a File Save beforehand just in case something goes wrong.

Note You can always perform a Query Find before doing a Query Delete, just to make sure that your criteria are working as intended.

Unique Records

When the Extract function is performed, Symphony copies every matching record to the output range. If some records are duplicates of each other, Symphony copies both. You can prevent this by using Unique rather than Extract from the Query menu. Symphony will only copy one of the duplicate records to the output. This helps to avoid reporting errors.

When you are creating large database tables, it is not unusual for exact duplicate records to occur, particularly if more than one person is using the database table. However, any time you sort the database you can use the Unique option to remove duplicates.

Sorting Extracted Data

Once you have extracted data from a database table, you may well want to print it. Printing an output range is much like printing any other part of the worksheet. You can use the Print Settings Source

Range command to show Symphony which cells you want printed. However, you might want to sort the extracted information before printing it. Extracted data is a series of consecutive rows and named columns. In fact, it constitutes a new database. This database can be sorted by using a new settings sheet. To produce an alphabetical list by company name from the output created in the sample database shown in Figure 5-20, follow these steps:

1. Select MENU Query Settings Name, and choose Create. Type the name **LIST** and press (ENTER).
2. Select Name again, and choose Initial-Settings. This will clear the previous settings from LIST.
3. Choose Basic Database, and then define the range as B25..D30. Select Quit and then Sort-Keys.
4. Choose 1st-Key and choose cell B25. Use Ascending order. Choose Quit to get back to the Query menu, and choose Record-Sort followed by Unique. The effects on the output range are shown in Figure 5-21.

You now have a settings sheet that will allow you to sort the output range with a minimum of effort. As a final step, at this point you should save the file under a new name, **COMPANY4**, for use later in the chapter.

THE FORM ENVIRONMENT

So far, you have seen how the Query commands on the SHEET menu allow you to sort, search, and report database information. However, the data you have been working with is arranged in a table, and a fairly small one at that. As you work with larger tables

```
Sort data records                                                                MENU
Settings  Find  Extract  Unique  Delete  Record-Sort  Parse  Quit
┌─────A─────────────B──────────────C──────────D──────────E──────────F──────────┐
21  Record#         Company        Profit      Issue       Buy
22                                          +ISSUE>=@D Yes
23
24
25           Company               Issue     Profit
26           DuoPri Partners       05/14/91     $220
27           GrandPro Inc.         03/24/91      $35
28           SuperEra Corp.        03/25/91     $201
29           SuperGrand Group      05/13/91     $750
30           TeraByte Company      05/27/91     $536
```

FIGURE 5-21 Sorted output range

that extend across several screens, locating specific data to edit can get difficult.

In the FORM environment Symphony provides a streamlined method of entering data and issuing search commands. Records are presented one at a time like cards in a file. The actual data entered through the FORM environment is still stored in the worksheet, and Symphony still uses database, criterion, and output ranges to manage the data, but the FORM environment provides a simplified "front end" that many users will appreciate.

Creating a Database In the FORM Environment

Creating a database in the FORM environment requires a little bit of planning. You need to decide the names of the fields, what type of information they will contain, and how long the entries in each field will be. You then define the database, using this information. You begin with a series of labels, one for each field in the database. Each label consists of three parts: the name of the field, a single-letter code for the type of data in the field, and the length of the field in characters. The type codes are: Label (L), Number (N), Date (D), Time (T), and Computed (C).

To build a database like the one used previously in this chapter, but using the FORM environment, follow these steps:

1. In a new worksheet, enter a series of five labels in column A, one for each field in the database. Each label consists of three parts connected with colons, as shown here:

```
A1: 'Record#:L:9                                                    SHEET
┌────A────────B─────────C─────────D─────────E─────────F─────────G─────────H────┐
1  Record#:L:9
2  Company:L:20
3  Profit:N:9
4  Issue:D:9
5  Buy:L:4
6
7
```

   Enter them in A1 through A5, just as they appear here.

2. Press the TYPE key ((ALT-F10)) and choose FORM. A fairly blank screen will appear, as shown in Figure 5-22.

3. Press MENU and note the different set of choices. Select Generate. You will be asked for a field type. This is the default type that Symphony will assume if you do not define each field type separately. Since you have already defined each type, just choose Label.

4. You will be asked for a field length. This is the length that Symphony will assume if you do not define each field length separately. Since you have already defined each length, just press (ENTER) to accept the default of 9.

5. Now you need to choose a name for the database settings sheet that Symphony will generate. Press (ENTER) to accept the default choice: MAIN.

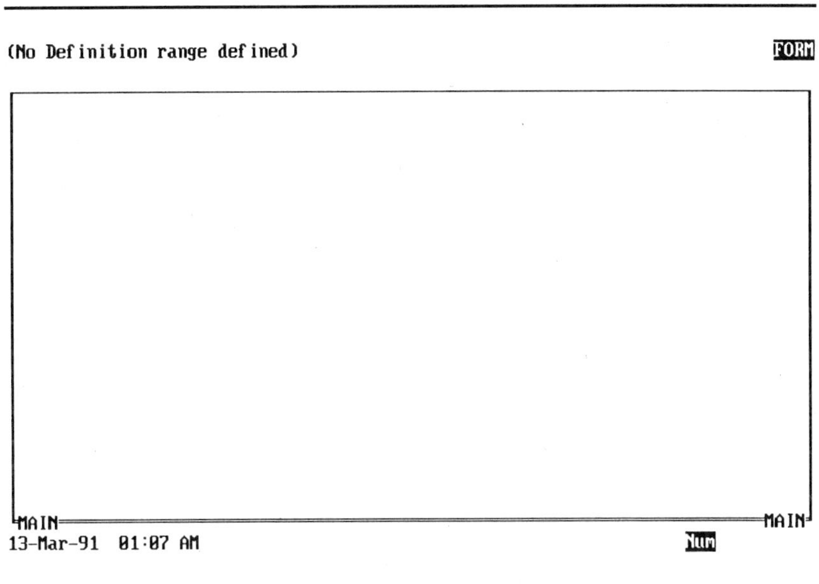

FIGURE 5-22 First view of the FORM environment

6. Symphony now asks for the range where the field names are located and shows you the worksheet. Indicate the range A1..A5 and press (ENTER). Symphony presents a database form like the one in Figure 5-23.

The first line of the screen tells you that you are creating a new record; you are inserting record 1. The second line prompts you to make an entry in the Record# field, where the cursor is flashing. Each field that you have defined is presented with enough spaces to accommodate entries of the length you specified.

Data Entry Commands

To enter a new record in a database using the data entry form, you type in data in each field in turn. After typing an entry you press

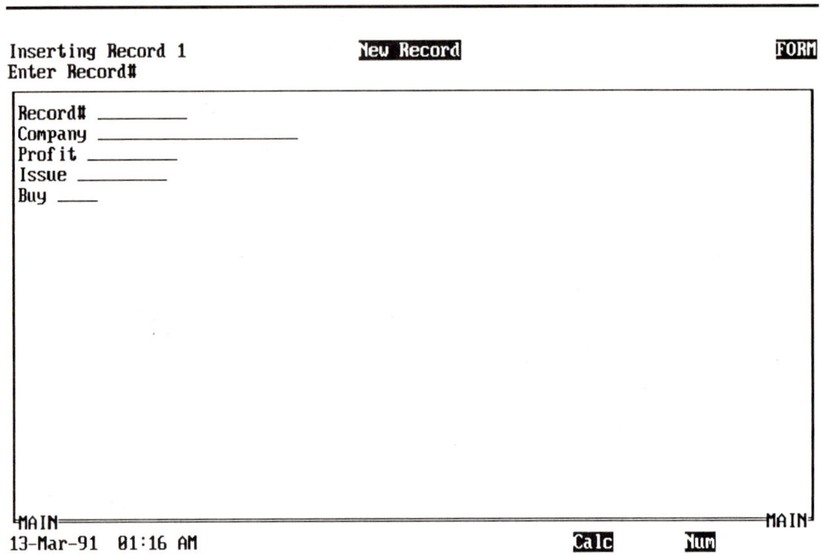

FIGURE 5-23 The Symphony data entry form

ENTER, which inserts the entry and moves the cursor to the next field. Go ahead and type the record number, **1001**, and note that the characters appear in normal text. If you make a mistake, just press BACKSPACE to erase it and try again. When you have typed the entry correctly, press ENTER. You will see the data you have entered is now shown in boldface.

Now type the company name, **MegaDyna Inc.**, and press ENTER. When you have filled in at least one field in a record, you can move through the record from field to field. If you want to move to the next field of the current record, four different keys can be used: DOWN ARROW, RIGHT ARROW, ENTER, and TAB. To move the edit cursor to the previous field, you should use either the UP ARROW or LEFT ARROW. Use CTRL-LEFT ARROW (Big-Left) to move the cursor to the first noncomputed field of the record and

```
Editing Record 1 of 1                                                  FORM
Enter Record#

Record# 1001_____
Company MegaDyna Inc._______
Profit 350______
Issue 01-Jan-91
Buy Yes_

MAIN                                                                   MAIN
13-Mar-91  01:50 AM                                  Calc        Num
```

FIGURE 5-24 First record entered

use (CTRL-RIGHT ARROW) (Big-Right) to move the cursor to the last noncomputed field of the record.

Go ahead and type the profit figure of **350** and note that when you press (ENTER), the number is not formatted. The formatting will be added later. To enter the issue date just type **1/1/91** and press (ENTER). You will see that the form uses date format 1 as a default format for dates. Go ahead and enter **Yes** in the last field. Note that when you press (ENTER), the cursor moves back to the first field, which allows you to edit the record if you need to. Editing will be dealt with in a moment. At this point, the data in the fields will appear as shown in Figure 5-24. To add the first record to the database and create a second one, you press (INS).

To go back to the previous record, press (PGUP) and you will see that the top status line now says "Editing Record 1 of 1." Press

(PGDN) and you will be back at the second record. Complete it with the following information:

1002 GrandVia United 405 1/12/91 No

Press (INS) to enter the second record and create a third. Complete the third record with this information:

1003 Quad Ultra Partners 446 1/24/91 No

Now press (PGUP), which will add the new record to the database and display the previous record. Other keys that you can press while adding new records are (END), which adds the record to the database and leaves it in as the current record, and the (HOME) key, which adds the record to the database and displays the first record in the database. You can now press (HOME) to see record 1 and (END) to see record 3. Press GOTO ((F5)), type **2**, and press (ENTER). This will take you to record 2.

(Don't worry: You won't be adding any more records in this manner. The records in the previous file, COMPANY4, will be added to this database shortly).

Editing Records

Once you are viewing a record, you can examine, edit, or delete it. Bear in mind that entries in boldface characters have been entered into the database. Pressing (DEL) when all entries are in boldface will tell Symphony you want to delete the complete record. Symphony will ask you to confirm this with a message at the top of the screen and a No/Yes choice.

To alter an entry in any field except a computed field, use the movement keys to move the cursor to the field you want to change. To make a new entry that replaces the existing contents of the field, simply type the new entry and press (ENTER). To edit the field, press

EDIT ((F2)), make your changes, and press (TAB) or (ENTER) when you are done.

While you are in EDIT mode, you can press (DEL) to remove one character at a time, as when you are editing worksheet cell entries. The (HOME) and (END) keys work in EDIT mode to move the cursor to the beginning and end of the entry. The Big-Left and Big-Right keys move the cursor within the entry five characters to the left and right, respectively.

To clear the entry completely while you are in EDIT mode, you can press (ESC). Pressing (ESC) a second time will restore the contents of the field to the way they were before you edited them. To restore the entire record to the values it contained before you edited it, press (ESC) a third time. To delete the contents of a field once they have been entered, move to the desired field and press (BACKSPACE).

Editing records can be a little confusing at first, since the actions of the keystrokes are different enough from those in the SHEET or DOC environment to cause hesitation. The two main points to remember are as follows:

- Records in boldface are already entered, and you need to press EDIT to change them.

- To delete an entry from a field, the sequence is (F2), then (ESC), then (ENTER).

You can add edited records to the database with one of several keys. The (INS) key adds the record and leaves the cursor in first field. The (PGUP) key adds the record and displays the previous record. The (PGDN) key adds the record and displays the next record. The (HOME) key adds the record and displays the first record in the database, and (END) adds the record and displays the last record in the database. The keys used to move between records are summarized in Table 5-2.

UP ARROW or LEFT ARROW	Moves cursor to previous field
DOWN ARROW	Moves cursor to next field
RIGHT ARROW	Moves cursor to next field
TAB	Moves cursor to next field
ENTER	Moves cursor to next field
Big-Left	Moves cursor to first noncomputed field
Big-Right	Moves cursor to last noncomputed field
PGUP	Displays previous record (also adds record to database if you are entering a new record)
END	Displays last record (if you are entering new record it also adds record to database)
HOME	Displays first record in database (also adds record to database if you are entering new record)
GOTO	Asks for specific record number and displays the record you request
INS	Adds new record to the database and lets you enter another one
ESC	Pressed once, clears the current field; twice, clears all the fields and restores any default values; three times, clears the record and displays previous record

TABLE 5-2 Keys to Navigate Records in the FORM Environment

Performing a Sort In the FORM Environment

To sort records in the FORM environment, you define sort keys, just as you did in SHEET mode. Although this is a very small database, try an alphabetical sort by company name.

1. Press MENU and notice that a blank data entry form replaces the record you were viewing. From the menu, select Settings.

```
Database, Criterion, Output ranges                                              MENU
Basic  Form  Underscores  Sort-Keys  Report  One-Record  Name  Cancel  Quit
┌──────────────────────────────────────────────────────────────────────────────┐
│Basic Ranges                               Report Ranges                      │
│  Database:        MAIN_DB                   Main:          MAIN_MA           │
│  Criterion:       MAIN_CR                   Above:         MAIN_AB           │
│  Output:                                    Below:                           │
│Form Ranges                                  Type           Single            │
│  Entry:           MAIN_EN                     Entry list:                    │
│  Definition:      MAIN_DF                     Input cell:                    │
│Underscores:       Yes                     One-Record:      No                │
│Sort-Keys                                                                     │
│  1st-Key:                   2nd-Key:                  3rd-Key:               │
│    Order:                     Order:                    Order:               │
└════════════════════════════════════════════════Database Settings: MAIN┘
```

FIGURE 5-25 Database settings sheet

Note that many sections of the settings sheet have already been completed, as shown in Figure 5-25. When you used the Generate command, Symphony assigned names to various ranges in the worksheet, including the database range and criterion range. These will be examined in more detail later.

2. Select Sort-Keys and then 1st-Key. Symphony presents the part of the worksheet it is using to store the records you entered through the form. At this point you want to highlight the field name "Company" in B28 and press (ENTER).

3. Select Ascending for the sort order, and then press (ESC) (not Quit) to move back to the main menu, where you can select Record-Sort followed by Unique.

After a sort, Symphony returns you to the data entry form you were viewing before pressing MENU. When you are using the FORM environment's Settings menu, remember that the Quit option takes you back to the form, not one step back in the menu system as it did in the SHEET environment.

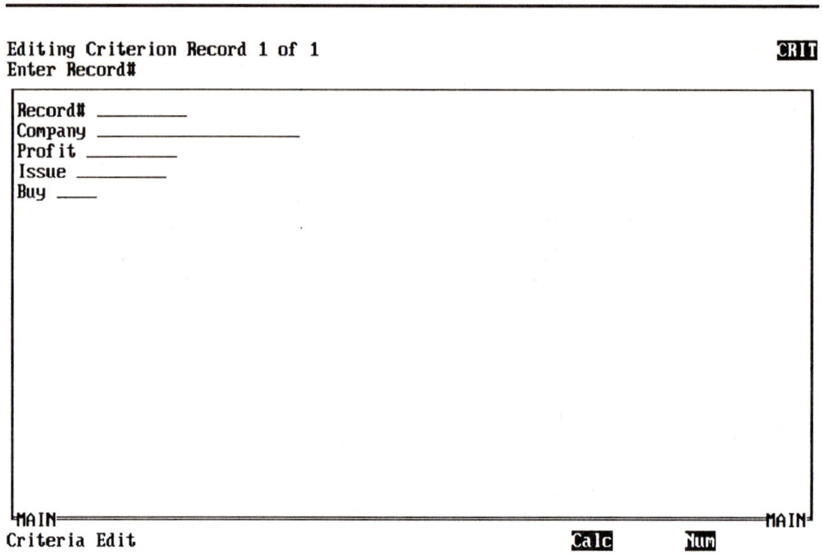

FIGURE 5-26 Editing criterion record 1 of 1

Setting Criteria

Sorting records in the FORM environment is much the same as in the SHEET environment, but the way you set up criteria in the FORM environment is somewhat different. Suppose you want to find record 1002:

1. Press MENU and select Criteria. You have three choices: Use, Ignore, and Edit. Select Edit, and you will be editing criterion record 1 of 1, as shown in Figure 5-26. Note that you are now in Criterion mode, indicated by the message "CRIT" in the mode indicator.

2. You use this form as though it were a data entry record, but you only enter information that you want to match. In this case you type **1002** in the Record# field and press (ENTER).

3. Now you press (INS) to insert the criterion record and then (PGUP) to return to the form. Press MENU and select Criteria Use, and you will be presented with any records that match the entry you made in the criterion record, as shown here:

```
Editing Record 1 of 3 (1 Match)                                    FORM
Enter Record#

Record# 1002____
Company GrandVia United____
Profit 405_____
Issue 12-Jan-91
Buy No__
```

Symphony tells you which record you are viewing (1 of 3) and how many records match your criteria (1 match). If there is more than one matching record, you can move from record to record with the regular movement keys listed in Table 5-2. When you select Criteria Use, Symphony groups matched records in a minidatabase or subset of records. To return to the entire database, use Criteria Ignore. To change or add criteria, use Criteria Edit.

Entries in the criterion records of the FORM environment work much the same way as the criterion range in the SHEET mode. You enter simple numbers and text for exact matches. For a range of text values, you use the wildcards. For a range of numeric values, you use formulas. Formulas are slightly easier to enter in the FORM environment. For example, to find all companies with a profit figure greater than 500, you would enter **+?>500** in the Profit field of the criterion record. The use of the question mark rather than a range name or cell reference simplifies matters.

Note If you issue the Criteria Use command and then use Criteria Edit to alter the criteria, you do not have to reissue the Criteria Use command. The criteria will already be in effect when you press (PGUP) to finish editing the criterion record.

To use multiple criteria, you enter each additional criterion in the appropriate field of criterion record 1 if you want the criteria to have the AND relationship. For example, this criterion record has been edited to find all companies with over 400 in the Profit field and issue dates after 1/15/91:

```
Editing Criterion Record 1 of 1                                    CRIT
Enter Record#

Record# ________
Company ________________
Profit +PROFIT>4
Issue +ISSUE>@D
Buy ____
```

The full formulas cannot be seen, but they are +?>400 and +?>@DATE(91,1,15), respectively.

To set up an OR relationship between criteria—for example, to find all companies that begin with "C" or "G"—you will use a second criterion record. This is created automatically when you press (PGDN) while using the Edit Criteria command. In this case, the first criterion record would contain C* in the Company field, while the second record would contain G* in the Company field.

To remove a criterion from a field, you move the cursor to the field, press (F2), then (ESC), and then (ENTER). To remove unwanted criterion records, you press (DEL) and answer Yes. If you use criteria and there is no match, Symphony will give you an error message and you must press (ESC) to return to the data entry form.

THE WORKINGS OF THE FORM ENVIRONMENT

At this point, you might want to see how Symphony is using the underlying worksheet to store the entries you make through the data entry form. To see the worksheet, just press (ALT-F9). This is the key that switches you between the current environment and the

```
A1: 'Record#:L:9                                                          SHEET

   A             B                C          D      E       F         G
1  Record#:L:9
2  Company:L:20
3  Profit:N:9
4  Issue:D:9
5  Buy:L:4
6
7  Record# ________
8  Company ___________________
9  Profit ________
10 Issue ________
11 Buy ___
12
13 Name      Value               Type      Default  FormValidity Input
14 Record#   1002                L:9
15 Company   GrandVia United     L:20
16 Profit                    405 N:9
17 Issue               12-Jan-91 D:9
18 Buy       No                  L:4
19
20 Record#   Company             Profit    Issue    Buy
                                                                         MAIN
13-Mar-91  11:38 AM                                                Num
```

FIGURE 5-27 The SHEET view

previous one. In the case of the sample database, the view in the SHEET environment looks like Figure 5-27.

The Database Ranges

The collection of information in the worksheet in Figure 5-27 defines the database and the entry form, beginning with the entries you made to set up the database. The information is arranged in several different groups and extends beyond one screen. The entire area of the worksheet used by the Generate command in the FORM environment can be seen in Figure 5-28, where the different sections are pointed out.

Note The asterisks in the database area result from the storage of formatted dates in a column that is only nine characters wide. The width of the columns in the SHEET environment is determined by

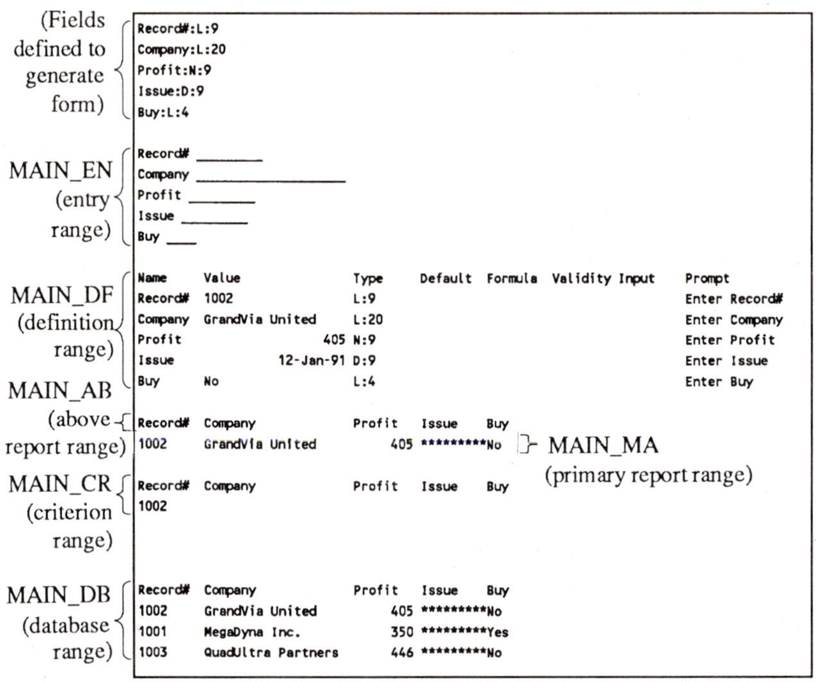

FIGURE 5-28 The data management ranges

the lengths you specify for the fields, so that column A is the width of the first field, column B is the width of the second field, and so forth.

Symphony assigns range names to each piece of information it needs for the FORM environment. Some of these names use the name you chose for the FORM settings when you generated the database (in this case, MAIN). You saw in Figure 5-25 that these names are automatically used in the database settings sheet; for example, the database range is called MAIN_DB. The full set of range names created by Symphony is listed in Figure 5-29. (The table in Figure 5-29 was created using the worksheet command

```
P1: 'BUY                                                                   SHEET

    ---P--------Q---------R---------S---------T---------U---------V---------W----
1   BUY      E29        A field name, used in criteria
2   COMPANY  B29        A field name, used in criteria
3   ISSUE    D29        A field name, used in criteria
4   MAIN_AB  A20..E20   The Above range, stores text used for report headings
5   MAIN_CR  A23..E24   The Criterion range, stores the criteria you set
6   MAIN_DB  A28..E31   The Database range, stores the records you enter
7   MAIN_DF  A14..H18   The Definition range, stores field definitions
8   MAIN_EN  A7..A11    The Entry range, stores the text of the data entry form
9   MAIN_MA  A21..E21   The Main range, used in producing reports
10  PROFIT   C29        A field name, used in criteria
11  RECORD#  A29        A field name, used in criteria
12
13
14
15
16
17
18
19
20
                                                                           MAIN
13-Mar-91  12:30 PM                                                 Num
```

FIGURE 5-29 Range name table

Range Name Table. The cell pointer was placed in P1 before the command was issued. The command produced the list in columns P and Q; the notes in column R were added manually.)

```
A7: 'Record# : _______                                                  SHEET

    ---A-------------B-------------C---------D---------E---------F---------G---
1   Record#:L:9
2   Company:L:20
3   Profit:N:9
4   Issue:D:9
5   Buy:L:4
6
7   Record# : _______
8   Company : ________________
9    Profit : _______
10    Issue : _______
11      Buy : ___
12
```

FIGURE 5-30 Edited entry form in SHEET environment

The Entry Range

This is a series of labels used to create the data entry form. Each field has a label consisting of the field name and a series of underlines. The number of underlines is equal to the field length. You can edit these labels to alter the appearance of the form. For example, in Figure 5-30, you can see that the labels in the entry range have been edited to line up flush-right. The effect of this back in the FORM environment is shown here:

```
Editing Record 1 of 3                                        FORM
Enter Record#

Record# : 1002____
Company : GrandVia United____
 Profit : 405_____
  Issue : 12-Jan-91
    Buy : No__
```

You can also change the names of fields as they appear in the data entry form. For example, in a name and address database you might have fields called Last and First, but the names in the entry form can be edited to read Last Name and First Name without affecting the operation of the database.

Definition Range

The definition range is a very powerful part of the database system. Each column of this area performs a special function.

NAME This column lists the names of the fields used in the database. The field names are listed in the order in which they appear in the data entry form.

VALUE This column lists the values of the record that was current when you switched to the SHEET environment. The values are listed to help you establish formulas and formats. If you want to add formatting to values stored in the database, you do so by formatting the appropriate cells in this column. For example, you would format B16 as Currency, zero decimal places, and B17 as Date format 4 if you wanted to match the formatting of the earlier sample database. To create formulas for computed fields, see the following section on formulas.

TYPE This column stores the field type and length. When you set up the database, you specified both of these parameters; however, you need only specify parameters that vary from the defaults you select. Thus, you could have chosen Label as the default type and 9 as the default length and used the following in cells A1..A5 for the Generate command: Record#, Company:20, Profit:N, Issue:D, Buy:4. Where parameters are not stated, Symphony supplies the defaults. Note that when you edit the entry range, you can use less underline characters than the number of characters specified in the field length. When you do this and are entering data, Symphony will scroll any entry longer than the underlined field space to enable you to complete the entry or edit it later.

DEFAULT This column stores values that you want Symphony to enter automatically in every new record. For example, when compiling a name and address list of customers, most of whom live in the same city, you could enter the city name in the default area, on the appropriate row for the city field. Any data that is entered automatically in this way can always be edited to something else later. Also, you can switch to the SHEET environment at any time and either remove or change the default values.

FORMULA This column contains any calculations you need in each record. For example, if an employee database contains a field called Hours and a field called Rate, you could have a field called Pay that is the contents of Rate times the contents of Hours. You would set this up by creating Pay as a computed field, using a definition like this: Pay:C:9. The field would be empty until you entered the formula in the Formula area of the definition range. The formula would use the cell coordinates of the sample values in the Value column, so that it might read +B15*B16. As soon as a formula is entered in the Formula column, it is calculated for all of the records in the database if you press (F8), the CALC key.

VALIDITY This column can contain what are sometimes referred to as "data entry checks," tests that determine if the operator has entered acceptable data in a field. Symphony already performs a check of this type, making sure that all entries match the field type. You can complement this with a conditional formula. For example, in the sample database the Buy field must contain either Yes or No. You would enter this formula in cell F18 to check entries in the Buy field:

+B18="No"#OR#B18="Yes"

If you return to the FORM environment and try to enter anything other than Yes or No in the Buy field, you will get an error message and be told that the entry is invalid.

This technique helps prevent extra zeros from being added by mistake in numeric fields. In the employee pay example, if the Hour field is represented in cell B15 of the definition range and the field should contain no value greater than 60, the formula +B15<60 would be entered on row 15 of the Validity column.

INPUT This is a temporary holding column for entries. What you are typing as a fresh entry is stored here while the entry is being created.

PROMPT This column holds the text displayed when you are entering data in the form. As you can see, the default text is the word "Enter" plus the name of the field. This can be made much more helpful. For example, in the case of the Profit field, you could change the prompt text to

```
Enter the profit figure, in 1000s, as listed on form K2
```

The prompt text is one area in which you can easily customize the data entry form and make it easier for others to use.

The Criterion Range

This stores the criteria you create in the FORM environment with the Criteria Edit command. The criterion range will have as many lines in it as there are criterion records. You can alter criteria in the SHEET environment, but it is safer to use the Criteria Edit command in the FORM environment.

The Database Range

This is simply the area used to store the records. The field names are used as column headings, and the range extends as far down the worksheet as needed to accommodate the entries you make. You can add records to the database in the SHEET environment as long as you remember to expand this definition of the database range name to include the new records.

Combining Records In the SHEET Environment

If you created the sample SHEET environment database earlier in this chapter, the one with the Record# field that was last saved as COMPANY4, you can use records from that file to expand the sample FORM database. This is a fairly common operation when you are combining information from several worksheets into a

```
Replace cells in worksheet with cells from file                              MENU
Copy  Add  Subtract
  ----A--------B---------------C--------D--------E--------F--------G---
21  1002     GrandVia United           405 *********No
22
23  Record#  Company              Profit    Issue    Buy
24  1002
25
26
27
28  Record#  Company              Profit    Issue    Buy
29  1002     GrandVia United           405 *********No
30  1001     MegaDyna Inc.             350 *********Yes
31  1003     QuadUltra Partners        446 *********No
32
33
34
35
36
37
38
39
40
                                                                        MAIN
File Combine                                                       Num
```

FIGURE 5-31 Using the Combine command

single database. To prepare for this, first save the FORM database file, using the name **COMPFORM**.

1. In SHEET mode, place the cell pointer in A32, the cell just below the last entry in the database range. Press SERVICES and select File Combine Copy, as shown in Figure 5-31.

2. Select Entire-File, and then Ignore, followed by Values. Symphony will present a file list.

3. Select COMPANY4, the name you used for the previous database file the last time you saved it. The cells in the COMPANY4 file are read into the current worksheet, as shown in Figure 5-32.

4. As you can see, there is some extraneous material that needs to be removed. To delete the row containing the field names, issue the Delete Rows command and press (ENTER).

```
A32: 'Record#                                                           SHEET

     A          B                   C          D       E        F        G
21  1002      GrandVia United          405 *********No
22
23  Record#   Company               Profit    Issue    Buy
24  1002
25
26
27
28  Record#   Company               Profit    Issue    Buy
29  1002      GrandVia United          405 *********No
30  1001      MegaDyna Inc.            350 *********Yes
31  1003      QuadUltra Partners       446 *********No
32  Record#         Company            Profit     Issue     Buy
33        1001 MegaDyna Inc.          $350 01/01/91 No
34        1002 GrandVia United        $405 01/12/91 No
35        1003 QuadUltra Partners     $446 01/24/91 No
36        1004 DuroCalc Inc.          $714 01/16/91 Yes
37        1005 DuoPri Partners        $220 05/14/91 Yes
38        1006 GrandPro Inc.           $35 03/24/91 Yes
39        1007 TeraOri Partners       $231 03/10/91 Yes
40        1008 UnoExe United          $783 05/01/91 No
                                                                        MAIN
13-Mar-91  02:37 PM                                              Num
```

FIGURE 5-32 Completed combine operation

5. Using (END) and (DOWN ARROW), move to the last record, and then press (DOWN ARROW) to go one row further down. You want to delete this row and all others below it. Press MENU, select Delete and then Rows, and press (END) followed by (HOME). This will remove all of the extra rows in the worksheet.

6. Now you want to redefine the MAIN_DB range to include the new records. Select Range Name Create and press (F10) to see all of the range names. Select MAIN_DB and press (END) and (DOWN ARROW) to include all of the cells. Press (ENTER) to confirm the new range.

7. You can now press (ALT-F9) to switch back to the FORM environment. There should be a lot more records—21 in total.

By using the File Combine command, you can bring data from one file into another. Be sure that you issue this command from a safe location, such as below all the active rows of the database. This will ensure that the incoming data does not overwrite existing information.

Report Ranges

When you want to create a report from a database stored in the FORM environment, you use the SERVICES Print command. You must select Settings and then Source to select Database as the source of the information to be printed. If you have several databases in the same worksheet, you will see the names listed and you can choose the one you want to print from.

When you ask Symphony to print with Database as the source, it will print all records that are currently available, which will be the entire database unless you have issued the Criteria Use command to select a subgroup of records. When Criteria Use is in effect, only the matching records will be printed.

When Symphony prints with Database as the source, the area of the worksheet known as the above range is printed first, followed by the records, one per line. You can set headers and footers for the report by using the same print commands as in Chapters 3 and 4. Beyond this, you can expand the above range to include additional text. For example, to include a memo with the report, you would do the following:

1. To locate the above range, switch to the SHEET environment and press (F5). Press (F10) twice to show the full list of range names. Select MAIN_AB, the above range for the MAIN database. Your cell pointer is now in the first cell of this range.

2. Select Insert and Row. Then press (DOWN ARROW) five times and press (ENTER). This will provide some space for the memo. Now type the text shown here as a series of labels in column A, pressing (ENTER) at the end of each line:

```
A22: 'From: Marketing                                              SHEET
 ┌──────A───────────B───────────C─────────D─────────E─────────F─────────G───┐
21
22  From: Marketing
23  To: Sales
24  Re: Current Issues
25
```

3. Now you need to expand the MAIN_AB range so that it stretches from A20 through E26. Choose Range Name Create and press (F10) to see the list of names. Select MAIN_AB, and use (UP ARROW) to include the rows up to 20 as shown in Figure 5-33. Press (ENTER) to confirm the new range.

4. To print the report, press SERVICES and select Print Settings Source Database. Then choose MAIN. If all of the other settings are in place, such as margins and destination, then you can use the Print Go command to print the report.

```
Range name: MAIN_AB                     Specify range: A20..E26        POINT
 ┌──────A───────────B───────────C─────────D─────────E─────────F─────────G───┐
8   Company ___________________
9   Profit ________
10  Issue ________
11  Buy ___
12
13  Name      Value               Type      Default  Formula  Validity Input
14  Record#   1001                L:9
15  Company   MegaDyna Inc.       L:20
16  Profit              $350      N:9
17  Issue           01/01/91      D:9
18  Buy       Yes                 L:4
19
20  MEMO
21
22  From: Marketing
23  To: Sales
24  Re: Current Issues
25
26  Record#   Company             Profit    Issue     Buy
27  1001      MegaDyna Inc.            350 *********Yes
                                                                        MAIN
Range Name Create                                               Num
```

FIGURE 5-33 Expanding the MAIN_AB range

MEMO

From: Marketing
To: Sales
Re: Current Issues

Record#	Company	Profit	Issue	Buy
1001	MegaDyna Inc.	$350	01/01/91	No
1002	GrandVia United	$405	01/12/91	No
1003	QuadUltra Partners	$446	01/24/91	No
1004	DuroCalc Inc.	$714	01/16/91	Yes
1005	DuoPri Partners	$220	05/14/91	Yes
1006	GrandPro Inc.	$35	03/24/91	Yes
1007	TeraOri Partners	$231	03/10/91	Yes
1008	UnoExe United	$783	05/01/91	No
1009	SuperGrand Group	$758	05/13/91	Yes
1010	TeraByte Company	$536	05/27/91	Yes
1011	EraUno Corp.	$745	03/29/91	No
1012	QuadStar Partners	$591	03/26/91	No
1013	CalcByte Inc.	$56	05/18/91	No
1014	SuperEra Corp.	$201	03/25/91	Yes
1015	QuadPluto Associates	$239	03/13/91	No
1016	EraUlt Company	$409	03/12/91	No
1017	SoftSync Corp.	$450	05/26/91	No
1018	PlutoQuest Group	$78	02/03/91	Yes

FIGURE 5-34 Printed report

The results will look something like Figure 5-34. If you want to use extensive text, you can create a DOC window to type it. You can also use a DOC window to create a form letter that is addressed to records stored in the FORM environment. This technique is described in Chapter 11.

SUMMARY

Symphony has a complete range of database commands in both the SHEET and FORM environments. Which environment you use for your database work will depend on the quantity and complexity of your data. The SHEET environment is fairly easy to use for small tasks. The FORM environment offers the sort of automation and convenience you will need for large-scale data entry.

Both the SHEET and FORM environments make extensive use of range names and named settings to manage information and options. By using named settings, you can quickly change the way you look at data and even manage several different sets of data within one file.

In addition to sorting, searching, and printing database information, Symphony can analyze data with formulas. This ability is discussed in Chapter 10, where you can also learn about the @BASE add-in application, which provides yet another technique for managing data in Symphony.

6

BUSINESS GRAPHICS

This chapter describes how to create graphs with Symphony. Graphs are visual representations of numeric data and can be an effective means of communicating facts and figures. Symphony has an extensive range of commands to help you design a wide variety of graphs. Indeed, to show all of the possible combinations of features would take up far more room than is available here. Furthermore, since graphs are visual in nature, many aspects of their design are subject to aesthetic judgment. Opinions differ as to what makes a good-looking graph, and the data being graphed imposes restrictions on the graph maker. This chapter presents the basics of graph making with Symphony and touches upon some of the accepted guidelines for effective graph design. Note that the terms "chart" and "graph" are treated as interchangeable.

THE BASIC GRAPH

In Figure 6-1, you can see a graph printed by Symphony from data stored in a Symphony spreadsheet. The main areas of the graph have been indicated. The following section discusses the terms used when graphing with Symphony.

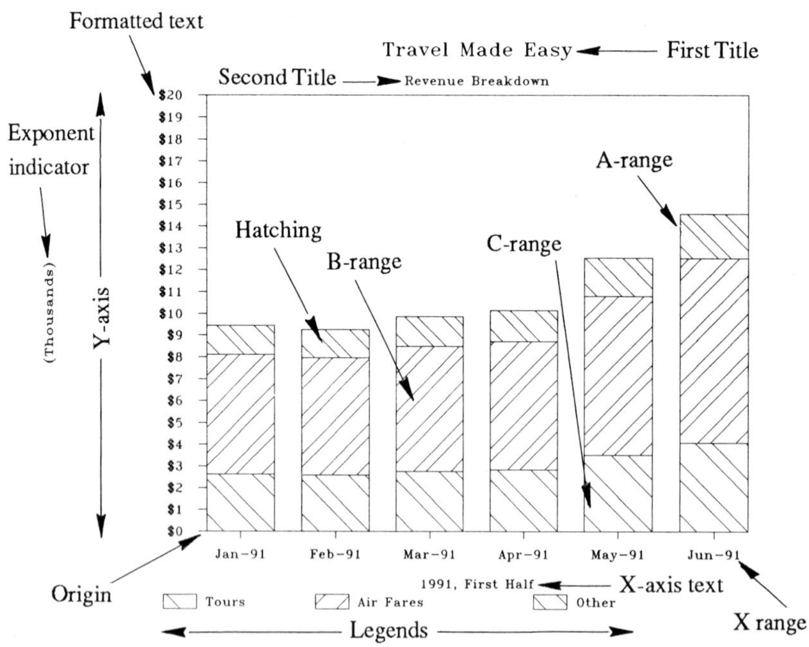

FIGURE 6-1 Sample graph

Graph Terms

Most graphs, with the notable exception of pie charts, depend on two or more *axes:* not wood-chopping tools, but the plural of "axis." The maximum number of axes in Symphony graphs is two: the Y-axis, which is normally the vertical left edge; and the X- axis, normally the horizontal bottom edge. The program also scales the numbers on the Y-axis, based on the minimum and maximum values included in the cells being plotted. Symphony automatically provides tick marks for both axes.

Every point plotted on a graph has its own *X,Y location.* The X variable is the horizontal position corresponding to the category associated with the data point, such as Sales, Revenue, or Jan-91. The Y variable in the graph coordinate represents the vertical position corresponding to the second value associated with the data point, such as Units Sold or Profit %. In Figure 6-1, for example, the X variable is month and the Y variable is a dollar value.

The intersection of the Y-axis and the X-axis is referred to as the *origin.* The origin for the Y-axis in Figure 6-1 is thus zero. The values on the X-axis are just labels for the data, so there is no mathematical origin for the X-axis. In Figure 6-2, you can see a different graph that has mathematical values on both axes. You could say that the origin point on this graph is 0,0.

Graphs can be plotted with a nonzero origin to emphasize various aspects of the numbers. For example, graphs of the recent performance of the Dow-Jones Industrial Average rarely show the entire size of the reading, just the top third or quarter, so that the day-to-day variations are more clearly visible. Later in this chapter you will learn how to manually adjust the upper or lower limits of the scale initially set by Symphony.

The Graph Menus

Symphony generates graphs from numbers and text in worksheet cells. Each graph is a combination of settings, and each can be

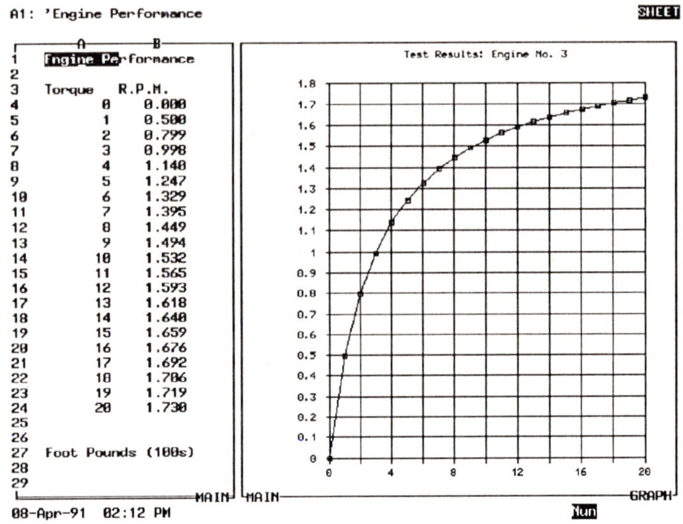

FIGURE 6-2 Graph showing 0,0 origin

named, so you can create a selection of graphs from a single worksheet. Graphs can be viewed on screen in place of the worksheet or next to the worksheet using a GRAPH window. For example, the travel agency revenue worksheet shown in Figure 6-3 can be graphed to show the relative importance of the three categories of revenue or the relative month-to-month performance of the agency as a whole.

There are two ways to access the commands that create the graph settings. While in the SHEET environment, you can press MENU and select Graph. You get this menu:

```
Draw graph (may be Attached to GRAPH window)                              MENU
Preview  1st-Settings  2nd-Settings  Image-Save  Quit
     A          B          C          D          E          F          G          H
1  Travel Made Easy
2
3  Revenue Breakdown:
```

The first item on the menu, Preview, is used to view a graph on-screen once you have defined one. The 1st-Settings and 2nd-Settings commands are what you use to define a graph.

A5: SHEET

	A	B	C	D	E	F	G	H
1	Travel Made Easy							
2								
3	Revenue Breakdown:							
4								
5		Jan-91	Feb-91	Mar-91	Apr-91	May-91	Jun-91	TOTAL
6								
7	Tours	2,642	2,589	2,758	2,839	3,513	4,078	18,420
8	Air Fares	5,472	5,364	5,714	5,882	7,277	8,447	38,155
9	Other	1,321	1,295	1,379	1,420	1,757	2,039	9,210
10								
11	Total	9,434	9,248	9,851	10,141	12,547	14,564	65,785
12								
13								
14								
15								
16								
17								
18								
19								
20								
21								
22								
23								
24								
25								
26								
27								
28								
29								

MAIN

07-Mar-91 07:48 PM Num

FIGURE 6-3 Sample worksheet

\- GRAPH

	A	B	C	D	E	F	G	H
1	Travel Made Easy							
2								
3	Revenue Breakdown:							
4								
5		Jan-91	Feb-91	Mar-91	Apr-91	May-91	Jun-91	TOTAL
6								
7	Tours	2,642	2,589	2,758	2,839	3,513	4,078	18,420
8	Air Fares	5,472	5,364	5,714	5,882	7,277	8,447	38,155
9	Other	1,321	1,295	1,379	1,420	1,757	2,039	9,210
10								
11	Total	9,434	9,248	9,851	10,141	12,547	14,564	65,785
12								

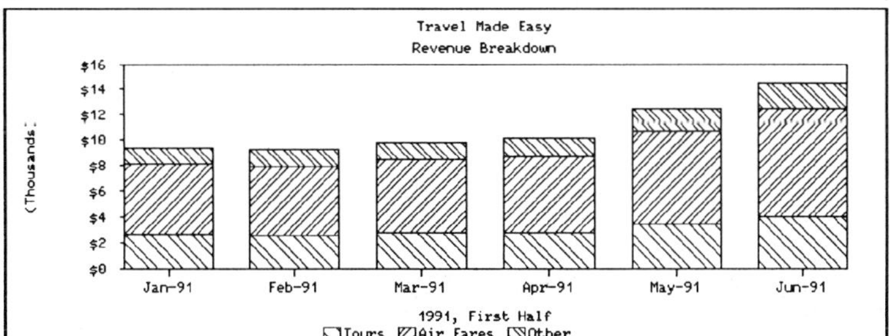

REV-BAR1000 REV-BAR

15-Mar-91 08:35 PM Num

FIGURE 6-4 Using a GRAPH window

When you define a graph and use the Preview command, the graph display takes up the whole screen. As an alternative, a graph can be attached to a GRAPH window. The advantage of a GRAPH window is that it allows you to view a graph on the screen at the same time as the underlying worksheet, using a special window, as shown in Figure 6-4.

You can also use the GRAPH environment to build a graph. While viewing the worksheet to be graphed, you press (ALT-F10) and select GRAPH. The first time you do this, when you have not yet created a graph, you get the response shown in Figure 6-5. Simply press MENU, and you will see the commands shown in Figure 6-6. You use the 1st-Settings and 2nd-Settings commands to define or create the graph.

There are so many different features of a graph that can be adjusted that Symphony has divided the settings into two groups. When you select 1st Settings, you see the menu and settings sheet

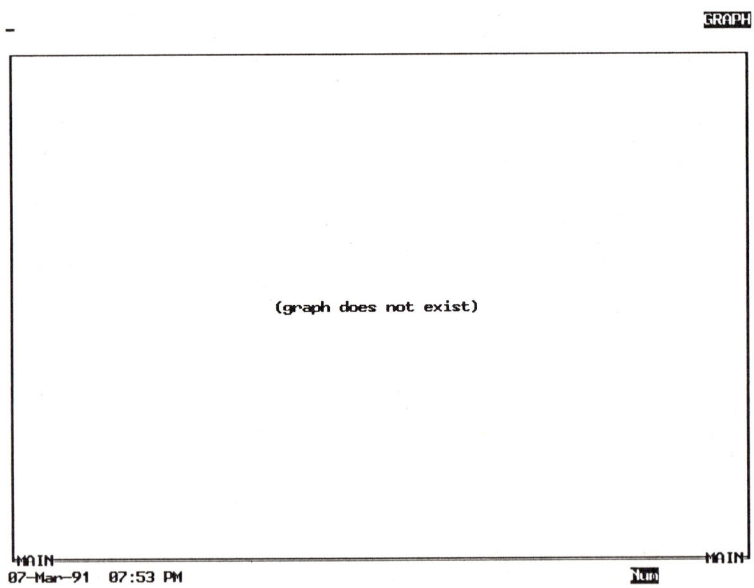

FIGURE 6-5 Switching to the GRAPH environment

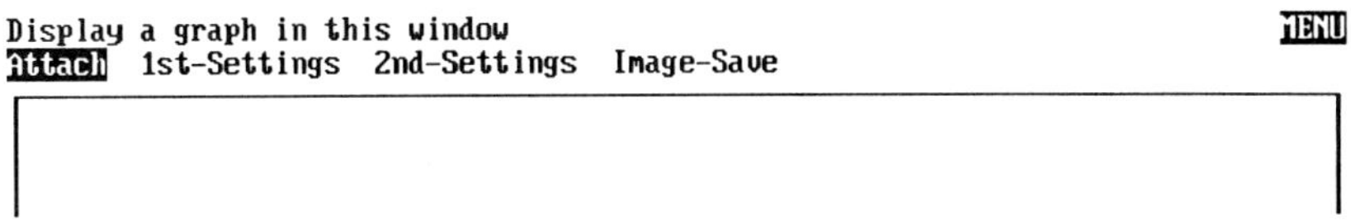

FIGURE 6-6 The main GRAPH menu

shown in Figure 6-7. The first option is to switch to the 2nd-Settings sheet. Similarly, when you are using the 2nd-Settings sheet, the first option on the menu is to switch back to the 1st-Settings sheet. The basic settings that are required to build a graph are Type and Range. The Type command determines the kind of graph created; the default graph type is Line. The Range settings include

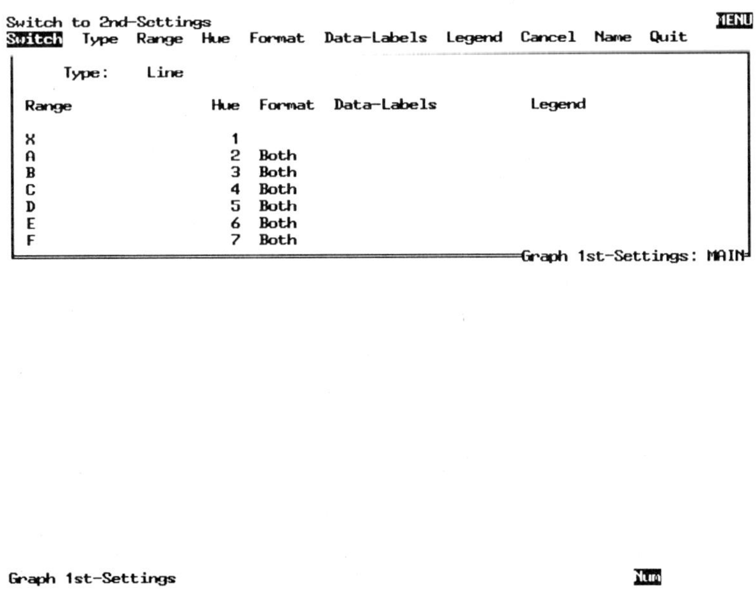

FIGURE 6-7 Blank settings sheet

- The X range, cells that supply labels or values for the X-axis
- One or more data series, up to a total of six, called A range, B range, and so on

You can see these ranges marked on the graph in Figure 6-1. The A range is also called the first data range, the B range is the second data range, and so on.

The Sample Worksheet

If you have data of your own to graph, you can probably apply the steps given in this chapter to your own worksheet. However, if you want to exactly follow the examples in this chapter, the worksheet used as a basis for the graphs can be created as follows. The results will be shown in Figure 6-8.

1. In a fresh worksheet, enter the labels in column A. The line drawn in A6 and A10 is simply the label \-.
2. In B5, enter **@DATE(91,1,1)**, and in B6, enter the label \-. In C5, enter **31+B5**. Enter the label \- in C6. Use MENU Format to assign Date format 3 to cells B5..C5.
3. Copy cells C5..C6 to D5..H6. In H5, replace the date with the label **TOTAL**. Enter the numbers in cells B7 through G9, and use the Format command to assign the Punctuated format, zero decimal places to B7..G9.
4. In B10, enter the label \-, and in B11, enter the formula **@SUM(B7..B9)**. Use the Format command to assign the Punctuated format, zero decimal places to B11. Copy cells B10..B11 to C10..H11.

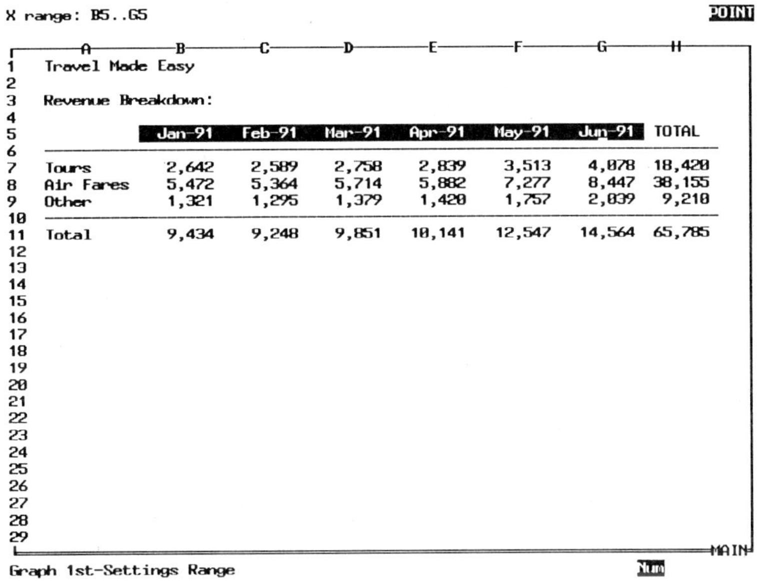

FIGURE 6-8 Selecting the X range

5. In H7, enter the formula **@SUM(B7..G7)**. Use the Format command to assign the Punctuated format, zero decimal places to H7. Copy cell H7 to H7..H9.

6. Save the file with SERVICES File Save and the name **TMEREV01.WR1**.

The Sample Graph

To graph revenue from this worksheet, you first press ALT-F10 and select GRAPH. You will see a screen like the one in Figure 6-5. Do not worry about the message in the middle of the screen; just follow these steps:

1. Press MENU to display the commands shown in Figure 6-6, and choose 1st-Settings. You will see a menu like the one in Figure 6-7.

2. Select Range. The first seven main items on the Range menu are X, which is the range for labels along the X-axis, the horizontal axis; and A, B, C, D, E, and F, which are data ranges that are plotted along the Y-axis, the vertical axis. You can plot as many as six sets of data.

3. To provide the graph with an X-axis, select X from the menu and you will be shown the worksheet. Select cells B5..G5, as shown in Figure 6-8. When you press (ENTER) to confirm the range, you will be returned to the Range menu.

4. To enter the first data range, choose A and then select B7..G7. Note that you do not include the totals for the data being graphed. If your graph needs totals, they will be calculated by Symphony. You will be returned to the Range menu, where the range coordinates will be listed in the settings sheet.

5. Now select B and enter **B8..G8**. Select C, and enter **B9..G9**. There are just three data ranges in this graph.

6. Select Quit to leave the Range menu, and select Quit again to leave the 1st-Settings menu. The graph will be drawn on the screen, as shown in Figure 6-9.

This is a line chart with one line for each of the ranges A, B, and C. Each point on the line represents a value in the data range cells of the worksheet. Each point is referred to as a *data point*. The labels along the X-axis are the months from the worksheet. The numbers along the Y-axis represent thousands. Symphony has automatically scaled the Y-axis from 0 to 8500 to accommodate the data points.

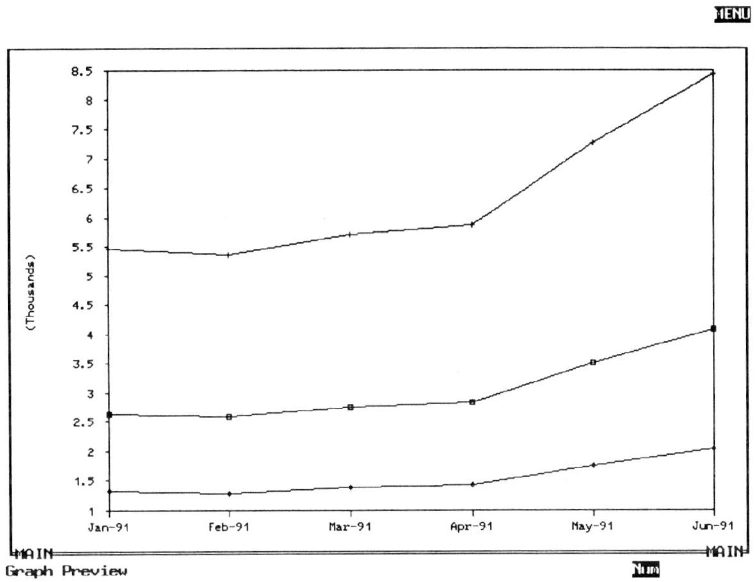

FIGURE 6-9 The first graph

Note Your monitor may show a graph slightly different in appearance from this one. If you have a color display system, Symphony will probably show the graph with color.

Basic Improvements

A line chart is the default graph type used by Symphony. However, it is not always the most appropriate way to represent the data being graphed. Symphony provides six types of graphs. When you change the type, Symphony uses the current data ranges to make a new chart with the type you have selected.

CHANGING TYPE To return to the menu and alter the graph type, just press (F10), choose 1st-Settings, and pick Type. Select

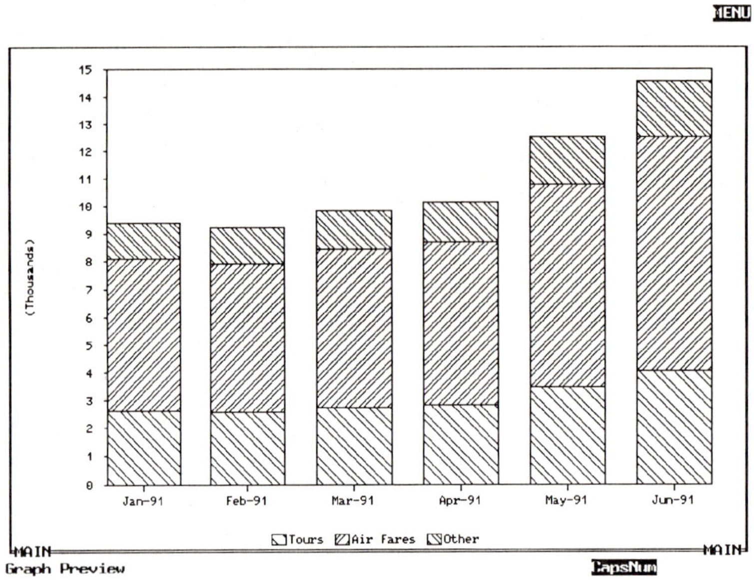

FIGURE 6-10 A stacked bar chart

Stacked-Bar. Now select Quit, and you will see each month's revenue as a single bar, with the value of each of the three categories of revenue as a portion of the bar, as shown in Figure 6-10. You can see that the Y-axis has been changed to accommodate the fact that the bars are totals for each month. Automatic scaling of the Y-axis takes a lot of the work out of making graphs.

Note Note that the bars are shaded or hatched. If you have a color display system, the bars may be shaded in different colors or hues. Symphony lets you shade graphs either with hatching or hues. See the section on "The Hue Factor" for more on how this affects the graph's printed appearance.

ADDING A LEGEND Another improvement in Figure 6-10 is the addition of a legend explaining what each section of the bars represents. This is not automatically added; the Legend command on the 1st-Settings menu must be used to create this part of the graph. When you select Legend, you get a simple listing of the data ranges of the graph: A, B, C, D, E, and F. To assign a legend to data range A, you select A. You can type text for the legend, or you can enter the address of a cell that contains a label that you want to use for the legend. In this example you would enter **\A7** to use the label in cell A7. Note that you use a backwards slash (\) before the cell address. The advantage of the worksheet cell approach is that it is dynamic: Change the text in the worksheet, and it will automatically change the text in the legend.

Caution Legend text supplied by a worksheet cell is only partly dynamic: If you move the cell, the Graph command will not know and the text will disappear from the graph.

When you have entered the text for legend A, you can do B and C, using **\A8** and **\A9**, respectively. When you select Quit to leave the Legend menu, you can choose Quit again to view the results, which should appear as in Figure 6-10.

ADDING TITLES All your graph lacks at this point is a title. You are allowed two lines of title text at the top of the graph, plus one line for each of the axes. You title your graphs with the 2nd-Settings menu. Use Switch on the 1st-Settings menu to get to 2nd-Settings, or choose 2nd-Settings from the main GRAPH environment menu. Figure 6-11 shows the 2nd-Settings menu.

All of the text added to a Symphony graph can be supplied by worksheet cells. Thus, to supply the first line of the title, **Travel**

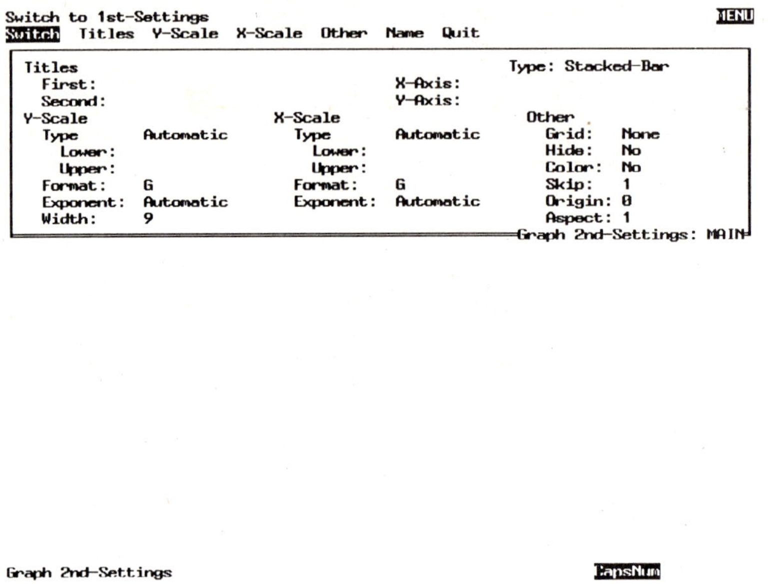

FIGURE 6-11 The 2nd-Settings menu

Made Easy, you would select Titles, then First, and then enter **\A1**. Note that there is no facility for pointing to cells to enter their coordinates in the text menu. As you are typing title or legend text, you can use (BACKSPACE) to correct any errors. If you want to edit the title, the (LEFT ARROW) and (RIGHT ARROW) keys move the cursor through the text of the title. You can insert new characters to the left of the cursor by typing them. Pressing (ESC) while you are typing a title removes the text you have entered. Pressing (ESC) with the title edit line blank returns you to the Titles menu. When you have typed the title correctly, press (ENTER) to confirm it.

Note: When you use a cell reference for text, the cell reference and not the text itself is visible in the Titles setting.

You can add a second title line, **Revenue Breakdown**, by selecting Titles and then Second. If you were to use cell A3 for the title, you would get the colon at the end of the label as well, which some people might object to. Text for the X-axis is entered by selecting Titles X-Axis. In the case of the example graph, this could be **1991, First Half**. The Y-Axis item on the Titles menu labels the Y-axis, and the example graph should explain what units of measurement are displayed; in this case, dollars. However, as an alternative to a Y-axis title you can format the numbers on the Y-axis to show that they are dollars.

FORMATTING THE Y-AXIS You can alter the appearance of the X and Y axes in several ways using the Y-Scale and X-Scale commands on the 2nd-Settings menu. One of the most useful features is the ability to control the appearance of numbers on the axes. For example, in Figure 6-9, the lack of consistency in decimal places on the Y-axis is untidy.

To alter the appearance of the numbers on the Y-axis in Figure 6-10 so that they all have dollar signs, you first choose Y-Scale from the 2nd-Settings menu. Then choose the Format command. The options are the same as those for the Format command used on cells in the SHEET environment. Choose Currency and specify zero decimal places (the numbers shown are thousands, so using decimal points would be confusing). If the format you use makes the numbers wider than the default width allowed (9 characters), you will get asterisks instead of numbers. If this happens, alter the format or use the Y-Scale Width command to allow more room (you can select from 1 to 40 characters). Before quitting the Y-Scale menu to see the results of this change, consider the proportions of the Y-axis in Figure 6-10.

SCALING THE AXIS Normally, the proportion of the scaling on the Y-axis is decided by Symphony. However, there may be times when you want to change this scaling. For example, the graph in Figure 6-10 gives the impression that the company has done very well. This is because the total revenue for June is close to reaching the upper limit of the Y-axis scale. If management were hoping to reach $20,000 in total sales by mid-year, the actual performance would not be so impressive. By altering the upper limit of the Y-axis, you can alter the impression given by the graph.

When you want to alter the scaling of the Y-axis, you choose Type from the Y-Scale menu. Then you choose Manual-Linear so that you can set the scale yourself. Symphony prompts for the lower limit and suggests 0. Press (ENTER) to accept this, and Symphony will suggest an upper limit. To override this, type a new number—in this case, **20000**—bearing in mind that the numbers shown in Figure 6-10 are thousands. When you press (ENTER), you will see the change recorded in the settings sheet. Now you can select Quit twice to see the effect of the changes. The graph should appear like the one in Figure 6-12. (Notice the name of the graph in the lower left of Figure 6-12. This is added by the Name command, discussed in a moment.)

THE HUE FACTOR Whether the graph you see on your monitor is shaded with colors or hatch patterns depends on your display system. If you install Symphony for a color display system, you will normally see color shading, or hues. If you install a monochrome system, sometimes called a "black and white display," you will see hatching. (If you have only the old-fashioned IBM monochrome display system, you will not be able to display graphs). If you have a color system, you can use the 2nd-Settings Other command to change the display from hues to hatching. This is done by selecting Color and choosing No. Indeed, if you have a monochrome printer, one that can only print a single color (usually black), you *must* make this change before the graph is prepared for printing. Later in this chapter the commands for changing the

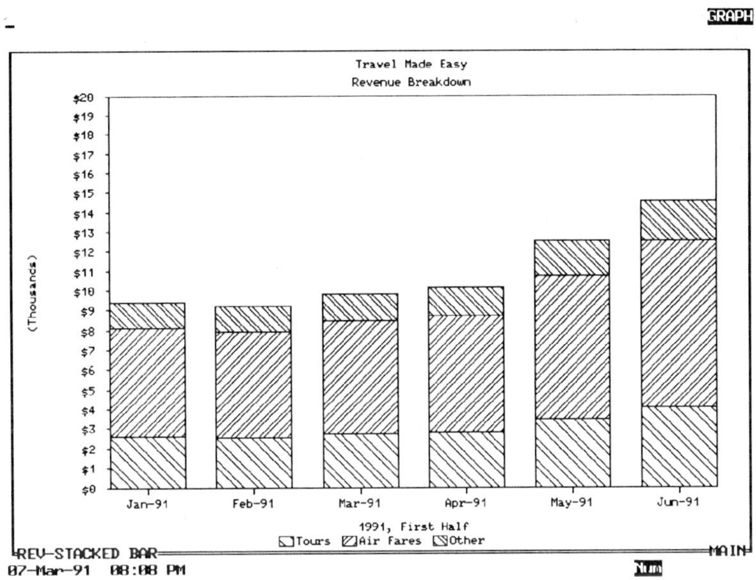

FIGURE 6-12 Improved graph

actual colors and hatching patterns assigned to the different data ranges will be reviewed. At this point, it is time to consider storing the graph before printing it or making any further changes.

SAVING AND NAMING GRAPHS

Although there are several commands that can be used to further enhance the graph in Figure 6-12, it is important at this point to understand the commands used to preserve the work done on the graph so far. Symphony makes it fairly easy to build a graph, but having to rebuild the graph whenever you want to print or display it on-screen would be frustrating.

Saving Strategy

You can preserve your work in two ways: by saving a snapshot of the graph on disk with the Image-Save command, and by naming the settings within the worksheet, using the Name Create command, and then saving the worksheet. If you have designed one graph from a worksheet and want to design a second graph from the same worksheet, you can capture the image of the first graph on disk and then name the graph so that its settings are preserved before creating the second graph.

In Symphony, you cannot design a graph and print it without leaving the main program. You must issue two file storage commands to successfully design and print a graph. You should use the SERVICES File Save command on a regular basis while designing graphs, just as you do when designing worksheets. When you save the worksheet file in which you are designing the graph, the current graph settings are stored in the file, including any settings you have named. Furthermore, in order to print a graph, which is a fairly complex process for your computer/printer to perform, Symphony requires that the graph be saved as an image in a special file on disk before printing.

There is an exception to this: If you use the Allways program, provided with Symphony 2.2, you can print graphs together with spreadsheet data from within Symphony. However, you must still save the graph in an image file. The Allways program is described in Chapter 11.

Image Storage

To save an image of a graph for printing, select Image-Save from the main GRAPH environment menu or from the Graph menu in the SHEET environment. When you select Image-Save, you are prompted for the filename. You either can use the arrow keys to highlight an existing name or type a name of up to eight characters.

To save the sample graph, type **REVBARS** and press (ENTER). Symphony will supply the file extension PIC. If a file by the same name already exists in the current directory, you will see a No/Yes menu. To overwrite the contents of the existing file, select Yes; select No to abandon the save process. Remember that the current graph is the one you would see by switching to the GRAPH environment or by selecting Preview from the Graph menu in the SHEET environment.

If you have set up subdirectories for disk storage, you can store the current graph in a subdirectory other than the current one without first having to issue a Services File Dir command to change directories. To store the graph, select MENU Graph Image-Save. To store it in a subdirectory of the current directory, highlight the subdirectory name at the end of the filename list and press (ENTER) to see a list of files in that directory and to store the current graph there. To store it in a completely different directory, press (ESC) twice at the file list to remove current directory information, and then type the name of the new subdirectory in which you want to store this particular graph, followed by the filename.

Naming Graphs

Graphs saved to PIC files cannot be recalled into Symphony and are essentially frozen images that are used in the PrintGraph part of the program (discussed in a moment). However, you can save the settings for one or more graphs in a worksheet and recall them later by using the Name command. This works like the Name commands in the FORM, DOC, and SHEET environments. As you design a graph, adding new ranges, labels, and so forth, Symphony continues to use each addition in the next version of the same graph, unless you specifically cancel that addition. You can see the cumulative changes to the 2nd-Settings sheet in Figure 6-13.

To name the current graph settings, you issue the Name command, which can be found on both the 1st-Settings and the 2nd-

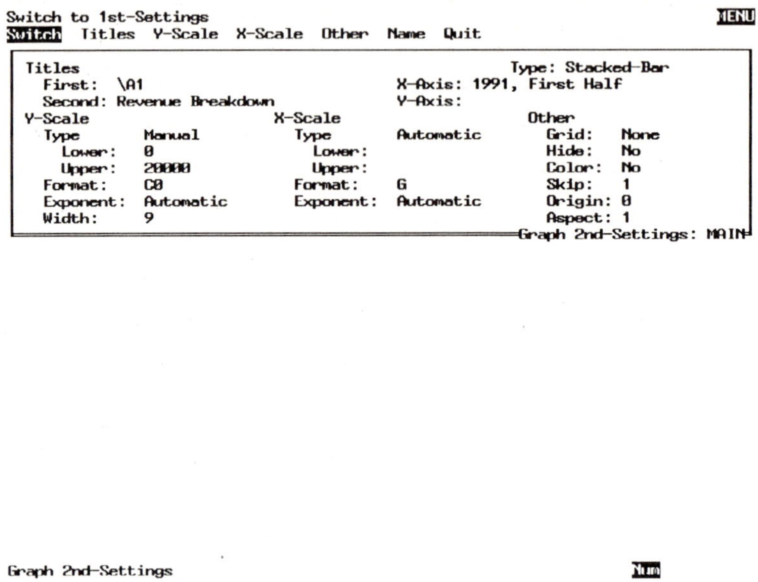

FIGURE 6-13 Settings sheet showing changes

Settings menus. When you select Name, you get the following menu, which should be familiar by now:

Use Create Delete Previous Next Initial-Settings Reset Quit

The Create command stores the current graph setting under a name, up to 15 characters long, that you provide. When you select Create, you can type a name and press (ENTER). This ensures that the current graph, the one you see when you view the graph, is stored under that name. For the sample graph, use the name **REV-STACKED BAR**. Having assigned a name to the current graph, you can then alter the graph settings and save the altered graph under a new name. However, this name itself is not yet saved. You must issue the SERVICES File Save command to record the addition of a name into the worksheet file on disk. For the worksheet file, use the name **TMEREV02**.

When you have created and named more graphs, you can select Use from the Name menu to display a list of named graphs. When you highlight a name on the list and press (ENTER), that graph becomes the current graph and is displayed. Do *not* execute the Use command unless you have named the existing current graph. The Delete command removes a single named graph from the list. As in other Name menus, the Previous and Next commands activate the named settings on either side of the current one in the list of named settings. The Initial-Settings command returns the original settings to the current sheet, and Reset removes all named graph settings.

Altering Graph Settings

When you have named a graph and saved the worksheet, you can be sure that the graph settings will be there when you need them. However, if you want to change a graph and keep the original version, you should—as with database settings—create a new graph settings name before making the changes. The Create command will copy the current settings to a new named sheet, and the new sheet can then be altered while the original stays unchanged.

If you want to make just a few changes to a graph's design, you can do so with the various graph options. However, if the next graph you will construct is substantially different from the current one, you may want to use the Cancel command from the 1st-Settings menu. Selecting Cancel produces a menu with the following items:

Entire-Row   Range   Format   Data-Labels   Legend   Hue

The Entire Row option refers to the fact that the 1st-Settings sheet stores several settings for each range of information on a separate row. Each row holds settings for Range, Hue, Format, Data-Labels and Legend. When you select Entire-Row you can choose Graph to cancel all Range/Hue/Format/Data-Labels/Legend information for the entire graph. As an alternative, you can choose one of the lettered ranges (X, A, B, C, D, E, or F) to cancel the Range/Hue/Format/Data-Labels/Legend information for just that range.

The second option on the Cancel menu, Range, allows you to cancel all range settings for the graph or select a specific range (X, A, B, C, D, E, or F) to cancel. The last four items on the Cancel menu allow you to cancel Format, Data-Labels, Legend, and Hue settings for any one of the ranges (X, A, B, C, D, E, or F) or for the entire graph.

GRAPH PRINTING

So far, you have created Symphony graphs that are displayed on the screen. Screen graphs give you an idea of what the graph will look like when printed and can be used when making a presentation with your computer. However, you usually need to create printed versions of your graphs to distribute to coworkers, use in business presentations, or keep on file. To print graphs you use the PrintGraph program, which is separate from the main Symphony program.

Basic Graph Printing

In a moment, the operation of the PrintGraph program itself will be reviewed, but before that it will be helpful to look at the ten basic steps involved in printing a Symphony graph.

1. Design the graph, defining the ranges, legends, and titles. Adjust the Y-axis if necessary.

2. If you are going to print the graph on a color printer, make sure the Other Color setting in the 2nd-Settings sheet says Yes. If you are going to print the graph on a normal printer, make sure the Other Color setting in the 2nd-Settings sheet says No.

3. View the graph to make sure it is correct.

4. Save the graph to a PIC file using Image-Save.

5. Name the graph with Name Create from the 1st- or 2nd-Settings menu.

6. Save the worksheet, using the SERVICES File Save command.

7. Exit Symphony and load PrintGraph. (If you loaded Symphony by using the Symphony Access System you can select PrintGraph from the Access menu; otherwise, you can load PrintGraph by entering **PGRAPH** at the DOS prompt in the Symphony dircctory.)

8. Use the Settings Hardware command to make sure that the Graphs Directory setting matches the directory in which you have stored your PIC file(s), and that the Fonts Directory setting matches the Symphony program directory.

9. Use the Image-Select command to choose the PIC file to be printed. Make any adjustments to the final appearance of the graph by using the Settings Image command.

10. Select Align and then Go.

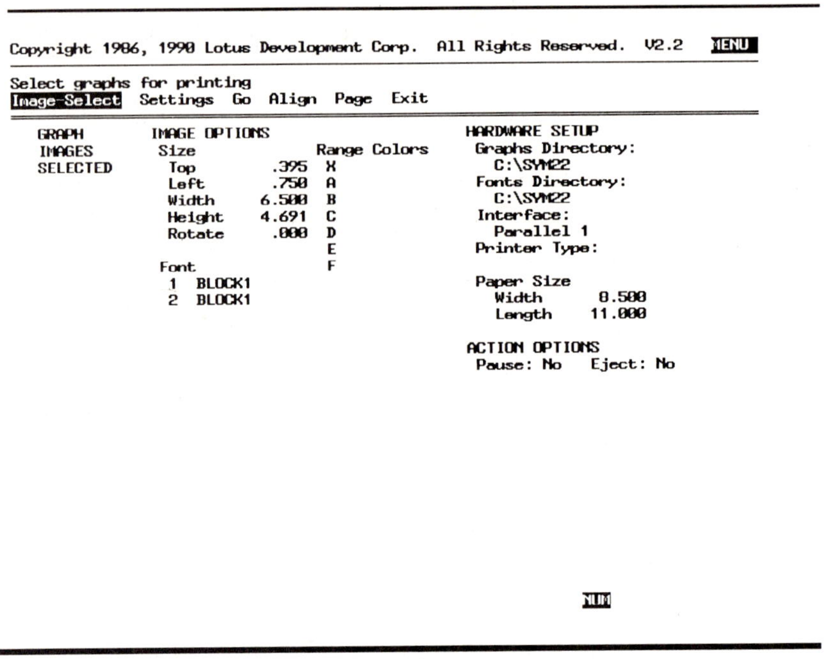

FIGURE 6-14 PrintGraph menu

When you load the PrintGraph program, the menu in Figure 6-14 appears. The menu operates in much the same way as the regular Symphony menus, with one or two new features.

Checking the PrintGraph Settings

When you first load PrintGraph, it is a good idea to make sure that the directories used for fonts and PIC files are correct and that PrintGraph is properly informed about the printer you will be using. The column on the right of the PrintGraph screen, headed "HARDWARE SETUP," lists the current settings, but the full names of the directories are often hard to read. To check the hardware setup, you select Settings. You will see these options:

Image Hardware Action Save Reset Quit

When you select Hardware you see the following options:

Graphs-Directory Fonts-Directory Interface Printer Size-Paper Quit

The first two options are self-explanatory: You simply pick them and type in the correct name of the directory in which you stored the PIC files—for example, **C:\SYM22\DATA**. The Fonts-Directory entry is the same as the Symphony program directory (for example, **C:\SYM22**).

The Interface setting is used to tell PrintGraph how your graph printing device is connected. Although many popular printers use a parallel interface and are typically connected to parallel port 1, some color plotters are connected to a serial port. Check that the selection is correct for the device you will be using to produce your graph.

You may notice that the Printer Type field in the HARDWARE SETUP column is empty. Select Printer from the Hardware menu, and you will see which printers you have to choose from. These are the ones you selected when you installed Symphony. Note that some printers have several entries in the list, as shown in Figure 6-15. This is because the printer can print in several different densities.

A Special List

The list used by the Printer command is of a type not found in the main part of Symphony, but it is used extensively in the PrintGraph menu. The keys used to operate the menu are listed on the screen. Essentially, you use the arrow keys to move the highlight bar to the item you want and then press the spacebar to select the item. This puts a check mark (#) by the item, and when you press (ENTER) that item is recorded as your choice. What distinguishes this type of list is that it allows you, in some cases, to choose more than one entry, although in the case of printers, only one can be selected at a time.

```
Copyright 1986, 1990 Lotus Development Corp. All Rights Reserved. V2.2   POINT
Select graph output device
==============================================================================
          Type of Graphic Output
 ---------------------------------------- [SPACE] turns mark on and off
  HP-LaserJet+ or LaserJet II-Med den.    [RETURN] selects marked device
 # HP-LaserJet+ or LaserJet II-High den.  [ESCAPE] exits, ignoring changes
                                          [HOME] goes to beginning of list
                                          [END] goes to end of list
                                          [UP] and [DOWN] move cursor
                                              List will scroll if cursor
                                              moved beyond top or bottom

                                                                  NUM
```

FIGURE 6-15 Multiple Printer entries

Paper Handling

After selecting the right directories and printer, you need to make sure that the paper size is correct. As you can see from Figure 6-14, the default size is regular American letter-size paper (8 1/2 by 11 inches). The size of your paper is entered with the Width and Length options. You must provide measurements in inches. European users of A4 paper should note that it is 8.27 inches wide by 11.69 inches long.

When you have checked the Paper Size setting, you can select Quit twice to leave the Size-Paper and Hardware menus and review the Action options. These are Pause and Eject. You select Pause if you need PrintGraph to wait while you manually load paper. You select Eject if you want PrintGraph to feed out the page when the graph is printed. This is helpful for plotters and laser printers when you have several graphs to print, one per sheet.

```
Copyright 1986, 1990 Lotus Development Corp.  All Rights Reserved.  V2.2  POINT
Select graphs for output
===============================================================================
   PICTURE      DATE      TIME      SIZE
   ---------------------------------------      [SPACE] turns mark on and off
   REVB1000  03-14-91  10:43      2461          [RETURN] selects marked pictures
 # REVBAR    03-14-91  10:30      2781          [ESCAPE] exits, ignoring changes
                                                [HOME] goes to beginning of list
                                                [END] goes to end of list
                                                [UP] and [DOWN] move cursor
                                                    List will scroll if cursor
                                                    moved beyond top or bottom
                                                [DRAW] displays selected picture




                                                                  NUM
```

FIGURE 6-16 Image-file listing

When you have made your Action selections, it is time to store the settings so far. This will ensure that they are in place the next time you load PrintGraph. Simply select Save from the Settings menu to write the information to the configuration file.

Image Selection

Now it is time to tell PrintGraph which PIC file(s) you want printed. When you choose Image-Select from the main PrintGraph menu, you are presented with a list of PIC files in the current Graphs directory, as shown in Figure 6-16. This list works like the one for printers, except you can choose more than one graph. This allows you to select a group of graphs to be printed one after another using the same basic settings. Highlight the graph you want to print, and press the spacebar. When the graphs you want to print are selected, as shown by the # sign next to their names, press

(ENTER). The selected graphs are listed in the main PrintGraph menu.

Note When you are using PrintGraph for the first time, it is a good idea to select just one graph. Graph printing can take quite a long time on some printers.

FIGURE 6-17 Font samples

Image Options

Now it is time to think about how large you want your graph, where on the page you would like it printed, and what fonts and colors you would like PrintGraph to use. As far as size is concerned, you can see that the default setting is 4.691 inches high by 6.5 inches wide. This graph is essentially a half page graph. The program will start printing the graph .395 inches from the top of the page and .75 inches from the left edge. The rotation on the graph is 0, meaning it will appear upright on the page. You can change these settings, but it is a good idea to print at least one graph with the default settings to see how it looks. If you want a full-page graph that is sideways on the page you can try these settings: Top 0.5, Left 0.5, Width 10.0, Height 7.0, and Rotate 90.0.

After size comes shape: the shape of the letters in which the graph text is to be printed. You have a choice of 7 fonts, examples of which are shown in Figure 6-17. The default font is BLOCK1. Some fonts are available in regular or boldface; BLOCK1 is regular, BLOCK2 is boldface. You can see ROMAN1 in effect in Figure 6-1. The actual size of the letters is determined by PrintGraph in proportion to the size of the graph.

You can assign one font to the first title line and another to the rest of the text. These are referred to as Font 1 and Font 2. You choose fonts by using the Font option in the Settings Image menu. Choose 1 to assign a font to the title text. This activates a list, as in Figure 6-18. This list works like the Printer list—you use the spacebar to check the font you want and press (ENTER) when you have made your choice. When you have assigned a font to area 1, you choose area 2 and select a font for it. The choices are recorded on the Settings menu, as shown in Figure 6-19.

Unless you have a color printer, the only tasks remaining are to check that your printer is connected, turned on, and loaded with paper, and then issue the Align command followed by the Go command. PrintGraph will tell you that it is generating a picture, and after a while you will see the printer start to react. If you have

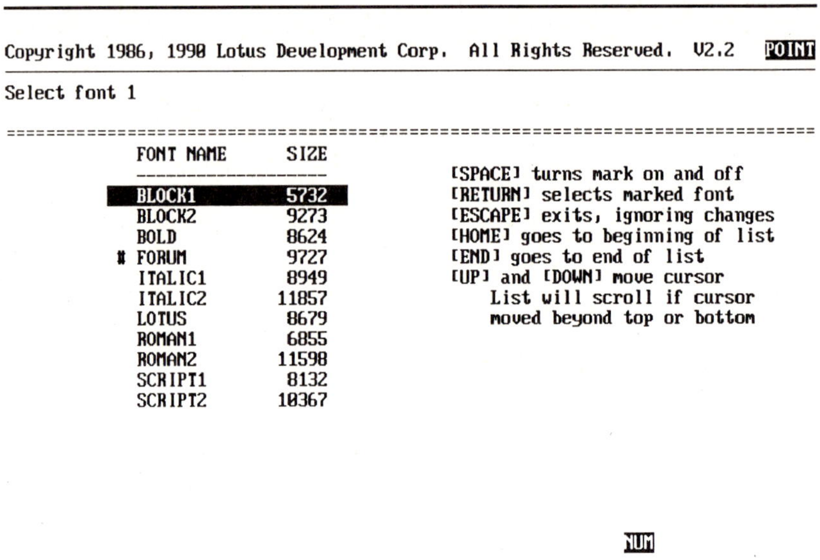

FIGURE 6-18 Font list

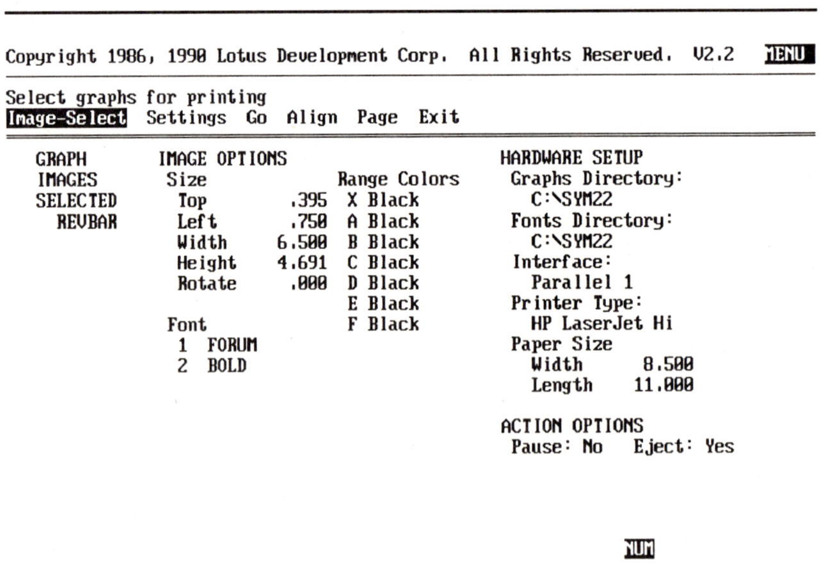

FIGURE 6-19 Completed settings and image selection

set the Eject option to Yes, the printed graph will be fed out by the printer, which will be ready for the next graph.

The actual look of a printed graph may differ somewhat from the image on the screen, particularly with regard to the appearance of fonts and, if you are using a color printer, colors. The printed appearance of fonts and colors depends to a large extent on the capabilities of your printer, which is the same situation you face with spreadsheet printing.

Color Printing

When it comes to using color, PrintGraph recognizes seven areas of the graph, referred to as X, A, B, C, D, E, and F. The color you choose for X will be the basic color, used for the frame around the graph, titles, text, and any grid lines. The colors assigned to A, B, C, D, E, and F are used to shade the corresponding data ranges. If you have not selected a color printer, then PrintGraph uses your printer's primary color, which is black in most cases. If you have a color printing device and want to use color, select Range-Colors from the Settings Image menu. When you select a range to color, you can choose from a range of colors available on your printer.

For an example, if you are using the HP7475A plotter, Symphony will present the 10 most common plotter-pen colors. When you have chosen the colors and go to print, Symphony will ask you to load certain colors in certain pen positions. In other words, if you have chosen Black for the X area, Symphony will ask you to load the black pen into position 1.

Graph-Printing Tricks

You can combine graphs and spreadsheet data by sending one item after another to the printer without using the Align command between them. In Figure 6-20 the sample graph is printed following the data it is based on. This was done by first printing in the SHEET

Travel Made Easy

Revenue Breakdown:

	Jan-91	Feb-91	Mar-91	Apr-91	May-91	Jun-91	TOTAL
Tours	2,642	2,589	2,758	2,839	3,513	4,078	18,420
Air Fares	5,472	5,364	5,714	5,882	7,277	8,447	38,155
Other	1,321	1,295	1,379	1,420	1,757	2,039	9,210
Total	9,434	9,248	9,851	10,141	12,547	14,564	65,785

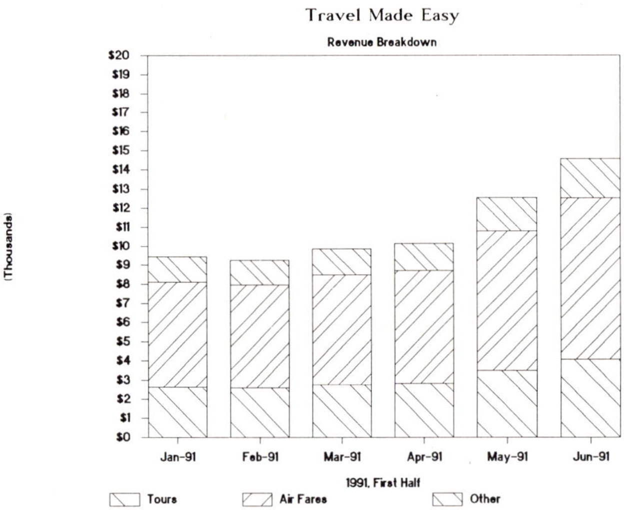

FIGURE 6-20 Combined graph and data

environment of Symphony, and then leaving the page in the printer and switching to the PrintGraph program, where the graph was printed.

Note that the print range in the worksheet was set as A3..H13 to include blank lines above and below the actual numbers and to exclude the label in A1. The centered heading, "Travel Made Easy," is actually a print header, entered in the Print settings sheet as |**Travel Made Easy** with the Header command. The page number is a footer created with the entry |**Page #**, using the Footer command.

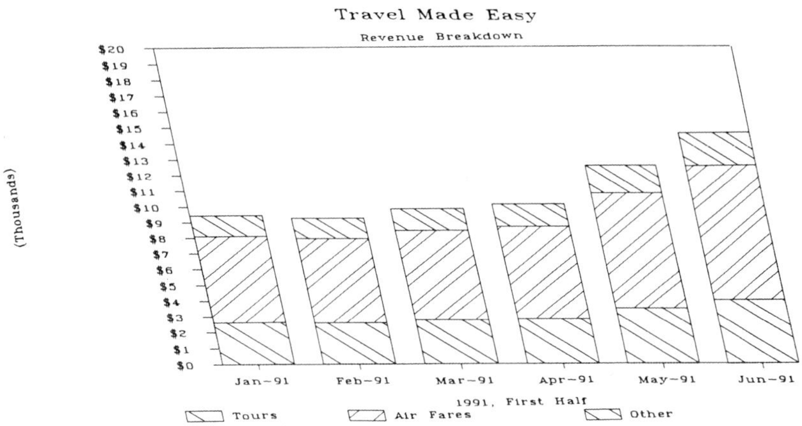

FIGURE 6-21 Low wide graph

To print a series of graphs, one after the other, you can select multiple graphs in the PrintGraph program. However, you must bear in mind that when you issue the Go command, each graph you have selected will be printed using the same settings. There is no system for attaching image settings to a particular graph and storing them. You can store a standard set of image settings by issuing the Settings Save command after selecting image options.

You work on the basic graph design when you are displaying the graph on screen. Such features as data ranges and titles are specified at this point, as well as such details as grid lines and hatch patterns, which are dealt with in a moment. You cannot modify these features when you get into the PrintGraph program. However, you can alter the overall size and proportions of the graph with PrintGraph commands. Figure 6-21 shows a graph altered by changes in the settings. This low, wide graph, printed with a width of 7.5 inches and a height of 4.5 inches plus a slight rotation (15.0), gives a different slant to the figures being presented.

GRAPH TYPES

You will want to make your graphs as readable and effective as possible. To do this, you need to choose the right graph type for the data you are graphing. You have already seen that choosing one of the seven available graph types is easy: You use Type and pick one of the options. When you change graph types, the current data series is retained but presented in a different arrangement.

When you select Type, the following items are available:

Line   Bar   Stacked-Bar   XY   Pie   High-Low- Close-Open

By selecting one of these options, you set that graph type. Of the six Symphony graph types, all but the pie graph display both X and Y axes. The line, bar, stacked-bar, and high-low-close-open display numbers (centered on the tick marks) along the Y-axis only. The X-axis for these graph types can optionally display user-defined labels centered on the tick marks. The XY graph displays numbers on both axes.

In Table 6-1, you can see the types of graphs and their normal settings, together with the default assignments for line symbols, bar shading, and color for each data range. The following sections should help you decide which graph to use for a particular set of data.

Line Graphs

You can use up to six sets of data in ranges A, B, C, D, E, and F. Symphony creates one graph line for each range; each point on a line represents one value in the range. The data points in each data

Line

- X data range is used as the X-axis labels and A through F data ranges are used as the lines in the graph.
- Symbols are used to differentiate data ranges. Choices for symbols cannot be changed, and all lines connecting data points are always solid.
- Default settings:

First data range	Squares connected by lines
Second data range	Plus signs connected by lines
Third data range	Diamonds connected by lines
Fourth data range	Upward triangles connected by lines
Fifth data range	Crosses like X's connected by lines
Sixth data range	Downward triangles connected by lines

Use 1st-Settings Format to turn off Lines or Symbols for a particular data range. Use Neither to hide the data range and then reveal specific points with Data Labels.

Bar

- Graphs up to six sets of data as bars. The X data range is used as the X-axis labels, and the A through F data ranges are used as the sets of bars in the graph.
- You can alter the hatching or coloring used in the bars.

XY

- Also called a scatter chart, shows correlations between two types of numeric data. Uses the A through F data ranges as points in the graph and the X data range as the X-axis scale.
- Only XY graphs use a numeric X data range.
- Initially uses same symbol settings as LINE, with data points marked by symbols connected by lines.
- Use 1st-Settings Format to turn off Lines or Symbols for a particular data range or the entire graph.
- Use Neither to hide the data range and then reveal specific points with Data Labels.

Stack-Bar

- Graphs up to six sets of data as stacked bars. Used to compare values by stacking them one on top of another.
- The X data range is used as the X-axis labels and the A through F data ranges are used as portions of the bars.

TABLE 6-1 Types of Graphs

	• The A-range values form the bottom portion of the bars, B-range values form the next-highest portion of the bars, and so on. • Initially uses same hatch and color settings as Bar type.
Pie	• A circular chart, each slice of which represents a single value. Used to relate two or more positive values to one another. • Uses the A data range as the pie slices and the X data range as labels for the pie slices. • Uses a D data range to get colors or hatch patterns for the pie slices, entering values in cells of the worksheet corresponding to the hatch/color choice. • Hatch patterns and colors correspond to those for BAR, with the first value in the A data range taking the hatch pattern/color normally used by the entire A data range. • To explode slices away from the pie, add 100 to the B-range.
High-Low-Close-Open	• Graphs four sets of data as high-low-close-open lines. Tracks fluctuation in stock prices (or any other type of data) over time. • The high and low data for each time period is depicted as a vertical line between two points in the graph. Option close and open figures are graphed as horizontal lines. • Uses the X data range as the X-axis labels and the A, B, C, and D ranges as the sets of high, low, close, and open values, respectively.

TABLE 6-1 Types of Graphs (*continued*)

range are marked by a unique symbol and/or color when graphed. The example graph as a line chart was shown in Figure 6-9.

Bar Graphs

In a bar graph you can chart as many as six data ranges: A, B, C, D, E, and F. Symphony creates one set of bars for each range; each bar in a set represents one value in the range. The bars for multiple data ranges appear within each X-axis group on the graph in alphabetical (A-F) order from left to right. When you have selected

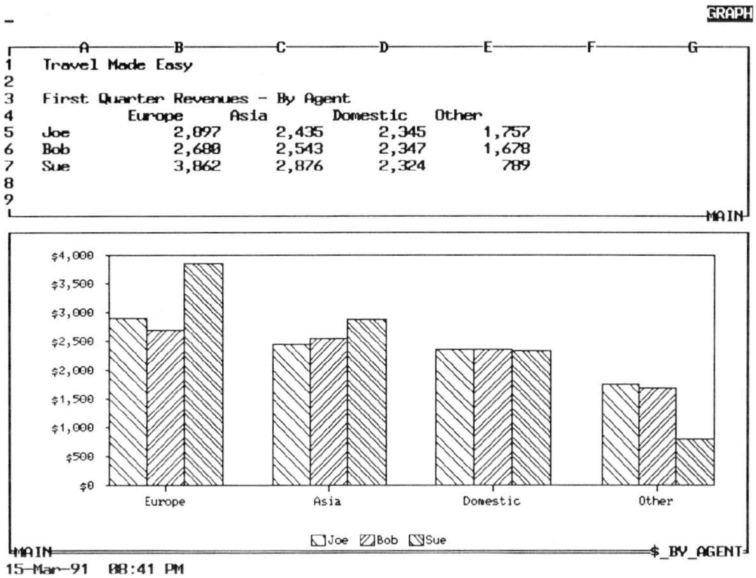

FIGURE 6-22 Basic bar chart

Other Color No, the bars for each data range are displayed with a unique shading. When you have selected Other Color Yes, the bars are displayed with a unique color (limited by the maximum number of colors possible on your display system). You can see a basic bar chart in Figure 6-22, along with the data it is based on. Note that in this example the X-axis is non-numeric, being a set of labels from the worksheet. The display of charts next to worksheets in Symphony will be discussed toward the end of this chapter.

XY Graphs

This graph type is the only one that treats values in the X-axis as values rather than labels. Used for statistical charting, the XY graph takes an independent variable as the X-axis data. You can enter as many as six dependent variable ranges to plot against the

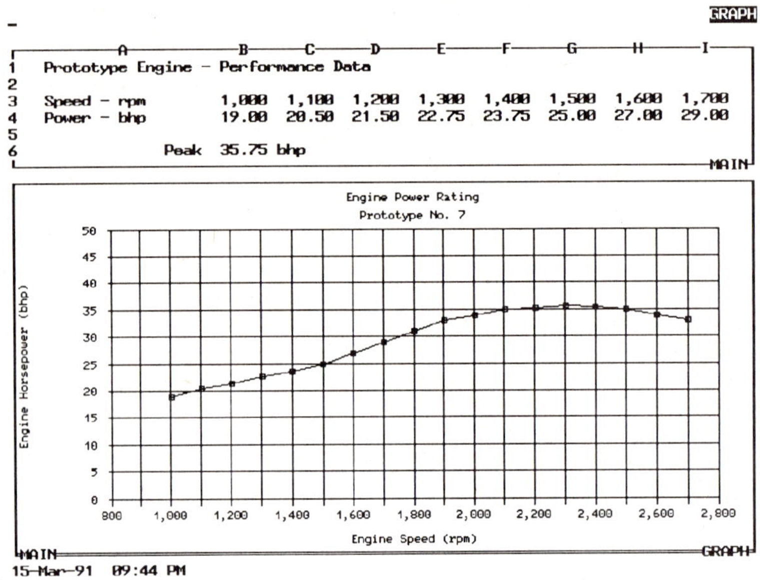

FIGURE 6-23 Engine XY graph

X-axis: A, B, C, D, E, and F. Symphony creates one set of points for each dependent variable range, as you can see from Figure 6-23, which graphs engine power (bhp) against engine speed (rpm). In this case, there is one dependent variable: power. Note that when more than one data range is shown in an XY graph, the data points for each data range are marked by a unique symbol when graphed. The symbols are the same as the line symbols shown in Table 6-1. The grid lines used on this graph are created with the 2nd-Settings Other Grid option, described later in this chapter.

Stacked Bar Graphs

This type is similar to the bar graph in most respects; however, in a stacked bar graph, multiple data ranges appear from bottom to top in alphabetical order. The financial review example was shown as a stacked bar chart in Figure 6-1. For some data that would not normally be summed, this is not really an appropriate chart. For example, if you were graphing revenue and expenses, you would want a bar and not stacked bar chart, since the latter would show revenue and expense as a breakdown of a single figure.

Pie Charts

A pie chart is a one-dimensional graph. For a pie chart you enter only one data series. You do this by selecting A from the main Graph menu. For each value in the A range, Symphony creates a pie "slice." You can use a pie chart to show the percentage breakdown of a single total, as in Figure 6-24. To shade and "explode" pieces of the pie, also select a B range, as explained later in this section. To label sections of the pie you can choose a range

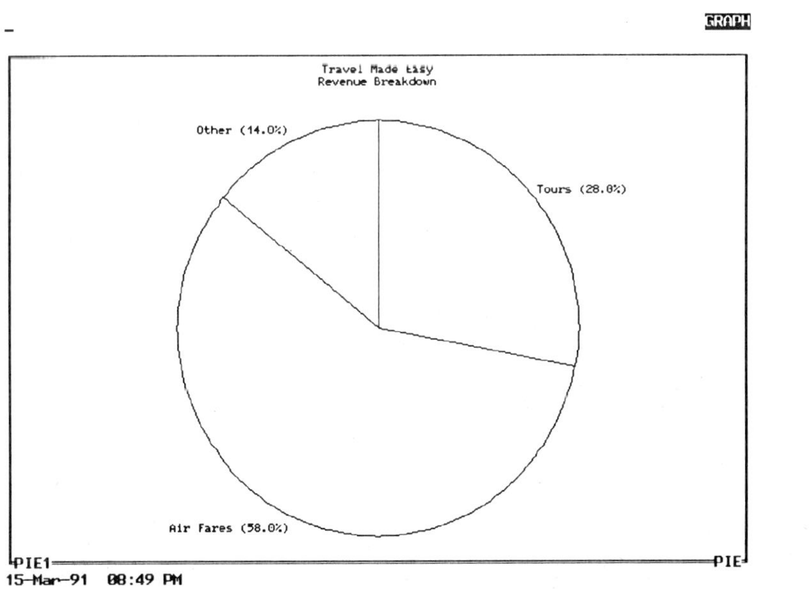

FIGURE 6-24 Pie chart example

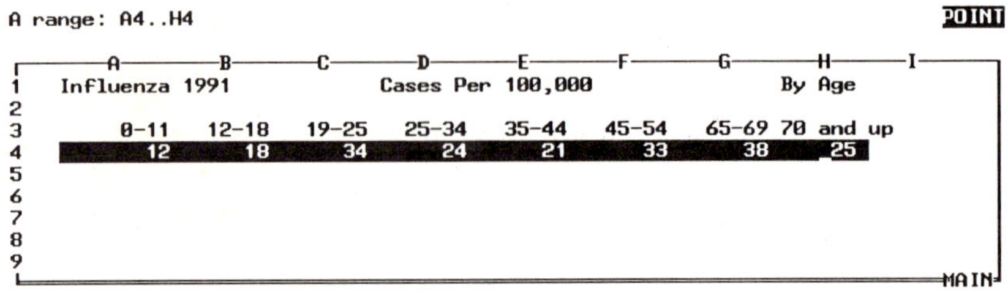

FIGURE 6-25 Influenza table

of data labels as an X range. The sample worksheet produces the pie chart in Figure 6-24 if you define the A range as H7..H9 and the X range as A7..A9. The total figures for the six-month period are used for the pie chart in Figure 6-24. Using figures in columns B through G would only give a breakdown of a particular month.

The limit to the number of slices in a pie arises from considerations of clarity. In Figure 6-25, for example, you can see a worksheet containing medical statistics about the incidence of influenza. You want to see a pie chart of the breakdown of the incidence of the disease by age group. If you select cells A4..H4 as the A range and choose Pie as the graph type, you get the eight-slice chart seen in Figure 6-26, which is about the limit on readable slices that you can create. Notice how the percentage of each slice is displayed.

The chart in Figure 6-26 is not very clear despite the first and second titles that are displayed. The chart needs explaining. As an alternative to legends, pie charts use a range of data labels as an X range to label sections of the pie. In Figure 6-25, you can see that category headings for the figures being graphed consist of labels on row 3. Thus, the range A3..H3 is set as the X-axis to label the pie slices. You can see the results of this in Figure 6-27. Note that one slice is "exploded," meaning that it is displayed a short distance from the rest. Also note that the shading of pies in Figure 6-27 is different from that in Figure 6-26.

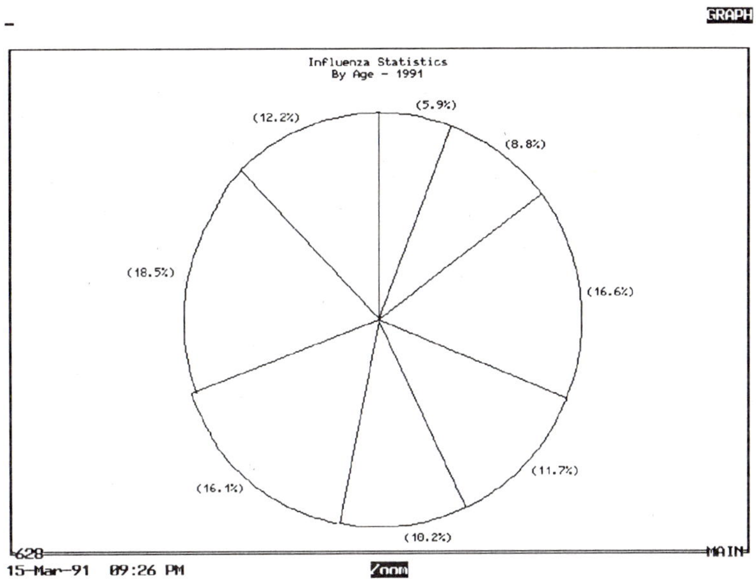

FIGURE 6-26 Influenza pie chart

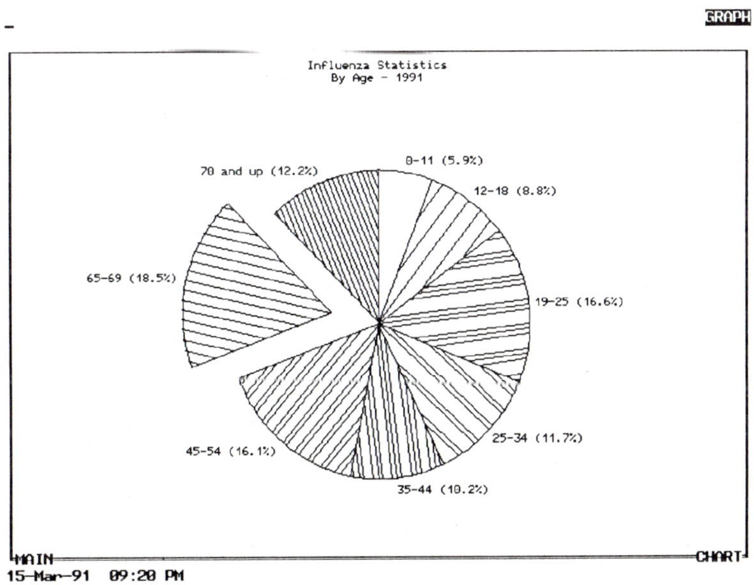

FIGURE 6-27 Pie with labeled slices

```
A1: 'Influenza                                                              SHEET
        A          B          C          D          E          F          G          H          I
1  Influenza 1991                     Cases Per 100,000                          By Age
2
3       0-11      12-18      19-25      25-34      35-44      45-54      65-69 70 and up
4         12         10         34         24         21         33         38        25
5          0          7          6          5          4          3        102         1
6
7
8
9
                                                                                     MAIN
```

FIGURE 6-28 B range codes

To alter shading of slices and explode pieces of the pie, you select a B range in which you enter special numeric codes. The codes 0 through 7 are used for the hatch patterns or colors you desire. These are entered in the worksheet and defined in the graph as the B range, as shown on row 5 of the worksheet in Figure 6-28. Hatch patterns are shown on monochrome displays, and colors are shown on color displays. Note that without careful selection of shading, the results can be deceptive, failing to distinguish all of the slices uniquely. By changing pattern settings you can overcome this problem.

You add 100 to any code in the B range to explode the corresponding section of the pie chart. For example, in Figure 6-28 you can see that the value of 102 is used in cell G5, causing the explosion of the seventh slice. (The first slice in a Symphony pie chart is the one that extends clockwise from the 12:00 noon position.)

You do not have to place these "cosmetic" ranges next to the real data. You can place the information columnwise or rowwise in another part of the worksheet. However, you need to make sure that the number of cells in the B range matches the number of cells in the A range. By using conditional formulas to supply the values for the B range, you can have the pie chart's appearance depend on conditions in the worksheet.

High-Low-Close-Open Graphs

When a stock or commodity is traded, the highest price it fetches in a given period is called "the high." The lowest price that the item is traded for in a period is called "the low." The going price for an item at the end of the trading period is called "the close." The term "open" is used for the price the item traded at when the trading period opened. You can see a worksheet of such figures, based on a fictitious stock, in Figure 6-29. High-Low-Close-Open, or HLCO, is a special type of graph used in charting information about the price of any stock or other traded commodity over time. In Figure 6-30, you can see an example of this type of graph, based on the worksheet of fictitious stock. The chart shows the various price levels of the stock during the trading period. HLCO graphs

```
A1: "Company:                                                    SHEET
      A          B          C          D          E          F          G          H
1   Company: MegaPrix
2
3    Trading: OTC
4
5       Code: MGPX
6
7   Date       Open       High       Low        Close
8       02/04    23.750     24.125     23.375     23.750
9       02/05    23.750     24.250     23.000     23.667
10      02/06    25.000     25.188     24.188     24.792
11      02/07    21.875     22.125     20.500     21.500
12      02/08    23.500     23.750     22.250     23.167
13      02/11    23.000     23.125     21.625     22.583
14      02/12    22.250     22.688     20.938     21.958
15      02/13    25.875     26.250     25.125     25.750
16      02/14    25.750     26.313     25.063     25.708
17      02/15    28.125     28.313     27.438     27.958
18      02/18    24.875     25.438     23.813     24.708
19      02/19    29.125     29.250     28.375     28.917
20      02/20    25.250     25.500     23.750     24.833
21      02/21    27.000     27.063     25.563     26.542
22      02/22    25.625     26.063     24.188     25.292
23      02/25    29.875     30.063     28.938     29.625
24      02/26    27.875     28.313     26.688     27.625
25      02/27    30.875     30.938     29.813     30.542
26      02/28    27.625     27.625     25.750     27.000
27
28
29
                                                                 MAIN
15-Mar-91   09:38 PM                     Zoom
```

FIGURE 6-29 HLCO worksheet

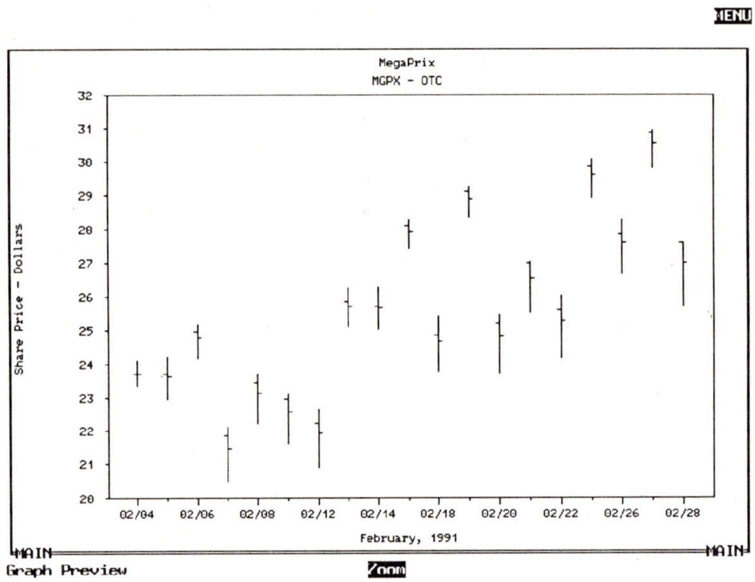

FIGURE 6-30 HLCO graph

are specialized for commodity market information, but they also can be used to track other kinds of fluctuating data over time, such as daily temperature or currency exchange rates.

Each set of data in an HLCO graph consists of four figures representing high, low, close, and open values. The X-axis is the time period of trading (in this case, the dates in worksheet column A, which are all the trading days in February, 1991). The range of the values for any given day is represented on the graph as one vertical line. The vertical extent of the line—its length—is from the low value to the high value. The close value is represented by a tick mark extending right from the line, and the open value by a tick mark extending left. The total number of lines on the graph depends on the number of time periods included.

Data ranges for an HLCO graph are assigned as follows:

A The high values (column C in the example)
B The low values (column D in the example)
C The closing values (column E in the example)
D The opening values (column B in the example)

You can specify just a few of these ranges, and only the corresponding part of the graph will be plotted. The minimum requirements are the X and A ranges. Enhancements, such as titles and axis labels, are added as with the other graph types.

DATA LABELS

After selecting the right graph type and setting up the data ranges and titles, you may want to create labels on the graph itself in order to explain one or more of the data points. Data labels are either labels or numbers entered in the worksheet from which you are graphing. You can use the cells you are graphing as both data ranges and data labels to fully document a graph.

Creating Data Labels

You add data labels to a graph by selecting Data-Labels from the 1st-Settings menu and selecting from the letters that correspond to the data ranges of the graph. First select the data range to which you are assigning data labels. You cannot type the data labels directly; instead, you must specify a worksheet range that contains the labels. For example, consider the data that was charted in Figure 6-23 as an XY graph. Suppose you want the actual horsepower values to be shown next to the corresponding data points on the chart, as shown in the lower part of Figure 6-31 (the worksheet that produces the graph is shown in the upper part of the figure). The actual numbers stretch off the right of the screen to column S. To assign data labels, you first select Data-Labels from the 1st-Set-

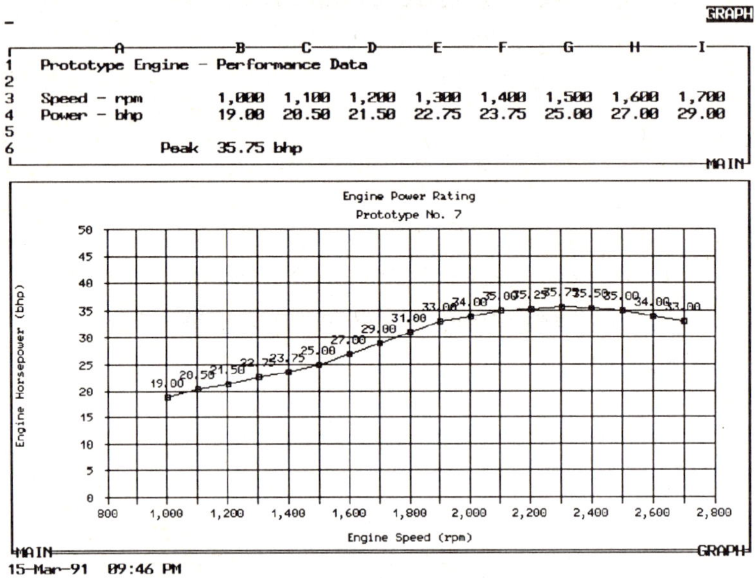

FIGURE 6-31 Using data labels

tings menu, and then select A, the first data range. You include cells B4..S4 as the range of data labels (these are the same cells that are graphed as the first data range).

You can give the range for the data labels as a cell address by pointing or by entering a range name. After you specify the data label range, the choices Center, Left, Above, Right, and Below appear. The selection you make from this menu determines where each data label will be displayed in relation to the corresponding data point. For example, in Figure 6-31, the labels are above the data points (the Above option). The labels or numbers in the data label range are then assigned to data points in the order in which the labels appear in the worksheet.

As you can see from Figure 6-31, placing a lot of labels within a graph often produces rather crowded results. You can solve the overcrowding problem by using the technique described in the next section. Other problems also arise, particularly on line and XY graphs, where the first and last labels tend to overlap the frame of the graph and be truncated. To solve this problem with a line graph, you can expand any data ranges defined for a line graph by including blank cells at each end of the defined ranges, including the X range. The solution for an XY graph is to manually set the scale for the X-axis to ensure that it is large enough to clearly show the beginning and ending values.

Individual Data Labels

When you want a data label for each data point, you simply assign a range full of values or numbers as the data label range. But when you want to label only certain points, you need to do more planning.

Suppose that you do not want data labels all over the graph as they are in Figure 6-31. Instead, you just want the peak of the power curve, which is 35.75 b.h.p. at 2,300 r.p.m., to be identified on the chart, as shown in Figure 6-32. You have the label "Peak" in cell A6. However, you cannot use this label as a data label. If you did, Symphony would not know which data point it should display the label beside. The data label range should contain as many cells as the graphed data range that is being labeled. Thus, you enter the label **Peak** in row 5, beneath the cell that actually contains the peak value—in this case O5—and redefine data label range A as B5..S5.

After the range for the labels is identified, the position of the labels relative to the data point must be chosen. To give the effect seen in Figure 6-32, the Above option was used. Remember that when you want to label just a few points of a graph, you can set up a range of cells parallel to the data range and just fill in the cells corresponding to the values you want to label; for example, the first cell contains the label for the first cell, and the last cell contains the label for the last value. The blank cells won't appear on the graph.

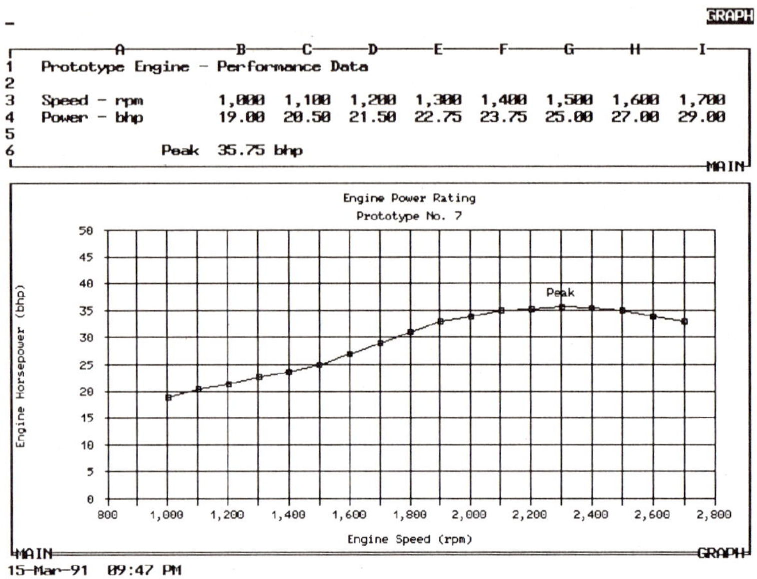

FIGURE 6-32 Labeled peak

Free-Form Labels

You can use the Data-Labels command to add text just about anywhere on a graph. This is because data label text itself can be a plotted point. To display data labels without the data points themselves, you use the 1st-Settings Format command and select the Neither option. This results in neither lines nor symbols being plotted for the specified data range, leaving you with just the data labels. For example, if you were to create a B range for the graph in Figure 6-32 and assign data labels to it, you could display the data labels rather than the values, giving you what are in essence free-floating labels. You can see an example of this in Figure 6-33.

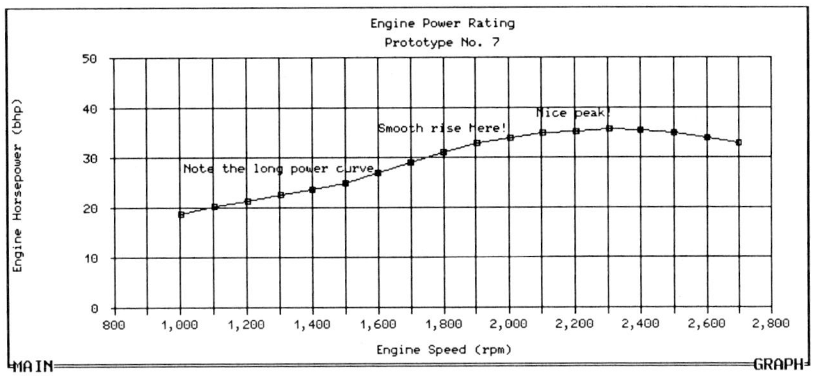

FIGURE 6-33 Floating text

To create the text on the graph in Figure 6-33, the three labels were entered into a special row of the worksheet, adjacent to values that form the second data range, as shown here:

```
E6: 'Note the long power curve                                                  SHEET
        A                  B        C        D        E        F        G        H        I
1  Prototype Engine - Performance Data
2
3  Speed - rpm           1,000    1,100    1,200    1,300    1,400    1,500    1,600    1,700
4  Power - bhp           19.00    20.50    21.50    22.75    23.75    25.00    27.00    29.00
5  Second data range:                               25.00
6  Data labels:                                     Note the long power curve
7
8
9
                                                                                        MAIN
```

The second or B data range was defined as B5..S5, and the third or C range of data labels was defined as B6..S6. The position of data labels with respect to the X-axis is determined by the position of the label cells relative to the data range. For example, placing a label in the fourth cell of the range positions the label at the fourth data point along the X-axis. That is how the label "Note the long power curve" was placed, since E6 is the fourth value in the range B6..S6.

The position of the label with respect to the Y-axis is determined by the value associated with the label. The label in E6 is associated with the value 22.75 in E4. This causes the label to be placed at position 22.75 on the Y-axis. You can select Center for the data label position, which centers the labels over the positions where the data points would have appeared; or you can use one of the other positions, such as Right, which will show the labels to the right of the data points. By using this technique of a special data range, you can place labels anywhere on the graph.

To change the range or position of the data labels, use the same command sequence you used to create them. Enter a different data label range or specify a different position. You can remove data labels by using the Cancel command and selecting Data-Labels.

The X-Axis As Labels

The X data range in many graphs is a means of placing descriptive information within a graph. With all graph types except pie charts and XY graphs, the main Graph menu's X option can be used to position labels below the X-axis. The cells you specify for the X range or for a data label range can contain either labels or values. If values, they are displayed on the graph in the same format as they are displayed on the worksheet. If a label used for a data label does not fit on the graph, the label is truncated. If a value used as a data label does not fit on the graph, it will overlap other values, as seen in Figure 6-34.

One command that can help a great deal when displaying long values or labels on the X-axis is the 2nd-Settings Other Skip command. This allows you to specify that only every other cell in the X range be displayed on the chart. For example, consider the biorhythm chart in Figure 6-34. The X-axis on this chart covers

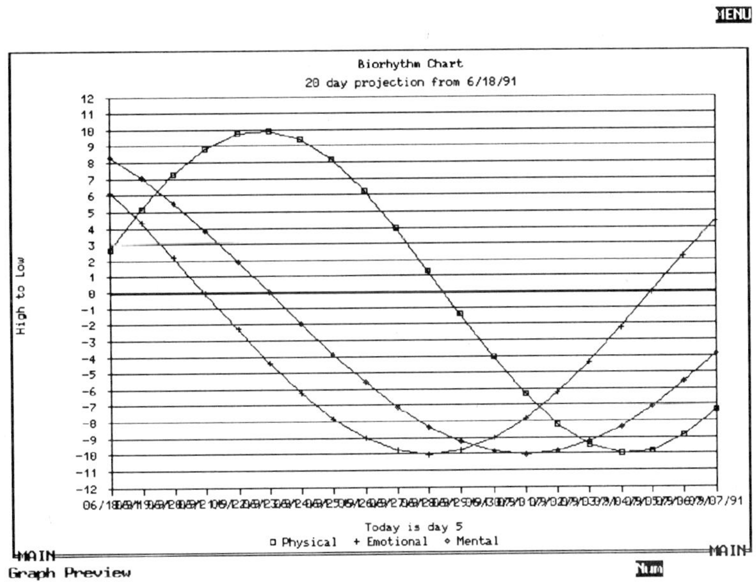

FIGURE 6-34 Biorhythm chart

the dates 6/18/91 through 7/07/91, but displaying a date value for each point across the axis makes it very crowded.

If you look at the worksheet in Figure 6-35, which produced this graph, you can see that the date values are important to the calculation of the biorhythm curve and so cannot be eliminated from column D. You could format the dates with a shorter format, or you could number the days with a series of numbers (1, 2, 3, and so on) and use these numbers as the X-axis range. You might go to the trouble of setting up a dummy X-axis range with every other date included, but this is a lot of work. Instead, you can use the Skip command. The command asks for a skip factor, the default being 1, which means "display all X-axis labels." Entering a factor of 2 means "skip every other label." A factor of 3 means "display every third label," and so on. By using a factor of 2 with the graph in Figure 6-34, you can achieve the results shown in Figure 6-36.

D5: 10*@SIN(C5*@PI/11.5) SHEET

	A	B	C	D	E	F
1	BIORHYTHM CHART		Period Projected:		Birthday:	10/17/52
2	Fred Smith		20 days		Today:	06/22/91
3						
4	Day	Date	Date-Birthday	Physical	Emotional	Mental
5	1	06/18/91	14,123	2.70	6.23	0.31
6	2	06/19/91	14,124	5.20	4.34	7.07
7	3	06/20/91	14,125	7.31	2.23	5.56
8	4	06/21/91	14,126	8.88	0.00	3.83
9	5	06/22/91	14,127	9.79	(2.23)	1.95
10	6	06/23/91	14,128	9.98	(4.34)	0.00
11	7	06/24/91	14,129	9.42	(6.23)	(1.95)
12	8	06/25/91	14,130	8.17	(7.82)	(3.83)
13	9	06/26/91	14,131	6.31	(9.01)	(5.56)
14	10	06/27/91	14,132	3.98	(9.75)	(7.07)
15	11	06/28/91	14,133	1.36	(10.00)	(8.31)
16	12	06/29/91	14,134	(1.36)	(9.75)	(9.24)
17	13	06/30/91	14,135	(3.98)	(9.01)	(9.81)
18	14	07/01/91	14,136	(6.31)	(7.82)	(10.00)
19	15	07/02/91	14,137	(8.17)	(6.23)	(9.81)
20	16	07/03/91	14,138	(9.42)	(4.34)	(9.24)
21	17	07/04/91	14,139	(9.98)	(2.23)	(8.31)
22	18	07/05/91	14,140	(9.79)	(0.00)	(7.07)
23	19	07/06/91	14,141	(8.88)	2.23	(5.56)
24	20	07/07/91	14,142	(7.31)	4.34	(3.83)
25			/	/	/	/
26			This column	Each of these columns calculates a point		
27			takes birth-	on a curve, using @SIN and @PI, and a cycle		
28			date away	of 22 days for Physical, 28 for Emotional,		
29			from Date	and 32 for Mental.		

MAIN

15-Mar-91 10:15 PM

FIGURE 6-35 Biorhythm worksheet

MENU

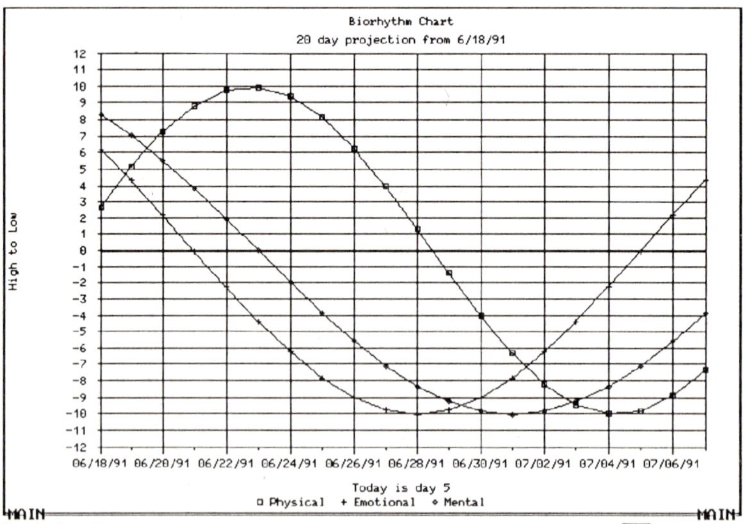

Graph Preview Num

FIGURE 6-36 Improved X-axis

You may need to make some other adjustments to your graph to get the correct appearance with a skip factor. For example, in Figure 6-36 a vertical grid has been added to make the graph clearer. However, while the first date of the range is displayed, the final value is not, making the right end of the graph difficult to read accurately. To get the final value displayed you would need to change the skip factor or the number of data points in the X-range.

OTHER ENHANCEMENTS

There are a few other options that you might want to explore as you look to improve the appearance of your graphs. You can add grid lines to make data points easier to identify and change the appearance of lines in a line chart. You can alter the hatch patterns and colors used to print/display your graphs.

Background Grids

The default background for Symphony graphs is clear, as seen in Figure 6-1. At times, however, you may want to impose a grid on a graph so that the data-point values are easier to read. In Figure 6-36, you can see gridwork of vertical and horizontal lines. In Figure 6-34, there are horizontal grid lines. To set lines, you select 2nd-Settings Other Grid, using the Horizontal, Vertical, Both, or None choices.

The Horizontal option draws a series of horizontal lines across the graph, spaced according to the tick marks on the Y-axis. The Vertical option draws a series of vertical lines on the graph, spaced according to the tick marks on the X-axis. The Both option draws both horizontal and vertical lines. The None option removes any grid lines from the graph.

Graph Formats

The 1st-Settings Format selection is where you specify the format of the data displayed in graphs that include lines (Line, XY, and HLCO graphs). When you select Format, the data range letters A, B, C, D, E, and F appear. You select the data range whose format you want to specify according to its letter. After selecting a range, the Lines Symbols, Both, and Neither choices appear.

Choose Lines if you want the data points connected by lines, with no symbols displayed. Select Symbols to have a symbol displayed at each data point, but no lines connecting the symbols. Choose Both to display both symbols and connecting lines, which is the default setting. Choose Neither to suppress both symbols and lines. This option is used with floating data labels, as described previously.

Assorted Scale Options

You have already seen that the Y-Scale and X-Scale commands allow adjustment of the X and Y scales by changing the scale type to manual and setting the lower and upper values. You have also seen that you can adjust the format and width of numbers on the axes. Two options not yet covered are Exponent and Origin.

EXPONENTS The Exponent setting determines the power of 10 by which scale numbers must be multiplied to reflect the actual values in the graph. In the graph in Figure 6-1, Symphony automatically selected an exponent of 3. The scale values (for example, 10 and 15) must be multiplied by 1000, which is 10 to the third power. You can manually select a scale exponent if you wish. Your choices are -9, -6, -3, 0, 3, and 6. To change the exponent, select Y-Scale Exponent Manual and enter the desired figure. Table 6-2 shows the text used by Symphony at the available exponent settings. By choosing the appropriate exponent, together with a suitable format and width setting, you can customize the display

Setting	Displays 1999 As
-2 (hundredths)	199900
-1 (tenths)	19990
0	1999
1 (tens)	199.9
2 (hundreds)	19.99
3 (thousands)	1.999
4 (times 10E4)	0.1999
5 (times 10E5)	0.01999

TABLE 6-2 Examples of Text at Different Exponent Settings

of numbers on the axes to a considerable degree. Bear in mind that numbers on the X-axis can only be altered by these commands if the graph type is XY. Otherwise, numbers in the X range are just treated as labels.

ORIGINS AND LIMITS You have seen that when you create a graph with Symphony, the program automatically sets the scale, or minimum-maximum range, of the Y-axis, based on the smallest and largest numbers in the data plotted. For XY graphs, Symphony also automatically establishes the X-axis scale based on values in the X range. To specify an axis range manually, you first select Type from the Scale menu and then Manual-Linear. You are prompted to enter the lower limit or minimum axis value. When you have done that, you are prompted for the upper limit or maximum axis value. For example, in Figure 6-36, the Y-Axis Lower setting is -12 and the Y-Axis Upper setting is 12.

Selecting Automatic from the Scale menu returns Symphony to its default automatic scaling. Note that although you can change the minimum and maximum axis values, you cannot determine the size of the tick-mark increment; this is set automatically by Symphony. Also note that there is nothing to prevent you from setting

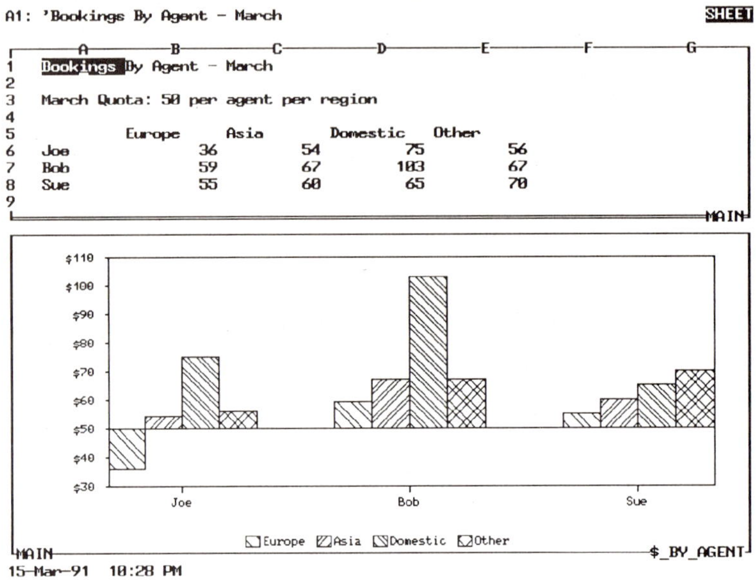

FIGURE 6-37 Graph showing an origin other than zero

an axis range that is too small to include all the data points. Symphony does not warn you when all data points cannot be plotted, so you must watch for this when using Manual-Linear settings.

By altering the origin of a graph, you can achieve several different effects. You can make sales figures look less impressive by setting an origin that is above zero, perhaps representing sales quota, as shown in Figure 6-37. This gives a graph a different perspective. To alter the origin you use the 2nd-Settings Other command and type in the number you want to use. For Figure 6-37, the origin is set at 50. Bear in mind that if you set an origin higher than the lowest value in the data ranges, you will not see all of the values on the graph.

LOG AND LINEAR Symphony normally graphs your data on a linear scale in which equal distances on the axis correspond to equal increments in value: 10, 20, 30, and so on. The Type command on the Scale menu lets you specify whether the graph axis will have a linear scale or a logarithmic scale. On a logarithmic scale, equal distances on the axis correspond to logarithmic (base 10) increments in value: 10, 100, 1000, and so on. Although you generally use linear scales, logarithmic scales are appropriate for graphing data sets that span a wide range of values when small fluctuations at the lower end of the data range must be visible.

Using Color and Hatching

In the earlier section on color printing, you saw that printed colors are determined by the settings in the PrintGraph program. This is because only a few printers can produce colored output. Colors used to display graphs on the monitor are separate from printed colors and are determined by the 1st-Settings Hue command.

When you select Colors, a menu of letters from A through F appears. Select the letter of the range whose color you want to specify. After you specify the range, a menu with the numbers 1 through 8 is displayed. These choices let you pick the color that corresponds to the selected number. The color is used for all values in the specified data range. The particular colors that correspond to the numbers 1 through 8 depend on your graphics hardware and your printer.

The Hatches option is used to specify the hatch patterns used for the bars in bar, stacked bar, mixed, and HLCO graphs, and for the slices in pie graphs. You use this option in much the same way as you set colors. Select Hatches, and then select the desired data range A through F. Next, select 1 through 8 or Range. The options 1 through 8 assign the corresponding hatch pattern to the selected data range. Displayed hatch patterns 1 through 8 are the same for all monitors, but printed hatch patterns may differ, depending on your printer.

GRAPH WINDOWS

A very useful feature of Symphony is that it allows you to view a chart in a GRAPH window next to the figures that produced the chart in a SHEET window. This option has been shown in several graphs in this chapter. The only limits on the display of graphs along with other information are the hardware you are using and the size of the windows.

Text/Graph Display

In the installation of Symphony, you are asked if you want to display graphs and text on the same screen. If you answer Yes and your display system supports this mode of operation, you can follow the steps given here to arrange a text/graph display. If your system does not support text/graph display, you may still be able to create and view graphs in a window that shares the screen with a SHEET, DOC, or FORM window, but the graph will disappear when you use one of the other windows.

Setting Up Text/Graph Display

Displaying a graph in a window can be extremely useful during graph development. You can instantly view the effects of changes in data ranges, options, or graph types. To create a graph below the SHEET window in the TMEREVO2 worksheet,

1. In SHEET mode, make the MAIN window smaller by pressing SERVICES and selecting Layout. Press (UP ARROW) to move the bottom edge of the window up to row 12.
2. Now press SERVICES and select Window. Select Create and enter the name **CHART**. Select Graph as the type.
3. To define the screen area for this window, press the period key (.) twice to move the active corner to the top left of the window. Press (DOWN ARROW) to move the top edge of the window down to line 12. Press (ENTER) and then select Quit.
4. If your display can show text windows and GRAPH windows together, then the window called CHART will be visible, displaying the current graph, as shown in Figure 6-5 earlier in this chapter.
5. To show a different graph in the CHART window, press MENU while the CHART window is active. Select Attach, and select one of the graphs you have named from the list provided.

Remember that you can zoom the active window to full screen size by pressing (ALT-F6). Press (ALT-F6) a second time to reduce the window. Use (F6) to change the active window.

Note that Figure 6-5 and some of the other figures in the chapter were taken from a high-resolution display that shows more than 20 lines on the screen at once. If you have a lower-resolution display, you may not get the legend or other graph text with your graph in smaller GRAPH windows. Symphony does not lose this material; it simply suppresses its display to keep the graph legible.

SUMMARY

Symphony's graphing commands provide a simple way to chart facts and figures that you are storing and organizing in Symphony. Using a series of settings menus, of a type that by now should be familiar, you can control many aspects of a graph's appearance. Using a system of named settings, you can create many different charts from one worksheet. Although Symphony does not offer all of the "bells and whistles" found in dedicated charting programs, it *does* help you keep to the golden rule of good graphics: "Keep It Simple." The key elements of a good graph are unity, balance, contrast, and meaning. If your graphs contain all four elements, they will be an effective means of communicating information.

In some situations there is no substitute for what is sometimes called a number chart or data table. This is essentially a printed spreadsheet, the numbers and labels arranged in columns and rows with titles and totals. When you need to provide extensive detail as well as summary information, then a spreadsheet printout is the best type of report to use. In Chapter 11, you will learn how to print out enhanced Symphony charts together with spreadsheet data by using the Allways program that is provided with Symphony 2.2.

7

COMMUNICATIONS

This chapter explores how Symphony's COMM environment enables you to use special hardware to communicate with other computers. In the COMM environment Symphony acts as a communications program, providing a way for you to exchange information between computers without leaving the Symphony program. Using the COMM environment, you can access files on electronic bulletin boards, obtain news and data from information services, and use electronic mail to communicate with other computer users. Symphony lets you control your communications hardware to work with a wide variety of remote computers, from other personal computers to large mainframe systems. You can communicate over the telephone lines with a device called a modem, or directly through a special cable.

DATA COMMUNICATIONS IN PERSPECTIVE

Symphony can be used to send data files across telephone lines to other computers around the world. You can send and receive Symphony worksheets or "capture" information from another computer into a worksheet where you can use it. You can capture commodity and stock prices and then analyze them and graph them. When you send an entire worksheet to another computer, Symphony will check the file for errors and alert you if any bits of information are lost.

The communications settings you need to control, such as the speed at which data will be sent, can be stored by Symphony using a system of special files called communications configuration files. In practice, this system works somewhat like the Name system used in the GRAPH and FORM environments. Symphony can also store the commands you use to establish contact when calling large computer systems that require identification numbers and passwords, as well as the phone numbers of the computers you regularly call.

Given these features, there is an inherent efficiency to intercomputer communications with a program like Symphony, and many potential benefits. However, the practical realities of establishing connections between different systems can be very frustrating. Much of the frustration comes from the widespread perception, fostered by the media, that calling up another computer is child's play, something that every teenager with a home computer can do at the touch of a button. The fact is that successful computer-to-computer communication requires a great deal of planning, as well as a good understanding of the specialized terminology of data communications. Consequently, any phrase like "communications made easy" is a relative one. Although it is possible to lay out the steps to building a spreadsheet model and guarantee that they will work, communications cannot be presented in such a format. You must understand the many factors that need to be coordinated in order to successfully connect two computers before you can explore this area of Symphony with any hope of success.

The rewards of communicating with your personal computer can be significant, in terms of both productivity and personal satisfaction. However, if you are using Symphony to explore data communications for the first time, be prepared to spend some time learning the basics. If you are using Symphony as part of your work and someone has already set up the necessary connections and equipment for modem communications, you may want to ask that person for specific instructions on how to use Symphony with the equipment. For more on the possibilities offered by information services, see the section towards the end of this chapter called "A Good Example."

INTERCOMPUTER COMMUNICATIONS 101

So far, you have learned how to use Symphony to enter, edit, and store your own information, as a spreadsheet, a document, or a database. Sometimes the information you want to work with is stored on another computer. There are several ways to get this information and to share your information with other users. A communications program such as Symphony, with the right hardware, offers you one way of sharing computerized information.

The Need to Communicate

When you need to use information stored on another computer, you can have someone send you a printout. However, this means that the information will have to be re-entered into the computer—a time-consuming, laborious, and error-prone process, not to mention the length of time it takes to ship the printout. A more sophisticated approach is to send the information in a file on disk. This saves some time and effort but is still limited by shipping methods. Furthermore, using disks for exchanging information requires that the two computers be able to read from and write to the same disk. This is not always the case. There are considerable differences in disk dimensions, with the sizes most commonly used by personal computers being 5 1/4-inch and 3 1/2-inch disks. Even when sizes are the same, there are significant variations in the physical arrangement of information stored on disks. This arrangement is called the disk format, and there is no universal disk format.

When used for purposes of intercomputer communication, printouts and disks are examples of intermediate media, temporary storage places for information. The most efficient method of exchanging information between computers is to eliminate this intermediate step and communicate electronically, using cables between the computers. The data can then go straight from one computer to the other. When the two computers that want to exchange information are on the same desk or in the same room, you can use a special cable between them and software known as a *file transfer utility*. Products such as LapLink, Brooklyn Bridge, and MacLink fall into this category. Symphony can be used as a limited file transfer program, as described later in the section called "Local Connections."

When there are more than two computers that need to share information within the same room or building, you can use a network of special cables between the computers. Called a *local area network,* or *LAN,* such an arrangement is increasingly common in offices today. Networks such as TOPS, Novell, and Ethernet allow different brands of computers to share information. However, there are many situations in which the computer you want to contact is not in the same state, let alone the same building. When it is not feasible to install your own cable to connect to another computer, that computer is described as *remote*. To communicate with a remote computer, you do not use your own cable; instead, you rent one: the telephone line. Establishing a connection with a remote computer is sometimes referred to as going *on-line*. Information you receive from the remote computer is said to be *downloaded* to your computer. Information you send to the remote computer is said to be *uploaded.* A computer that can receive calls from other computers is called a *host* computer. A computer that has called another computer is said to be acting as a *terminal* for the host computer.

Your computer can use the existing network of phone lines to communicate with other computers if you use a *modem.* A modem can convert electronic information into sound so that it can travel down the phone line, and convert received sound into electronic information. "Modem" is short for "modulator-demodulator." There has to be a modem at each end of a computer-to-computer phone call. The three methods of communicating—file transfer cable, network, and modem—are diagrammed in Figure 7-1.

These days, most modems are *auto-dial,* which means that when they are given the proper instructions, they will dial the telephone for you. Some modems do not have this facility; you use them by dialing the number on a phone unit and then switching over to the modem. Typical of this manual type are modems that use acoustic

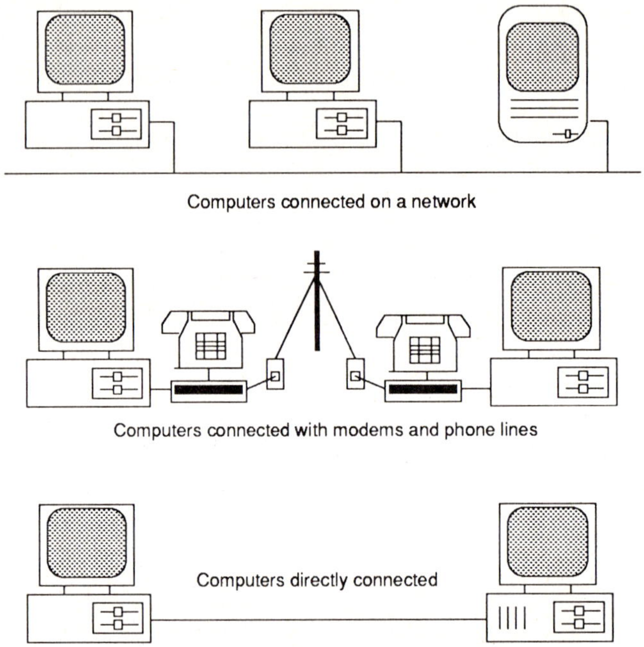

FIGURE 7-1 Intercomputer communications

couplers, which are soft cups that fit over the mouthpiece and earpiece of the handset.

Most modems not only allow you to initiate calls to other computers, but also permit your computer to answer the phone. This feature is called *auto-answer*. However, there is no danger of someone gaining access to your computer through your modem unless you specifically program it to answer calls. With Symphony this means using the Wait-Mode command and leaving both the computer and modem turned on. The Wait-Mode command is described later in the section on receiving calls.

Working with Modems

When you purchase a modem for your personal computer, you have to decide between internal and external models. An *internal*

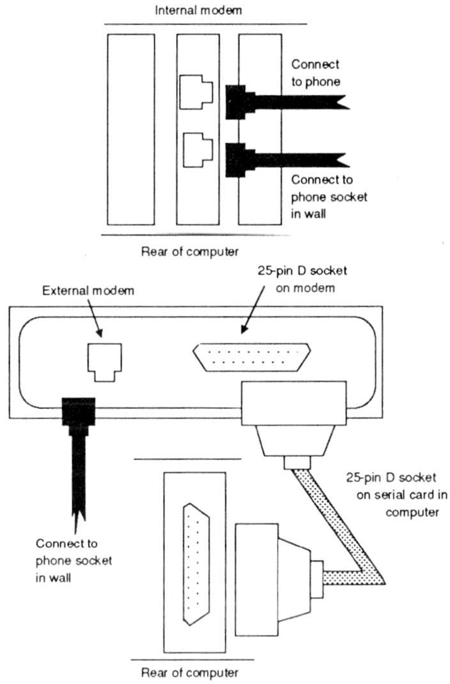

FIGURE 7-2 Connecting a modem

modem is a printed circuit board or card that fits into an expansion slot inside your machine, so a prerequisite to installing one is a spare slot. When the internal modem is installed, you plug a cable from the telephone wall socket into the modem through the back of the computer, as shown in Figure 7- 2. You can usually plug the telephone handset into the modem as well, to give you the ability to use the same phone line for either voice or data. Most internal modem cards have a small speaker on them so that you can hear the calls being made, a very helpful feature when you are trying to solve problems in computer-to-computer connections.

An *external* modem consists of a small box attached to the outside of your personal computer, usually by means of a cable. The telephone line is plugged in to the modem, and a telephone handset can usually be connected as well. Some external modems have a set of lights on the front that show you the progress of calls between computers, as well as a speaker to let you listen to calls. An external modem attaches to a socket on the back of your computer. This socket is either a 9-pin or 25-pin male D socket. It is called a D socket because it is shaped like the letter "D" to prevent connections from being reversed. The term "male" implies that it has the pins sticking out, waiting for a plug that has holes in it. This socket, referred to as a serial port or COM port, for reasons described in a moment, may be part of your computer's standard equipment, or it may need to be added, in which case you will need to install a serial expansion card in your system.

An internal modem gets the electricity it needs to operate from within the computer, but an external modem is usually powered by a battery or transformer. Whereas an internal modem offers a simple and compact way to connect your computer to the telephone lines, an external modem can easily be transferred from one computer to another, and the ones with lights on them give you a clearer picture of what is happening when you are connecting with a computer.

Symphony operates on personal computers that are designed to the IBM PC standard. Within this design, provision has been made for several communication channels through which information can be fed into the computer from outside sources, and through which the computer can send out information. These channels can be used by either internal or external modems. The channels used for telephone communications are referred to as *COM ports* and are numbered COM1, COM2, and so on. These designations can refer to either the physical socket that you plug the modem in to, or the channel within the operating system that the modem uses.

Although some modems can be installed as COM3 or COM4, Symphony works with either COM1 or COM2. These channels are also referred to as *serial ports* because they transmit information in a series of characters. (This distinguishes them from the parallel ports, used by most printers, which send information as several characters at once. Think of "serial" as marching in single file and "parallel" as marching eight abreast.)

If you have an internal modem card, you will set switches on it to tell the computer it is either using COM1 or COM2. If you have an external modem, it will be connected to your computer with a D connector, shown in Figure 7-2, that is either part of the computer's main circuit board or installed on a serial expansion card. In either case, this socket will have been set up as either COM1 or COM2 by means of switches on the card itself or elsewhere inside the computer. You will sometimes see a serial socket referred to as an *RS232* or *RS232C port,* an allusion to the set of standards governing serial connectors, although in practice there is very little that is standard about serial ports on personal computers.

For your modem to work properly with Symphony, it must be installed as or connected to either COM1 or COM2, and there must be nothing else using this port number. For example, suppose you install an internal modem that has its switches set to COM1. You cannot, at the same time, install a plotter that is attached to a port on a serial card that has been set up as COM1.

Cables and Chaos

Few subjects in the history of computing have caused so much anguish and frustration as those that go by the deceptively innocuous name of "serial cables." The simple truth is this: If you use the wrong cable to connect your external modem to your personal computer, your attempts to communicate via the modem are doomed.

Note

One advantage of using an internal modem is that you do not have to worry about using the right cable. If you want to buy an external modem, get cable from the same supplier and make sure you have a guarantee that it is the correct cable.

The problem with serial cables is that there is no such thing as a "standard serial cable" or a "standard modem cable." This may come as a surprise if you have heard the serial port referred to as the RS232C port, a reference to a set of standards. What has happened in practice is that serial ports have been used for such a variety of tasks besides modem connection that variations have arisen. For example, some printers and plotters use the serial port, as do some mice (the pointing devices used for computer input). This problem is further compounded by the existence of two distinctly different types of serial cable that are referred to with the word "modem."

The following notes are provided so that you can discuss this subject intelligently with your dealer or coworkers. There are two factors to consider: the plugs on the end of the cable, and the pins within the plug.

PLUG SIZE The first IBM PCs used serial connectors with room for 25 pins. The socket on the computer had the pins sticking out (male), and so the plug on the serial cable had holes in it (female). This distinguished it from the parallel connector used by most printers, since that had holes in it. However, both connectors were type D so that they could only be inserted one way (see Figure 7-2). It may come as a surprise to find out that to communicate with a modem, only three wires are absolutely necessary: one to send signals, one to receive, and a common ground wire. In effect, this meant that for most uses the 25-pin socket was overkill. This was remedied on later models, beginning with the IBM PC AT, which adopted a 9-pin serial socket. The smaller socket was quickly copied on laptop computers. However, by this time most external modems (as well as other serial devices) were in production with 25-pin ports. Consequently, there was a big boom in 25-pin to 9-pin converters.

The existence of two sizes of serial connector means that you must get a cable with the right size of socket at each end or use a converter in order to actually plug the cable in. You must also make sure that the cable has a female connector on the end that connects to the PC, and a connector of the correct gender where it connects to the modem (most modems have female sockets on them, so the cable will be female-to-male).

Note These remarks apply to "typical" PC systems. There may be proprietary connectors on your personal computer or modem that differ from any of these "standards."

PIN CONNECTION If you look closely at the male D plug on a serial cable, you may see that the holes are numbered. Hole number 1 receives pin number 1 and so on. In what is sometimes referred to as a "straight" serial cable, pin 1 on one end connects to pin 1 on the other, pin 2 to pin 2, and so on. A serial cable in which all pins are connected in this manner might be referred to as a "full straight." Some serial cables save money by only connecting some of the pins, producing a "thin" cable.

As mentioned earlier, there are only three essential wires in a modem cable. These connect pins 2, 3, and 7. Typically, pin 2 is for characters leaving the computer, pin 3 is for characters arriving at the computer, and 7 is a ground signal. However, an IBM PC with a 25-pin serial connector also uses pins 5, 6, and 20 for modem connection. If the modem is to answer the phone, then pin 22 is used as well. Unless a thin cable is guaranteed to work with your particular modem and personal computer, you are better off with a full cable.

NULL MODEM CABLES One final area of serial cable confusion is the so-called "null modem cable." This cable gets its name from its role in connecting two computers directly, *without* modems. It stands to reason that you do *not* want a null modem cable to connect your modem to your personal computer. In a null modem, the wires connecting pins 2 and 3 are crossed, so that what is sent from one computer on pin 2 reaches the other on pin 3. If you are using Symphony to directly connect two computers through their serial ports, you will need one of these cables. If you already have a straight modem cable, you can buy a small connector, called a modem eliminator, that fits between a straight serial cable and a serial port. This device crosses wires 2 and 3 to create a null modem connection.

How Data Is Sent

You may see references in your modem's documentation to *asynchronous* communications. This refers to how the actual data being communicated is packaged. To explain this term, and some of the mechanics of data communication, it is necessary to look at how information is represented by computers.

As you may know, information on computers is stored in binary form, where a collection of 1s and 0s represent characters. Each 1 or 0 is called a *bit,* short for "binary digit." With eight bits you can have 256 different combinations (2 to the power of 8). These combinations can be depicted in this way:

00000000
00000001
00000010
00000011

On personal computers each one of these 256 combinations is assigned a character, known as an *ASCII character* (short for American Standard Computer Information Interchange). A collection of eight bits is known as a *byte,* the unit of measurement which the disk operating system uses when showing you the size of files stored on disk.

You do not need 256 characters to write most messages and represent numbers. If you use just seven bits, you can have 128 characters (2 to the power of 7). Using seven bits saves space when storing information and time when transmitting it. In data communications the term *word* is used for one character of data. Many information services use words that are seven bits long. Some computer bulletin boards use eight-bit words, which gives them the ability to handle data that contains the full range of ASCII codes, including the other 128 characters known as the *upper ASCII codes.*

Using a modem, data may be transmitted directly from your computer's keyboard, or, in larger amounts, from memory or disk. The method of transmission known as asynchronous is most suitable for the former, whereas a method known as *synchronous* is sometimes used for larger data volumes. The serial ports in most personal computers are asynchronous.

Note Synchronous boards are usually installed only for special operations. Symphony does not support synchronous communications.

Asynchronous transmission sends data in units of one character, with a variable time interval between each one. This method was developed for direct keyboard use and is able to cope with differing time gaps between each transmitted character. The receiving terminal therefore needs some way of determining when a character begins and ends. This is achieved by inserting a start bit before the main character string, and either one or two stop bits at the end.

Remember that each bit is either a 1 or a 0. On the phone, you can think of these as high tones or low tones. A personal computer working as an asynchronous terminal almost always maintains a mark bit set to 1, a high tone, when it is idle during a communication session. In fact, when a modem answers a call you can hear this high tone on the line. When a character is transmitted, the start bit, set to 0, alerts the receiving terminal, which then begins

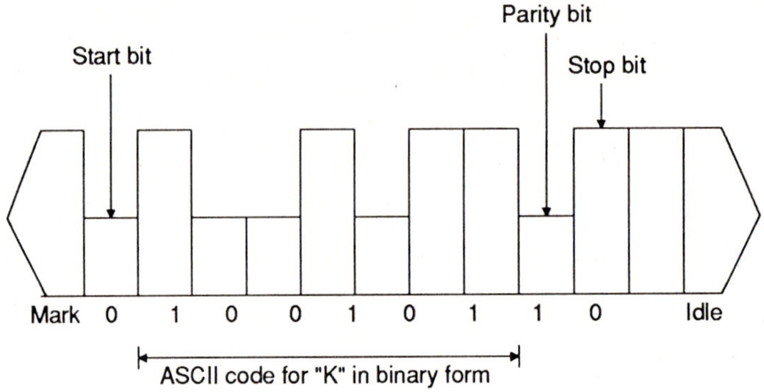

FIGURE 7-3 Transmitting a character

sampling the incoming data. This is why you hear the high tone of the modem switch to a lower tone as the connection is made.

After the seven-bit code for the character is sent, followed by the parity bit (described in the next section), there is a stop signal consisting of one or two bits to indicate the end of the character or the return to idle state. The diagram in Figure 7-3 illustrates the data stream and line activity during transmission of the letter "K." The start bit is always a change to the opposite of the idle state for one bit's duration. While the line is idle, it remains at a static or "mark" condition until the start bit of the next character. The stop bit or bits are the same line condition as the idle state for 1 or 2 bits' duration.

Although Symphony does not support synchronous transmission, it is worth noting that this method of communicating sends data as a continuous stream at a constant rate, thus making maximum use of the available line capacity. The terminal equipment at each end (usually the modems) is synchronized before transmission begins, enabling the receiving terminal to detect the beginning of the data stream and thereafter pick off each character by counting the number of bits. This usually saves two or three bits per character—the start bit and one or two stop bits—and can be 25% faster than asynchronous transmission. Taking the example in

Figure 7-3, only 8 bits would be needed to transmit the letter "K" synchronously, instead of the 10 bits needed for asynchronous transmission. At a transmission speed of 2400 bits per second, characters in this form would be transmitted at a maximum rate of 240 per second asynchronously or 300 per second synchronously. If you are planning large-scale exchanges of information, you might want to explore a synchronous system, but you will not be able to use Symphony for this mode of communication.

A Question of Parity

A technique known as *parity checking* is used by computers when communicating to determine if characters have been corrupted by line interference during transmission. To indicate if line corruption has occurred, an additional bit, the parity bit, is added to each character. When parity is even, the number of ones (including the parity bit) adds up to an even number; when parity is odd, the total will be an odd number. A setting referred to as "Ignore parity" means that the computer ignores the parity setting. A setting of None or No for parity means that no parity bit has been added. You must set the parity at your end of the call to be the same as that of the distant computer you are calling. Note that parity checking does not really guarantee error-free transmission, because it offers no protection against two bits in a character string being corrupted at the same time.

The Duplex Question

Data can usually be transmitted in both directions between computers acting as terminals. In the mode of operation known as half duplex this is possible, but only in one direction at a time. In full duplex mode, data can be transmitted in both directions simultaneously. Duplex is the transmission mode normally used for communicating data between two personal computers and for accessing central computer systems. Data can be sent in both directions at once, providing efficient operation when error correction is used. The duplex mode is divided into two subcategories: either full duplex or asymmetrical duplex.

Full duplex means data transmission in both directions at the same speed simultaneously. Full duplex can be used for keyboard data transmission, to echo back the transmitted data from the receiving terminal for error checking. Keyboard transmission can then take place if necessary. For direct data transmission between computers, the receiving machine can request the retransmission of data if errors have occurred. It can also send acknowledgements when data has been received correctly, without interrupting the flow of data from the sending terminal. Full duplex is therefore ideal for interactive and file transfer applications.

Asymmetrical duplex provides high-speed data transfer one direction and slower transmission in the reverse direction. This makes it suitable for accessing database services, where the bulk of information comes in one direction from a distant database, but allows you to send instructions the other way without interrupting the flow of data. Symphony does not support asymmetrical duplex operation.

A Good Line

To originate phone calls in the COMM environment, you must have your modem correctly connected to your computer and to the phone line. Slipshod and faulty connections are a major source of problems when working with data communications; also, the telephone line itself can be a source of trouble because noise on the lines affects data that is being transmitted. If you see strange and unexpected characters on your screen while communicating, or if characters you have typed inexplicably disappear, then you probably have a poor phone line. You might want to have your telephone company check the line for worn insulation and other faults. You can sometimes have the signal on your line boosted or strengthened. If you are in an office with a multiple-line phone system you may want to get a dedicated telephone line, one that is not shared with other telephone users. If someone picks up your line while you are connected to another computer they will just hear a fuzzy noise, but when they hang up it will probably break your connection.

A particular problem arises when you are using a modem on a line that has call-waiting installed. When you are communicating with another computer and someone calls on the line, the call-waiting signal will disrupt the connection. In some phone systems, call-waiting can be turned off by entering a special code from the telephone dial. Ask your phone company if you can do this.

INTO COMM MODE

To use Symphony's communications capability, you must be in the COMM environment. This is where Symphony displays what you type to the other computer and the response that the other computer makes.

Moving to the COMM Environment

To explore the COMM environment, load Symphony and in a fresh worksheet press TYPE (ALT-F10) and select COMM. The columns and rows of the worksheet will be replaced by an empty rectangle. The environment indicator in the upper-right corner of the screen reminds you that you are in the COMM environment. The cursor is just an underscore that appears near the upper-left corner of the screen. Whereas in other work environments, such as DOC or FORM, you can immediately get down to work at the cursor location, when you first activate the COMM environment, you cannot type anything. You must establish a connection with another computer before you can enter information.

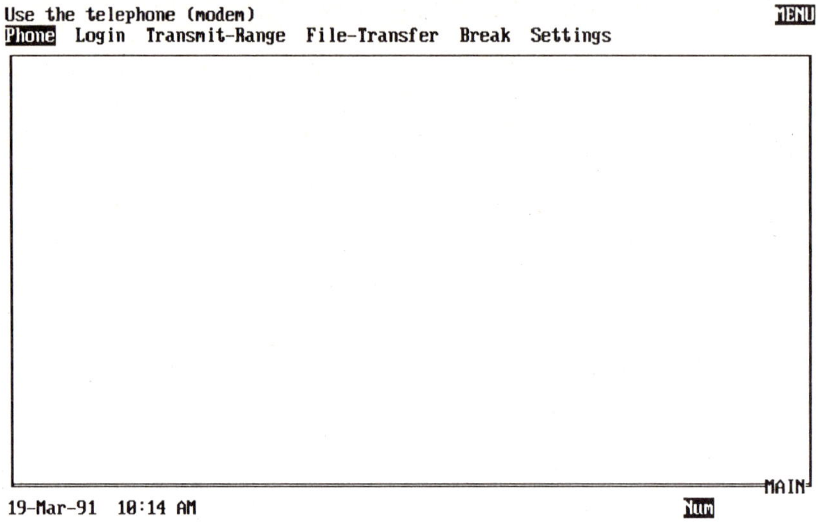

FIGURE 7-4 The COMM environment with MENU

Note — Intercomputer communications is a lot like housc-painting: nine tenths preparation, one tenth execution.

Most activity in the COMM environment is controlled by the menu you get when you press (F10), referred to as the main COMM menu. You can see this and the rest of the initial COMM environment screen in Figure 7-4.

Note — If Symphony does not respond when you type on your keyboard in a COMM window, try pressing (CTRL-Q) before you talk to your dealer or technical resource person.

What You Need to Know

There are preparations to make and questions to answer before you try calling another computer with Symphony. To connect to another computer system over the telephone lines, you need a modem that is supported by Symphony, a phone cord to connect the modem to the telephone line, and, if you are using an external modem, possibly a cable to connect it to your computer's communications port. (Some external modems attach directly to the communications port without a cable.)

You also need to know what type of telephone service you have. This does not mean Sprint versus AT&T, or even good versus mediocre—it means pulse versus tone. If you lift the receiver on your phone and dial a number, you will hear a series of clicking sounds if you are using pulse service. If you hear a single beep for each number you dial, you are using tone service. Some phones can be switched between tone and pulse; some older phones cannot generate tones. This means that your computer may be able to use tone service even if your phone cannot. Check with your local phone company, since tone service is definitely preferable.

About Settings

Communications between two computers requires that both systems transmit data in the same way. This means both computers must use the same *communications settings*. These settings include baud rate, parity, word length, and stop bits, all of which are further described in a moment. The operator of the computer you want to connect to should be able to furnish you with a list of the communications settings you must use to establish a connection with that computer.

Obviously, the computer you are going to connect with has a phone number and you will need to know it. Large information services such as CompuServe can be reached through a local phone number in larger cities. These local numbers are actually part of a special telephone network designed to provide less expensive access to distant computers.

To use most information services, you need an account number and a password. You are asked to supply these at the beginning of

```
Speed and type of transmission                                                      MENU
Interface  Phone  Terminal  Send  Break  Handshaking  Capture  Login  Name  Quit

 Interface            Terminal                  Send
    Baud:      110      Screen:     Window        EOL:       \m
    Parity:    None     Echo:       No            Delay:     0
    Length:    7        Linefeed:   No            Response:  \j
    Stop bits: 1        Backspace:  Backspace     Format:    No
    Comm Port: COM1     Wrap:       Yes         Break:       60
  Phone                 Delay:      0           Handshaking
    Type:      Pulse    Translation:              Inbound:  Yes
    Dial:      60         (none)                  Outbound: Yes
    Answer:    15                               Capture:
    Number:                                       Range:    No
                                                  Printer:  No
                                              Communications Settings:
```

FIGURE 7-5 Communications settings sheet

a communication session for billing and identification purposes. The process of providing such information is known as *logging in.*

Using Settings Sheets

Before you can use Symphony's COMM commands to communicate with another computer, you must select Settings from the main COMM menu and define a number of settings on the sheet, shown in Figure 7-5. The Communications settings sheet describes how data will be sent and received, what kind of telephone equipment you have, and where the data retrieved from the remote computer system is to be stored. At first, the sheet contains the default settings, shown in Figure 7-5, which you can accept or change. Since communication between two computer systems requires that both systems transmit data in the same way, you must change any communications settings that do not match those required by the host computer you are planning to call.

Because many of the settings depend on the characteristics of the remote computer and these vary from computer to computer, Symphony lets you store a Communications settings sheet in a communications configuration file on disk with the special extension (CCF). You can have a number of these, each with settings for a different host computer. In fact, Symphony provides a collection of preconfigured settings sheets with sample settings for connecting with various services.

Suppose you have signed up with CompuServe, one of the largest general-purpose electronic information systems for personal computer users. From CompuServe you have received your account number, initial password, and a list of local phone numbers you can use to reach the service. Instead of defining all of the settings yourself, you can choose Name from the Settings menu and then Retrieve. A list of available CCF files appears, as shown in the following example:

```
Configuration file name: C:\SYM22\*.ccf                                          FILES
ADP.CCF           COMPUSRV.CCF      DOWJONES.CCF      MCI.CCF          SOURCE.CCF
| Interface            Terminal                Send                              |
```

You select COMPUSRV.CCF, and Symphony displays the settings sheet you have selected. The name of the settings sheet appears in its lower-right corner, as shown in Figure 7-6. The CCF files supplied by Symphony are listed in Table 7-1.

```
Maintain Communications configuration files (.CCF)                                MENU
Interface  Phone  Terminal  Send  Break  Handshaking  Capture  Login  Name  Quit

 Interface              Terminal                    Send
    Baud:       1200      Screen:      Window         EOL:        \m
    Parity:     None      Echo:        No             Delay:      0
    Length:     7         Linefeed:    No             Response:
    Stop bits:  1         Backspace:   Backspace      Format:     No
    Comm Port:  COM1      Wrap:        Yes          Break:        60
  Phone                   Delay:       30           Handshaking
    Type:       Tone      Translation:                Inbound:    Yes
    Dial:       60          (none)                    Outbound:   Yes
    Answer:     30                                  Capture:
    Number:                                           Range:      No
                                                      Printer:    No
===================================Communications Settings: C:\SYM22\COMPUSRV.CCF
```

FIGURE 7-6 The COMPUSRV.CCF settings

File	Service	Description
COMPUSRV.CCF	CompuServe	General on-line information service
DOWJONES.CCF	Dow Jones News Retrieval	On-line financial news service
MCI.CCF	MCI Mail	Electronic mail service
SOURCE.CCF	The Source	General on-line information service
ADP.CCF	General Purpose	On-line information service

TABLE 7-1 CCF Files Supplied with Symphony

As you can see by comparing Figures 7-5 and 7-6, there are considerable differences between the default settings and those used for calling CompuServe. The only item you need to adjust before calling CompuServe is the Number entry under the heading "Phone," which is left blank in the COMPUSRV.CCF file that Symphony provides, since users in different parts of the country access CompuServe through different numbers. If you add a phone number, as described in a moment, you can use the Name Save command to store the updated CCF file either under the old name or a new name.

You can automatically load a communications configuration file into the Communications settings sheet each time you start a Symphony session or every time you work with a specific worksheet, as described later in the section on "Storing Communications Settings." After you load a CCF file, the settings sheet can only be returned to the default values by exiting the current worksheet or creating a new one.

In practice, you will probably not want to use the default settings. Most of your communication sessions will be conducted with your own versions of the CCF files that Symphony supplies. The following sections describe each of the aspects of the settings that you can adjust for specific services not covered by the supplied CCF files.

Interface Settings

The first item on the Settings menu is Interface. The settings listed in this category are Baud, Parity, Length, Stop bits, and Comm Port. These control what are referred to as communications *protocols*. For data communications to be successful, the sending and receiving computers have to transmit data according to the same rules, or protocols. If these protocols do not match, you will have difficulties. The following elements, described in the order in which they are found on the Communications settings sheet, make up the communications protocols and can be changed with the Interface command.

BAUD The speed at which data transmission between computers occurs is referred to as the *baud rate*. One baud is roughly equal to one bit per second (bps). Thus 1200 baud, a popular rate used by many personal computer modems, is about 1200 bits per second or approximately 120 characters. Typically, a modem can only handle certain rates, and the higher the rates a modem can handle, the more expensive the modem. The baud rate that you select must be one that your modem can handle as well as one the other computer is expecting. Many large host computers support 300, 1200, and 2400 baud and will adjust their rate according to the one you use. Some host computers in Europe support two speeds, one for information coming from the host and another for information going to the host. Written as 1200/75, such a rate indicates asymmetrical duplex operation, which is not supported by Symphony.

The highest rate supported by Symphony, 9600, is generally used when directly connecting two computers. When you select Baud, you choose the appropriate rate, numbered 1 through 8:

1	110	5	1200
2	150	6	2400
3	300	7	4800
4	600	8	9600

PARITY As mentioned earlier, the parity bit is the single bit that the computer uses to perform error checking. Typical choices are Odd, Even, or No parity. Set this to whatever the other computer is expecting. When you select Parity, you choose one of the three numbered settings:

1	None
2	Odd
3	Even

If you set the parity incorrectly, the data that you receive back from the host may be hard to read, due to strange-looking characters. You will not see it, but the data you transmit will also be incomprehensible to the host. Strange received characters, such as ¶<?}{[*¿, can mean either a poor phone line or incorrect parity setting. If the host computer appears to understand most of what you type to it, then it is probably the phone line that is at fault.

LENGTH Each character communicated by a computer is made up of bits. A group of bits is referred to, in data communications terms, as a word. Typically data words are seven bits in length, but some host computer systems use eight-bit words. The Length settings should match the word length used by the host. When you select Length from the Interface menu, you choose either of these settings:

1	7
2	8

STOP BITS As mentioned earlier, in asynchronous transmission, each word is followed by one or two stop bits, signaling the end of the word. The number of stop bits depends on the system that you're talking to. One stop bit is usually sufficient. When you select Stop bits from the Interface menu, you choose either of these settings:

1	1
2	2

COMM PORT While not strictly speaking a protocol, selecting the proper communications port is essential to using a modem. Symphony allows you to select either of these settings:

1	COM1
2	COM2

The COM port you select must be the one used by the serial card to which your external modem is connected or the one assigned to your internal modem card.

Phone Settings

There are several important settings that may need to be adjusted under the second item on the Settings menu, Phone. The Phone settings only work with modems that can automatically dial and answer telephone calls. You will have to dial and answer telephone calls manually if your modem does not perform these functions. The Phone settings are Type, Dial, Answer, and Number.

TYPE When using telephone lines for communications with Symphony, as opposed to a direct-wire connection, you may need to choose Type from the Phone menu to change the setting to Pulse or Tone to match the type of phone service you are using (this is determined by your phone, not the host computer's).

DIAL You can control how much time Symphony spends trying to call a number with the Dial option. The Dial setting is the maximum amount of time Symphony allows to elapse while trying to make a phone call. If the receiving computer does not answer the call within this period, Symphony automatically hangs up. Do not alter this from the default of 60 seconds unless you are having problems establishing a connection.

ANSWER You can control how much time Symphony waits before telling the modem to answer a call using the Answer option. Do not change this from the default of 15 seconds unless you are having problems getting an auto-answer arrangement to work.

NUMBER If you want a settings sheet to be dedicated to a particular computer-to-computer connection, you can use the Number option to enter the telephone number of the computer that the sheet is to be used for. This will save you entering the number each time you want to make a call. When entering a telephone number, the only punctuation you can use is a comma (,). You cannot include hyphens or spaces; they would confuse Symphony. The comma is only used when you need to tell the modem to pause briefly before dialing the numbers that follow.

Suppose you are going to call the number 555-4568. You would select Number, type **5554568**, and then press (ENTER). If you need to add a 9 to get an outside line, you would enter **95554568**. If you need a pause after dialing 9 for the outside line, you would enter **9,5554568**. If you are in New York and the number 555-4568 is in San Francisco, you would enter **4155554568**.

Terminal Emulation

When your personal computer is connected to a host computer, it is working as a terminal on that computer system. Terminals have particular methods of handling the entry and display of information on their screens. Host computers expect all terminals, including personal computers, to behave in specific ways. Symphony lets your computer behave like, or *emulate,* a variety of common computer terminals. You control this aspect of a communications connection with the Terminal option back on the COMM Settings menu. The areas you can control with options are Screen, Echo, Linefeed, Backspace, Wrap, Delay, Translation.

SCREEN Emulating some terminals requires full screen operation. For example, the host computer will assume that there is room for nearly 80 characters across a line and that about 25 lines can be placed on one screen. In this case, your COMM window must be full size or you may not be able to read everything that the host computer communicates to you. Other terminals do not need to use the entire screen, so the COMM window can be any size you like. The Screen choices are Full-Screen or Window.

ECHO When you press a key on the keyboard, a character generally appears on the screen. This is referred to as *screen echo.* In the Communications settings sheet you must specify whether the host computer will echo the characters you type back to your screen, or whether Symphony will do this. When you select Echo, you choose No or Yes in response to the question "Echo characters locally?" For most information services the choice is No. The choice is Yes when you communicate with another system that is using Symphony. The Echo settings correspond to two terms described earlier: duplex and half duplex. When Echo is set to Yes, you have half duplex. Full duplex is Echo set to No.

LINEFEED When you press (ENTER) on most terminals, the cursor moves to the beginning of the next line. On some terminals, however, pressing (ENTER) moves the cursor to the beginning of the current line, so what you type keeps appearing on the same line. To avoid this problem, you can ask Symphony to issue a linefeed—that is, move the cursor to the next line—each time you press (ENTER). To do this, choose Linefeed and then Yes.

BACKSPACE The (BACKSPACE) key usually deletes the character to the left of the cursor. On some terminals it works like the (DEL) key, which deletes the character at the cursor. When you select Backspace from the Terminal menu, you can choose either Backspace or Delete to have the (BACKSPACE) key operate normally or like the (DEL) key.

WRAP As your typing gets to the end of the line on some terminals, the characters that exceed the length of the line move to the next line, just as they do in the DOC environment. This word wrap feature is not supported by all terminals. On some terminals, you must press (ENTER) to move to the next line, or characters will disappear off the right edge of the screen. Choose Wrap and then Yes when you want the text to wrap on your screen.

DELAY When you send data to another computer, the other computer generally receives the data in a temporary storage location, or buffer. This buffer is generally of limited size. If you send the information too quickly, you can exceed the size of the buffer and lose information. To help prevent this, Symphony lets you pause, or delay, transmission between characters. When you select Delay, you can enter the period as a number of seconds.

TRANSLATION Used in communicating with computers in other countries, the Translation setting lets you translate the characters you type on your keyboard into the correct characters for the country you are calling. For example, there is no £ symbol on an American personal computer keyboard. This could be a problem if you want to communicate about financial matters with someone in Britain. Symphony's translation facility allows you to type a character that is on the U.S. keyboard and have this translated, as it is sent, into a £. This facility is also available for reading text files into Symphony worksheets, as described in Chapter 11.

When you select Translation, the choices are Default, National, Custom, and Generate. When you choose Default, there is no translation and you see "(none)" in the Translation portion of the settings sheet. The National option gives you a choice of ten countries, listed as A through J. Select the correct letter for the country whose character set you want your typing to be translated to. As an alternative, you can choose Translate Custom to load a customized character translation file. This is a special file with the extension CTF, in which the required character translation is defined. You use the Translate Generate command to create a CTF file, using the codes described in Appendix A.

Storing Communications Settings

In the COMM environment, as well as everywhere else in Symphony, the golden rule is save, save, and save again. You can go to a lot of trouble getting the settings just right, but unless you save them they will be lost as soon as you exit from Symphony. Exiting can happen sooner than you expect if there is a power cut, or if you get stuck trying to connect another computer and have to restart your system. To avoid having to change the communications settings every time you place a call, save them in a CCF file. To do this you select Name from the Settings menu. Enter a name for the Communications settings sheet. Do not add the .CCF suffix; Symphony will do this for you. Choose a mnemonic name, one that reminds you of the name of the information service. This makes it easier to retrieve the file that contains the settings you need the next time you call the service.

The CCF file is separate from and not automatically connected to the current worksheet file. To make this connection, so that whenever you retrieve a particular worksheet a specific CCF file is also retrieved ready to use, press SERVICES and choose Settings, followed by Communications. Select Set and choose the CCF file from the list provided by pressing (ENTER). Now press (ESC) to return to the main SERVICES menu, and choose File Save to store the worksheet. This procedure is useful if you are using the Capture Range feature described later in this chapter. You can create a worksheet that you use every time you contact a particular on-line service. Screen data from the service is stored in the same range of the worksheet every time.

If there is one computer service that you contact more than any other, you can establish a CCF file as the default for all worksheets. This is done with the SERVICES Configuration Communications Set command. You specify a CCF file that will always be used unless you specifically retrieve another one, either with the Name Retrieve command or by loading a worksheet that has a default CCF file attached to it. As long as you use the Update command on the Configuration menu after selecting a CCF file, this setting will remain in place the next time you load Symphony.

GOING ON-LINE

Now that you have taken care of the matter of settings, you are ready to make a call. Make sure that you have handy any account numbers, ID numbers, passwords, and command lists from the information service that you will be calling. Check that you have the correct settings in place, either by altering the defaults or by loading a stored settings sheet.

Making the Connection

Communicating with a remote computer is usually a two-stage process. First, you make the telephone connection so that you can send characters to the host computer; then you identify yourself to the host. The second stage is known as logging in. Since it comes immediately after the initial connection is established, you should read both this section and the next before making your first call.

To establish a connection, follow these steps:

1. Make sure that nobody else is using the phone line or planning to use it for the duration of your session. Also make sure that no urgent calls are expected on the line you will be using, since you cannot receive calls while connected to the other computer. (If you have call-waiting, an incoming call can terminate your connection, so temporarily disable this feature if you can). If you are using an external modem, make sure that it is turned on and connected properly (internal modems are on whenever your computer is on).

2. Use MENU Settings to review the settings and make sure they are correct, changing any parameters that need adjusting and saving the altered settings in a CCF file with the Name Save command.

3. Escape from the Settings menu and select Phone from the main COMM menu (*not* the Phone command you use to change the Phone settings on the Communications settings sheet). You will see the menu shown in Figure 7-7.

4. Select Call, and the phone number you entered on the Communications settings sheet will appear in the control panel. If you did not enter a number in the settings sheet, you can type the number now, using no spaces or punctuation such as hyphens

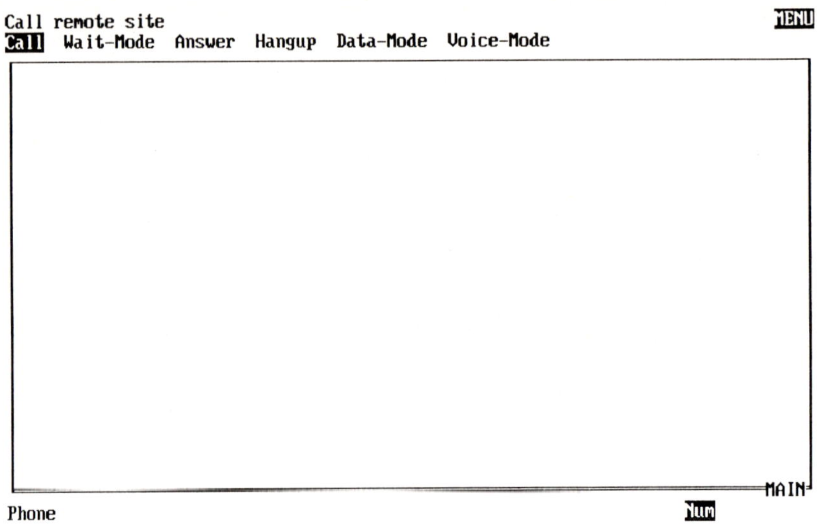

FIGURE 7-7 Using the Phone command

and brackets. If you do not have an auto-dial modem, you will have to dial the number yourself on the telephone, as described later in this section.

5. Press (ENTER), and Symphony tells the modem to dial the number. If the modem connection is correct, you will see the message "Dialing..." in the control panel, and you may hear a series of beeps and tones. On modems with lights on the front, some of the lights will flash.

6. When the modem finishes dialing, the message disappears. You may be able to hear the telephone ring at the other end of the line. If an error message appears, press MENU, then (ESC), and start the call over again. For example, the message may indicate that the number you are calling is busy.

7. Listen for a click as the other computer's modem picks up the phone, followed by the high-pitched sound described earlier. This is called the *carrier* tone and it tells you that you have connected with the information service. Symphony displays the message "OnLine" at the bottom of the screen, meaning that every character you type will now be sent through the telephone lines to the other computer. Any characters sent by the other computer will appear on your screen.

8. Press the key required to begin the log-in procedure. Many information services expect you to press (ENTER) one or more times to begin logging in. You must do this fairly quickly after the other computer answers, or the information service will assume there is nobody on the line and hang up, terminating the connection.

9. After you press the required key, the information service will display some sort of response on your screen (if nothing happens, refer to the "Troubleshooting" section). You are now ready to perform the log-in sequence.

Logging In

The process of identifying yourself as a legitimate user of the information service is known as logging in. After your computer has connected with the information service, a message of some kind will appear on the screen. This may be just a few characters with a cursor, rather like the DOS prompt. The service will probably want you to identify yourself. In some cases you will need to say which area of the service you want to access. Type the appropriate pieces of log-in information, pressing (ENTER) after each piece. What you type will appear in the COMM window.

If you have to enter a password, be sure to type it accurately, down to the use of matching upper- and lowercase letters. What you type for a password may not appear on the screen. This is a security measure. Most systems will give you a couple of chances to enter the password before hanging up.

When your log-in procedure is complete, instructions for using the information service will probably appear on the screen. Some services will want account information the first time you log in. If you have logged in with a temporary password you should follow the service's instructions to change the password to one of your own choosing. Keep this password from others, change it frequently, and do not lose it.

Once you have seen how a particular system handles logging in, you can automate the log-in procedure by using a Login settings sheet, as described in a moment.

Logging Off from The Information Service

When you want to break a connection with another computer you can press the (BREAK) key. This will break the connection. However, on-line etiquette states that you should announce your departure and make an orderly exit. This helps the service manage multiple users more efficiently and bill you accurately (simply breaking the connection may result in you being charged for using the service past the time when you hung up).

To make a proper exit, issue the quit command recognized by the service. This could be Quit, Off, Lo, Exit, Bye, or something similar. The service should display a message confirming that you have ended the communications session. Some services will also display a message telling you how long you were connected.

After you log off, the telephone must be hung up. With auto-dial modems this is done by the modem. If you do not have an auto-dial modem, you must hang up the telephone using Symphony. Press MENU and select Phone and then Hangup.

TROUBLESHOOTING

The following guidelines for solving common communications problems cannot cover all possible situations. When trying to connect to an information service for which you are paying fees, do not hesitate to call the service's customer assistance number to get help.

Cannot Make a Connection

If nothing happens when you attempt to call the information service, you should first make sure that the modem is correctly installed in your computer or properly attached to the communications port and that the modem is properly connected to the telephone. Next check the Baud and Length settings on the Communications settings sheet. These settings must match the settings the information service requires. Check the Comm Port setting on the Communications settings sheet. If the wrong communications port is specified, Symphony will not be able to talk to the modem.

Cannot See What You Type

If you do connect but the COMM environment screen does not display the characters you type, you can probably correct the problem by changing one of the terminal settings on the Communications settings sheet. Press MENU and select Settings, followed by Terminal and then Echo. Select Yes and then choose Quit to return to the COMM mode.

Characters in Stereo

If every character you type appears twice, you can probably correct the problem by changing the Terminal Echo setting on the Communications settings sheet. Press MENU and select Settings followed by Terminal. Select Echo and choose No. Then select Quit to return to COMM mode.

Received Data Garbled

An incorrect Parity or Length setting can cause incoming data to be garbled. Check the Parity and Length settings on the Communications settings sheet. These settings must match the settings the information service requires. If necessary, change these settings.

CREATING A LOGIN SETTINGS SHEET

Suppose that you regularly call an on-line service called InfoBase. The following steps will show you how to automate the log-in procedure required by this imaginary service, using a Login settings sheet. By entering the information necessary for identifying yourself to InfoBase, such as your ID number and password, into a Login settings sheet, you will avoid supplying this information manually every time you start a communications session with InfoBase.

To create a Login settings sheet, press MENU and select Settings followed by Login. You will see the Login Settings screen shown in Figure 7-8. First you select Maximum-Time, which specifies how many seconds Symphony will spend trying to log in to InfoBase before giving up. Set it for 30 seconds by typing **30** and pressing (ENTER).

Now select Repeat-Time, the setting that determines how many seconds Symphony allots to receive confirmation information from InfoBase. If the information is not received before the Repeat-Time setting has expired, Symphony automatically re-sends

```
Number of seconds to wait for log-in to succeed                              MENU
Maximum-Time  Repeat-Time  A  B  C  D  E  F  G  H  I  J  New  Quit

  Count  Send (maximum time 0)              Receive (repeat time 0)
A 1
B 1
C 1
D 1
E 1
F 1
G 1
H 1
I 1
J 1
                              Login Settings: C:\SYM22\COMPUSRV.CCF
```

FIGURE 7-8 Login Settings screen: the default settings and those used for calling

the last part of the log-in procedure it sent. Set this for 10 seconds by typing **10** and pressing (ENTER).

The rest of the Login settings sheet consists of rows lettered A through J, each of which is divided into three columns: Count, Send, and Receive. The Send column contains the log-in information you want to send to InfoBase. The Receive column contains the anticipated InfoBase response. The Count column limits the number of times the same Send column is transmitted in the event that you do not get the response specified in that row's Receive column.

In this example, select A, followed by Count, and type **4** and then press (ENTER). Now select Send, and Symphony asks you to enter a string of characters that will be sent to the host computer. The maximum length for a string in either the Send or Receive column is 30 characters. Receive strings are case- sensitive. In this case you want to tell Symphony to send the equivalent of (CTRL-C) (that is, holding down (CTRL) and pressing the C key), which the InfoBase computer recognizes as a signal that another computer is trying to get its attention. You type this as **\c\c** and press (ENTER).

The response that InfoBase makes when you send (CTRL-C) is to display a prompt, "User ID:," which you will now enter in the

Receive column for row A. You do this by selecting Receive, typing the text of the response, and pressing (ENTER). Now select Quit to leave the settings for row A. Type **B** to enter the settings for row B. Select Count, type **2**, and press (ENTER). Now you need to enter the user identification number that InfoBase has supplied to you. Suppose this is 75671@102. You select Send, type the number, and press (ENTER). Now select Receive and type **Password:**, which is the prompt that the InfoBase's computer system gives you after it has received your user identification. Press (ENTER) to confirm the Receive text, and select Quit to complete the row B settings.

In row C you will enter a Count value of 2, and the Send text will be your password. This verifies your identity to the InfoBase computer system. There is no need to enter any Receive text for the last row of the Login settings sheet, so the sheet is now complete, as shown in Figure 7-9. However, in order to retain your work for the next session, you must quit back to the Settings menu and issue the Name Save command to store the log-in settings

```
Number of seconds to wait for log-in to succeed                                MENU
Maximum-Time  Repeat-Time  A  B  C  D  E  F  G  H  I  J  New  Quit

   Count  Send (maximum time 30)              Receive (repeat time 10)
 A 4      \c\c                                User ID:
 B 2      75671@102                           Password:
 C 2      Commadeasy
 D 1
 E 1
 F 1
 G 1
 H 1
 I 1
 J 1
                                   Login Settings: C:\SYM22\INFOBASE

Settings Login                                                            Num
```

FIGURE 7-9 Completed Login settings sheet

along with the communications settings for the InfoBase service in a suitably named CCF file, such as INFOBASE.CCF.

The next time you want to connect with InfoBase, you can use Name Retrieve to load the INFOBASE.CCF file and proceed to dial the service with the Phone Call command. Symphony will automatically log you in. This feature saves you having to remember ID numbers, passwords, and other trivia. Apart from being a more efficient way of connecting, automatic log-in is a boon to clumsy typists.

You can actually take the system a step further if you want and use the other lines of the Login settings sheet to issue commands to the information service. As long as you know the commands and the response that the service makes, you can even automate information retrieval and log off.

ON-LINE ACTIVITY

There are various activities you can engage in when connected to another computer. Information services usually have a series of menus that allow you to navigate from one collection of information to another. For example, you might be logging in to check stock prices. After that, you could check the latest news. You might leave a message for another user of the same service, or engage in an on-line conversation with that user. What you type to each other will be shown on the screen. You might want to send a file to the computer or copy a file to your system.

Capture Versus File Transfer

There are several ways of exchanging information with another computer and several types of information you can send and receive. You can send text to the screen of the other computer by typing it in the COMM window while on-line. This is referred to as *text transfer*. You can receive information sent to you on the screen by capturing it to a worksheet range or sending it straight to your printer. You can compose messages in a worksheet and transmit them to the other computer as text with the Transmit-Range command.

You can use the File-Transfer Send command to transmit a data file produced by programs such as 1-2-3 or Symphony, or even a software program file. Such files are called *binary files,* since they consist of more than just a string of ASCII characters. You use the File-Transfer Send command to transmit a file of this kind from disk to the other computer.

On-line Printing

You can send or *dump* information from the screen to your printer. The easiest way is to press the (PRTSC) key on your keyboard. Provided the printer is turned on and is ready to receive information, the current screen will be printed.

Of course, you would have to do this for each screen you wanted to capture, so Symphony has provided the Capture facility to help you out. You can turn the Capture facility on and off any time during a communications session with the (F4) key. When you press (F4) in the COMM environment, you can choose between capturing data to a range of the worksheet or sending it to the printer. Select Printer, and then Yes. All incoming data displayed in the COMM environment will now be printed on the printer. The Capture indicator at the bottom of the screen shows that the Capture facility is on. You can turn off the Capture facility at any time during a communications session to stop printing. Press CAPTURE, select Printer, and then select No.

Capturing to a Worksheet Range

If you want to capture what you see on screen as data that you can later manipulate with Symphony, you can give Symphony a range of worksheet cells to be used for this purpose. You must set this up before initiating the call, using the Capture option on the Settings menu and choosing Range. This will allow you to select a range of cells in the underlying worksheet into which the information will be recorded, much like changing the print destination to "worksheet" with the SERVICES Print command.

Since you may have to set the range without knowing how much data will be received, you can simply use A1..IV8192 as the range, provided you have no other information in the worksheet that you want to keep. To select this range you do the following after selecting Range from the Settings Capture menu:

1. Press (HOME) to make sure the cell pointer is in A1. This is the default starting position of the Capture range.
2. Press (TAB) to anchor the range at A1.
3. Press (END) and then (HOME), which takes you to the junction of the last column and row that has been used in the worksheet. This will only move the cell pointer if you have already used the worksheet. If you want to keep any of your work so far, you can press (ESC) and change the beginning point of the range.
4. Having anchored the beginning point of the range, press (END) and then press (DOWN ARROW), followed by (END) and then (RIGHT ARROW). This will include all of the worksheet to IV8192.
5. Press (ENTER) to confirm the range.
6. Before using the range, issue the Name command on the Settings menu to store the Capture Range setting. Whenever you use this named setting, the specified range of the underlying worksheet will be used for captured data.

When you have defined a range of cells to use, you can call up the other computer and use the CAPTURE key to begin capturing screen data to the worksheet. When you press CAPTURE, Symphony will ask you if you want to use Range or Printer. Select Range and answer Yes to confirm. You can turn off the capturing of data to the worksheet during a session by pressing CAPTURE and selecting Range followed by No.

When a communication session is over, you can switch to the SHEET environment and review the information there. The information will be stored as a series of labels in the leftmost column of the range you select. You can use the Query Parse command, described in Chapter 11, to convert columns of captured information into data cells.

To store the captured information on disk, you can save the file with SERVICES File Save. You may want to use a different filename from the existing one—a name that describes the data you have downloaded.

File Transfer

To exchange files between your computer and a remote system, you first establish the connection so that you are on-line. The host computer will have a set of commands necessary for sending or receiving a file. You begin the send process by issuing a host computer command that prepares the host to receive the file. The host computer will then issue a prompt telling you when to send the file.

If there is an operator controlling the other computer, you begin a file exchange by sending a message informing the operator that you are ready to begin transferring files. The other computer user has to execute a command in order to receive or send a file. In some cases, the other user may also have to start a file transfer program.

Sending Files

When the other computer is ready to receive your file, you press MENU and select File-Transfer followed by Send. Symphony displays a list of the files in the current directory. You can either select a filename from the list or type the name of a file in another directory. When you have selected the file you want to send, Symphony displays a message in the control panel telling you that it is sending the file you selected and is waiting for a response. As soon as the other computer acknowledges the start of transmission, Symphony displays another message, such as:

```
Sending file: BUDGET.DOC
2048 bytes out of 4095 sent 0 errors corrected
```

The first number increases as Symphony sends the file. When the entire file is sent, the message disappears.

Sending Worksheet Data

When you want to send lengthy messages (such as letters or reports) to another computer, you can compose them in a worksheet, using the DOC environment, before you place the call. Then you can use the Transit-Range command to identify the range of cells to be sent to the other computer. Bear in mind that the other computer will not receive this information as cells, but as a stream of text. To transmit operational worksheets you would send them as files.

Special Protocols

In order to make sure that files transmitted over phone lines are complete and not affected by the transmission, and also to speed up the transfer process, special rules have been developed. Just to confuse matters, these sets of rules are sometimes called "communications protocols," although they are quite different from the baud/parity/stop-bit protocols. The term *file transfer protocols* will be used to make the distinction.

Symphony supports three popular protocols: XMODEM, CompuServe B, and BLAST. You can configure Symphony so that it will use either of the first two or BLAST. This choice is made through the Install program, described in Appendix A. Fortunately, the XMODEM/CompuServe B option is the default and will serve you well on most on-line services. You do not have to issue any commands to choose between XMODEM and CompuServe B, as Symphony will use XMODEM by default and switch to CompuServe B automatically if you are using CompuServe.

XMODEM The popularity of this widely used file transfer protocol is a major triumph for the pioneering spirit of personal computing. Developed by a man called Ward Christianson and sometimes eponymously referred to as the "Christianson protocol," XMODEM is so popular because Christianson released the original software to the public domain. Versions of this software have been developed for a wide variety of computer systems.

COMPUSERVE B This protocol is provided by Symphony for performing file transfers between Symphony and the CompuServe network. When you use CompuServe B protocol with Symphony, the CompuServe host computer controls the file transfer. This means that if there is a problem with a file transfer, Symphony does not display an error message. If the transfer stops, Symphony displays the message, "Transfer aborted." If the CompuServe computer stops a file transfer, you should check for problems. Your receiving disk might be full or have a read/write error. You might have specified the filename incorrectly, attempting to use a file that does not exist.

BLAST Using BLAST with Symphony allows you to communicate with a mainframe computer that also uses the BLAST protocol. You cannot use BLAST with Symphony for communication between two microcomputers. There are some special rules that need to be followed when using BLAST. The BLAST driver has a 10-kilobyte internal buffer. When you perform a file transfer, the BLAST driver does not update the status indicator in Symphony until it transmits 10 kilobytes of information. This means that Symphony displays the message "Waiting for connection" until the BLAST driver transmits the first 10 kilobytes. BLAST updates the byte counter each time it transmits an additional 10 kilobytes. Once the file transfer is complete, the message "Transfer complete" appears.

When you are using BLAST, the file you send must be in the directory that is current. You cannot specify another drive or a path name for the file. You cannot select a file by highlighting it. When specifying a file, you first press (ESC) to clear the file menu and the drive specifier from the control panel. Then you type the name of the file you want to send. If you are sending a binary file, you need to type the name of the file twice, separated by two colons. For example, to send a binary file called MY.DOC you enter **MY.DOC::MY.DOC**. The first filename is the name of the file as it is stored on your system; the second filename is the name as it will be received by the host computer. If you are sending a text file, you must type the name of the file followed by **%t-txt**. For example, if you are sending a text file called MY.TXT and you want the mainframe to receive it as YOUR.TXT, you would type

MY.TXT%t-txt::YOUR.DOC%t-txt

Symphony will replace a copy of a file you have saved on your computer with a new file that has the same name. You should use unique filenames if you do not want to write over the file that is already on the mainframe. You must restart BLAST on the mainframe computer for each file you transfer. Once BLAST completes a file transfer on the mainframe, it returns your computer to the operating system.

Receiving Files

When you are on-line and tell the other computer that you want to receive a file, the other computer will tell you to begin receiving. At this point you press MENU and select File-Transfer and then Receive. Type a name for the file you are going to receive, or choose an existing filename. Symphony displays a list of the files in the current directory. You can either select a filename from the list or type the name of a file in another directory. Symphony displays a message in the control panel telling you that it's waiting for a connection so it can receive the file. When the entire file has been received, the message disappears and the file will be on your disk.

RECEIVING CALLS

As well as allowing you to call other computers, Symphony allows other computers to call you. Although your personal computer certainly contains nothing like as much information as the rooms full of disk drives used by CompuServe, you may have just the information that another user needs. By having another user call you at a particular time and having Symphony answer the phone call, you can establish a connection that will allow information to be exchanged.

One advantage of this is to allow someone else to pay for the call. Suppose you are a remote sales office. You prepare reports on Symphony that need to go to headquarters. They send you the latest price lists, prepared with Symphony. You can have a computer at headquarters call you at a particular time and have Symphony answer the phone. You can then send the report file to headquarters, and receive the price list worksheet.

To have Symphony answer the phone when you know a call is about to come in, you turn on your modem, load Symphony, switch to COMM mode, and load the settings that the remote computer will expect. Then select the Phone command from the main COMM menu and select Answer. The "WAIT" message will flash in the upper right of the screen, and the word "Answering" will appear in the top left. Symphony will maintain this mode for as many seconds as you have set with the Settings Phone Answer-Time command. If a call comes in, Symphony will issue a connect message. If a call does not come in before the answer time expires, Symphony gives you an error message and you must press (ESC) to return to normal operation.

If you do not know exactly when a call is coming in, you can tell Symphony to wait for a call by using the Phone Wait-Mode command. This tells Symphony to answer any and all phone calls until you press (BREAK) and use the menu to turn this mode off. Wait mode should be used with care: Symphony does not provide password control over remote access. Wait mode leaves your computer open to access by anyone with a modem and a lot of curiosity.

VOICE AND DATA MODE

The Data-Mode and Voice-Mode commands on the Phone menu allow you to use the same phone call to exchange data and talk to someone. This involves some coordination because both parties must switch to the same mode at more or less the same time. However, it is fairly simple to initiate a voice call, have a conversation, and then switch to data mode for the rest of the call. You can actually use Symphony as an automatic dialer. Use the Phone Call command to have Symphony call a number; then switch to Voice mode as soon as the phone starts ringing at the other end.

To change modes at any time during a call, press MENU, select Phone, and choose the desired mode. Bear in mind that changing to Voice mode during a file transfer will damage the file.

LOCAL CONNECTIONS

Symphony's COMM commands can be used to establish a direct connection between two computers through their serial ports. The need for this type of connection arises when you want to share information between two machines but they have no disk size or format in common. The procedure is to run a null modem cable between the serial ports of the two machines and then load a communications program on each computer. (The null modem cable was described earlier in the section on cables.)

You set matching communications parameters on each machine, using the highest baud rate that both communications programs support. If you are using Symphony as the communications program, the highest baud setting is 9600.

Instead of dialing a number to connect the two computers, you run the communications programs and have them check for a direct connection. For example, when you switch to COMM mode in Symphony and there is a direct physical connection in place, Symphony proceeds to establish contact. You can then type messages between the two computers or use the File-Transfer and Transmit-Range commands to exchange information.

This method of sharing information may sound attractive: You already have Symphony, a null modem cable is inexpensive, and you can share data without disks. However, there are some serious limits to this approach to data sharing, the principal one being speed. The popularity of computers with 3 1/2-inch disk drives that still need to share files with computers using 5 1/4-inch drives means that many programs dedicated to the task of PC-to-PC file transfer are available. They come with special cables and have top speeds far greater than Symphony's 9600 baud. For example, LapLink, shown in Figure 7-10, supports 115200-baud file transfers. If you regularly need to transfer files or need to move large files, you might want to consider a dedicated package like LapLink.

```
LAP-LINK (2.04) Copyright 1986, 87   Traveling Software Inc.          M207145
══ Local Drive (C:)10342400 Free ═══╦═══ Remote Drive ( :)       0 Free ═══
 .                <DIR>  2-06-91 12:43a ║
 ..               <DIR>  2-06-91 12:43a ║
 1PROR1   .WR1     1041  3-18-91  3:50p ║
 1PROR2   .WR1     1041  3-18-91  3:52p ║
 1PROR3   .WR1     1041  3-18-91  4:01p ║
 1PRORA   .WR1     1457  3-18-91  4:03p ║
 ADD      .WK1     6793  2-06-91 12:33a ║
 ADD      .WR1     6793  2-06-91 12:32a ║
 BINARY   .WR1   108514  2-15-91 12:15p ║  Attempting link to remote system...
 BUILD1   .WR1     1166  2-25-91 11:40p ║     Remote system not active...
 BUILD2   .WR1    11096  2-26-91  2:15p ║               Press →
 BUILD3   .WR1    11287  2-26-91  2:52p ║
 BUILD4   .WR1    10626  2-26-91  5:37p ║
 BUILD5   .WR1    17958  2-27-91  1:03p ║
 BUILD6   .WR1    18313  2-27-91  1:51p ║
 BUYSELL  .WR1     6058  3-05-91  4:25p ║
 CARDATA1.DBF      4729  2-17-91 11:08p ║
 CARDATA1.WK1      7730  2-17-91 11:05p ║
 CARDATA1.WR1      8988  2-17-91 11:25p ║
 CARLOAN1.WR1       842  2-05-91  8:24p ║
= C:\SYM22\DATA ════════════════════╩═══  : ═══════════════════════════════
                                                    T COM1: 115200  NUM
COMMANDS: Help Log Tree Copy Wildcopy Group Options View Erase Rename Dos Quit
```

FIGURE 7-10 LapLink in action

A GOOD EXAMPLE

Until there are significant improvements in hardware capabilities, communications standards, and telephone services, the goal of consistently successful computer-to-computer connections will remain a challenging one. Nobody is well served by glossing over the limitations that beset this area of personal computing. However, it is also important not to lose sight of the tremendous potential of data communications. A good example of this is the CompuServe Information Service, known among users as CIS. This one of the largest on-line information networks and one of the most popular with PC users. A typical session on CompuServe might go like this:

1. *Log on.* This can be automated within Symphony, as described earlier, by using a Login settings sheet.

2. *Check mail.* If you have any electronic mail waiting, CIS tells you and allows you to go straight to the mail section to read it.

3. *Read and reply.* Having read a message from another user, you can immediately post a reply without having to address the message, since CIS knows who it is from. You can also tell CIS to let you know when the recipient reads the message.

4. *Check clippings.* You can have CIS run a clipping service for you, scanning a wide variety of news sources (such as the Associated Press and McGraw-Hill Business News) for any items that match your search criteria. When you check this area, you can read some or all of the articles selected, which can be listed by subject or by-line.

5. *Check stocks.* You can get a current quote on any listed stock or a price history. Historical figures for all commodities and indicators are also available. If you have signed up with an on-line brokerage, you can issue buy/sell instructions on-line.

6. *Ask questions.* You can ask just about any question regarding personal computers and get a reply within hours. By moving to a special-interest area and posting a message, you can ask other users for assistance. This could be a software or hardware question. Dozens of computer product companies run "help" services on CIS, and with hundreds of experienced "power users" using the service at any one time, the chances are good that someone will be able to help. Answers can be posted for all to read or sent direct to your mailbox. Of course, if you see questions from other people that you can answer, go right ahead.

7. *Download a file.* Many sample data files and program files are stored on CIS. You can download these free of charge. You

might find just the utility program you need, or a spreadsheet design that will be helpful.

8. *Upload a file.* If you have messages for others or files you want to share, you can upload these to CIS from Symphony with the procedure described earlier.

9. *Check your account.* You pay for your use of CompuServe based on the length of time you are connected. You can use the customer service area free of charge to check your account, change your password, and read about CompuServe services.

10. *Log off.*

TIPS

There is much to learn when it comes to exploring data communications. It is still a pioneering personal computer activity, one that is less well established than spreadsheet modeling or word processing.

Modems and the Global Network

One of the great unfulfilled promises of data communications is the creation of a global electronic network that you can tap into from anywhere in the world. The obstacles are a lack of standards and the limited capabilities of current phone lines.

PLUG-IN The plugs that connect phone lines to phones or modems are different in different countries. You cannot take your U.S. modem to the U.K. and plug in the phone line directly. You'll need a phone-line adapter. You will also need a voltage adapter for your external modem unless it runs on batteries.

INTERNATIONAL STANDARDS There are two main groups of standards used in basic data transmission. Those referred to as the CCITT Recommendations are the most universal and are widely used throughout Europe and the rest of the world. Bell Standards originated in the USA and are popular for data transmission within the Americas. If you plan to use a Bell Standard modem to communicate with the rest of the world, you will need to check compatibility. The Bell standards are as follows:

Bell 103/113	Transmits asynchronous data at 300 bits per second full duplex, but is incompatible with CCITT V21.
Bell 201C	Used for 2400-bit/second data transmission at half duplex. Modems based on this standard are usually compatible with those based on the equivalent CCITT V26 bit standard at 2400 bits per second.
Bell 202C	Used for 1200-bit/second half-duplex transmission, which is generally not compatible with equivalent CCITT V23 modems.
Bell 212A	Similar to CCITT V22 and generally compatible at 1200-bit/second synchronous transmission at full duplex, and also for asynchronous data when the character length is 9 or 10 bits. The 300-bit/second fall-back facility provided with Bell 212A modems is not compatible with CCITT V series modems.

Two CCITT standards frequently used in modems designed for personal computers are as follows:

V21	Provides full-duplex asynchronous transmission at speeds of up to 300 bits per second. They are generally used for low-speed asynchronous transmission from teletypes, visual display units, and personal computers. V21 is incompatible with the US Bell Standard 103/113, which works at the same speed.
V22	Provides full-duplex transmission at 1200 bits per second, with an optional lower speed of 600 bits per second. Modems will accept either synchronous or asynchronous data from the computer. V22 is used for both file transfer and interactive working from personal computers, and is generally compatible with the parallel Bell Standard 212A.

As you can see, there is a measure of compatibility between CCITT V Series Recommendations and some Bell Standards, and calls may be made between compatible modems. However, some services in Europe require the receiving modem to transmit a guard tone to protect the telephone network from interference. Check that a modem you plan to use in Europe can provide a guard tone in the Receive mode. (Since CCITT is an agency of the International Telecommunications Union, you might expect that its standards were universally accepted; however, this is not likely to happen for some time. The fact that the agency is based in Geneva and the acronym "CCITT" stands for International Telegraph and Telephone Consultative Committee in French is one clue as to why this might be the case.)

CABLES VERSUS SATELLITES Much of the phone traffic across the Atlantic uses satellites. The beaming of your voice into space and back results in a short time gap before you are heard on the other end. This is merely annoying in conversation, but it can be fatal for data communication. Dialing the U.S. from the U.K., you can precede the phone number with a two-digit code that routes your call through the undersea cables, resulting in a better-quality connection. For example, to dial a New York data service you might normally dial 12125559876 while in the U.S. From the U.K., you could dial 01012125559876 to reach this number, but you can use 0101**83**2125559876 to route your call through the cable system (83 uses the RCA cables, 84 uses the ITT cables). There is no extra charge for this service. There does not seem to be an equivalent feature available on U.S. phone service to Europe.

A Good Line

One benefit enjoyed by American modem users is the ability to choose between carriers. If you try a long-distance modem connection and get a poor line, you can force the phone call through one of the following services, using the code shown:

AllNet	10444
AT&T	10288
ITT	10488
MCI	10222
U.S. Sprint	10777
Western Union	10220

For example, to force a call to a database in San Francisco through U.S. Sprint, you would dial 1077714155559876. The call will be billed through your local phone company.

Dedicated Software

Symphony is a good basic communications package and offers the advantages of a familiar command system plus the convenience of both manipulating and exchanging documents within the same program. However, Symphony lacks features found in most dedicated communications software. Since many modems come with such software, you may wonder whether to use Symphony or a dedicated program.

Having explored Symphony's COMM environment, you are now in a good position to evaluate the alternatives. Try the dedicated modem program and see if you feel comfortable with it. You will probably find that it offers an on-screen list of phone numbers for "point and shoot" dialing of different services, a more automated log-in system, and a wider range of file transfer protocols.

What most dedicated modem programs offer that Symphony does not is direct access to the modem's features, such as volume control, redial, timed dialing, and so on. Many packages support a complete command language with which you can create extensive scripts that the modem will follow for unattended file transfer. If you want to extend your data communications to this level, it may be worth exploring a dedicated package. Such programs can receive text files that Symphony can read directly and worksheet files that Symphony can load, as well as program files. For more on reading and manipulating text files, see Chapter 11.

If you are using CompuServe, a very specialized type of software is available that lets you plan a session in advance and then make a call in the shortest possible time. This program, called TAPCIS, can greatly reduce your connect time and thus your CIS bills. You can download TAPCIS from CIS, and a special support group is available to help with using the program.

One final factor in choosing between programs intended for more advanced operations will be your experience and comfort level with Symphony macros. These are groups of commands that you put together to have Symphony carry out several operations in a sequence. Creating macros is described in Chapter 9. If you get on well with macros, you may want to apply them to the COMM environment, where they can be used to provide further automation.

SUMMARY

Data communications is an exciting field and Symphony's COMM environment offers a good way to explore it. You need to take the time to learn the basic vocabulary, as well as the commands Symphony uses to handle the various data communication functions. For direct connections or more extensive features, you may want to consider a dedicated package to compliment Symphony. In the end, successful data communications will depend on two things:

- Proper connections between computer and modem, modem and phone, and between phones
- Correct protocols that match the settings of your system with those of the host computer

8

FILES, LINKS, VIEWS, AND ADD-INS

Now that you have explored each of the five Symphony environments, you need to learn more about how to manage your Symphony files. This chapter reviews more advanced aspects of Symphony files, such as linking worksheet files together for more practical spreadsheet modelling and accessing the power of Symphony add-ins. You will learn how to view files from within Symphony without having to retrieve them, how to protect your files with passwords, and how to translate files from other formats. The chapter begins with a review of the basics of file management on PCs.

DISK OPERATIONS 101

To explore file management with Symphony, load the program and press (F9), the SERVICES key. From the SERVICES menu, select File. The SERVICES File menu appears, as shown in Figure 8-1. As you have seen, the commands on the SERVICES File menu are consistent from one Symphony environment to another. This is one of the most important menus in Symphony.

The Current Directory

You use the SERVICES File menu to store and retrieve your worksheet files, whether those files contain spreadsheet models, word processing documents, databases, or graphs. Select Dir from the File menu, and Symphony will respond by displaying what it calls the current directory. This is the area of disk that Symphony is currently using to store your worksheet files. A typical response to the Dir command might be C:\ SYM22\ DATA, as shown here:

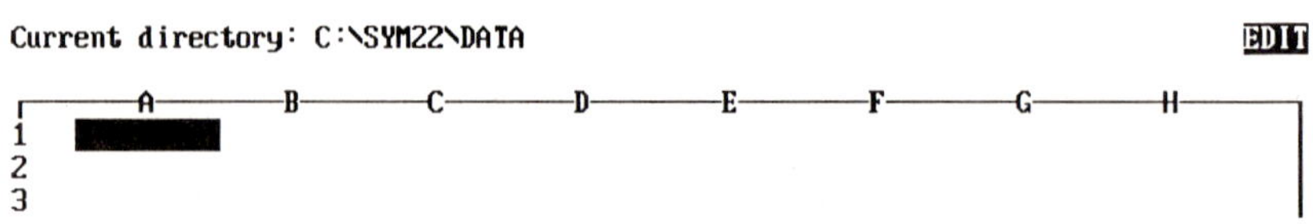

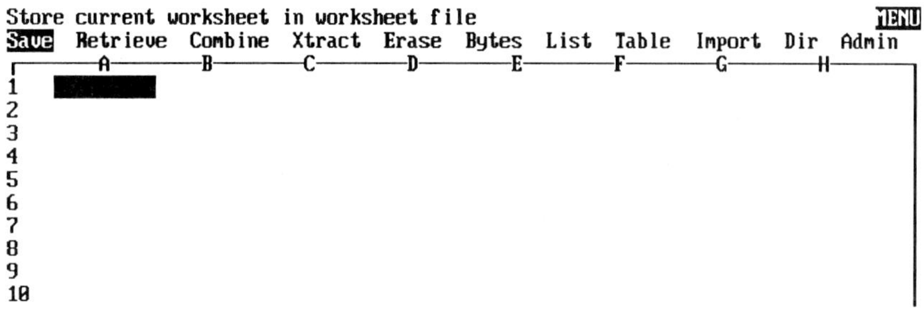

FIGURE 8-1 The SERVICES File menu

You can use the SERVICES Configuration File command to change this setting, as described later in this chapter. For now, you should make a note of this setting and then press (ENTER) to confirm it. The Dir setting will be referred to in some of the examples in this chapter, as the meaning of "the directory" is explained.

Memory and Storage

You have seen that the data you enter into a worksheet is not immediately stored in a worksheet file on disk: At first, it is temporarily retained in the computer's memory. The memory area, called *random access memory* (*RAM*), is like an electronic desktop. Because it is electronic, the work that you do there, such as entering and calculating, is performed very quickly. By retaining most of your worksheet in memory while you manipulate it, Symphony can provide fast responses and rapid calculations.

Unfortunately, even an electronic desktop has its disadvantages. The problem with RAM is that everything you have entered into it is erased when the power to your PC is turned off or interrupted. Thus, it is important to use the SERVICES File menu on a regular basis to transfer a copy of the worksheet from memory to storage in a disk file.

How the Operating System Works

To understand how a computer manipulates disk storage and memory operations, consider the following description of what happens when you turn on your PC. The first thing a computer does when you flip on the switch is to look to the disk drives to find information stored on disks. Disks are made of the same material as cassette tapes and video cassettes. On a disk, the magnetic storage medium is laid out flat and divided into a series of concentric circles. Information is both read from and written to a disk by a moving head. This head is essentially the same as a head in a cassette tape player.

The first piece of information that the computer looks for is the operating system. On an IBM PC or PC compatible, the operating system is called the disk operating system, or DOS. This system can be either PC-DOS, distributed by IBM, or MS-DOS, which is the version licensed by Microsoft to many other computer manufacturers.

When the computer finds DOS, it reads the essential parts from the disk and loads them into memory. Whereas the disk and disk drive use a combination of electronic and mechanical components, the computer's memory is purely electronic. It is a place where information can be changed much faster than on a disk. Symphony takes good advantage of this speed. Most of the program is loaded into memory. This is done automatically by Symphony so that you do not have to worry about it.

The role of DOS is twofold. First, DOS is a flow manager that manages the flow of information in and out of the computer. When you type the letter **q**, DOS makes sure that a "q" appears on the screen and that the character is stored and printed as a "q." Although you may give Symphony a command to print out data, Symphony actually passes that request on to DOS for execution. Second, DOS is a file manager. The information your computer uses is stored in either program files or data files. The arrangement of these files on the disk is managed by DOS. Thus, DOS—not Symphony—executes your request to Symphony that data be stored on the disk.

Once the computer has loaded DOS, it can start handling your information. Two important pieces of information that are usually supplied to the disk operating system at this point are the date and the time, which can be entered manually or read automatically from a clock within the computer. The date and time information is stored in memory until the computer is turned off or reset. Symphony uses the date and time for the on-screen clock display and for applications that require time and date information.

Note The @NOW function can be used in the SHEET environment to read the current time and date from memory.

When DOS stores a file on disk, the file is date- and time-stamped. DOS can display this date and time when files are listed. This information will help you manage files.

Loading Programs

After the date and time have been entered into memory, the computer wants to know what programs you wish to execute. It asks you this by displaying the system prompt. Also known as the DOS prompt, the system prompt can consist of several pieces of information. The first is usually the name of the drive that the computer is using (normally C for a hard drive). The second is the cursor. The cursor points out where you are and where the next character you type will appear. Here are three typical DOS prompts:

```
C>
C:\>_
Thu 3-21-1991 C:\>_
```

To start running a program, you usually type the name of the program at the system prompt and press (ENTER) to send the request to the disk operating system. DOS will then look on the disk for the program and begin to load it into memory. For Symphony, this probably means you type **SYMPHONY** and press (ENTER). However, there is another way to load Symphony, and that is to type **ACCESS** and press (ENTER). This takes you to the Symphony Access menu, discussed later in the chapter.

You do not have to worry about whether to use upper- or lowercase letters when sending information to the disk operating system—DOS does not distinguish between the two. For example, when you ask Symphony to store information on the disk and Symphony passes this request on to DOS, the name of the file in which the information will be stored can be typed in either uppercase or lowercase. However, DOS will store the name in uppercase.

Disks and Directories

Just as Symphony comes to you stored on disks, the data you create with programs is also stored on disks. Information is stored on disks in files. As you work with your computer, you quickly create many files. To keep these files manageable, there is a practical limit to how many files should be stored on a disk. An actual limit of 512 files per directory exists in some versions of DOS.

Large-capacity disks, particularly hard disks, are often divided into small, manageable parts called *subdirectories*. This division is much like that used in the telephone directory of a large company. The directory may list departments in its main section, but not list every single person in the company; each department might have its own subdirectory listing each staff member. Subdirectories are an important part of organizing your Symphony work on your hard disk.

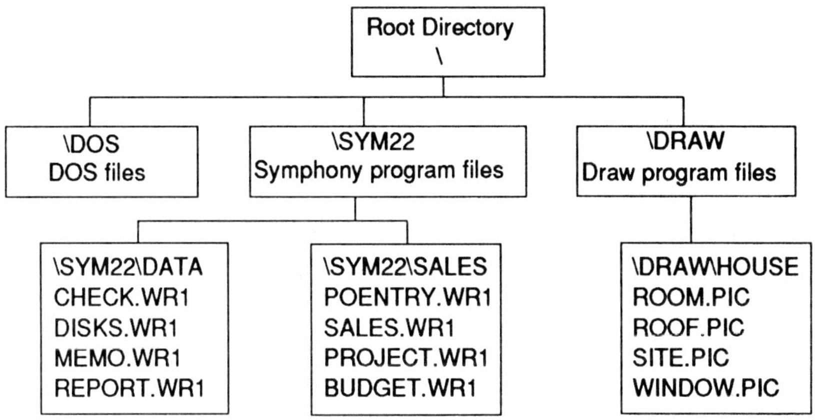

FIGURE 8-2 Hard drive map

A hard-disk directory system for a computer running Symphony and a drawing program might look like the one in Figure 8-2. For your computer to find either a program file or a data file, you must specify a *path* for it to follow. For example, the path to the ROOF.PIC file is \DRAW\HOUSE\. The path to the purchase-order entry worksheet in the SALES subdirectory of the SYM22 directory is \SYM22\SALES\. You can have more than one file with the same name on the same hard disk if you keep them in separate directories. It is generally safer, however, to give each file a unique name. To identify files on a hard disk accurately, include the path to the file as part of the file name. Thus, the full name of the ROOF.PIC file is

C:\DRAW\HOUSE\ROOF.PIC.

When using a hard disk, you cannot be in two places at once. Normally, you begin working with a hard disk in the *root* directory. You are said to be in the root directory of a drive when you are at the top level, which is signified by A:\, B:\, C:\, and so on. The directory you are in at any particular time is called the current or default directory.

Issuing DOS Directory Commands

To experiment with DOS commands, particularly those that relate to hard-disk management, enter the following commands from the DOS prompt, either before or after using Symphony. (You can temporarily exit Symphony to use DOS commands by using the DOS add-in, described later in this chapter.) This example assumes that you are using a hard disk called drive C. If your hard disk is called D, E, or another letter, just substitute that letter for C in the examples. You can also carry out these steps using a floppy disk, although it is less common to use directories on floppy disks because of their smaller storage capacity.

1. Begin by making sure that you are in the root directory: type **CD** and press (ENTER). This command tells DOS to change the directory to the root directory.

2. Type **DIR** and press (ENTER). This tells DOS to list the files in the current directory. There are five columns of information. The names of the files are split into name and extension. The third column is the size of the file measured in bytes (see Chapter 7 for more on bytes). The last two columns show the date and time each file was last saved onto the disk.

3. If there are more than 20 files in the directory, the listing will scroll off the top of the screen. Type **DIR/P** and press (ENTER) to tell DOS to pause the list so that you can read each screen before pressing a key to see the next one.

4. To see more files at once, type **DIR/W** and press ENTER. This lists just the names, and spreads them across the screen. Note that each DIR command ends with a count of the files in the current directory and the number of bytes of unused space on the current disk.

The instructions you add to DIR, such as /P for Pause and /W for Wide, are known as *switches* because they turn on features of the DIR command. You can also modify the results of the DIR command by using parameters. For example, to list files in the Symphony program directory instead of in the root directory, type **DIR C:\SYM22** and press ENTER. The path C:\SYM22\ is a parameter that qualifies the DIR command.

You can also qualify the DIR command with something called a *file specification*. This can be the name of a file that you want to know more about. For example, if you enter **DIR FRED.WR1**, DOS will list the file called FRED.WR1, along with its size and date/time stamp, if such a file exists in the current directory. If this is not the case, DOS will tell you "File not found." Alternatively, a file specification can use a wildcard character to refer to a group of files, as described in the following section on copying files.

Identifying Directories

At the top of the listing it provides, the DIR command tells you which directory you are viewing. This is the current directory unless you add something to the DIR command to tell it to look at a different directory. All DOS commands operate on the current directory unless you instruct them otherwise. There are other ways of telling which is the current directory.

1. At the DOS prompt, type **CD** without the backslash and then press ENTER. DOS responds by telling you the name of the current directory.

2. The simple C> prompt is relatively uninformative; it just tells you that you are using drive C. You can change this to a prompt that will always tell you what subdirectory you are in (for example, C:\> tells you that you are using drive C and are currently in the root, or main, directory). To change the prompt to this more informative version, type **PROMPT PG** at the C> prompt. When you press ENTER you will see the drive letter and the path of whatever subdirectory you are in. The path is displayed by the $P following the PROMPT command. The greater-than sign is represented by $G.

The new prompt remains in effect until you turn off or reset your computer. To get around having to re-enter the command each time you turn on your computer, you might want to add the prompt command to your AUTOEXEC.BAT file, as described in Appendix A.

To see the path prompt in action and to explore the directory commands, follow these steps:

1. Change your location to a subdirectory such as the one used for the Symphony program files. Type **CD\ SYM22** and press ENTER. You will see your prompt change. (If you use a directory name other than SYM22 for your Symphony program files, substitute that name in these examples.)

2. To change your current location back to the root directory, type **CD** and press ENTER.

3. To make a subdirectory called XAMPLE directly below the root directory, type **MD \XAMPLE** and press ENTER.

4. To make a subdirectory of the XAMPLE directory called MINE, type **MD \XAMPLE\MINE** and press ENTER.

File and Directories

At the DOS prompt you can copy files from one disk to another, from one subdirectory of a disk to another, and from one file name to another. If you want to copy a group of files, you use special characters called wildcards to denote more than one file, as in

```
COPY *.WR1 A:
```

This command tells the system to copy all spreadsheet files in the current directory of the current disk to the disk in drive A. The asterisk is used to represent any number of characters. The *.WR1 portion of this statement is a file specification.

You can get more particular in your commands by using the question-mark wildcard. The command

```
COPY SALES??.WR1 A:
```

tells the system to copy all of the worksheet files related to the SALES database (including SALES01.WR1, SALES02.WR1, and so on) to drive A. The question mark is used to represent a single character. Thus, SALES?T.* includes SALES1T.WR1 and SALES2T.WR1, but not SALES3.WR1.

By now, you probably have some Symphony worksheet files in at least one directory of your disk, the one that Symphony shows you when you use the SERVICES File Dir command. This might be C:\SYM22\DATA or something similar. Suppose you want to move the files to another directory. There is no DOS command for MOVE. However, there is a COPY command that makes copies of files in another directory. This can be followed by a delete command applied to the original files, thus effecting a move from one location to another.

In order to create copies of all of the worksheet files that are in C:\SYM22\DATA in the new directory you have created, you could do the following:

1. Move into the subdirectory by typing **CD \XAMPLE\MINE** and then pressing (ENTER).

2. Enter **COPY C:\SYM22\DATA*.WR1**. This command tells DOS to copy all files that have the extension WR1 *from* C:\SYM22\DATA\ *to* the current directory, which in this case is C:\XAMPLE\MINE.

3. Alternatively, you could enter the following while you are still in the root directory:

   ```
   COPY C:\SYM22\DATA\*.WR1 C:\XAMPLE\MINE
   ```

In the second approach you have to specify both the FROM and TO locations, whereas the first method allows DOS to assume that the TO location is the current directory.

The commands just given create copies of files in a different directory. To permanently move files from one directory to another, you would follow the COPY command with a DEL or ERASE command to remove the copied files from their original location. However, in this example you do not want to complete this process; it would upset your current filing system. Instead of deleting the original files from the Symphony data directory, you will delete the copies from the sample directory and remove the directories you made. Using the knowledge you gain in this exercise, you can then proceed to create your own arrangement of directories for your work.

To remove all files from a subdirectory, you use the command DEL *.*. This will only delete files in the current subdirectory, not across the whole disk. You can delete the files in a subdirectory from anywhere if you specify the path. For example, if you are in the root directory, you could enter

```
DEL \XAMPLE\MINE\*.*
```

to delete all files in the MINE subdirectory of the XAMPLE subdirectory.

In some situations, you may want to delete just a set of files. For example, entering

```
DEL \XAMPLE\MINE\*.WR1
```

will delete all files with the .WR1 extension in the MINE subdirectory of the XAMPLE subdirectory.

To remove a subdirectory, you must first remove all data and program files from it. To remove an empty subdirectory, you remove the lowest levels first.

1. Type **DEL \XAMPLE\MINE*.*** and press ENTER.
2. Type **DEL \XAMPLE*.*** and press ENTER.
3. Type **RD \XAMPLE\MINE** and press ENTER. RD stands for Remove Directory.
4. Type **RD \XAMPLE** and press ENTER.

The directory system you created in the example has now been removed.

Help with DOS

Since DOS commands are not the easiest to learn and apply accurately, you may sometimes make mistakes. One of the worst is to delete the wrong file. Fortunately, there is a remedy for this.

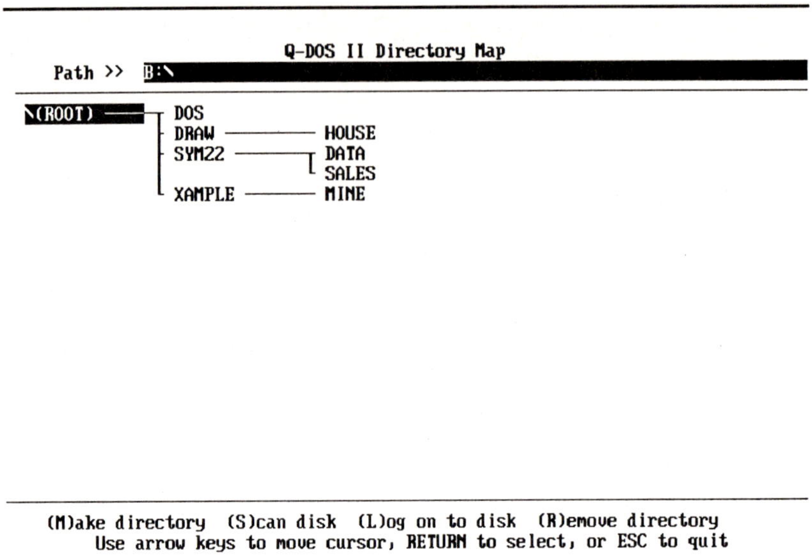

FIGURE 8-3 QuickDOS directory

If you realize you have erased a file that you wanted to keep, do not continue to move or store additional files. Instead, reach for a program called The Norton Utilities or another called Mace Utilities. These programs will, among other things, enable you to restore the file in most cases.

If the DOS directory commands seems difficult to grasp, you may want to use a hard-disk organizing program like QuickDOS II from Gazelle Systems of Provo, Utah. This program draws a picture of your directory system, as shown in Figure 8-3, which shows the directories created in the previous example. QuickDOS II also provides lists of files with a menu of commands to copy, erase, rename, and otherwise manipulate them. The list can be changed quickly from alphabetical to chronological. QuickDOS II uses menus similar to those in Symphony for all of the DOS commands. You can also use a Lotus product for hard-disk management. The Magellan program, which is discussed later in this chapter, offers similar features to QuickDOS II plus the ability to view file contents.

SYMPHONY FILES

When you type **ACCESS** and press (ENTER) at the DOS prompt in your Symphony directory, you enter the Lotus Access System. This provides access to four programs: the main Symphony program, the PrintGraph program (described in Chapter 6), the Install program (discussed in Appendix A), and the Translate program (described later in this chapter). The programs are presented in a menu, as shown in Figure 8-4. The fifth item on the menu, Exit, takes you back to DOS.

You select items from the Access menu with the first letter or by highlighting the item and pressing (ENTER), using the arrow keys to move the highlighting across the row of menu items. When you

```
Start Symphony
Symphony  PrintGraph  Install  File-Translate  Exit

                        Symphony Access System

                       Copyright (C) 1986, 1990
                    Lotus Development Corporation
                         All Rights Reserved
                             Release 2.2

The Access system lets you choose Symphony, PrintGraph, the Install
program, or the Translate utility from the menu at the top of this
screen.  If you're using a diskette system, the Access system may prompt
you to change disks.  Follow the instructions below to start a program.

o  Use [RIGHT] or [LEFT] to move the menu pointer (the highlight bar at
   the top of the screen) to the program you want to use.

o  Press [RETURN] to start the program.

You can also start a program by typing the first letter of the menu
choice.  Press the [HELP] key for more information.
                          Press [NUM LOCK]
```

FIGURE 8-4 The Access System

select one of the programs, it is loaded into memory. When you exit that program, you are returned to the menu in Figure 8-4. This is simply a convenience. You can run PrintGraph, Install, and Translate from the DOS prompt simply by typing the program name (PGRAPH, INSTALL, or TRANS) and pressing (ENTER).

Naming Files

When you have loaded Symphony, you are ready to enter worksheet data. When you first type entries, the data is held in RAM. The program does not store the worksheet on disk as you build it; you must issue a File Save command later to tell Symphony to store the worksheet in a disk file. Every file in the same directory of a disk must have a unique name, composed of three parts: a file name, a period, and an optional extension.

The file name consists of one to eight letters or numbers without spaces. You can use some punctuation marks in a file name, but it is usually easier to use numbers and letters rather than trying to remember which punctuation marks are acceptable. Valid punctuation characters in a file name are shown here:

( ) ! @ # $ % & - _ ‘ { } ~ ’ ^

If you use invalid characters, DOS responds with the message "Invalid File Name."

When you try to use a file name that does not conform to the rules, Symphony normally responds with "Cannot create file." However, you need to be careful of file names longer than eight characters, because Symphony does not object to them. Instead, Symphony truncates the name. However, if you happen to enter ALLOFTHESALES as a file name when saving a file, Symphony saves the file as ALLOFTHE.WR1.

One piece of punctuation has a special role in file names: the period. It connects the file name with its extension. The extension is usually three characters long and follows the same rules as those for file names. Extensions are often used to distinguish between types of files. For example, Symphony worksheets have the extension WR1. Earlier versions of Symphony used the extension WRK. Symphony Release 2.2 can read spreadsheet files created by Lotus 1-2-3, which have the extension WKS (1-2-3 Release 1) or WK1 (1-2-3 Releases 2.0, 2.01, and 2.2).

Symphony normally assigns an extension to the file name you create, depending on what kind of data you are saving in the file. For example, worksheets are saved in WR1 files, and graph images are saved in PIC files. Table 8-1 lists the Symphony files with their extensions and a description of each file's use.

File Size

As shown in Table 8-1, the size of files is measured in bytes. One byte is about the amount of space it takes to store one character, numeral, space, or piece of punctuation. However, you cannot directly relate the size of a data file to the number of characters you type into it. For example, files may contain information about how the data is arranged. Symphony stores a typical worksheet of 480 active cells in about 10,000 bytes of disk space.

Since one byte is a minute unit of measurement, you will often see bytes measured in units of kilobytes (abbreviated as K). Each kilobyte is 1024 bytes. Don't worry about the extra 24 bytes; just use 1000 when converting from bytes to kilobytes. Thus, a worksheet that contains 10,244 bytes can be described as 10 K in size. When files get really big, they occupy megabytes. One megabyte, or MB, is 1024 K, or roughly a million bytes (1,048,576 to be exact). The capacity of your disks is usually measured in kilobytes and megabytes. The standard 5 1/4-inch floppy disk stores 360 K. The special "high density" 5 1/4-inch disks used in the IBM PC AT can store 1.2 megabytes. The hard-jacketed 3 1/2-inch disks used in many laptop PCs and the PS/2 series from IBM can store 720 K, or 1.4 megabytes, depending on how they are formatted.

File Name	Extension	Size	Description
ACCESS	COM	5,653	The Access program
ALLWAYS	APP	13,482	The Allways application program
ALLPELWP	APD	3,312	A printer driver
BLOCK1	FNT	5,732	A font for graph printing
COMPUSRV	CCF	1,427	A communication configuration file
HERC	SET	51,070	Customized installation settings
LOTUS	SET	51,896	The standard installation settings
PGRAPH	EXE	65,344	The PrintGraph program
SPELLER	APP	141,248	The Spelling application
SYMPHONY	CNF	1,143	The Symphony configuration file
SYMPHONY	EXE	50,096	One of the Symphony program files
SYMPHONY	HLP	156,965	The Symphony Help file
TRANS	COM	35,588	The Translate program
VIEWER	APP	29,266	The Viewer application
WR1DCA	XLT	62,416	A Translation file (WR1 to DCA)
MYFILE	WR1	10,071	A user-created Symphony worksheet
MYFILE	PRN	9,688	A user-created print or text file
MYFILE	PIC	6,733	A user-created graph image file
MYFILE	MLB	7,430	A user-created macro library file
MYFILE	DBF	14,060	A user-created @BASE or dBASE database
MYFILE	WK1	11,017	A user-created 1-2-3 Release 2 worksheet

TABLE 8-1 Files Used with Symphony

Most hard disks hold at least 20 megabytes, and some exceed 100 megabytes in capacity.

Saving Worksheets

When you want to save a worksheet, you use the SERVICES File Save command. If the worksheet is new—that is, it has not previously been saved onto disk—the File Save command presents a list of worksheet files that have already been stored in the current directory. This list is created by the file specification *.wr1 together with the path of the default directory, as in

C:\SYM22\DATA*.wr1

At this point you can store the current worksheet over an existing file by selecting one of the names on the list (highlight it and press (ENTER)), although you will rarely want to do this, since it erases the previous contents of the file. You are more likely to want to give a new file a new name. You do this simply by typing the name at the C:\SYM22\DATA*.wr1 prompt.

When you start typing the desired name, the file list disappears. As you type the name, you can press (BACKSPACE) to erase mistakes or use the other editing keys listed in Table 8-2. You can press the

Key	Action
(ESC)	At File Save or File Retrieve: prompt places you in EDIT mode. When in EDIT mode, removes all prompt text. When no prompt text is displayed, cancels command.
(LEFT ARROW)	Moves cursor 1 character left.
(RIGHT ARROW)	Moves cursor 1 character right on edit line.
(HOME)	Places cursor under first character of the prompt text.
(END)	Moves cursor to the right of the last character of the prompt text.
(CTRL-RIGHT ARROW)	Moves cursor 5 characters to the right.
(CTRL-LEFT ARROW)	Moves cursor 5 characters to the left.
(DEL)	Deletes character at cursor.
(BACKSPACE)	Deletes character to left of cursor.
(ENTER)	When prompt text ends in \, tells Symphony to look for files matching *.wr? specification. When prompt text ends in other than \, tells Symphony to save/retrieve worksheet with a name that matches prompt text.
(CTRL-ESC)	Clears all prompt text from edit line.
(CTRL-[)	Same as (CTRL-ESC).

TABLE 8-2 Keys to Edit File Save/Retrieve Prompt

```
Name of file to retrieve: C:\SYM22\DATA\*.wr?                                FILES
          CARLOAN1.WR1   02/05/91      20:24          842

 1PROR1.WR1     1PROR2.WR1     1PROR3.WR1     1PRORA.WR1     ADD.WR1
 BANKS.WR1      BINARY.WR1     BUILD1.WR1     BUILD2.WR1     BUILD3.WR1
 BUILD4.WR1     BUILD5.WR1     BUILD6.WR1     BUYSELL.WR1    CARDATA1.WR1
 CARDATA2.WR1   CARLOAN1.WR1   CARLOAN2.WR1   CARLOANX.WR1   CARPRICE.WR1
 COMP1.WR1      COMPANY1.WR1   COMPANY2.WR1   COMPANY3.WR1   COMPANY4.WR1
 EXPENSES.WR1   FORM2GO.WR1    FORM3GO.WR1    FORMDES.WR1    FORMLAST.WR1
 FORMREPO.WR1   FRED.WR1       GRAFCHAP.WR1   GXBHP.WR1      GXBIO.WR1
 GXBIO1.WR1     GXBIO2.WR1     GXDEM.WR1      GXGRF.WR1      GXHLC.WR1
 GXHP1.WR1      GXHP2.WR1      GXHP3.WR1      GXHP4.WR1      GXHP5.WR1
 GXHP6.WR1      GXPIE.WR1      GXSIM.WR1      GXSMT0A.WR1    GXSMT0B.WR1
 GXSMT0C.WR1    GXSMT0D.WR1    HOUSECAL.WR1   INVENTDS.WR1   LETTER01.WR1
 LETTER02.WR1   LETTER03.WR1   LETTER04.WR1   LETTER05.WR1   LETTER06.WR1
 MAILMERG.WR1   OHMJAN91.WR1   OHMPRO91.WR1   PAR1.WR1       PCUSERS.WR1
 PVF01.WR1      PVF02.WR1      PVF03.WR1      ROTATE.WR1     SAMPLE.WR1
 SORTORD.WR1    TEMP.WR1       TEST.WR1       TME01.WR1      TME02.WR1
 TMEALL01.WR1   TMEPREAL.WR1   UKMAG.WR1      XTAB1.WR1

File Retrieve                                                          Num
```

FIGURE 8-5 Full-screen file list

(INS) key to get into Overstrike mode, indicated by "OVR" in the status line. If you start to edit the file name and then press (ESC), the entire file name and path disappears and you can type any path and file name that you like.

When listing file names in a single-line list, you can press the MENU key ((F10)) to get a full screen list, as shown in Figure 8-5. This places you in FILES mode, where you can move the highlighting to any file name and see that file's date and time stamp plus file size. The keys listed in Table 8-3 will help you navigate the file lists. Remember that if you select a file from this list for the SERVICES File Save command, you will be asking Symphony to destroy the existing disk file that uses the chosen name, replacing it with the current file that you are saving. When the name is typed correctly, press (ENTER) to confirm the Save command.

In All Lists:	
MENU ((F10))	Switches between full-screen and single-line lists
(END)	Moves highlighting to last file in list
(HOME)	Moves highlighting to first file in list
(BACKSPACE)	Moves prompt one directory level closer to the root
(ESC)	Places prompt text in EDIT mode to change directory and file specification
In Single Line Lists:	
(RIGHT ARROW)	Moves highlighting one file to the right
(LEFT ARROW)	Moves highlighting one file to the left
(UP ARROW)	Moves highlighting exactly five files to the left
(DOWN ARROW)	Moves highlighting exactly five files to the right
(CTRL-RIGHT ARROW)	Pressed once, moves highlighting to last currently displayed file on the right; successive presses move highlighting five files to the right
(CTRL-LEFT ARROW)	Pressed once, moves highlighting to first currently displayed file on the left; successive presses move highlighting five files to the left
(PGUP)	Same as (UP ARROW)
(PGDN)	Same as (DOWN ARROW)
MENU ((F10))	Switches between full-screen and single-line lists
In Full-Screen Lists:	
(RIGHT ARROW)	Takes highlighting one column to the right until it reaches the last column, then moves highlighting back to the first column, one line down; will eventually scroll through all files back to the first
(LEFT ARROW)	Takes highlighting one column to the left until it reaches the first column, then moves highlighting to the last column one line up; will eventually scroll through all files back to the last
(UP ARROW)	Moves highlighting up one row
(DOWN ARROW)	Moves highlighting down one row
(CTRL-RIGHT ARROW)	Pressed once, moves highlighting to last column on the right; successive presses move highlighting one row down the last column on the right

TABLE 8-3 Keys Used for Navigating File Lists

(CTRL-LEFT ARROW)	Pressed once, moves highlighting to first column on the left; successive presses move highlighting one row up the last column on the left
(PGUP)	Moves highlighting up 20 files or to the first row, whichever comes first
(PGDN)	Moves highlighting down 20 files or to the last row, whichever comes first

TABLE 8-3 Keys Used for Navigating File Lists (*continued*)

Save Confirmation

If you happen to have typed a file name that is already in use, Symphony warns you with this message:

A file with this name already exists -- replace it?

You can select No, the default response, to avoid saving the new file over the old one, or you can select Yes to proceed with the replacement of the old information.

Changing the Directory

If you want to save your new file to a directory other than to the current directory, then you can press (BACKSPACE) at the prompt C:\SYM22\DATA*.wr1. This shows you a listing of the next level up in the directory system. For example, if you have a directory structure like that shown in Figure 8-2 and you have the default directory set to C:\SYM22\DATA, pressing (BACKSPACE) at the *.wr1 prompt would result in the following display:

```
Name of file to retrieve: C:\SYM22\*.wr?                                        FILES
DATA\              SALES\
  ------A------B---------C---------D---------E---------F---------G---------H-----
1
2               Sales Figures
3
4                 Jan-91    Feb-91    Mar-91    Apr-91    May-91    Jun-91    Jul-91
```

This tells you that there are no worksheet files in the SYM22 directory, but there are two subdirectories, SALES and DATA. If you highlight one of these and press (ENTER), you will see a list of files for that directory. In this case, if you press (BACKSPACE) again you will see a list of subdirectories in the root directory of the disk, the level above C:\SYM22.

The Directory Setting

Symphony always needs to know the directory and drive in which you want the worksheet stored. Initially, Symphony assumes that you want to save the data to the drive and directory from which you started the program. You can change this temporarily by using the File Dir command.

Suppose you have Symphony installed on drive C in a directory called SYM22. The full name of this storage area, its path, is C:\SYM22\. However, you would like Symphony to store a series of worksheets on drive A. You select the Dir command from the SERVICES File menu and are prompted "Enter current directory:" as you saw earlier in the chapter. The currently selected directory is shown—in this case, C:\SYM22. The cursor is flashing under the first letter of this path name. Simply type the path name of the new storage area (in this case, **A:**) and it will replace the current one. If you want to specify a particular directory you have created on A, you would add a backslash (\) and the name of the directory, as in A:\WORK. When you have typed the new directory, press (ENTER). From now until you end the current session with Symphony, or until you use the File Dir command again to select a different area, Symphony will store files to and retrieve files from the new directory.

To make a more permanent change to the data directory setting, use the SERVICES Configuration File command and specify the directory you want Symphony to use. You must then use the Configuration Update command to add this preference to the program's configuration file that is read each time Symphony is loaded. To store just one file to an area other than the default directory, use the File Save command and edit the path and file name to include the desired path.

RETRIEVING FILES

When you want to bring back into memory a copy of a worksheet that you have stored on disk, you use the Retrieve command from the SERVICES File menu. The command assumes that you want to retrieve a worksheet from the drive and directory currently selected.

File Listing

When you select SERVICES File Retrieve, Symphony helps you identify the file you want by displaying a list of files similar to the one displayed during the SERVICES File Save operations just described. You can press the MENU key to show a more complete list. Use the movement keys described in Table 8-2 to move through these lists and highlight the file you want. If there are too many worksheet files in the current storage area to fit on one screen, you will need to scroll down the list. To see the date and time the files were saved, as well as their size, highlight the file you want and check the second row of the screen. When you find the file you want to retrieve, press (ENTER), and Symphony will read that file into memory.

If you want to retrieve a file from a storage area other than the current one, you have several options. When you select File Retrieve and are prompted for a file name, you can press (ESC) and then edit the path of the area you want to retrieve from. You press (ENTER) to see a list of the files in that area. For example, suppose you want to see all of the worksheets in the SALES subdirectory of the SYM22 directory, but the DATA subdirectory is the current directory. The initial prompt is C:\SYM22\DATA*.wr1. When you press (ESC) this changes to C:\SYM22\DATA\. You can then press (BACKSPACE) five times so that you remove the DATA subdirectory. Now you can type in the new directory, as in C:\SYM22\SALES\, and press (ENTER) to see all of the worksheets in this directory.

Another way to edit this prompt is to press (CTRL-LEFT ARROW) to move the cursor left five characters and then press (INS) to get into Overstrike mode, typing the next directory over the existing prompt. When you press (ENTER), Symphony will automatically add the *.wr1 specification for you. Note that you must use the backslash at the end of the edited prompt. If you do not include this, Symphony will assume that you are looking for a file called SALES.WR1 in the SYM22 directory.

File Retrieve Restrictions

Symphony will not permit you to have more than one worksheet in memory at a time. When you read a file from disk with the File Retrieve command, the data from the file is placed in memory. If you already have data in memory, Symphony assumes that you want to replace the current data with data you are going to read from disk. The data read from the file will replace all that was there before it, from cell A1 through cell IV8192.

There is the considerable potential to lose work when issuing the File Retrieve command. To prevent accidental loss of data, make sure you save your current work before issuing the File Retrieve command. Even if your work is not saved, Symphony will not ask you if you want to lose your changes when you use the Retrieve command.

Automatically Loading Files

You may find that your work with Symphony involves heavy use of one particular worksheet. You can have Symphony retrieve a specific file automatically whenever the program is loaded. To activate this feature, use the SERVICES Configuration Auto command to enter the name of the worksheet file you want Symphony to load automatically. You must type in the file name; Symphony does not provide a list of files. If the file is not in the default directory, you must include the full path name of the file.

Note Remember to use the Configuration Update command to store this setting.

Suppose you enter the name **BUDGET**. Whenever you load Symphony, the program looks for a worksheet file in the current directory called BUDGET.WR1. If such a file is present, it is loaded into memory as soon as the Symphony program has finished loading. This works well with the automatic macro feature described in Chapter 9. You can automatically load a file, and then Symphony will run a specially named macro in that file.

If you need to turn off the automatic loading feature, simply select SERVICES Configuration Auto and press (ESC) to remove the file name before pressing (ENTER). Then use the Update command to record this change.

A New File

If you want to clear the current worksheet from memory, you use the SERVICES New command. It erases the current worksheet and all associated settings from memory, essentially cleaning out your work area. Whenever you execute this command, you must select Yes to complete it. The command is not intelligent: it does not know if unsaved changes exist in any of the worksheets. If you execute New and then answer Yes, there is no way Symphony can recall what you were working on.

MANAGING FILES

As you accumulate files on your computer, you may need help in organizing them. Symphony provides such help with three commands: File Erase, File List, and File Table.

The File List Command

When you want to see what files are in your data directory but are not interested in retrieving or saving a file, you can select File List, which shows you these choices:

```
File with .WRK or .WR1 extension                                      MENU
Worksheet  Print  Graph  All  Linked
┌──────A──────B──────C──────D──────E──────F──────G──────H──────┐
1
```

When you select Worksheet, you are shown the files included by the file specification *.wr?, which is the same one used by Symphony when showing you a list of files to retrieve.

The list of files is in the same format as that used by the (F10) key, with four columns of up to 21 names per column on a normal display. You can use the arrow keys to scroll through the list. The file whose name you highlight has its details displayed at the top of the screen.

The File List commands initially present the files in the current dircctory, but you can press (ESC) to edit the file-list prompt to the path and file specification that you want. For example, if you edit the prompt to C:\SALES\ and press (ENTER), Symphony will show you all files encompassed by *.wr? in the directory SALES on drive C.

The Print option on the File List command shows files in the current directory with the extension PRN. The Graph option shows files with the extension PIC (for more on graph files, see Chapter 6). The All option lists all files, using the *.* specification, which includes program files and worksheets. The last item on the File List menu is Linked, which shows all files that have links to the current file.

File Erasing

When you have been working with Symphony for a while, there may be old files that you no longer need—perhaps early versions of models, small worksheets that are now redundant, or experimental files no longer required. To clean up your disk you can use the File Erase command, bearing in mind that this command actually erase files from the disk and so is fairly drastic. The File Erase command presents files in four categories: Worksheet, Print, Graph, and Other. The last option is particularly useful as well as dangerous. You can use it to delete any file from the disk.

When you choose one of the four file categories, you are shown a single-line list of file names. You can press MENU ((F10)) to make the list full screen. Highlight the name of the file you want to get rid of, and press (ENTER). Fortunately, Symphony prompts you to confirm the action before completing it. You are taken out of the menu system when you select Yes to delete the file or No to cancel the command.

File Tables

Your efforts at file management with Symphony can be greatly assisted by the File Table command. This command places file information into a worksheet as a series of labels and values. When you select File Table, you are prompted to tell Symphony which directory you want listed. Then you get a menu of file categories like the one used by the List command.

Suppose that you want a list of worksheets in the current directory. You select Worksheet. Symphony prompts you for a location for the table. This should be an unused area of a worksheet that is three columns wide and has no data below it. When you point to the top left corner of such an area or type in a cell location and press (ENTER), the table is placed in the worksheet.

If you do not have much room in your worksheet, you can define a location that is a complete range, three columns wide and as many rows long as you think there will be files in the table. For example, if you think that there will be about 20 files, you can use a specific area of the worksheet, such as J1..L20. If there are more files than will fit, Symphony will not overflow the area you have defined as it does when you give a single cell as the table coordinate.

You can see a typical file table in Figure 8-6. The first column is a set of labels, and the other two columns are numeric values. Note that the files are listed in alphabetical order, and the first

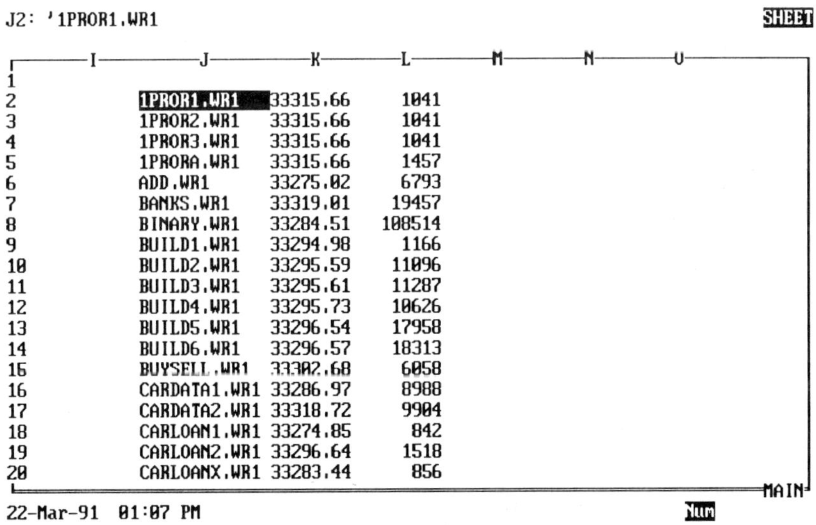

FIGURE 8-6 Results of the File Table command

```
J2: '1PROR1.WR1                                                    SHEET

     I         J            K          L        M          N         O
1              Name        Date       Size
2          1PROR1.WR1    03/18/91     1,041 Region 1 sales
3          1PROR2.WR1    03/18/91     1,041 Region 2 sales
4          1PROR3.WR1    03/18/91     1,041 Region 3 sales
5          1PRORA.WR1    03/18/91     1,457 Combined sales, all regions
```

FIGURE 8-7 Formatted file table

column needs to be 13 characters wide for the full names of files to be clearly visible. Also note that the date/time stamp is listed as a combined serial number, such as 33315.66 for 3:30 P.M. on 3/18/91. The third column is the size of the file in bytes.

To dress up the table, you can apply the D4 date format to the second column. This will give you the date stamp in readable form. Format the third column with the Punctuated format, zero decimal places. Add a line of centered labels, and you have the very attractive display as in Figure 8-7. Note that the user has added comments in a fourth column to document the files.

Note The results of the File Table command are not interactive, meaning that changes made to disk files are not automatically read into the table. However, you can manually update the table very quickly by reissuing the File Table command.

To create a printed list of files, you can read the table into a worksheet and use the SERVICES Print command. You can also print a file list by using DOS. For example, to print a list of the files on a floppy disk in drive A, you can exit Symphony and enter **DIR A: > PRN** at the DOS prompt. The > PRN parameter will send the directory of files to the printer. However, this does not give you the chance to sort the files or annotate them. The file table in Figure 8-7 can be sorted according to any of the columns, as described in Chapter 5. Comments can be added, and the table can become part of a report, printed with headers and footers if it is more than one page long. Such reports can be used to help keep track of files that are being copied off the hard disk onto floppy disks for storage, or worksheets that go together to make up an application.

PASSWORD PROTECTION

To prevent unauthorized access to a worksheet stored on disk, you can assign a password to the worksheet while you are saving it. The procedure is very simple and well worth using if you are nervous about other people reading your worksheets.

Creating Password Protection

To assign a password to a file, you select File Save from the SERVICES menu as if you were going to perform an ordinary file save. However, when Symphony presents the current file name, you type a space followed by **P**. If the file does not yet have a name, just type a name followed by a space and **P**. When you press (ENTER), Symphony prompts you for a password. The password can be several words, numbers, and spaces, up to a total length of 15 characters. Pick a password that you can remember—neither Lotus nor anyone else can retrieve the data if you forget the word. No one can see the letters of the password as you type, because Symphony shows blanks for each letter, as shown here:

```
Enter password: ■■■■■■■■                                          EDIT
┌────────I──────────J──────────K──────────L─────────M─────────N─────────O──────────┐
1                 Name       Date       Size
```

When you have typed the password, press (ENTER). You are then asked to verify the word by typing it again. The theory is that if you can type the word twice, you know what it is and did not make a mistake the first time you entered it. After typing the word a second time, you press (ENTER). The file-saving process continues as usual. If you replace an existing file with a password-protected file, the file is then password protected.

Working with Password-Protected Files

When you attempt to retrieve or open a password-protected file, you are prompted for the password. This time, you only need to type the password once and then press (ENTER) to access the file. If you type an incorrect password, Symphony beeps and gives you the message "Invalid password."

When you save a file with password protection, Symphony encrypts the file; that is, it scrambles the data to make it unintelligible even to a sophisticated, well-trained programmer. Do not expect to be able to get the data back if you forget the password. Trying to get around the password by using the partial file retrieval command, File Combine, does not work either. You cannot even use the Translate program to translate a password-protected file to a different format.

Note: Keep a copy of the password in a secure place, such as a locked desk drawer or in another password-protected Symphony file.

When you want to remove password protection from a file, you must first open the file and then use the File Save command. Symphony will remind you that the file is password protected:

```
Save file name: C:\SYM22\DATA\LIST [PASSWORD PROTECTED]                 EDIT
┌────────I──────────J──────────K──────────L──────────M──────────N──────────O──────────┐
1                  Name       Date       Size
```

You can press (BACKSPACE) to remove the protection message. Then press (ENTER) to complete the file save, and the file is no longer protected. Unless you remove the password protection during a file save, the file will continue to be password- protected.

Designing Passwords

Using passwords can be a nuisance, so you should decide if the need for security is real. If it is, then you will want to make sure you use proper passwords. There is no point in using a password if it is a useless password such as "password," "pass," your first name, the filename, and so on. The serious data thief is likely to guess most words that do not have the following features:

At least eight characters
A mixture of text and numbers
Some odd characters, like @, spaces, and commas
A mixture of upper- and lowercase
A lack of obvious logic

Although a determined thief could simply try one password after another to retrieve a password-protected worksheet, the number of possible combinations of characters is staggering. If the number of different characters from which you can compose a Symphony password is 100 and you use 5 characters, there are 10,000,000,000 combinations (100^5). In fact, there are more than 100 possible characters you can use in a password.

Although some programs that use passwords do not distinguish between upper- and lowercase in password characters, Symphony does, which is an important point to remember when recording your passwords. The password "Fred's File" will not be accepted if it is supplied as "FRED'S FILE," and even "Fred's file" will be rejected.

To create passwords that lack a logical connection between the contents of the file and the password protecting it, you need to be imaginative. For example, a banker might use the names of birds to protect a series of salary recommendation files. Combined with the other features, something like this would be difficult to guess:

```
Crow@576
```

Since such a name would also be difficult to remember, you must make proper provision for recording and securing passwords. A sheet of paper locked in a drawer is a good technique. You can also use a spreadsheet or word processor to list files and their passwords. The more paranoid might want to code the passwords on the printed listing. One method for assigning and remembering passwords is to use the first word on a particular page of a book that you have in your office. If you use the page number in the file name, it will help you find the password.

WORKING WITH ADD-IN APPLICATIONS

With its five environments and extensive range of commands, Symphony provides many of the features you need for your work. However, you might find yourself wishing for added features in one or two areas. If Lotus had included in Symphony every feature that users have asked for, the program simply would not fit on most personal computers. Instead, Lotus created add-in applications to augment Symphony's power without making the main program too large. Later in this chapter, two add-ins are discussed: DOS and Viewer. Both of these add to your ability to manage files.

Attaching an Add-In

Symphony comes with about a dozen add-ins, and there are others available from third-party software developers. You can pick and choose which add-ins you want to use; you do not have to use any, or you can use several at once. Add-in applications are attached to Symphony through the SERVICES Application command. They can be attached to Symphony during a session to provide extra functions without removing Symphony or the current worksheet from memory. However, because add-ins make additional demands on memory, you may not be able to load all of the add-ins at once.

The DOS add-in application gives you the ability to temporarily suspend Symphony and issue commands at the DOS prompt. Use the following steps to attach the DOS add-in, bearing in mind that the procedure is similar when attaching other add-ins:

1. Press SERVICES and select Application.
2. Select Attach, and Symphony will present a list of files from the program directory, each of which has the extension APP.
3. Press (F10) to see the entire list, shown here:

```
Application name: C:\SYM22\*.app                                              FILES
          ALLWAYS.APP    01/04/90        19:43           13482
 ALLWAYS.APP    BASE.APP       BASEFUNC.APP   BASEUTL.APP    DOS.APP
 INPUT.APP      MACROMGR.APP   NETFILE.APP    OUTLINER.APP   SPELLER.APP
 STAT.APP       VIEWER.APP     VT100.APP      DATA\          SALES\
```

4. Select the file called DOS.APP. You will be returned to the Application menu.
5. At this point you could select Invoke to use the DOS applications, but instead, select Quit to leave the menu system. Using SERVICES Application Invoke is a long-winded way of using an application. Most applications are actually attached to existing menus as new menu items.
6. To see the DOS application as a menu item, press SERVICES. You will see the DOS command at the far right of the menu line, as shown here:

```
Modify current window or use another window                                  MENU
Window  File  Print  Configuration  Application  Settings  New  Exit  DOS
 --------A--------B--------C---------D---------E---------F---------G--------H--------
1
```

Invoking an Add-In

To use an add-in application, you can use SERVICES Application Invoke and select the application you want to use from the list that Symphony provides of all attached applications. Alternatively, you can select the application as a menu item. In the case of the DOS application, the menu item is called DOS and it appears on the main SERVICES menu. After you review the rest of the Application commands, the correct use of the DOS application will be examined.

Eliminating the Attachment For an Add-In

Once an add-in is attached, it will remain attached until you exit Symphony. This means that you can invoke it again and again, whenever you want. It also means that some of your computer's memory is allocated to the add-in. If you know you are not going to use the add-in again, the best approach is to eliminate its attachment to Symphony. This can be accomplished in two ways.

If you only want to eliminate the attachment for one add-in, select Detach from the Application menu. To eliminate all attached add-ins with one command, select Clear from the Application menu. This removes all currently attached applications. Any remaining applications are detached when you quit Symphony.

Permanent Attachments

If you find that you are using a particular application on a regular basis, you can tell Symphony that you would like it to be loaded every time. Using the menu shown here allows you to select up to eight applications that will be automatically loaded each time you start Symphony:

```
Select an application to be automatically loaded, and attach it          MENU
Set  Cancel  Quit

 1:                         Auto-Invoke: No
 2:                         Auto-Invoke: No
 3:                         Auto-Invoke: No
 4:                         Auto-Invoke: No
 5:                         Auto-Invoke: No
 6:                         Auto-Invoke: No
 7:                         Auto-Invoke: No
 8:                         Auto-Invoke: No
                                             Application settings
```

Suppose that you want the DOS application to be loaded all the time. You choose the Set option, and Symphony presents a list of numbers 1 through 8, corresponding to the eight application slots available. Select 1, and a list of applications appears:

```
Application name: C:\SYM22\*.app                                            FILES
ALLWAYS.APP    BASE.APP       BASEFUNC.APP    BASEUTL.APP     DOS.APP

 1:                         Auto-Invoke: No
```

Select DOS.APP from the list. Symphony then asks, "Automatically invoke add-in when it is loaded?" In this case, you answer No since you do not want the DOS command executed as soon as Symphony starts up. Some other applications are more suitable candidates for Auto-Invoke.

After answering No, you will see the DOS application listed on the Application settings sheet, as shown here:

```
Select an application to be automatically loaded, and attach it          MENU
Set  Cancel  Quit

 1: DOS                     Auto-Invoke: No
 2:                         Auto-Invoke: No
```

Symphony also loads the application if it is not already loaded. To record this change for the next session, you must select Quit from the Other Application menu and select Update from the main Configuration menu to update the configuration file on disk.

To remove an application from the Applications settings sheet, you use the Cancel command. This command also removes the application from memory. Although you can set up to eight applications to be loaded with Symphony, you will need a lot of memory in your computer to accommodate more than two or three at once. Try to reserve the Configuration Other Application command for applications you need all the time.

OPERATING SYSTEM ACCESS

While you are working in Symphony, you may have need of a disk operating command such as COPY to duplicate some files, or FORMAT to prepare a new floppy disk for data storage. Or, you might want to use the MD command to make a new directory area on your data disk. You can do this without unloading Symphony by using the DOS command, supplied by the DOS add-in application. The Symphony worksheet you are working on will be retained in memory until you return to Symphony.

The DOS command leads you to a screen that has a modified version of the DOS prompt, as shown in Figure 8-8. You are reminded that to return to Symphony you must type **EXIT** and press (ENTER). Note that the active or current directory is the one from which you started Symphony. You can move to other directories to perform DOS operations. For example, you can copy a Symphony worksheet file to a new name to make a working copy. This is an alternative to retrieving the file into Symphony and then saving it under a new name. Using DOS is sometimes quicker when the file is large.

While using the DOS command to access DOS, you should not use programs or commands that alter the DOS environment or leave code in memory. For example, you should not load a terminate-and-stay-resident program, such as Borland's SideKick, at this point. You should also avoid using the PRINT command, which can interfere with Symphony. Some file management utility programs, such as Norton Utilities and QuickDOS, can be run

```
(Use the EXIT command to return to Symphony)

Microsoft(R) MS-DOS(R)  Version 3.30
             (C)Copyright Microsoft Corp 1981-1987

C:\SYM22>
```

FIGURE 8-8 Using DOS from Symphony

while using the Symphony DOS command, since these programs are cleanly removed from memory when you leave them.

Because there is a possibility that an error will occur when you are using DOS, you should save your Symphony work before using the DOS command. Also, you must remember that you are using DOS through the Symphony DOS command, since Symphony does not remind you. The message in Figure 8-8 disappears after you use a command that clears the screen. It is possible to forget that you got to DOS through Symphony, and thus forget to exit back to Symphony to quit the program correctly.

You can also use the DOS application by selecting SERVICES Application Invoke. This command presents a list of currently attached applications, and you can select DOS from the list. Symphony responds with this prompt:

```
Press [RETURN] or enter program name:                                    EDIT
 ┌───────A─────────B─────────C─────────D─────────E─────────F─────────G─────────H────────┐
 1
```

Just press (ENTER) to use the DOS application and get to the DOS prompt. Type **EXIT** and press (ENTER) when you are ready to return to Symphony.

USING THE VIEWER

Another Symphony add-in application that helps with file management is the Lotus Magellan Viewer, called the Viewer for short. You attach the Viewer by pressing SERVICES, selecting Application Attach, and then choosing VIEWER.APP from the list of application program files. When you have attached the Viewer, it offers a new option on the SERVICES File menu, called View.

Exploring the Viewer

When you select View from the SERVICES menu, you have three choices: Retrieve, Link, and Browse. All three options list your worksheet files in the same way. In Figure 8-9 you can see how this file listing differs from the normal file list: the contents of the highlighted file are shown on the screen.

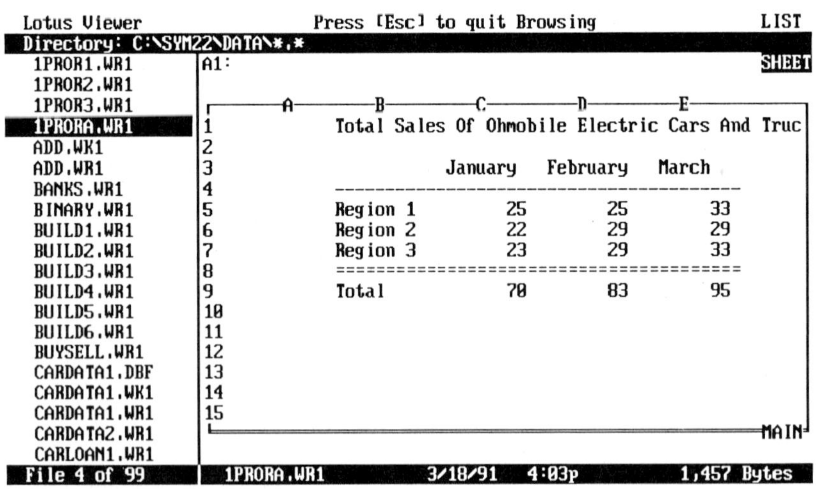

FIGURE 8-9 The Viewer in action

The difference between the three View commands is the action they perform with files that you select. The Retrieve command lists files so that you can select a file to be retrieved; it is a sophisticated alternative to the File Retrieve command. The Link command lists files so that you can establish links between them, a Symphony worksheet facility described in more detail in the next section. The Browse command, shown at work in Figure 8-9, simply lists files so that you can explore your disks and does not allow you to do anything with the files besides view them.

The Viewer can show you the contents of four different types of file: Symphony worksheets, 1-2-3 worksheets, dBASE files, and text files. You can also view the titles of a PIC graph file, but you cannot view the graph itself. The Viewer lets you identify files by their contents, rather than just by the name. In most cases the view of the file is very similar to what you would see if you were in the original application itself.

The text-file Viewer is the default, used if the file does not match one of the other three Viewer file formats. The text-file Viewer displays only alphanumeric characters, skipping any graphics in the file.

To view other types of files, including non-Symphony word processing and graphics files, you can use the full Lotus Magellan program. This software offers other features besides file viewing. Magellan has a fast file search either by file name or by words or phrases within files. Magellan can launch applications corresponding to the file you are viewing (similar to the document-launching facility on the Apple Macintosh). Magellan also provides a variety of utilities for such tasks as file deletion, backup, and file compression (to save disk space), plus a file integrity checking function that can alert you to computer viruses.

As you can see from Figure 8-9, the Viewer screen efficiently conveys information about the files in your current Symphony directory. The Viewer screen consists of the status line, the directory path, the List and View windows, and the information line. The status line at the top of the Viewer screen displays user prompts for the retrieving, linking, and browsing commands. In the top right corner is the current mode indicator, which tells you what is happening. The following messages may be displayed there:

LIST	You have entered the Viewer and have the highlight bar in the List window.
VIEW	You have moved the highlight into the View window.
WAIT	You have asked the Viewer to retrieve a file or display the contents of another file (it sometimes takes a moment for the View screen to be redrawn).
ERROR	You have used a keystroke that caused an error.
HELP	You pressed (F1) for HELP.

The directory path just below the status line is the default directory, the one listed when you use the SERVICES File Dir command. You cannot change the directory path from within the Viewer. To change the directory, you have to quit the Viewer and use the File Dir command.

The window on the left is the List window. It contains a list of files in alphabetical order. You can use the cursor movement keys to scroll through the list. When a file name is highlighted, that file is the current file and is thus selected for the next command. The window to the right of the List window, the View window, displays the contents of the file currently highlighted in the List window.

The line directly beneath the List and View windows is called the information line. It is divided into two areas. The left area relates to the List window, and the right area to the View window. The List window area gives the total number of files in the current directory and the number of the currently selected file name. The View window area gives you DOS information for the current file (date and time stamp, and file size in bytes).

In the List Window:	
ENTER	Retrieves currently highlighted file when using View Retrieve
DOWN ARROW	Moves highlighting one file down the list
UP ARROW	Moves highlighting one file up the list
PGDN	Moves highlighting to top of next screenful of files going down the list
PGUP	Moves highlighting to top of next screenful of files going up the list
LEFT ARROW	Moves highlighting into View window
HOME	Moves highlighting to first file in directory
END	Moves highlighting to last file in directory
In the View Window (Action Depends on Type of File Viewed):	
UP ARROW	Worksheet: Moves highlight up one cell Database: Moves highlight up one record Text: Moves highlight up one line
DOWN ARROW	Worksheet: Moves highlight down one cell Database: Moves highlight down one record Text: Moves highlight down one line
RIGHT ARROW	Worksheet: Moves highlight right one cell Database: Moves highlight right one field
LEFT ARROW	Worksheet: Moves highlight left one cell Database: Moves highlight left one field
CTRL-RIGHT ARROW	Worksheet: Moves highlight right one window
CTRL-LEFT ARROW	Worksheet: Moves highlight left one window
END	Database: Moves highlight to the last record Text: Moves highlight to last line of the window
HOME	Worksheet: Moves highlight to the first cell Database: Moves highlight to the first record Text: Moves highlight to the first line of the window
PGDN	Moves highlight down one screen
PGUP	Moves highlight up one screen
In All Windows:	
CTRL-BREAK	Takes you out of Viewer and back to Symphony environment

TABLE 8-4 Keys Used with the Viewer

ESC	Backs you out of Viewer one step at a time until you reach the current worksheet
HELP	Displays the Viewer Help screen
ENTER	Retrieves currently highlighted file when using View Retrieve

TABLE 8-4 Keys Used with the Viewer (*continued*)

Note: You cannot resize the List and View windows, or change the display of the directory path or status line.

Using the Viewer

You can move around the List and View windows with the cursor movement keys, as listed in Table 8-4. The pointer movement keys act according to which Viewer is active, and these are also listed in Table 8-4. The three View commands perform as follows.

BROWSE The File View Browse command displays all the files in the current directory in the List window. You can scroll through the list of files and view their contents in the View window. Press ESC to quit browsing. Each time you press ESC, the Viewer backs you out one step at a time until you reach the current worksheet. Press CTRL-BREAK to quit browsing. The Viewer returns you directly to the Symphony worksheet. In Figure 8-10, you can see how the Viewer displays the contents of a dBASE (DBF) file. In Figure 8-11, you can see how the Viewer displays the contents of a PIC file. Note that only the graph text is visible.

LINK File linking is a new feature in Symphony 2.2; it is fully explained in "Linking Worksheet Files" later in this chapter. The main reason for doing file linking with the Viewer is that you can

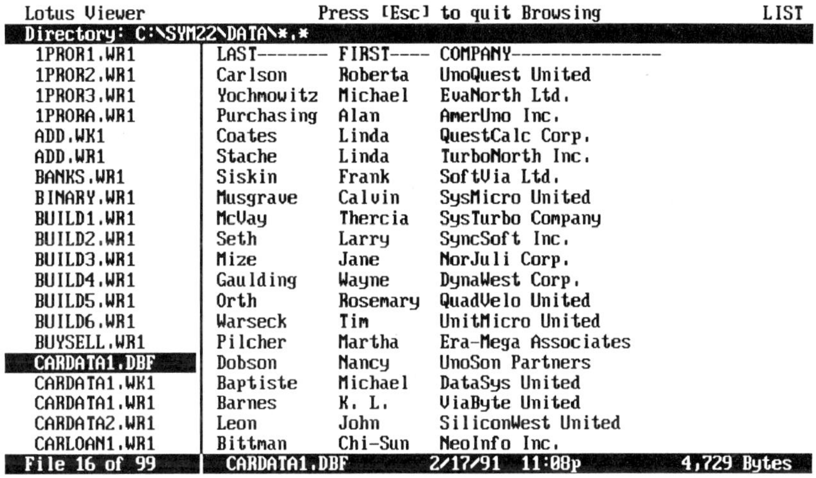

FIGURE 8-10 Viewing a database file

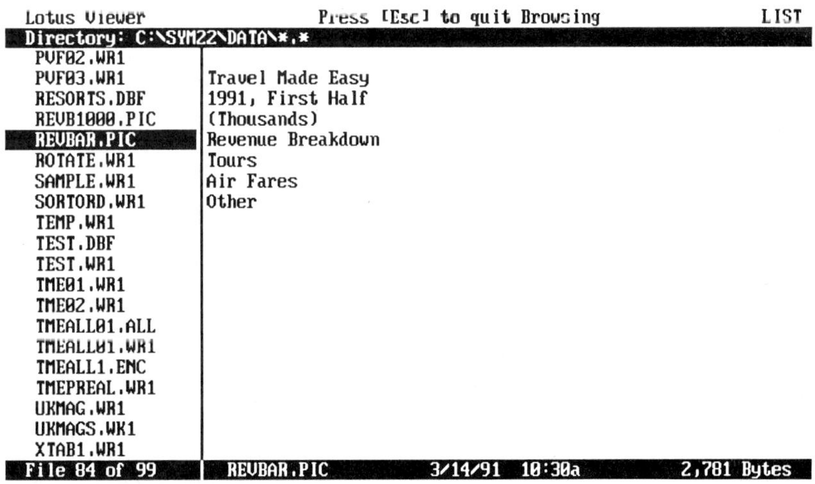

FIGURE 8-11 Viewing a PIC file

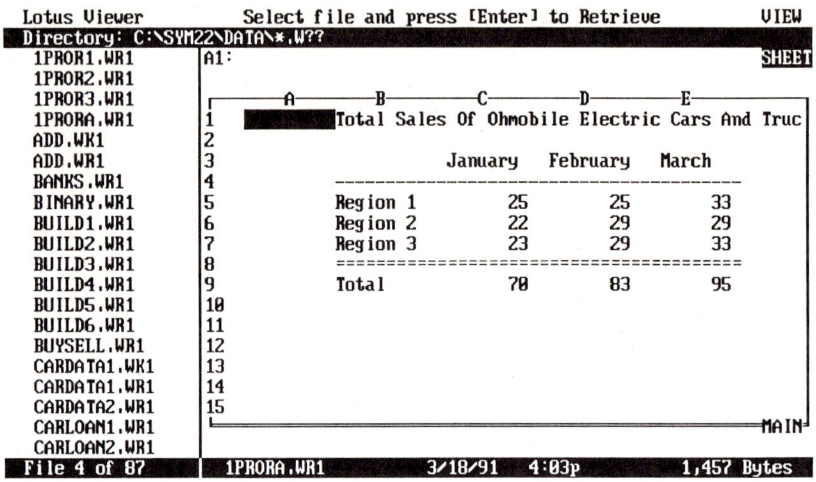

FIGURE 8-12 The View Retrieve command

see the contents of the source file, which supplies the data for the link to the current file, called the target file. Because you see the contents of the source file, you can make sure you are selecting the correct cell as the source cell. The Viewer automatically writes the correct linking formula in the target cell of the current worksheet. When you leave the Viewer and return to the target cell, the cell contains the linking formula.

RETRIEVE As you can see from Figure 8-12, the File View Retrieve command displays the Symphony and 1-2-3 worksheet files in the current directory in the List window and prompts you to select and retrieve a file from the list. You can scroll through the list of files and view their contents. Bear in mind that the View Retrieve command will replace any file in memory with the file you select for retrieval, so make sure you have saved the file in memory before using this command. Highlight the file you want

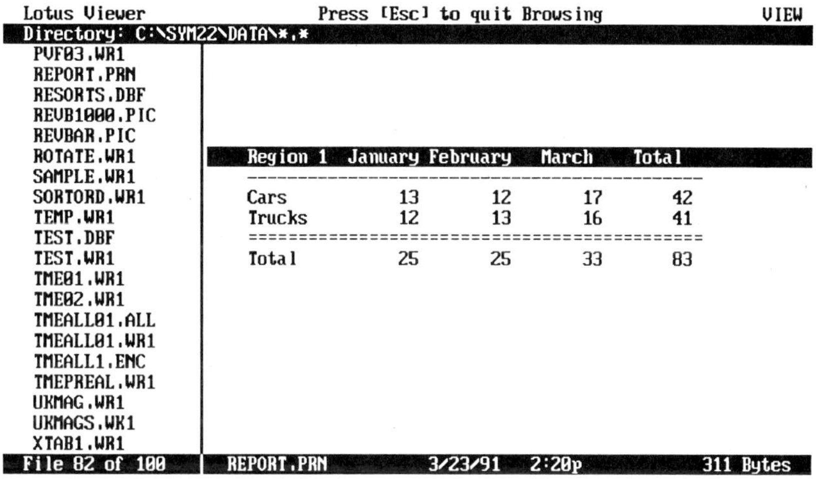

FIGURE 8-13 Viewing a text file

to retrieve and press (ENTER) from either window. The Viewer retrieves the file and returns you to the Symphony environment.

Note that when you select File View Retrieve, the Viewer lists Symphony and 1-2-3 worksheet files and any other files that have "W" as the first letter of their extension. Most files display as worksheet files in the View window, except for 1-2-3 Release 3.0 files and nonworksheet files, both of which display as text files. You can see a worksheet as a text file in Figure 8-13. Note that the highlight bar runs the entire width of the line. This particular file is a PRN file, created with the print-to-disk feature described in Chapter 11.

The Viewer makes a useful addition to Symphony's file management tools. The limit of eight user-selected letters in a Symphony worksheet name makes it hard to come up with descriptive names, so the ability to see what is in a particular file before retrieving it is very handy. If you want to have the Viewer attached to Symphony every time you use the program, see the earlier section on permanent attachments.

SPACE PROBLEMS

When you are building a large worksheet, it is surprising how fast the worksheet can grow in size. The Copy command, in particular, quickly generates a lot of data. This can result in space problems, both on disk and in memory.

Disk Space

When you attempt to save a file that is too large to fit in the remaining free space on your disk, Symphony responds with a "Disk full" error message. You can respond to this in several ways.

SAVE TO A FLOPPY DISK If you have been saving to a floppy disk and the current disk cannot accommodate the worksheet you are trying to save, you can retry the save after inserting a disk with a greater amount of free space on it. If you have attached the DOS application, you can use the DOS command to temporarily exit to DOS and format a fresh floppy disk if you need one. The DOS command, which was described earlier in this chapter, does not affect your unsaved work. If you have been saving to a hard disk that has now filled up, you might consider saving to a floppy disk as a temporary measure. Remember that some floppy disks can now store over a megabyte of information.

CLEAN UP YOUR HARD DISK If you are trying to save to a hard disk that has run out of space, you can use the DOS command or the SERVICES File Erase command to erase unwanted files from your hard disk. This will make more room available and help to accommodate the worksheet you are trying to save.

CONVERT VALUES The amount of space required by formulas in a worksheet is greater than that taken up by values. If you convert numbers that are generated by formulas into their values, using the Range Values command, then the worksheet can be stored in less space.

DIVIDE THE WORKSHEET When you attempt to save a worksheet and get a "Disk full" message, you may want to consider splitting the worksheet into separate, smaller worksheets. To do this you can use the File Xtract command, described later in this chapter.

Memory Space

Symphony displays a "memory full" message when you attempt to retrieve a file that is too large to fit in currently available memory. You get a similar message when you expand the current worksheet beyond the limits of available memory. If you want to check on the amount of memory you have available, use the SERVICES Settings command and read the current status of memory from the screen. A typical display might show this:

```
Conventional Memory: 99573 of 128528 Bytes (77%)
Expanded Memory: (none)
```

The first line tells you that 99,573 bytes are unused, out of a total memory area of 128,528 bytes. The total memory figure of 128,528 is how much memory you have left on your system after loading DOS plus Symphony and any add-in applications. The difference between 128,528 and 99,573 is how much space the current worksheet occupies.

The first line of the memory listing shows *conventional memory*. This is normal memory, the first 640 K of RAM in your system. If you have more than 640 K of RAM, Symphony can use this, but it needs to be configured as *expanded memory*. For more on these terms, see Appendix A. If you have expanded memory, then Symphony shows how much of it is used. The percentage figure is a helpful guide to how much more work you can fit into the remaining memory.

If you have a worksheet loaded when you read the settings screen, you can see how much room there is for expansion. If you have a blank worksheet, you can tell how large a file you can retrieve. Symphony needs enough free memory to read in the file from disk and to manipulate the data within the worksheet. Thus, if you have 82,944 bytes available, it would be unwise to try to retrieve anything larger than 80,000 bytes.

When you use a command that causes Symphony to run out of memory, you should save parts of the worksheet to separate files using the SERVICES File Xtract command. This will allow you to store the data safely so that you can redesign the worksheet, perhaps free more memory, or add more memory to the system. You can free memory by saving the current worksheet, exiting Symphony, and removing any memory-resident programs you might have loaded.

If it was a Copy command that caused Symphony to run out of memory, you will probably find that only part of the range was copied. However, the data you had before the copy operation should still be intact. If you tried to retrieve a file that was too large, only part of the file will be in your worksheet, but the entire file will still be safely stored on disk.

Data Loss

The best approach to prevent data loss is the same one you use for steady monetary accumulation: Save on a regular basis. That means saving every 15 minutes. You should also save your files

Before you perform a file retrieve
Before you turn off your PC

Before you leave your PC unattended
Before a large move or copy
Before a data sort or extract or range fill operation
Before a file combine

However, even if you live by these rules, there is always a possibility that something will go wrong between saves. Regularly timed file saving is the best guarantee against data loss. When a problem occurs, the saved version of the file can be retrieved intact.

LINKING WORKSHEET FILES

Symphony gives you the ability to link several worksheets, making data in one dependent on data from another. This ability really opens up a new realm of spreadsheet design possibilities. In some cases, you will want to use this feature to split large and cumbersome worksheets into more manageable, interrelated units. Knowing that Symphony supports links between files allows you to approach new projects in a different way, following more closely the traditional accounting model of consolidated sheets and supporting sheets.

Creating a Linked File Model

Consider the situation faced by the sales manager at the headquarters of Ohmobile, the fledgling electric car company. Each quarter, she receives a sales worksheet like the one in Figure 8-14 from each of three regional offices. She would like to consolidate these figures to obtain an overall sales picture, but they are in separate files. To see how file linking works, you will use it to solve the sales manager's problem. First you will create the three regional sales worksheets. (These will also be used later in the chapter to demonstrate file combining.)

```
A1: 'Region 1                                                    SHEET
      A         B         C         D         E        F        G        H
1  Region 1  January February   March     Total
2  -------------------------------------------------
3  Cars           13        12       17        42
4  Trucks         12        13       16        41
5  =================================================
6  Total          25        25       33        83
7
8
9
10
```

FIGURE 8-14 Region 1 sales worksheet

1. In a new worksheet, enter the following information in cells A1 through E6, using the worksheet commands you learned in the first three chapters:

A1: Region 1	B1: ^January	C1: ^February	D1: ^March	E1: ^Total
A2: \-	B2: \-	C2: \-	D2: \-	E2: \-
A3: Cars	B3: 13	C3: 12	D3: 17	E3: @SUM(B3..D3)
A4: Trucks	B4: 12	C4: 13	D4: 16	E4: @SUM(B4..D4)

2. To save time, you can copy the formula from E3 to E4 with the MENU Copy command. With the cell pointer in E3, you press MENU, choose Copy, and press (ENTER) to confirm E3..E3 as the FROM range. Press (DOWN ARROW) and (ENTER) to confirm E4 as the TO range.

3. Enter the label \= in cell A5, and copy it to B5 through C5 using the MENU Copy command. With the cell pointer in A5, you press MENU, choose Copy, and press (ENTER) to confirm A5..A5 as the FROM range. Type a period to anchor A5 as the beginning of the TO range. Press (UP ARROW) once, and then press (END). Press (RIGHT ARROW) and then (DOWN ARROW). Press (ENTER) to confirm A5..E5 as the TO range.

4. In A6, enter the label **Total**, and in B6 enter the formula **@SUM(B3..B4)**.

5. To complete the model, copy the formula from B6 to C6 through E6 using the MENU Copy command. With the cell pointer in B6, you press MENU, choose Copy, and press (ENTER) to confirm B6..B6 as the FROM range. Type a period to anchor B6 as the beginning of the TO range. Press (UP ARROW) once, and then press (END). Press (RIGHT ARROW) and then (DOWN ARROW). Press (ENTER) to confirm B6..E6 as the TO range. The worksheet will now look like the one in Figure 8-14.

6. Use the SERVICES File Save command to store the worksheet on disk, using the name **1PROR1**.

To create the second and third regional worksheets, you will simply alter the current worksheet and then save it using a different name.

1. Having made sure that step 6 in the previous exercise was carried out, change the worksheet label in A1 and the numbers in B3 through D6 so that the worksheet matches the following. Note that the formulas remain the same although the results are different.

```
A2: \-                                                           SHEET

    ------A--------B---------C---------D---------E---------F---------G---------H------
1   Region 2  January February   March     Total
2   ---------------------------------------------
3   Cars           11       11       16        38
4   Trucks         11       18       13        42
5   =============================================
6   Total          22       29       29        80
```

2. Save the altered file using the name **1PROR2**.

3. Change the entries one more time for Region 3 so that they match the following and save this worksheet as **1PROR3**:

```
A1: 'Region 3                                                      SHEET
 ------A--------B--------C--------D--------E--------F--------G--------H----
1  Region 3  January February   March    Total
2  ----------------------------------------------
3  Cars           12       16       17       45
4  Trucks         11       13       16       40
5  ==============================================
6  Total          23       29       33       85
```

To create the consolidation worksheet, you can alter the 1PROR3 worksheet so that it looks like Figure 8-15. Follow these steps, which show how one worksheet can easily be edited into something different:

1. You need to move the model from its current location. With the cell pointer in A1, press MENU and select Move. Press (END) and then (RIGHT ARROW), followed by (END) and then (DOWN ARROW). This selects A1..E6 as the move FROM range. Press (ENTER). Move the cell pointer to B3 and press (ENTER). This completes the Move command.

```
A1:                                                                SHEET
 ------A--------B-----------C-----------D-----------E-----------F--------G----
1          Total Sales Of Ohmobile Electric Cars And Trucks
2
3                     January    February    March      Total
4          ------------------------------------------------
5          Region 1                                        0
6          Region 2                                        0
7          Region 3                                        0
8          ================================================
9          Total              0          0          0      0
10
```

FIGURE 8-15 Consolidation worksheet

2. Move the cell pointer to B1 and enter the following:

   Total Sales of Ohmobile Electric Cars and Trucks

3. You will now enter an extra row in the model. Move the cell pointer to B6, and press MENU. Select Insert followed by Row, and press (ENTER) to insert a blank row.

4. You will now copy the label from B3 to B5..B7. Move the cell pointer to B3 and press MENU. Select Copy and press (ENTER). Move the cell pointer to B5. Press (TAB) to anchor the TO range coordinates. Press (DOWN ARROW) twice. Press (ENTER) to confirm B5..B7 as the TO range.

5. With the cell pointer still in B3, press MENU, select Erase, and press (ENTER). By now the model will look like Figure 8-16.

6. To change the region labels in column B, first move the cell pointer to B5 and edit the label to read "Region 1." Press (F2), then (BACKSPACE). Type **1** and then press (DOWN ARROW). Press (F2) again and press (BACKSPACE). Type **2** and press (ENTER).

7. To remove the sales figures from the model, move the cell pointer to C5. Press MENU and select Erase. Type **C5.E7** as the erase range and press (ENTER).

```
B3:                                                              SHEET
     A        B         C        D        E        F        G        H
1          Total Sales Of Ohmobile Electric Cars And Trucks
2
3                    January February   March    Total
4          ------------------------------------------
5          Region 3       12       16       17       45
6          Region 3
7          Region 3       11       13       16       40
8          ==========================================
9          Total          23       29       33       85
10
```

FIGURE 8-16 Partially completed consolidation worksheet

8. All that remains is to copy the formula from F5 to F6. Regardless of the cell occupied by the cell pointer press MENU and select Copy. Type **F5** and press ENTER. Type **F6** and press ENTER.

Before you add the link formulas that will allow this converted model to act as a consolidation worksheet, use the SERVICES File Save command and enter **1PRORA** as the file name.

Establishing Links

At this point, you have the consolidation worksheet in memory and the three regional worksheets on disk. This is the situation faced by the sales manager after she has received the floppy disks containing the worksheets from the regional managers and copied the files to her hard disk. You will now create file links that supply values to the consolidation worksheet from the regional worksheets.

If you refer to Figure 8-14, you can see that the total number of units sold in January in Region 1 is in cell B6 of the file you stored as 1PROR1. You will use both the file name and cell coordinate in the link formula. The cell coordinate follows the name of the file, which is enclosed in double angle brackets.

1. Move the cell pointer to C5. Type the file link formula **+<<1PROR1>>B6** and press ENTER.

2. The resulting value is 25, and the resulting formula is stored by Symphony as +<<1PROR1.WR1>>B6, as you can see from Figure 8-17. You can enter a link formula that refers to a Symphony worksheet without using the WR1 extension, but Symphony adds this when recording the formula.

```
C5: +<<1PROR1.WR1>>B6                                              SHEET
 ───────A────────B────────C────────D────────E────────F────────G────────H──
1          Total Sales Of Ohmobile Electric Cars And Trucks
2
3                   January February   March    Total
4          ----------------------------------------------
5          Region 1        25                    25
6          Region 2                               0
7          Region 3                               0
8          ==============================================
9          Total           25        0         0     25
```

FIGURE 8-17 The file link formula in place

3. Like other Symphony formulas, the one in C5 can be copied. You want D5 and E5 in this worksheet to reflect C6 and D6 in the Region 1 worksheet. To achieve this, you simply copy the formula from C5 to the block D5..E5. The results are shown here:

```
D5: +<<1PROR1.WR1>>C6                                              SHEET
 ───────A────────B────────C────────D────────E────────F────────G────────H──
1          Total Sales Of Ohmobile Electric Cars And Trucks
2
3                   January February   March    Total
4          ----------------------------------------------
5          Region 1        25       25        33       83
```

Note that the formula +<<1PROR1.WR1>>B6 is translated to +<<1PROR1.WR1>>C6 when it is copied from column C one column to the right.

4. The link formulas on rows 6 and 7 need to refer to a different file, so you cannot copy them from row 5. In C6, enter **+<<1PROR2>>B6** and copy to D6..E6. In C7, enter **+<<1PROR3>>B6** and copy to D7..E7.

5. The model is now complete and should look like this:

```
C7: +<<1PROR3.WR1>>B6                                                    SHEET

      A       B        C        D        E        F        G        H
1            Total Sales Of Ohmobile Electric Cars And Trucks
2
3                    January February   March     Total
4            ----------------------------------------------
5            Region 1       25       25       33       83
6            Region 2       22       29       29       80
7            Region 3       23       29       33       85
8            ==============================================
9            Total          70       83       95      248
```

Note that there was no need to adjust the formulas in column F or those in row 9 because they are @SUM formulas based on the columns and rows of the model. Use SERVICES File Save to store the completed worksheet as **1PRORA**.

In the future, when this file is retrieved, it will look to the files named in the link formulas and read the latest values from the linked cells. To see how this works, follow these steps:

1. Having saved 1PRORA, use the SERVICES File Retrieve command to recall 1PROR1.

2. Place the cell pointer in B3 and enter **23**.

3. Press SERVICES, select File followed by Save, and press (ENTER) to resave the file. Answer Yes to the Save confirmation prompt.

4. Use SERVICES File Retrieve to recall 1PRORA. Note that the figure in C5 has changed to reflect the change you made to the supporting file.

Working with Linked Files

Obviously, the preceding is a fairly simple example of what can be done with linked files, but the principles are the same, even with much larger models. Bear the following points in mind as you experiment with file linking.

References to cells outside of the current file are called *dependent file links*. Worksheets like the one just created in this model, that depend upon other files for values, are called *dependent files*. Values that are supplied to another file are called *supporting values*. A worksheet that supplies values to a dependent worksheet is called a *supporting file*.

When you establish a file link with a supporting Symphony file that is stored in the same directory as the dependent file, then the formula will only need to use the name of the supporting worksheet, enclosed in angle brackets, as in <<1PROR1>>. If the file is in a different directory, you must use the full path and worksheet name, as in

```
<<C:\SYM22\SALES\1PROR1>>
```

Symphony will not let you create a link formula if it cannot find the file you want to link to. If you create a link to a file and later move the file, then the link formula will return ERR, indicating that there is an error.

You can establish links to files from other Lotus programs, such as 1-2-3 worksheets with the WK1 extension. However, if the file you are linking to is not a WR1 file, your link reference will need to include the extension. For example, suppose that you want to link with cell B6 in a 1-2-3 file called REGION1.WK1. Entering **+<<REGION1>>B6** will not work, since Symphony will be looking for a file called REGION1.WR1. You must enter **+<<REGION1.WK1>>B6**.

You must take care with the file names you use for supporting files. For example, if you save a dependent worksheet with a link to SALES.WR1 and then edit and save the file SALES.WR1 as SALES1.WR1, Symphony will not know that you have changed the reference and will continue to read the supporting data from SALES.WR1 and not SALES1.WR1.

When you open a dependent file, Symphony reads all of the link formulas in the file and recalculates them, reading the appropriate values from files on disk. If you think that the data in a supporting file might have been changed (perhaps by another user) since you opened the dependent file, you can tell Symphony to update the links to other files. To do this you issue the SERVICES File Admin command while the dependent file is the current file. From the File Admin menu, you select Link-Refresh. Symphony will look to all the supporting worksheet references and read the needed data from them. This can take several seconds.

The SERVICES File Admin Link-Refresh command should be used before printing reports from a dependent file and before basing critical decisions on the file. Another possible problem arises when a supporting file is not found. When you load a dependent file or issue the Link-Refresh command, Symphony looks for the supporting files. If a file is not found, perhaps because it has been moved to a different directory, Symphony returns the ERR message in cells referencing the missing file. You can either find the missing file or alter the link formula to refer to a correct and available file.

You cannot treat the references to cells in other worksheets as part of larger formulas. For example, if you want to use cells in another worksheet, you either have to refer to a cell in the other worksheet that contains a sum formula, which is what you did in the example, or use several link references to pull the numbers to be summed into the dependent worksheet.

File Links with the Viewer

The Viewer add-in can be used to create file links. This method circumvents a problem you may have encountered in the previous example: verifying the address of the cell to which you wanted to link. This is difficult to do if you have no diagram of the supporting file and are not familiar with its layout. To see how the Viewer add-in assists you in creating file links, you can follow these steps:

1. First make sure that the Viewer add-in is attached. Press SERVICES and select Application, followed by Attach. Select VIEWER.APP. The application will be attached (if it is already attached, Symphony will tell you to press (ESC) to return to SHEET mode).

2. Now you will remove the links to 1PROR3 on line 7 of the consolidation worksheet so that you can create them with the Viewer. With the 1PRORA file loaded, move the cell pointer to C7 and press MENU. Select Erase and press (RIGHT ARROW) twice to create an erase range of C7..E7.

3. Leave the cell pointer in C7. To create a link with the Viewer, you first place the cell pointer in the cell of the dependent worksheet that is to receive the link.

4. From the SERVICES File menu, you now select View. Choose the Link option and scroll the list of files that is displayed until the supporting worksheet you want to link to is highlighted—in this case, 1PROR3.WR1.

5. Following the instruction at the top of the screen, press (RIGHT ARROW) to move the highlighting into the righthand window. As you can see from Figure 8-18, the file you selected is still marked in the file list.

6. Move the highlighting, which now acts like a cell pointer, to the cell you want to link with—in this case, B6. Note that the top left corner of the righthand window tells you the address of the current cell and its contents. Press (ENTER) to confirm the link.

7. You are immediately returned to SHEET mode with the link formula in place. Notice that Symphony records the full path of the file you are linking to when you create the link with the View Link command.

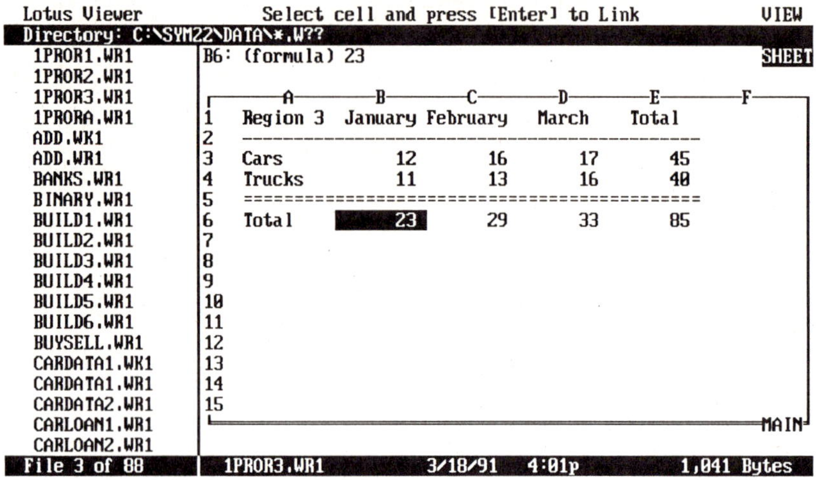

FIGURE 8-18 Using the View Link command

You can use the Copy command to copy the link formula from C7 to D7 and E7. The View Link command saves any guesswork for correct file names and cell addresses, since you can clearly view the file you are linking to.

FILE COMBINING

When you issue the SERVICES File Retrieve command, the file you specify completely replaces the current file. This is the command to use when you first start a Symphony session and go to work on a file, or when you have been working on one file and want to access another. However, there may be times when you want to read data from one worksheet without overwriting the data you are working on. This is the case if you want to create one large worksheet out of several smaller ones. For this you use the SERVICES File Combine command.

Mastery of the File Combine command, together with its partner File Xtract, is less of a necessity in Symphony 2.2 because you can link two files together to share data. However, there are times when File Combine comes in handy, so a simple example is presented here, using the sample files created in the preceding section.

Using File Combine

To bring the contents of another file into the current worksheet without overwriting the current file, use the File Combine command. As an example, consider the sales manager at Ohmobile who needs to consolidate sales figures from three regions. You have seen that this can be done with file linking, which reads selected values from one worksheet to another. However, if the sales manager wants to analyze all of the figures in one file, she can combine the separate files sent to her by regional managers. The only real limit to this approach is the need for plenty of memory to accommodate the large worksheet on her computer.

In order to use the File Combine command, you need to answer five questions that provide Symphony with the information it needs to execute the command. These will be explained in the following paragraphs, after which a file-combining exercise will be carried out.

COPY, ADD, OR SUBTRACT Do you want the incoming worksheet to be copied over the current worksheet? The alternatives are to have Symphony mathematically relate the incoming values—that is, you can have the new value cells that overlay existing value cells actually added to those values or subtracted from them. This is useful when accumulating year-to-date information.

ENTIRE FILE OR NAMED-AREA Do you want to combine the entire contents of the incoming file? The alternative is to bring in a copy of a part of the other worksheet, a range of cells that you have previously named in the external worksheet.

IGNORE OR READ Do you want Symphony to keep (read) range names that apply to the cells or file you are combining? If you want Symphony to forget range names in the incoming data, choose Ignore.

FORMULAS OR VALUES Do you want Symphony to read the results of formulas in the file that is being combined, or the formulas themselves? If you select Values, the calculated values from the combined file, such as totals, will no longer be active formulas in the current worksheet.

FILE NAME What is the name of the incoming file? This does not have to be in the current disk and directory. Symphony uses a file list like the one for the File Retrieve command to allow you to select the file.

A Combine Example

The simplest method of file combining is to bring in the other file in its entirety. You can see the File Combine command in action with the 1PRORA worksheet created in the previous section. After making sure that file is saved, follow these steps:

1. Move the cell pointer to A11 and enter the label **Report Detail:**.
2. Move the cell pointer to B12.
3. Press SERVICES and select File, then Combine. Choose Copy followed by Entire-File. Choose Ignore and then Formulas.
4. Highlight the file called 1PROR1 from the list provided. You can see the list in Figure 8-19, where the Combine command is

```
Name of file to combine: C:\SYM22\DATA\*.wr?                                    FILES
1PROR1.WR1         1PROR2.WR1        1PROR3.WR1        1PRORA.WR1       ADD.WR1
      A         B         C         D         E         F         G         H
1          Total Sales Of Ohmobile Electric Cars And Trucks
2
3                   January February   March     Total
4          ---------------------------------------------
5          Region 1     35       25        33        93
6          Region 2     22       29        29        80
7          Region 3     23       29        33        85
8          =============================================
9          Total        80       83        95       258
10
11   Report Detail:
12
13
14
15
16
17
18
19
20
                                                                                MAIN
File Combine                                                              Num
```

FIGURE 8-19 Selecting a file to combine

about to be completed. Press (ENTER) to select the file. This completes the command.

The data in the other file is read into the current file, beginning at the cell pointer location. The results can be seen in Figure 8-20, where the cell pointer has been moved to C17 in order to show how the @SUM formula has been translated in accordance with its new location.

To complete this worksheet you could combine the contents of the other two regional files, at B19 and B26, respectively. (There is no need to do this with your sample file.) In Figure 8-21, you can see the other data added; the link formula in C5 was manually replaced by the simple reference +C17. With all of the data in one file, the sales manager could work out totals by category and other useful figures.

```
C17: @SUM(C14..C15)                                                    SHEET

     A        B         C         D         E         F         G         H
1             Total Sales Of Ohmobile Electric Cars And Trucks
2
3                       January February   March     Total
4             ---------------------------------------------
5             Region 1         35        25        33        93
6             Region 2         22        29        29        80
7             Region 3         23        29        33        85
8             =============================================
9             Total            80        83        95       258
10
11   Report Detail:
12            Region 1  January February   March     Total
13            ---------------------------------------------
14            Cars             23        12        17        52
15            Trucks           12        13        16        41
16            =============================================
17            Total            35        25        33        93
18
19
20
                                                                        MAIN
24-Mar-91  07:56 PM                                                 Num
```

FIGURE 8-20 The combined results

```
C5: +C17                                                               SHEET

     A        B         C         D         E         F         G         H
1             Total Sales Of Ohmobile Electric Cars And Trucks
2
3                       January February   March     Total
4             ---------------------------------------------
5             Region 1         35        25        33        93
6             Region 2         22        29        29        80
7             Region 3         23        29        33        85
8             =============================================
9             Total            80        83        95       258
10
11   Report Detail:
12            Region 1  January February   March     Total
13            ---------------------------------------------
14            Cars             23        12        17        52
15            Trucks           12        13        16        41
16            =============================================
17            Total            35        25        33        93
18
19            Region 2  January February   March     Total
20            ---------------------------------------------
                                                                        MAIN
24-Mar-91  09:21 PM                                                 Num
```

FIGURE 8-21 After combining all files

Working with File Combine

In an entire file combine such as the one you have just performed, as many as possible of the occupied cells from A1 through IV8192 of the incoming file are copied into the cells of the current worksheet. The copying starts at the cell highlighted by your cell pointer when the command is issued. This would be cells A1 through IV8192 if you issued the File Combine Entire command from cell A1. The incoming file is controlled just like a range of cells, by its top left corner cell, A1.

Cells of the incoming file that are not occupied by data do not affect entries in the existing worksheet, but you can see that if you are not careful, a worksheet being combined into the current one could disrupt existing data. To avoid losing data when file combining, you should position your cell pointer at some point below the lowest row used in the current worksheet, or to the right of the rightmost column used, *before* you issue the command.

The Named-Area Option

Since there is considerable potential for accidental loss of data from an incorrectly performed file combine when an entire file is brought in, you can opt to bring in just a select group of cells by using the File Combine Named-Area command.

To use the Named-Area option for your file combining, you must first name the range of cells to be selected in the incoming worksheet. You cannot use range coordinates instead of a range name when executing the command. For example, if you refer to Figure 8-14, the cell range B6..D6 could be given the name REG1TOTAL. You will recall that to name a range you place the cell pointer on the first cell in the range, press MENU, select Range Name Create, and then type the range name. When you press (ENTER), you are prompted for the cell location, which you can highlight or type. You then press (ENTER) and the range is named, but you *must* save the worksheet after attaching a name to a range in order for Symphony to remember the range name setting.

If the name REG1TOTAL had been applied in the 1PROR1 file, you could then perform a consolidation using the File combine command and a worksheet like the one in Figure 8-17. Ignoring the link formula in that figure, you would place the cell pointer in C5, press SERVICES, and select File Combine Copy Named-Area. You would enter **REG1TOTAL** as the range name and then select Ignore, followed by Values. Finally, you would select the 1PROR1 file. Symphony would read into the current file just the values in the named range.

Note: Bear in mind that cell-pointer placement prior to the command is still important when using File Combine Copy with a range. The incoming cells will overwrite the current contents of the cells, and the only way to recover from such an error is to retrieve a copy that you saved prior to the combine operation.

The Add Option

You can save a lot of time and effort in some circumstances by using the File Combine Add command. This adds overlying cells together, as you might do when adding together the total sales reports for several different regions. The Add option only brings in numeric data from the combined file. For example, the sales manager's worksheets seen earlier were for all vehicles, and she might want to list sales for each of the two categories: Cars and Trucks. In Figure 8-22 you can see a worksheet set up to accumulate data from each region in the two categories. With the cell pointer in B3, the File Combine Add Entire-File Ignore Values command is issued. The 1PROR1 file is selected. The numeric values in the 1PROR1 are read into the current worksheet. The

```
B3:                                                                  SHEET
      A        B        C        D        E        F        G        H
1          Total Sales Of Ohmobile Electric Cars And Trucks
2
3                   January February   March    Total
4          ---------------------------------------------
5          Cars                                     0
6          Trucks                                   0
7          =============================================
8          Total           0        0        0      0
9
10
```

FIGURE 8-22 Alternative consolidation worksheet

labels and formulas in the current worksheet are unaffected. The command is repeated using 1PROR2 and 1PROR3, with the results shown in Figure 8-23.

```
B3:                                                                  SHEET
      A        B        C        D        E        F        G        H
1          Total Sales Of Ohmobile Electric Cars And Trucks
2
3                   January February   March    Total
4          ---------------------------------------------
5          Cars           46       39       50     135
6          Trucks         34       44       45     123
7          =============================================
8          Total          80       83       95     258
9
10
11
12
13
14
15
16
17
18
19
20
                                                                  MAIN
24-Mar-91  09:44 PM                                        NUM
```

FIGURE 8-23 Effects of Combine Add

The Subtract Option

The Subtract option in a combine operation is the reverse of the Add option. It is useful if you are tracking goals or quotas; you can have the actual sales figures subtracted from the quota and show the remaining sales needed.

Note In the File Combine Subtract command, as well as the File Combine Add command, it is important to keep track of the combining process to make sure that you do not forget which files' numbers have already been combined.

FILE EXTRACT

When you do not want to save an entire spreadsheet or when you would like parts of a large spreadsheet saved into smaller, separate files, possibly for later combining with another worksheet, you use the File Xtract command.

Note This command is not called "Extract" because it shares a menu with the Erase command, and Symphony needs to have each menu item begin with a different letter. Do not confuse Xtract with Erase—the latter can permanently remove files from your disk.

Using File Xtract

The SERVICES File Xtract command takes a copy of a range of cells and places it in a new file; it does not actually remove cells from the current worksheet. To perform this command, Symphony needs to know whether you want to extract formulas or values. The merits of both options will be discussed in a moment. After you have chosen between the two, Symphony will prompt you for a

```
A1: 'Sales of Ohmobile Vehicles in January                                    SHEET

      A         B          C          D        E        F        G        H
1   Sales of Ohmobile Vehicles in January
2
3    Invoice  Model       Net        Auto     Power    Solar   Stereo   Private
4       1101 Truck    $13,309.54      N        Y        N        Y        N
5       1102 Truck    $11,576.23      N        N        Y        Y        N
6       1103 Truck    $10,186.80      N        Y        Y        N        N
7       1104 Truck    $11,584.95      Y        Y        N        Y        N
8       1105 Truck     $9,422.75      Y        N        Y        N        Y
9       1106 Truck    $11,261.24      N        N        Y        Y        N
10      1107 Car      $12,917.42      N        N        Y        Y        N
11      1108 Truck    $12,711.20      Y        N        Y        N        Y
12      1109 Car       $9,938.54      N        N        Y        N        N
13      1110 Car      $11,005.45      Y        N        N        N        N
14      1111 Car      $11,070.67      N        Y        N        N        N
15      1112 Car       $9,207.90      Y        N        Y        N        Y
16      1113 Truck    $10,500.10      Y        N        Y        Y        Y
17      1114 Truck    $11,694.81      N        N        Y        N        Y
18      1115 Truck    $12,932.23      N        Y        N        N        Y
19      1116 Truck    $13,445.28      N        Y        Y        N        N
20      1117 Truck    $13,162.39      N        Y        N        N        Y
                                                                          MAIN
25-Mar-91  01:50 PM                                                 Num
```

FIGURE 8-24 Sales statistics

file name to use. When you have specified a file name, you will be asked to point out the range of cells to be extracted.

The File Xtract command is much like the Copy command or the Range Values command, except the destination or TO cell range is cell A1 of another file, not another area of the current worksheet. Consider the worksheet of sales statistics shown in Figure 8-24. Suppose that, as sales manager at Ohmobile, you are working with this data and need to send a colleague a list of all sales in which the net was more than $13,000. The File Xtract command can help you do this.

First, you sort the list, based on the Net column. Then you place the cell pointer in A3. The File Xtract command is then issued. Symphony presents the choice between Formulas and Values, as shown in Figure 8-25.

Preserve formulas MENU
Formulas Values

	A	B	C	D	E	F	G	H
1	Sales of Ohmobile Vehicles in January							
2								
3	Invoice	Model	Net	Auto	Power	Solar	Stereo	Private
4	1139	Car	$13,804.97	Y	Y	Y	N	Y
5	1122	Truck	$13,778.56	N	N	N	Y	Y
6	1171	Car	$13,703.41	Y	Y	N	N	Y
7	1135	Car	$13,651.68	N	N	Y	N	N
8	1116	Truck	$13,445.28	N	Y	Y	N	N
9	1101	Truck	$13,309.54	N	Y	N	Y	N
10	1150	Truck	$13,277.85	N	Y	N	N	N
11	1167	Truck	$13,223.32	Y	N	Y	Y	Y
12	1123	Truck	$13,205.64	N	Y	Y	N	Y
13	1118	Truck	$13,204.14	Y	N	N	N	Y
14	1117	Truck	$13,162.39	N	Y	N	N	Y
15	1174	Truck	$13,131.56	Y	Y	N	N	N
16	1124	Truck	$12,975.56	Y	Y	Y	Y	Y
17	1115	Truck	$12,932.23	N	Y	N	N	Y
18	1107	Car	$12,917.42	N	N	Y	Y	N
19	1130	Truck	$12,906.30	Y	Y	N	Y	Y
20	1164	Car	$12,857.11	N	N	Y	N	Y

MAIN

File Xtract Num

FIGURE 8-25 Using File Xtract

Formulas and Values

When you select Xtract from the File menu, you must choose between Formulas and Values. Choosing Formulas means that any cells in the range that you extract that contain formulas will be preserved in the new file you are about to create. Their relative references will be adjusted for the fact that the top left corner of the cell range you extract will become cell A1 in the file you extract to. However, if you extract a range of cells that contains one or more formulas that refer to cells outside the extracted range, Symphony will have a hard time making sense of the formulas in the new file.

Choosing Values is a lot like using the Range Values command to convert cells to their values. The File Xtract Values command stores the cells as their current values. You will want to use this option when you plan to combine the values you are extracting into another file using the Add or Subtract option. You will also need to use it when the formulas in the range being extracted refer to cells outside the range. The Values option is appropriate in this case, since none of the numbers are formulas.

Note that when you use the Values option, the full value of the cells is saved—not just the displayed value—and unseen decimal places are stored. Also note that the worksheet should be recalculated prior to a file extract to ensure that correct values are saved. Once saved, the values in the new file are no longer interactive with the original worksheet and no longer reflect changes to the file from which they were extracted.

Completing the Extract

In this case, all of the cells are values, so you would choose Values. Symphony then presents a list of worksheet files and asks you to enter an extract file name. You can either enter a new name to create a fresh file or reuse an existing name, bearing in mind that the contents of the file will be overwritten.

Having entered the file name, you are prompted for the cell coordinates in the current file—in this case, A3..H15. You can highlight the desired range of cells in the usual way. When you press (ENTER) to confirm the cell coordinates, the new file is created and you are returned to SHEET mode. (If you selected a file name that already exists, Symphony will ask you to confirm overwriting the file.) You may want to retrieve the file to check what it looks like. You can see the results of this example in Figure 8-26.

Note that cell formatting, label alignment, and column widths are copied from the parent file. However, a file extract is not dynamic: The contents of the new file are not permanently linked in any way to the parent file. The sales manager can now dress this file up with some more labels and pass it on.

A1: ^Invoice SHEET

	A	B	C	D	E	F	G	H
1	Invoice	Model	Net	Auto	Power	Solar	Stereo	Private
2	1139	Car	$13,804.97	Y	Y	Y	N	Y
3	1122	Truck	$13,778.56	N	N	N	Y	Y
4	1171	Car	$13,703.41	Y	Y	N	N	Y
5	1135	Car	$13,651.68	N	N	Y	N	N
6	1116	Truck	$13,445.28	N	Y	Y	N	N
7	1101	Truck	$13,309.54	N	Y	N	Y	N
8	1150	Truck	$13,277.85	N	Y	N	N	N
9	1167	Truck	$13,223.32	Y	N	Y	Y	Y
10	1123	Truck	$13,205.64	N	Y	Y	N	Y
11	1118	Truck	$13,204.14	Y	N	N	N	Y
12	1117	Truck	$13,162.39	N	Y	N	N	Y
13	1174	Truck	$13,131.56	Y	Y	N	N	N
14								
15								
16								
17								
18								
19								
20								

MAIN

25-Mar-91 01:59 PM Num

FIGURE 8-26 The extracted file

DEFAULT SETTINGS

Several references have been made in this and previous chapters to the default settings in Symphony. For example, the default Page-Length setting is 66 lines, the default name for windows is MAIN, and the default symbol in the currency format is $. These and other settings can be changed by using the SERVICES Configuration menu. The commands on this menu are reviewed here.

The Default Areas

When you use the SERVICES Configuration menu command, you are shown a menu like the one in Figure 8-27. Some of these commands have been examined earlier. For example, you saw that the File command allows you to change the default directory for worksheet files. The Printer command reveals ten different aspects of printer control that can be set as defaults; these were dealt with

```
Directory to become current at start of session                              MENU
File  Printer  Communications  Document  Window  Help  Auto  Other  Update  Quit

File: C:\SYM22\DATA                Document                 Window
Printer                              Tab interval:    5        Type: SHEET
  Type:        Parallel 1            Justification:   1        Name:
  Auto-LF:     No                    Spacing:         1          MAIN
  Wait:        No                    Left margin:     1      Help: Removable
  Margins                            Right margin:           Auto-Worksheet:
    Left:  4       Top:      2       Blanks visible:  No
    Right: 76      Bottom:   2       CRs visible:     Yes    Clock on Screen:
  Page-Length: 66                    Auto-Justify:    Yes      Standard
  Init-String:                       Hard-Tabs:       Yes    File-Translation:
  Name: HP 2686 LaserJet Series                            IBM PC or Compatible
Communications name:                                           AEM: Yes
                                                   Configuration Settings
```

FIGURE 8-27 The default configuration settings

in Chapter 3. The Communications command, covered in the last chapter, allows you to name a CCF file to be loaded automatically. The Document command covers default settings for the DOC environment, discussed in Chapter 4.

Configuration Update

The Update command is treated out of turn because it is so important. This is the command used to write the current settings to the special configuration file that Symphony uses (normally, SYMPHONY.CNF). After you alter defaults, you *must* select Update to make sure that the defaults are in effect the next time you load Symphony.

Window Defaults

The Window command on the Configuration menu allows you to set a default window type and name. So far, you have seen that when you load Symphony or issue the File New command, you get a fresh worksheet with the name MAIN of type SHEET. If you mainly use Symphony for word processing, you might want to change the default type to DOC. You might want a different name from MAIN, such as LETTER. Use the Configuration Window command for this.

The Type option presents a list of the five environments to choose from. The Name option prompts you to enter a name. This will be stored and displayed in capitals only.

Getting Help

Whenever you press (F1) while using Symphony, you get a screen of helpful hints about the action you are currently performing. You can navigate this excellent system of notes by using the arrow keys to move the highlighting to different topics and then pressing (ENTER). The screens remind you of the details of the different commands when you are working with Symphony. They are stored on disk in a file called SYMPHONY.HLP.

Symphony offers two forms of access to help. Using the Configuration Help command, you can choose Instant if you have a hard disk. This is the fastest way of getting a response to (F1). The other method is the Removable option, which is used if you have a floppy-disk system and sometimes need to take out the disk that contains the help file. Choosing Removable ensures that Symphony prompts you to insert the Help disk when it is needed.

The Auto Option

Unfortunately, the Configuration Auto option does not get Symphony to automatically create your files for you. What you *can* do with this command is specify a file that is loaded every time that Symphony is loaded. This is very helpful if most of your work with Symphony revolves around one particular file, or if you always want a worksheet of appointments to be loaded when you start

Symphony. You can combine this feature with an auto-executing macro, described in the next chapter, to set in motion a whole series of commands just by loading Symphony.

To activate the Auto feature you simply select Auto, enter the name of the worksheet you want Symphony to load, and press (ENTER). Be sure to use the Update command before exiting Symphony to try this command. The next time you load Symphony, the file you specified will be loaded in place of a blank work area.

The Other Defaults

The Other command reveals a five-item menu of additional default items:

Clock File-Translation International Application Memory

The Application item was dealt with earlier in the section on permanent attachments. The Memory option is used to alter the way that Symphony uses expanded memory on your system; it is covered in Appendix A. The File-Translation option is used to control how Symphony deals with foreign characters when reading text files and is also discussed in Appendix A.

The Clock option determines the format of the on-screen clock and determines whether or not it is displayed. The normal setting is Standard, meaning that Symphony will display the clock in this format:

DD-MMM-YY HH:MM AM/PM

which appears as

01-Apr-91 01:33 PM

As an alternative, you can use the International setting, which presents the date and time in the currently defined D4 and T4 formats, usually

MM/DD/YY HH:MM

which appears as

04/01/91 13:33 PM

If you find the clock annoying, you can turn it off by selecting None.

International Defaults

The International option on the Configuration Other menu covers several areas of Symphony's operation that can be fine- tuned for use in countries other than the U.S. The Other International menu contains the Punctuation, Currency, Date, Time, and Negative options. These give users the ability to make Symphony more closely follow local conventions in presenting date and time information, punctuating and presenting numbers, and translating text files. For example, you can set a worksheet with currency stated in English pounds and dates in European fashion, as in the following, where the date June 15, 1991, is shown:

```
B1: (D4) @DATE(91,6,15)                                          SHEET

   ----A-----------B-----------C--------D--------E--------F--------G---
1   Show Date:       15.06.91
2       Venue: Wembley Stadium
3        City: London
4   Gross Rev:    £3,432,547.00
5    Expenses:       £45,345.00
6     Net Rev:    £3,387,202.00
```

To get a pound sign for currency, select Currency from the International menu and then hold down (ALT) and type **156** from the numeric keypad. Release the (ALT) key, and the pound sign will appear. The number 156 is the ASCII code for the pound sign. ASCII codes for other symbols are shown in Appendix C. When you have typed a symbol, press (ENTER), and Symphony will ask you to choose the symbol placement, either Prefix or Suffix (use Prefix for pounds and dollars):

```
Currency sign precedes value                                          MENU
Prefix  Suffix
Punctuation:   A                               Date format D4:  A (MM/DD/YY)
      Point Dot
   Argument Comma                              Time format T3:  A (HH:MM:SS)
  Thousands Comma

Currency sign: £               (Prefix)        Negative:        Parentheses
                                                      International Settings
```

When you have selected the position of the symbol, all currency-formatted values in the current worksheet are altered to show the chosen symbol. Furthermore, all worksheets created or retrieved hereafter will have their currency-formatted values shown with the chosen sign. You cannot use this feature to mix currency symbols within a single worksheet.

You can use currency symbols that are suffixes like the French franc symbol shown here, created with (ALT) and 159:

```
B1: (D4) @DATE(91;6;15)                                               SHEET
    A                B            C         D         E         F         G
1     Show Date:      15.06.91
2         Venue:  Palais De Rock
3          City:  Paris
4     Gross Rev:     3.432.547,00ƒ
5      Expenses:        45.345,00ƒ
6       Net Rev:     3.387.202,00ƒ
```

The numeric punctuation used here was effected by issuing the International Punctuation command and selecting style B from the menu of possibilities shown here:

```
Decimal: DOT    Argument separator: COMMA         000 separator: COMMA    MENU
A (.,,)  B (,..)  C (.;,)  D (,;.)  E (., )  F (,. )  G (.; )  H (,; )
Punctuation:   A                               Date format D4:  A (MM/DD/YY)
      Point Dot
   Argument Comma                              Time format T3:  A (HH:MM:SS)
  Thousands Comma

Currency sign: $               (Prefix)        Negative:        Parentheses
                                                      International Settings
```

This requires that arguments in function statements and multiple range settings be separated by periods rather than commas.

The Date options, shown here, affect the D4 and D5 formats in both Default and Range Format commands:

```
Format D4 will be MM/DD/YY      Format D5 will be MM/DD                    MENU
A (MM/DD/YY)  B (DD/MM/YY)  C (DD.MM.YY)  D (YY-MM-DD)

Punctuation:   A                            Date format D4:  A (MM/DD/YY)
       Point Dot
    Argument Comma                          Time format T3:  A (HH:MM:SS)
   Thousands Comma

Currency sign: £                (Prefix)    Negative:        Parentheses
                                                 International Settings
```

They also affect the appearance of the calendar when the International option is chosen from the Clock menu. The Time options are shown here:

```
Format T3 will be HH:MM:SS      Format T4 will be HH:MM                    MENU
A (HH:MM:SS)  B (HH.MM.SS)  C (HH,MM,SS)  D (HHhMMmSSs)

Punctuation:   A                            Date format D4:  C (DD.MM.YY)
       Point Dot
    Argument Comma                          Time format T3:  A (HH:MM:SS)
   Thousands Comma

Currency sign: £                (Prefix)    Negative:        Parentheses
                                                 International Settings
```

These affect the T3 and T4 formats, as well as the appearance of the clock when the International option is chosen from the Clock menu. Table 8-5 summarizes the Punctuation, Currency, Date, and Time options.

The International Negative option allows you to select either Parentheses or Minus to alter the display of values less than zero in the Punctuated and Currency formats. The Parentheses option places negative values in parentheses. The Minus option uses a leading minus sign.

FILE TRANSLATION

In the highly computerized world of today's office, information is often the lifeblood of the company. Information must flow for the

Punctuation

Options A - H determine the combination of symbols for the decimal point, argument separator in @functions and command language statements, and separator between thousands:

	A	B	C	D	E	F	G	H
Decimal point	.	,	.	,	.	,	.	,
Argument separator	,	.	;	;	,	.	;	;
Thousands separator	,	.	,	.				

Date

Options A-D establish full (D4) and partial (D5) international date formats, used in setting range or global formats. They are listed here representing April 1, 1991 as an example:

	Full (D4)		Partial (D5)	
A:	MM/DD/YY	04/01/91	MM/DD	04/01
B:	DD/MM/YY	01/04/91	DD/MM	01/04
C:	DD.MM.YY	01.04.91	DD.MM	01.04
D:	YY-MM-DD	91-04-01	MM-DD	04-01

Time

Options A-D establish full (T3) and partial (T4) time formats, used in setting range or global formats. They are listed here representing one-forty-five in the afternoon as an example:

	Full (T3)		Partial (T4)	
A:	HH:MM:SS	13:45:00	HH:MM	13:45
B:	HH.MM.SS	13.45.00	HH.MM	13.45
C:	HH,MM,SS	13,45,00	HH,MM	13,45
D:	HHhMMmSSs	13h45m00s	HHhMMm	13h45m

TABLE 8-5 International Punctuation, Date, and Time Options

company to function effectively and compete successfully. A lot of that information is "on the computer." However, the kind of computer that the information is on can vary from a mainframe to a minicomputer to a variety of microcomputers. This means that connections between computers are vital links in the chain. At the microcomputer level, the information may be on the computer but stored through a variety of different programs.

Although you may think that Symphony is the best program and the one that you and your company should use for all of its information processing needs, only sole proprietorships have the benefit of being the sole judge of what's best for the company. But even sole proprietors have to interact with the rest of the business community. If you are receiving computer information from others that is not in the form of Symphony worksheets, you will need to be aware of how Symphony handles "foreign" information.

The more you use Symphony, the more likely you are to encounter situations in which you want to use Symphony to access data stored in files that were not created by Symphony. You might have worksheets that were created by an earlier release of Symphony, or by a completely different program such as dBASE or Excel. There are several techniques you can use to bring data into Symphony, from SERVICES File Retrieve to the special Translate program.

Files from Other Lotus Products

Files from previous releases of Symphony and from some releases of 1-2-3 are read directly by Symphony with no special translation process. This includes files with the extensions WKS, WK1, WRK, and WR1. Since a whole host of other programs can save files into one of these formats (usually into WK1), this gives Symphony a great range of data files that it can read with no particular effort besides correctly naming the file.

When you want to load a WK1 file, you use the SERVICES File Retrieve command and type ***.WK1** to replace the usual file specification of *.wr1. When you press (ENTER), Symphony will list all WK1 files. Alternatively, you can use ***.W??** as the file specification to see both Symphony and 1-2-3 files. When you have worked on a WK1 file in Symphony and then go to save the file, Symphony warns you that the file is being saved in the WR1 format, as shown here:

```
Save file name: C:\SYM22\DATA\CARDATA1.WR1                                        EDIT
File will be saved as .WR1
┌───────A──────────B─────────────C───────────────────────D─────────────────────┐
1  Last        First     Company               Address
2  Carlson     Roberta   UnoQuest United       163 West 125th Street
3  Yochmowitz  Michael   EvaNorth Ltd.         Box 1000
```

There is no two-way street between Symphony files and 1-2-3 files. You cannot read a WK1 file into Symphony and then save it as a WK1 file with SERVICES File Save. You cannot use SERVICES File Save to create a 1-2-3 file. You must use the Translate program to send data back to 1-2-3 from Symphony.

The Translate Program

There may be times when you need to pass the data stored in a WR1 file along to a colleague or client who does not have access to Symphony. This means you need to translate your WR1 file to another format. To handle the translation of files both within and beyond the Lotus formats, Lotus provides Symphony with a program called Translate.

The Translate program can be loaded from the Lotus Access menu described earlier in the chapter. Simply select the File-Translate option to start the Translate program, or load it from the DOS prompt by typing **TRANS** and pressing ENTER. Figure 8-28 shows the initial Translate program screen that appears. To convert files, you first select the type of translation you want by highlighting the desired formats in the FROM box. If you highlight Symphony 2.2 in the FROM list, you get a range of options in the TO list, as shown in Figure 8-29.

When you have highlighted your choice in the TO list, you press (ENTER) to move to the next screen. This may be a help screen of information about the translation process you have selected. You may be told to press (ESC) to continue the translation or (ENTER) to read more warnings about the process.

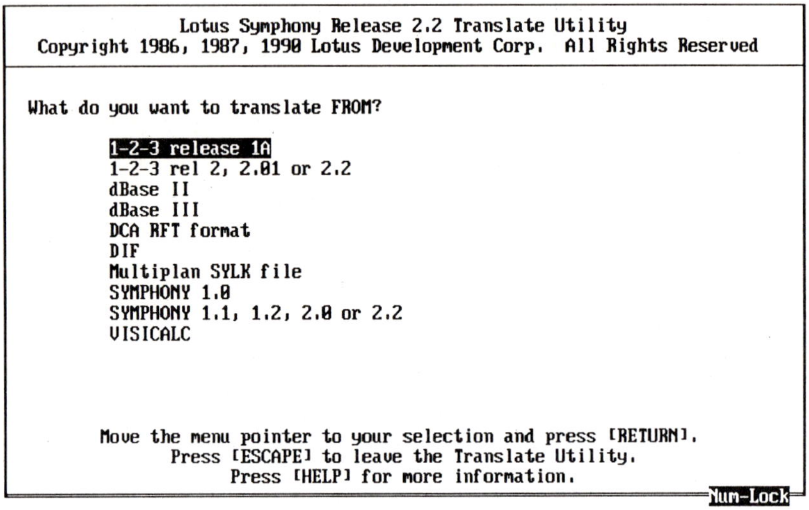

FIGURE 8-28 Translate program

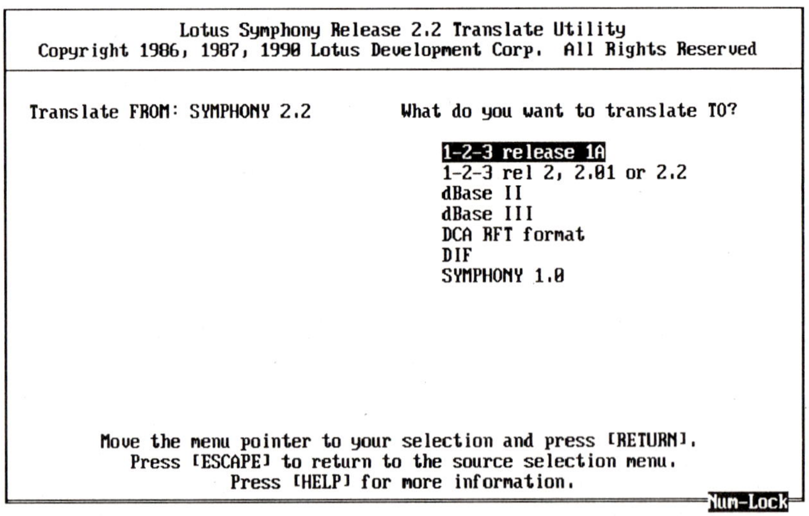

FIGURE 8-29 The TO options

When you press (ESC) to get to the file selection screen, you will see a list of files meeting the criteria you imposed when you selected the FROM format. These are files in the *program* directory, so you may need to press (ESC) to edit the directory prompt in order to specify the correct directory.

You need to highlight the source file you want to translate and press (ENTER). When you do this, Translate assumes that you will want to use the same file name for the target file as for the source file, with just the file extension changed. For example, the file CUSTOMER.WR1 would be translated to CUSTOMER.DBF. However, you are given a chance to alter the file name by using the edit keys. After making any adjustments to the file name, you press (ENTER) to continue. Translate gives you one more chance to change your mind, presenting a Yes/No/Quit box. In some cases you are also asked to decide between translating the entire worksheet or just a named range.

Answering the Yes/No/Quit question will complete the process. After a few moments, Symphony will present the message "Translation Successful" or an error message explaining why the translation was not successful. At the "Translation Successful" message, you press (ENTER) to continue and are returned to the file list in case you want to perform further translations from the same group of files.

Unlisted Programs

You or your associates may be working with a program that has not been mentioned yet. Some popular programs are not specifically listed in Translate's file formats, such as the databases R:base and Paradox, or the spreadsheets VP Planner and SuperCalc 5. Can these programs share data with Symphony? Yes, if they use one of the listed formats as an intermediate format. For example, the spreadsheet Quattro Pro can save files in both WK1 and DBF format, as well as its own format. To transfer data from Quattro Pro to Symphony, save the file as WK1 in Quattro Pro and then retrieve it into Symphony. To pass data back to Quattro Pro, save the worksheet as WK1, which can then be read by Symphony.

Many other programs have this multiple file-format capability, thus allowing fairly easy exchange of data. However, the limitations of file translation, discussed in a moment, also apply in these other "save as" situations.

Symphony and 1-2-3 Files

When translating from Symphony to 1-2-3, the Translate program discards the Symphony file's Window settings. Documents created in Symphony's DOC environment appear in 1-2-3 as they do in Symphony's SHEET environment. Owing to the smaller size of Release 1A worksheets, rows below 2048 are lost and formulas that refer to cells outside the range A1..IV2048 will cause unpredictable answers when translating to WKS format. You will not be able to translate password-protected Symphony files to 1-2-3 format, and you cannot use Symphony command-language macros in 1-2-3 Release 1A.

Symphony and dBASE Files

When translating from dBase to Symphony, the Translate program does not include deleted records from the dBASE source file in the Symphony destination file. Database entries that would produce labels longer than 240 characters are truncated. Records after record number 8191 will not be translated. Translate does not include memos from a dBASE text file (DBT) in the Symphony destination file.

When translating from Symphony to dBASE, you can translate an entire file only if it consists of nothing more than a database; otherwise, you must name the database range within the worksheet. The file or range you want Symphony to translate must meet the following criteria:

- The first row of the file or range must consist of field names. These field names must be ten characters or less; otherwise, they will be truncated. The field names should be label cells beginning with a letter and containing no spaces (use ADDRESS_1 instead of ADDRESS 1 or 1 ADDRESS).

- The second row must be the first data record. Each cell in this row must contain data or at least be formatted.

- Columns must be wide enough to display the data, or the data will be truncated.

- The Scientific format should not be used, since dBASE has no equivalent format (the General format is acceptable, as are Punctuated, Fixed, and Currency).

The database records exported to dBASE may consist of up to 128 fields. Each field will be assigned a field type such as label or number. Translate matches the field types in each dBASE record with the field types in the first data record of the worksheet/range. The format found in each field of the first data record is used for the entire database, regardless of the contents of subsequent records. Numbers used in the worksheet should be valid dBASE III numbers. Numeric columns should be no wider than 19 characters, but wide enough to allow for the decimal point and two digits that dBASE adds to whole numbers.

Before translating the Symphony file, Translate displays a menu with two options: Worksheet and Range. Select Worksheet to translate the entire Symphony file. Choose Range to translate a named range of the Symphony file. Ranges cannot be referred to by cell coordinates.

All cells in the active worksheet or range will be translated, including blank cells. Special characters entered in the DOC window, such as the hard carriage return, the hard tab, and the indent character, will be deleted when the dBASE file is created. If you are using tab stops in a Symphony document, choose No on the Configuration Document Hard-Tabs menu to save tabs as spaces. Resave the file before translating the file to dBASE. An alternative method of transferring Symphony data to a dBASE file is to use the @BASE add-in, discussed in Chapter 10.

Symphony and the DCA RFT

The term *DCA RFT* stands for "Document Content Architecture Revised Text Format," which was developed by IBM. The word processing programs DisplayWrite 3 and DisplayWrite 4 use this format, and many other word processors can create files in DCA RFT, called RFT for short. Translate specifically supports the RFT format as implemented in IBM DisplayWrite 3/4 and Lotus Manuscript 1.0/1.1 . Support for RFT formats in other products will depend on how they implement RFT.

When translating from the RFT format to Symphony, the Translate program creates Symphony DOC window settings based on the RFT values. When translating data to RFT from Symphony, the Translate program uses the Symphony Document window settings as a basis for the RFT document. The formatting information is taken from the printed format of the Symphony document. If no document settings are present, Translate uses the default print settings.

When you are converting to RFT, the Translate program presents a three-part menu that asks you to choose between the default page format (8 1/2 x 11), or alternate formats. If you select Alternate, you can choose from six different paper sizes. You can select Update to make any selected format the default for future translations. Symphony uses WR1DCA.CNF, the configuration file, to maintain information about the different page formats, and this file must reside in the current directory for the translation to be successful.

Symphony and DIF

When translating to Symphony from the DIF format, the Translate program displays a menu with the options Columnwise and Rowwise. Like 123, Symphony creates columnwise DIF files. To preserve the original format, select Columnwise. To transpose rows and columns, select Rowwise.

When translating from Symphony to the DIF format, the Translate program creates columnwise DIF files. Translate will only accept Symphony worksheet files created with the File Save command. If you wish to translate a file created with the File Xtract command, you must first retrieve the file and save it with File Save.

Special characters entered in a DOC window in Symphony, such as the hard carriage return, the hard tab, and the indent character, will be deleted when the DIF file is created. If you have used hard tabs in a DOC window, specify saving hard tabs as spaces on the Configuration settings sheet and then resave the file.

Symphony and the SYLK Format

When translating to Symphony from the SYLK format, there are several limitations. The term *SYLK* stands for "Symbolic Link" format, used by Microsoft in the Multiplan spreadsheet. Symphony only recognizes rectangular groups of cells as ranges, whereas Multiplan permits range names for irregularly shaped groups of cells (unions). These will be ignored in the Symphony file. Range names with more than 15 characters will be truncated. If this creates a duplicate range name, only the first occurrence is translated; others are ignored. Window settings in the Multiplan worksheet will be ignored.

Both Symphony and Multiplan support linked worksheets, but only the current value of cells in the Multiplan file can be translated. If the linked worksheet has been modified since the Multiplan file was saved, values may be out of date.

Translate replaces characters above ASCII code 127 with LICS (Lotus International Character Set) characters. Characters that are not available in LICS are replaced by the "unknown character" symbol (LICS code 153). Formulas containing the following Multiplan functions are converted to labels:

SIGN
DELTA
CURRENCY
ITERCNT
MIRR

The two functions COLUMN and ROW are converted to @CELL("*col*", *location*) and @CELL("*row*", *location*) in Symphony. The Multiplan LOOKUP function translates to @VLOOKUP or @HLOOKUP, depending on the dimensions of the range argument in the Multiplan worksheet.

Note that the result of the COUNT function may differ between Multiplan and Symphony. In Multiplan, cells are only counted if they contain number values. In Symphony, all cells that are not empty are counted.

The five Multiplan financial functions, PV, FV, NPER, PMT, and RATE, may or may not have Symphony equivalents, depending on the arguments used. If there is no Symphony equivalent, the formula will be converted to a label in the target worksheet. After translation, the result of a formula that uses any of these financial functions may have the reverse sign, so that 150 may appear as (150). This is because Multiplan calculates items like payments as negative cash flows.

Since Multiplan takes up less memory than Symphony, you may not be able to load very large worksheets you have translated. If this is the case, Symphony will present a "Memory Full" message.

You will have to go back to Multiplan, where you can divide the worksheet into smaller files and then translate again.

SUMMARY

You have seen that Symphony gives you a considerable range of tools to deal with files. The full-screen file list makes it easy to manage larger groups of files. The DOS application allows you access to DOS to carry out directory management tasks. The Viewer application lets you look at files so that you can be sure what they contain.

Using file linking, you can create separate files for parts of a project and then consolidate information in another file. When you need to separate a large file into parts or pull parts together, you can use File Xtract and Combine. If you need to work with information from another program, you can use the Translate program to place it in a Symphony-readable format.

Even with Symphony's help, managing files can become a chore, but it is one that you ignore at your peril. The following tips will help you keep track of your files and make the most out of computerizing your data:

- Make sure that your computer's clock and calendar are set correctly. This will allow you to use date stamps when looking for files and tidying up disks.

- Organize your hard disk into directories and segregate files according to project. Never mix program and data files in the same directory.

- Use meaningful file names. Assign parts of the name to different pieces of information, as in ACCFTD14.WR1, where ACC is the three-letter department code (ACCounting); F and T are the initials of the person creating the file; D is a single-letter code for the main environment in the worksheet (D for DOC); and 14 is the two-digit code for the project dealt with in the worksheet.

- Use the DOS wildcards in file lists to look at groups of files. If you use a structured approach to file names like the one in the previous tip, you can use specifications like ACC???14.W??, which will list all worksheets from the accounting department, of any type, pertaining to project 14.

- Use the Viewer to check file contents before retrieving.

- Keep an annotated list of files on paper, showing the contents of files. You can easily create the list in a Symphony worksheet with the File Table command.

- Regularly back up your entire hard disk with the DOS BACKUP command or a commercial backup program like Backit from Gazelle Systems. Perform incremental backups of data files even more regularly.

- If you have a large hard disk, consider investing in a tape backup unit or a disk cartridge system like the Bernoulli Box from Iomega.

9

SYMPHONY MACROS

As you become familiar with Symphony and apply it to more and more tasks, you will want to take advantage of macros to reduce repetitive typing. In this chapter you will learn how to record, edit, use, and organize macros. You may be somewhat in awe of macros, since they have traditionally been in the realm of power users and spreadsheet aficionados. Fortunately, with Symphony's Learn command it is easy to create and use macros.

Macros are not more complex than other Symphony tasks, and they do not require that you be highly proficient with everything else in the book to this point. If you plan on using more than a few macros, you should have a good grasp on naming ranges, described in Chapter 3. However, the most important requirement for using macros is that you are already using Symphony for a task that you want to simplify or speed up.

BASIC MACROS

When you find yourself repeating the same keystrokes over and over, you need the power of macros. Originally developed for word processing programs as a way to record and play back frequently used phrases, *macros* store multiple keystrokes under a single key or name. Symphony allows you to use macros in all of the five environments, although macros themselves are always stored and edited in the SHEET environment.

The Learn Feature

The macro recording feature in Symphony, called Learn, enables you to record and play back any series of keystrokes, including labels, numbers, formulas, and menu choices. For example, you can record a macro for entering the current date in your worksheet. In addition to simply entering the @NOW function in a cell, the macro can also select the Format Date command from the menu. The macro can even convert the @NOW function into its result.

If you have to format a lot of separate cells in the SHEET environment using the % format, you can create a macro to perform that action. A macro can complete the whole command including selection of decimal places, without your having to go through the menus every time. If you are using the DOC environment and need to enter the same phrase many times, you can create a macro that will type the phrase for you.

Recording Keystrokes

As you work with Symphony, you can have the program "learn" what you are doing—that is, it can record your keystrokes in a designated area of the worksheet. After you have told Symphony the learn range, you turn on Learn mode at any time—for example, before you begin a frequently used series of commands. While in Learn mode, Symphony keeps a record of your keystrokes in the learn range. When you have completed an action that you want recorded, you turn off Learn mode.

Using the following steps, you can test the Learn command by creating a macro that enters the current date into a worksheet cell:

1. Before recording a macro, you must tell Symphony which cells to record the macro in. In a new worksheet, with the cell pointer in A1, press SERVICES and select Settings, followed by Learn. You will see the menu shown in Figure 9-1.

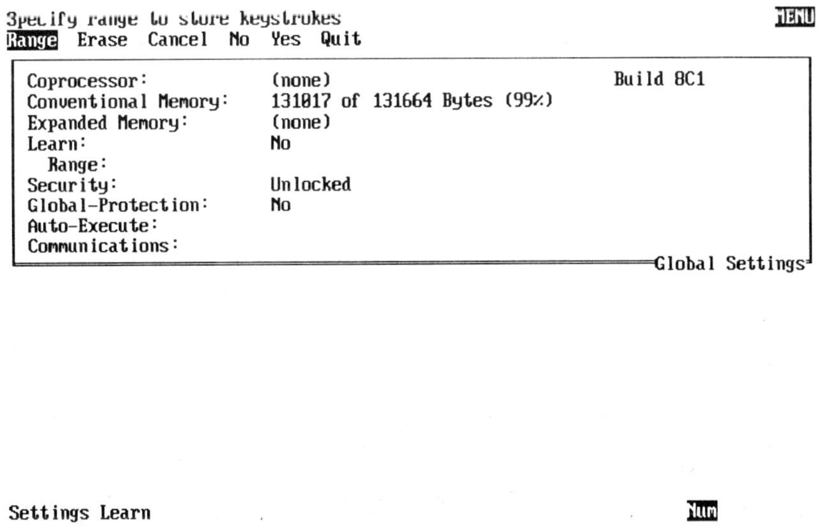

FIGURE 9-1 Learn menu

2. From the Learn menu, select Range. Press (PGDN) to move the cell pointer to A21. Press (TAB) to anchor A21 as the beginning point of the range, and then press (PGDN) twice more, highlighting A21..A61 as the learn range. Press (ENTER) to complete the range selection.

3. Select Quit from the Learn menu and Quit from the Settings menu. You are now back in SHEET mode.

4. To begin macro recording, press LEARN ((ALT-F5)). Notice the "Learn message" on the bottom status line. This reminds you that you are in Learn mode.

5. At cell A1, type **Today is:** and press (RIGHT ARROW) to enter the label and move the cell pointer to B1.

6. At cell B1, type **@NOW** and press (ENTER). The result should be a number greater than 33,000. This is the date serial number for the current date according to DOS (33,000 was the 7th of May, 1990).

7. With the cell pointer still at B1, press MENU and type **F** for Format followed by **D** for Date. Type **4** to select date format 4 (Full International). Press (ENTER) to format B1. The results will look like this:

```
B1: (D4) @NOW                                                    SHEET
┌───────A─────────B─────────C─────────D─────────E─────────F─────────G─────────H──────┐
1   Today is:03/25/91
2
```

8. Press LEARN ((ALT-F5)). This turns off Learn mode. The macro has been recorded.

```
A21: 'Today is:{RIGHT}                                                    SHEET

  ┌───────A───────B───────C───────D───────E───────F───────G───────H───────┐
21  Today is:{RIGHT}
22  @NOW~
23  /FD4~
24
25
```

FIGURE 9-2 Macro recorded in the learn range

9. To see what the recording looks like, press (HOME) followed by (PGDN). As you can see from Figure 9-2, the first line of the macro is in the first cell of the learn range, A21.

Note: If you press the (F10) key for MENU instead of typing /, you will find "{MENU}" instead of "/" in your recording.

Having recorded a macro, you can see that it is a set of keystrokes or instructions stored as a series of labels in a column. The numbers and letters you type are stored as numbers and letters, but within labels. For example, in Figure 9-2 you can see that the label "Today is:" was stored literally. Keys like (ENTER), (RIGHT ARROW), and (F5) are stored as special symbols or words within braces. For example, (RIGHT ARROW) is stored as {RIGHT}, and the (ENTER) key is represented by the tilde (~). Commands are usually stored by the characters used to select them; for example, /FD4 records the selection of Format Date 4 from the menu. Note that there are no spaces between the different commands in the macro.

If you use the arrow-key method to select commands, Symphony will record the arrow keys. The effect will be the same, but the recording will be longer and more difficult to decipher. If you use lowercase letters to select commands, Symphony will record them as lowercase letters. This does not affect the execution of the macro.

Using a Macro Recording

The labels that represent recorded keystrokes are called *macro code*. Now that you have macro code in your worksheet, you can execute or "run" it. However, before you can use the macro you have recorded, you must give it a name. Macros are named with the Range Name Create command (see Chapter 3 for more on this command). The range name is given to the first cell of the macro (in this case, A21). To name the macro, follow these steps:

1. Press MENU and select Range Name Create.
2. Type **\T** and press (ENTER).
3. When prompted to specify the range, type **A21** or move the cell pointer to A21 and then press (ENTER). You are returned to SHEET mode.

To execute the macro, you first move the cell pointer to the area in which you want to enter the date—say, A2—and then hold down (ALT) and type the letter "T" (otherwise known as pressing (ALT-T)). Symphony reads and executes the instructions in A21, and then looks to the cell below, A22, and executes the instructions there. Symphony continues reading and executing instructions until it reaches an empty cell. Using the (ALT) key plus a single letter is just one method of executing macros.

Note that you must use the SERVICES File Save command to save the worksheet into which you have placed the macro in order for the macro and its name to be properly stored. The macro is then available whenever the file in which it is stored is loaded. For information about sharing macros between worksheets, see the section on macro libraries later in this chapter. At this point, press

SERVICES, select File, select Save, and use the name **MACRO1** to store the sample worksheet.

Macro Naming

The name you give to your macro can be any valid range name, but there are several conventions for macro names. The convention you follow depends on how you want to invoke the macro.

- Use backslash together with a letter, as in \T. This name means that you can execute the macro by holding down (ALT) and pressing whatever letter was used in the name; in this case, "T." You can use \A through \Z for key names.
- Use a descriptive or mnemonic name like TODAY. Macros named like this are executed by pressing USER ((F7)) and then typing in the name and pressing (ENTER). You can also use descriptive names when you use a macro within a macro, as described later in this chapter.
- Use the names \1 through \9. Macros named like this are executed by pressing USER and then the function key that corresponds to the number, such as (F2) to execute a macro named \2.
- Use a single-letter name, such as T, which means that the macro can be executed by pressing USER, typing the letter, and pressing (ENTER).

You can assign more than one name to a macro. For example, in the macro example worksheet you could name cell A21 as \T, TODAY, \1, or T. The method you use to name macros depends on your style of working and the purpose of the macro. Regularly used macros are best named with the *letter* method (\T), as this allows them to be executed with a single keystroke ((ALT-T)). You can have 26 of these macros, one for each letter of the alphabet. The *number* method (\2) provides nine macros that only need two keys to execute (USER, F2). The single-letter method of naming (T) gives you a second string of 26 macros that can be executed with just three keystrokes (USER, **T**, ENTER). The descriptive name method (TODAY) requires more keystrokes (USER, **TODAY**, ENTER) but is perhaps clearer.

When you press the USER key to execute a macro, the word "User" appears in the lower-right corner of the screen. What you type for a macro name then appears in this box as you type it, allowing you to check that you have pressed the correct keys before you press ENTER to execute the macro. This gives the USER method of execution a level of safety that the *letter* method does not have. If you press USER and type the wrong letter and press ESC before you press ENTER, the macro is cancelled.

Expanding Macros

Macros can consist of much longer instructions than the three lines in Figure 9-2. When a macro contains many instructions, the instructions are placed on successive rows of the same column. A macro that consists of more than one line of instructions is executed by naming the first cell in the macro. Symphony reads the instructions in that cell, then the instructions in the next cell down, and so on, until a blank cell is encountered.

Suppose you want the sample macro to convert the @NOW function to a permanent serial number, so that the cell remains today's date even if you load the worksheet tomorrow. (You will recall that the @NOW function returns the current date from your system clock. If you load the same spreadsheet the next day, the @NOW date changes. If you want a permanent date that does not change, use the EDIT/CALC keys.)

To add instructions to the sample macro, you can use the Learn mode. Each time you use Learn mode without altering the learn range, Symphony adds the new recording directly below any code that is already recorded in the learn range. Follow these steps to expand the \T macro:

1. With the cell pointer in an empty cell, such as A3, press (ALT-T) to execute the macro. Move the cell pointer to the cell that now contains a date, B3.

2. Press LEARN ((ALT-F5)) to turn on macro recording. Notice the "Learn" message at the bottom of the screen.

3. Press EDIT ((F2)) to edit the cell and then CALC ((F8)) to calculate the @NOW function. On the second line of the screen, you will see "@NOW" change to a number.

4. Press (ENTER) to complete the editing. As you can see from the top of the screen, the cell now contains a fixed date.

5. Press (ALT-F5) to stop the macro recording.

6. Move the cell pointer to the learn range. The results will look like this:

```
A21: 'Today is:{RIGHT}                                              SHEET

     A         B         C         D         E         F         G         H
21  Today is:{RIGHT}
22  @NOW~
23  /FD4~
24  {EDIT}{CALC}~
25
```

Symphony has added the code {EDIT}{CALC}~. This means "Press the EDIT key, followed by the CALC key, followed by (ENTER)." Move the cell pointer to a blank cell, such as A4, and try the \T function. Note that it executes the entire code, including the EDIT/CALC step. This is because the new macro code comes directly after the first code.

Managing the Learn Range

You have seen that Symphony continues to use the same learn range each time you use LEARN ((ALT-F5)). There is an exception to this: When you save a file and then retrieve it, Symphony "forgets" the learn range. This might strike you as inconvenient, but in fact there will be situations in which you want Symphony to either forget the learn range or use a different area of the worksheet for the Learn command.

Suppose you want to create a completely new macro in the same worksheet as the \T macro. If you record the new macro in the sample worksheet without adjusting the learn range, the new code will follow immediately after the \T macro, and Symphony will not be able to distinguish the two. This is why Symphony provides you with the Erase and Cancel commands on the SERVICES Settings Learn menu. The Erase command deletes any entries in the cells of the learn range, and Cancel removes the learn range coordinates, allowing you to define a different learn range.

There are three different ways to go about creating a new macro after you have already set up a learn range and recorded one macro:

- Change the learn range. Use SERVICES Settings Learn Cancel, followed by Learn Range, to indicate the area in which you want to store the new macro.

- Reuse the same area. Copy the macro you have recorded in the learn range to a new part of the worksheet. Then use SERVICES Settings Learn Erase Yes to clear the learn range and ready it for the next recording.

- Record the new macro below the old one. Then move the new code to a new location before naming and using.

The last option might seem easiest, but it requires a greater understanding of macros in order to spot where one macro ends and another begins.

Suppose you want to create a macro that saves the current worksheet without your having to use the SERVICES menu or answer the "Replace it?" prompt. You want to record this macro in the sample worksheet, the one with the \T macro.

1. Press SERVICES and select Settings Learn Cancel.
2. Select Learn Range and move the cell pointer to A27, several rows below the last line of the previous macro.
3. Press (TAB) to anchor the beginning point of the learn range. Press (PGDN) twice; this will give you plenty of room in the learn range. Press (ENTER) to confirm A27..A67 as the learn range.
4. Select Yes from the Learn menu. This is an alternative to (ALT-F5) as a way of turning on the recording feature. Symphony returns you to SHEET mode with the Learn indicator displayed.
5. Press SERVICES, type **F** to select File, and then press (ENTER) to select Save. If you have already saved the worksheet, the name of the worksheet appears. Press (ENTER), and type **Y** for Yes to confirm replacement of the old version of the file with the new.
6. Symphony places you back in SHEET mode, where you press (ALT-F5) to turn off the recording (alternatively, you can use SERVICES Settings Learn No to turn off recording).
7. Symphony will place the following code in the first cell of the learn range: {SERVICES}F~~Y. You can see this in Figure 9-3. Note that lowercase characters were recorded in the figure; this does not affect the execution of the macro.

```
A27: '{SERVICES}f~~y                                                SHEET

  ---A---------B---------C---------D---------E---------F---------G---------H---
21  Today is:{RIGHT}
22  @NOW~
23  /FD4~
24  {EDIT}{CALC}~
25
26
27  {SERVICES}f~~y
28
```

FIGURE 9-3 New macro added

Note: If you end a macro recording session and Symphony does not enter code in the learn range, move the cell pointer or press CALC ((F8)). This prompts the program to place the recorded code in the worksheet.

You can now place the cell pointer in A27 and use the Range Name create command to assign a name such as \S to the new macro. This will enable you to store the current worksheet at any time simply by pressing (ALT-S). Of course, all macros should be used with care. Bear in mind that this one will overwrite the previous version of the current worksheet.

MANAGING MACROS

Because macros are such powerful and useful tools once you start to develop them, you will probably begin to accumulate many of them. The placement of macros within a worksheet, the conventions used for assigning names, and the sharing of macros between worksheets are important factors to consider when organizing macros.

```
B21: '\T                                                         SHEET

   A         B           C                 D          E         F         G
21           \T          Today is:{RIGHT}  Enters text
22                       @NOW~             Enters @NOW
23                       /FD4~             Formats with D4
24                       {EDIT}{CALC}~     Fixes date value
25
26
27           \S          {SERVICES}f~~y    Saves file over old
28
```

FIGURE 9-4 Macros rearranged and labeled

Arranging Macros

Although the \T and \S macros work just fine as they appear in Figure 9-3, you might want to move them to a new location, and organize them according to popular macro conventions. In Figure 9-4, you can see a typical arrangement of macros. This arrangement follows the three-column convention that has been widely adopted by many spreadsheet users. The first column contains the range names of the macros. The second column contains the actual lines of macro instructions. The third column contains a series of labels briefly describing what each macro does.

One reason for the popularity of this arrangement is that it works well with the Range Name Labels command, which assigns names to ranges based on labels in adjacent cells. To see how this works, follow these steps:

1. With the worksheet still as it appears in Figure 9-3, move the cell pointer to A21. Press MENU and select Move. Select A21..A27 and press (ENTER). Move the cell pointer to C21 and press (ENTER) to complete the move.

2. Enter the labels shown in Figure 9-4 into column D, noting that this will appear to truncate some of the entries in column C. This will not affect the execution of the macros.

3. To make the code in column C more readable, move the cell pointer into column C, press MENU, and select Width. Choose Set and type **18** for the column width. Press (ENTER) to complete the column widening.

4. Press MENU and select Range Name Create. You will see the two range names listed. Select \S, and you will see that Symphony has kept track of the new location of the \S macro, which is now in C27. Press (ENTER) to confirm this location.

5. Press MENU and select Range Name Reset. This command will remove all range names from the worksheet so that you can see how the Range Label command works. Type **Y** to confirm the Reset command. Now press MENU and select Range Name Create to see that there are no names listed. Press (CTRL-BREAK) to return to SHEET mode.

6. With the cell pointer in B21, type **'\T** and press (ENTER). This creates a label, \T, which will be used to name cell C21.

Note: Note that you must use a label prefix (', ^, or ") before the backwards slash (\), since this is the cell fill character; Symphony reads \T by itself as "Fill the cell with T's".

7. Enter **'\S** in B27 and press (ENTER). This creates a label, \S, which will be used to name cell C27.

8. With the cell pointer in B21, press MENU and select Range Name Labels Right. Press the (DOWN ARROW) key several times so that you include B27. Press (ENTER). This command uses any labels in B21..B27 to assign range names to all cells in C21..C27 that are to the right of a label entry in B21..B27. Thus, C21 is once again named \T, and C27 is \S.

The Range Name Labels Right command works very nicely to create macro names. You can use Range Name Labels Down to assign labels in one row to cells in the next row down. There are also Left and Above options.

When using the Labels command to assign names, you must include all the cells on the row or in the column that contains the names you want to use, whether or not they contain labels. Blank cells do not create blank names; they are simply ignored. In the example, cell B22 does not name C22, because there is no label in B22. Note that any cells within B21..B27 that may already be established as range names are reassigned by this command.

Editing and Altering Macros

Suppose you decide that you do not always want the last line of the \T macro to be executed when you type \T. Furthermore, the {EDIT}{CALC}~ part of the code you recorded as part of the \T macro is useful for tasks other than converting @NOW to a fixed serial number. You might want to use this code within another macro, or on its own. To accomplish this, you can further rearrange your macro code.

1. Place the cell pointer on the EDIT/CALC code (C24).
2. Press MENU and select Move. Press (RIGHT ARROW) to include the label in D24. Press (ENTER) and move the cell pointer to C30. Press (ENTER) to complete the move.
3. Move the cell pointer to B30 and enter '\V (so that the macro can be executed with (ALT-V)).
4. With the cell pointer still in B30, press MENU and select Range Name Labels Right. Press (ENTER). Cell C30 is now called \V.

```
D30: 'Fixes current cell value                                         SHEET

   ----A--------B---------C---------------D---------E--------F--------G---
21          \T        Today is:{RIGHT}  Enters text
22                    @NOW~             Enters @NOW
23                    /FD4~             Formats with D4
24
25
26
27          \S        {SERVICES}f~~y    Saves file over old
28
29
30          \V        {EDIT}{CALC}~     Fixes current cell value
```

FIGURE 9-5 New arrangement

5. Move the cell pointer to D30 and edit the cell to read **Fixes current cell value**.

The new arrangement should appear as in Figure 9-5, and the (ALT-V) macro is ready to use. You can now enter **@NOW** with the \T macro and then convert to a value with (ALT-V) if you want to. You can use (ALT-V) on any cell to convert a formula in that cell to the resulting value.

Moving or copying parts of macros is very useful, but it can pose problems if you are working with the first line of a named macro. For example, if you were to decide that the first step of the \T macro was not needed, you could not simply erase cell C21. If you tell Symphony to execute the code in cell C21 and it is empty, Symphony simply does nothing. You must move new code into the cell and check that the range name is correctly assigned. Try this procedure:

1. With the cell pointer in C22, press MENU and select Move.
2. Include C22..D23 in the FROM range and press (ENTER).
3. Move the cell pointer to C21 and press (ENTER) to complete the move.

```
C21: '@NOW~                                                          SHEET
 ─────A────────B──────────C──────────────D──────────E──────────F──────────G──────
21          \T      @NOW~               Enters @NOW
22                  /FD4~               Formats with D4
23
24
25
26
27          \S      {SERVICES}f~~y      Saves file over old
28
29
30          \V      {EDIT}{CALC}~       Fixes current cell value
```

FIGURE 9-6 Altered \T macro

4. Press MENU and select Range Name Create. Choose \T, and you will see that the location is not correct; it should be C21, as it was before. Enter **C21** as the range location.

The \T macro simply enters @NOW and formats the current cell. The worksheet should now look like Figure 9-6. Whenever you change the first line of a macro, you should check that the range name is correctly assigned.

Macro Writing

Instead of recording macro code as you have done so far, you can enter the macro code into the worksheet directly. Macro code is entered as labels. Suppose that you want a macro that will widen a column by one character. If you think this action through, or try it on your sample worksheet, you can see that it consists of typing **/ W S** and pressing RIGHT ARROW and ENTER. To write a macro to do this, you are faced with the problem of entering a label that consists of **/ W S RIGHT ARROW and ENTER**. If you begin by typing /, then the menu will be displayed; if you press RIGHT ARROW or ENTER while typing a label, the label is placed into the current cell. To see how you get around these problems, follow these steps:

1. You will create the macro in cell C25, so move the cell pointer there.

2. You must begin the macro with a label prefix character. Normally, the apostrophe is used. Thus, you would begin the macro with **'/WS**, which gets you as far as selecting the Width Set command.

3. To incorporate (RIGHT ARROW) in your macro, you enter **{RIGHT}**. To incorporate (ENTER) in your macro, you type the tilde (~). The completed label will be

   /WS{RIGHT}~

   Enter this in C25 and move the cell pointer to D25.

4. In D25, enter the label **Widens column 1 character**.

5. In cell B25, enter '**W** (so that the macro can be executed with (ALT-W)).

6. With the cell pointer still in B25, press MENU, select Range Name Labels Right, and press (ENTER). Cell C25 will now be called \W.

The completed macro you have written can be seen in Figure 9-7. You can test this in any column by pressing (ALT-W). You will see the column increase in width. This is handy when making final adjustments to a spreadsheet design. A useful companion macro could narrow the column one character and be called \N. If you

```
B25: '\W                                                          SHEET

    ----A-------B-----------C---------------D---------E---------F---------G----
21          \T          @NOW~               Enters @NOW
22                      /FD4~               Formats with D4
23
24
25          \W          /WS{RIGHT}~         Widens column 1 character
26
27          \S          {SERVICES}f~~y      Saves file over old
28
29
30          \V          {EDIT}{CALC}~       Fixes current cell value
```

FIGURE 9-7 The \W macro added

follow these steps, you can copy some of the code you already have to make this macro:

1. To make room for the new macro below the \W macro, place the cell pointer in B26. Press MENU and select Insert Row. Press (DOWN ARROW) three times to insert a total of four rows. Press (ENTER). The \S macro is now on row 31.

2. Place the cell pointer in B28. Press MENU and select Copy. When prompted for the range to copy from, press (ESC). Move the cell pointer up to B25 and press (TAB) to anchor the beginning point of the range. Press (RIGHT ARROW) twice to include B25..D25 in the FROM range. Press (ENTER) twice to complete the copy to row 28.

3. With the cell pointer still in B28, press EDIT ((F2)) and then (BACKSPACE), and type N to alter the label to '\N. Press (ENTER).

4. Press MENU, select Range Name Labels Right, and press (ENTER). Cell C28 is now called \N.

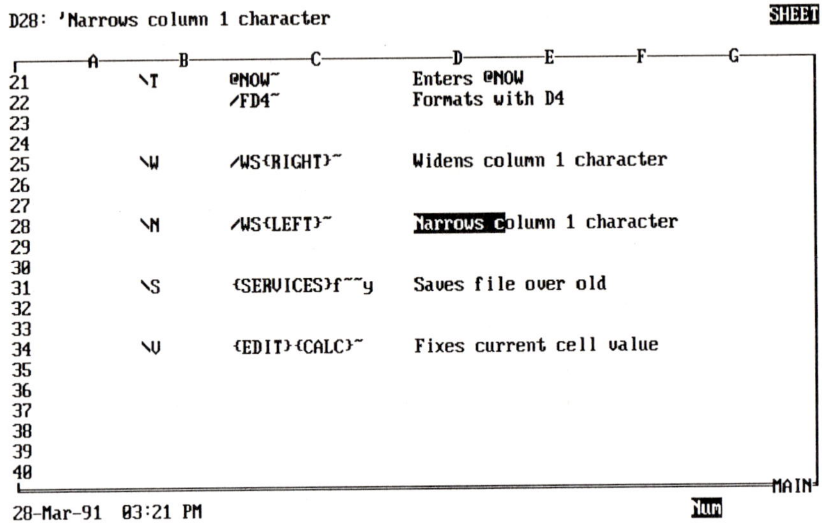

FIGURE 9-8 The \N macro added

5. Now edit cell C28 to **{LEFT}** instead of {RIGHT}, and edit cell D28 to **Narrows column 1 character**. The results can be seen in Figure 9-8.

You can see that macro code, like other entries in a worksheet, can be copied and reused. In order to preserve your latest changes, use the (ALT-S) macro to perform a File Save using the name **MACRO1**.

When writing rather than recording macros, there is a whole system of codes for actions that cannot simply be typed as labels. You can see them listed in Table 9-1.

If you plan carefully, you can write macros that work the first time. However, you should save the worksheet before trying any new macro, just in case it does not work as expected. Bear in mind that the simplest method of creating useful macros is to record them. This avoids the need to memorize the codes in Table 9-1.

Key Name	Equivalent
{ABS}	F3
{AUTO} justify	CTRL-J
{BACKSPACE} or {BS}	BACKSPACE
{BIG LEFT}	CTRL-LEFT ARROW
{BIG RIGHT}	CTRL-RIGHT ARROW
{BREAK}	CTRL-BREAK
{CALC}	F8
{CAPTURE}	F4
{CASE} change	CTRL-X
{CENTER}	ALT-F4
{COPY} text	CTRL-C
{DLEFT}	CTRL-T
{DLINE}	CTRL-D
{DRIGHT}	CTRL-Y
{DWORD}	CTRL-BACKSPACE
{DELETE}	DEL
{DOWN}	DOWN ARROW
{DRAW}	ALT-8
{EDIT}	F2
{END}	END
{ERASE}	F4
{ESCAPE} or {ESC}	ESC
{FORMAT} line	CTRL-F
{GOTO}	F5
{HELP}	F1
{HOME}	HOME
{INDENT}	F3
{INSERT}	INS
{JUSTIFY}	F2
{LEFT}	LEFT ARROW
{MENU} or {M}	F10
{MOVE} text	CTRL-M
{NEXTPAGE}	CTRL-PGDN
{PAGE UP}	PGUP
{PAGE DOWN}	PGDN
{PAGE} break	CTRL-N

TABLE 9-1 Macro Key Names

Key Name	Equivalent
{PASTE} text	CTRL-P
{REPLACE} text	CTRL-R
{RIGHT}	RIGHT ARROW
{SEARCH} for text	CTRL-S
{SERVICES}	F9
{SPLIT}	ALT-F3
{STEP}	ALT-F7
{SWITCH}	ALT-F9
{TAB}	TAB
{TOPPAGE}	CTRL-PGUP
{TYPE}	ALT-F10
{UP}	UP ARROW
{WHERE}	ALT-2
{WINDOW}	F6
{ZOOM}	ALT-6

* DOC environment only

TABLE 9-1 Macro Key Names (*continued*)

Note: To see a list of macro key names while writing macros, press F1, and then select Help Index followed by Macro Key Names.

Macro Writing Tips

Before composing a macro, you will find it helpful to make notes of the operations you want the macro to perform and sketch out the required steps. When you enter the macro instructions into the worksheet, remember that you use direct keystrokes for menu selections and code words or "key names" for keystrokes such as cursor movement and function keys.

Often, you will be able to put together a macro from several sources. For example, you can use the record method to capture the keystrokes for part of an operation, and then add those recorded keystrokes to the rest of the macro with the Move command. When combining macro instructions, you may want to use several of the techniques described here.

Sometimes your macros can accumulate rather cumbersome lines of instructions like this one:

```
/C{DOWN}{DOWN}{DOWN}{DOWN}{DOWN}{RIGHT}{RIGHT}
```

There is nothing technically wrong with repeating the keystroke representation over and over. However, you can refer to a series of repeated keystrokes by the name of the key and a number. The key name takes a numeric argument enclosed within braces, as in {DOWN 5} or {RIGHT 2}. You can use this system with all of the cursor key macro names. Thus, the line of code just shown becomes

```
/C{DOWN 5}{RIGHT 2}
```

This abbreviated version is easy to read and much more compact. However, you will probably want to look carefully at the use of multiple cursor movement keystrokes in your macros. In general, you will find macros more reliable if you use range names wherever possible, instead of the pointing method of identifying cell coordinates.

The number used as the argument with a repeated macro key name can be a number you enter directly or a number supplied by a cell reference. Thus, {DOWN A1} causes the DOWN ARROW action to be repeated five times if A1 contains the number 5 or a formula that results in 5. Likewise, the instruction {DOWN TIMES} causes the DOWN ARROW action to be repeated five times if the range TIMES contains the number 5 or a formula that results in 5.

Note You can further shorten your macros if you use the abbreviations shown in Table 9-1. Use {ESC} instead of {ESCAPE} and {BS} instead of {BACKSPACE}.

At times, you may not be able to reduce the length of recorded macro instructions by using the abbreviation method. However, you may still want to split the macro line into more manageable sections. One way to do this is to copy the line that needs to be split and then edit both versions. For example, you might want to split the following line:

```
/QSBD{BS}.{END}{RIGHT}{END}{DOWN}
```

To split this line, you first copy the line from its current cell to the one below it (assuming that the cell you are copying to is empty or contains expendable data). Then highlight the original instruction and press (F2) to edit it. Use the (BACKSPACE) key to erase all the text to the right of the first {END}. Then press (ENTER) to return the edited line to the cell. Move your cell pointer to the copy of the original line, and press (F2) to edit it. Press (HOME) and then (DEL) to remove all of the text up to and including the first {END}. Press (ENTER) to return the edited contents to the cell. The resulting cells will look like this:

```
/QSBD{BS}.{END}
{RIGHT}{END}{DOWN}
```

You now have the macro instruction in two short labels, rather than one long one. This technique often helps make macro instructions more manageable.

There may also be times when it is prudent to combine lines of macro code. For example, Symphony might record a single tilde or period on one line at the end of a macro. Such "orphan" characters are best added to the line above to make the macro easier to read, copy, and keep together.

Macro Design Factors

Whenever you create a macro, you need to give some thought to what the role of the macro will be. For example, SHEET environment macros can be used to enter values and labels, to select menu items, and to activate function keys. They can be executed in SHEET mode, in EDIT mode, and from within the menu system. Of course, if you make a macro that works from SHEET mode, it should be executed in SHEET mode and not in the middle of a menu.

Be careful about the action of the macro and the data it will affect. For example, if the macro is designed to perform a particular action on a cell, you must remember to move your cell pointer to a suitable cell before executing the macro. There is a possibility of losing data through any of these SHEET environment actions:

Copy
Move
Erase
Query
Extract
Range Fill
Range Name Table
Range Transpose
Range Value
File Table

If you want to store additional macros close to the ones already entered into the worksheet, but you do not want them to become part of the existing macros, you should make sure that at least one blank cell separates macros.

Where you place macros on your spreadsheet not only affects how they relate to other macro instructions, but also how they affect the rest of your work. One possible location is to the right of the main work area. This location is acceptable until you decide to delete a row from the work area. Since the macros and the work area are probably not going to be in view at the same time, it is all too easy to delete a row from the work area and accidentally delete a row of macro code. Because macros run until they encounter a blank row, even inserting a new row can cause problems for macros stored to the right of the work area.

One way to avoid inadvertently deleting rows is to use the full movement of the cursor when using the Delete Row or Insert Row command. You can press not only the DOWN ARROW key when deleting or inserting rows, but also the RIGHT ARROW and Big Right keys. Doing so allows you to move to the right of your work area to check for macros before deleting or inserting the rows.

Another way to avoid macro problems caused by deleting rows is to store macros below the work area. You are less likely to delete columns, and adding columns is less likely to disrupt a macro, since the instructions are stored in single columns.

Macro Propagation and Navigation

Some users like to place their macros above the main work area and to the left of the spreadsheet—that is, around the home position. Here, they are relatively safe from column and row deletion and easy to find. This approach works well with another technique employed by macro users. In the worksheet in Figure 9-8, which you have saved with the name MACRO1, you have a number of general-purpose macros. Suppose you want to use these macros in a new worksheet. You can extract the macros to another file and use that file as the basis for your new worksheet. To do this, follow these steps:

1. Place the cell pointer in B21 and press SERVICES.
2. Choose File Xtract Formulas and type **MACRO2** as the file name. Press ENTER.

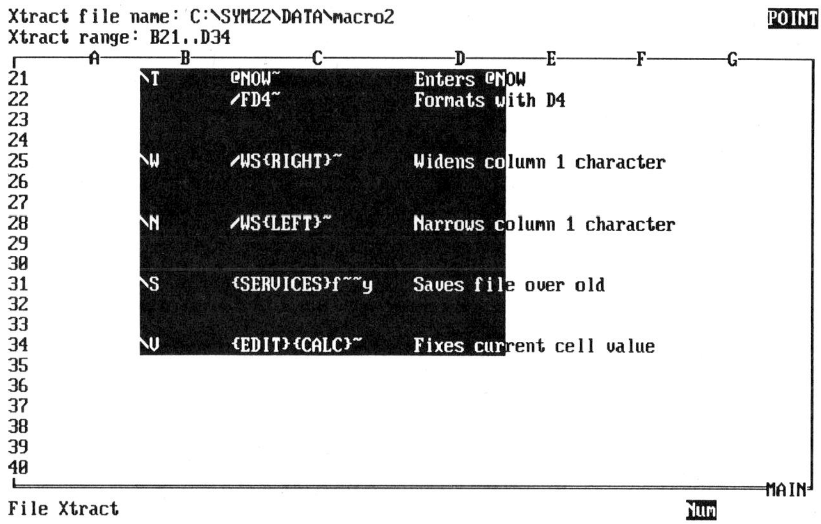

FIGURE 9-9 Saving macros to a new file

3. Select B21..D34 as the Xtract range, as shown in Figure 9-9, and press (ENTER).

4. To examine the new file, press SERVICES, select File Retrieve, and select MACRO2. The file will appear, containing the macros beginning at A1, as shown in Figure 9-10.

The range names will still be attached to the macros, and they are ready to use. You could now proceed to create your worksheet model below and to the right of the macros, leaving them relatively unaffected by ongoing changes in your worksheet design. However, perhaps the most elegant solution for protecting macros is to store them in a macro library, described later in this chapter.

When you locate a group of macros away from the main work area in order to protect them, you might find it difficult to locate

```
A1: '\T                                                              SHEET

     A           B                   C          D          E         F         G
1   \T          @NOW~               Enters @NOW
2               /FD4~               Formats with D4
3
4
5   \W          /WS{RIGHT}~         Widens column 1 character
6
7
8   \N          /WS{LEFT}~          Narrows column 1 character
9
10
11  \S          {SERVICES}f~~y      Saves file over old
12
13
14  \V          {EDIT}{CALC}~       Fixes current cell value
15
16
17
18
19
20
                                                                            MAIN
29-Mar-91  10:24 AM                                                  Num
```

FIGURE 9-10 The extracted file

them for editing purposes. If you use the "above and to the left" approach, you can always find them with (HOME). However, if you use the "below and to the right" design, they are more difficult to find quickly. An easy way of moving to a specific area of your worksheet is to use the GOTO key ((F5)) with a range name. To make it easier to move directly to the area where you have stored the macros, you could assign the name MACROS to the entire macro storage area. Then you could move to the named range by pressing Goto ((F5)), typing **MACROS**, and pressing (ENTER). You could also use (F5) followed by (F10) to list the existing range names and then select the area you want to move to from the list. In fact, you can always move to the first cell of any macro by pressing (F5), typing the name of the macro, and pressing (ENTER).

Using cursor movement keys to move to a specific location can be a problem when recording the macros themselves. When you write cell-pointer movement into a macro, the best approach to locating a specific area is to first name the cell in the top left corner of the area you want to get to, and then, in the macro instruction, use Goto and the range name. Subsequent changes to the location or size of the range will not affect the macro instruction.

MACRO CONTROL AND CORRECTION

Symphony contains numerous features for controlling macro execution. There are also tools to help you understand why a macro does not work the way you expect it to.

Stopping Macros

If you give the command to execute a macro and the effects immediately appear to be different from what you expect, you may want to stop the macro. You do this with (CTRL-BREAK). When you press (CTRL-BREAK) during macro execution, Symphony responds by displaying the word "Break" at the bottom left of the screen and flashing "ERROR" in the mode indicator. Press (ESC) to remove the "ERROR" message and return to SHEET mode.

Debugging Macros

Symphony macros execute quickly, so it may be hard to tell what goes wrong when a macro misbehaves, and it may be hard to stop the macro before it is completed. For this reason, you sometimes need to undertake a procedure known as *debugging*. This is a combination of operations, all of which have the goal of figuring out what has gone wrong. The first step is to check the troubleshooting list in Table 9-2 for clues on what is wrong.

To help you in the debugging process, Symphony provides a DEBUG mode for macro execution. This mode is a simple way of seeing your macro run one step at a time. As an example of how

1. Use the Range Name Create command to check that the macro name is correctly assigned; it should apply to the first cell in the macro.

2. Check that there are no gaps in the macro; no blank cells within the code of a single macro.

3. Use (F5) and then (F10) to select the macro you want to inspect.

4. Check that macro key names and keywords are spelled correctly.

5. Check that all { have a matching }.

6. Check for missing tildes (~). This is the most common problem when writing macros, since the (ENTER) key is the most commonly used key.

7. If you are using a lot of range names in a worksheet, use the Range Names Table command to list them in the worksheet and check that they are correct.

8. Check that references to range names and cell coordinates within macros are correct.

9. Save the worksheet and take a short break. Many macro problems are easier to solve after a few moments relaxation.

10. Ask a colleague to review your macro. Sometimes you can fail to see an error while staring at it, whereas someone taking a fresh look can see the problem clearly.

TABLE 9-2 Macro Troubleshooting List

the macro debug feature can help in a relatively simple macro, consider the worksheet in Figure 9-11. This is the revenue breakdown you created in Chapter 6. The revenue figures are listed in columns by month. The columns are about to be summed on row 11. Two macros are visible on the worksheet. The first one, \C, is used to copy the contents of a cell across the model to the last column. This macro uses the (END) and (RIGHT ARROW) sequence to do this.

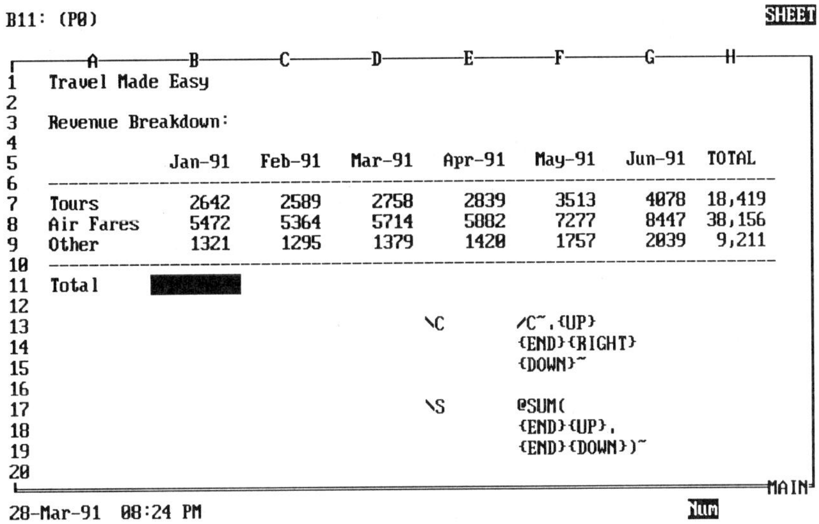

FIGURE 9-11 Sample worksheet

The second macro, \S, is designed to sum a column. The macro is supposed to do this by first typing the @SUM function and the opening parenthesis. Then the macro moves the cell pointer to the top of the column, anchors the range to be summed at that point with a period, and then includes all the cells down to the bottom of the column. Finally, a closing parenthesis is added and the formula is entered in the cell with a tilde.

The idea behind the \S macro is that the user will place the cell pointer in B11 and press (ALT-S) to activate the macro and sum the column. But as you can see from Figure 9-12, the results are not as expected. Cell B11 contains the formula @SUM(B10..B8192), which is not only incorrect but also a circular formula, one that refers to itself, as noted by the message "Circ" at the bottom of the screen. The debug feature should help show where the problem lies by stepping through the macro.

```
B11: (P0) @SUM(B10..B8192)                                              SHEET

    A          B          C          D          E          F          G          H
1   Travel Made Easy
2
3   Revenue Breakdown:
4
5                Jan-91    Feb-91    Mar-91    Apr-91    May-91    Jun-91   TOTAL
6   --------------------------------------------------------------------------------
7   Tours          2642      2589      2758      2839      3513      4078  18,419
8   Air Fares      5472      5364      5714      5882      7277      8447  38,156
9   Other          1321      1295      1379      1420      1757      2039   9,211
10  --------------------------------------------------------------------------------
11  Total             0
12
13                                          \C        /C~.{UP}
14                                                    {END}{RIGHT}
15                                                    {DOWN}~
16
17                                          \S        @SUM(
18                                                    {END}{UP}.
19                                                    {END}{DOWN})~
20
                                                                             MAIN
28-Mar-91  08:24 PM                        Circ                     Num
```

FIGURE 9-12 Error after using (ALT-S) in B11

To activate STEP mode, press (ALT-F7) and select Step. The STEP indicator appears at the bottom of the screen. From this point until you reissue the Step command, any macro you execute will run in STEP mode. Before executing the macro you want to debug, however, you should make sure that the conditions are correct. For example, in the case of the worksheet in Figure 9-12, the incorrect formula needs to be deleted from cell B11 before the macro is retried. If you then issue the command to run the sample macro \S that needs to be debugged, Symphony shows the macro code in the bottom status line as you press the spacebar to run the macro one step at a time. Each time you tap the spacebar, another character or command in the macro is executed.

In Figure 9-13, you can see that the problem with this macro has become apparent. The (END-UP ARROW) combination took the cell pointer only to cell B9, and the (END-DOWN ARROW) combination

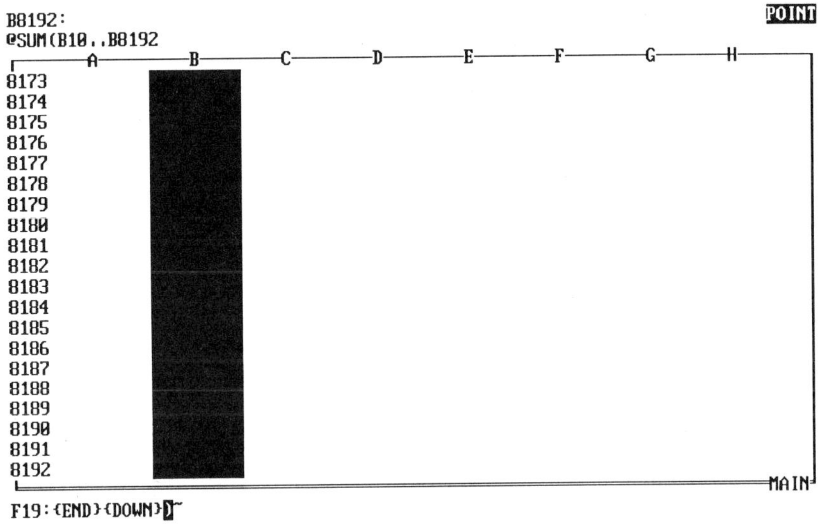

FIGURE 9-13 Macro problem

has thus taken the cell pointer to the bottom of the worksheet. The macro can be aborted at this point by pressing (CTRL-BREAK). You then press (ESC) to return to READY mode without completing the macro. Note that simply ending the macro does not reverse the effect of Step, which will continue to cause macros to be executed in STEP mode until you press (ALT-F7) again. To correct this particular macro, you need to amend the second line so that it reads

{UP}{END}{UP}{DOWN}

with the added {UP} command causing the cell pointer to anchor the beginning point of the sum range at B6. The resulting formula is @SUM(B6..B10), which works fine (adding the rows of hyphens does not affect the result of the formula). This formula can then be copied across the rest of the model, by using the \C macro.

THE MACRO COMMAND LANGUAGE

In addition to using macros for a fixed set of instructions, replicating the keystrokes that might otherwise be entered manually from the keyboard, Symphony allows the use of special macro commands, called *keywords*. Collectively know as the *macro command language* or just the *command language* for short, these keywords provide access to features and functions not available from the keyboard. The following sections discuss the theory of macro keywords and provide examples of how they can be applied. Appendix C includes a review of the individual keywords. These range from {BEEP}, which sounds your computer's beep to alert the user, to {GETLABEL}, which prompts for user input, and {MENUBRANCH}, which enables custom menu development.

A Command Language Example

The basic purpose of macro keywords is to add logic to macros, thus enabling you to create macros that evaluate conditions and choose between different courses of action based on parameters you specify. For this reason, the macro commands are a lot like programming statements. This does *not* mean that macro commands are just for programmers. If you are reasonably familiar with Symphony, you will be quite capable of taking advantage of this powerful facility, either to simplify your own work or to prepare Symphony applications for others to use.

One of the most commonly used keywords is {BRANCH}. Earlier, you saw that when executing a macro, Symphony keeps looking to the next cell down for further macro code until a blank cell is reached. If Symphony encounters a {BRANCH} command in a macro, it continues executing macro code at another location, one specified by the {BRANCH} command. Like many keywords, {BRANCH} takes an argument. The argument is the cell address or range name of the macro code you want Symphony to branch to. The argument is placed within the braces but separated from the keyword by a space, as in

{BRANCH C9}

This tells Symphony to continue the macro by executing code in cell C9.

You can use the sample worksheet MACRO2, last shown in Figure 9-10, to see how the {BRANCH} command works. Suppose that you have decided you really would like the \T macro to convert the @NOW function to a value. The code that performs this action is now the macro called \V. You could copy the code from \V to cell B3, the one directly below the last line of code in \T. Alternatively, you could use the {BRANCH} command, as shown in Figure 9-14. This instruction simply directs Symphony to the cell called \V when it reaches the third line of the \T macro.

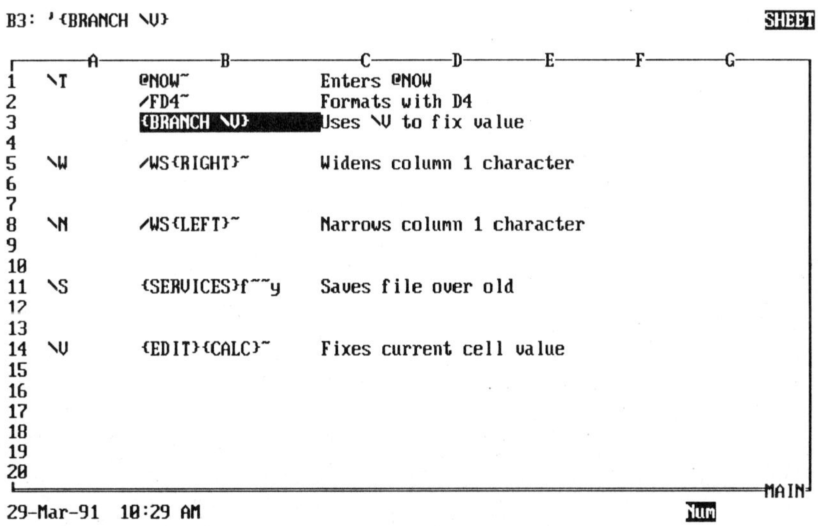

FIGURE 9-14 Using the {BRANCH} command

As you can see, the macro keywords allow you to recycle useful sections of macro code. Keywords also allow you to make room for user input in a macro. This means that you can have the \T macro ask whether the date should be converted to a value or not. One way of doing this is to use the {GETLABEL} command, which asks the user a question and then places the user's response in a designated cell of the worksheet. Macro code to enhance the \T macro in this way will be developed over the next few paragraphs.

A {GETLABEL} statement needs two pieces of information, supplied as arguments separated by a comma. The first argument is the text of the prompt or question. This is enclosed in quotes. The second argument is the location into which to place the response. This location can be a cell coordinate or a range name. Range names are preferable since they are more constant than cell references. A typical {GETLABEL} statement might read

```
{GETLABEL "Convert @NOW to a fixed date (Y/N)? ",ANSWER}
```

The range name for the response is ANSWER. Note the space between the question mark and the quotes. This ensures that the cursor is not right next to the question mark when the command is issued.

Once you have a response to a question, you must find a way of evaluating that response. One keyword that is useful for this is {IF}, which works like the @IF function. You use a conditional statement as the argument for the {IF} command, as in

```
{IF ANSWER="N"}
```

When Symphony encounters such a statement in a macro, it does one of two things. If the conditional statement is true—in this case, if the cell called ANSWER contains the letter "N"—then Symphony executes whatever macro code is immediately to the right of the {IF} statement. If the conditional statement is false—for example, if ANSWER contains the letter "Y"—then Symphony ignores any code to the right of the {IF} statement and proceeds to the code below the statement. In the example, you could use these two lines to evaluate the response to the {GETLABEL} command:

```
{IF ANSWER="N"}{QUIT}
{BRANCH \V}
```

The first line uses the {QUIT} keyword to tell Symphony to stop executing the macro if the ANSWER is N; otherwise, it proceeds with the {BRANCH} command.

To try these keywords in the MACRO2 worksheet, follow these steps:

1. Move the cell pointer to row 3.
2. Issue the Insert Row command and press (DOWN ARROW) once to insert a total of two rows. Press (ENTER).
3. In cell B3, enter this code:

   ```
   {GETLABEL "Convert @NOW to a fixed date (Y/N)? ",ANSWER}
   ```

4. In cell B4, enter this code:

   ```
   {IF ANSWER="N"}{QUIT}
   ```

   The code {BRANCH \V} will now go in B5.
5. In cell F1, enter the label **ANSWER** and issue the Range Name Label Right command. Press (ENTER) to name G1 as ANSWER.

The macro is now ready to run. Move the cell pointer to an empty cell and press (ALT-T). The user input question will appear on the first line of the screen, as shown in Figure 9-15, where the user has typed **y** as a response. Note the "Macro" message in the bottom

```
Convert @NOW to a fixed date (Y/N)? y                                    SHEET

        A          B                    C           D           E          F           G
1   \T        @NOW~                Enters @NOW                       ANSWER
2             /FD4~                Formats with D4
3             {GETLABEL "Convert @NOW to a fixed date (Y/N)? ",ANSWER}
4             {IF ANSWER="N"}{QUIT}
5             {BRANCH \V}          Uses \V to fix value
6
7   \W        /WS{RIGHT}~          Widens column 1 character
8
9
10  \N        /WS{LEFT}~           Narrows column 1 character
11
12
13  \S        {SERVICES}f~~y       Saves file over old
14
15
16  \V        {EDIT}{CALC}~        Fixes current cell value
17
18
19
20                                                                    03/29/91
                                                                            MAIN
29-Mar-91  11:06 AM                         Macro                        Num
```

FIGURE 9-15 Using the {GETLABEL} keyword

status line, reminding you that a macro is running at this point. Answering **y** causes the macro to perform the \V macro; the results can be seen in Figure 9-16, where the user response can be seen in cell G1. Note that upper- or lowercase response is treated the same by the {IF} command.

You probably want to erase the contents of the cell in which you tested this macro. You might also want to reset the range format of the cell. A good macro to do both of these things is

```
/E~/FR~
```

Enter this code in cell B19. Enter the label **'\E** in A19. With the cell pointer in A19, issue the Range Name Labels Right command, and press (ENTER) to name B19 as \E. This macro is now ready to use. At this point you should save the improved macro file, using the name **MACRO2**. This file will be used again later.

```
G20: (D4) 33326.463206                                                    SHEET

    ----A--------B-------------C----------D----------E----------F----------G----
1   \T       @NOW~               Enters @NOW                  ANSWER   y
2            /FD4~               Formats with D4
3            {GETLABEL "Convert @NOW to a fixed date (Y/N)? ",ANSWER}
4            {IF ANSWER="N"}{QUIT}
5            {BRANCH \U}         Uses \U to fix value
6
7   \W       /WS{RIGHT}~         Widens column 1 character
8
9
10  \N       /WS{LEFT}~          Narrows column 1 character
11
12
13  \S       {SERVICES}f~~y      Saves file over old
14
15
16  \U       {EDIT}{CALC}~       Fixes current cell value
17
18
19
20                                                            03/29/91
                                                                        MAIN
29-Mar-91  11:07 AM                                           Num
```

FIGURE 9-16 After the macro

More Keyword Examples

Another situation in which a macro keyword can be very effectively applied is when you need to repeat a series of operations. Suppose that you have a column of values that need to be rounded to two decimal places. In order to develop a macro that does this, you can create a set of test figures, like those in Figure 9-17, by following these steps:

1. In a new worksheet, enter the label **Test Results** in A1.

2. Move the cell pointer to B2 and enter the formula **@RAND*1000**. The @RAND function picks a random number between 0 and 1, so the result of this formula will be a number between 1 and 1000 with at least four decimal places.

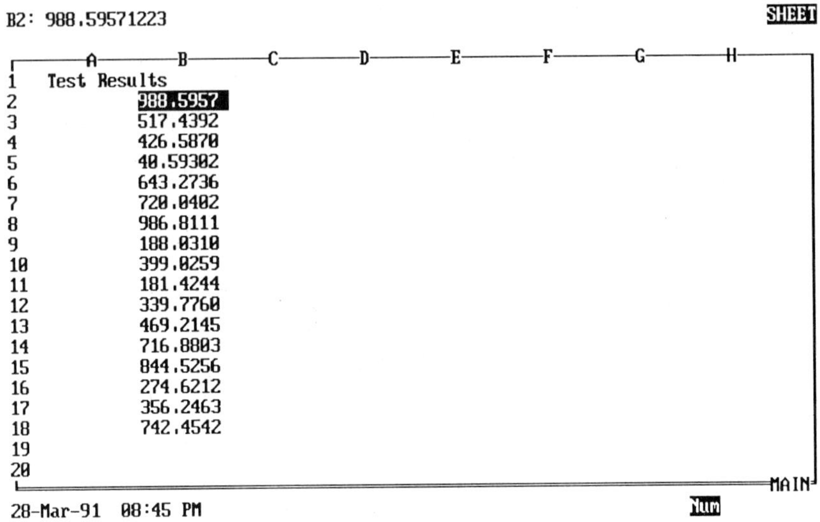

FIGURE 9-17 Test figures

3. Copy cell B2 to B2..B18. You now have a column of imaginary test results.

4. To convert the cells from formulas to numbers, press MENU and select Range Values. Select B2..B18 as the FROM range and B2 as the TO range. The numbers are now just numbers, as in Figure 9-17. (Your numbers will differ, since they are supposed to be random numbers).

5. You can save this file as **RESULTS1** and use it in the following examples.

The first task is to design a macro that will round these purposefully long numbers to two decimal places. You could edit the first cell and place **@ROUND(** in front of the value. Then you could place **,2)** at the end of the value and enter the new information into the cell. A macro called \R designed to do this might look like this:

```
\R {EDIT}{HOME}@ROUND({END},2)~
```

Go ahead and enter this in the worksheet, as shown here:

```
D2: '\R                                                          SHEET

┌───────A──────────B──────────C──────────D──────────E──────────F──────────G──────────H──────
1   Test Results
2              988.5957              \R         {EDIT}{HOME}@ROUND({END},2)~
3              517.4392
4              426.5870
```

With the cell pointer in D2, issue the Range Name Labels Right command and press (ENTER) to name E2 as \R. After performing this action on one value, you would move down to the next. You can add this movement to the macro. Since the (DOWN ARROW) key enters data from EDIT mode, you could amend the macro to

```
\R {EDIT}{HOME}@ROUND({END},2){DOWN}
```

This macro will round the current cell and then move the cell pointer to the next cell down.

If the column of values you want to round is a long one, you may want to repeat the macro many times. Instead of repeatedly executing the same macro, you can incorporate the repetition into the macro by means of the {BRANCH} keyword. When reading macro instructions, Symphony normally proceeds straight down a column, one cell after another. However, you might want Symphony to branch back to the first cell of the macro and begin over again. Note that there are two movements being discussed here: the progress of the actual cell pointer as it works its way down a column of values being edited in the spreadsheet, and the progress of Symphony as it reads the macro code. The latter movement can be referred to as the macro pointer, the current cell of macro code.

As you saw earlier, the {BRANCH} command alters the course of the macro pointer. From moving straight down a column, the pointer is diverted to a different location. The following \R macro tells Symphony to go back and repeat the macro. When the first line of code is read, the macro pointer moves to the second line. This tells Symphony to branch to the cell named \R:

```
\R   {EDIT}{HOME}@ROUND({END},2){DOWN}
     {BRANCH \R}
```

In this case, the argument for the {BRANCH} command is \R. Once you place the cell pointer in a cell containing a value and then execute \R, the macro will loop continuously, attempting to round cell values until you stop it. You can stop the macro with CTRL-BREAK followed by ESC. Although this is a fairly crude way of controlling macro execution, it is simple enough to implement for general purposes.

In actual fact, what happens is that the cell pointer moves down the column of values being edited. When the cell pointer reaches an empty cell, an error occurs, which is then repeated until the macro is stopped.

Using @CELL in Macros

Instead of using CTRL-BREAK to end your macro, you might want to have the macro stop as soon as it reaches the bottom of the column. The @CELL function and its companion, @CELL-POINTER is very useful in macros when you need to get information about a cell. For an example, say you want to know if a cell is a blank. There are several methods of determining this, but the simplest is to use @CELL or @CELLPOINTER, together with a special term that describes the type of information that is required.

The @CELL function takes two arguments. The first is the term for the category of information, in this case "type," and the second argument is the name of the cell about which you are inquiring. For example, the statement

```
@CELL("type",A1)
```

returns the code **b** if cell A1 is blank, **v** if it contains a value, and **l** if it is a label. The @CELLPOINTER function works the same as @CELL, except that the second argument is not required. This is because @CELLPOINTER returns information about the cell currently occupied by the cell pointer.

The categories of information that can be returned by the @CELL function include: address, row, column, contents, type, prefix, protection status, width, and format. The codes used in the @CELL commands are listed in Appendix B, where the function is described in more detail. Bear in mind that the @CELL result is a label, so an {IF} or @IF statement using @CELL may need to refer to the result as a string in quotes. For example, the result **"b"** in the following formula is placed in quotes. This formula returns **VACANT** if A1 is blank:

```
@IF(@CELL("type",A1)="b","VACANT","OCCUPIED")
```

The same formula with the @CELLPOINTER function would appear as

```
@IF(@CELLPOINTER("type")="b","VACANT","OCCUPIED")
```

This is a rather interesting formula to enter, since @CELLPOINTER returns information about the current cell. When you type this formula and press ENTER, the immediate response is **OCCUPIED**, because you have just entered the formula. However, if you type the formula and press DOWN ARROW, then the result will depend upon whether or not the cell below the formula is blank.

Using the {IF} Command

Having seen that you can get information about the current cell with the @CELLPOINTER function, you need to look at how you can incorporate that information into a macro. This is where the {IF} command comes in. As you have seen, {IF} is the macro keyword equivalent of the @IF function. The {IF} command is used to present the macro with a conditional statement, one that is either true or false. The macro's response to a true condition is to continue processing instructions on the same line as the {IF} statement. The response of the macro to a false condition is to skip the rest of the current line of macro code and go on to the next line.

The condition for an {IF} command statement is a Symphony formula that evaluates to true or false, such as

```
A1>100
```

or

```
@CELLPOINTER("type")="b"
```

Note that the result returned by both of these formulas can be true or false, and nothing else. The condition is then enclosed within the {IF} command braces, as in

```
{IF A1>100}
```

Let's examine a typical arrangement of the {IF} statement in a macro. For example, suppose that you have a cell, called GREEN, that contains macro code and another cell, called RED, that contains different code. You have a macro that you almost always want to branch back to the cell called GREEN. The only exception is when the value of cell A1 reaches or exceeds 100, in which case you want the macro to branch to RED. The following lines of code will do the trick:

```
{IF A1<100}{BRANCH GREEN}
{BRANCH RED}
```

The first line of code tells Symphony to evaluate the contents of A1. If that value is less than 100, the conditional statement is true and the macro will continue reading the instructions to the right of the {IF} statement; that is, it will branch to GREEN. If the value of A1 is 100 or greater, the macro will ignore the instructions to the right of the {IF} statement and proceed to the next line, branching to RED.

As a variation on this scenario, suppose you want the macro to either branch to GREEN or quit. The following line of code will accomplish this:

```
{IF A1<100}{BRANCH GREEN}
```

This code will work *if* the cell below it is empty. The line of code tells Symphony to evaluate the contents of A1. If that value is less than 100, the conditional statement is true and the macro will branch to the location called GREEN. If the value of A1 is 100 or greater, the macro ignores the instructions to the right of the {IF} statement and proceeds to the next line, which is blank and thus terminates the macro.

The {QUIT} Command

The method of programming in the previous example is a little risky, because the cell below the {IF} statement might become occupied and thus do something other than cause the macro to terminate smoothly. To make termination of macros more precise and professional, you can use the {QUIT} command.

When you want a macro to either branch to a specific location or quit, these two lines of code will work nicely:

```
{IF A1>100}{BRANCH GREEN}
{QUIT}
```

This code does not require any empty cell below it. The first line of code tells Symphony to evaluate the contents of A1. If that value is less than 100, the conditional statement is true and the macro will branch to the location called GREEN. If the value of A1 is 100 or greater, the macro ignores the instructions to the right of the {IF} statement and proceeds to the next line, {QUIT}, which tells the macro to end.

You can turn this macro around, if you want, and have the {QUIT} command as the default action—the one that is carried out if the conditional statement is true. Consider this code:

```
{IF A1>100}{QUIT}
{BRANCH GREEN}
```

Here, the macro performs almost the same action as the previous one, quitting if the value of A1 exceeds 100. Note that the conditionals here do not exactly match those in the previous macro; the effect of A1 being exactly 100 would be different. To match the previous example, the conditional statement should be altered to read

```
{IF A1=>100}{QUIT}
{BRANCH GREEN}
```

A Controlled Loop

If you combine the {BRANCH}, {IF}, and {QUIT} commands together with the @CELLPOINTER function, you can make a well-behaved looping macro. Let's return to looping a macro that rounds a column of values. The following macro was suggested.

```
\R    {EDIT}{HOME}@ROUND({END},2){DOWN}
      {BRANCH \R}
```

The effect of executing this macro was that when the cell pointer reached a blank cell at the bottom of the column of values, errors began to occur until the macro was halted with CTRL-BREAK. The following macro halts automatically when it reaches a blank cell:

```
\R    {EDIT}{HOME}@ROUND({END},2){DOWN}
      {IF @CELLPOINTER("type")="b"}{QUIT}
      {BRANCH \R}
```

At the {IF} statement, Symphony evaluates the contents of the cell currently occupied by the cell pointer. If the cell type is **b** or blank, then the action {QUIT} is carried out. If the type is not **b**, the macro loops to repeat itself.

A problem can occur with this macro, since there is nothing to stop it from trying to round a label cell. By altering the macro, you can avoid this problem. Here, you can see the code required to have the macro check for the type **v** or value. When the cell is found to be a value, the macro loops. When the current cell is not a value, the macro quits.

```
\R    {EDIT}{HOME}@ROUND({END},2){DOWN}
      {IF @CELLPOINTER("type")="v"}{BRANCH \R}
      {QUIT}
```

With this macro entered into the RESULTS1 file, as shown here, you can go ahead and resave the file. The \R macro will be used again later in the chapter.

```
E3: '{IF @CELLPOINTER("type")="v"}{BRANCH \R}                        SHEET

     A         B         C         D         E         F         G         H
1  Test Results
2              988.6               \R        {EDIT}{HOME}@ROUND({END},2){DOWN}
3              517.44                        {IF @CELLPOINTER("type")="v"}{BRANCH \R}
4              426.59                        {QUIT}
```

Testing Commands

To look up information about commands and the arguments that they take, you can use the help feature. In SHEET or EDIT mode, you can press the HELP key (F1) and select Help Index followed by Macro Keywords to display a list of the macro commands, as shown in Figure 9-18.

Note A quick way to get to the Help Index is to press F1, then END, and then ENTER. The Help Index is the last item on all of the help screens.

Highlight the command about which you would like more information and press ENTER to get detailed help and a description of the command. For example, the {BEEP} command is about to be looked up in Figure 9-18; in Figure 9-19, you can see the results.

The {BEEP} command is a very useful one because it allows you to program sound from your computer into your macros—beeps like the ones you get when you make an error in Symphony. This is helpful when you want to alert users of your macros to

```
E2:                                                                    HELP

Command Language Keywords

Symphony's command language includes keywords with which you can build
statements. The description of each keyword shows any arguments it takes.
Square brackets ([]) indicate an argument is optional.  Uppercase and
lowercase are equivalent.  Keywords are as follow:

BEEP      FORBREAK   MENUCALL   RECALCCOL
BLANK     GET        ONERROR    RESTART
BRANCH    GETLABEL   OPEN       RETURN
BREAKOFF  GETNUMBER  PANELOFF   SETPOS
BREAKON   GETPOS     PANELON    WAIT
CLOSE     HANDSHAKE  PHONE      WINDOWSOFF
CONTENTS  IF         PUT        WINDOWSON
DEFINE    INDICATE   QUIT       WRITE
DISPATCH  LET        READ       WRITELN
FILESIZE  LOOK       READLN     ?
FOR       MENUBRANCH RECALC

Command Language Syntax          Help Index

28-Mar-91  08:56 PM                                             Num
```

FIGURE 9-18 Macro help

```
E2:                                                                    HELP

Command Language Keywords

{BEEP [number]}         Sounds computer's bell or tone. [number] specifies the
                        tone.

{BLANK location}        Erases the location.

{BRANCH location}       Macro continues at location.

{BREAKOFF}              Disables use of [BREAK] key to interrupt macro
                        execution.

{BREAKON}               Enables use of [BREAK] key to interrupt macro
                        execution.

{CLOSE}                 Closes a file that was opened with the {OPEN}
                        macro keyword.

Other Keywords          Command Language Syntax      Help Index

28-Mar-91  08:56 PM                                             Num
```

FIGURE 9-19 The {BEEP} command

errors. Another use of {BEEP} that benefits developers of macros is as a test command.

Suppose that you are testing the commands needed to loop a macro. To test the design of the earlier example of a macro that rounded a column of values, you would have to repeatedly enter a fresh series of values in a worksheet in order to experiment on them. This is easy enough to do with the Copy and Range Values commands, but some macro designs can require elaborate steps just for testing. If you use the {BEEP} command instead of an actual worksheet action, the logic of the macro is more quickly put to the test.

For example, this macro tests the {BRANCH} and {IF} commands and the @CELLPOINTER function, without altering the contents of the worksheet:

```
\B    {BEEP}{DOWN}
      {IF @CELLPOINTER("type")="b"}{QUIT}
      {BRANCH \B}
```

If you execute \B at the top of a column of values, it will beep, then move to the next cell, and beep again, unless the cell is blank. Likewise, you can use the following code to test a macro that checks for the type **v** or value. When the cell is found to be a value, the macro loops and beeps. When the current cell is not a value, the macro quits.

```
\B    {BEEP}{DOWN}
      {IF @CELLPOINTER("type")="v"}{BRANCH \B}
      {QUIT}
```

You may have noticed in Figure 9-19 that the {BEEP} command takes a tone-number argument: 1, 2, 3, or 4. The command {BEEP 1} gives a high note, whereas {BEEP 4} gives a low note. This allows you to test branches very effectively. For example, you can enter in a cell called LOW

```
{BEEP 4}{BEEP 4}{BEEP 4}
```

and then enter in a cell called HIGH

```
{BEEP 1}{BEEP 1}{BEEP 1}
```

Now you can test conditional statements and branches by using code like this:

```
{IF A1>100}{BRANCH HIGH}
{BRANCH LOW}
```

With this code, a macro can be told to perform one action if the conditional statement (in this case A1>100) is true, and a different action if it is false. Instead of having to invent actions to test your conditional statement, you can hear the result immediately. If the value of A1 is greater then 100, you will hear three high notes; otherwise, you will hear three low notes.

The Syntax of Macro Keyword Commands

The macro commands can be categorized in several ways. There are those that do not have arguments, like {QUIT}, and those that do, like {IF *condition*}. Both types include a keyword in braces. The Subroutine command is an exception, since it invokes another macro, making the name of the macro you want to use (rather than a keyword) the item that is placed in the braces, as in {\R}. The format of the non-argument commands is simply a keyword enclosed in braces. These characters are recognized as label indicators by Symphony.

The format of the commands that take arguments consists of the keyword followed by a blank space and a list of arguments separated by commas. As with @function arguments, no spaces are allowed between or within arguments. The entire statement, complete with arguments, is enclosed in the curly braces. Some commands have optional arguments. For example, the {BEEP} command can be entered as is or with a tone-number argument, as in {BEEP 3}.

A Simple but Powerful Question

In creating branched and looped macros, it is easy to overlook the simplest way to get user input in a macro: the {?} command. This pauses the macro until the user selects from the program menu, moves the cell pointer, or presses (ENTER). For example, suppose that you want a macro that formats the current cell with the percentage format. Your macro might look like this:

```
\Q /F%~~
```

However, this macro simply accepts the default decimal place setting of 2, which might not be appropriate. If you want the macro to give you the chance to select a decimal place setting, then you can use

```
\Q /F%{?}~~
```

This macro pauses at the "Enter number of decimal places" prompt. The user can then type in a suitable number. After this, the user must press (ENTER) to confirm that he or she has finished replying to the pause. Alternatively, the user can accept the default entry of 2 by pressing (ENTER) without typing anything. Pressing (ENTER) causes the macro processing to continue. Indeed, the macro will not continue until (ENTER) has been pressed. After the user presses (ENTER), the next macro instruction is carried out—in this case, the pair of tildes.

You may wonder why there are two tildes. One is to enter the user's response, the other is to confirm the range to be formatted (in this case, the current cell). You must bear in mind that the user pressing (ENTER) is responding to the {?} command, confirming that the selection has been made. The (ENTER) key must be pressed by the macro to confirm the response to Symphony. You can see this more clearly in the next example.

Suppose that you want a macro to apply a date format to a range of cells named RESULTS. You would like the macro to provide the user with a choice of formats. You can do this with a macro such as

```
\D /FD{?}~RESULTS~
```

This macro pauses at the Range Format Date menu. When the user selects a format by highlighting it and pressing (ENTER), the macro continues by applying the format command to the range called RESULTS. Note that there is a tilde after the {?} and another after the range name.

Problems can arise when you use the {?} command for menu selection. If the user selects a menu item by its first letter, the macro will not proceed. The {?} command is better for entering simple command responses, menu settings, and data. For example, you will find that {GOTO}{?}~ is useful code for getting a user response for a cell location. To prompt the user to select a range to go to from the list of names, use the following:

```
{GOTO}{MENU}{?}~
```

The addition of {MENU} means that the macro shows the user the short list of range names, together with the prompt "Enter address to go to." To save space, you can use the abbreviation for MENU:

```
{GOTO}{M}{?}~
```

You can use {?} to create a simple macro that makes an entry and moves the cell pointer down one cell. Consider this macro:

```
\Y {?}{DOWN}{BRANCH \Y}
```

When you press ALT-Y, nothing appears to happen. However, in the lower status line you can see the message "Macro," telling you that a macro is running. You type a cell entry and then press ENTER. Your entry is made at the current cell, and the cell pointer is moved to the next cell down. The macro then repeats to wait for another entry. You will need to press CTRL-BREAK followed by ESC to terminate the macro. Notice that there is no tilde in this macro, because the {DOWN} command takes care of entering what you have typed.

This type of macro was popular when keyboards did not have separate numeric and cursor movement keypads. When you have a column of numbers to enter and no separate numeric keypad, the macro can be very convenient, avoiding the use of the NUM LOCK key. You can avoid the need for this macro by judicious use of the SHIFT key. Make sure that NUM LOCK is off, then simply hold down SHIFT with your left hand, type a number with your right, release the SHIFT key, and press DOWN ARROW. The SHIFT key lets you switch between numbers and arrows without using NUM LOCK.

You can even use the {?} command for simple prompted input. You can have the macro present a message asking for input by putting a false entry on the input line. The user presses ESC to clear the message, and then types the response, as in this line of code:

```
Press Escape then type amount and press Enter{?}~
```

If users follow the instructions, the amount that they type will be entered for them.

AUTOMATIC MACROS

You can have Symphony activate a macro as soon as the file in which it is stored is retrieved. You do this with the SERVICES Settings Auto-Execute Set command. When you issue this command, Symphony asks you to specify the starting cell of the code you want executed when the file is retrieved. You can either enter a cell coordinate or a range name, such as the name of a particular macro. When you specify the code and then save the worksheet, the feature is activated. To deactivate, use the SERVICES Settings Auto-Execute Cancel command and then save the file.

The auto-execute macro works well with the Configuration Auto command, whereby a worksheet file is designated to be retrieved from disk as soon as Symphony is loaded. If you establish an auto-execute macro in a worksheet named as the Auto file, you can initiate any series of events that macros can control.

A simple application of the auto load/macro feature is to have Symphony show you a list of files every time you load the program. To do this, enter the label **{SERVICES}FR{MENU}** into cell A1 of an empty worksheet and set the cell as the auto-execute macro. Save the file as **AUTOFILE**. Then use the Configuration Auto command to name the file as the one to be retrieved on startup. Use the Configuration Update command to record this setting. The next time you load Symphony, the first thing you will see is a list of files from which to select.

THE MACRO LIBRARY MANAGER

Having seen how powerful macro command language can be, and having developed several useful macros recorded in the MACRO2 file, you are ready to use the Macro Library Manager, a very useful Symphony add-in application that allows you to share macros between worksheets.

Macro Limits

When you apply macros to real worksheets, you will invariably develop and use favorite macros—macros that you like to use all the time. You will find that having to recreate the macros you want in each new file is cumbersome. Earlier, you saw how you could extract macros to a separate file, but there is no method of accumulating macros in a separate file that can be used at any time, without disturbing the current worksheet—unless you attach the Macro Library Manager. This application allows you to copy macros from current worksheets into a special file, called a *macro library*. The file can be loaded "in the background" while you are using other worksheets, and you can execute any macros that are in the library.

Attaching the Macro Library Manager

To attach the Macro Library Manager, you use the SERVICES Application Attach command and select the MACROMGR.APP file. This creates an extra item, called Macros, at the end of the SERVICES menu. To make sure that the Macro Library Manager is always attached when you load Symphony, use SERVICES Configuration Other Application Set and assign the file called MACROMGR.APP to one of the auto-load slots. Use the Yes option of the Auto-Invoke feature if you want to load macros whenever you start a Symphony session. Remember to use SERVICES Configuration Update to record your application choices.

Using the Macro Library Manager

The Macro Library Manager is operated by means of the menu you see here:

```
Copy macro library from disk to memory                                         MENU
Load  Save  Edit  Remove  Name-List  Quit
  ------A---------B---------C---------D---------E---------F---------G---------H------
1
2
3
4
5
```

This menu appears whenever you

- Attach the Macro Library Manager and then select Macros from the SERVICES menu
- Attach the Macro Library Manager and then select MACROMGR.APP from the list of attached applications, after issuing the Invoke command from the SERVICES Application menu
- Load Symphony with the Macro Library Manager configured as an Auto-Invoke Application

Before you can load a macro library, you must create one. To create a macro library you do the following, after attaching the Macro Library Manager:

1. Retrieve a worksheet in which you have created useful macros—for example, the MACRO2 worksheet you created earlier in this chapter, shown in Figure 9-20.
2. Press SERVICES and select Macros. Select Save. Enter a name for the library file, such as **MYLIB1**. Symphony will automatically add the extension MLB.
3. Now select the range of cells that contain the macros you want stored in the library. This range should include descriptions and any cells needed for the macros to execute—in this case, A1..G19.

```
A1: '\T                                                              SHEET

   ----A--------B------------C---------D--------E--------F--------G----
1  \T          @NOW~           Enters @NOW              ANSWER   y
2              /FD4~           Formats with D4
3              {GETLABEL "Convert @NOW to a fixed date (Y/N)? ",ANSWER}
4              {IF ANSWER="N"}{QUIT}
5              {BRANCH \V}     Uses \V to fix value
6
7  \W          /WS{RIGHT}~     Widens column 1 character
8
9
10 \N          /WS{LEFT}~      Narrows column 1 character
11
12
13 \S          {SERVICES}f~~y  Saves file over old
14
15
16 \V          {EDIT}{CALC}~   Fixes current cell value
17
18
19 \E          /E~/FR~         Empties current cell and resets format
20
                                                                   MAIN
29-Mar-91  11:59 AM                                          Num
```

FIGURE 9-20 The MACRO2 file

4. Symphony asks if you want to use a password to lock the library. If you select Yes, you must type the password and press (ENTER) (you will have to use this password when loading the library file). If you select No, Symphony proceeds immediately to the next step, moving the macros out of the current worksheet into the library file.

You are left with an empty space in the current worksheet. A copy of the macro code is now stored in the file MYLIB1.MLB. To retain the macros in the MACRO2 file as well, simply do not resave the altered worksheet using the MACRO2 name.

When you create a library file, it is immediately active. You can test this by pressing (ALT-T) in a fresh worksheet. The macro will run immediately. However, the next time you load Symphony you will need to load the library file for it to be active. To do this, you first attach the Library Manager, and then choose Load from the Library Manager menu. Select the library file you want to load from the list provided. You can create any number of different libraries if you like; perhaps one for each different type of Symphony work.

If you find that you have loaded the wrong library file, you can simply load a different library to replace the currently loaded one. Alternatively, you can remove the currently loaded library from memory using the Remove command from the Macro Library menu.

If you need to alter macros that are in a library, you can edit them in any current worksheet. Select the Edit command from the Macro Library menu and designate a free area of the worksheet into which Symphony can place the contents of the library file. You can then edit the macros and return them to the library with the Save command. To check which macros are in a library file without editing them, use the Name-List command. This produces a list of the library macros in the current worksheet.

Expanding the Library

One of the big advantages of the Macro Library Manager is that you can keep adding macros. Suppose you want to add the looping macro, the one you created in the RESULTS1 file, to the macro library. You would follow these steps:

1. Retrieve the RESULTS1 file. Press (END) and (HOME) to move the cell pointer away from the rest of the cell entries. This will probably be cell E18.

2. Press SERVICES, select Macros, and choose Edit. Select the MYLIB1 file. Enter the password if you have used one. Select Overwrite to preserve the range names in the library. Press (ENTER) to read in the library entries at the current cell. The results appear in Figure 9-21.

```
E18: '\T                                                                  SHEET
   A          B          C          D          E          F          G          H
1  Test Results
2              988.6              \R         {EDIT}{HOME}@ROUND({END},2){DOWN}
3              517.44                        {IF @CELLPOINTER("type")="v"}{BRANCH \R}
4              426.59                        {QUIT}
5               40.59
6              643.27
7              720.04
8              986.81
9              188.03
10             399.03
11             181.42
12             339.78
13             469.21
14             716.88
15             844.53
16             274.62
17             356.25
18             742.45                        \T         @NOW~      Enters @NOW
19                                                      /FD4~      Formats with D4
20                                                      {GETLABEL "Convert @NOW to a fix
                                                                                   MAIN
29-Mar-91  01:05 PM                                                          Num
```

FIGURE 9-21 The library entries

3. Move the cell pointer to D2, where the \R macro is entered. Use MENU Move to move cells D2..E4 to an area below the library macros—say, E39—as shown in Figure 9-22.

4. Now you can return the complete set of macros to the library file. Press SERVICES, select Macros Save, and choose MYLIB1.MLB. Choose Yes to replace the old version with the new. Select E18..L41 as the range (that is, all of the macro code, including \R).

5. If you want to use a password, select Yes and enter the word; otherwise, choose No. The macro library file now contains the \R macro.

If you would still like to keep the \R macro in the RESULTS1 worksheet, you can simply select New from the SERVICES menu. This will mean that the RESULTS1 file on disk is not changed.

```
E39: '\R                                                        SHEET
┌──────E─────────F─────────G─────────H─────────I─────────J─────────K─────────L──────┐
24  \W        /WS{RIGHTWidens column 1 character
25
26
27  \N        /WS{LEFT}Narrows column 1 character
28
29
30  \S        {SERVICESSaves file over old
31
32
33  \V        {EDIT}{CAFixes current cell value
34
35
36  \E        /E~/FR~  Empties current cell and resets format
37
38
39  \R        {EDIT}{HOME}@ROUND({END},2){DOWN}
40            {IF @CELLPOINTER("type")="v"}{BRANCH \R}
41            {QUIT}
42
43
└──────────────────────────────────────────────────────────────────────────────MAIN┘
29-Mar-91  01:34 PM                                               Num
```

FIGURE 9-22 The \R macro moved

However, a macro in the currently loaded library that has the same name as a macro in the current worksheet takes precedence. You can use macros in the current worksheet that have different names from those in the library.

The Macro Library Manager gives you the welcome ability to keep all related macros in the same place, accessible across different worksheets.

MENUS CREATED BY MACROS

The one aspect of macros that you have not yet explored is one of the most popular: creating customized menus within a spreadsheet to simplify its operation, either for yourself or for other users. You can place macro menus in macro libraries to make them available in any worksheet. At the top of Figure 9-23, you can see a menu that is activated by pressing ALT-M. This macro-generated menu

```
Saves the file                                                             MENU
Save  Widen   Narrow  Quit
 ---------A-----------B----------------C----------------D----------------E-------
17
18
19
20
21  MACMEN   Save               Widen            Narrow           Quit
22           Saves the file     Widens column    Narrows column   Exit macro menu
23           {BRANCH \S}        {BRANCH \W}      {BRANCH \N}      {QUIT}
24
25
26
27  \M       {MENUBRANCH MACMEN}
28
29
30
31
32
33
34
35
36
                                                                          MAIN
29-Mar-91  01:31 PM                              Macro                Num
```

FIGURE 9-23 Sample macro menu

offers the user a choice between some of the macros designed earlier in the MACRO2 file.

Menu Types

Before experimenting with macro-generated menus, it is important to understand that there are two types of menus in Symphony: menus you create with macros, and program menus that you access with the SERVICES and MENU keys. The program menus cannot be modified, except by add-in applications. They always remain constant between worksheets. The macro menus you create with the {MENUBRANCH} command shown in Figure 9-23 and the alternative keyword {MENUCALL} consist of a series of macro instructions in consecutive columns and are created in worksheets. They can be shared by making the worksheet that contains them into a macro library, but the library must be loaded for them to work, and they do not become part of the program menu system.

Writing Macro Menus

Macro-generated menus appear on screen in the same format as regular Symphony menus, with a horizontal list of options followed by descriptions of the options on the next line. You can browse through these items by moving the highlighting across the list, noting the corresponding description on the second line. You can select an item by pressing (ENTER) when it is highlighted or by using the first-letter method of selection. To let you know that you are still in the middle of a macro, not in a Symphony menu, the program displays a "Macro" message at the bottom of the screen.

When the user selects one of the items on the menu in Figure 9-23, macro commands are activated to carry out the item. You can easily create such a menu in your MACRO2 worksheet. All of the instructions that make up the menu macro in Figure 9-23 can be seen in the figure, except for the macros called by the menu choices (/S, /W, and /N).

Each menu item is arranged as a separate column, with the columns contiguous, listing the parts of the menu on consecutive rows. The first row is the name of the item as it is to appear on the menu. Each menu item at the same level should begin with a different first letter if you want to be able to use the first-letter method of picking them.

The length of menu items depends upon several factors. The total length cannot exceed 240 characters, but the limits of your screen, even in high-resolution mode, will make a menu of more than about 12 items a difficult thing to navigate. Symphony will automatically place two spaces between each item when the menu is displayed to help the user distinguish items. Although the standard spacing between menu items is two spaces, you can increase this by adding trailing spaces to the labels that make up the menu item names.

You can use whatever style you like for the menu item names. For example, regular Symphony menus use initial capitals and single words for most items. When two words are needed, as in Col-Width, abbreviation and hyphenation are used. You can also use an underline, as in Print_table. In fact, there is nothing to stop you from using two words for a menu item with a space between them, but this can make some menu items hard to read.

The second line of each menu item is the explanation of the item that appears when the item is highlighted. Longer descriptions are generally more helpful, but they are difficult to display in their entirety in the contiguous columns of the menu layout. Just as menu item names can be up to 240 characters long, so can explanation lines, but you will not be able to read the explanation if it is wider than your screen (the standard display is 80 characters wide). In normal practice you would make the menu name brief, the explanation lengthier.

Below the explanation text are the macro commands that are executed when an item is chosen. To refer to a menu like this in a {MENUBRANCH} command, the top left cell of the menu is named—in this case, B21. You can see from Figure 9-23 that the placement of macros in adjacent columns stipulated by the menu macro-command syntax could make it difficult to see all of the commands on a given line, particularly if you could not widen the columns. However, this is not a problem for the execution of the macro, since Symphony does not care if the entire command is visible.

Macro Menu Control

When the user selects any one of the menu items in the example in Figure 9-23, the commands beneath that item are executed and then the macro is over. Symphony returns to SHEET mode. An alternative to returning to SHEET mode would be to refer the macro back to the menu for more choices. You would accomplish this with the command

```
{MENUBRANCH MACMEN}
```

at the bottom of each item. If you take this approach, you will probably want to include one option that does not branch back to the menu; for example, a Quit Menu item.

Another command, {MENUCALL}, can bring up a menu, but it differs from the {MENUBRANCH} command in that the flow of the macro returns to the macro that issues the {MENUCALL} argument after the actions in the menu have been completed. The {MENUBRANCH} command passes control of the macro to the menu that is called. The {MENUCALL} command can reduce the repetition of macro code and help keep the user within the menu structure.

Macro menus offer considerable power when you want to simplify operations for novice users, or even to make life simpler for your own operation. Using macro menus, you can extend the menu-driven operation of Symphony to all types of custom operation.

SUMMARY

The macro facilities in Symphony provide you with a lot of opportunities to both speed up and simplify your work. Although you may find them difficult at first, macros quickly become a familiar tool, and you can explore the macro command language to write increasingly sophisticated macro code. Remember these points as you work with macros:

- Use Learn to record basic macros.

- Use labels to name macros and to explain them.

- Test all macros and save the worksheet before testing.
- Build macros in sections, testing each part as you go.
- Use macro key names and macro keywords to enhance basic macros.
- Use STEP mode to debug macros.
- Use the Macro Library Manager to organize macros.

10

@BASE AND ADVANCED DATA COMMANDS

This chapter explores some of the more advanced commands for manipulating data in Symphony: the What-If command for creating result tables and cross-tabulations; the Statistical Analysis add-in for performing distributions, regression, and matrix arithmetic; and Query Parse. There are examples of passing data from text files into Symphony and exporting data from Symphony by printing to disk. However, the main focus of the chapter is the @BASE add-in, which gives you the ability to work with large dBASE type data files from within Symphony.

DATA TABLES

Sometimes referred to as "what-if tables" or "result tables," *data tables* are columns and rows of possible results for one or more formulas in a worksheet. For example, when making projections, you often want to experiment with values to see what different actions will result in. This is called *what-if analysis*. After you have established the formulas that relate the different cells in a worksheet, you can change the numbers upon which the formulas are based. For example, you can set up a worksheet to calculate sales for the next 12 months based on a starting volume of 2000 units, increasing at 5% per month. By adding up the sales for the year, you can see what kinds of sales are possible with a 9% growth rate starting at 2000 units. By changing the starting figure, you can calculate sales beginning at 2500 instead of 2000. Then you might want to create a table of total sales achieved by different starting numbers. Such a table is sometimes referred to as a *one-way data table,* the list of results obtained from varying one factor in a calculation. You could create a two-way data table by varying both the beginning figure and the rate of growth. This kind of what-if analysis can be automated to a certain extent by using the Range What-If command. Using multiple worksheets you can even establish three-way data tables.

A One-Way Data Table Example

Suppose you are thinking of buying a car. You know that the amount you need to finance is $7000. The number of monthly payments you want to make is 36. Your bank has quoted 9.00% A.P.R. as a rate of interest on the loan, but the bank will take several days to complete the paper work. The car dealer is offering

```
B5: (C2) @ROUND(@PMT(7000,B2/12,36),2)                                    SHEET

 ---------A-----------B------------C------------D-----------E------------
1   Automobile Loan
2   Annual Interest         12.00%     <Input 1
3
4
5                        $232.50
6
7
8
9
10
```

FIGURE 10-1 Automobile loan worksheet

immediate financing at 12.00%, or at 14.00% with a $100.00 cash rebate. You want to compare the monthly payments. Using the worksheet in Figure 10-1, you can quickly create a one-way data table to show how the amount of the loan payment will vary based upon the interest rate. You can then tell what effect a higher interest rate will have on your monthly payments.

The spreadsheet shown in Figure 10-1 initially performs a simple payment calculation with the @PMT function in cell B5. Cell C2 is labeled Input 1 in preparation for creating a data table. To create the spreadsheet, follow these steps:

1. Starting with a new worksheet, you want to widen the columns. Press MENU and select Settings. Choose Width and type **15**. Then press (ENTER).

2. Enter the label **Automobile Loan** in A1 and the label **Annual Interest** in A2.

3. In B2, you want to enter 12%. You do this by typing **12** and then typing the percent sign. When you press (ENTER), Symphony divides 12 by 100 for you. The cell now contains .12. Press MENU, select Format, and then select %. Press (ENTER) twice to format B2 with 2 decimal places.

4. In C2 you can, enter the **""<Input 1**, although this is not required by the What-If command

5. In B5, enter the formula

   @ROUND(@PMT(7000,B2/12,36),2)

   Format the cell as Currency with 2 decimal places.

Symphony will calculate a table of results from the formula in cell B5 by feeding a series of values into the input cell, B2, and placing into the worksheet the result for each of the values produced by the formula in B5. Suppose that you have seen interest rates quoted from 9% to 14%. Values from .09 through .14 will be the input values, or variable values, for the table.

To set up a one-way table from the worksheet in Figure 10-1, you need to enter the varying percentages in column A. You can do this with the Range Fill command. Use A6..A11 as the fill range, .09 as the start value, .01 as the step value, and either .14 or a greater number as the stop value. Then you can format the numbers with the Format % command, to 2 decimal places.

When you select What-If from the Range menu, you have three choices: 1-Way, 2-Way, and Reset. In Figure 10-2, the Range What-If 1-Way command has been issued. Symphony is prompting you to enter the table range. As you can see, the table range is a rectangle that includes the formula whose results will fill the table, plus the column of varying values that will be fed into the formula. The blank cells in column B are where the results will be placed. Cell A5 will remain empty.

The Range What-If Table 1 command says "Replace the value in the input cell with values from the cells on the left edge of the table." This is what is needed to see the loan payment calculated for each rate of interest. When the table range has been entered, the program prompts you to enter input cell 1, meaning "Into which

```
Table range: A5..B11                                               POINT

  ──────A──────────────B──────────────C──────────────D─────────E──────
1   Automobile Loan
2   Annual Interest        12.00%      <Input 1
3
4
5                        $232.50
6              9.00%
7             10.00%
8             11.00%
9             12.00%
10            13.00%
11            14.00%
12
13
14
15
16
17
18
19
20
                                                                  MAIN
Range What-If 1-Way                                          Num
```

FIGURE 10-2 Entering table range for one-way table

cell do you want to read the values from the left column of the data table?" In this case, the Interest cell, B2, is the input cell, as shown here:

When you have confirmed input cell 1, the results are tabulated.

```
Input cell 1: B2                                                   POINT

  ──────A──────────────B──────────────C──────────────D─────────E──────
1   Automobile Loan
2   Annual Interest        12.00%      <Input 1
3
4
5                        $232.50
6              9.00%
7             10.00%
```

Symphony feeds each of the values from column A into cell B2 and reads the resulting answers from B5 into the table, creating the output shown in Figure 10-3. (Note that cells B6 through B11 are not automatically formatted by Symphony; the Format Currency

```
A5:                                                              SHEET

      A                    B                C                D          E
1   Automobile Loan
2   Annual Interest           12.00%        <Input 1
3
4
5                            $232.50
6              9.00%         $222.60
7             10.00%         $225.87
8             11.00%         $229.17
9             12.00%         $232.50
10            13.00%         $235.86
11            14.00%         $239.24
```

FIGURE 10-3 Results of Range What-If 1-Way command

command was applied to B6..B11 to improve the table's appearance.) You can see that a 9.00% loan saves you about $10 per month over a 12.00% loan, a savings of some $360 over the 36-month loan term. A 14.00% loan costs $6.74 per month more than a 12.00% loan, a total of $242.64 over the 36-month term of the loan.

Note: You can use Symphony as a calculator without entering figures in the worksheet. With the cell pointer in any cell, type the calculation, such as **239.24–232.5**, and press (F8). The result appears on the edit line. Do not press (ENTER). Either press (ESC) to clear the edit line or type more calculations, such as ***36**, followed by (F8). Press (ESC) twice to return to SHEET mode.

Using the One-Way Table

The output in cells B6..B11 of Figure 10-3 consists of numbers, not formulas, so it is not interactive. Changing the terms of the loan on the spreadsheet would not cause any immediate change in the cells of the data table. You must repeat the Range What-If command to take into account changes in the model. For example, if

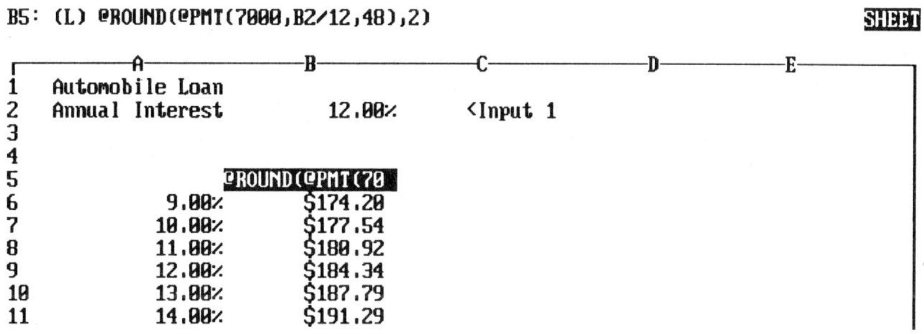

FIGURE 10-4 Updated table

you decided you wanted 48 monthly payments, you would alter the formula in cell B5 to

@ROUND(@PMT(7000,B2/12,48),2)

You would then press MENU, select Range What-If 1-Way, and repeat the settings, which Symphony retains, simply by pressing (ENTER). The table would be recalculated. The results in this case are shown in Figure 10-4, where cell B5 has been formatted in the Other Literal format to show the formula. As you can see, a data table is a very quick way to perform a repetitive series of calculations and list the results.

You can use a one-way table to produce the results of more than one formula just by adding the formulas to the right of the first one on the same row. When you include cell C5 in the table range in Figure 10-5, you can see the payments for a loan based on $8000 borrowed, as well as for $7000, based on interest rates from 9.00% to 14.00%.

As you can see, what defines a data table as "one-way" is the fact that only one factor is changed by the command. In other words, there is only one input cell. In a moment, you will look at using two input cells.

```
C5: (L) @ROUND(@PMT(8000,B2/12,48),2)                                    SHEET

   ----------A---------------B---------------C---------------D---------------E---
1  Automobile Loan
2  Annual Interest           12.00%          <Input 1
3
4
5                       @ROUND(@PMT(70 @ROUND(@PMT(80
6              9.00%     $174.20          $199.08
7             10.00%     $177.54          $202.90
8             11.00%     $180.92          $206.76
9             12.00%     $184.34          $210.67
10            13.00%     $187.79          $214.62
11            14.00%     $191.29          $218.61
```

FIGURE 10-5 Added formula in a one-way table

Data Tables and Databases

There is no getting around the fact that the term "data" is overused. The difference between a data table of results and a database of fields and records is fairly clear, but the two terms tend to get muddled when you look at using the data table commands to analyze a database. To recap, the terms are as follows:

- Data: Pieces of information.
- Database: Generic term for a collection of data organized in a meaningful way, and the Symphony term for a collection of data organized in a meaningful way in the columns and rows of a Symphony worksheet or in an external program.
- Data Table: A table of results in a Symphony worksheet from a calculation based on a range of input values.

When you apply data tables to databases, you can perform what is sometimes referred to as *cross-tabulation.* A table of results summarizes information according to categories that you specify. Consider the small collection of information in the top half of Figure 10-6. This is a list of customers that shows the state they

D16: (P2) @DSUM(A3..G13,4,A15..A16) SHEET

	A	B	C	D	E	F	G
1	Customer Database						
2							
3	Customer	Last	State	Model	Total	Ordered	Shipped
4	10005	Robinson	TX	Royal	$69.95	04/13/90	04/17/90
5	10004	Shovestull	IL	Royal	$69.95	04/13/90	04/24/90
6	10006	Lausterer	CA	Aristo	$105.73	04/15/90	04/27/90
7	10007	Ward	NY	Royal	$69.95	04/19/90	05/01/90
8	10009	Profenna	FL	Majestic	$49.95	04/21/90	05/02/90
9	10008	Depew	NY	Supreme	$359.80	04/21/90	05/03/90
10	10010	Morgan	PA	Aristo	$119.70	04/23/90	04/26/90
11	10011	Spensley	TN	Noble	$59.95	04/26/90	05/08/90
12	10012	Herring	TX	Noble	$419.65	05/01/90	05/05/90
13	10012	Herring	TX	Imperial	$39.95	05/04/90	05/14/90
14							
15	State			Total Sales			
16				1,364.58			
17			IL	69.95			
18			CA	105.73			
19			TX	529.55			
20			TN	59.95			

MAIN

30-Mar-91 06:38 PM Num

FIGURE 10-6 Sample database

are from, the model they ordered, the total amount they paid, and order/ship dates. Suppose you want to see the total sales broken down by state. You can do this with a one-way data table, as shown in the lower half of Figure 10-6.

Performing Cross-Tabulation

To perform the cross-tabulation seen in Figure 10-6, you need to set up a one-way data table consisting of a range of input values and a formula. The formula uses a database @function, @DSUM. The database functions take three arguments: the location of the database table containing the information to be cross-tabulated; the column of the table that will be the subject of the cross- tabulation (for example, the Total column); and the location of the cells used to specify the criteria. You can see the three arguments entered in the formula in cell D16 of Figure 10-6. The first argument is

A3..G13, the location of the database table. The second argument is 4, meaning column 4. Remember that the first column of the table is column 0, so 4 means column E in this case. The third argument is cells A15 and A16, the location of the criteria for the cross-tabulation.

You can see from Figure 10-6 that the only entry in the range A15..A16 is State. This is the name of the field that is the category by which the data is to be cross-tabulated—in this case, the State column. The cell below the word "State" is empty. This is actually the input cell; when the data table calculation is performed, Symphony will feed the state codes from the data table into cell A16. Thus, cell D17 is the result of the @DSUM function when cell A16 contains the state code IL, cell D18 is the result of the @DSUM function when cell A16 contains the code CA, and so on.

When you enter the formula that is the basis of your cross-tabulation, you place it at the top of the column where you want the results displayed—in this case, D16. The cell displays the result of calculating @DSUM with a blank criteria, which is actually the total sales for all states in the database table, since a blank criteria cell means "Include everything." In the column to the left of the formula, you enter the items you want to be fed into the criteria range. In this example, total sales are calculated for just four states, designated by the codes IL, CA, TX, and TN. These codes are in cells C17 through C20. After making sure that the criteria range is set up, either by using an existing criteria range or by creating a new one for the cross-tabulation, you can proceed to define the various elements with the Range What-If command.

From the Range What-If menu, you select 1-Way. You are prompted for the table range, which includes the formula and the column of input values, shown in this case in Figure 10-7. After the table range is defined, you are prompted for input cell 1, which is A16. When this is entered, the results are calculated. Symphony feeds the input values into the input cell and places the results of the formula into cells D17 through D20, as shown earlier in Figure

```
Table range: C16..D20                                                    POINT
┌─────A─────────B──────────C─────────D─────────E──────────F──────────G──────────┐
1   Customer Database
2
3   Customer Last        State  Model     Total    Ordered    Shipped
4      10005 Robinson    TX     Royal     $69.95   04/13/90   04/17/90
5      10004 Shovestull  IL     Royal     $69.95   04/13/90   04/24/90
6      10006 Lausterer   CA     Aristo   $105.73   04/15/90   04/27/90
7      10007 Ward        NY     Royal     $69.95   04/19/90   05/01/90
8      10009 Profenna    FL     Majestic  $49.95   04/21/90   05/02/90
9      10008 Depew       NY     Supreme  $359.80   04/21/90   05/03/90
10     10010 Morgan      PA     Aristo   $119.70   04/23/90   04/26/90
11     10011 Spensley    TN     Noble     $59.95   04/26/90   05/08/90
12     10012 Herring     TX     Noble    $419.65   05/01/90   05/05/90
13     10012 Herring     TX     Imperial  $39.95   05/04/90   05/14/90
14
15  State                       Total Sales
16                              1,364.58
17                       IL
18                       CA
19                       TX
20                       TN
└═══════════════════════════════════════════════════════════════════════MAIN┘
Range What-If 1-Way                                                   Num
```

FIGURE 10-7 Defining the table range

10-6. Note that database-related tables usually take longer to calculate than tables based on other types of calculations.

The label "Total Sales" in cell D15 is purely cosmetic, intended to describe the entries below. You could use the Format Other Hidden command to remove the formula in D16 from view. The results of a data table command can be used for a variety of reporting and analytical purposes. For example, the results in Figure 10-6 could be sorted, together with the input values, to show a table of sales by state ranked from highest to lowest. Note that the input values do not need to be in any special order.

You can use the other database functions with data tables. For example, suppose that you want to see the average of sales for the four states. You would change the @DSUM formula in D16 to @DAVG.The results are shown in Figure 10-8. Remember that changing the formula in D16, or the input values in C17..C20, does not alter the results in the cross-tabulation table until the Range What-If command is repeated. Also note that the Hidden format

```
D16: (H) @DAVG(A3..G13,4,A15..A16)                                     SHEET

     A          B          C       D          E          F          G
1   Customer Database
2
3   Customer Last          State  Model      Total    Ordered     Shipped
4      10005 Robinson      TX     Royal      $69.95    04/13/90    04/17/90
5      10004 Shovestull    IL     Royal      $69.95    04/13/90    04/24/90
6      10006 Lausterer     CA     Aristo    $105.73    04/15/90    04/27/90
7      10007 Ward          NY     Royal      $69.95    04/19/90    05/01/90
8      10009 Profenna      FL     Majestic   $49.95    04/21/90    05/02/90
9      10008 Depew         NY     Supreme   $359.80    04/21/90    05/03/90
10     10010 Morgan        PA     Aristo    $119.70    04/23/90    04/26/90
11     10011 Spensley      TN     Noble      $59.95    04/26/90    05/08/90
12     10012 Herring       TX     Noble     $419.65    05/01/90    05/05/90
13     10012 Herring       TX     Imperial   $39.95    05/04/90    05/14/90
14
15  State                         Avg Sales
16
17                         IL         69.95
18                         CA        105.73
19                         TX        176.52
20                         TN         59.95
                                                                        MAIN
30-Mar-91  06:44 PM                                              Num
```

FIGURE 10-8 Results with @DAVG

has been applied to the formula cell to make the table more attractive.

As with the earlier example of a loan payment table, you can add additional formulas to a one-way data table, placing them in the cells to the right of the first formula. Thus, you could enter the @DSUM formula in cell D16, the @DAVG formula in cell E16, and so on. Remember to alter the data table range to include the new formulas.

Two-Way What-If Calculations

There are times when you want to vary more than one value in a calculation. In Figure 10-5, for example, you saw a payment table with varying rates of interest used as the input values. A second formula was added to the one-way table to calculate payments based on a different principal amount. Adding formulas to a one-

```
A5: (C2) @ROUND(@PMT(B1,B2/12,B3),2)                                  SHEET

          A                  B               C               D          E
1   Amount Financed     $5,000.00
2   Annual Interest        12.00%      <Input 1
3   Number of Pymts            36      <Input 2
4
5           $166.07            24             36             48         60
6             9.00%       $228.42        $159.00        $124.43    $103.79
7            10.00%       $230.72        $161.34        $126.81    $106.24
8            11.00%       $233.04        $163.69        $129.23    $108.71
9            12.00%       $235.37        $166.07        $131.67    $111.22
10           13.00%       $237.71        $168.47        $134.14    $113.77
11           14.00%       $240.06        $170.89        $136.63    $116.34
12
13
14
15
16
17
18
19
20
                                                                       MAIN
30-Mar-91  06:52 PM                                               Num
```

FIGURE 10-9 Two-way data table

way table is one way to accommodate more than one variable. A cleaner approach is to use a two-way data table, an example of which is shown in Figure 10-9. This table shows the payments on the loan based on a variety of interest rates and four different payment terms. The table varies both the interest in B2 and the term in B3. The formula that is being calculated by the Range What-If command is entered in A5.

The two-way data table operation is performed by first setting the interest rates down a column that will be the left side of the data table—in this case, column A. These will be the first input values. Next, the terms of the loan, which will be the second input value, are entered across the row that will be the top of the data table. The Range What-If 2-Way command is then selected. The table is defined as the range formed by the column of variables and the row of variables—A5 through E11, in this case. You are then prompted for input cell 1, which is the interest rate in B2. This is the cell that will be fed with values from column A. Finally, you

A6: (H) +B4 SHEET

	A	B	C	D	E
1	Amount Financed	$5,000.00			
2	Annual Interest	12.00%	<Input 1		
3	Number of Pymts	36	<Input 2		
4	Monthly Payment	$166.07			
5					
6		24	36	48	60
7	9.00%	$228.42	$159.00	$124.43	$103.79
8	10.00%	$230.72	$161.34	$126.81	$106.24
9	11.00%	$233.04	$163.69	$129.23	$108.71
10	12.00%	$235.37	$166.07	$131.67	$111.22
11	13.00%	$237.71	$168.47	$134.14	$113.77
12	14.00%	$240.06	$170.89	$136.63	$116.34

FIGURE 10-10 Relocated formula

are prompted for input cell 2, the term, which is in cell B3. The results are then created by Symphony, as seen in Figure 10-9.

You can use this table to decide what terms are best suited to your budget. You could easily produce a different table with various prices and interest rates to see how expensive a car you could afford to finance. Also, you could move the formula from cell A5 to a more suitable location. For example, in Figure 10-10, you can see the payment formula more logically located at B4 and an extra row added. What you now have in cell A6, which must be the formula supplied to the Range What-If 2-Way command, is actually a simple cell reference formula, +B4. Symphony can still perform the payment calculation through this reference to the formula that is now in B4. In Figure 10-10, cell A6 has been formatted as Hidden, making the table more attractive.

You use the Range What-If Reset command to clear the current settings for the data table and input cells. Remember, the data table is not interactive and will not be updated when you change other factors in the model. You must reissue the Range What-If command to update the table.

```
C16: (H) @DSUM(A3..G13,4,A15..B16)                                          SHEET

      A          B          C        D          E          F          G
1   Customer Database
2
3   Customer Last       State  Model      Total      Ordered     Shipped
4      10005 Robinson   TX     Royal       $69.95    04/13/90    04/17/90
5      10004 Shovestull IL     Royal       $69.95    04/13/90    04/24/90
6      10006 Lausterer  CA     Aristo     $105.73    04/15/90    04/27/90
7      10007 Ward       NY     Royal       $69.95    04/19/90    05/01/90
8      10009 Profenna   FL     Majestic    $49.95    04/21/90    05/02/90
9      10008 Depew      NY     Supreme    $359.80    04/21/90    05/03/90
10     10010 Morgan     PA     Aristo     $119.70    04/23/90    04/26/90
11     10011 Spensley   TN     Noble       $59.95    04/26/90    05/08/90
12     10012 Herring    TX     Noble      $419.65    05/01/90    05/05/90
13     10012 Herring    TX     Imperial    $39.95    05/04/90    05/14/90
14
15  State      Model
16                             Royal      Aristo     Noble
17                      IL       $69.95      $0.00       $0.00
18                      CA        $0.00    $105.73       $0.00
19                      TX       $69.95      $0.00     $419.65
20                      TN        $0.00      $0.00      $59.95
                                                                            MAIN
30-Mar-91  07:02 PM                                                     Num
```

FIGURE 10-11 Two-way cross-tabulation

Two-Way Tabulations

The two-way data table can be applied to cross-tabulations in which a second criterion or category is required. For example, when you want total sales broken down by state and then by model, you have two categories to deal with, State and Model. By expanding the criteria range used by the @DSUM formula, seen earlier in Figure 10-6, you can accommodate both categories.

In Figure 10-11, you can see a two-way cross-tabulation. The formula in C16 refers to the database table in A3..G13, column E (signified by 4), and the criteria range which is now expanded to A15..B16 to include the Model field. The first input cell is A16. Into this cell Symphony will feed the values from C17 through C20. The second input cell is B16, into which will be fed the values in D16..F16. Note that the formula in cell C16 has been formatted with the Hidden format to disguise the formula entry in the table.

Although they can sometimes take several minutes to generate, two-way cross-tabulation tables are very valuable, especially when creating reports. You can produce summary tables that give a clearer picture of large collections of data. In many cases the input values used in the table help to document the table of results. In the example in Figure 10-11, you would only need to add a title for the table to be completed and ready for printing. If you create a two-way table and do not get the results you expect, such as the same value for each result, check that you have expanded the criteria range in the database function statement to include the second field.

TEXT FILES

In Chapter 8, you saw that the Translate program offered a way to transfer words and numbers from Symphony to other programs that cannot read worksheet files directly. In fact, there are some programs that cannot read any of the formats that the Translate program can produce. To transfer data to such programs, you can create a special type of file called a text file, using the Print command. Just about any program can read files that are stored in ASCII, the American Standard Code for Information Interchange. One reason that programs read information stored this way is that they communicate with printers in ASCII. Printers receive the letters and numbers of your documents as ASCII characters. In fact, that is how Symphony sends your worksheet to the printer. By diverting data intended for the printer to a file on disk, you can create an ASCII file, or print file, of worksheet data.

A Print File Example

Symphony creates ASCII files through the Print command using File as the Destination setting. This changes the target of the print range from the printer to a file. The file has the extension PRN to

A1: 'Sales of Ohmobile Vehicles in January SHEET

	A	B	C	D	E	F	G	H
1	Sales of Ohmobile Vehicles in January							
2								
3	Invoice	Model	Net	Auto	Power	Solar	Stereo	Private
4	1101	Truck	$13,309.54	N	Y	N	Y	N
5	1102	Truck	$11,576.23	N	N	Y	Y	N
6	1103	Truck	$10,186.80	N	Y	Y	N	N
7	1104	Truck	$11,584.95	Y	Y	N	Y	N
8	1105	Truck	$9,422.75	Y	N	Y	N	Y
9	1106	Truck	$11,261.24	N	N	Y	Y	N
10	1107	Car	$12,917.42	N	N	Y	Y	N
11	1108	Truck	$12,711.20	Y	N	Y	N	Y
12	1109	Car	$9,938.54	N	N	Y	N	N
13	1110	Car	$11,005.45	Y	N	N	N	N
14	1111	Car	$11,070.67	N	Y	N	N	N
15	1112	Car	$9,207.90	Y	N	Y	N	Y
16	1113	Truck	$10,500.10	Y	N	Y	Y	Y
17	1114	Truck	$11,694.81	N	N	Y	N	Y
18	1115	Truck	$12,932.23	N	Y	N	N	Y
19	1116	Truck	$13,445.28	N	Y	Y	N	N
20	1117	Truck	$13,162.39	N	Y	N	N	Y

MAIN

31-Mar-91 09:45 AM Num

FIGURE 10-12 Sales statistics

distinguish it from other files. The data in the file is simply strings of letters, numbers, and spaces. Formulas are converted to their values and the values become text, including any formatting such as the dollar signs of the Currency format.

Suppose that you have used Symphony to prepare a database like that in Figure 10-12, and you want to use it in an accounting program. Retyping the numbers from Symphony into the accounting program would be a chore, and errors could arise from inaccurate typing. Instead, you decide to export the figures as an ASCII file. To create the worksheet seen in Figure 10-12, which will be used in several of the examples in this chapter, follow these steps:

1. In a fresh worksheet, enter the label **Sales of Ohmobile Vehicles in January** in cell A1.

2. In A3, enter the label **Invoice** and enter the other labels across row 3: **Model, Net, Auto, Power, Solar, Stereo, Private**.

3. Press MENU and select Range Label-Alignment, followed by Center. Select A3..H3 as the range of labels, and press (ENTER).

4. To create the invoice number, place the cell pointer in A4 and press MENU. Select Range Fill. Select A4..A83 as the fill range. Enter **1101** as the start value, **1** as the step value, and **1180** as the stop value.

5. In B4, you will enter a formula that creates one of two labels: Car or Truck.

   @IF(@RAND>0.46,"Truck","Car")

   Copy this formula from cell B4 to the range B4..B83.

6. With the cell pointer in C4, press MENU and select Width followed by Set. Type **12** and press (ENTER) to set the width of this column to 12.

7. In cell C4, you will enter a formula that creates a value with two decimal places, between 9000 and 14,000.

   @ROUND(9000+@RAND*5000,2)

8. Before you copy this formula, format the cell. Press MENU, select Format Currency, and press (ENTER) to accept 2 decimal places. Press (ENTER) to format C4.

9. Copy cell C4 to the range C4..C83.

10. In cell D4, you will now enter a formula that creates one of two labels: Y or N.

    @IF(@RAND>0.52,"Y","N")

11. Copy this formula from cell D4 across to column H and down to row 83. Use D4..H83 as the TO range.

12. To convert the formulas you have entered into values, press (HOME), then MENU. Select Range Values and press (END)

followed by (HOME) to include all cells of the worksheet. Press (ENTER) and then (ENTER) again to convert all formula cells to their values.

13. Using the Range Label-Alignment Center command, adjust the labels in D4 through H83 so that they are centered. The results will appear as in Figure 10-12.

14. You can now store the file using the SERVICES File Save command. Use the name **OHMSALES**.

Preparing for Print

To place the data from this file into an ASCII text file, you use the SERVICES Print command.

1. The first item to select from the Print menu is Settings. Choose Source and select Range to tell Symphony which cells of the worksheet are to be placed in the file.

2. The choice of cells to place in the print file depends on the program that will use the file. Some programs will use just the data; that is, A4..H83. Others will want column heading/field name information as well (A3..H83). Some programs will make sense of the whole file (A1..H83). In this case, select A1..H83 as the range to be printed.

3. Now select Destination and choose File. Enter a print file name, such as **OHMSALES**. Symphony will automatically add the extension PRN.

4. When you have entered a print file name, you are returned to the Print Settings menu. The text file you are creating will be difficult to read if it has space at the left margin or is split into pages. You should remove margin settings prior to printing to disk. Do this by selecting Margins and then No-Margins. This

```
Maintain a catalog of Print settings sheets                                      MENU
Page  Source  Destination  Init-String  Margins  Other  Name  Quit

 Page                        Source:      Range A1..H83
   Length:      66           Destination: File C:\SYM22\DATA\OHMSALES
   Spacing:     1            Init-String:
   Number                    Margins                   Other
     Print-Number: 1           Left:   0                 Space Compression: No
     Start-Page:   1           Right:  240               Attributes:          Yes
     End-Page:     999         Top:    0                 Format: As-Displayed
   Breaks:      No             Bottom: 0                 Top-Labels:
   Wait:        No                                       Left-Labels:
   Header:
   Footer:
                                                  Print Settings: PRINT2DISK
```

FIGURE 10-13 Settings ready for printing to disk

will also tell Symphony to use single spacing with no page breaks and no headers or footers.

5. You might want to use the Name Create command to store these print settings under a name like PRINT2DISK so that you can reuse them for further text-file printing. The settings sheet should look like Figure 10-13.

6. Select Quit from the Settings menu and choose Go from the main Print menu. This tells Symphony to open a file on disk and place in it the cells you have selected. However, Symphony does not close the file right away. This means you can select further groups of cells and print them to the same file. Only when you select Quit from the main Print menu does Symphony close the file. Do this now.

Checking the Results

To see the OHMSALES.PRN file that you created, you can either exit Symphony (resaving the worksheet file before you do so) or use the DOS command described in Chapter 8 (attaching the DOS add-in application first, then invoking it). Once you are at the DOS prompt, you can use this command to view the file, substituting the name of your default directory for SYM22\DATA:

```
TYPE \SYM22\DATA\OHMSALES.PRN | MORE
```

This command presents the file contents one screen at a time. After one screen, you get the message "--More--," which means you can press any key to see the next screen. The results will look like Figure 10-14. Note that each record is a single line of data spaced exactly as it was laid out in the worksheet.

Note If you get the message "Bad command or file name" in response to this command, it means that DOS cannot find the small program file called MORE.COM. You can still see the print file by leaving out the "| MORE" part. Use CTRL-S to stop the file from scrolling too quickly, then CTRL-S again to resume scrolling.

```
    1160 Truck     $9,365.21    Y        N        N        Y        N
    1161 Truck    $11,673.47    N        N        Y        N        N
    1162 Car      $10,611.17    Y        Y        Y        N        N
    1163 Car      $10,475.32    N        N        N        Y        Y
    1164 Car      $12,857.11    N        N        Y        N        Y
    1165 Car       $9,340.96    N        N        Y        N        N
    1166 Truck    $11,491.27    Y        Y        Y        Y        Y
    1167 Truck    $13,223.32    Y        N        Y        Y        Y
-- More --

    1168 Truck    $12,734.06    Y        N        N        Y        Y
    1169 Truck    $11,280.90    Y        Y        N        Y        Y
    1170 Truck    $10,521.28    N        N        N        Y        N
    1171 Car      $13,703.41    Y        Y        N        N        Y
    1172 Truck     $9,815.21    N        N        Y        N        N
    1173 Car      $10,094.45    Y        Y        Y        N        N
    1174 Truck    $13,131.56    Y        Y        N        N        N
    1175 Truck    $11,128.21    N        N        N        Y        Y
    1176 Car      $10,297.28    Y        N        Y        Y        N
    1177 Truck    $11,217.59    N        Y        N        N        N
    1178 Car      $12,533.79    Y        Y        Y        Y        Y
    1179 Car      $10,521.99    Y        Y        N        N        N
    1180 Car       $9,952.94    N        N        N        N        N

C:\SYM22>
```

FIGURE 10-14 Viewing the file in DOS

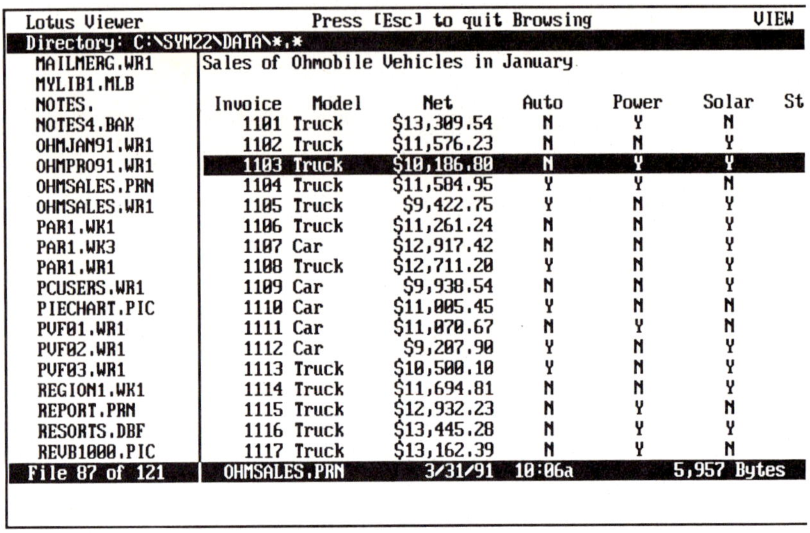

FIGURE 10-15 Using the Viewer

Another way to see the contents of the OHMSALES.PRN file is to use the Viewer application, described in Chapter 8. When you attach the Viewer, you can use the File View Browse command to see the contents of text files, as shown in Figure 10-15.

If you are using the text-file export technique to transfer data to a program that will manipulate the data as values, you might want to check the way the receiving program handles values and dates. For example, writing to disk a worksheet that has dates in the format 09/01/90 will create the text string 09/01/90. The receiving program may not be able to understand this as a date. However, it may understand 33117, the date's serial number, and you can write this to the text file if you first format the date in General or Fixed format. Some programs will not understand values that are preceded by dollar signs, so you may want to format numbers in Fixed format before printing them to disk.

Note that when you select Destination File, Symphony shows a list of existing PRN files (if any) in the current directory. You can choose one of these names as the destination of the print range. If you select an existing name, Symphony does not ask if you want to replace the data in the existing print file with new data. Instead, Symphony allows you to add data to an existing print file. This means that there are two ways to print additional data to a text file: before exiting the Print menu, redefine the print range and select Go, or choose an existing print file name.

TEXT INTO SYMPHONY

Having seen how Symphony creates a text file, you can now see how Symphony reads text files into a worksheet file. At times you may have useful information stored in files created by another program, but Symphony cannot read the format of those files. You might like to bring this information into a Symphony worksheet. One way of doing this is to convert the data into a text file by using the other program's equivalent of Symphony's Print Destination File command.

Importing ASCII Text Files

Suppose your company has an order processing program from which you can get sales information. You would like to make a database of the sales information. The order processing program should be able to print a text file to disk. The command that you use in Symphony to read this text file is File Import. This command works in conjunction with the Query Parse command to read imported information into a database.

To begin, you place your cell pointer at the top left corner of the area into which you want to import the data. Imported data will overwrite existing data if they overlap. When you select File Import, there is a choice between Text and Structured. The Text option imports each line of the file as a long label and enters it in one cell of the worksheet. For example, a line in a text file might look like this:

```
1101  Truck  $13,309.54  N  Y  N  Y
```

Out of this, Symphony would make a long label that consisted of the following characters:

```
'1101  Truck  $13,309.54  N  Y  N  Y
```

The text would not be split into separate items. The fact that each part of this line is a different piece of data is not clear to Symphony. Each successive line of data is entered in the same column below the cell pointer's initial location. If a line is longer than 511 characters, Symphony will truncate the line.

The Structured option is used for bringing in data from programs that create files in which the pieces of information are separated by commas, quotes, or both. A line of data in this arrangement of information is sometimes called *comma delimited,* and might look like this:

```
1101,"Truck",13309.54,"N","Y","N","Y"
```

Some databases and accounting programs can create files in this format, which makes it easier for the importing program to distinguish between separate items of data. The separate pieces of data can be discerned by Symphony and placed into separate cells across a row, one row for each line of data in the imported file. The Structured option can also be used with files that are not delimited, in which case it reads only numbers from the file and omits the text. Numbers in delimited files must not have commas in them, and Symphony will not know that 33117 is a date; you will have to add formatting after importing.

```
A5: '     1101 Truck      $13,309.54      N          Y          N          Y          SHEET
 ┌─────────A─────────B───────────C───────────D──────────E──────────F──────────G──────────H──────────┐
1
2   Sales of Ohmobile Vehicles in January
3
4     Invoice    Model          Net          Auto       Power      Solar     Stereo     Private
5        1101 Truck       $13,309.54       N          Y          N          Y           N
6        1102 Truck       $11,576.23       N          N          Y          Y           N
7        1103 Truck       $10,186.80       N          Y          Y          N           N
8        1104 Truck       $11,504.95       Y          Y          N          Y           N
9        1105 Truck        $9,422.75       Y          N          Y          N           Y
10       1106 Truck       $11,261.24       N          N          Y          Y           N
11       1107 Car         $12,917.42       N          N          Y          Y           N
12       1108 Truck       $12,711.20       Y          N          Y          N           Y
13       1109 Car          $9,938.54       N          N          Y          N           N
14       1110 Car         $11,005.45       Y          N          N          N           N
15       1111 Car         $11,070.67       N          Y          N          N           N
16       1112 Car          $9,207.90       Y          N          Y          N           Y
17       1113 Truck       $10,500.10       Y          N          Y          Y           Y
18       1114 Truck       $11,694.81       N          N          Y          N           Y
19       1115 Truck       $12,932.23       N          Y          N          N           Y
20       1116 Truck       $13,445.28       N          Y          Y          N           N
 └═══════════════════════════════════════════════════════════════════════════════════════MAIN┘
31-Mar-91   10:41 AM                                                           Num
```

FIGURE 10-16 Imported file

When you issue the File Import command and select either Text or Structured, you must then specify the name of the file. Symphony lists all files in the current directory using the *.* file specification. The file you select is then read into the worksheet at the current position of the cell selector. In the example shown in Figure 10-16, the OHMSALES.PRN file was imported. The cell pointer was in cell A2 when the command was issued.

This information looks a lot like a spreadsheet, but if you carefully observe the contents of cell A5, you will see that it is one long label. There is no data in columns B, C, D, and so on. There are two techniques you can use to help Symphony make sense of data like this. The first is called *parsing*, which consists of breaking up the lines of data according to a set of interpretation rules. The second approach, which is more complex, is to use the string functions, described in Appendix B.

Using the Parse Command

To turn a single line of data into separate cells of information, Symphony uses a set of rules by which it reads, or parses, the long labels of data. To import the OHMSALES.PRN text file and parse it into database values, follow these steps:

1. In a new worksheet, place the cell pointer in A2. Press SERVICES and select File Import Text. Select OHMSALES.PRN.

2. Move the cell pointer to I1. Here, you will describe the database into which the imported data will be parsed. Enter the definition labels as shown here:

```
I1: 'Invoice:N:9                                                      SHEET
 ---------I---------J---------K--------L--------M---------N---------O---------P-----
1   Invoice:N:9
2   Model:L:9
3   Net:N:12
4   Auto:L:9
5   Power:L:9
6   Solar:L:9
7   Stereo:L:9
8   Private:L:9
```

3. Press TYPE and select FORM. You will get the "No definition range" message. Press MENU and select Generate. Press (ENTER) to accept Label as the default field type, and press (ENTER) again to accept 9 as the default field length. Press (ENTER) to accept the name MAIN.

4. For the range of field names, select I1..I8. This will produce a blank form like the one in Figure 10-17. You will parse the imported data into this database.

5. Switch to SHEET mode and place your cell selector on the first cell containing a label to be parsed: A5. For Symphony to break up the long label into separate values, the width of underlying columns must match the field lengths used when defining the

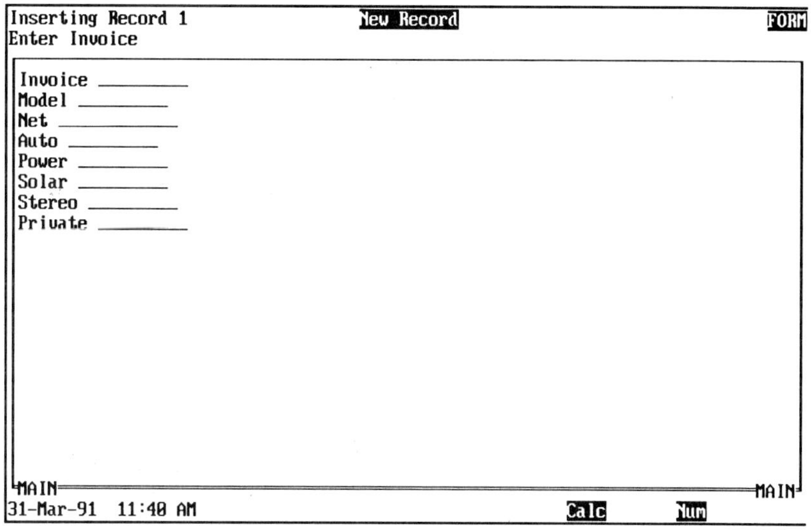

FIGURE 10-17 A blank form in the new database

database. Since most of the fields are 9 characters wide, you only need to widen column C to 12 characters.

6. Still in the SHEET environment, press MENU and select the Query Parse command. This prompts for the range to be parsed—actually, the column of labels that will be broken into values. Press TAB to anchor the range at A5, and press END, then DOWN ARROW, and then RIGHT ARROW to include A5..H84.

7. Symphony needs a range of cells in which to place values that do not fit the definitions you have set up. For the review range, use cell A86, below the main database. When you confirm the review range, Symphony completes the Query Parse command. You can quit from the menu and use the SWITCH key to move into the FORM environment and examine the results, which should appear as in Figure 10-18.

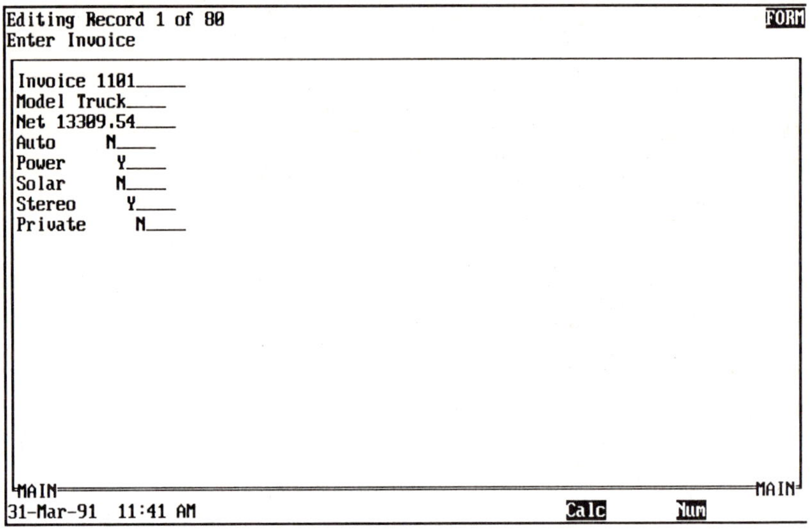

FIGURE 10-18 Record parsed into the form

If there were any records that did not "parse" the test, they will be in the review range where you can examine them. These may be incorrectly entered records that must be manually corrected and added to the database through the FORM environment.

STATISTICAL ANALYSIS

There are several statistical analysis features that are not built in to Symphony but are available through the Statistical Analysis add-in application. These features are Distribution, Regression, and Matrix. When you attach the Statistical Analysis application, these commands are added under the Range menu as Distri, Regres, and Matrix. Under Matrix, you will actually find two commands: Multiply and Invert. As a group, these commands are not necessarily more complicated or less used than other aspects of Symphony, but they have specialized uses, particularly the

Regression and Matrix commands. (The menu items Distri and Regres will be referred to here by their full names, Distribution and Regression.)

Before you can use the Statistical Analysis add-in application, you must use the SERVICES Application Attach command to select STAT.APP. Do not use SERVICES Application Invoke to access the statistical commands; instead, use the MENU Range command. You can use the SERVICES Configuration Other Application command to set up STAT.APP as one of the applications that is automatically loaded with the main Symphony program. Do not set the application to be automatically invoked. Remember to use the SERVICES Configuration Update command to record your choice.

Relating with Regression

When you have a large collection of related facts, you may want to see how strong the relationship is between them. For example, you may want to evaluate the relationship between goods sold and the amount of money spent on advertising the goods, or see the connection between earnings and levels of education, and so on. One method of analyzing the connection between such facts is called *linear regression.* The subject of regression analysis is complex, and a complete discussion is beyond the scope of this book. A reference such as *Modern Business Statistics* by Ronald L. Iman and W. J. Conover (New York: John Wiley & Sons, 1983) can provide complete coverage of all aspects of the field as they relate to typical business situations.

A REGRESSION EXAMPLE Regression is a measurement of how different factors relate to each other. For example, how does the amount of advertising done by a company relate to its sales? Standard business philosophy states that the amount of advertising a company does is related to the sales level it achieves. Regression

```
A5: (D3) @DATE(91,1,1)                                             SHEET
  ---A-------B-------C-------D-------E-------F-------G-------H---
1   Ohmobile - Marketing Figures
2
3          Actual   Actual
4   Month: Pages:   Sales:
5   Jan-91       4       39
6   Feb-91       5       51
7   Mar-91       6       58
8   Apr-91       5       51
9   May-91       6       61
10  Jun-91       7       67
11  Jul-91       5       49
12  Aug-91       6       59
13  Sep-91       5       49
14  Oct-91       6       56
15  Nov-91       7       69
16  Dec-91       8       80
17
18
19
20
                                                                MAIN
31-Mar-91  12:10 PM                                         Num
```

FIGURE 10-19 Marketing data to be analyzed

can help you determine how strong this relationship is in the case of your company.

Suppose you have compiled the marketing data you see in Figure 10-19. In column B is a list of the number of pages of newspaper advertising placed by Ohmobile in 1990, listed by month. The numbers in column C represent sales, in thousands, for those same months. You want to try to determine how these two sets of numbers relate. Once you measure the relationship, you may be able to use that measure to predict future sales based on different levels of future advertising.

SETTING UP REGRESSION When you press MENU and select Range followed by Regres, you see a menu that lists the following items:

X-Range Y-Range Output-Range Intercept Reset Go Quit

The first two items on the Regression menu refer to the variables used in the regression calculation. The correlation of the independent or X-axis variable to the dependent or Y-axis variable is what you want to calculate. In this case, Actual Pages are the independent variables, so the X range is cells B5..B16. The strength of correlation with Sales, the dependent variable, is what is to be calculated, so the Y range is cells C5..C16. The pairs of variables must be situated in matching columns and rows of the worksheet and contain an equal number of pieces of data, as is the case in this example. When you select X-Range and Y-Range, you can enter the cell coordinates either by typing them in or pointing to them. (There can be more than one independent variable, as will be discussed later.)

The Regression command produces a table of results that occupies an area of the worksheet defined as the output range. Initially, this is a range of blank cells set apart from the data being analyzed. For the example in Figure 10-19, you could begin the output range at cell E3. The results of the calculation will occupy four columns and nine rows. You only need to define the top left corner of the cells of the output block.

After setting the X range, Y range, and output range, you can select Go, which tells Symphony to perform the regression analysis and place the results in the output range. If you need to change the Range Regression settings (say, to analyze a different set of figures), you can use the Reset command, which clears the current settings.

REGRESSION RESULTS As you can see from Figure 10-20, the result of a regression calculation is a column of numbers that represent the numeric relationships between the variables and columns of labels describing these numbers. Note that outputting to columns any narrower than the default width of 9 will make the data difficult to read.

Interpreting these results involves understanding numerous concepts about statistics. The results are best explained in order of

```
E3:                                                                     SHEET
   ----A-------B--------C--------D--------E--------F--------G--------H-----
1   Ohmobile - Marketing Figures
2
3          Actual   Actual              Regression Output:
4   Month: Pages:   Sales:              Constant                      0.719512
5   Jan-91       4       39             Std Err of Y Est              1.687528
6   Feb-91       5       51             R Squared                     0.980377
7   Mar-91       6       58             No. of Observations                 12
8   Apr-91       5       51             Degrees of Freedom                  10
9   May-91       6       61
10  Jun-91       7       67             X Coefficient(s)  9.719512
11  Jul-91       5       49             Std Err of Coef.  0.434837
12  Aug-91       6       59
13  Sep-91       5       49
14  Oct-91       6       56
15  Nov-91       7       69
16  Dec-91       8       80
17
18
19
20
                                                                      MAIN
31-Mar-91   12:12 PM                                            Num
```

FIGURE 10-20 Regression results

complexity. "No. of Observations" is simply how many data points were observed for the variables—in this case, 12, one for each month. Degrees of freedom represent the number of observations minus one for each variable observed—in this case, 10. The value R squared is sometimes referred to as the coefficient of determination, a measure of the extent to which the variables are related, with 1 being the highest possible value. In this example, where the sales are clearly very closely related to the pages, the value of R squared is nearly 1.

"Std Err of Y Est" is the estimated standard error of the Y values. With this, you measure the certainty with which the independent variables predict the dependent variables. In general, the larger this measure, the less reliable the relationship is between the independent and the dependent variables. This measure, like R squared, is useful when deciding between different independent variables as predictors of the dependent variables. "Std Err of Coef" gives an error measurement of the coefficients. The larger this measurement, relative to the X coefficient, the less certain the relationship between the variables. This measurement will often be smaller when more observations are included in the calculation.

Probably the most useful numbers in the regression output are the constant and the X coefficient. The Constant can be described as the Y-axis intercept of the regression line that describes the relationship between Pages and Sales. The X coefficient tells how much the dependent variable, Sales, will change for a single unit increase in the independent variable, Pages. As you can see in the output in Figure 10-20, this is close to 10, and most of the Sales figures are, in fact, about 10 times the Pages figures.

USING REGRESSION RESULTS The Constant and X Coefficient readings can be used to predict the value of sales based on different numbers of pages. In Figure 10-21, you can see a series of numbers added to the model in column D. Headed "Predicted Sales," these figures represent what Symphony would predict the

```
D5: @ROUND($H$4+$G$10*B5,0)                                          SHEET
   A        B        C          D          E        F         G        H
1  Ohmobile - Marketing Figures
2
3          Actual   Actual   Predicted         Regression Output:
4  Month:  Pages:   Sales:   Sales:     Constant                    0.719512
5  Jan-91       4       39         40   Std Err of Y Est            1.607528
6  Feb-91       5       51         49   R Squared                   0.980377
7  Mar-91       6       58         59   No. of Observations               12
8  Apr-91       5       51         49   Degrees of Freedom                10
9  May-91       6       61         59
10 Jun-91       7       67         69   X Coefficient(s)  9.719512
11 Jul-91       5       49         49   Std Err of Coef.  0.434837
12 Aug-91       6       59         59
13 Sep-91       5       49         49
14 Oct-91       6       56         59
15 Nov-91       7       69         69
16 Dec-91       8       80         78
17
18
19
20
                                                                     MAIN
31-Mar-91  12:15 PM                                             Num
```

FIGURE 10-21 Checking predicted figures

sales to be, based on the number of pages in column B and the relationship analyzed by the regression output, using the formula

Constant + X Coefficient * Independent Variable

In this case, cell D5 contains the formula

@ROUND($H$4+$G$10*B5,0)

This formula was then copied down the column, producing the numbers shown, which are fairly close to the real results. The value of this calculation is seen when the numbers in column B are changed from actual pages in 1991 to planned pages in 1992, as shown in Figure 10-22. Column D now shows the sales predicted for 1992.

Remember that the prediction seen here is only a statistical inference, not a guaranteed basis for a business decision. Although

```
D5: @ROUND($H$4+$G$10*B5,0)                                                  SHEET

      A        B        C        D         E         F         G         H
1   Ohmobile - Marketing Figures
2
3            Planned             Predicted          Regression Output:
4   Month: Pages:                Sales:   Constant                    0.719512
5   Jan-92         7                    69 Std Err of Y Est            1.607528
6   Feb-92         7                    69 R Squared                   0.980377
7   Mar-92         7                    69 No. of Observations               12
8   Apr-92         8                    78 Degrees of Freedom                10
9   May-92         8                    78
10  Jun-92         8                    78 X Coefficient(s)  9.719512
11  Jul-92         9                    88 Std Err of Coef.  0.434837
12  Aug-92         9                    88
13  Sep-92         9                    88
14  Oct-92        10                    98
15  Nov-92        10                    98
16  Dec-92        10                    98
17
18
19
20
                                                                           MAIN
31-Mar-91   12:19 PM                                                   Num
```

FIGURE 10-22 Calculating next year's figures

there appears to be a strong relationship between the pages of advertising and the amount of sales, you cannot directly infer that more advertising causes more sales. Other factors, such as seasonal patterns, must be considered. However, there is a suggestion that more advertising will produce more sales.

MULTIPLE VARIABLES You can include more than one independent variable in the regression calculation. This allows you to examine relationships between a variety of different factors.

Frequency Distribution

When handling large quantities of data, you often need to analyze the distribution of the data. For example, consider the sales statistics in Figure 10-12. Someone might ask, "How large are the net invoices?" You could say that they range from around 9000 to almost 14000, based on a quick review of the values in column C. If you were to sort the statistics based on column C, you could easily find the largest and smallest values, but this response is rather vague. If you were to categorize the invoices based on net value and count how many fell into each category, you would get a better understanding of the statistics. This is the role of the Distribution command added to the Range menu by the Statistical Analysis application.

PERFORMING A DISTRIBUTION To perform a frequency distribution with Symphony, you need to supply two pieces of information. The first is the range of values that are to be categorized. In this case, you want to analyze sales statistics according to the size of the invoice, so the values range is C4..C83. The second piece of information is the column of numbers representing the range over which the values are to be distributed: the categories, as it were. The cells containing these category numbers are called the bin range, as though each number in the values range

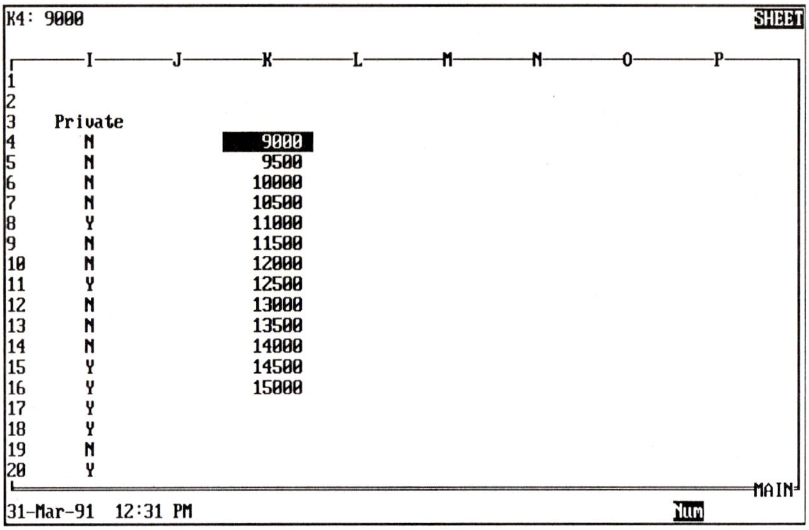

FIGURE 10-23 Range of bin numbers

was tossed into the appropriate bin for counting. The result of the Distribution command is a list of the totals of that count placed in the column to the right of the bin numbers.

Before using the Range Distribution command, you must enter a series of numbers for the bin range. The first number will represent from 0 to that number, so that 9000 would represent from 0 to 9000. For the invoices, you could use numbers 9000 through 15000 in intervals of 500, as seen in Figure 10-23.

This series of numbers can easily be entered with the Range Fill command using these settings:

Range: K4..K24
Start: 9000
Step: 500
Stop: 15000

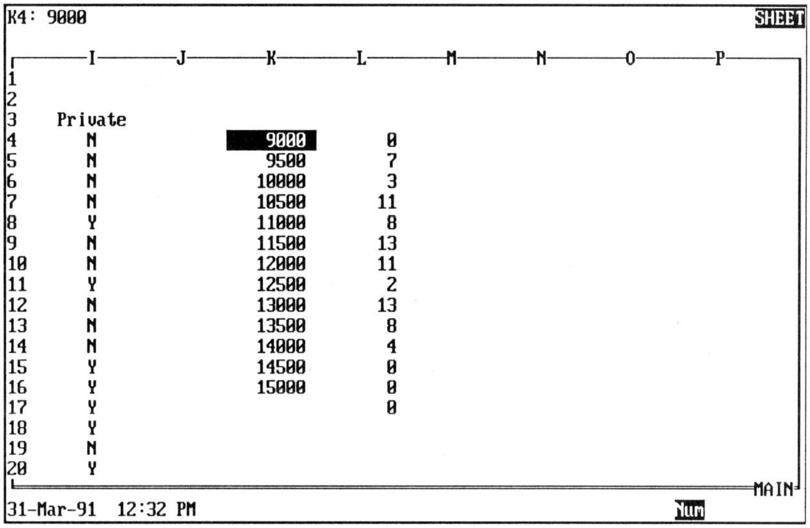

FIGURE 10-24 Distribution results

Be sure that the cells used for the bin range have empty cells immediately to the right of them. When you select Distribution, you are first prompted for the range of values to analyze—in this case, cells C4..C83. As soon as this is entered, you are prompted for the bin range: K4..K16. When the bin range is entered, Symphony immediately responds with the count of numbers, as in Figure 10-24. From this result you can see that none of the invoices were from 0 to 9000. There were seven invoices of 9001 to 9500, and so on. The results provide a valuable picture of the sales data. Frequency distributions are a good basis for many graphs.

IMPROVING THE DISTRIBUTION Since the bin numbers are somewhat difficult to interpret, you can add a second column, as shown in the worksheet in Figure 10-25. The bin numbers are still shown in column K. The numbers in column J are added to

```
J4: +"From "&@STRING(K3,0)&" to"                                        SHEET
 ───────I──────────J──────────K────────L─────────M─────────N─────────O─────────P───
1
2
3    Private
4       N     From 0 to          9000      1
5       N     From 9000 to       9500      6
6       N     From 9500 to      10000      3
7       N     From 10000 to 10500         11
8       Y     From 10500 to 11000          8
9       N     From 11000 to 11500         13
10      N     From 11500 to 12000         11
11      Y     From 12000 to 12500          2
12      N     From 12500 to 13000         13
13      N     From 13000 to 13500          8
14      N     From 13500 to 14000          4
15      Y     From 14000 to 14500          0
16      Y     From 14500 to 15000          0
17      Y     Over 15000                   0
18      Y
19      N
20      Y
                                                                              MAIN
31-Mar-91  12:41 PM                                                    Num
```

FIGURE 10-25 Enhanced results

show the range of numbers implied by each "bin" or interval value in column K.

Note the use of a string formula to make the labels in column J. This formula was copied from J4 to the range J5 through J16, to automatically produce the correct labels. The label "Over 15000" in J17 was added to account for the final frequency measurement, which always goes one cell beyond the actual bin range.

Matrix Arithmetic

Two items on the Matrix menu, Invert and Multiply, provide you with tools for performing matrix arithmetic. If you know what the inverse of a matrix is and need to perform matrix arithmetic in your work, the following account of the Invert and Multiply commands will get you started in applying Symphony to the task. If you are not familiar with inverting matrices, the following example will give you an idea of how they are used to solve practical problems.

Matrix arithmetic is used in linear programming, a technique for determining the optimal allocation of limited resources. This has practical application in many areas—notably, in economics, which has been defined as "the science that studies human behavior as a relationship between ends and scarce means which have alternative uses." Although a discussion of economic theory and linear programming concepts is clearly beyond the scope of this book, you can get an idea of how matrix commands work and how linear programming is applied with Symphony from a relatively simple example.

The manager at an airline needs to determine the optimal mix of cargo on a plane, choosing between packages and people. The data from which this mix must be calculated is the amount of fuel needed to fly each package and each person, plus the amount of handling time involved for each package and each person. The data is laid out in the worksheet in Figure 10-26. The profit per package and person is also listed in the worksheet. The numbers are values, not formulas.

You can set up a similar worksheet very easily. Column A is set to 16 characters wide, and all other columns are 9 wide. In cell E3, enter **Matrix Output** to label the results of the first set of calculations, which will be created by Symphony's Invert command.

The calculation that must be performed to determine the optimal mix of packages and persons involves the following equations:

2,750 * Packages + 9,250 * Persons = 80,000 Gallons
3 * Packages + 2 * Persons = 40 Hours

These equations will yield the number of packages and persons you should load to optimize the allocation of the given resources. Once you have entered the data in the worksheet, you can have Symphony calculate an inverse of the matrix of numbers in B4..C5.

```
B4: (P0) 2750                                                        SHEET
 ┌──────────A──────────B──────────C──────────D──────────E──────────F──────
 1  Cargo/Passenger Analysis
 2
 3                    Package    Person    Resources Matrix Output
 4  Fuel (gallons)      2,750     9,250     80,000
 5  Handling (hours)        3         2         40
 6  Profit Per Unit        50        25
 7
 8
 9
10
```

FIGURE 10-26 The Cargo worksheet

MATRIX INVERT When you select Invert from the Range Matrix menu, you are prompted for the range of cells to invert. In this case, the range is B4..C5. The cell coordinates can be pointed out or typed in, just as at other Symphony range prompts. The matrix to be inverted must be square; that is, it must have the same number of columns as rows. When you have entered the range to invert, you are prompted for an output range. In this case, E4 will be used. The destination block will be the same size as the source block, so you must use an adequate area of your spreadsheet for this. However, you need only point out the top left corner of the output range. When the output range coordinate is entered, the inverse matrix is produced. You can see the results in Figure 10-27.

MATRIX MULTIPLY Having calculated the inverse matrix of the numbers, you can use the Matrix Multiply command to multiply the original resources of 80,000 gallons and 40 hours by the inverse matrix. The resources, which were the constants in the equations, constitute a matrix. The Multiply command allows you to multiply two matrices together. In this case, the results will be the number of packages and persons that make the most efficient use of your limited resources.

```
E4: -0.0000762943                                                    SHEET

    A                  B          C          D          E          F
1   Cargo/Passenger Analysis
2
3                      Package    Person     Resources Matrix Output
4   Fuel (gallons)       2,750      9,250      80,000 -0.000076 0.4032697
5   Handling (hours)         3          2          40 0.0001307 -0.119891
6   Profit Per Unit         50         25
7
8
9
10
```

FIGURE 10-27 Matrix Invert results

When you select Multiply from the Matrix menu, you are prompted for the first range to multiply, which will be the inverse matrix, cells E4..F5. When these coordinates are entered, you are prompted for a second range to multiply, which will be the resources in D4..D5. After entering the 2nd Matrix coordinates, you are prompted for an output range. In this example, cell B10 is used. You can see the resulting numbers in Figure 10-28, where some additional labels have been added to identify the results.

When you enter the destination coordinate, the results of the calculations are seen. In this case, a mix of approximately 10.03 packages and 5.67 persons is the most efficient use of the resources available. You might want to format cells B10 and B11 with less decimal places. Since you cannot have 5.67 persons, you might want to display the result without any decimal places. However, if you are going to use the result in another calculation, you may want to use the @ROUND function to eliminate the decimal places.

In cell B13 of Figure 10-29, you can see a calculation added to the worksheet to show the amount of profit made by the mix determined in B10 and B11, using the profit figures from row 6. The formula used to multiply per-unit profit by optimal number of units is

```
+B6*@ROUND(B10,0)+C6*@ROUND(B11,0)
```

```
E4: -0.0000762943                                                        SHEET

      A           B          C          D          E          F
1  Cargo/Passenger Analysis
2
3                   Package    Person     Resources Matrix Output
4  Fuel (gallons)      2,750      9,250     80,000 -0.000076 0.4032697
5  Handling (hours)        3          2         40 0.0001307 -0.119891
6  Profit Per Unit        50         25
7
8  Optimum Mix Calculation
9
10 Packages         10.027247
11 Persons          5.6675749
```

FIGURE 10-28 Results of Matrix Multiply

Note that the @ROUND function means that the formula uses whole units of packages and persons.

USING @BASE

As you learned in Chapter 5, programs designed to handle large amounts of information are called database management software. There are three levels of database management in Symphony:

```
B13: +B6*@ROUND(B10,0)+C6*@ROUND(B11,0)                                  SHEET

      A           B          C          D          E          F
1  Cargo/Passenger Analysis
2
3                   Package    Person     Resources Matrix Output
4  Fuel (gallons)      2,750      9,250     80,000 -0.000076 0.4032697
5  Handling (hours)        3          2         40 0.0001307 -0.119891
6  Profit Per Unit        50         25
7
8  Optimum Mix Calculation
9
10 Packages             10.03
11 Persons               5.67
12
13 Profit                 650
14
```

FIGURE 10-29 Enhanced matrix results

SHEET-based, FORM-based, and disk-based. The first two were dealt with in Chapter 5, while the third is the subject of this section. Disk-based database features are provided within Symphony by the @BASE add-in application.

@BASE and Other Programs

Many different software packages offer some level of database management abilities. These programs can be divided into two groups: relational and simple, the latter sometimes called "flat-file." The SHEET and FORM environments in Symphony are examples of simple, flat-file database management. In these environments, you can work on one database at a time. On the other hand, in relational database management you can relate the data in several different files based on common elements. These programs can handle large amounts of data. The Ashton-Tate programs dBASE III and IV offer this kind of database management. In fact, attaching @BASE to Symphony is rather like merging dBASE III with an electronic spreadsheet. You have the functional equivalent of dBASE III plus direct access to database files from the SHEET environment.

Another term used to describe such programs as dBASE is "disk-based". This contrasts with Symphony, which, as you have seen, is memory-based. All of the information in a Symphony worksheet is in memory at once, whereas a disk-based program like dBASE leaves most of the information in a file on disk until it is needed (for example, for editing). This gives disk-based programs a big advantage in terms of file size, since files are limited by disk space, not memory space.

Symphony uses the @BASE add-in program to provide features identical to those of a disk-based relational database. @BASE allows you to design, create, sort, and query databases in the dBASE format (that is, files with the DBF extension). You can use @BASE as a bridge between Symphony and files created by dBASE or compatible programs. This allows Symphony to offer the best of both worlds. When dealing with smaller databases that will fit in memory, Symphony's SHEET and FORM environments perform operations like sort and find very quickly. If a database grows too large for memory-based operation, then @BASE can be invoked to provide disk-based database management. When you are working with databases in Symphony, you have all the power of Symphony's built-in functions and graphics on hand to help analyze your data. Plus, the macro command language of Symphony makes possible customized, menu-driven database management applications.

A Sample Database File

To see how @BASE loads and manipulates a dBASE database file, you need to create a sample file to work with. You can use the OHMSALES worksheet described earlier in this chapter as the basis for a DBF file. The Translate program, described in Chapter 8, can convert a Symphony worksheet to a DBF file. (Note that once you become familiar with @BASE, you can use @BASE commands to quickly create DBF files from Symphony databases.)

1. Load the OHMSALES file, the one shown in Figure 10-12. Use the Range Name Create command to name the database portion of the worksheet, cells A3..H83, as **DATABASE**. You can see this being done in Figure 10-30. You will use this range name when converting the data to DBF format. Save the file.

2. Exit Symphony and load the Translate program. Either choose File-Translate from the Access system or enter **TRANS** at the DOS prompt. Select SYMPHONY 2.2 in the list of FROM formats. Select dBase III as the TO format. Press (ESC) to clear the file translation message.

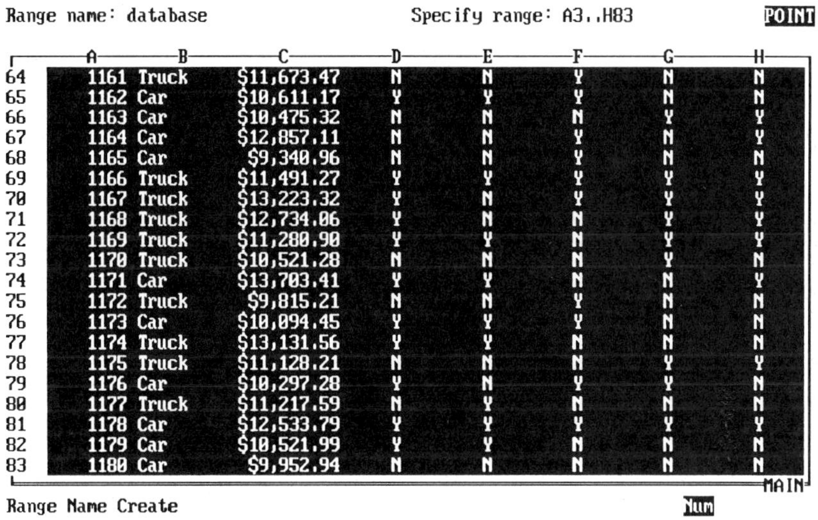

Range name: database　　Specify range: A3..H83　　POINT

	A	B	C	D	E	F	G	H
64	1161	Truck	$11,673.47	N	N	Y	N	N
65	1162	Car	$10,611.17	Y	Y	Y	N	N
66	1163	Car	$10,475.32	N	N	N	Y	Y
67	1164	Car	$12,857.11	N	N	Y	N	Y
68	1165	Car	$9,340.96	N	N	Y	N	N
69	1166	Truck	$11,491.27	Y	Y	Y	Y	Y
70	1167	Truck	$13,223.32	Y	N	Y	Y	Y
71	1168	Truck	$12,734.06	Y	N	N	Y	Y
72	1169	Truck	$11,280.90	Y	Y	N	Y	Y
73	1170	Truck	$10,521.28	N	N	N	Y	N
74	1171	Car	$13,703.41	Y	Y	N	N	Y
75	1172	Truck	$9,815.21	N	N	Y	N	N
76	1173	Car	$10,094.45	Y	Y	Y	N	N
77	1174	Truck	$13,131.56	Y	Y	N	N	N
78	1175	Truck	$11,128.21	N	N	N	Y	Y
79	1176	Car	$10,297.28	Y	N	Y	Y	N
80	1177	Truck	$11,217.59	N	Y	N	N	N
81	1178	Car	$12,533.79	Y	Y	Y	Y	Y
82	1179	Car	$10,521.99	Y	Y	N	N	N
83	1180	Car	$9,952.94	N	N	N	N	N

MAIN

Range Name Create　　Num

FIGURE 10-30 Naming the database

3. If your worksheet file is not in the program directory, you may have to press (ESC) to edit the path to match the data directory in which you have stored the file OHMSALES.WR1. Select OHMSALES.WR1 as the source file, as shown in Figure 10-31.

4. Press (ENTER) to confirm OHMSALES.DBF as the destination file.

5. Select Range from the Worksheet/Range prompt seen in Figure 10-32, and enter **DATABASE** as the name of the range. Choose Yes to proceed, and Translate will show you the progress of the translation process.

```
Lotus Symphony Release 2.2 Translate Utility
Copyright 1986, 1987, 1990 Lotus Development Corp.  All Rights Reserved

Translate FROM: SYMPHONY 2.2          Translate TO: dBase III

Source File: C:\SYM22\DATA\*.wr1

 OHMSALES WR1   3/31/91   3:57p      9344

        OHMSALES WR1
        PAR1     WR1
        PARSED   WR1
        PCUSERS  WR1
        PVF01    WR1
        PVF02    WR1
        PVF03    WR1
        —More—

Move the menu pointer to the file you want to translate and press [RETURN].
              Press [ESCAPE] to edit the source specification.
                     Press [HELP] for more information.
                                                               Num-Lock
```

FIGURE 10-31 Selecting the source file

```
Lotus Symphony Release 2.2 Translate Utility
Copyright 1986, 1987, 1990 Lotus Development Corp.  All Rights Reserved

Translate FROM: SYMPHONY 2.2          Translate TO: dBase III

Source File: C:\SYM22\DATA\OHMSALES.WR1

Destination: C:\SYM22\DATA\OHMSALES.DBF

     Translate a range within the worksheet
     Worksheet  Range

                                                               Num-Lock
```

FIGURE 10-32 Selecting Range

6. After you successfully translate the data to a DBF file, it can be read directly by dBASE or by @BASE. Exit the Translate program and load Symphony.

You are now ready to attach the @BASE add-in and use it to work with the DBF file. Later, you will learn how to create DBF files directly through @BASE.

Attaching @BASE

@BASE consists of three add-in files. This lets you attach only the parts of @BASE you need to use, which is helpful when your computer is low on memory. (You may find that Symphony flashes the "Mem" message in the bottom status area as you carry out the following exercises. If that happens, try unloading all unnecessary programs and applications before attaching @BASE and loading a DBF file.) The @BASE files are

BASE.APP	Adds the BASE environment to Symphony and lets you use all @BASE commands except the Utility commands; takes up approximately 64 K of RAM
BASEUTL.APP	Adding BASEUTL.APP as well as BASE.APP lets you use the @BASE Utility commands; takes up approximately 10 K more RAM
BASEFUNC.APP	Adding BASEFUNC.APP as well as BASE.APP lets you use the @BASE @DB functions. It takes up approximately 10K more RAM. The @DB functions are listed in Appendix B, along with the regular Symphony functions

The @BASE program also uses a file named BASE.TXT, which contains the @BASE program text. Before you attach any of the @BASE add-in files, make sure BASE.TXT is either in your Symphony program directory or in a directory on your DOS path.

You attach the @BASE add-ins the same way you attach any other Symphony add-in, such as the STAT.APP described earlier in the chapter. Press SERVICES and select Application Attach. Then specify the add-in you want to attach, either by highlighting the name or by typing it, and press (ENTER).

As described in Chapter 8, you can also use SERVICES Configuration Other Application Set to attach the @BASE add-ins automatically whenever you start a Symphony session. If you do this, be sure to set the Auto-Invoke setting for the @BASE add-ins to No.

If you are using expanded memory, you should attach the @BASE add-ins, as well as any other Symphony add-ins that you intend to use, at the beginning of a Symphony session before retrieving any Symphony worksheet files. This optimizes the use of expanded memory. If you plan to use BASEFUNC.APP, attach it before attaching any other Symphony add-ins, including BASE.APP and BASEUTL.APP. Attaching BASEFUNC.APP first ensures that if you later detach the other add-ins, you will regain the maximum amount of usable memory. You can detach BASE.APP and BASEUTL.APP with SERVICES Application Detach. However, as with most @function add-ins, you can detach BASEFUNC.APP only by leaving Symphony.

Once you attach the @BASE add-ins, they are immediately available for use. You do not have to invoke them after attaching them. However, you can use the Invoke command to check that the requisite parts of @BASE are attached. Here, you can see all three parts attached:

```
Application to invoke:                                              NAMES
DOS            BASE           BASEFUNC        BASEUTL
------A---------B---------C---------D---------E---------F---------G---------H-------
1
2
```

The @BASE Menu

To access the @BASE program, you use the new environment added to the list presented by the TYPE command ((ALT-F10)). You should use a fresh worksheet to experiment with the @BASE commands. When you press TYPE after attaching @BASE, you see the following list:

```
@BASE database                                                        MENU
SHEET  DOC  GRAPH  FORM  COMM  BASE
 ------A--------B--------C--------D--------E--------F--------G--------H-------
1
2
```

When you select BASE, you are presented with an almost empty window. The headings "Alias" and "Field Name" appear, and the mode indicator says "BASE." When you press MENU, you see the @BASE commands shown in Figure 10-33.

The @BASE menu system works just like regular Symphony menus, with one exception. Whereas Symphony generally uses

```
Open  Close  Use  Define  Modify  Extract  Field-Rename  Post            BASE
File  Data  Criteria  Settings  Utility
 Alias          File name



                                                                     MAIN
31-Mar-91  04:03 PM                                              Num
```

FIGURE 10-33 The @BASE menu

(ESC) to let you back out of commands step by step, and in most @BASE commands @BASE uses (ESC) the same way, at certain points in some @BASE commands, (ESC) works as an Accept or Continue key. For example, during Data Browse (explored in a moment), pressing (ESC) ends the Data Browse command instead of taking you to the previous step. During File Modify, when @BASE is in FIELD mode, pressing (ESC) tells @BASE to accept the current field definitions and continue to the next step of the command. As you learn @BASE, be aware that the effect of the (ESC) key depends on the command you are using.

Accessing DBF Files with @BASE

Like a Symphony database, an @BASE database can include up to 256 fields. However, each record in an @BASE database can include up to 4000 characters, far more than the limit in Symphony. Furthermore, the number of records you can include in an @BASE database is not limited to 8191 as it is in Symphony. An @BASE database is limited only by available disk space.

Since @BASE is compatible with dBASE, you can use @BASE to process files you create with dBASE, and you can use dBASE to process files you create with @BASE. The terms "@BASE database file" and "@BASE file" refer to files you create with @BASE as well as to dBASE files you are processing with @BASE. The number of @BASE files you can have open at one time is limited to 15.

To use @BASE to work with a database file, you select File from the @BASE menu and choose Open. This prompts @BASE to list all DBF files in the current directory. @BASE database files are subject to the same name rules used for any other type of DOS file (from one to eight characters long; any combination of letters, numbers, underscores, and hyphens; and no spaces). @BASE automatically assigns the DBF extension to files you create using @BASE. In addition, to open an existing database file in @BASE, the file must have the extension DBF.

When you select the file you want to work with, @BASE asks you for an *alias*. A file's alias is the name that @BASE uses to identify the file internally. You use this alias to specify the file in almost all @BASE commands and @DB functions. By default, @BASE uses a file's name, sans extension, as its alias, in this case, OHMSALES. Press (ENTER) to accept this default.

You can override the default alias assignment and use any name between 1 and 15 characters as the alias. An alias can include any combination of characters, but it cannot include spaces, nor can it duplicate an alias you already specified for another open file.

When you open a database file, you must specify the type of access you want for that file. You can select one of three types of access: exclusive, primary, or read-only. The type you choose determines the kind of work you can do with the file and, if the file is on a network, whether other users can access it simultaneously.

EXCLUSIVE FILE ACCESS When you have exclusive access to a database file, you can do any type of work you want with the file, including altering the file structure. This means you can change field names or the order of records. You can also change data in the file, create new records, and delete old ones. With exclusive access, no one else on a network can open the file until you close it.

PRIMARY FILE ACCESS When you have primary access to a database file, you can view and edit records in the file, but you cannot change the file structure. With primary access, other users can open the file simultaneously but only with read-only access.

READ-ONLY ACCESS When you have read-only access to a database file, you can view the file's records but you cannot change the records or the file's structure. When you have read-only access, another user can open the same file with primary access and modify records while you are viewing the file.

When you have chosen the type of access you require, @BASE returns you to the main menu, where you can see the open file listed by name and alias, as shown here:

```
Open  Close  Use  Define  Modify  Extract  Field-Rename  Post          BASE
File  Data  Criteria  Settings  Utility

Alias          File name
OHMSALES       C:\SYM22\DATA\OHMSALES.DBF
```

Accessing Data

To see the records in the OHMSALES file, you select Data from the @BASE menu. You then select Browse. All open files are listed by their aliases. Select the alias of the file you want to browse (since you use this alias to specify the file in almost all @BASE commands and @DB functions, selecting the file by its alias will be assumed). When you select the file, @BASE asks if you want to see all of the fields in the file or just selected fields. If you choose Selected, you are shown a list of the fields:

```
                                                                BASE

Name            Type       Length    Decimals
INVOICE         Numeric       9        2
MODEL           Char          9
NET             Numeric      12        2
AUTO            Char          9
POWER           Char          9
SOLAR           Char          9
STEREO          Char          9
PRIVATE         Char          9
```

To select the fields you want @BASE to show when browsing records, you move the highlighting up and down the list with the (UP ARROW) and (DOWN ARROW) keys and press (ENTER) when you are highlighting a field that you want selected. When you press (ENTER), @BASE marks the field as selected, as shown here:

BASE

Name	Type	Length	Decimals	
INVOICE	Numeric	9	2	1 Selected
MODEL	Char	9		2 Selected
NET	Numeric	12	2	3 Selected

Pressing (ENTER) while highlighting a field that is already selected de-selects that field. When you have selected all of the fields you want, you press (ESC). You are presented with a view of the records like the one shown in Figure 10-34. If the number of fields selected results in records extending beyond the right edge of the window, you can use the cursor movement keys to view different parts of each record. Likewise, you can scroll more records into view. The keys to use are listed in Table 10-1.

You can see that @BASE numbers each record, in effect adding another field to the record. However, you cannot edit this record number; it is used exclusively by @BASE to keep track of records.

BROWSE

File OHMSALES

Record	INVOICE	MODEL	NET	AUTO	POWER	SOLAR
1	1101.00	Truck	13309.54	N	Y	N
2	1102.00	Truck	11576.23	N	N	Y
3	1103.00	Truck	10186.80	N	Y	Y
4	1104.00	Truck	11584.95	Y	Y	N
5	1105.00	Truck	9422.75	Y	N	Y
6	1106.00	Truck	11261.24	N	N	Y
7	1107.00	Car	12917.42	N	N	Y
8	1108.00	Truck	12711.20	Y	N	Y
9	1109.00	Car	9938.54	N	N	Y
10	1110.00	Car	11005.45	Y	N	N
11	1111.00	Car	11070.67	N	Y	N
12	1112.00	Car	9207.90	Y	N	Y
13	1113.00	Truck	10500.10	Y	N	Y
14	1114.00	Truck	11694.81	N	N	Y
15	1115.00	Truck	12932.23	N	Y	N
16	1116.00	Truck	13446.28	N	Y	Y
17	1117.00	Truck	13162.39	N	Y	N
18	1118.00	Truck	13204.14	Y	N	N
19	1119.00	Car	10739.37	Y	N	Y

MAIN

Mem Num

FIGURE 10-34 Browsing records

In General:	
LEFT ARROW	Moves the highlight left one character on the screen
RIGHT ARROW	Moves the highlight right one character on the screen
UP ARROW	Moves the highlight up one character on the screen
DOWN ARROW	Moves the highlight down one character on the screen
ESC	Backs out of a prompt;cancels the current command and moves back one level in the command sequence (can cancel back to the @BASE main menu); for commands and modes in which you select or edit fields, indicates that you are finished selecting or editing and displays the next prompt
ENTER	Selects what is highlighted; processes keyed-in data
In a Browse Table:	
LEFT ARROW	Moves the highlight left one field
RIGHT ARROW	Moves the highlight right one field
UP ARROW	Moves the highlight to the same field in the previous or next record
DOWN ARROW	Moves the highlight to the same field in the previous or next record
CTRL-LEFT ARROW	Moves the highlight left one screen
CTRL-RIGHT ARROW	Moves the highlight left or right one screen
DEL	Toggles between marking and unmarking records for deletion
END LEFT ARROW	Moves the highlight to the first or last field in the current record
END RIGHT ARROW	Moves the highlight to the first or last field in the current record
END UP ARROW	Moves the highlight to the first record, keeping the highlight in the current field

TABLE 10-1 @BASE Keys

END DOWN ARROW	Moves the highlight to the last record, keeping the highlight in the current field
ESC	Returns you to the @BASE main menu
GOTO (F5)	Moves the highlight to the record whose number you specify
HOME	Moves the highlight to the first field of the first record
PGDN	Moves the highlight down one screen
PGUP	Moves the highlight up one screen
In Form Mode:	
UP ARROW	Moves the highlight to the previous field in the same record
DOWN ARROW	Moves the highlight to the next field in the same record
END	Displays the last active record
ESC	Returns you to the @BASE main menu
GOTO (F5)	Displays the record whose number you specify (this applies even if the record is marked for deletion or does not match the active criteria)
HOME	Displays the first active record in the database file
PGDN	Moves the highlight to the same field in the next active record
PGUP	Moves the highlight to the same field in the previous active record
When Adding Records in Data Browse and Data Form:	
ESC	If you are using Data Browse, returns you to the browse table without adding the new record; if you are using Data Form, returns you to the record that was current when you displayed the blank record entry form
INS	Adds the new record to the database and displays another blank record entry form
+ (plus)	Adds the new record to the database and displays another record entry form that contains the same, that is, duplicated, data

TABLE 10-1 @BASE keys (*continued*)

The number is assigned according to the original order in which the records were entered or translated into the database. The only way to reassign record numbers is to re-sort the database to a new file, as described later in this chapter.

Database Fields

Databases created with @BASE, or that are recognized by @BASE, can include five types of fields: character, numeric, floating-point, date, and logical. There are rules governing the typing of fields and their length.

CHARACTER FIELDS These are used to store text entries, which can consist of any combination of alphanumeric characters.

NUMERIC AND FLOATING-POINT FIELDS These are used to store numbers. Entries in these fields can include any series of digits and a decimal point, but they cannot include thousands separators. The field's decimal-place setting determines the number of decimal places allowed for entries in a numeric or floating-point field.

DATE FIELDS These are used to store dates. @BASE actually stores dates in YYYYMMDD format, as in 19910401 for April 1, 1991. However, you enter dates in an @BASE record using the 04/01/91 format. This matches the format used by Symphony in the Format Date 4 command (Full Intn'l), so if you change the Symphony format with the International setting it will alter the way you have to enter dates in @BASE. You can tell @BASE to use two digits or four digits to represent the year portion of dates by using the @BASE Settings Year command and choosing either 2-Digit or 4-Digit.

LOGICAL FIELDS To store the logical values true or false, you use the field type Logical. @BASE uses T for true and F for false.

FIELD LENGTHS The length of an @BASE database field determines the maximum length of entries in that field. For character and numeric fields, you can specify the field length. For logical and date fields, @BASE sets the length automatically. Character fields can be up to 254 characters long. Numeric and floating-point fields can be up to 19 characters long and can include up to 15 decimal places. Date fields are always 8 characters long, and logical fields are 1 character long.

FIELD NAMES Each field name in an @BASE database must conform to the following requirements: it can be from 1 to 10 characters long; it can include any combination of letters, numbers, and underscores (_), but it must begin with a letter; it cannot include spaces; it must be unique within the database.

@BASE displays entries in numeric and floating-point fields the same way. Both Symphony and dBASE III use floating-point arithmetic to process entries in both types of fields. The distinction between these field types applies only to dBASE IV, which uses packed-decimal arithmetic to process numeric fields and floating-point arithmetic to process floating-point fields. For information on the difference between these types of fields for dBASE IV processing, see your dBASE IV manual.

Since @BASE converts the contents of date fields to Symphony date numbers when performing statistical calculations and transferring records to the Symphony worksheet, dates before January 1, 1900 and after December 31, 2099 are not valid for these operations. This is a reasonable limitation, since these are dates to which Symphony cannot assign a date number.

Although databases you create with @BASE cannot include memo fields, you still use @BASE to work with dBASE files that include memo fields. In memo fields that contain an entry, @BASE displays the word "Memo" (uppercase "M"); in memo fields that do not contain an entry, @BASE displays the word "memo" (lowercase "m"). Deleting memo fields with the @BASE File Modify command does not delete or change the associated dBASE text (DBT) file.

The @BASE Environment

When you are working in the BASE environment, you can press SERVICES and use some of the commands on the menu. However, the File Save and Retrieve commands apply to worksheets and not to DBF files. You must use the @BASE Menu File commands to store and retrieve database files. Also, the SERVICES Application commands are not available from the @BASE environment. To use these commands, for example, to attach an additional @BASE add-in, you must switch to one of the other environments before issuing the Application command.

You can use SERVICES Window Create to create as many @BASE windows as you want. However, the work you do with @BASE is only shown in the current @BASE window; any other @BASE windows continue to display the main @BASE screen as in Figure 10-33. To move to another Symphony environment from the @BASE environment, press ESC to remove the @BASE main menu from the control panel and then use either TYPE (ALT-F10) or SWITCH (ALT-F9) to change environments.

Mode	Action You Can Perform
BASE	Display a Symphony or an @BASE menu
BROWSE	View a database file in a browse table
EDIT	Add or change data
ERROR	Press (F1) to display help, or press (ESC) to perform another activity
FIELD	Define fields
FILES	Specify a file or directory
FORM	View a database file record by record
HELP	View help text
INSERT	Insert a new record
MENU	Select a command from the displayed menu
NAMES	Make a selection from the displayed list of field or range names
POINT	Specify a range
WAIT	Wait while @BASE completes a command or process

TABLE 10-2 @BASE Modes

@BASE has a set of indicators it displays to provide information about the program or about keys you are using with the program. @BASE has two types of indicators: mode and status. These are listed in Tables 10-2 and 10-3, respectively. The mode indicator is located at the far right of the first line of the control panel. It tells you what mode, or state, @BASE is currently in. Status indicators appear in the status line at the bottom of your screen when you use certain keys and when particular conditions exist.

Indicator	Meaning
Calc	@DB and other formulas in the worksheet may need to be recalculated
Caps	The CAPS LOCK key is on
Draw	One or more windows need to be updated
End	In browse mode, you pressed END and must press a pointer movement key to move to another field or record
Learn	Symphony is recording your keystrokes in the learn range
Link	Links in the worksheet may need to be refreshed
Macro	Symphony is executing a macro
Mem	Less than 4096 bytes of memory are still available
Num	The NUM LOCK key is on
Online	Symphony communications are in use
Pause	A macro is being executed in STEP mode
Scroll	The SCROLL LOCK key is on
Step	The STEP (ALT-F7) key is on, meaning that macros will execute one step at a time
User	The USER (F7) key is on; you can enter the name of a macro
Zoom	You have enlarged the current window to full-screen size

TABLE 10-3 @BASE Status Indicators

There are a number of function keys specific to the BASE environment. In addition to using some of the function keys that work in other Symphony environments, @BASE uses the function keys shown in Table 10-4 from within the BASE environment. In @BASE commands, the effects of pointer movement keys and special keys (such as INS, ESC, and DEL) are specific to the command you are using. For information about how to use pointer movement keys and special keys with a specific command, see Table 10-1.

Key	Purpose
COMPOSE (ALT-F1)	Lets you create a special character from two standard keyboard characters
CRITERIA (F3)	In browse or FORM mode, displays the Criteria menu
DRAW (ALT-F8)	In BASE mode, updates all windows
EDIT (F2)	Switches to EDIT mode so you can enter or change data
GOTO (F5)	In FORM mode, displays the record you specify; in browse mode, moves to the specified record or, if that record is inactive, to the next-higher active record
HELP (F1)	Displays a context-sensitive help screen
LEARN (ALT-F5)	Switches LEARN mode on and off for recording macros
MENU (F10)	In BASE mode, displays the @BASE main menu; in POINT or FILES mode, displays a list of range names or file names
SERVICES (F9)	In BASE mode, displays the Symphony SERVICES menu
STEP (ALT-F7)	Switches STEP mode on and off for macro execution
SWITCH (ALT-F9)	In BASE mode, switches a window between current and previous environments
TYPE (ALT-F10)	In BASE mode, displays the menu of environment types so you can change the current window type
USER (F7)	Lets you invoke a macro by typing its name and pressing ENTER
WINDOW (F6)	In BASE mode, makes the next window current
ZOOM (ALT-F6)	Switches the current window between original size and full-screen size

TABLE 10-4 @BASE Function Keys

@BASE includes four global settings, which affect all database files you work with. These settings appear in the global settings screen which @BASE displays whenever you use the Settings command from the @BASE menu:

```
Skip-Deleted  Use-Deleted                                          BASE
Deleted  Year  Blanks  File-Directory  Update  Quit


Deleted records          Skip
Year                     2-Digit
Blanks                   Zeros
@BASE file directory

Symphony data dir        \SYM22\DATA
```

The Deleted Records setting specifies whether @BASE skips records marked for deletion (the default) or includes records marked for deletion during record processing. The Year setting determines how the year portion of dates is displayed in date fields, and how dates are entered. The default setting is two-digit numbers (such as 91) or four-digit numbers (such as 1991). The Blanks setting specifies how @BASE handles blank numeric, logical, and date fields in calculations. The default is for blank fields to have a value of zero. Alternatively, you can change this to None or NA. The @BASE File Directory setting tells @BASE which directory to look in for database files. By default, @BASE uses the current Symphony directory, but you can use Settings File-Directory Set to specify a different directory.

@BASE stores the global settings in a configuration file called BASE_SYM.CFG. This file must be in the directory from which you start Symphony or a directory that is in your DOS path. When you use Settings Update to update the global settings, @BASE updates this file. The settings are read from the file and used in successive @BASE sessions until they are changed again.

Viewing Records

The Data Browse command is one of two ways you can view an @BASE database. In a browse table, @BASE displays the field

Criteria NET>13000 BROWSE
File OHMSALES

Record	INVOICE	MODEL	NET	AUTO	POWER	SOLAR
1	1101.00	Truck	13309.54	N	Y	N
16	1116.00	Truck	13445.28	N	Y	Y
17	1117.00	Truck	13162.39	N	Y	N
18	1118.00	Truck	13204.14	Y	N	N
22	1122.00	Truck	13778.56	N	N	N
23	1123.00	Truck	13205.64	N	Y	Y
35	1135.00	Car	13651.68	N	N	Y
39	1139.00	Car	13804.97	Y	Y	Y
50	1150.00	Truck	13277.85	N	Y	N
67	1167.00	Truck	13223.32	Y	N	Y
71	1171.00	Car	13703.41	Y	Y	N
74	1174.00	Truck	13131.56	Y	Y	N

FIGURE 10-35 Browsing specified records

names across the top of the table and the record numbers on the left hand side. Each database record occupies one row of the browse table. When you set selection criteria for a database (as explained next), @BASE displays the selection criteria in the control panel and includes only those records that match those selection criteria in the browse table. In Figure 10-35, the selection criteria for the database is NET>13000, so the browse table includes only those records in which the value of NET is greater than 13000.

Another way to display an @BASE database is with Data Form. Data Form displays a database one record at a time, as shown in Figure 10-36. As you move between records, the field names remain the same but the record number and data change. As with browse tables, @BASE displays in this database form only those records that match the active criteria.

Using Selection Criteria

At times, you need to work with only those database records that match a certain condition. To do this, you create selection criteria

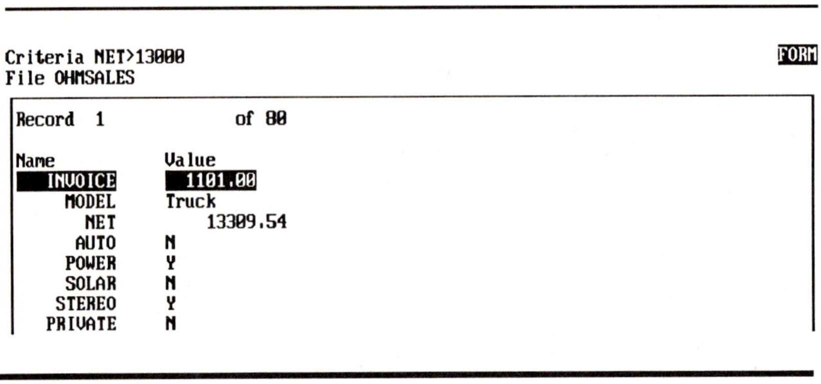

FIGURE 10-36 Browsing with Data Form

for the database. Like the entries in a criterion range in the SHEET environment, the @BASE selection criteria define the condition that a record must match for @BASE to display and process that record. However, in @BASE you use the Prompt command to develop criteria through a series of menus.

Suppose you want NET>13000 selection criteria. In Figure 10-35, you can see that @BASE displays a database in a browse table after you establish selection criteria for the database. Most @BASE commands and @DB functions work only with records that match the current selection criteria for a database. In BASE mode, with the sample database loaded, you establish selection criteria like this:

1. Press MENU and select Criteria. Choose Prompt and select the OHMSALES file.

2. @BASE presents a list of the fields in the database, as seen earlier while using the Browse command. To choose a field you want to include in your criteria, press the (DOWN ARROW) key to highlight the field name—in this case, NET—and press (ENTER).

3. @BASE presents a list of logical operators from which to choose, as shown here:

```
                                                              BASE
NET
=   (Equal)
<>  (Not equal)
>   (Greater than)
>=  (Greater than or equal)
<   (Less than)
<=  (Less than or equal)
```

Note that the name of the field you are working with, NET, is shown in the top left of the screen.

4. When you select the appropriate operator for your criteria (in this case, >), @BASE prompts you to enter the comparison value you want to use in the criteria (in this case, 13000), which is typed in as shown here:

```
Enter value: 13000                                            BASE
NET>
```

5. When you press (ENTER) to confirm the value, @BASE offers you a chance to add further qualifications to the criteria, as shown here:

```
                                                              BASE
NET>13000
Quit
And
Or
```

You can use And as well as Or. If the criteria is complete at this point, you can select Quit.

6. When you select Quit, you are returned to the main @BASE menu and the selection criteria is in effect. If you select Data Browse, choose the OHMSALES file, and choose All Fields, you will see a display like the one in Fig. 10-35. Note that All Fields means each field in a record will be displayed, not that all records will be displayed.

You can use the Prompt command again to create new criteria, or alter existing criteria with the Criteria Edit command. This presents the criteria on the first line of the screen as a statement to be edited, just like a worksheet cell entry is edited with the (F2) key. You can also use the Criteria Edit command to create criteria from scratch, without prompts, if you are comfortable with logical operators.

Use the Cancel command to remove criteria completely. To retain frequently used criteria, use the Save command. This allows you to paste a copy of the current @BASE criteria statement into the underlying Symphony worksheet. You can choose which cell to use for the criteria, which are entered as one-cell labels. When you save the worksheet, the criteria are saved. To use previously saved criteria, use the Criteria Retrieve command and select a criteria statement from the worksheet.

Records that meet criteria are referred to as *selected records*, and it is important to remember that many @BASE commands apply to selected records rather than to the entire set of records. The Data Browse, Form, Crosstab, Transfer, and Delete Mark commands all apply to selected records only.

Criteria Functions

Since criteria are so important, @BASE provides a special set of functions that can be used when creating criteria. For example, the RECNO function can be used to refer to record numbers in a criteria statement. To locate records 5 to 49, you would use this statement:

```
RECNO()>=5#AND#RECNO()<=49
```

The full range of criteria functions is listed in Table 10-5.

You can include the following in @BASE criteria strings: database field names and values, worksheet cell addresses and range names, the * and ? wildcards, and the following operators and these criteria functions:

ABS(*number*)
: Returns the absolute value of a number or numeric field.

CTOD(*string*)
: Converts a string into the date represented by the string.

DAY(*date*)
: Returns the day portion of a date.

DEL( )
: Checks whether a record is marked for deletion.

DTOC(*date*)_
: Converts a date to a string in the current date format.

IF(*conditionresult1,result2*)
: Returns one of two results, depending on whether the specified condition is true or false.

INSTR(*substring,string*)
: Checks whether a string includes the specified substring.

INT(*number*)
: Returns the integer portion of a number.

LEFT(*string,number*)
: Returns the specified number of characters at the beginning of a string.

LEN(*string*)
: Returns the length of a string.

LOWER(*string*)
: Converts a string to lowercase.

LTRIM(*string*)
: Removes spaces from the beginning of a string.

MONTH(*date*)
: Returns the month portion of a date.

RECNO( )
: Returns the number of the current record.

TABLE 10-5 @BASE Criteria Functions

RIGHT(*string,number*)

Returns the specified number of characters, starting at the end of the string or field.

ROUND(*number,decimal-places*)

Rounds a number to the specified number of decimal places.

RTRIM(*string*)

Removes spaces from the end of a string.

STR(*number,length,decimal-places*)

Converts a number to a string of the specified length and with the specified number of decimal places.

SUBSTR(*string,start-number,count-number*)

Extracts a substring of the length specified by *count-number*. The substring starts *start-number* of characters from the beginning of the string.

TODAY( )

Returns the Symphony date number that corresponds to the current system date.

UPPER(*string*)

Converts a string to uppercase.

VAL(*string*)

Converts a string that consists entirely of numeric characters to a number.

YEAR(*date*)

Returns the year portion of a date in four-digit format.

Valid operators in @BASE criteria strings are as follows:

= equal	< > not equal
> greater than	>= greater than or equal to
< less than	<= less than or equal to
#AND# and	.AND. and
#OR# or	.OR. or

TABLE 10-5 @BASE Criteria Functions (*continued*)

Note that when you use text in criteria, you must enclose it in quotes. When you use the Criteria Prompt command to compose text criteria, you do not have to type the quotes; they are placed around the text for you. The Edit Criteria command requires you to type in the quotes yourself.

Updating Existing Records

To update records in an @BASE database you can use the Data Browse or Data Form command to display the database and edit the appropriate records. To edit data in an @BASE database, you use the same keys that you use for editing data in the Symphony worksheet. For example, suppose that you have to change, from Truck to Car, the entry in the MODEL field of the record with invoice number 1101. First you would locate invoice number 1101. You can either do this by using Data Browse to move through the records, or you can use Criteria Edit to set a criteria of INVOICE=1101. Then you use Data Form to present the record. In Figure 10-37, you can see invoice number 1101 being edited. The highlighting was moved with (DOWN ARROW) to the MODEL field. The (F2) key was pressed to place the contents on the edit line at the top of the screen. You press (ENTER) to return the edited data to the field. Bear in mind that as soon as you leave this record, by pressing (ESC), the change is permanently recorded in the database.

You can also use the Data Replace command to perform large-scale editing. This command replaces data in selected fields in a group of selected records. For example, suppose you want to change the term "Car" to "Auto" in all records referring to cars.

1. Use the Criteria command to set up MODEL="Car" as the criteria to select the records to be altered. You *must* check that

```
MODEL: Truck                                                    FORM

Record  1             of 80

Name             Value
   INVOICE          1101.00
     MODEL       Truck
       NET              13309.54
      AUTO       N
     POWER       Y
     SOLAR       N
    STEREO       Y
   PRIVATE       N
```

FIGURE 10-37 Editing a record

you have performed this action correctly; otherwise, @BASE will alter all records, not just the ones that relate to cars. Note that when you create this criteria with the Criteria Prompt command, you do not need to type the quotes yourself.

2. Now select Replace from the Data menu and confirm the file name. @BASE lists the fields for you to select which one to alter. When you highlight the MODEL field and press (ENTER), @BASE prompts you to enter a field value. Type **"Auto"** including the quotes. This tells @BASE to use the string of characters between the quotes; if you just enter Auto, @BASE will copy the contents of the AUTO field into the MODEL field for the selected records.

3. When you have typed the replacement value, press (ENTER). @BASE retains the list of fields for you to make further changes if need be. Press (ESC) to return to the main menu, and you will have to choose between Cancel and Execute to complete the Replace command. When you select Cancel or, in this case, Execute, you will be returned to the main menu.

BROWSE

File OHMSALES

Record	INVOICE	MODEL	NET	AUTO	POWER	SOLAR
1	1101	Auto	13309.54	N	Y	N
2	1102	Truck	11576.23	N	N	Y
3	1103	Truck	10186.80	N	Y	Y
4	1104	Truck	11584.95	Y	Y	N
5	1105	Truck	9422.75	Y	N	Y
6	1106	Truck	11261.24	N	N	Y
7	1107	Auto	12917.42	N	N	Y
8	1108	Truck	12711.20	Y	N	Y
9	1109	Auto	9938.54	N	N	Y
10	1110	Auto	11005.45	Y	N	N
11	1111	Auto	11070.67	N	Y	N
12	1112	Auto	9207.90	Y	N	Y
13	1113	Truck	10500.10	Y	N	Y
14	1114	Truck	11694.81	N	N	Y
15	1115	Truck	12932.23	N	Y	N
16	1116	Truck	13445.20	N	Y	Y
17	1117	Truck	13162.39	N	Y	N
18	1118	Truck	13204.14	Y	N	N
19	1119	Auto	10739.37	Y	N	Y

MAIN

02-Apr-91 03:47 PM Num

FIGURE 10-38 Altered records

Use the Criteria Cancel command followed by the Data Browse command to see the changes. They should appear as shown in Figure 10- 38. You can also use the @DBUPD function, described in Appendix B, to update data in an @BASE file.

Adding Records

Once you have opened an @BASE file, there are several ways of adding records to it. Use the method that is most appropriate to the type of work you are using @BASE for.

THE (INS) KEY You can insert new records by pressing the (INS) key either in browse mode or FORM mode. This presents a new record form to be filled in, as shown in Figure 10-39. New records

```
                                                                  INSERT
File OHMSALES
Record  81            of 80

Name           Value
 INVOICE
   MODEL
     NET
    AUTO
   POWER
   SOLAR
  STEREO
 PRIVATE
```

FIGURE 10-39 Adding a new record

are automatically added to the end of the file and given new record numbers. When you have typed the field entries, press (INS) again. This inserts the new record and presents a further blank form. Fill in this form or press (ESC) to just enter the one new record.

DATA TRANSFER EXPORT You can use the Data Transfer Export command to add records to an @BASE file from the Symphony worksheet. (In what seems to be a contrary piece of nomenclature, bringing data into @BASE from Symphony is called exporting, meaning that @BASE sees this as exporting from Symphony.) For example, suppose that you have two further invoices in a Symphony worksheet, as shown here:

```
A1: ^Invoice                                                        SHEET

       A        B          C          D        E       F       G        H
1   Invoice   Model       Net        Auto    Power   Solar   Stereo  Private
2      1181  Car     $13,221.99      N        Y       N       N        N
3      1182  Car      $9,552.94      N        Y       N       N        N
4
5
```

You want to update the @BASE file using this information.

1. Switch to the @BASE environment and issue the Data Transfer Export command.

Sorting Records

To sort records you use the Data Sort command, which allows you to sort up to 256 fields at one time. The Sort command affects all records in the database, not just those selected by the current criteria.

When you select Sort from the Data menu, you are presented with a list of fields. Select the field that is the primary basis for the sort. For example, if you want to sort the sample records from highest net to lowest, you would highlight the NET field and press (ENTER). @BASE prompts you to choose between Ascending or Descending, as shown here:

```
Sort from low to high (numbers last)                                    BASE
Ascending  Descending

Name            Type       Length     Decimals
INVOICE         Numeric       9          0
MODEL           Char          9
NET             Numeric      12          2
AUTO            Char          9
POWER           Char          9
SOLAR           Char          9
STEREO          Char          9
PRIVATE         Char          9
```

In this case, you would choose Descending. @BASE records your choice next to the field name and uses the number 1 to indicate that this is the primary sort key.

If you wanted to sort on two levels—for example, to sort by model and then by net amount—you would select the primary field first (that is, MODEL), and then the secondary field (that is, NET). To deselect a sort field, you simply press (ENTER) again while still highlighting the field. If you go on to select a second field, you can no longer deselect the first field. To reselect multiple sort fields, you press (ESC) twice to clear all the sort settings and try again.

After you have made the correct settings, you press (ESC) just once. This causes @BASE to present a choice between Overwrite or Create-File. The latter option allows you copy the sorted data to a new file, whereas the former simply sorts the data within the current file. If you select Create-File, you must provide a name for the new file. Both options require you to confirm the command by choosing Cancel or Execute. When you tell @BASE to go ahead and execute the Data Sort command, the records are reordered, both in memory and on disk.

CREATING AND MODIFYING @BASE FILES

The previous sections explained some of the ways you can use @BASE to work with records within an existing database file. The following sections look at how you create new files and change the structure of existing files.

Creating New @BASE Files

There are several ways of creating a new @BASE file. The method you use will depend on the source of the information being used in the database.

UTILITY FILE TRANSLATE When you want to create a DBF file based on a Symphony database, you can use the Utility File Translate command. Earlier, you saw how Symphony's Translate program can turn a WR1 file into a DBF file. In fact, @BASE provides a quicker method. Having loaded @BASE, you load the Symphony worksheet that contains the data you want to place in the DBF file. You then issue the @BASE Utility File Translate command. @BASE switches to the SHEET environment in POINT mode for you to indicate the database cells. If you have already defined a database range in the worksheet using the FORM environment commands or the SHEET environment Query Settings commands, then @BASE suggests this range. You can accept the range as presented by @BASE or define a different area using the normal Symphony range definition methods.

When you press (ENTER) to confirm the range, @BASE prompts you for a name for the new DBF file. When you have entered a name, you must provide an alias. Having done this, you are shown the field definitions to review them. You can alter field names, types, and lengths if you want to. You press (ESC) when you have finished reviewing and altering the field definitions. @BASE asks you to confirm that you want to save the data on disk. When you do so, the DBF file is created and loaded into @BASE. At first, it may not look like @BASE has opened the new file, but if you press SWITCH ((ALT-F9)) to move to the SHEET environment and then again to come back to @BASE, you will find the file listed in the @BASE window.

FILE DEFINE To create a DBF file from scratch with @BASE, you use the File Define command. After you provide a name for the new file, @BASE leads you through a series of prompts for field names, types, and lengths. When you have finished defining fields, you press (ESC) to return to the main menu, where you can use Data Form to start entering records.

FILE EXTRACT To create a DBF file from an existing @BASE file, you use the File Extract command. When you use this command, you must provide a name for the new file and choose between Copy-Records or No-Records. The latter creates a new database that is a clone of the existing one, but without any records. The Copy-Records command clones an existing file complete with records.

You can also use the Data Sort Create-File Command to make a new database out of an old one, altering the sort order of the records as you do so. If you want to take data from a DBF file and place it into a Symphony worksheet, you use the Data Transfer Import command, described in a moment.

Changing the Structure of Existing Files

At the heart of an @BASE file are the field definitions. These consist of the field name, type, length, and, in the case of numeric and floating-point fields, the number of decimal places. To modify an @BASE file, you change the field definitions. To change a field name, you use the Field-Rename command. To change a field type, length, or number of decimal places, you use File Modify. You can also modify an existing database by adding or deleting fields in the file. To add or delete a field, use File Modify.

Any time you create a new @BASE database file or modify an existing one, @BASE displays a field definition screen so you can enter or edit the field definitions for that database. For example, suppose that you want to add a new field called COLOR to the OHMSALES database. You select File Modify, and @BASE presents the field definition screen shown in Figure 10-41. At first you just have a list of the fields used so far, but if you press (DOWN ARROW) to move the highlighting below the last field, in this case, PRIVATE, you are prompted to define a new field, as shown in Figure 10-41.

When you have typed the name of the field and pressed (ENTER), @BASE lists the choices for field type, as shown in Figure 10-42.

```
Enter field name:                                                FIELD

Name           Type       Length     Decimals
INVOICE        Numeric       9          0
MODEL          Char          9
NET            Numeric      12          2
AUTO           Char          9
POWER          Char          9
SOLAR          Char          9
STEREO         Char          9
PRIVATE        Char          9
```

FIGURE 10-41 Field definition screen

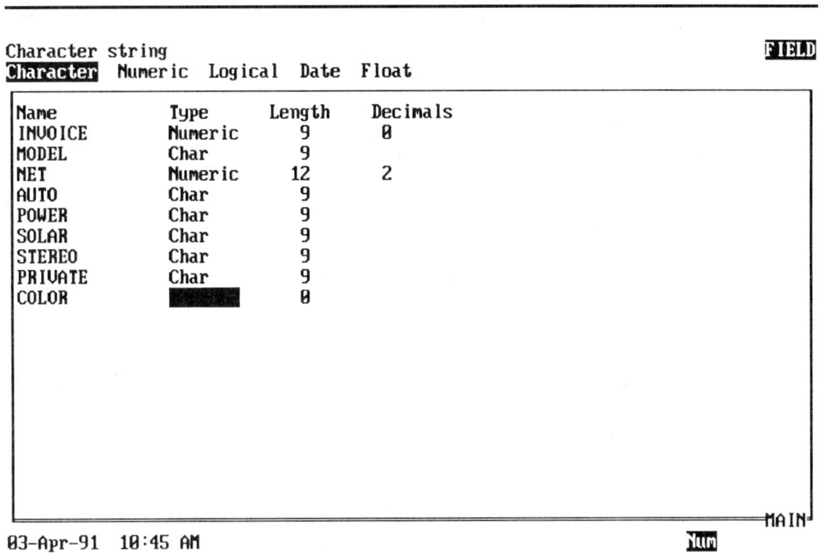

FIGURE 10-42 The field type prompt

In this case, you would choose Character. Since character fields can be any length from 1 to 4000 characters, selecting this type leads to the field length prompt. When you enter a length, the definition of the new field is completed. You press (ESC) to leave the field definition screen and choose between Cancel and Save, the latter option causing @BASE to write the changes to disk.

When you have confirmed changes to the database, you can use the Data Form command to see the new field in place. As you can see from Figure 10-43, the field has been added and is ready for the color information to be entered.

Saving Your Work

You have seen that at certain points, @BASE asks you to choose between Save and Cancel. The Save option confirms that you want @BASE to write to disk the changes you have made or the data

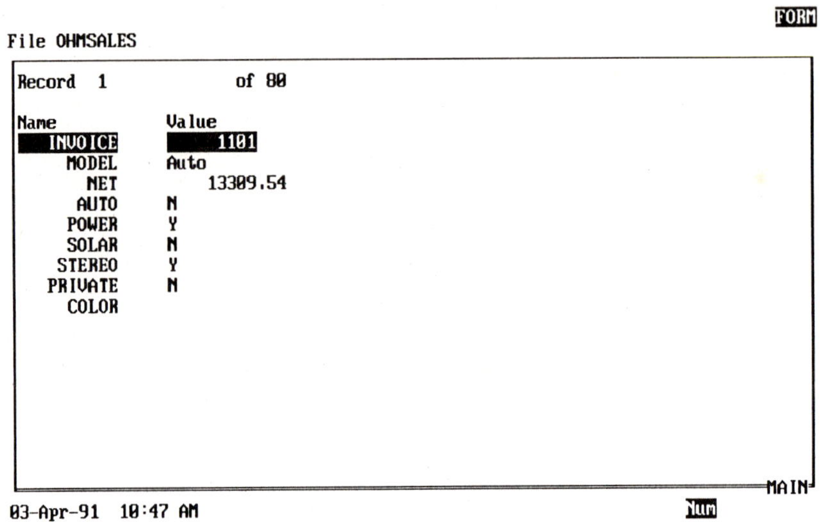

FIGURE 10-43 The new field in record 1

you have entered. However, this is not the only saving to disk that @BASE performs. As a disk-based application, @BASE automatically saves most work on disk for you, rather than waiting like Symphony does for you to issue a File Save command.

Whenever you make a change to the contents or structure of an @BASE database file, @BASE immediately attempts to write the change to disk. However, because it is really DOS that does the writing of files to disk, and DOS is sometimes busy, @BASE temporarily stores the change in a buffer in memory rather than writing it straight to disk. For this reason, @BASE periodically writes any data stored in file buffers to the appropriate file or files on disk. In addition, @BASE writes to disk any data stored in file buffers when you do one of the following:

- Close the corresponding file or files with File Close or @DBCLOSE
- Detach @BASE
- Use SERVICES Exit to end the Symphony session

The @BASE File Post command is used to force @BASE to save the contents of all open file buffers to disk. By using this command regularly, as you do the Symphony File Save command, you can further minimize the chances of data loss from a power failure or any other event that might occur before @BASE has had a chance to write the latest file buffer contents to disk.

Using @BASE with Symphony

One of the most powerful features of @BASE is its close integration with Symphony. As you have seen, @BASE provides facilities for processing database files from within the SHEET environment and for transferring @BASE database records to and from the Symphony worksheet. There are a number of procedures you can use when working with @BASE and Symphony.

THE @DB FUNCTIONS You can enter @BASE functions, referred to as the @DB functions, in a Symphony worksheet. The @DB functions are built-in @BASE formulas that let you open and close @BASE databases, perform calculations on individual @BASE database records or groups of records, and add or edit records from within the SHEET environment. The functions are classified as statistical, logical, and file manipulation functions.

As an example of an @DB file manipulation function at work, consider this example:

```
A7: @dbapp("OHMSALES",A3,A4,B3,B5,C3,C5,D3,D5,E3,E5,F3,F5,G3,G5,H3,H5)       SHEET

      A         B          C            D         E         F         G         H
1  Sales of Ohmobile Vehicles in January
2
3   Invoice  Model      Net          Auto      Power     Solar     Stereo    Private
4      1184 Truck     $11,342.00      Y         Y         N         N         N
5      1185 Car       $11,645.00      N         N         N         N         N
6
7        85
```

The @DBAPP functions adds, or "appends," data to an open @BASE file. When you enter the function it adds a new record to the file and returns the number of the record. The function takes three basic arguments. The first is the alias of the @BASE file you want to add the record to, enclosed in quotes. The second argument is the name of the field you want to place a value in, and the third argument is the field value. As you can see, cell references can be used to indicate field names and values.

DATA CROSSTABS You can use the @BASE Data Crosstab command to create statistical reports in the Symphony worksheet based on data in an @BASE database. Crosstab reports can either tabulate the number of records containing the same entry in one or more fields or sum numeric data in one or more fields. For example, suppose you want to find the total net amount from the invoices in the OHMSALES database, broken down by model. In such a cross-tabulation, the MODEL field is referred to as the key field and the NET field is referred to as the sum field. The values within the MODEL field—that is, the different models—are referred to as the key values.

1. First make sure that you have the OHMSALES file open and no criteria in place (Data Criteria Cancel).

2. In the BASE environment, issue the Data Crosstab command and select the OHMSALES file.

3. @BASE presents a list of fields. You must choose the key field, the field that is the basis of the cross-tabulation. In this case, you select the MODEL field. Press (ESC) to leave the field selection screen.

4. @BASE asks you to choose between three different ways of defining the key values to be used in the cross-tabulation: Generate, Exact, and Range. In this case, choose Generate to have @BASE choose the key values for you.

5. @BASE now presents the worksheet and asks you to indicate a starting place for the table, referred to as the key values label row. If you are using an empty worksheet, indicate cell B2; otherwise, any cell below and to the right of existing entries will do.

6. When you have indicated the cell to be used, you must choose between a count or a sum cross-tabulation. In this case, you want to see the total amount generated by the invoices, so select Sum.

7. Now @BASE asks you to select the field you are going to sum. This must be a numerical field, in this case, NET. When you have selected the field, you press (ESC), and @BASE generates the table and returns you to the menu.

A temporary file appears in the file list. This is used by @BASE when making the cross-tabulation. When you press (ESC) to clear the menu and press SWITCH to move to the SHEET environment, the results appear as shown here:

```
B2: 'MODEL                                                  SHEET
      A        B           C         D       E       F       G
1
2              MODEL             NET
3              Auto        341812.67
4              Truck       556833.82
5
6
7
```

The results can be dressed up with cell formatting. The two numbers represent the total of the NET field in the two categories Auto and Truck. You can repeat the command with the Count option to get a count of the different models, as shown here:

B2: 'MODEL SHEET

	A	B	C	D	E	F	G	H
1								
2		MODEL	Count					
3		Auto	30					
4		Truck	48					
5								

Note that there is no field name for the right column of the table. Instead, the label "Count" is entered by @BASE. This is because the Count option only adds up the number of entries in the NET field; it does not do any math with the entries. In Figure 10-44 you can see the results of cross-tabulating three fields (AUTO, POWER, and SOLAR). This shows how many vehicles were sold with the different combinations of options.

When you use more than one key field, @BASE asks you to choose between Down and Across for listing the values in the fields. In Figure 10-44, the Down option was used so that the possible key values, created by the Generate command, would be listed down the column.

B2: 'AUTO SHEET

	A	B	C	D	E	F	G
1							
2		AUTO	POWER	SOLAR	Count		
3		N	N	N	8		
4		N	N	Y	11		
5		N	Y	N	9		
6		N	Y	Y	6		
7		Y	N	N	10		
8		Y	N	Y	11		
9		Y	Y	N	12		
10		Y	Y	Y	11		
11							

FIGURE 10-44 Multiple cross-tabulation

A11: 'Trucks only: SHEET

	A	B	C	D	E	F	G
1	All vehicles:						
2		AUTO	POWER	SOLAR	Count		
3		N	N	N	8		
4		N	N	Y	11		
5		N	Y	N	9		
6		N	Y	Y	6		
7		Y	N	N	10		
8		Y	N	Y	11		
9		Y	Y	N	12		
10		Y	Y	Y	11		
11	Trucks only:						
12		AUTO	POWER	SOLAR	Count		
13		N	N	N	4		
14		N	N	Y	6		
15		N	Y	N	5		
16		N	Y	Y	5		
17		Y	N	N	8		
18		Y	N	Y	7		
19		Y	Y	N	8		
20		Y	Y	Y	5		

MAIN

03-Apr-91 02:02 PM Num

FIGURE 10-45 Further cross-tabulation

Using criteria prior to performing a cross-tabulation considerably improves the command's flexibility. In Figure 10-45, you can see a second cross-tabulation performed below the one in Figure 10-44. Prior to using the Crosstab command, the criterion MODEL="Truck" was established. This resulted in the cross-tabulation applying only to the selected records. Note that you must label such results yourself; @BASE will not do it for you. Also note how the labels in the results have been centered with the Range Label-Alignment Center command to improve the worksheet's appearance.

DATA TRANSFER IMPORT To transfer @BASE database records to the Symphony worksheet for querying, analyzing, printing, and performing other tasks with Symphony commands and formulas, you can use the @BASE Data Transfer Import command. This command gives you three ways of determining which fields of information are placed into Symphony. The options are All Selected and Labels. The last of these allows you to set up names of desired fields as labels in a worksheet prior to the Data Transfer Import command. When you use the Selected option you pick the desired fields from a field list.

You also get to determine which records will be transferred by using a set of criteria before the command. The command will only transfer the records that meet the criteria. When you have issued the Data Transfer Import command and selected the fields, all that remains is to point out the top left cell of the worksheet range in which you want the data placed. When you do this, the data is written to the worksheet. Note that the record number is included, as shown in Figure 10-46, where you can see the results of Data Transfer Import with just the INVOICE, MODEL, and NET fields selected and the criteria statement MODEL="Trucks" in effect.

A21: "Recno SHEET

	A	B	C	D	E	F	G
21	Recno	INVOICE	MODEL	NET			
22	3	1103	Truck	10186.00			
23	4	1104	Truck	11584.95			
24	6	1106	Truck	11261.24			
25	8	1108	Truck	12711.20			
26	13	1113	Truck	10500.10			
27	14	1114	Truck	11694.81			
28	15	1115	Truck	12932.23			
29	16	1116	Truck	13445.28			
30	17	1117	Truck	13162.39			
31	18	1118	Truck	13204.14			
32	20	1120	Truck	11177.15			
33	22	1122	Truck	13778.56			
34	23	1123	Truck	13205.64			
35	24	1124	Truck	12975.56			
36	25	1125	Truck	10421.14			
37	26	1126	Truck	12525.29			
38	27	1127	Truck	10042.71			
39	28	1128	Truck	11939.79			
40	29	1129	Truck	12788.19			

MAIN

03-Apr-91 02:18 PM Num

FIGURE 10-46 The results of Data Transfer Import

MACROS You can use Symphony macros to work with @BASE databases. For example, you can create a mailing label macro that prints mailing labels from data in a name and address database, or a data entry macro that appends records entered in the Symphony worksheet to an @BASE database file.

SUMMARY

This chapter clearly demonstrates the power of add-in modules to enhance Symphony in specialized areas such as statistics and database management. As you become experienced with the various add-ins, you can develop the right combination for your work, bearing in mind that you may need additional memory in your computer to accommodate all of the modules you want to use.

- When you have large database files to work with, consider using the @BASE application to place the data in a DBF file rather than storing it in a worksheet.
- Use worksheets to compliment DBF files for reporting, graphing, cross-tabulation, and other data analysis.
- For analysis of data in worksheets, you can use the statistical add-in as well as cross-tabulations generated by the Range What- If command. You can also use @BASE Data Crosstab to perform cross-tabulations on DBF files.
- For a table of results from a what-if scenario, use the Range What-If command.

11

THE OUTLINER, THE SPELLING CHECKER, AND ALLWAYS

This chapter looks at how Symphony's word processing powers are augmented by the Outliner and Spelling Checker add ins, and how the Allways program brings desktop publishing features to all Symphony documents. The ways you can share data between different environments will also be reviewed, so that you can start to make the most of Symphony's integration.

THE SYMPHONY SPELLING CHECKER

One of the add-ins provided with Symphony 2.2 is called the Spelling Checker. It is a great help when you are word processing with Symphony. You can use it to weed out typos from your writing.

About Spell-Checking

Computers are great tools for working with words. This book was written on a computer and typeset by a computer. Word processing programs, like Symphony's DOC environment, make editing a lot easier than in the days of white-out. However, the actual writing of the book was not done by a computer. We humans still do the writing, and, as humans, we tend to make mistakes. When we type, we find it hard to get our fingers around certain words. For example, "formula" might come out as "formual" and "answer" might come out as "anwser." To help us avoid the embarrassment of presenting documents to others that contain spelling errors, programmers came up with a genre of software called spell-checkers (or spelling checkers). This software usually consists of three files:

- A large data file, called a dictionary, containing tens of thousands of commonly used words
- A smaller data file, called a user dictionary, containing words that are not in the dictionary file but are nevertheless acceptable to you, the user
- A program file that compares the words in your document with the words in the two dictionary files and indicates discrepancies

The spelling checker provided by Lotus as a Symphony add-in is arranged in this way. The main dictionary file is called AMERICAN.LEX. The personal user dictionary is called PERSONAL.DCT. The spelling program is called SPELLER.APP.

Before you learn the joys of spell-checking, you need to have clearly in mind the principle behind the program: It does not actually check spelling, it merely compares the words in your document with those in the dictionary and spots discrepancies. If you use correctly spelled words in the wrong place or misspell a word in such a way as to produce a different but correctly spelled word, the spelling checker is none the wiser. For example, the following phrase gets a clean bill of health: "Hear toady butt gong to morrow." Until programmers develop "context-sensitive" programs that can make sense of what we are trying to say, spelling checkers will remain no more than a tool, a useful way of correcting typos and other obvious errors. Spell-checking is no substitute for human copyediting, and you should not assume that just because you spell-checked it your document is correct.

Preparing To Spell-Check

To use the Spelling Checker add-in, you must first attach it. This may require some planning, since it takes up a considerable amount of memory. Unless you have expanded memory, you will probably not want to run any other add-ins along with the Spelling Checker. This means you may need to unload other add-ins before attaching the Spelling Checker. To attach the Spelling Checker for a single session, press SERVICES and select Application Attach and then choose the file called SPELLER.APP. To attach the Spelling Checker so that it is loaded for each Symphony session, press SERVICES, select Configuration Other Application Set, choose an add-in number, and select the file called SPELLER.APP. Do not set SPELLER.APP to Auto-Invoke.

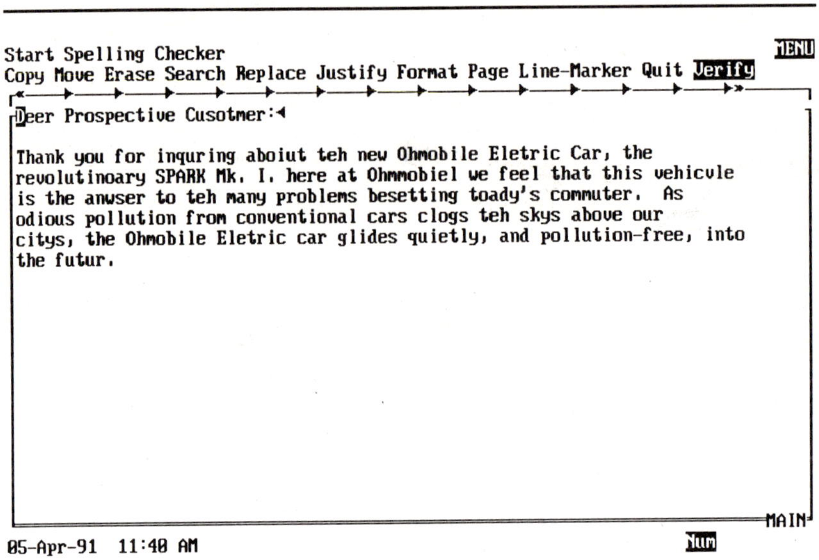

FIGURE 11-1 The Verify menu item

Attaching SPELLER.APP adds a new item, Verify, to the main menu in the DOC environment, as shown in Figure 11-1. Before you use this item, you should create some text to be checked. In a fresh worksheet, press TYPE ((ALT-F10)) and select DOC as your environment. Then carefully type the text shown in Figure 11-1.

Having typed the text and pressed (HOME) to place the cursor at the beginning of the document, press MENU and select Verify. The following menu items appear: Go, Maintenance, Settings, and Quit. Before you use the Go command to start checking the document, you need to make sure that the Spelling Checker is properly configured for your system. This is not something you need to do every time you use the program—just the first time and whenever you want to alter the spelling options.

To configure the Spelling Checker, you select Settings from the Verify menu. You will see a settings screen like the one in Figure 11-2. The main items to check at this point are the location settings

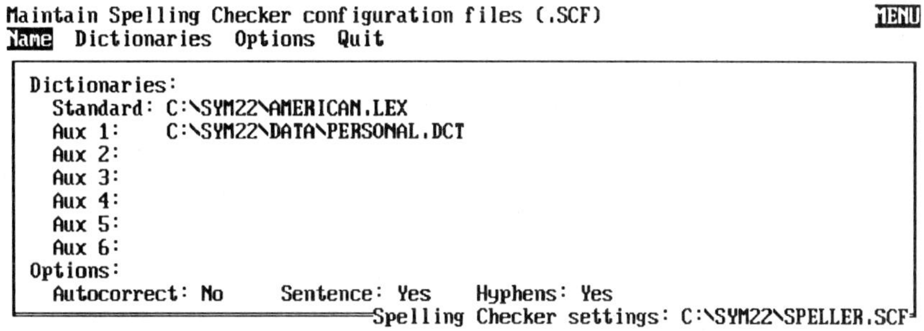

FIGURE 11-2 Spelling settings

for the dictionaries, both Standard and Aux 1, the latter being the file used for your own list of acceptable words. Although your screen might list AMERICAN.LEX under Standard and PERSONAL.DCT under Aux 1, the file name alone is not good enough. You must include the drive letter and path for each dictionary file in order for Symphony to be able to find it when spell-checking. The AMERICAN.LEX file is usually stored in the Symphony program directory. The PERSONAL.DCT file can be stored in the program directory or in a data directory. (Later, you will learn how to use foreign dictionary files and multiple auxiliary dictionaries.)

To include the drive/path information in the Dictionaries setting, choose Dictionaries followed by Set. Select Standard and enter the full path and file name. Symphony will check to make sure that this is correct by looking in the directory you specify. If Symphony does not find the file using the path information you have provided, you will need to try again. Press (ENTER) to confirm the correct setting. Repeat the process for the Aux 1 setting. A file called PERSONAL.DCT is placed in the Symphony program directory by the Symphony installation procedure, but this is an empty file, ready for you to add your own words. You can use this file as your personal dictionary file or use a different file name. Symphony will create the file for you.

Having used the Dictionaries command on the Verify Settings menu to properly identify the dictionaries you want to use, you can use the Name command to save the settings in a file named with the SCF extension (short for "Spelling Configuration File"). Usually, this file is called SPELLER.SCF. It is the spelling configuration file that is normally loaded by Symphony. Of course, you can create several different configuration files and load the one you want with the Verify Settings Name Retrieve command. However, to store your settings in the normal SCF file—that is, SPELLER.SCF—select Save from the Verify Settings Name menu and press (ENTER) to confirm the name. If necessary, type **y** to confirm that you want to replace SPELLER.SCF. Quit from the Settings menu back to the main Verify menu.

Starting the Check

When you have properly configured the Spelling Checker, you can select Go from the main Verify menu to begin checking your document. You will be asked to enter the spell-check range. This is expressed in terms of lines and characters, as in 1,1..1,1, which is the initial range (if you have placed the cursor at the top of the document before pressing MENU). Being able to spell-check a range of the document rather than the whole document is sometimes very useful if you have areas of the document that would be tedious or pointless to check. However, if you want to check the whole document, press (END) and then (HOME). Press (ENTER) to confirm the range, and the Spelling Checker goes to work. After a brief wait, the List menu will appear, as shown in Figure 11-3.

So far, the Spelling Checker has read through your document word-by-word, comparing each word with those in the dictionaries until it encountered a word in your document that was not in the dictionaries. This is why it did not object to "Deer," since "Deer" is in the dictionary. Such errors will have to be corrected later. The

```
Display corrections list for Cusotmer                                    MENU
List  Edit  Resume  1  2  3  4  5  6  Quit
Deer Prospective Cusotmer:

Thank you for inqurning aboiut teh new Ohmobile Eletric Car, the
revolutinoary SPARK Mk. I. here at Ohmmobiel we feel that this vehicule
is the anwser to teh many problems besetting toady's commuter.  As
odious pollution from conventional cars clogs teh skys above our
citys, the Ohmobile Eletric car glides quietly, and pollution-free, into
the futur.

                                                                      MAIN
Verify Go                                               Ovr     Num
```

FIGURE 11-3 List menu

word "Cusotmer" is the first "spelling" error, and the word is highlighted in the document.

The choices on the List menu, shown in Figure 11-3, allow you to handle most eventualities. The first option is List, which shows you a list of correctly spelled words that the Spelling Checker thinks might be what you were trying to type when you created the erroneous word that is highlighted. Select List and, after a brief wait, the choices are displayed, as shown here:

```
Select replacement for Cusotmer                                          MENU
Customer  Customary  Customers  Custom  Customs  Customize
Deer Prospective Cusotmer:

Thank you for inqurning aboiut teh new Ohmobile Eletric Car, the
revolutinoary SPARK Mk. I. here at Ohmmobiel we feel that this vehicule
is the anwser to teh many problems besetting toady's commuter.  As
odious pollution from conventional cars clogs teh skys above our
citys, the Ohmobile Eletric car glides quietly, and pollution-free, into
the futur.
```

Note that the list is capitalized to match the erroneous word. Also note that the correct word is the first on the list and so is already highlighted. The Spelling Checker manages to accomplish this level of response quite frequently, allowing you to replace the erroneous word with the correct one simply by pressing (ENTER).

When you press (ENTER), the misspelled word is replaced with the word you selected from the list, with no chance to change your mind. Make sure that you have highlighted the correct word in the list before you press the (ENTER) key. Use the (LEFT ARROW) and (RIGHT ARROW) keys and the (END) and (HOME) keys to navigate the list. You cannot select from the list with the first-letter method as you can in menus, but you can move the highlighting with the spacebar.

Corrections and Additions

When you have chosen Customer from the list, the Spelling Checker moves on to "inquring," correctly guessing the correct word and placing it at the front of the list presented when you choose List. Press (ENTER) to make the correction, and the highlighting moves on to "aboiut." When you select List this time, the correct word is the only word suggested. Press (ENTER) to select it.

The next problem is "teh," which List correctly guesses as "the." Make the correction, and you will find the word "Ohmobile" is highlighted. The Spelling Checker knows about some proper nouns, like America, but it does not recognize this fictitious brand name. Even though it is unlikely to solve the problem, try the List command to see what happens. The list shows "Homebodies." This is not the right word: in fact, the word is fine as it is. To leave the list without selecting a word, press (ESC) once.

Your options with a word that the Spelling Checker does not recognize but which you find acceptable are to skip the highlighted word, which is done by selecting Resume, or to add the word to your personal dictionary. You do this by choosing one of the numbers on the List menu. These numbers correspond to the personal dictionaries you have installed. Since you only have the one personal dictionary installed (Aux 1) you would type **1** to add this word to it. You can take the word out later, so go ahead and choose 1 to add it to the dictionary. The advantage of this over Resume is that the next time the Spelling Checker encounters "Ohmobile," it will accept it as spelled correctly.

Capitals and Other Conventions

The next problem word is "Eletric." which is correctly guessed as "Electric," and is presented with the correct capitalization. After making the correction with List, you find "revolutinoary," again guessed correctly. When you make the change, the Spelling Checker stops at "here," which is not spelled incorrectly but begins a sentence and so should be capitalized. Your choices are Capitalize, Resume, or Quit. Select Capitalize, and "here" becomes "Here." This feature performs a very useful copyediting function, making sure that all of your sentences begin with capital letters.

Another copyediting task performed by the Spelling Checker is the removal of spaces. When the Spelling Checker has completed checking a section of text, it will remove all double spaces between words except for double spaces after a period, question mark, or exclamation mark. If you have three spaces after a period and before the next word, it will reduce the three spaces to two.

The next problem is "Ohmmobiel," which is an incorrectly spelled proper name. Try the List command and you will see that the Spelling Checker now knows the correct spelling because you added the correct version of the word to your personal dictionary. Press (ENTER) to select the correct spelling.

The next word is "vehicvle," which is guessed correctly, so after you select List press (ENTER). This takes you to "anwser," a simple transposition of letters. However, when you select List you will see several words ("amuser," "amusers," "nastier," and so on) but no "answer." This is just one of those situations in which simple human error is not simple for a computer to unravel. When the correct word for your misspelling is not in the list, you must press (ESC) to leave the list and then use the Edit command. This places the word on the first line of the screen for you to edit, as shown here:

```
Edit: anwser                                                       EDIT

Deer Prospective Customer:

Thank you for inquiring about the new Ohmobile Electric Car, the
revolutionary SPARK Mk. I. Here at Ohmobile we feel that this vehicle
is the anwser to teh many problems besetting toady's commuter.  As
odious pollution from conventional cars clogs teh skys above our
citys, the Ohmobile Eletric car glides quietly, and pollution-free, into
the futur.
```

After you have edited the word properly, you can press (ENTER) to place the edited version into the document in place of the incorrect text. As a safety measure, the Spelling Checker checks what you have entered. If it is still not recognized, the Corrections menu will appear again.

Automatic Corrections

Now you come to another "teh," which you can correct with List. You may think that this is a tedious repetition of the action you took before to correct the same mistake. In fact, there is an option you can adjust within the Spelling Checker to avoid this problem. Back in Figure 11-2, you saw the Verify Settings screen. In future sessions you may want to select the item called Options on the Verify Settings menu and set the Autocorrect option to Yes. This will tell the Spelling Checker to automatically correct repeated misspellings, such as "teh" in the example.

This feature applies to corrections you make through Edit as well as List commands and can save a lot of time and effort if you tend to be consistent in your typos. As with all time-saving features, however, there is a trade-off. Suppose that you think you have typed "I will alter this sentence later." However, what you actually typed was "I will atler this sentence atler." With the

Autocorrect feature active, this type of error presents a problem: Using either Edit or List to correct the first "atler" to "alter" will result in the second instance being automatically corrected to the same word, making nonsense of your sentence.

There is no real cure for this shortcoming. In a long document you will not be able to see all of your typos at once, so the Autocorrect feature can have unexpected results. The best defense is to look at the correction you are making and decide if it could possibly be ambiguous. If it could be, then skip the correction by selecting Resume and fix the problem later with Autocorrect disabled. Alternatively, you can select Quit to end the Spell-check and this will leave the cursor at the beginning of the word you were highlighting when you picked Quit. Correct the word manually and then restart the spell-check with Verify Go, selecting an area that excludes the manual correction. Bear in mind that Autocorrect remembers all changes for an entire Symphony session, not just for the duration of the current Verify operation. Until you are familiar with the Spelling Checker program, you may want to leave the Autocorrect option at the default setting of No.

Further Corrections

When you come to "skys" and choose List, you will find that the Spelling Checker does not have the correct word in the list, so press (ESC) to return to the List menu to choose Edit. Alter the word manually and press (ENTER) to proceed. The erroneous "citys" is treated in the same way. The second occurrence of "Eletric" also would have been corrected automatically if Autocorrect had been in effect.

When you get to "pollution-free," you will find that the List command is no help. In fact, you get an error message: "No correction words found." Press (ESC) or (ENTER) to remove the ERROR indicator and return to the menu; since the phrase is acceptable, you select Resume to skip it. The hyphenated word "pollution-free" is a problem to the Spelling Checker, because by default the Verify Settings Options Hyphens option is set to Yes. This tells the Spelling Checker to treat hyphenated words as one word. If you set this option to No, then "pollution-free" is not a problem—it is checked as two words, "pollution" and "free."

After Checking

The last word to be dealt with is "futur," for which the correct spelling is the first suggestion when you choose List. When the Spelling Checker finds no more errors, it returns the cursor to the position in the document it occupied when the Verify command was issued. If you use the Quit command to leave the spell-checking operation before it is complete, the cursor is left at the beginning of the last word identified as misspelled.

So far, you have seen most of the tasks performed by the Spelling Checker; however, there are several wrinkles that have not yet been covered. There is a possibility that you will accidentally add a "wrong" word to your personal dictionary. For example, suppose that when the Spelling Checker highlighted "Eletric," you typed **1** by mistake. This adds the word to your personal dictionary and tells the Spelling Checker that the word is acceptable. How do you check for this? After all, you cannot spell-check the dictionary! You must watch for situations in which the Spelling Checker fails to spot an error. If this happens, you can use the Verify Maintenance command.

When you select Verify Maintenance, you have these options: Add, Delete, Modify, and Quit. The Add option allows you to enter a word in a personal dictionary. This is handy when you are about to check a large document that has a lot of words (such as proper nouns) that the Spelling Checker is not likely to accept. The more you use the program, the better sense you will have of what words the program accepts. Entering words with the Add option speeds up the actual checking. To remove words that should not be in the dictionary, you select the Remove command, type the word, and

```
Set standard dictionary name                                              MENU
Standard  1  2  3  4  5  6

 Dictionaries:
   Standard: C:\SYM22\AMERICAN.LEX
   Aux 1:    C:\SYM22\DATA\PERSONAL.DCT
   Aux 2:
   Aux 3:
   Aux 4:
   Aux 5:
   Aux 6:
 Options:
   Autocorrect: No     Sentence: Yes    Hyphens: Yes
                        Spelling Checker settings: C:\SYM22\SPELLER.SCF
```

FIGURE 11-4 The Verify Settings Dictionaries Set command

press (ENTER). The Modify command prompts you to type the word you want to modify. When you enter the word, the Spelling Checker makes sure it exists in the dictionary and then prompts you for a replacement.

The Spelling Checker allows you to use more than one personal dictionary. In Figure 11-4 you can see that the Verify Settings Dictionaries Set command has been issued. This allows you to specify the files that you want for your Standard and personal dictionaries. Users of foreign versions of Symphony may have access to main dictionaries other than AMERICAN.LEX, which they can specify as the Standard dictionary file. To use a personal dictionary, you select a number and then specify a DCT file. The file can be an existing dictionary that you have created or a new dictionary, which is created when you enter a new name. Because you can attach up to six different personal dictionaries, you have a lot of flexibility. For example, you might want one personal dictionary for correspondence and another for technical reports. If you are sharing a system with other users, you can each have your own dictionary. What you need to bear in mind is that attaching dictionaries 1 through 6 increases the number of words that are accepted. To just use one personal dictionary at a time, select 1 and change the file to the one you want to use.

Double Trouble

In addition to capitalizing the first characters of a sentence and removing double spaces between words, the Spelling Checker performs one other copyediting chore: double-word checking. With deleting and copying made so easy by word processing programs, it is all too easy to end up with duplicate words. When the Spelling Checker spots a situation like this, it highlights the second word and provides a choice of three actions: Erase, Resume, or Quit. Choose Erase to remove the duplicate. Choose Resume to ignore the duplicate, a situation that arises in some lists where words are repeated. Choose Quit to leave the duplicate in place and end the Verify procedure.

There are one or two quirks in the operation of the Spelling Checker that you will discover. For example, suppose you are writing about a person called Fred Smith. The Spelling Checker highlights "Fred" as an error, but when you select List the first offering is Fred. If you select Fred, you immediately get the Erase/Resume/Quit menu that suggests you have two Freds. In fact, if you select Erase you end up with no Fred, so the correct choice is Resume. There may be other words that give rise to this anomaly.

When you accidentally type a punctuation character or number as the first character of a word, the Spelling Checker ignores it. This means that the following are accepted: 2GO, /Red, -ink. Also, along with many other programs of this type, the Symphony Spelling Checker finds no fault with single characters. Thus, there would be no objection to this sentence:

```
The p ink 1 is 7my /favor it w.
```

Despite these limitations, the Spelling Checker is a great tool for weeding out typos and other errors. Any reports or correspondence you prepare in the DOC environment will benefit from a quick once-over with the Verify command.

TEXT OUTLINING

Most people find that the powers of a word processing program assist them in producing readable and legible documents. The ability to electronically change words and their order both quickly and neatly means that you no longer have to weigh the desire to change wording against the pain of retyping an entire page. However, word processing alone does nothing to help you organize your thoughts or present information in an orderly fashion. This is where the category of software known as outliners comes in. One of the add-in applications that comes with Symphony 2.2 is called the Text Outliner, which consists of the file called OUTLINER.APP. This file contains a complete outlining program that works together with the DOC environment to supplement basic word processing.

What an Outliner Does

An outliner provides a flexible system of headings and sub-head ings by means of which you can create an outline for a document prior to filling in the details. You can see a typical application of this in Figure 11-5. When you attach OUTLINER.APP to Symphony, it offers a further environment type, OUTLN. An OUTLN window gives a different perspective on the Symphony word processing environment. You create headings for the various parts of your document in the OUTLN window and then flesh out the headings with the body of the text in the regular DOC window.

Only the outline headings appear in the OUTLN window, whereas both outline and text appear in the corresponding DOC window. In Figure 11-6 you can see the DOC environment version of the outline shown in Figure 11-5. You can move back and forth between an OUTLN window and its corresponding DOC window at any time with one keystroke (press F5 in an OUTLN window

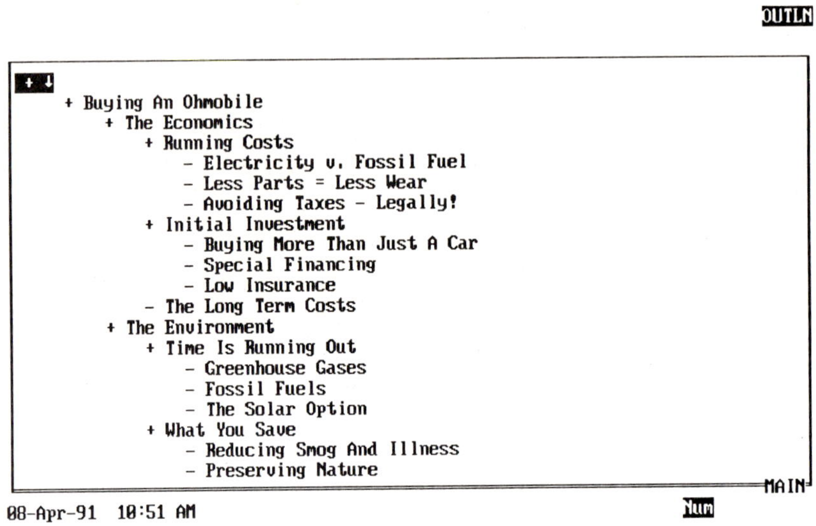

FIGURE 11-5 A sample outline

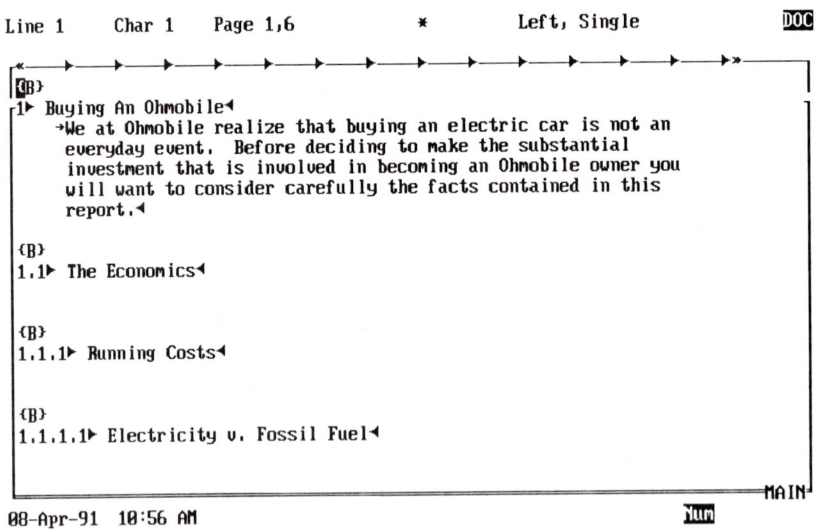

FIGURE 11-6 The DOC view

to go to the DOC window; press ALT-F9 to switch from DOC to OUTLN).

The OUTLN window provides the tools to create multilevel outlines with headings and subheadings to a depth of 32 levels. In Figure 11-5 you can see three levels of heading below the main heading. The plus signs (+) indicate a heading that has subheadings below it. The minus signs (-) indicate headings that have no subheadings. You can move or copy headings and subheadings. You can also add or delete headings and subheadings. You can display all headings, as in Figure 11-5, or just major headings, as shown here:

```
                                                    OUTLN
+ ↓
 + Buying An Ohmobile
   + The Economics
   + The Environment
   + The Enjoyment
- ↑
```

You can print summary documents consisting of headings alone, or print headings plus body text for a full document.

The OUTLN Commands

When you are in the OUTLN mode, you can select outline-specific commands from the F10 menu. Press MENU, and you will see the following commands:

Copy Move Insert Delete Join Numbering Tables Print-Range Attributes

The Copy command copies outline entries and associated text. The Move command moves outline entries and associated text. Insert is used to add outline entries, and Delete removes outline entries and associated text. The Join command merges a section with the preceding section. The Numbering command controls outline

Moving Around in an Outline:	
UP ARROW	Moves up within the same level of entry
DOWN ARROW	Moves down within the same level of entry
LEFT ARROW	Moves up one entry regardless of entry level
RIGHT ARROW	Moves down one entry regardless of entry level
PGDN	Moves down one screen
PGUP	Moves up one screen
Big-Left	Moves to the previous entry at a higher level
Big-Right	Moves to the next entry at a higher level
GOTO (F5)	Switches from an OUTLN window to the corresponding DOC window (Outliner moves you to the line below the entry that was highlighted when you pressed GOTO)
Command Keys:	
INS	Inserts outline entries
DEL	Deletes outline entries *and* associated text from DOC window
EDIT (F2)	Edits outline entries
TAB	Changes outline numbering
–	Hides all subheadings under highlighted entry
+	Exposes all subheadings one level under highlighted entry
*	Exposes all subheadings under highlighted entry
1 through 9	Changes indentation between outline levels (default setting is 4)
Symbols in the OUTLN window:	
↓	Indicates the top of the outline
↑	Indicates the bottom of the outline
+	In front of a heading, indicates that subheadings follow
–	In front of a heading, indicates that no subheadings follow

TABLE 11-1 Outliner Keys and Symbols

Symbols in the DOC Window:

{B}	Indicates the beginning of a section (section-begin marker)
{-B}	Indicates the beginning of a section that is hidden in the OUTLN window
{E}	Indicates the end of a section (section-end marker)
{N}	Indicates a nonprinting heading

TABLE 11-1 Outliner Keys and Symbols (*continued*)

numbering and indentation. You can create a table of contents from an outline with the Tables command, which can also be used to copy an outline into a worksheet. The Print-Range command specifies a text range for printing. The last command, Attributes, sets the print attributes for some or all of the selected headings.

Some keys perform special functions in the OUTLN window. They permit you to edit or change the appearance of the outline, or to switch to the corresponding DOC window. The OUTLN keys are shown in Table 11-1.

A Basic Outline

To see how outlining works, you can create the example shown in Figure 11-5. You should attach OUTLINER.APP before beginning the exercise (use SERVICES Application Attach). In a fresh worksheet, press TYPE ((ALT-F10)) and select OUTLN. You should see a blank outline screen, as shown in Figure 11-7.

The minus signs indicate that there are no headings in place. The downward-pointing arrow indicates the beginning of the outline, and the arrow pointing upward indicates the end of the outline. These indicators will become clearer as you proceed to create the sample outline. First, you will create the main headings.

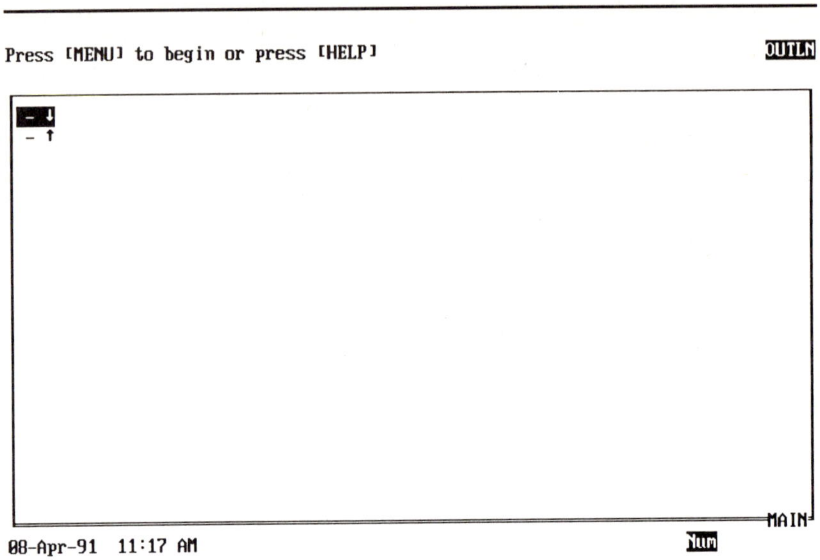

FIGURE 11-7 Blank outline screen

1. Press MENU and select Insert, or simply press the (INS) key. The first minus sign moves one line down and several spaces away from the left margin. The minus sign on the first line has become a plus.

2. Type **Buying An Ohmobile**. This is the main heading, or the title of the outline. As you type the heading, you can use the (BACKSPACE) key, the (LEFT ARROW) and (RIGHT ARROW) keys, and the (DEL) key to edit what you type.

3. When you have typed the heading correctly, press (ENTER). This produces what is called the Insert menu, shown here:

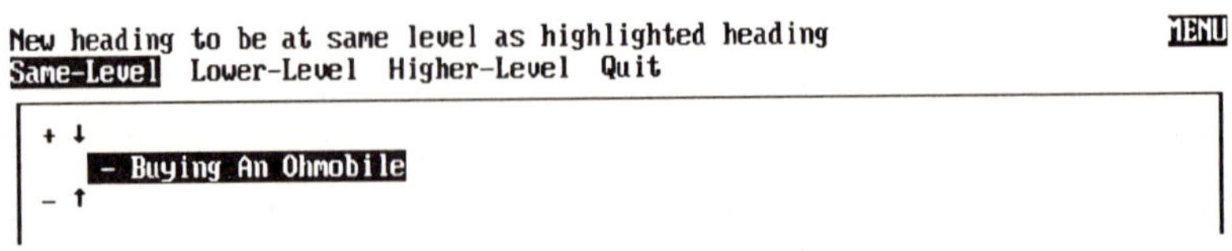

From this menu you choose Lower-Level, because you want to insert a series of headings below the main heading. When you choose Lower-Level, the minus sign in front of the first heading changes to a plus sign to show that there is a subheading. The subheading is marked by a minus sign, to show that there are, as yet, no headings below this.

4. Type **The Environment** and press (ENTER). Select Same-Level from the Insert menu.

5. Type **The Economics** and press (ENTER). Select Same-Level from the Insert menu.

6. Type **The Enjoyment** and press (ENTER). This is the last heading you need at this level, so you select Quit from the Insert menu. The results will look like this:

```
                                                              OUTLN
+ ↓
    + Buying An Ohmobile
        - The Environment
        - The Economics
        - The Enjoyment
- ↑
```

When you select Quit to leave the Insert menu, you are said to be in the "work environment." This means that the cursor is now a highlight bar that can be moved around the headings, allowing you to edit a specific heading or select a point at which to insert subheadings. You move the highlight bar using the arrow keys. The (UP ARROW) and (DOWN ARROW) keys move the highlighting vertically, within the same level. The (LEFT ARROW) and (RIGHT ARROW) keys move the highlighting through the outline from top to bottom, through all levels. The (END) key takes the highlighting to the end of the outline, and (HOME) takes it to the beginning. The OUTLN keys are summarized in Table 11-1.

To edit an existing heading, you highlight it and press EDIT ((F2)). This places you in EDIT mode, and you can use the usual

Symphony editing keys to make changes to the heading. Note that pressing (ESC) while in EDIT mode removes the text of the heading. Pressing (ESC) again replaces the text and takes you out of EDIT mode into work mode. However, if you press (ENTER) when you have removed the text from a heading, you will end up with a blank heading. You cannot actually remove a heading from an outline in EDIT mode; you must use the (DEL) key or Delete command (described shortly).

From OUTLN to DOC

To see what your outline looks like so far in the DOC environment, move the highlighting to the heading that reads "The Economics" and press GOTO ((F5)). As you can see from Figure 11-8, this key takes you directly to the DOC environment, with your cursor immediately below the heading you were highlighting in the OUTLN environment. Note that the headings are numbered, and there are special codes ({B} and {E}) attached to them. These codes are used to keep track of outline levels while you are editing outlined documents in the DOC environment. The {B} stands for "Begin outline level" and the {E} stands for "End outline level." The codes are not printed when you print the document, and you cannot edit them.

The numbering of the headings should not be altered in the DOC environment, but the text of the headings can be edited. This means that you can use the Spelling Checker to check the spelling of heading text. Changes that you make to heading text in the DOC environment will remain in effect when you switch back to the OUTLN environment.

```
Line 12    Char 1    Page 1,13                    Left, Single          DOC

{B}
1▸ Buying An Ohmobile◂

{B}
1.1▸ The Environment◂

{E}
{B}
1.2▸ The Economics◂
█

{E}
{B}
1.3▸ The Enjoyment◂

{E}
{E}
                                                                      MAIN
08-Apr-91  01:28 PM                                              Num
```

FIGURE 11-8 The DOC view of basic headings

The main reason to switch from OUTLN to DOC environment is to flesh out the document you are outlining. For example, you can add this text below the heading numbered 1.2:

```
1.2▸ The Economics◂

There are numerous economic factors to be considered when purchasing a
car.█

{E}
```

The text is automatically attached to the heading above it. As you will see, this allows you to move text along with headings if you need to rearrange the outline.

Expanding an Outline

To add further headings to an outline, you first switch from DOC mode into OUTLN mode. Do this by pressing the TYPE key ((ALT-F10)) and choosing OUTLN, or simply by pressing the SWITCH key ((ALT-F9)). Notice that the text you typed in the DOC environment disappears. Also notice that you are highlighting the entry that was above the text you were typing when you switched to the OUTLN environment. Now you can use the pointer movement keys to highlight the entry after which you want to insert new outline entries. In this case, you want to expand the heading about economics. The following steps produce this outline:

OUTLN

```
+ ↓
    + Buying An Ohmobile
        - The Environment
        + The Economics
            - Running Costs
            - Initial Investment
            - The Long Term Costs
        - The Enjoyment
- ↑
```

1. When you are highlighting "The Economics," either press MENU and select Insert from the OUTLN menu or press the (INS) key. This presents the Insert menu so that you can select a level for the new entry.

2. Select Lower-Level, type **Running Costs**, and press (ENTER). Select Same-Level, type **Initial Investment**, and press (ENTER). Select Same-Level, type **The Long Term Costs**, and press (ENTER).

3. After you finish entering outline headings at a particular point, you select Quit from the Insert menu or press (ESC) while viewing the Insert menu. Press (ESC) now.

Warning: Do not press ESC before pressing ENTER when you are creating a new heading. If you do so, you will lose the heading text and cancel the insert operation.

Displaying the Outline

By default, outlines in the OUTLN window are displayed with indentation between entry levels and with no numbering. You can use the TAB key to add sequential or multilevel numbering to your OUTLN display.

1. Press TAB to add sequential numbering at each level in the outline (1, 2, 3, and so on) as shown here:

OUTLN

```
+ ↓
    + 1 Buying An Ohmobile
        - 1 The Environment
        + 2 The Economics
            - 1 Running Costs
            - 2 Initial Investment
            - 3 The Long Term Costs
        - 3 The Enjoyment
- ↑
```

2. Press TAB again to obtain multilevel numbering (1, 1.1, 1.1.1, and so on). This type of numbering, shown here, is also referred to as absolute numbering:

OUTLN

```
+ ↓
    + 1 Buying An Ohmobile
        - 1.1 The Environment
        + 1.2 The Economics
            - 1.2.1 Running Costs
            - 1.2.2 Initial Investment
            - 1.2.3 The Long Term Costs
        - 1.3 The Enjoyment
- ↑
```

This is the type of numbering that appears on the outline in the DOC environment.

3. Press (TAB) a third time to return to the default display (that is, with no numbering).

You can also change the indentation between entry levels. You do this by pressing any number from 1 to 9 while in OUTLN mode. You will see the headings move across the screen. The default setting, used in the illustrations so far, is 4.

If you want to turn off the outline numbering that appears in the DOC environment, you can use the Numbering command on the main Outliner menu. When you select Numbering, your choices are Delete-Numbers and Renumber. The Delete-Numbers option results in the Outliner temporarily lining up the headings flush with the left of the window. When you press (F5) to go to the DOC environment, you will see that the numbering has been removed. This remains the case until you issue the Numbering Renumber command or any of these Outliner commands: Insert, Delete, Copy, or Move.

If the outline becomes large, you may want to display only major headings so that the entire outline or an entire section of the outline appears on the screen at once. You type a minus sign (–) to hide all subheadings of the highlighted heading. Type a plus sign (+) to expose all subheadings one level under the highlighted heading. Type an asterisk (*) to expose all subheadings at all levels under the highlighted heading. For example, if you press (HOME) to move to the top of the outline (marked by the downward arrow, ↓), and type a minus sign, the Outliner hides all headings. If you then type a plus sign, the Outliner exposes only the top level headings, in this case "Buying An Ohmobile." If you highlight this exposed heading and type a plus again, you will expose the next level headings, as seen here:

OUTLN

```
+ ↓
   + Buying An Ohmobile
        - The Environment
        + The Economics
        - The Enjoyment
- ↑
```

The plus signs in the display act as useful reminders that further subheadings exist. From the top of the outline, you can type an asterisk to expose all headings.

Outline Editing

There are several commands that help you rearrange headings. The great advantage of these commands is that they move all subheadings plus any text that has been added to the outline in the DOC environment. For example, the Move command moves outline entries and associated text. Suppose you want to move the section on economics so that it is the first heading below the main heading.

1. First contract the headings so they appear as in the last illustration. You do not have to contract headings to move them, but it is sometimes easier to work this way. Now highlight the heading "The Economics."
2. Press MENU and select Move. The prompt at the top of the screen asks, "Move what?" You respond by highlighting the block of entries that you want to move and pressing (ENTER). In this case you are already highlighting the block, so press (ENTER).
3. The prompt now changes to "Move after what heading?" Position the pointer on the heading below which you want to place

the block being moved, in this case, "Buying An Ohmobile." Now press ENTER.

4. The Outliner asks at what level you want to place the block you are moving, relative to the highlighted heading. In this case you want to choose Lower-Level. When you do so, the move is completed.

Press HOME and then type an asterisk to expand all of the headings, and you will see that the subordinate headings related to "The Economics" have also been moved. If you switch to the DOC environment, you will see that the associated text has also been moved.

The Copy command works in a similar fashion to copy outline entries, subordinate headings, and associated text. The Delete command, chosen from the Outliner menu or activated by pressing the DEL key, removes outline entries *and* any associated text. Although the Delete command requires that you confirm the deletion, you should always use this command with care: It removes text that you cannot see—that is, text associated with the heading in the DOC environment.

The Join command merges a section of outline with the preceding section. This also merges text associated with the two headings. You select Join from the OUTLN menu and then move the pointer to the section you want to merge with the preceding section. When you press ENTER, the Outliner asks you to confirm your selection before it merges the sections. Select Yes to confirm; otherwise, select No. When you select Yes, the Outliner joins the second section to the first and removes the second section's heading. It also exposes any subsections of the merged section that were hidden and renumbers the outline. You can only merge a section if the preceding section is at the same level or higher.

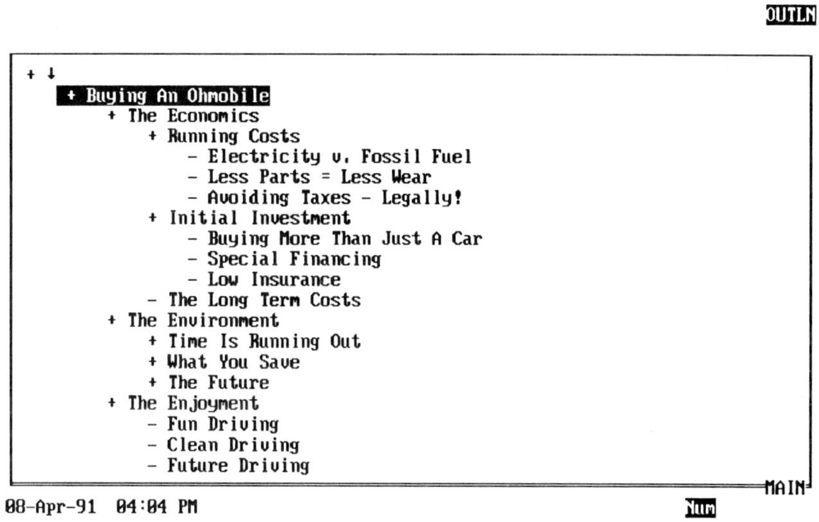

FIGURE 11-9 Added headings

Outline Tables

If you want to complete the sample outline, you will need to add several more headings, as shown in Figure 11-9. The section on the environment has further headings, as shown in Figure 11-10. After you have created this outline, you may want to save it. Any outline you create is saved whenever you issue the SERVICES File Save command.

By creating an outline for a document before writing the text of the document, you arc better able to map out its direction and structure, ensuring that the document has a consistent design and covers all of the areas that need to be addressed. The Outliner allows you to go into detail in the DOC environment while retaining access to an instant overview.

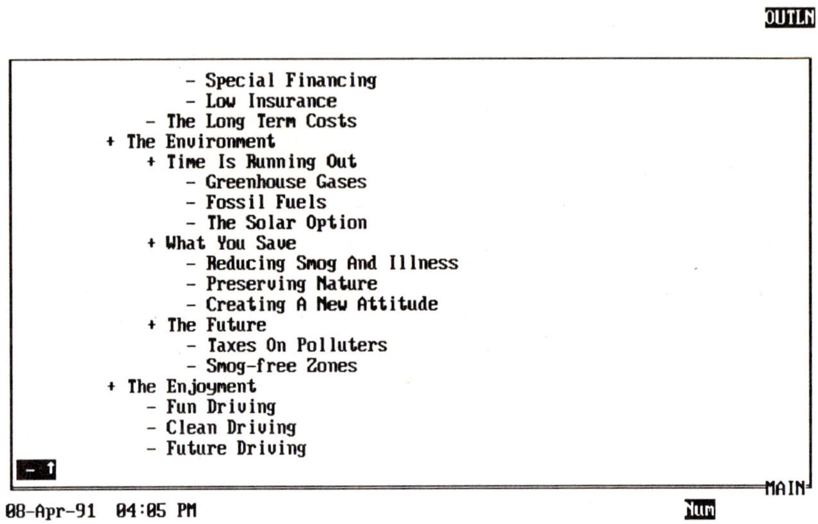

FIGURE 11-10 More headings

There may be times when you want to use the text of an outline in other documents, or as a table of contents. The Tables command generates a table of contents or a copy of an outline. Select Tables from the OUTLN menu, and select either Table-of-Contents, which generates a table of contents on the worksheet based on your current outline, or Outline, which copies the outline to an area of the underlying worksheet.

In Figure 11-11 you can see an example of a table of contents generated by the Tables command, based on the sample outline. When you select Tables from the OUTLN menu and choose Table-of-Contents, the Outliner asks you to specify the width of the table of contents, the indentation between entry levels, and the maximum number of entry levels to include in the table. The default settings are a width of 72, 4 characters for indentation, and 32 entry levels. The table in Figure 11-11 was created with these settings.

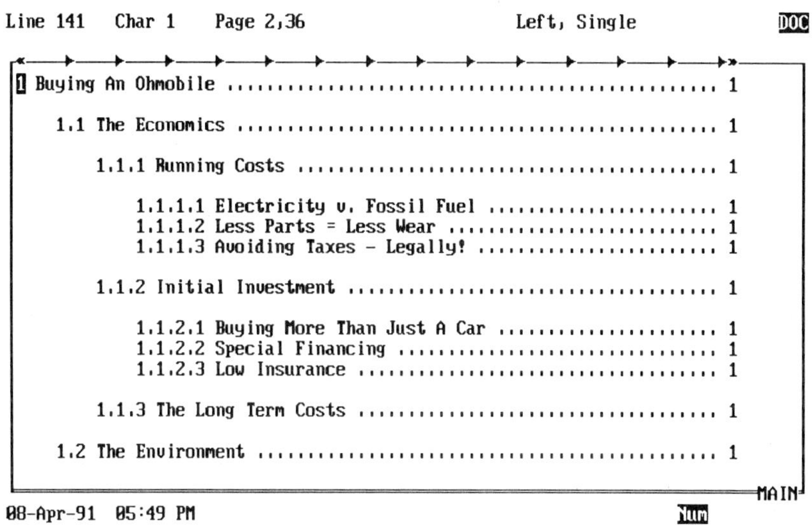

FIGURE 11-11 Table of contents

When you have provided the settings to be used for the table, you are presented with the worksheet and must provide a cell coordinate for the table. This marks the area into which the table is to be placed. Use an area with plenty of free cells below it; the table can get quite large. In this example, the outline text itself occupies almost 140 rows, so cell A141 was used for the table. When the table is generated, you are returned to the OUTLN environment. From there you can switch to the DOC environment, where the table will be visible below the body of the document. You can then use the Move and paste (CTRL-P) commands to place the table of contents at the beginning of the document.

The page numbers are placed in the table based on the current state of the underlying document in the DOC window. If you then add text to the different headings, the page numbers will be different. However, the table is not dynamic, and you must reissue the Table command to get an up-to-date listing.

When you generate a table of contents or a copy of an outline, do not use an area of the worksheet already occupied by either the outline or other parts of the document. Tables overwrite existing text that gets in their way.

If you do not need an entire table of contents complete with page numbers, you can use the Table Outline command to copy just the outline text from the OUTLN window to the worksheet. When you select this command, you simply move the cell pointer to an empty area in the worksheet where you want to copy the outline and press (ENTER). The Outliner copies the outline as it currently appears in the OUTLN window. If the outline is contracted, you get just the visible headings, as shown in Figure 11-12. You can display the copy of the outline in either a SHEET or a DOC window.

```
Line 201   Char 1   Page 3,40                  Left, Single            DOC

+ Buying An Ohmobile
    + The Economics
    + The Environment
        + Time Is Running Out
            - Greenhouse Gases
            - Fossil Fuels
            - The Solar Option
        + What You Save
            - Reducing Smog And Illness
            - Preserving Nature
            - Creating A New Attitude
        + The Future
            - Taxes On Polluters
            - Smog-free Zones
    + The Enjoyment
                                                                      MAIN
08-Apr-91  05:52 PM                                                Num
```

FIGURE 11-12 Outline copied to DOC environment

Printing Outlines

The Tables Outline command is useful when you want to print just the outline of a document. After you copy the outline to the worksheet, you can print it with the Print command, setting the source range to include the cells occupied by the outline.

The Print-Range command on the Outliner menu is another method of printing an outline, together with the related document text. This command prompts you to select the section of the outline you want to print by highlighting it. Place the cursor on the highest level heading that you want to print before you issue the Print-Range command. The headings you select are set as the current print source. After making a selection, you use the SERVICES Print command to print the document. Text that is associated with the headings of the outline is also printed.

Print Attributes

The Attributes command on the main Outliner menu allows you to set special print attributes for all or some headings to distinguish them from the document text and from each other in a printed report. First, you select Attributes from the OUTLN menu. Then you choose Global to set the attributes for all headings or Level to set the attributes for all headings at a given level. When you choose Level, you will need to move the pointer to any heading at the level you want to alter and press (ENTER). You can also choose Single if you want to set the attributes for a particular heading.

After telling the Outliner which headings to affect, you select an attribute. The choices are listed in Table 11-2. Choose Non-Printing if you do not want the headings to appear in the printed copy of the document. Choose Clear to remove attributes that you have already set.

B	Bold	0	Bold italic	5	Italic superscript
I	Italic	1	Bold underlined	6	Bold subscript
U	Underlined	2	Bold italic underlined	7	Italic subscript
+	Superscript	3	Italic underlined	8	Bold italic subscript
-	Subscript	4	Bold superscript	9	Bold italic superscript

Non-Printing means heading will not appear when outline is printed.
Clear removes assigned attributes.

TABLE 11-2 Outliner Attributes

The DOC Outline Commands

The Outline-Section command offers a way to create a new section and heading for an outline in the DOC window. You can use this feature to add an outline to an existing document or to subdivide an already existing outlined section of the document. This command does not appear on the Outliner menu but is an item added to the Format menu in the DOC environment when you attach OUTLINER.APP.

To use the Outline-Section command, you select Format from the DOC menu. Select Outline-Section, and move the highlighting to cover the text you want to include in the new section. Be sure to include any subsections that belong under this section. When you press (ENTER) to confirm your selection, you are prompted for the text of the heading. Type the heading and press (ENTER). Outliner inserts section-begin and section-end markers around the text and places the new heading in the appropriate place.

OUTLINER.APP adds one other command to the DOC environment: Format Location. This displays, in the lower left of the DOC window, the current location of the cursor in the outline, as in "Section 1.1.2."

Travel Made Easy

Revenue Breakdown:

	Jan-91	Feb-91	Mar-91	Apr-91	May-91	Jun-91	TOTAL
Tours	2642	2589	2758	2839	3513	4078	18,419
Air Fares	5472	5364	5714	5882	7277	8447	38,156
Other	1321	1295	1379	1420	1757	2039	9,211
Total	9,435	9,248	9,851	10,141	12,547	14,564	65,786

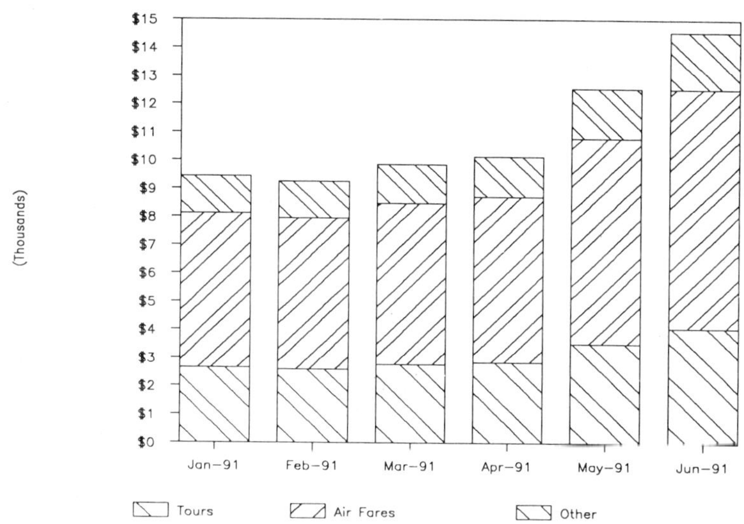

FIGURE 11-13 Enhanced revenue spreadsheet and graph

USING ALLWAYS

When you explored the SERVICES Print menu in Chapter 3 and the PrintGraph program in Chapter 6, you may have noticed that they did not make the most of your printer's features. Although you can create presentable reports and graphs with SERVICES Print and PrintGraph, you will also want to explore the Allways add-in application that comes with Symphony 2.2. Using Allways makes possible such reports as the one in Figure 11-13.

The Purpose of Allways

When Symphony was first introduced, most personal computer printers were slower and less versatile than those commonly available today. Back then, the first laser printer designed for personal computers, the HP LaserJet, had only just come onto the market, and there was very little software that could use its more advanced features, such as graphics and fonts. Many users still relied on daisywheel printers for "letter-quality" text. Slow and noisy, these printers could not produce graphics. Dot-matrix printers were used for graphics, but many could only produce "draft-quality" print.

Much has changed since then. In today's offices laser printers are commonplace, as are dot-matrix and ink-jet printers that can produce high-quality text and graphics. Personal computer users now have access to print features previously associated with professional typesetting hardware, features that are collectively referred to as *desktop publishing* or *DTP*. The software needed to control such capabilities is complex and requires extensive computing power. Through the Allways add-in, Symphony 2.2 provides DTP features for those who need them, without making the main Symphony program too large. (To use Allways with Symphony, you will need a hard disk and at least 640 K of RAM in your PC.)

Just as the Outliner provides a different view of the DOC environment, Allways provides a different view of the SHEET environment. When you have built a spreadsheet in the SHEET environment, you can look at it through an Allways window and alter its appearance. With a system of menus similar to those in the main Symphony program, Allways enables you to change the appearance of the characters that are used to print different cells.

The overall style or design of a character is known as its *typeface*. In Figure 11-14, you can see examples of a typeface called Times. As you can see, typefaces can be produced in different sizes, measured in *points*. The term *font* is used for each

Times 6 point (an Allways soft font)
Times 8 point (an Allways soft font)
Times 10 point (an Allways soft font)
Times 12 point (an Allways soft font)
Times 14 point (an Allways soft font)
Times 20 point (an Allways soft font)
Times 24 point (an Allways soft font)

FIGURE 11-14 Examples of Times typeface

set of characters in a particular size. For example, "Times 14 point" is a font. Allways allows you to use up to eight different fonts on one printout.

Most printers come with the built-in ability to produce several fonts. The font resources of some printers can be expanded by the use of additional cartridges. However, rather than rely on everybody installing the same set of fonts on their printer, Allways provides its own set of fonts. Instead of being a part of your hardware, these are *soft fonts,* meaning that the definition of each of the characters is stored on disk. This allows the same fonts to be used with a wide variety of dot-matrix and laser printers. In addition, you can still use the hardware fonts that come with your printer or that you have added by means of font cards or cartridges.

A spreadsheet report that is enhanced by Allways can also use shading, lines, and boxes to highlight important information in a report. The height of rows can be varied. You can also print graphs and worksheet text on the same page. If you have a graphics monitor, the effects of Allways commands are immediately visible on screen, a feature known as WYSIWYG ("What You See Is What You Get"). This instant feedback means that the features of Allways are relatively simple to master, enabling you to produce presentation-quality reports without a lot of trial and error. (If you do not see changes in screen fonts when you invoke Allways, use the Display command in Allways to set the mode to Graphics).

Using Allways does not alter the normal methods of spreadsheet and graph preparation you have learned so far. What Allways does alter is the method of printing information stored in worksheets and graph image files. Rather than printing with the Print and PrintGraph commands, you switch to Allways, enhance the worksheet entries, and then print them through the Allways menu.

You still have to save graphs into image files to print them with Allways, but unlike PrintGraph, Allways does not require that you exit Symphony to start another program when you want a printout of a graph. Allways makes it easy to print a graph on the same page as text entries from a worksheet and allows you to change the fonts and colors of the graph.

Starting Allways

The first step to using Allways is to install it. This was probably done when Symphony 2.2 was installed on your computer. Refer to Appendix A if you do not have Allways installed. The next step is to attach Allways, which is attached like any other add-in. To attach Allways for a single session, press SERVICES, select Application Attach, and choose the file called ALLWAYS.APP. To attach Allways so that it is loaded for each Symphony session, press SERVICES, select Configuration Other Application Set, choose an add-in number, and then select the file that is called ALLWAYS.APP. Do not set ALLWAYS.APP to Auto-Invoke.

Attaching ALLWAYS.APP adds a new item, Allways, to the end of the main menu in the SHEET environment. However, before you use this item, you might want to load a worksheet to be enhanced. The examples in the rest of this chapter will use the worksheet created in Chapter 6 and saved as TMESALES.WR1. This worksheet is featured in the report in Figure 11-13. After retrieving this file and attaching Allways, you can press MENU while in the SHEET environment and select Allways. The work-

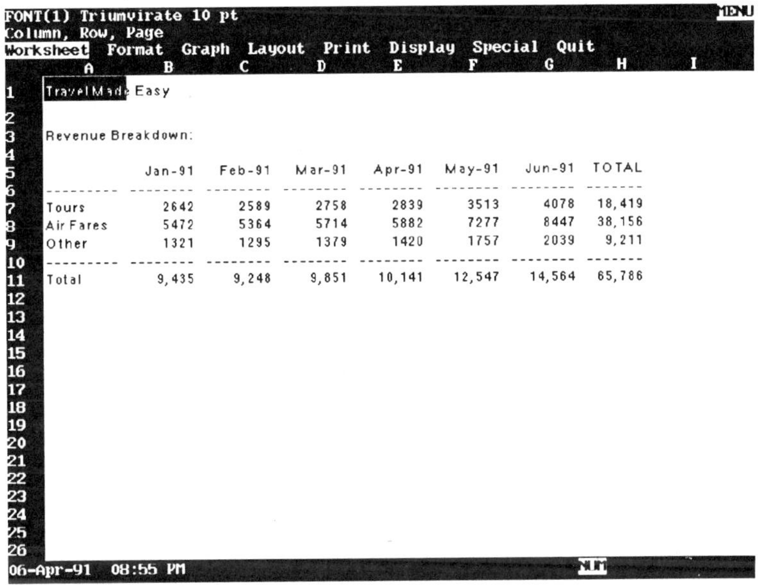

FIGURE 11-15 The worksheet in Allways

sheet will then be presented on the Allways display, as shown in Figure 11-15. Although it is the same information found on the worksheet, it looks a little different in Allways because the display simulates the appearance of the information on a printed page. The default font, FONT 1, is applied to all of the cells.

Like Symphony, Allways has a menu that is displayed at the top of the screen after you press the MENU key. This is shown in Figure 11-15. Menu selections are made by entering the first letter of the desired selection or by highlighting the desired selection and pressing (ENTER) to choose it. Allways has other similarities to Symphony that help you to gain familiarity with the product very quickly. One distinct difference is that you can select cells prior to altering them. In the SHEET environment, you issue a command (such as Format) and then specify the cells to be affected. In Allways, you can specify cells and then issue the command. Cells

Indicator	Meaning
ALLWAYS	Allways is ready for you to perform an action
ANC	In the lower status line, indicates that you have pressed (TAB) or typed a period (.) to anchor a range, ready to select a range of cells prior to issuing a command
EDIT	You pressed (F2) to edit an entry
ERROR	An error has occurred; press (ENTER) or (ESC) to clear the error
FILES	You need to specify a file
HELP	You pressed (F1) and a help screen is being displayed
MENU	A menu of commands is displayed
POINT	You need to specify a range of cells
WAIT	A procedure is in progress and will take a moment to complete
WARN	Allways is warning you of a possible problem

TABLE 11-3 Allways Mode Indicators

then remain selected after the command has been issued, allowing you to use several commands on the same range without reselecting the range each time.

A familiar sight in the Allways display is the mode indicator in the upper-right corner, telling you what Allways is doing at any given moment. The possible messages in the mode indicator are listed in Table 11-3. When the mode indicator is ALLWAYS, you can move the cell pointer around the display to highlight cells prior to issuing commands.

Another difference between Allways and other Symphony environments is the use of the (ESC) key. In other Symphony environments, you can leave menus and cancel commands by repeatedly pressing the (ESC) key. This also works in Allways, with the exception that pressing (ESC) when the mode indicator is ALLWAYS takes you out of Allways and back into the SHEET environment. This means that you should use (ESC) more sparingly in Allways.

Function Keys:

HELP	F1	Displays Allways help
EDIT	F2	Edits the current cell
ENLARGE	ALT-F4	Zooms in to increase the size of entries on the screen (keep pressing to achieve maximum enlargement)
REDUCE	F4	Zooms out to reduce the size of entries on the screen (keep pressing to achieve maximum reduction)
DISPLAY	F6	Toggles between graphics display mode and text display mode
GRAPH	F7	Toggles the display of graphs on and off
MENU	F10	Displays the Allways menu

Accelerator Keys:

ALT-B	Boldface (choose Set/Clear)
ALT-G	Gridlines (choose On/Off)
ALT-L	Lines (choose Outline/All/None)
ALT-S	Shading (choose Light/Dark/Solid/None)
ALT-U	Underline (choose Single/Double/None)
ALT-1 to ALT-8	Set font 1 through 8

Note: To affect a single cell, press accelerator key. To affect a group of cells, select a range first and then press accelerator key.

Movement Keys:
Allways uses all of the cell-pointer movement keys used in the SHEET environment.

Editing Keys:
Allways uses all of the editing keys used in the SHEET environment.

TABLE 11-4 Keys Used with Allways

Note: You can always use CTRL-BREAK to quit menus and cancel commands.

Like Symphony, Allways uses function keys to perform some tasks. As in Symphony, you can invoke the help feature by pressing F1. The F3 key displays a list of range names or file names for your selection. The F5 key is the GOTO key. The Allways function keys are given in Table 11-4. Like the DOC environment in Symphony, Allways provides a set of accelerator keys that you can use to request features without the need for many selections. These accelerator keys change the format of the current cell or the range selected before you press the accelerator key. Table 11-4 also lists the accelerator keys. You press a key combination at the location where you want to begin the special feature and again at the point where you want to stop using it.

Commands in the Allways Format menu selection will allow you to change fonts and use boldface, underlining, and other features. Allways will display the text on the screen as it will print, using a WYSIWYG interface. Also, format changes will appear in the top line of the control panel as you move the cell pointer around on the worksheet. As you can see from Figure 11-16, Allways gives full format descriptions rather than the coded entries you get in the SHEET environment. Cell A1 in Figure 11-15 is formatted with FONT 1, which is Triumvirate 10 point.

Another difference between the menu selections in Allways and Symphony is that you will not find a File option for saving and retrieving files. The effects of actions you perform with Allways will only be saved if you return to Symphony and save your Symphony file with SERVICES File Save. When you do this,

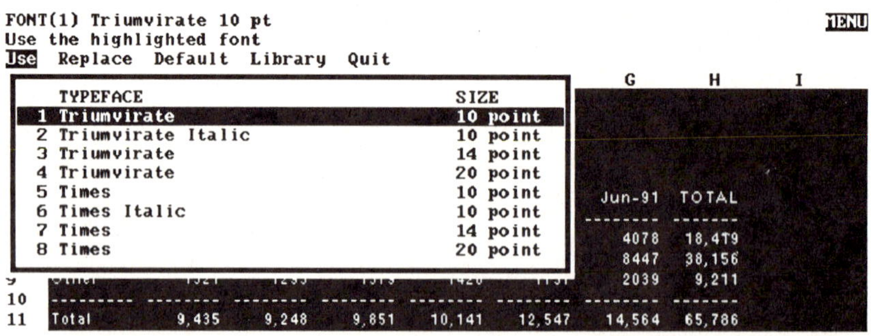

FIGURE 11-16 The Font selection menu

Allways stores your formatting settings in a file with the same name as the worksheet but with the extension ALL. Since there is no way you can end Allways without returning to Symphony, this should help you remember to save your changes. When you retrieve your Symphony file at another time, all of your Allways changes will be available if you attach Allways, and if the ALL file is in the same directory as the worksheet file it formats. You cannot retrieve ALL files, only the worksheet files that they format.

Working with Fonts

As a first step towards enhancing the rather plain worksheet in Figure 11-15, you will alter the font of some of the entries. Fonts are sometimes divided into two groups: fonts without embellishments, like Triumvirate, are referred to as *sans serif fonts;* fonts with embellishments at the ends of the lines that form the letters are known as *serif fonts*. The eight default fonts use a serif font called Times and a sans serif font called Triumvirate. Figure 11-16 shows the default fonts that are part of the Allways package. These are the fonts that you see initially when you select a font for your worksheet. However, you can use any of the other fonts that come with Allways, plus any of the fonts that your printer or a cartridge provides.

The size of the characters is another important component of a font. Size is measured in points. Each point is 1/72nd of an inch. Normally, 10- or 12-point fonts are used for regular spreadsheet entries. Headings may use 14- or 20-point fonts, and fine print may be displayed with a 5- or 7-point font.

You can use as many as eight fonts on any output created with Allways. The fonts available at any one point are part of a selectable font set. For different worksheets you might have different sets of fonts. The first font in any set is always the font used as the default, which means that it will be used for all entries unless you select a different font with the Format Font command or an accelerator key. When you format part of the worksheet to use a different font, the column widths may need to be resized to fit all of the characters. When worksheet entries are printed with the default font, you do not have to change the column width, because Allways defines the column widths according to the size of the default font.

Assuming you have the sample worksheet loaded and Allways attached, you invoke Allways by choosing it from the SHEET menu. You can then press the MENU key (either (F10) or /). The Allways menu will be displayed, as in Figure 11-15. Select Format and then Font to tell Allways that you want to use a different font for a range. Allways will display eight font selections that are part of its font set, as shown in Figure 11-16.

Note As you become familiar with the default fonts, you will make use of the accelerator keys to set the font of a worksheet range. Allways uses (ALT-1) through (ALT-8) for each of the eight fonts.

Select Times 14 from the font list by using the (UP ARROW) and (DOWN ARROW) keys to move to Times 14 and pressing (ENTER). If you try typing a letter to select a font, Allways interprets the letter as trying to select another menu option from the Format Font menu. To choose an option from a box like the one on the screen, you must point to it with the arrow keys or type the number beside the described option.

When you highlight a font and press (ENTER), Allways prompts you for the range you want to format with this font. In this example you just want to format the one cell, A1, so you can press (ENTER). If you need to alter the range highlighting to include more cells, you can use the normal SHEET environment commands for range selection.

When you press (ENTER) to confirm the range selection, your screen will show the cell in the new format, as in Figure 11-17. Notice that the entire entry for A1 is displayed in the new font, including the portion of the entry that borrows space from the cell

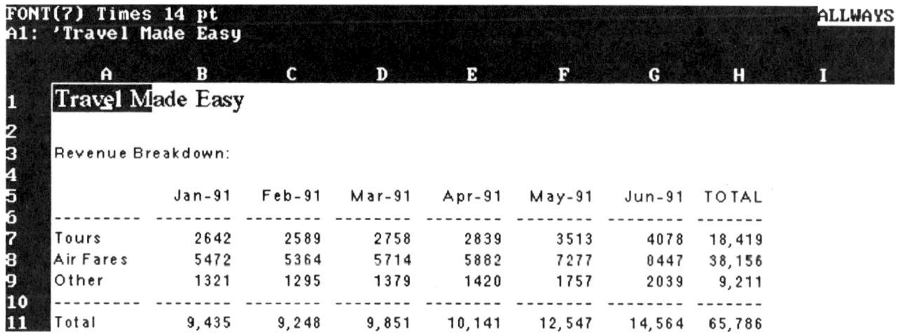

FIGURE 11-17 The new font

in column B. The control panel also shows your font selection. (If the screen font does not change, use the MENU Display Mode Graphics command.)

Allways has other alternatives for selecting ranges to format and keys to press to select the format. You can also select a range by moving to the first cell that you want to format and typing a period before moving the cell pointer to the opposite side of the range. Then you can use the accelerator keys to format the range. To try this with the sample worksheet, follow these steps:

1. Move the cell pointer to B5 and type a period (.). As you can see in Figure 11-18, the second line of the control panel changes to show that you are selecting a range instead of a single cell, and the ANC indicator (short for "anchor") appears in the bottom status line.

2. Press **END** and **RIGHT ARROW** to select B5..H5. Allways highlights the range that you have selected.

3. Press **ALT-5** to select Times 10 point. Note that the range remains highlighted.

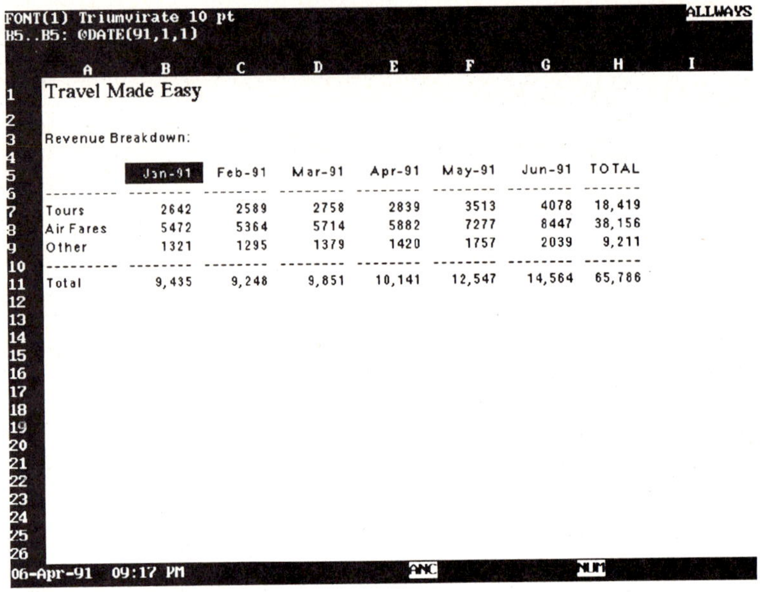

FIGURE 11-18 Anchoring a range

4. Press (ALT-B) for the accelerator key to make the range boldface. Again note that the range remains highlighted.

5. Press (ESC) to remove the range selection.

Your screen will look like the one in Figure 11-19. At this point, you may want to save your changes so far. To do this, you must return to the SHEET environment. To return to the SHEET environment from Allways, you either press (ESC) when the mode indicator is ALLWAYS or press MENU and select Quit. Note that the worksheet shows no sign of the formatting changes you made in Allways. These are confined to the Allways display. Use SERVICES File Save to store the worksheet.

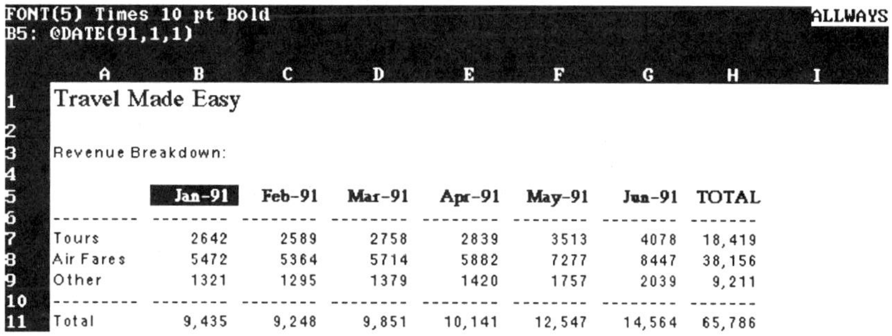
FONT(5) Times 10 pt Bold ALLWAYS
B5: @DATE(91,1,1)

	A	B	C	D	E	F	G	H
1	Travel Made Easy							
2								
3	Revenue Breakdown:							
4								
5		Jan-91	Feb-91	Mar-91	Apr-91	May-91	Jun-91	TOTAL
6	---------	--------	--------	--------	--------	--------	--------	-------
7	Tours	2642	2589	2758	2839	3513	4078	18,419
8	Air Fares	5472	5364	5714	5882	7277	8447	38,156
9	Other	1321	1295	1379	1420	1757	2039	9,211
10	---------	--------	--------	--------	--------	--------	--------	-------
11	Total	9,435	9,248	9,851	10,141	12,547	14,564	65,786

FIGURE 11-19 Further formatting changes

Line Formatting and Worksheet Editing

In addition to changing fonts and using boldface anywhere in the worksheet, you can alter the appearance of cell entries in other ways. For a range as small as one cell or as large as your entire spreadsheet entries, you can use single or double underlining, color selections, shading, and an outline around each cell. You can add lines at any side of a cell or a range of cells. If you use the outline feature, you can completely outline all the walls of each cell in a range. However, you may need to alter your worksheet to incorporate some of these options.

When you first created the sample worksheet in the SHEET environment, you used a row of labels to underline the dates and another one to separate the row of column totals from the rest of the model. If you want to use the underlining features in Allways, you will probably want to remove the underlining labels. To do this you must move to the SHEET environment and make the changes there. To move to the SHEET environment from Allways, you either press (ESC) when the mode indicator is ALLWAYS or press MENU and select Quit.

To see how you would replace the label rows with Allways format lines, follow these steps:

1. In the SHEET environment, place the cell pointer in any cell on row 6.

2. Press MENU, select Delete, and select Rows. Press (ENTER) to confirm the deletion of one row.

3. Move the cell pointer to the @SUM formula in what is now cell B10. If this formula reads "@SUM(B6..B9)," deleting row 9 will create an error. Edit the formula so that it now reads **@SUM(B6..B8)** and then copy it from B10 to C10..H10.

4. Press (UP ARROW) to place the cell pointer on row 9, and then press MENU and select Delete followed by Rows. Press (ENTER) to confirm the deletion of one row.

5. Press MENU and select Allways. Move the cell pointer to A5 and type a period (.) to anchor the cell pointer. Now press (RIGHT ARROW) and (END) followed by (RIGHT ARROW) to select A5..A5.

6. Press MENU to activate the Allways menu, and select Format and then Lines. The menu appears as in Figure 11-20. Select Bottom. The menu disappears and a line is drawn along the bottom of the highlighted cells.

7. Press (DOWN ARROW). This will unlock the cell pointer and move it to H6. Press (END) and (DOWN ARROW) to move the cell pointer down to H9. Type a period (.) and press (END) followed by (LEFT ARROW). This selects all of the cells (H9..A9) that you want to format with another line.

8. Press MENU and select Format Lines Top. Press (BACKSPACE) to unlock the cell pointer, and move the cell pointer to the

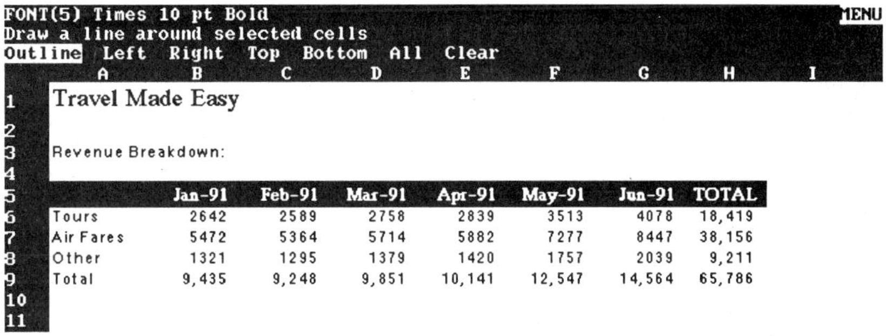

FIGURE 11-20 Format Lines menu

current cell, A9. Press (ALT-B) to add boldface to the font in A9. The results will appear as in Figure 11-21.

The Format Lines command is very flexible, allowing you to draw lines in these locations: Outline, Left, Right, Top, Bottom, and All. These options refer to the edges of the selected range of cells. If you want to draw a line around the edge of the selected cells, outlining them, then you choose Outline. If you want to

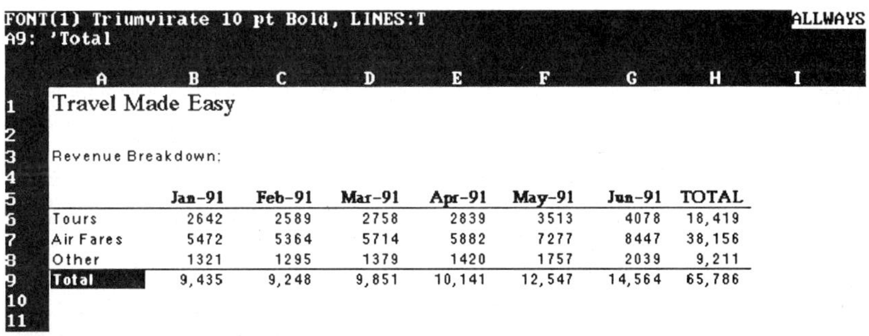

FIGURE 11-21 Lines added with Format Lines command

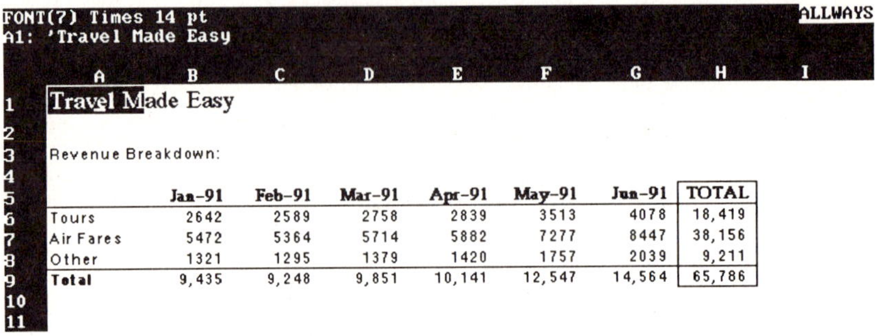

FONT(7) Times 14 pt
A1: 'Travel Made Easy
ALLWAYS

Travel Made Easy

Revenue Breakdown:

	Jan-91	Feb-91	Mar-91	Apr-91	May-91	Jun-91	TOTAL
Tours	2642	2589	2758	2839	3513	4078	18,419
Air Fares	5472	5364	5714	5882	7277	8447	38,156
Other	1321	1295	1379	1420	1757	2039	9,211
Total	9,435	9,248	9,851	10,141	12,547	14,564	65,786

FIGURE 11-22 Use of Outline

outline every cell in the selected range, you use All. To outline the end-of-period totals in column H, follow these steps:

1. Move the cell pointer to H5 and type a period (.). Then press (END) followed by (DOWN ARROW). This selects H5..H9.
2. Press MENU and choose Format Lines Outline. Press (HOME) to unlock the cell pointer. The results can be seen in Figure 11-22.

In addition to drawing lines at the edges of cells, you can underline text with either single or double underlining. Single underlining differs from a line at the bottom of the box in that it is only added for the length of the cell entries, not the entire cell width. Double underlining underlines the entire cell's width. To underline the titles at the top of the screen, move the cell pointer to A1, press MENU, and select Format Underline Single. Press (ENTER). Your screen will display underlining beneath the entire entry in A1 and into B1. If you decide to remove the underlining but want to leave other format changes such as the font intact, use the Format Underline Clear command.

The ALT-U accelerator key quickly underlines text. Pressing ALT-U once adds single underlining to the current cell or selected range. Pressing ALT-U again changes single underlining to double underlining. Pressing ALT-U a third time removes the underlining.

Changing Formats

You can remove any format that you add to a worksheet range. The Format Reset command strips away any format changes and displays the entries in FONT 1 format. To change cells from one format to another, you select the cells to be affected and issue a new Format command which then overrides the previous formatting. The formatting of lines is controlled very precisely using the Format Lines Clear command. This allows you to clear lines produced by the Left, Right, Top, Bottom, and All selections.

Shading

You can add any of three levels of shading to one or more cells in the worksheet. This helps to set entries apart or visually divide the print area. Allways supports light, dark, and solid black shading levels. You can use the Format Shade command to add shading either to a preselected range or to a range you select when prompted. The ALT-S accelerator key will lightly shade the current cell or selected range. If you press ALT-S again, Allways uses medium shading instead. If you press ALT-S a third time, Allways uses dark shading. Press it one more time, and you will remove any shading.

To add shading to the grand total in H9, follow these steps:

1. Move the cell pointer to H9.

2. Press ALT-S once. This is light shading.

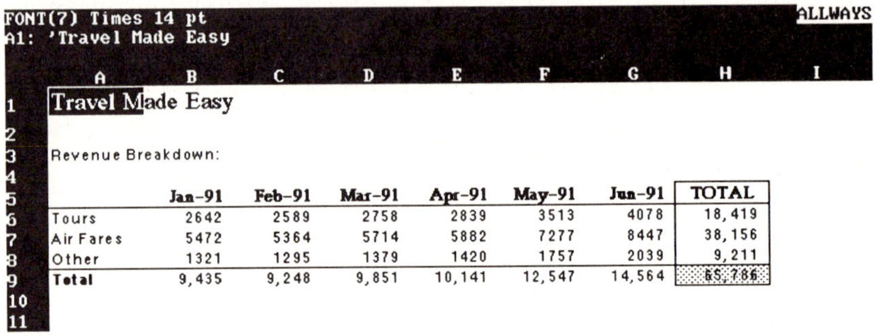

FIGURE 11-23 Range formatted with light shading

3. Keep pressing **ALT-S** to see the different options. Do not worry if your number seems to disappear; the underlying formula will not be affected by the command. Leave the shading at light and press **HOME**. The results will appear as in Figure 11-23.

Although the exact effect of shading can be difficult to see as you apply it, and although it can make cell entries slightly harder to read in the Allways display, the printed results are very effective, as you can see from Figure 11-13, where light shading was used in H9 and solid shading was applied in row 11 to create the thick line.

Label Alignment

Allways does not have an option for changing the alignment of labels. You must either return to the SHEET environment to change it with the Range Label-Alignment command, or you must edit the individual label prefixes. You can edit label prefixes in either SHEET or ALLWAYS mode by pressing **F2** and then **HOME**.

You may have noticed that in the SHEET environment, labels that exceed the width of the cell will seem to be left-aligned even if they are actually centered or right-aligned. This is not true in Allways, since Allways can allow such entries to flow into adjacent cells. Thus, part of a centered label may be displayed to the right of its cell, and part to the left. This allows you greater flexibility when aligning labels over numbers.

To see how this works, you can adjust the title of the sample worksheet.

1. Press (HOME) and then (F2). Press (HOME) again and then press (INS). This invokes the Overstrike mode of typing, which you can use for editing cells in Allways, although this is not available in the SHEET environment.

2. Type ^, which is the center label prefix. Press (ENTER). The label is now only partially visible.

3. Press (ESC) to move to the SHEET environment.

4. Press MENU and select Move. Press (ENTER) to move A1..A1 and then (RIGHT ARROW) to place the cell pointer in D1. Press (ENTER).

5. Press MENU and select Allways. Notice that the label now located in D1 is actually spread evenly across three columns, as shown in Figure 11-24.

Changing Column Widths and Row Heights

You can change the width of a column in the Allways display and the resulting printout without affecting the column width in the SHEET environment. Row heights are normally adjusted for the font size you have selected, but they can also be changed to a custom height. To change the column width, use the Worksheet

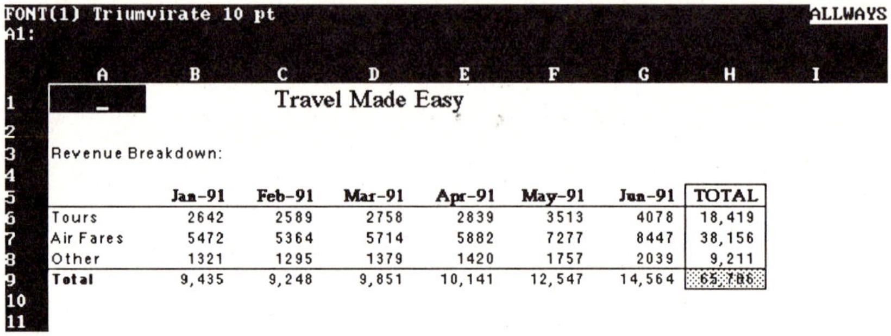

	Jan-91	Feb-91	Mar-91	Apr-91	May-91	Jun-91	TOTAL
Tours	2642	2589	2758	2839	3513	4078	18,419
Air Fares	5472	5364	5714	5882	7277	8447	38,156
Other	1321	1295	1379	1420	1757	2039	9,211
Total	9,435	9,248	9,851	10,141	12,547	14,564	65,786

FIGURE 11-24 Centered label

Column Set-Width command to select a specific size. The row height is changed with the Worksheet Row Set-Height command.

The column width can be adjusted more precisely in Allways than in the SHEET environment. The columns are measured in terms of the number of characters of the default font, which is initially a 10-point font. You can change to fractional sizes like 12.26 if you wish to accommodate the exact width needed for a different font.

To change the column width for column H, follow these steps:

1. Move the cell pointer to column H. In the worksheet, this column had been set to 8 characters wide.

2. Press MENU and select Worksheet Column Set-Width. Note the current setting of 8.00. Also note the vertical line on the screen that acts as a guide to the width setting.

3. Press the (RIGHT ARROW) key twice. This increases the width to 10. Press (LEFT ARROW), which changes the width to 9. You decide you want something in between 9 and 10. Type **9.5** and press (ENTER). The TOTAL column is now slightly wider than the month columns.

To reset the column width to the width used in the SHEET environment, you can use Worksheet Column Reset.

When you first view a worksheet in Allways, the row heights are uniform, but as you select different fonts Allways automatically adjusts the height to properly display the data. You can establish a specific height for a row by selecting Worksheet Row Set-Height and pressing (DOWN ARROW) or (UP ARROW) to alter the vertical spacing. Try this now:

1. Move the cell pointer to A11 and press MENU. Select Worksheet Row Set-Height. Note the current height setting, measured in points, and the horizontal line used to help you set the height.

2. Type **6** and press (ENTER). You will see the row is now much thinner than it was. The row number is partly occluded to accomodate this change.

3. To see an effective use of row-height variations, select cells A11..H11. Press (ALT-S) three times, and then press (HOME). As you can see from Figure 11-25, this adds solid shading below the model in a thickness that is determined by the row height.

To return control of the row-height setting to Allways so that it is adjusted automatically, you can select Worksheet Row Auto.

Changing Page Layout

Allways has several options that control what a printed page of your output will look like. With the Layout menu shown in Figure 11-26, you can control page size, margins, titles (headers and footers), and borders. You can even maintain a collection of named layout settings, referred to as a "library."

With the PageSize command, you can select one of the standard sizes that Allways supports or enter your custom measurements.

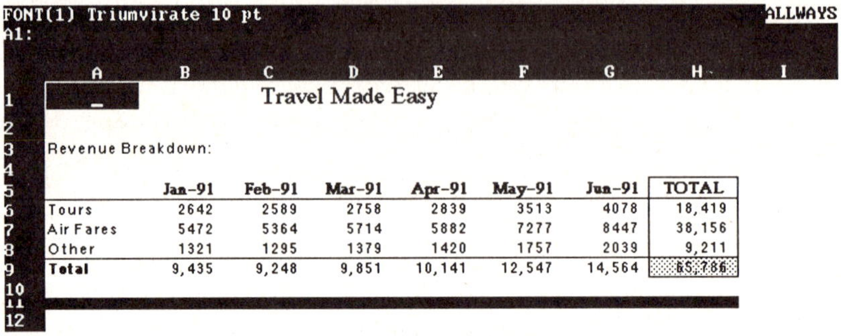

FIGURE 11-25 Added shading

The Margins command supports changes to the left, right, top, and bottom margins. Note that these are measured in inches. The Titles command allows you to enter single-line headers and footers. These can use the same codes as the headers and footers used in the SHEET and DOC environments, described in Chapter 3. When you enter a header or footer, it is shown in the Layout settings box. The header and footer text is printed in the default font for the worksheet; that is, FONT 1. To change the font used for the header

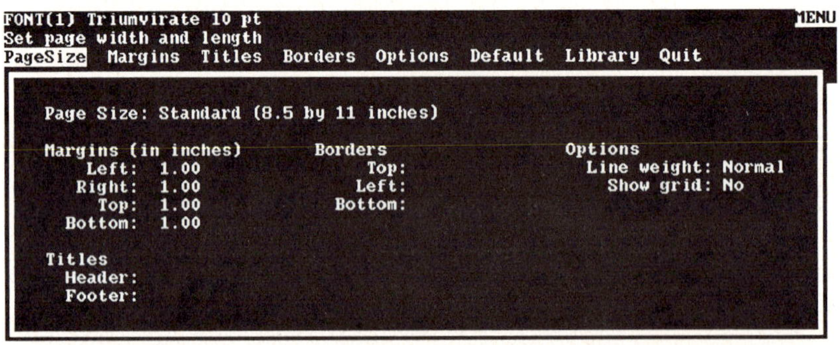

FIGURE 11-26 The Layout menu

or footer you must change FONT 1 to the font you want the header or footer printed in and format worksheet cells accordingly (see the later section on changing fonts for more details).

The Borders command allows you to set columns and rows as borders to the main print area, much the same as the Top-Labels and Left-Labels commands in the SERVICES Print Settings Other menu, described in Chapter 3. However, Allways permits bottom border rows as well as top border rows and left border columns.

The Options command offers you control of two special areas of Allways printing. The LineWeight option allows you to adjust the printed thickness of the lines you created with the Format Lines command. The choices are Normal, Light, and Heavy. The Layout Options Grid command offers a simple No/Yes choice between printing the worksheet with a grid of lines that match the column-and-row grid of the spreadsheet, or not. The default setting is No, but you can see the effect of the Yes setting in Figure 11-27. This is useful for documenting spreadsheet models. Also note that Figure 11-27 uses the LineWeight Heavy setting so that the lines added by the Format Lines command stand out more clearly from the grid lines. The grid lines also appear in the Allways display when Layout Options Grid is set to Yes.

Travel Made Easy

Revenue Breakdown:

	Jan-91	Feb-91	Mar-91	Apr-91	May-91	Jun-91	TOTAL
Tours	2642	2589	2758	2839	3513	4078	18,419
Air Fares	5472	5364	5714	5882	7277	8447	38,156
Other	1321	1295	1379	1420	1757	2039	9,211
Total	9,435	9,248	9,851	10,141	12,547	14,564	65,786

FIGURE 11-27 Worksheet with grid

The Layout Default command allows you to restore the original default settings to the various Layout options or to store the changes you have made as the new default. This saves you from having to make the same basic adjustments for every worksheet. If you feel uncomfortable replacing the original defaults with your own settings, then you might want to use the Library command to save the current settings in a named file (the file will have the extension ALS for "Allways Layout Settings"). The Library Retrieve command can then be used to update the current settings from a file on disk. You can use the Library Erase command to remove Allways layout settings files from disk.

As you make the layout changes you need, you can see them in the Layout settings sheet. Figure 11-28 shows the completed settings sheet used when creating Figure 11-13. If you store the worksheet at this point, back in the SHEET environment, these layout settings are stored in the Allways file. (This is the file that has the same name as the worksheet, except that the extension is ALL instead of WR1.)

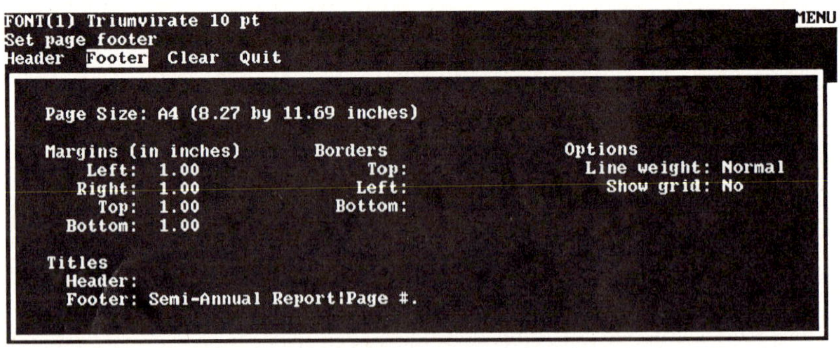

FIGURE 11-28 Completed settings sheet

Printing Your Allways Document

Once you have made all the changes you need, you can print the document. You must print it from Allways in order for the enhancements you have made to be present in the printout. All of the Allways options for printing can be accessed by selecting Print from the Allways menu. Using the Print Range Set command, you can define any range of cells you wish and send this range, with all its enhancements and the current layout settings, to the printer with the Go command. You can direct output to a file with the Print File command (the file will have the extension ENC, indicating that it is an encapsulated file, one that contains all of the print settings and not just the text of the document). If you need to alter the printer configuration, use the Configuration command and adjust various print settings with the Settings command.

To specify the print range, select Print Range Set, highlight the desired range, and press ENTER. You can use the Print Range Clear command to eliminate a print range. Try this now with the sample worksheet:

1. Press MENU and select Print Range Set.
2. Press the HOME key to move the cell pointer to A1.
3. Type a period (.) and then use the cursor keys to move the highlighting to H11. Press ENTER. Notice the dotted line placed around the print area, which helps you visualize what will be printed.
4. Select Go from the menu to print a copy. Allways gives you a progress report as the document is being printed.

The results, produced on an HP LaserJet II, appear in Figure 11-29. If you want to remove the dotted line of the print range from your display, use the Print Range Clear command.

Travel Made Easy

Revenue Breakdown:

	Jan-91	Feb-91	Mar-91	Apr-91	May-91	Jun-91	TOTAL
Tours	2642	2589	2758	2839	3513	4078	18,419
Air Fares	5472	5364	5714	5882	7277	8447	38,156
Other	1321	1295	1379	1420	1757	2039	9,211
Total	9,435	9,248	9,851	10,141	12,547	14,564	65,786

FIGURE 11-29 Worksheet printed with Allways

Allways has print settings that allow you to further customize your output. You can use these options to print multiple copies of your output or to print a selected range of pages. For example, to print two copies of the report, you select Print Settings Copies, type **2**, and press ENTER. Select Quit to exit the Settings menu. To print a selected range of pages, you select Print Settings Begin, type the number of the first page you wish to print, and then press ENTER. Next, you select End, type the number of the last page you want to print, and press ENTER.

To return print settings to the defaults, you use Print Settings Reset. If you need Allways to pause between sheets for you to insert paper in the printer, select Print Settings Wait.

You can also adjust the configuration of your printer in Allways, using the Print Configuration menu shown in Figure 11-30.

Graphs on Display

Allways supports the display of graphs saved as image files from the SHEET or GRAPH environments by placing the graphs in a range of the worksheet. Allways automatically sizes the graph for the size of the selected range. You can then print the graphs on the same page as worksheet text, because Allways uses the same print

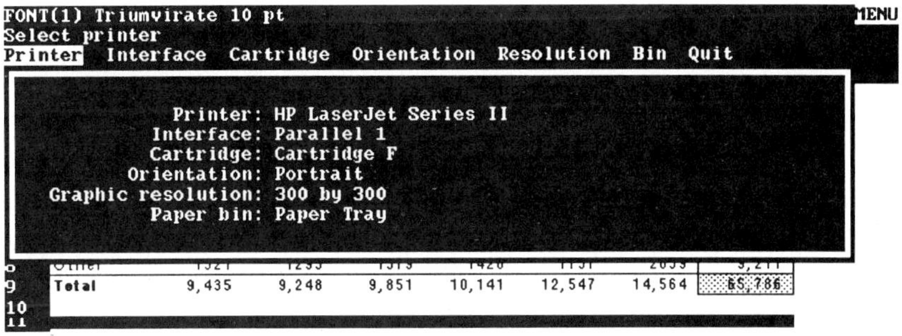

FIGURE 11-30 Print Configuration menu

commands to print a worksheet whether it consists of worksheet entries, graphs, or a combination of both.

To display a graph on the worksheet, you will need to have a copy of the desired graph saved as a PIC file on disk. These graph files are created with the Image-Save command when a graph is displayed in Symphony. Once you have stored the graph files on disk in Symphony, displaying them in Allways is a simple matter: Just select Graph Add and choose the name of the PIC file.

To add a graph to the current display, follow these steps, which include building the graph. If you have already created a graph, using the steps described in Chapter 6, then you can skip to step 7.

1. Select Quit from the Allways menu to return to the SHEET environment. Move the cell pointer to B5.

2. Press MENU and select Graph. If have never created a Symphony graph before, you will want to be sure to review details of the process in Chapter 6.

3. Select 1st-Settings and then Type. Choose Stacked-Bar.

4. Select Range and then X. Symphony presents the worksheet in POINT mode. Select cells B5..G5. Now choose A and select

B6..G6. Choose B and select B7..G7. Choose C and select B8..G8. Select Quit from the Range menu.

5. Select Legend and then A. Enter **\A6**. Select B and enter **\A7**. Select C and enter **\A8**. Select Quit from the Legend menu.
6. Select Switch to get to the 2nd-Settings menu. Choose Y-Scale and then Format. Select Currency and enter **0** for the decimal places. Select Quit to return to the main Graph menu. Choose Image-Save and type **BARALL** for the image file name. Symphony will add the extension PIC.
7. To add the graph to the Allways display, return to SHEET mode and invoke Allways. Move the cell pointer to A12.
8. Press MENU and select Graph Add. Highlight BARALL.PIC and press (ENTER).
9. Allways will prompt you for a range for the graph. This determines the size of the graph. Extend the range to A12..H33 and press (ENTER). Your stacked bar graph now appears on your Allways screen as in Figure 11-31.

If the graph does not appear but you get cross-hatching in the range you selected, use the Display Graphs command and change the setting to Yes. When this is set to No, only the X pattern shown will appear on your screen, allowing Allways to respond faster than when the graph is visible. You can use the (F7) key to toggle between the Yes and No settings for Display. If you get a graph area filled with "G's" then you are using Allways in Text mode. Use the Display Mode command to switch to Graphics mode. The (F6) key will toggle the display between Graphics and Text modes.

The graph is not only displayed on the Allways sheet, but can also be printed from it. The results in Figure 11-13 were created by selecting A1..H33 as the print range. Printing a graph with

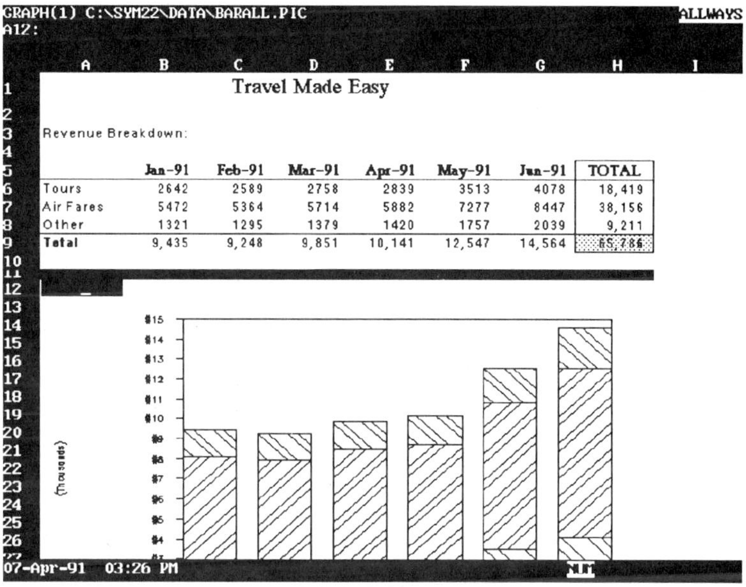

FIGURE 11-31 Graph added to worksheet

Allways is no different from printing a worksheet that contains text and numbers. You use the same menu selections to specify the range of the worksheet that Allways prints. You can use the Layout and Settings options to further adjust the report. When you are ready to print, select Go from the Print menu.

You can add more than one graph to a worksheet, which makes this feature particularly handy for placing multiple graphs on a single page. To remove a graph from the display, you select Graph Remove and choose the graph by name. The Graph Goto command allows you to move to a particular graph when any are displayed. The Graph Settings menu uses the settings sheet shown in Figure 11-32 to provide control over fonts used in the graph, the graph margins, and even the ranges being graphed.

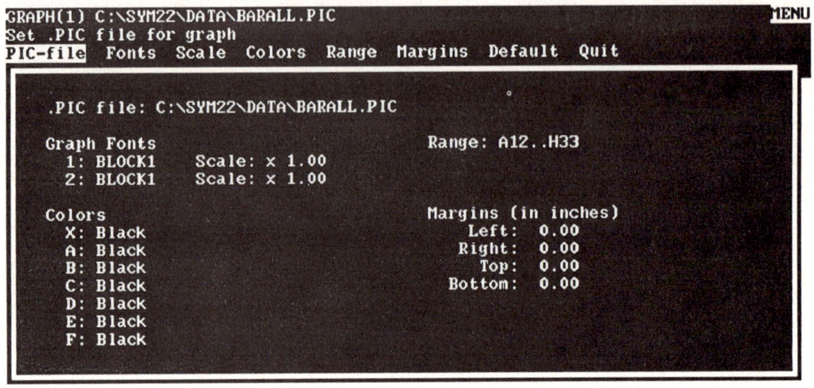

FIGURE 11-32 The Graph settings sheet

Changing Your Fonts

When you first install Allways, your font set is created from eight of the soft fonts provided with Allways. This means that you have access to four Triumvirate fonts and four Times fonts in the default font set. You also have the ability to replace any of these default fonts with fonts directly supported by your printer or another soft font. If you have a printer that supports font cartridges, you can tell Allways which of these fonts you are using and they will also be available for your selection.

To replace an existing font, follow these steps:

1. Press MENU and select Format Font.
2. Highlight the font you want to remove from the font set.
3. Select Replace.
4. Highlight the font in the list that you wish to use as the replacement, and press (ENTER).

5. Highlight the font size in the list that you wish to use as the replacement, and press (ENTER).

6. Select Quit.

Note that when you use the Format Font command, Allways assigns fonts to cells as FONT 1, FONT 2, and so on. If you have formatted a cell as FONT 2 and make a new selection for FONT 2, the cell is formatted with the new font.

If you select Format Font Replace and do not see your cartridge fonts in the list, follow these steps:

1. In ALLWAYS mode, press MENU and select Print Configuration Cartridge.

2. Highlight the desired cartridge in the list and press (ENTER).

3. Select Quit to leave the Configuration menu.

The cartridge fonts will now be included in the list of fonts to select from when you replace a font.

Further Uses of Allways

Apart from being a great way to dress up worksheets, print graphs, and combine graph images with text, Allways can be applied to other aspects of your work with Symphony. Having seen the power of Allways to control the display and printing of information, you can begin to appreciate the fact that Symphony stores all of your information—whether it is a spreadsheet calculation, a report you are writing, or a database you are sorting—in worksheet cells. By switching to the SHEET environment and then invoking Allways, you can dress up databases and documents, just as you can spreadsheets. In Figure 11-33, you can see a document that consists

Travel Made Easy

Memorandum

Date: August 15, 1991
To: Board Members
From: Controller

As you can see, there has been a steady improvement in all areas of revenue. We are particularly pleased to see a continued growth in Tour revenue, despite the recent recession in this area, felt by some of our competitors. Highlights in the first half of 91 include:

1 Improved revenue per agent
2 Better margins on air fare
3 Several new corporate clients

Revenue per agent:

5

65,786

13,157

Revenue Breakdown:

	Jan-91	Feb-91	Mar-91	Apr-91	May-91	Jun-91	TOTAL
Tours	2642	2589	2758	2839	3513	4078	18,419
Air Fares	5472	5364	5714	5882	7277	8447	38,156
Other	1321	1295	1379	1420	1757	2039	9,211
Total	9,435	9,248	9,851	10,141	12,547	14,564	65,786

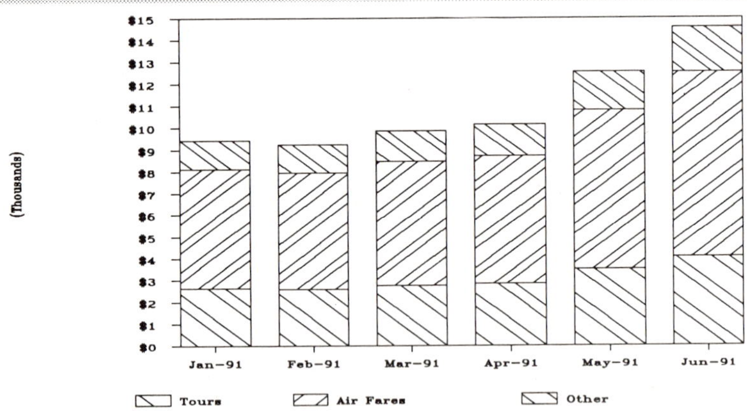

FIGURE 11-33 Full report

of spreadsheet cells plus text created in the DOC environment, formatted and printed with Allways.

An alternative approach to improving reports with Allways is to use the SERVICES Print command to designate a range of worksheet cells as the print destination, rather than the printer. This allows you to print complete reports to worksheet cells, which can then be formatted with fonts, lines, and shading, and then output with Allways.

A FORM LETTER EXAMPLE

Having seen how Allways can dress up all types of Symphony documents, you may want to begin integrating your Symphony data more closely. The following steps show you how to set up an employee database in the FORM environment and use it to customize a letter written in the DOC environment to inform employees about a bonus. You begin by defining the database, as follows:

1. In SHEET mode in a new worksheet, enter a series of labels in column A, one for each field in the database. Enter them in A41 through A45, just as they appear here:

   A41: Last:L:10
   A42: First:L:10
   A43: Dept:L:10
   A44: Salary:N:8
   A45: Bonus:C:10

2. Press the TYPE key ((ALT-F10)) and choose FORM. You will get the message: "No Definition range defined." Press MENU and select Generate.

3. Symphony asks you to select a default field type. Press (ENTER) to choose Label. You will then be asked for a field length. Press (ENTER) to accept the default of 9.

4. Now you need to choose a name for the database settings sheet that Symphony will generate. Press (ENTER) to accept the default choice: MAIN.

5. Symphony now asks where the field names are located and shows you the worksheet. Indicate the range A41..A45 and press (ENTER). Symphony presents a database form ready for you to fill in.

You are now ready to enter the data. You will enter four records to test the database. Note that you cannot make entries in the computed field, Bonus; this field will be calculated later.

1. In the First field of the first record, type **Smith** and press (ENTER). In the second field, that is, Last, type **Fred** and press (ENTER). In the DEPT field, type **Accounting** and press (ENTER). In the SALARY field, type **2300** and press (ENTER).

2. To add this record and create a new blank entry form press (INS). You should see a form like the one completed in Figure 11-34.

3. Complete the next three records as follows:

   Doe, Joe, Accounting, 2500
   Plane, Jane, Sales, 1800
   Rice, Don, Sales, 1750

   Remember to press (INS) after entering each record, except the last one. Press (PGUP) after entering the last record.

4. Press SWITCH to move to the SHEET environment. Move the cell pointer to B55. This is part of the Definition range. You

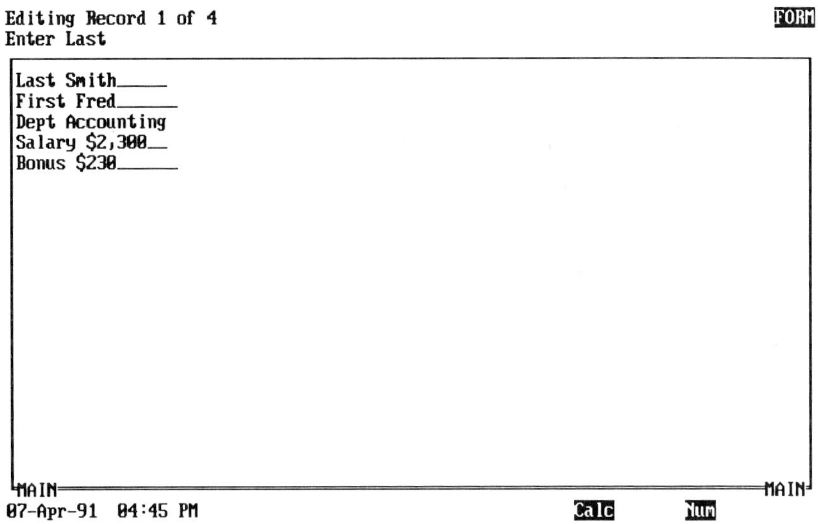

FIGURE 11-34 Record 1 completed

want to format the Salary and Bonus fields in Currency format, 0 decimal places. Use the MENU Format command and select B55 and B56 as the cells to be formatted.

5. You now need to enter the formula for the Bonus field. This is entered in the Formula column of the Definition range, cell E56 in this case. Enter **0.1*B55**.

6. The formula and format are not immediately added to each record, so press SWITCH to move back to the FORM environment and then view each record in turn, pressing CALC while viewing the record. When you have calculated each record, the database is ready to use.

You can now compose the letter to employees following these steps:

1. Press TYPE and select DOC. Press (HOME) to move the cell pointer to the top of the document. At line 1, character 1, type **April 1, 1991** and press (ENTER) twice.

2. At Line 3, Character 1, you want the employee's name to appear. To include information from a FORM database into a letter, you use the field name enclosed in ampersands (&). Type

   &FIRST& &LAST&

   and press (ENTER) once.

3. Type **Department:** and then a space. Type **&DEPT&** to include the employee's department. Press (ENTER) three times.

4. Type **Dear** and then a space. Type **&FIRST&** and then a colon (:). Press (ENTER) twice.

5. At line 9, character 1, type the following text, allowing Symphony to wrap the lines according to the current DOC format line:

   As a valued employee of Ohmobile you have helped us become Number One in electric car sales in North America! To celebrate this accomplishment, and to reward your efforts over the last twelve months, we have awarded you a bonus. Your bonus, which will be included in your next paycheck, is:

6. Now press (ENTER) twice and (TAB) twice. Type the following to include the salary and bonus fields:

Salary: &SALARY&	(then press (ENTER) once and (TAB) twice)
Bonus: &BONUS&	(then press (ENTER) twice)

7. Now type the following text:

   We trust that you will enjoy this bonus and see it as part of the caring approach to employee relations here at Ohmobile.

```
Line 1      Char 1     Page 1,6                      Left, Single            DOC

April 1, 1991◄

&FIRST& &LAST&◄
Department: &DEPT&


Dear &FIRST&:

As a valued employee of Ohmobile you have helped us become
Number One in electric car sales in North America!  To celebrate
this accomplishment, and to reward your efforts over the last twelve
months, we have awarded you a bonus.  Your bonus, which will be
included in your next pay-check, is:◄

►    ►    Salary: &SALARY&◄
►    ►    Bonus: &BONUS& ◄

We trust that you will enjoy this bonus and see it as part of the caring
approach to employee relations here at Ohmobile.◄
                                                                      MAIN
07-Apr-91  04:21 PM                                              Num
```

FIGURE 11-35 Completed letter

8. Press (ENTER) twice and type **Yours sincerely,** and then press (ENTER) twice more. Type **Ohmobile, Inc.** and press (ENTER).

9. Press MENU and select Page to insert a page break. Press (HOME) and the letter will appear as in Figure 11-35.

You are now ready to adjust the range names that will be used to merge the database and the letter. After that, you will be ready to print.

1. Switch to SHEET mode and use the Range Name Create command to name the cells that make up the letter as DOCUMENT. The range is A1..G24. This will be used as the print range by the FORM environment.

2. Switch to the FORM environment and press MENU. Select Settings and then Cancel. Select Report to clear any existing settings. Now select Report from the Settings menu, followed by Main. Type **DOCUMENT** and press (ENTER).

3. Select Quit once and press SERVICES. Choose Print and then Settings. Choose Destination and set this to Printer if you want to print the letters, or Range if you want to print to an area of the worksheet. Make sure that the range is large enough to accommodate one letter for each record (for example, you could use J1..IV8192).

4. Now select Source and specify Database. Select MAIN. Then choose Quit to return to the Print menu.

5. If you are printing to the printer, make sure it is on and loaded with paper. Select Align and then Go. Symphony prints the letter once for each record in the database.

If you print to the worksheet you can then format the resulting cells with Allways commands. You can see a sample letter in Figure 11-36. If you use criteria in the FORM environment, the letter will only be printed once for each record that meets the criteria.

SUMMARY

This book has taken you from the basics of spreadsheet operation to the sophistication of macros, outlining, and even desktop publishing. You should not expect to retain everything you have seen on first reading. In many ways, the tremendous power of a piece of software like Symphony 2.2 is equivalent to that of an entire programming language, which students may take several semes-

April 1, 1991

Fred Smith
Department: Accounting

Dear Fred:

As a valued employee of Ohmobile you have helped us become Number One in electric car sales in North America! To celebrate this accomplishment, and to reward your efforts over the last twelve months, we have awarded you a bonus. Your bonus, which will be included in your next pay-check, is:

Salary: $2,300
Bonus: $230

We trust that you will enjoy this bonus and see it as part of the caring approach to employee relations here at Ohmobile.

Yours sincerely,

Ohmobile, Inc.

FIGURE 11-36 Printed letter

ters to study. You should not expect to learn or use all of Symphony's capabilities right away. However, unlike many programming languages, Symphony is easily applied to practical tasks almost immediately.

You can also have fun with Symphony, designing graphs and charts, sorting lists, and creating helpful data tables. Many examples of Symphony at work are given throughout this book, but the best way to become familiar with Symphony is to consider the tasks you perform in your own work and try to apply Symphony to them. By using Symphony, you will get to know Symphony, and your work will become more productive, more professional, and more creative.

A

INSTALLATION

Symphony 2.2 uses sophisticated programming techniques to make installation a relatively simple process, despite the large size of the program and the wide variety of hardware on which the program runs. Using the Setup and Install programs, you can control aspects of the way in which the program runs on your hardware. This appendix begins by describing the basic installation process. It then discusses the hardware requirements of Symphony 2.2, as well as other aspects of installation, such as potential problems, upgrading older versions, and creating batch files for program startup.

BASIC INSTALLATION

Like all software programs, Symphony 2.2 requires a computer with a certain level of specifications before it can be installed and run. The minimum specifications are as follows:

- A PC running DOS 2.0 or later
- Monitor, keyboard, hard-disk drive, and floppy-disk drive
- At least 5 megabytes of unused storage space on the hard disk prior to installing Symphony 2.2
- At least 512 kilobytes of main memory (512 K of conventional RAM) just to run DOS and Symphony 2.2
- At least 640 K of conventional RAM to run DOS, Symphony 2.2, and any add-ins

To perform certain tasks with Symphony 2.2, you need hardware that meets certain specifications. Optional hardware specifications include the following:

- To display Symphony graphs, you need one of the display systems listed in Table A-1 or a close compatible.
- To use Symphony's communications features, you need a Hayes- or Popcom-compatible modem, or a direct connection to another computer.
- To create worksheets that use more than 7500 cells, you need expanded memory. Symphony 2.2 supports up to 4 megabytes of expanded memory. (Note that it is difficult to be precise about the size of worksheet files that Symphony 2.2 can create without

AT&T 6300
COMPAQ computer
COMPAQ Portable III
GRiDCase Series
Hercules card
IBM 3270-PC/GX
IBM 8514 adapter
IBM color card, color monitor
IBM MCGA
IBM/COMPAQ Enhanced Graphics
IBM/COMPAQ Video Graphics
Toshiba T1100 Plus
Toshiba T3100 (80 x 25)

TABLE A-1 Graphics Display Systems

using expanded memory, since many different factors determine just how much memory your work will use up. See the later section on memory management for more details.)

If you are unsure about your hardware specifications, hardware terminology, and the requirements of Symphony 2.2, you may want to review the section on hardware factors before beginning the installation procedure.

The Setup/Install Process

When you have passed the hurdle of determining whether or not you have the "right stuff" for running Symphony, the task of installing the program is a five-stage process, although the last two stages are optional.

1. You run the Symphony Setup program, which registers you as the owner of the software, makes the necessary directory on your hard disk, and copies the appropriate files onto your hard disk.

2. You work with the Install program to coordinate Symphony features with your hardware.
3. You work with the Allways Setup program to coordinate Allways features with your hardware.
4. You work with the AUTOEXEC.BAT and CONFIG.SYS files on your system, as well as directories, to facilitate/improve Symphony operation.
5. You tinker with additional files to integrate Symphony into your system, invoke other installation options, and make operation easier for novice users.

The completion of stage 4 requires some knowledge of the role of AUTOEXEC.BAT and CONFIG.SYS and may involve the ability to alter these files; they are discussed later in this appendix. In stage 5, you will need to have some understanding of batch files in general. Again, help with this subject is provided later in this appendix.

The five-stage process applies to fresh installations of Symphony. If you already have an earlier version of Symphony on your system, you may have some additional work to do, both to remove the old program and to upgrade existing files. The special steps in this upgrade process are described later in the appendix. A good place to start with all of this is to examine the slim volume entitled "Getting Started" that is included in the Symphony package.

Getting Started

You should use the Setup program provided by Lotus to install Symphony on your system. The files on the original Symphony program disks are not copy-protected: You can make copies of the master disks for safekeeping with the DOS command DISKCOPY (you should do this *before* installing the program). However, you cannot simply copy all of the files from the Symphony program disks to your hard disk to install the program.

Lotus has placed many of the program files on the master disks with a compression program that squeezes normal files so they occupy less disk space. If you look at a directory of the original program disks, there are many files with an exclamation point in the last three letters of their names, as in E!E. These files are compressed files. A program called INFLATE.EXE is used to inflate the files to normal size. This is done automatically when you use the Setup program. Thus, it is difficult to bypass the Setup program just by copying all of the files onto your hard disk. Instead, you are well advised to bear with the Setup program, which also takes care of registering your name on the program disk to discourage unauthorized copying of your program files.

Symphony comes to you on several disks. The exact number is determined by the size and type of disk you are using:

5 1/4 inch 360 K disks: 6 Symphony disks, 4 Allways disks
3 1/2 inch 720 K disks: 3 Symphony disks, 2 Allways disks

Most users will begin installation by placing the Symphony Setup disk in drive A. However, if you have a high-density 5 1/4 inch disk drive as your A drive (as on an IBM AT), you may want to use a low-density 5 1/4 inch drive, such as drive B, for the Setup program. This is because the installation procedure actually writes information on the Setup disk, and writing to a low-density 5 1/4 disk in a high-density drive sometimes causes problems reading the disk later.

After placing the Symphony Setup disk in a suitable floppy drive, you log on to the drive. Assuming the drive is A, this means making A the current drive, performed by entering **A:** at the DOS command line, or DOS prompt. You can now enter the command to start the Setup program. This command consists of three parts: the program name, the name of the directory that will store the

Symphony program files, and the name of the drive in which you have placed the Setup disk. Typically, you will enter

```
SETUP C:\SYM22 A:
```

Drives and Directories

Normally, your hard drive is drive C; however, some systems have a D drive. This often occurs when large drives are partitioned into C and D or when a second hard drive is fitted. You might even have a hard drive called E, which can be used just as easily as C or D. If you are using a drive other than C, substitute your drive letter for "C" in the following instructions and examples.

When you specify the directory Symphony will use to store the program files, there are several factors to consider. Lotus suggests that you use SYM22 as the directory name for Symphony Release 2.2. Many users of earlier versions of Symphony used SYMPHONY as the directory name, and you might be tempted to use this. However, there can be problems if you use a directory occupied by an existing copy of Symphony. You should either use a different directory for Symphony or make sure that you have followed the advice about upgrading in Chapter 3 of the "Getting Started" booklet. You might also want to review the section on upgrading later in this appendix.

The choice of a directory name is a personal one. Any valid DOS directory name can be used, but you might want to consider a couple of factors. The suggested SYM22 is probably easier to type than SYMPHONY, but perhaps harder to remember. There is a lot to be said for short directory names; they are easier to type and less likely to be typed wrong. When you start using subdirectories for data, as described later in this appendix, short names have the advantage of minimizing lengthy path names. You might want to use a name like S2, S22, or SYM. To learn more about directories, refer to Chapter 8 or read the section on disks and directories later in this appendix.

Whatever name you enter for a directory, the Setup program will check to see if it exists already on the drive you specified. If it does not, then the program creates the directory for you.

Setup in Action

When you start the Setup program with the desired drive and directory information, an information screen appears, telling you what is happening. The procedure used to record your name and that of your company writes a small file to the Setup disk. This means that the Setup disk must not be write-protected; otherwise, the installation will be prevented from continuing (the disk is not write-protected at the factory, so it should not be write-protected when you get it).

You press any key to move on from this first screen. Setup presents a copyright screen so you will know who owns what. At the bottom of the screen is one of Symphony's little quirks: You are requested to press the (RETURN) key. Very few PC keyboards have a key labeled (RETURN). What Symphony refers to as (RETURN)

```
The following information will be recorded:

Product:
        Symphony
Version:
        2.2
Serial Number:
        1L00012-4722563
Your name:
        Fred Smith
Your company's name:
        Ohmobile, Inc.


          Press RETURN to continue.
```

FIGURE A-1 Personalized information

is normally labeled (ENTER). For (RETURN), read (ENTER) in all Symphony instructions. When you press (ENTER), another information screen appears. You press (ENTER) to go past this, and Setup asks you to type your name. When you have done this (using the (BACKSPACE) key to correct any errors) you press (ENTER), type **Y**, and press (ENTER) again to confirm that it is correct. This takes you to the company name entry screen, which is treated the same way. After you confirm the company name, Setup reviews the information, as in Figure A-1. Press (ENTER) to move on from here.

When you press (ENTER) to continue, Setup creates the directory you specified when you started the program. You are then told that the Symphony files will be copied to this directory. Press any key when ready, check that the Setup disk is in drive A, and again press any key when ready. After copying files from the Setup disk, the program asks you to change disks.

A period of copying and disk switching follows until all of the Symphony files are copied, at which point the Allways Setup disk is called for. A series of decompressing commands are executed to inflate the files to normal size. After this, you will see the screen

```
                        Setup Completed

      Setup has completed transferring the Symphony 2.2 files
      to your C:\sym22 directory.

      To run the Symphony Install program, type install.
      (For more information on the Install program, see Chapter
      3 of Getting Started.)

      To run the Allways Setup program, type awsetup.
      (For more information on Allways Setup, see chapter 4 of
      Getting Started.)

      To run Symphony without printing, viewing graphs, using
      communications, or running Allways, type symphony.
      (For more information on starting Symphony, see Chapter 6
      of Getting Started.)

C:\SYM22>
```

FIGURE A-2 Information screen

shown in Figure A-2. You are now at the DOS prompt in the directory you specified for the Symphony files (in this case, C:\SYM22).

The screen in Figure A-2 tells you how to proceed to the next phase of the installation process, where you make specific choices based on your equipment. This stage uses the Symphony Install program and the Allways AWSETUP program to specify the correct software *drivers* for your system. A driver is a file that allows software to communicate correctly with a specific piece of hardware. For example, there are different drivers for different printer models, which allows Symphony and Allways to use the features specific to each printer. Instead of copying all of the drivers onto your disk, only those that you need are copied. If you later add or change equipment, you can update your drivers with the Install program.

The Install Program

To start the Symphony Install program, you enter **INSTALL** at the DOS prompt, in the directory to which you have copied the Symphony program files (the Symphony Setup program leaves you in this directory). Figure A-3 shows the opening screen of the Install program. This program is largely self-documenting, providing a lot of information about each step and a system of help screens accessed by pressing the (F1) key.

To select from among the many different combinations of equipment that are in use in PCs today, you use the Install program's menu system, the main menu of which is shown in Figure A-4. Unfortunately, the set of keystrokes used in this menu system and the arrangement of choices does not follow very closely the menu system used in Symphony itself. In most cases, (ENTER) does what you would expect: It selects the highlighted choice. However, you cannot select a menu item by typing its first letter, and there are some function key uses that are not immediately apparent. The best approach is to read each screen carefully, noting the message

```
                    Symphony Install Program

                      Copyright 1986,1990
                 Lotus Development Corporation
                      All Rights Reserved
                          Release 2.2


The Install program lets you tell Symphony what equipment you have.
Select your equipment from a list of options by moving the highlight
(the menu pointer) to your choice and pressing RETURN.  You can start
Symphony without using the Install program first, but you won't be able
to use a printer, see graphs, or communicate with other computers.

If you need more information to make a particular choice, press F1 to
see a Help screen.  Before you begin the Install program, make sure you
have completed the Hardware Chart that came on your Symphony package.

            Press RETURN to begin the Install program.
                                                           NUM
```

FIGURE A-3 Install program opening screen

```
                          M A I N   M E N U


                                             Select First-Time Installation
Use ↓ or ↑ to move menu pointer              if you want help making
                                             decisions about how to set up
 First-Time Installation                     Symphony for your equipment.
 Change Selected Equipment
 Advanced Options                            Press RETURN to select
 Exit Install Program                        First-Time Installation,
                                             or use ↓ to move the
                                             menu pointer.


↓ and ↑ move menu pointer.                   F1  displays a Help screen.
RETURN selects highlighted choice.           F9  takes you to main menu.
ESCAPE takes you to previous screen.         F10 shows current selections.
                                                           NUM
```

FIGURE A-4 Install Main Menu

```
Lotus supplies programs, called drivers, that let Symphony work with
different equipment.  Symphony comes with drivers that let you create
a spreadsheet, database, or word processing document immediately.  You
use the Install program to add drivers that allow Symphony to draw graphs,
print your work, and communicate with other computers.

When you use First-Time Installation, the Install program asks you
questions to help you decide which drivers you need to add.  Then, it
saves the drivers you select in a file, or driver set, called LOTUS.SET.
Each time you use First-Time Installation, you start over; Install doesn't
remember any choices you've made before.

If the NUM indicator appears on your screen, press NUM LOCK to turn it
off.  (The NUM indicator must be off when you use the Install program.)



                         Press RETURN to continue
                                                                    NUM
```

FIGURE A-5 What Install does

boxes and the keystroke guide at the bottom of the screen. Apart from its role in the initial configuration of Symphony, this menu system is used each time you alter basic hardware specifications.

When you first install Symphony, the top option on the Main Menu is the one you want: First-Time Installation. When you select this option, you are presented with a screen, like the one in Figure A-5, which explains the process. When you press (ENTER) to proceed, you come to the first equipment choice.

About Monitors

Symphony needs to know if your computer can display graphs. The ability to display graphs means that you can draw charts of your information with the Graph commands. This requires a graphics display adapter in your PC, one of the ones listed earlier in Table A-1 or a close compatible. If you have such an adapter, you can display graphs at one of two levels:

Text *and* Graph
Text *or* Graph

The first of these levels requires more work from your display system, and it may limit the colors used in your display as well as the flashing of the cursor. These options are discussed in a moment.

If your answer is Yes, you can display graphs, the next question is how many monitors you have. Symphony can operate two monitors at the same time, connected to the same computer; one is used for text and the other for graphics. However, most personal computers only have one monitor attached, and you should only select Two if your hardware has been set up with two monitors by your dealer or technical support staff. When you do select Two, you must choose which display system is used for graphics.

When you choose One, you are asked if you want to display graphs and text together. Choosing No means Text *or* Graph. You will not be able to see the contents of a GRAPH window at the same time as you are viewing a DOC, SHEET, or other window. The No option does produce faster operation and ensures that you have a cursor that flashes. Selecting Yes means Text *and* Graph, but your cursor may not flash and the number of colors displayed might be limited.

The next step is the selection of the specific display card you are using from the extensive list that appears in the next screen, shown in Figure A-6. To select the correct card, move the highlighting with the (UP ARROW) and (DOWN ARROW) keys and then press (ENTER). Note that some cards support two or more modes of operation. For example, the Hercules card can show you 80 characters and 25 lines, or 90 characters and 38 lines. Most of the screens used to illustrate this book use 80 x 25 display for clarity. However, some figures in Chapters 6 and 11 use the 80 x 34 mode of the VGA card to show more text and graphics on the screen.

When you have selected a display card, you are taken to the printer selection process, covered in the next section. If you answer No to the "Can your computer display graphs?" prompt, you move

```
                              C O M B I N E D
 AT&T 6300 (80 x 50)
 COMPAQ computer
 COMPAQ Portable III                          Select this if you have an IBM
 GRiDCase Series                              monochrome monitor with a
 Hercules card (80 x 25)                      Hercules card.  You can see
 Hercules card (90 x 38)                      more of the Symphony work area
 IBM 3270-PC/GX                               than with the standard size
 IBM 8514 adapter (85 x 38)                   (80 x 25), but characters are
 IBM 8514 adapter (128 x 54)                  smaller.
 IBM 8514 adapter (146 x 51)
 IBM color card, color monitor
 IBM MCGA
 IBM/COMPAQ Enhanced Graphics (EGA 80 x 25)
 IBM/COMPAQ Enhanced Graphics (EGA 80 x 43)
 IBM/COMPAQ Video Graphics (VGA 80 x 34)
Use ↓ to see more selections below.

↓  and  ↑  move menu pointer.             F1  displays a Help screen.
RETURN selects highlighted choice.        F9  takes you to main menu.
ESCAPE takes you to previous screen.      F10 shows current selections.
                                                                  NUM
```

FIGURE A-6 Screen selection

immediately to the selection of printers, since Install does not need to know the type of display card you have.

Printers

The first step in installing printers is to say whether or not you are using a text printer. This is the printer that will be used for printing with the SERVICES Print command, typically from the DOC and SHEET environments. When you select Yes, you must first select the brand from the list provided, as shown in Figure A-7. Even if your make of printer is not on this list, it may well be compatible with one of the ones shown. Otherwise, you can select the penultimate option, Unlisted.

When you select a particular make of printer, you are shown a list of specific models. For example, if you have an HP LaserJet, you choose HP from the brand list in Figure A-7, and then LaserJet in the next menu. When you have selected a model, you are asked if you have a second text printer. Install allows you to define up to

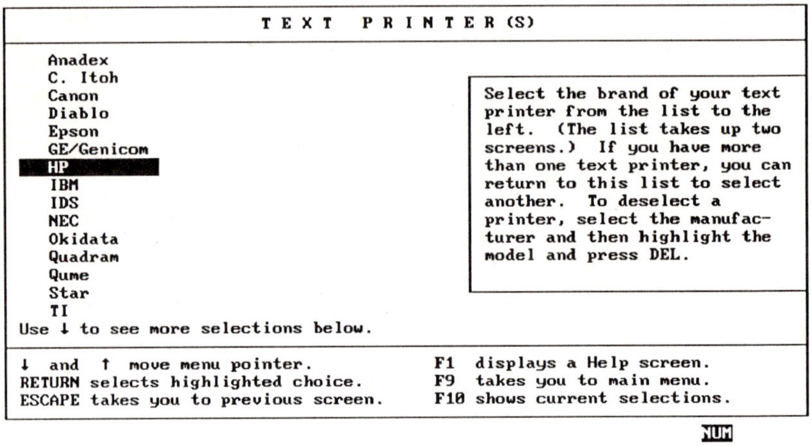

FIGURE A-7 Printer brand settings

eight text printers. You can then choose between printers while using Symphony, using the Configuration Printer Name. The printers will be numbered 1 through 8. To change which of the eight is the default printer, you use the Configuration Update command. To switch to a different printer temporarily, use the Configuration Printer Name command without using the Update command.

When you have finished selecting text printers, you are asked if you have a printer for graphs. You must select a graph printer, even if this is the same printer you will use for text, as in the case of an HP LaserJet, which can print both text and graphs. Again, you must choose the brand and then the model. You can select up to eight graph printers and choose between them when you are using the PrintGraph program to print graphs. The Settings Hardware Printer command will list the models by name.

Communications

After dealing with graph printers, Install asks if you plan to use communications. If you respond Yes, you must select the communications protocol you want to use: XMODEM/B protocol or BLAST protocol. See Chapter 7 for a discussion of these two protocols. If you are going to use Symphony's COMM environment mainly to call bulletin boards and on-line databases, select XMODEM/B. Select BLAST if you are going to be connecting with a mainframe that is using the BLAST program.

After choosing the protocol, you must say what type of modem you have: Hayes and compatible, or Popcom and compatible. Most personal computer modems are either made by Hayes or are Hayes-compatible. After selecting your communication options, you are ready for the next phase of installation: the driver set.

Driver Sets

Install now asks if you want to name your *driver set*. The driver set is a small file that is written to your hard disk when the Install program is complete. This file tells Symphony about the configuration of your particular system. It has the extension SET and is usually called LOTUS.SET. Every time the Symphony program is started, it looks for the LOTUS.SET file and reads the information in it. Choose No to avoid renaming the driver set and to accept this default name.

You choose Yes if you want a different name for this SET file. For example, you might call your SET file MY.SET. Several different configurations can be installed on the same machine and a particular configuration selected at the time the program is loaded. You might want to have different SET files for different display configurations, perhaps one for 80 x 25 display and another for 90 x 38 display, as described later in this appendix. (If you use a name other than the default, LOTUS.SET, you will need to specify the name when loading Symphony, as in SYMPHONY MY.SET, or ACCESS MY.SET if you want to load the Symphony Access System.)

When you choose No for the "Name your SET file" option, the file LOTUS.SET is created. If you choose Yes, you enter a name of up to eight characters, as instructed by the on-screen prompt. You can now quit the Install program (the process is complete), or you can press (F10) to review the settings you have chosen. You can see a typical listing in Figure A-8.

When you follow the on-screen prompts to exit from Install, you can load Symphony as described in the section on loading. Note that you may still need to adjust the memory management and operating system files on your machine before Symphony will provide maximum performance. These aspects are considered later in the appendix.

```
              Current selections in LOTUS.SET

Text Display          Hercules Card (90 x 38) - Combined·
Graph Display         Hercules Card (90 x 38) - Combined·
Keyboard              IBM Keyboard·
Port Intrface         IBM Port Interface·
Comm Port             IBM COM1/COM2 Asynchronous·
Modem                 Hayes and Compatible Modems·
Comm Protocol          XMODEM/B Protocol·
File Trnslate         IBM PC or Compatible·
Math Unit             Coprocessor Floating Point Driver·
                      Software Floating Point Driver·
Collating Seq         Numbers first·
Text Printer          HP·2686 LaserJet Series·
Graph Printer         HP·LaserJet+ or LaserJet II

                  Press ESC to continue
                                                   NUM
```

FIGURE A-8 The Install settings

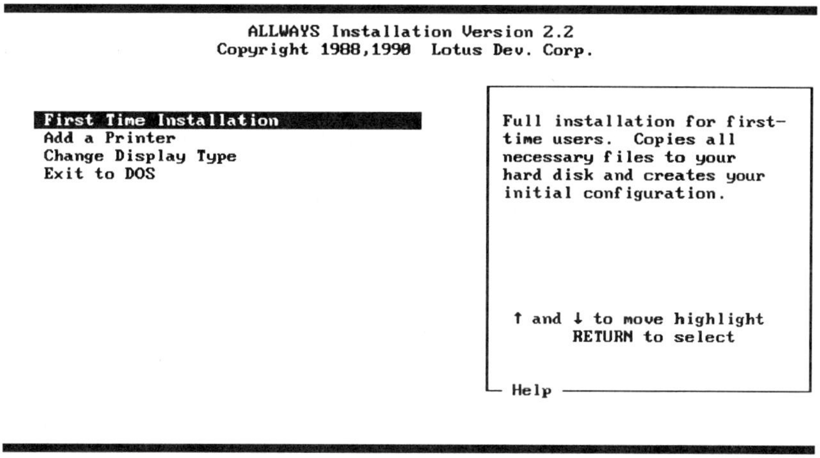

FIGURE A-9 Allways installation menu

Completing Allways Installation

If you plan to use Allways, you will need to specify the printing and display equipment you have before loading Symphony. When you exit the Install program, you will be at the DOS prompt in the Symphony program directory. To configure Allways, you enter **AWSETUP** at the DOS prompt. You will see the screen shown in Figure A-9. First you enter the drive and directory where the Symphony program files are stored. Allways suggests the current directory, so this should be correct. Press (ENTER). Allways can usually detect the type of display system you have, and you select Yes to confirm the choice. If the choice is wrong, select No and choose the correct type from the list.

Now you select your printer type from a make and model list. You can select another printer, as in Symphony. When you have selected printers, Allways copies files to your hard disk, prompting you to change disks until the installation is complete. You exit to DOS and are ready to load Symphony. Bear in mind that you may want to adjust other aspects of your system, such as data subdirectories and the AUTOEXEC.BAT file, as described later in this appendix.

LOADING SYMPHONY

If you do not need to alter any other aspects of your system, you can proceed to load—that is, start—the Symphony program. When you have completed the Install program and the AWSETUP program, you are in the correct location to start Symphony, in the directory in which the Symphony program files are stored. However, if you have restarted your computer since the installation, you need to make sure that you are in the correct location. First you need to be *logged on* to the hard disk; that is, the hard drive must be the current drive. If your hard disk is drive C, do this by typing **C:** and pressing (ENTER). To make sure the current directory is the one in which you stored the Symphony program files, type **CD \SYM22** and press (ENTER). If you used a different directory name, substitute it for SYM22. Now you can type either **SYMPHONY** or **ACCESS** and then press (ENTER).

Entering **SYMPHONY** takes you straight to a blank worksheet file, ready to work. The second approach, entering **ACCESS**, takes you to the Symphony Access System, shown in Figure A-10. As you can see, this menu lets you choose between running Symphony, PrintGraph, Install, or File-Translate, or exiting back to DOS. When you select a program from the Access menu and finish using that program, you are returned to the Access menu instead of to DOS. This is simply a convenience for users who need to do a lot of work with PrintGraph, File-Translate, or Install. When you select Symphony from the Access System, you are presented with a fresh worksheet and are ready to enter data or retrieve an existing worksheet file from disk.

An alternative approach to starting Symphony is possible if you have named a set of configuration defaults other than

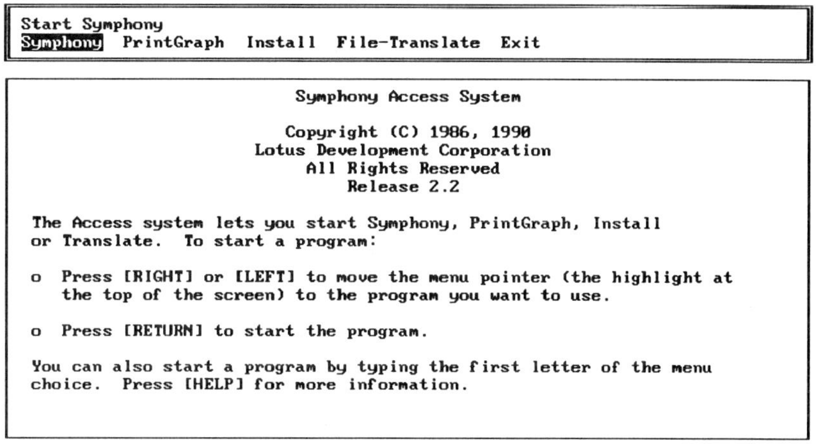

FIGURE A-10 Symphony Access System

LOTUS.SET. For example, suppose you have a set of defaults called HERC.SET. You can then enter **ACCESS HERC** to load Symphony and use the defaults in the HERC.SET file.

HARDWARE FACTORS

The equipment you use to run Symphony must meet certain minimum requirements. This section discusses these requirements, particularly the question of memory.

The Compatibility Factor

The first requirement for a computer that is going to run Symphony is that it fits the description "IBM-compatible." This term means that the computer must conform to certain design specifications, one of which is the ability to run the PC-DOS or MS-DOS operating system. Lotus actually tests computers to see if they will run Symphony and has pronounced certain makes and models to be "Lotus-certified." These include models from IBM, COMPAQ, and Toshiba. In fact, Symphony 2.2 appears to run very well on a wide range of IBM clones, including generic models assembled from off-the-shelf parts. However, with the number of different computer models that claim to be IBM-compatible now well into the thousands, Lotus will not guarantee the program's performance on anything other than Lotus-certified systems.

One further hardware fact you should know about your system is the type of *cpu chip* it contains. The central processing unit (cpu) is the microprocessor that is at the very heart of your PC. Almost all computers that run Symphony are based on cpu chips from a company called Intel. There have been a series of these chips, each more powerful than the one before. The first IBM PC was powered by a chip called the Intel 8088, after which came the 8086. The 80286 was introduced in the IBM PC AT, followed by the 80386, used in such systems as the Compaq 386 and IBM PS/2 Model 70. Most computer makers are selling, or at least planning to sell, systems based on the 80486 chip, and it is quite likely that Symphony will run on these machines as well.

About Memory

These days, your PC can come with several different types of random access memory (RAM). How much RAM and what kind of RAM it is makes a difference in how efficiently Symphony will run. Like file storage space on disk, RAM is measured in bytes and kilobytes. There are 1024 bytes in a kilobyte. One kilobyte is referred to as 1 K. There are 1024 K in 1 megabyte, referred to as 1 MB.

There are two basic types of memory in a PC, read-only memory (ROM) and random access memory (RAM). (Although some people refer to disks as memory, it is better to think of disks as storage.) The ROM in your computer holds instructions, permanently burned into the chips, that your computer uses immediately after the power is turned on, before even a disk is read. RAM is where all of the instructions, the programs that the computer is to execute, are held while being carried out. RAM is also where data is held while it is sorted onto disk. When you turn off the power to your computer, you wipe out the contents of RAM. When discussing RAM, further distinctions are made as to the type of memory. As you will see in a moment, there is extended RAM and expanded RAM in addition to normal RAM.

Memory in Action

Consider how memory works in a typical session with a typical piece of application software such as Symphony. (For the sake of clarity and brevity, this tale is simplified somewhat, but is basically a true story.) First, you turn on the computer. Almost immediately, instructions are read from ROM. This includes a test of memory that gives the numeric display in the top left of the screen, as well as the BIOS instructions (Basic Input Output System) that lay the ground rules for the exchange of information between different parts of the system, such as keyboard, display, disks, and so on.

The ROM instructions tell the computer to look to the drive(s) to find software on disk. When the computer finds a disk with an operating system on it—normally, DOS—the core of the operating system is read into memory. DOS actually consists of several parts, the two most important being the hidden system files and the command processor, which is called COMMAND.COM. After COMMAND.COM is loaded, DOS looks for two special files that tell it about the computer: CONFIG.SYS and AUTOEXEC.BAT. The CONFIG.SYS file is a list of settings for DOS to use, plus instructions about any special equipment that is part of the hardware configuration. The AUTOEXEC.BAT file is a list of instructions about what DOS should do first, like setting the date and time and displaying a menu of programs.

As manager of the flow and storage of information, DOS then allows you to issue an instruction that loads a program such as

Symphony. The program is read from disk into RAM. DOS remains in RAM as well. You enter some text from the keyboard, and this appears on screen. This information is held in RAM. You issue Symphony's File Save instruction, and a copy of the text in RAM is stored in a file on disk, but the text remains on screen as well for further editing. When you are done editing, you resave the file, replacing the old version on disk with the new one, and then exit Symphony, which removes both your entries and the program from RAM.

How Much Is Enough?

The preceding story is simple enough *if* you have enough RAM to hold both DOS and Symphony. How much is enough, and how much have you got? The basic rule is this: To run Symphony effectively, you need 640 K of normal RAM; to handle large worksheets and several add-ins at once, you need expanded RAM.

To explore how much RAM is in your computer, use the CHKDSK command from the DOS prompt. Simply type **CHKDSK** and press (ENTER). The results will look something like this:

```
Volume TOWER 386 created Jun 16, 1990 8:23a

33449984 bytes total disk space
  569344 bytes in 57 hidden files
   69632 bytes in 26 directories
26648576 bytes in 1139 user files
    2048 bytes in bad sectors
 6160384 bytes available on disk

  655360 bytes total memory
  146496 bytes free
```

Most of the information is about the files and space on the current disk, but the last section is about random access memory. You can see that according to DOS, this system has 655360 bytes, or 640 kilobytes, of total memory. The number of bytes free is the amount of the 640 K that is unused. Taking up the difference between the two figures are programs already loaded into memory, such as DOS and applications like Symphony.

The term "total memory" is very deceptive, since this is only the total that DOS can use directly. There may well be more memory in your computer. So where does this extra come from, and what kind of memory is it? The answer is fairly complex, and some background is necessary. When the IBM PC was first introduced, it came with 65,536 bytes, or 64 K of RAM. This was considered a lot of RAM at the time. Competing systems such as the Apple II had 48 K of RAM in standard configuration, and only the hottest CP/M machines had 64 K. WordStar, one of the most prevalent applications of the day, was only 32 K in size, so 64 K was more than enough. Since the "power users" back then had 64 K CP/M machines, the designers of DOS figured that ten times that much would be sufficient "user RAM" for DOS and any future applications; hence, 640 K is the maximum amount of user RAM that DOS can recognize.

This sounded like a reasonable limit at the time. However, users kept demanding more features from software, and each new wave of programs required more RAM. These days, a commonly used word processing program on PCs is WordPerfect, which takes up about 320 K. New functions have been added to DOS, which used to occupy less than 30 K but now requires some 80 K. In addition to DOS and regular application programs, a new breed of software, called TSRs or Terminate-and-Stay-Resident programs, gained popularity and consumed RAM. A TSR program, such as the original Borland SideKick, is loaded into memory after DOS but before application software and stays there as you unload one application and then load another. In this way a TSR program can offer the same features, such as a notepad or clipboard, within whatever application you are using. However, the TSR uses up additional memory.

There is also pressure on memory limits from the thirst for more exotic hardware. The designers of the original PC and DOS could not and did not anticipate every type of storage system, communications equipment, and hardware interface that was to be developed for PCs. Equipment like removable hard disks, FAX boards, and MIDI interfaces simply did not exist then. However, DOS was designed so that someone who created a new piece of equipment could also write a piece of software that told the PC how to relate to that equipment. This specialized software is called a *device driver*, and many products for the PC come with a device driver. The problem with device drivers is that they are loaded into memory when the computer starts up, right after COMMAND.COM. You cannot use such equipment as Bernoulli boxes without these drivers occupying space in memory. This is how the 640 K limit of DOS came to be such a squeeze: bigger and better applications and versions of DOS, plus TSR software and specialized equipment. Then along came networking to really put on the pressure, which has become known as "RAM-CRAM".

Memory Architecture

You might wonder why DOS has not been altered to recognize more than 640 K. The answer lies in the original design of the PC and what many users have seen as the necessity to keep each new wave of PC designs compatible with the last. Understanding the problem begins with understanding addresses. In order for a computer to keep track of the data it handles, it needs to know where it is. The location of each byte that is going to be processed needs to be defined. This is done by assigning a unique address to every byte. You can think of a delivery person attempting to make deliveries. If every customer has a unique address, the job of locating them is made much easier. In a computer, each piece of data that is processed has to pass through memory. Every address in memory has to be coded in binary code, which is the basis of all computer instructions. If you have 8 digits or bytes to work with, you can create 256 unique addresses. With 16 bits you can create 65,536 combinations or unique addresses. The 8088 chip used in the first PCs had the capacity to use 20 bits for addressing. This was a function of the physical design of the chip. This results in the maximum potential number of addresses of 1,048,576, which is exactly 1 megabyte worth of addresses or addressable memory. The 8088 chip can be said to have a 1-megabyte address space.

However, not all of this space can be used by programs that you load from disk. Some of the area needs to be reserved for information passing through memory to and from displays. There needs to be room to address the basic input/output system (BIOS) that controls how the pieces of hardware communicate with each other. To allow for these factors, IBM engineers allocated 640 K worth of addresses for programs and 384 K for system overhead. So, beyond the 640 K of user RAM, the rest of the PC's potential 1 MB total address space is reserved for system operations, a 384 K range of memory locations where the cpu finds data or instructions for its own use. Note that we are talking address space here, not actual memory chips. The 8088/8086 processors can see a total memory space no bigger than 1024 K, of which no more than 640 K can be RAM. Even if you have more than 640 K worth of RAM chips, DOS will not recognize it.

However, the address area above 640 K is rarely full. An 80-column, 25-line text display uses 4 K of video memory. The Monochrome Display Adapter occupies just the area from 704 K to 708 K. Only the most colorful EGA and VGA modes fill or exceed the 128 K assigned to video. Only IBM's PS/2 models, not PCs or ATs, use all the address space above 896 K for system ROM. Having vacant space in high memory can come in handy. Having a 64 K gap amidst the video buffers and BIOS routines makes possible something called expanded memory, described in a moment.

Although the 8088 cpu in the original PC runs out of addresses at 1 MB, the 80286 cpu found in the PC AT can address 16 MB, and the 80386 cpu can address as much as four gigabytes (4096

MB). Compared with the mess of addresses below it, RAM directly addressed above the 640 K boundary is fairly simple. It is known as extended memory, and is straightforward additional space for 80286 or 80386 systems running alternative operating systems such as OS/2, Xenix, or some 386-specific software. Unfortunately, a 286 or 386 using regular DOS runs in something called "real mode." This was designed into the chip for backward compatibility with earlier computers. The 8088-based PCs were around so long that hardware designers built their peripherals to take advantage of the addresses above 640 K. Altering the limit would affect your ability to use many popular hard-disk controllers, video boards, and so on.

Symphony and Memory Types

The real mode of 80286 and 80386 chips has the same 1 MB address limit as the 8088. There is an alternative mode that can be addressed by operating systems other than DOS. This is called "protected mode," and it can use large, extended memory spaces. Few DOS programs can actually do anything with extended memory. Many PC ATs come with 384 K of extended RAM memory installed in addition to the 640 K that DOS can use. This is largely used for utilities like RAM disks, print spoolers, or disk caches. Indeed, an AT with 1 MB of built-in RAM gives the same CHKDSK report of available memory as one with 640 K.

The memory limits of DOS have led to the development of a type of memory called expanded memory (also known as EMS memory, for "Expanded Memory Specification"). Symphony can use expanded memory to store larger worksheets than are possible with just 640 K. Since quite a lot of DOS programs can use expanded memory, but not extended memory, there is software to make your relatively useless extended memory appear as usable expanded memory.

About EMS Architecture

Compared with the simple linear addressing of extended RAM, expanded memory relies on a technical trick known as *paging*, or *bank-switching*: taking a "window" within the region visible to the processor (the 8088's 1 MB address space) and swapping different areas, or pages, of expanded memory in and out of that space as needed. What happens is that an unused 64 K section of the addressable space between 640 K and 1024 K is used as the address for a larger area—sort of like a mail drop that is one stop on the postal route but that has boxes for lots of customers. The cpu is fooled, busily operating within this virtual space on data whose real or physical address may be many megabytes away.

The bank-switching used by EMS is a sophisticated scheme. It involves hardware and software working together with the extra RAM and memory-mapping hardware on an EMS board, combined with a software driver added to your CONFIG.SYS file. This driver, the expanded memory manager (EMM), lets DOS and your applications recognize the paged memory. Given at least 64 K of contiguous, vacant address space above 784 K (one of the unused gaps), EMS creates a page frame holding at least four 16 K pages. The memory manager can map any 16 K segment, anywhere within expanded RAM, into any of these pages, fielding cpu while preventing collisions among multiple programs and data areas.

The original Expanded Memory Specification, EMS 3.2, supported 8 MB of expanded memory, mostly as work space for spreadsheets and other data files. AST and other firms modified that standard to create the Enhanced Expanded Memory Specification (EEMS), which can swap more pages, including some below the 640 K line as well as in the page frame above it. Now EMS 4.0 has surpassed the EEMS standard. With EMS 4.0, you get support for up to 32 MB at 8 MB per expansion slot. This is swapped into pages almost anywhere below 1 MB and it has many more functions and routines for executing program code as well as handling data. However, Symphony 2.2 can use no more than

4 MB of expanded memory, whatever standard that memory is designed to.

Organizing Memory

Now you know why memory is organized the way it is in a PC, and you have some basis for sorting out what Symphony needs for memory and how to arrange what you have to best fit those needs. If you do not need extended RAM for other applications, you will want all of your added memory configured as expanded memory so that Symphony can use it. If you do need extended RAM for another application, you will want all of your added memory configured as expanded memory after supplying enough extended memory for the other application to use.

The physical details of how you organize RAM in your computer depends on the type of computer and the type of memory cards you have to work with. Instructions for each piece of hardware vary considerably. However, beyond the physical installation of RAM chips, much of the manipulation of RAM depends on the CONFIG.SYS file used by DOS. The workings of this file are examined in some detail in the later section on configuration files.

ONGOING MEMORY MANAGEMENT

When you have installed Symphony and are using it, you may find that you sometimes run into memory constraints. There are several steps you can take to get around these limits. If you need to check the amount of memory available when working with Symphony, you can use the SERVICES Settings Status command. If you have installed expanded memory, make sure that it appears here. If not, check your installation.

Exactly how much information you can get into a worksheet before you run out of memory depends on many factors. Understanding these factors will help you manage memory better. Numbers take up less memory than formulas. Converting formulas to numbers with Range Values saves memory. Range names take up space in memory, as do named setting sheets. Default settings use less memory than changed settings or a collection of named settings. Add-in applications take up conventional memory space and can be removed to allow a larger worksheet.

To give you a rough idea of how large a worksheet you can create with Symphony 2.2, running under DOS 3.3, with no applications attached, 50 columns by 150 rows was about the limit with 640 K of conventional RAM and no expanded RAM. The worksheet used in this test had an entry in each cell, a mix of one-third labels, one-third numbers, and one-third formulas, with just a few range names.

The ability to use link formulas, new in Symphony 2.2, is probably the best way to avoid memory problems. Organize your work in small files, which can then be connected and consolidated through link formulas. This will make your work more manageable and less prone to exceed memory limits.

CONFIGURATION FILE ENHANCEMENT

To efficiently use Symphony on your system, you may need to fine-tune the way the system, not just Symphony, is configured. One file that greatly affects system performance is CONFIG.SYS.

The Role of CONFIG.SYS

When your computer starts up, it looks to the floppy disk in drive A for the disk operating system (DOS). If DOS is found on the disk in drive A, it is loaded into RAM. If the system does not find DOS on the disk in drive A, it looks to the hard disk, drive C, if you have one installed. If DOS is found on drive C, it is loaded into memory. The disk from which your system loads DOS is called the boot disk (this term comes from "pulling yourself up by your bootstraps").

DOS is the first piece of software loaded into memory. One of the first pieces of information DOS looks for when it is loaded is the configuration file, which is a file on the boot disk called CONFIG.SYS. The CONFIG.SYS file contains information about how your system is configured. This file is not essential for the boot disk, since DOS assumes certain default conditions if it does not find a CONFIG.SYS file. However, you will want to establish some settings with CONFIG.SYS when running Symphony.

The two settings that affect Symphony involve two aspects of the way DOS manages information in RAM: buffers and files. The number of buffers, temporary RAM holding areas into which DOS can put information your programs use, is normally 5. The number of open files that DOS can keep track of is normally 8. By increasing these settings with a CONFIG.SYS file, you can improve the speed with which DOS manipulates information in your system and help make sure that Symphony does not conflict with other programs that are opening files on your system.

A setting of 20 for buffers and 20 for files is often used. The settings are established by placing the following instructions in the CONFIG.SYS file:

```
BUFFERS = 20
FILES = 20
```

The instructions can be in upper- or lowercase letters. They are placed one instruction per line.

Other Settings in CONFIG.SYS

The CONFIG.SYS file may need additional information about your hardware. The CONFIG.SYS file for the author's system looks like this:

Entry	Use
BUFFERS = 20	Set buffers
FILES = 20	Set files
DEVICE = RCD.SYS	Support Bernoulli drive
DEVICE = HARDRIVE.SYS	Support hard-disk configuration
DEVICE = EMM.SYS	Support expanded memory board
DEVICE = RAMDRIVE.SYS	Support RAM disk

The instruction DEVICE = RCD.SYS is required to run the Iomega Bernoulli Box, a special high-capacity disk drive. The HARDRIVE.SYS instruction lets the system know that a large-capacity hard disk partitioned with the Speedstor program has been installed. The line DEVICE=EMM.SYS refers to expanded memory installed in the system. There may well be a set of numbers after EMM.SYS on this line. These are *parameters*, settings that determine how your EMM.SYS is set up.

The RAMDRIVE.SYS instruction sets up part of the added memory in your system to act like an extra disk drive. If you use memory to emulate a disk drive as a RAM disk, you can copy data or programs there very quickly since the disk is electronic and not mechanical. You may find additional information on this line, determining how large the RAM disk is and which part of your memory it is to occupy.

Checking and Changing CONFIG.SYS

You can check whether your system has a CONFIG.SYS file by using the command

```
DIR *.SYS
```

at the DOS prompt while in the root directory of your hard disk, or on the floppy disk with which you start your system. This will show you all of the device-driver files as well as any file called CONFIG.SYS. If you find a CONFIG.SYS file, you can examine its contents with the TYPE command, as in

```
TYPE CONFIG.SYS.
```

If you plan to change the CONFIG.SYS file or create a new one, you should copy the original file to another file, such as CONFIG.OLD. You do this at the DOS prompt with the command

```
COPY CONFIG.SYS CONFIG.OLD
```

A new CONFIG.SYS file can be created from scratch, from the screen, with the DOS COPY command. Type the following at the DOS prompt:

```
COPY CON CONFIG.SYS
```

Press (ENTER). The (ENTER) key gives you the first line for an instruction. Type the instruction—for example, **FILES = 20**—and then press (ENTER) for another line. After the last line of instruction, press (F6) and press (ENTER) again. The file will be written to the disk. (Pressing (F6) produces the CTRL-Z code, which DOS reads as meaning "end-of-file.") This CONFIG.SYS file is a pure ASCII file. You can also create one with SideKick's Notepad, WordStar in the nondocument mode, and many other word processors, such as SPRINT and WordPerfect, that can save text in ASCII.

HARD DISKS AND BATCH FILES

Symphony 2.2 should be installed on a hard disk. Lotus suggests that you store the Symphony program files in a subdirectory called SYM22. To make them easier to manage, Symphony data files should be kept in a directory separate from the program files. However, neither Setup nor Install deals with data directories, so steps for creating them are given here. If you need help with DOS and disk management commands, see the "Disk Operations 101" section in Chapter 8.

A Data Directory

To create and use a subdirectory called DATA directly below the Symphony program directory, you would enter the following at the DOS prompt. The example assumes that your hard disk is C and Symphony is installed in SYM22; alter these two components if this is not the case.

1. Type **CD** and press (ENTER). This changes the directory to the root directory (\\).

2. Type **MD \\SYM22\\DATA** and press (ENTER). This makes a directory below the Symphony directory.

3. Load Symphony and press SERVICES ((F9)). Select Configuration and then File. You will get a prompt that says "Initial current directory." If you have just installed Symphony, the name of the Symphony program directory will be entered here. Type **\\DATA**, and this will appear at the end of the program directory, as in

   C:\SYM22\DATA

4. Press ENTER to confirm the directory, and then select Update. This records your choice for future sessions. Now when you select File Retrieve from the SERVICES menu, Symphony will list the files in C:\SYM22\DATA.

If you wanted to copy any data files that were already placed in C:\SYM22 over to the new data directory, you would use the following commands:

```
COPY C:\SYM22\*.WR1   C:\SYM22\DATA
COPY C:\SYM22\*.PIC   C:\SYM22\DATA
COPY C:\SYM22\*.PRN   C:\SYM22\DATA
COPY C:\SYM22\*.DBF   C:\SYM22\DATA
COPY C:\SYM22\*.ALL   C:\SYM22\DATA
```

To remove copies of data files left in C:\SYM22, you would enter the following commands after making sure that the copies are in \DATA:

```
DEL C:\SYM22\*.WR1
DEL C:\SYM22\*.PIC
DEL C:\SYM22\*.PRN
DEL C:\SYM22\*.DBF
DEL C:\SYM22\*.ALL
```

Multiple Data Directories

You can have more than one data subdirectory—indeed, it makes sense to use multiple data directories to keep related files together. For example, if you are sharing a machine with other users, you could set up separate directories for each person, as in

```
C:\SYM22\FRED
C:\SYM22\JOE
C:\SYM22\DATA
```

Of Paths and Prompts

For DOS to find either a program file or a data file, you must specify a *path* for it to follow. For example, the path to the worksheet file called PROJECT.WR1 in the \SYM22\DATA subdirectory is \SYM22\DATA\PROJECT.WR1. To identify files accurately on a hard disk, which is normally referred to as C, the path to the file is joined to the file name. Thus, the full name of the PROJECT.WR1 file is

```
C:\SYM22\DATA\PROJECT.WR1
```

When you are using DOS, it is important to know which directory is current. To do this you normally modify the DOS prompt. The PROMPT command sets the prompt and uses a series of codes to supply information. For example, entering

```
PROMPT Hello Dan $G
```

results in a DOS prompt like this:

```
Hello Dan>
```

The $G code stands for the greater-than sign. Entering

```
PROMPT $P$G
```

results in

```
C:\>
```

when the root directory is the current directory, and in

```
C:\SYM22
```

when you are in the Symphony directory, because the $P code stands for "path." This prompt is very useful when working with directories.

Using Batch Files

Unfortunately, DOS forgets the helpful PROMPT command when you turn off the system. To solve this problem, you resort to *batch files*, collections of instructions to DOS that are delivered in a group or batch. A batch file has the extension BAT and is activated by typing the first part of the file name preceding the period. For example, the file P.BAT might contain the following lines:

```
PROMPT $P$G
DIR/W
```

Typing **P** and pressing ENTER would tell DOS to change the prompt and then list the files in the current directory, in the wide format.

The AUTOEXEC.BAT File

Every system can have a batch file called AUTOEXEC.BAT, which DOS looks for when the system starts up and automatically executes right after reading CONFIG.SYS. For example, you might want to go straight to work on Symphony every time you turn on your computer. The following AUTOEXEC.BAT file on the hard disk would accomplish this:

```
DATE
TIME
PROMPT $P$G
CD\SYM22
ACCESS
```

To create this batch file, you copy the instructions from the keyboard directly into a file by typing

```
COPY CON AUTOEXEC.BAT
```

at the DOS prompt. Pressing (ENTER) gives you the first line for an instruction. Type the instruction (for example, CD\SYM22), and press (ENTER) for another line. After the last line of instruction, press (F6) and press (ENTER) again. The file will be written to the disk. This file is a pure ASCII file. Note that you can add to the last line of this batch file items that cause Symphony to load specific configurations, as described shortly.

Paths Revisited

One command commonly found in the AUTOEXEC.BAT is PATH. This is used to tell DOS where programs can be found. When you issue a command at the DOS prompt—for example, if you enter **FRED**—DOS looks in the current directory for a program file called FRED.COM, FRED.EXE, or FRED.BAT. If there is no such file in the current directory, DOS looks for a PATH statement in memory to see if there are any other places that should be checked. For example, entering the command

```
PATH=C:\;C:\DOS
```

tells DOS to look in the root directory and the DOS subdirectory, in addition to whatever is the current directory. To check the current PATH setting on your computer, enter **PATH** on its own at the DOS prompt. DOS will tell you what the current path is.

The Symphony subdirectory can be added to the PATH statement. Indeed, if you have used a previous version of Symphony you may already have the path to the Symphony files in your

PATH statement. You do not have to have your Symphony directory in your system path for Symphony to run. However, including the Symphony directory allows you to start the program from anywhere on your hard disk. For example, you could load Symphony while still in the root directory. However, starting Symphony from somewhere other than the normal directory does not alter the program's default directory setting, once that setting is recorded with the Configuration Update command.

Batch-File Menu Systems

If you have a hard disk, you can easily move among different programs stored on the hard disk by using a series of small batch files and a *message file*. A message file is simply an ASCII file that contains text you want DOS to display. If you use the command TYPE together with the name of an ASCII file, DOS reads the text from the file to the screen. By preceding this command with the CLS command, which clears the screen in DOS, you can achieve a DOS screen display like this, which shows the contents of the MENU.MSG file:

```
              Main Menu
================================
1. Symphony             2. Drawing
2. Backit               3. QuickDOS
================================
Type number then press ENTER
```

You can display this message any time you return to DOS from another program by writing a batch file called Z.BAT, which changes the directory back to the root (CD\), clears the screen (CLS), and types the message (TYPE MENU.MSG).

If you write a batch file called 1.BAT that starts Symphony, you can load Symphony simply by typing **1** and pressing ENTER. If the 1.BAT file that starts Symphony runs the Z.BAT file after Symphony, you have created a loop from the menu to Symphony and back. The 1.BAT file would look like this:

```
ECHO OFF
CLS
CD\SYM22
ACCESS
Z
```

If you place the Z.BAT file and 1.BAT file in the \DOS subdirectory and then make sure that C:\DOS is in the PATH statement in your AUTOEXEC.BAT file, DOS will always be able to find Z.BAT. Thus, you will always be able to return to the root directory and the menu from anywhere on the disk by typing **Z** and pressing (ENTER) at the DOS prompt. You can easily adapt this system to your own needs by substituting commands for other software programs and expanding the list.

Multiple SETs and Parameter Passing

You could use a variation of the previous batch files to load Symphony in different configurations. For example, if Fred has stored his preferences in FRED.SET, he can load Symphony by entering

```
ACCESS FRED.SET
```

This can be part of a batch file that Fred uses to start Symphony, while the command

```
ACCESS JOE.SET
```

can be part of another batch file used by Joe to start Symphony with his preferences.

One technique that is useful in batch-file construction is to add a parameter to the file. This can be replaced by a value that you provide when you use the batch file. If you create a batch file called 1.BAT that looks like

```
ECHO OFF
CLS
ACCESS %1
Z
```

then you can load Symphony with a particular SET by entering

```
1 MY.SET
```

The %1 entry in the batch file is parameter 1 and will be automatically replaced with whatever you type on the command line after "1". The nice feature of parameters is that they do not need to be entered. Thus, you can enter **1** on its own just to load Symphony with the default SET of LOTUS.SET, or **1** followed by a space and a specific SET file name to load Symphony with that SET file.

DEALING WITH EXISTING VERSIONS OF SYMPHONY

Since many Symphony users are past users of previous versions of Symphony, you may encounter an existing directory of Symphony files when installing. This existing directory may well be called SYMPHONY. Although there is nothing preventing you from creating a new directory for Symphony 2.2, called something like S2 or SYM22, you may want to keep your existing directory structure and use the old SYMPHONY directory. Before you do this, there are some steps to consider.

Data Files

You should always try to keep program and data files in separate areas for better organization. If you have data files in your SYMPHONY directory, move them to another directory or create a new directory for them. For example, you could create a subdirectory of SYMPHONY called PREVIOUS and move the files there. Remember that data files may include files with these extensions: WR1, WKS, WK1, PIC, and PRN. The commands for this operation are shown here. You should press (ENTER) after each command.

```
MD \SYMPHONY\PREVIOUS
CD \SYMPHONY\PREVIOUS
COPY \SYMPHONY\*.W??
COPY \SYMPHONY\*.PIC
COPY \SYMPHONY\*.PRN
CD \SYMPHONY
DEL \SYMPHONY\*.W??
DEL \SYMPHONY\*.PIC
DEL \SYMPHONY\*.PRN
```

If you have been using any other types of data file, such as DBF or ALL files, then check for them in the SYMPHONY directory as well. If you created a personal dictionary file, such as PERSONAL.DCT, this should also be moved to the new directory.

Copy Protection

Some earlier versions of Symphony used a system of copy protection that checked a "key" file on your Symphony program disk. This key file was sometimes moved from the program on the hard disk. If you want to preserve the existing version of the program, you will need to take steps to preserve this file, moving it from the hard disk back to the program disk. If you used a special program to move the copy protection file to your hard disk, follow the instructions that came with it to reverse the process.

If the version of Symphony you are upgrading from is Release 1.2, you can remove the copy-protection file from your hard disk by using the ZAP program on the Symphony Setup disk (for users of 51/4 inch disks, it is on Disk 2). Place this disk in drive A and make sure the old Symphony program directory is the current directory on the hard-disk drive. Type **A: ZAP S** and press (ENTER). Type **y** to continue.

After dealing with any copy-protection situation, you can proceed to delete all of the remaining program files in the SYMPHONY directory and install Symphony. To delete all of the remaining files in the SYMPHONY directory, type the command **DEL C:\SYMPHONY*.*** and press (ENTER).

FINE-TUNING YOUR CONFIGURATION

There are several steps you may want to take to fine-tune your initial installation of Symphony. These involve the Install program and the PrintGraph program, both of which can be loaded from the Symphony Access System or from the DOS prompt (using INSTALL and PGRAPH, respectively).

Installation Changes

At any time after the initial installation of Symphony, you can load the Install program to change your configuration—for example, if you buy a different printer. When you load Install, you are shown the Main Menu, shown earlier in Figure A-4. Choose Advanced Options. This presents the menu shown in Figure A-11. When you modify an existing installation of Symphony, you need to think about which SET file you want to store your changes in. At any one time, there is just one current SET. If you do not specify a SET before loading Install, then LOTUS.SET is automatically the

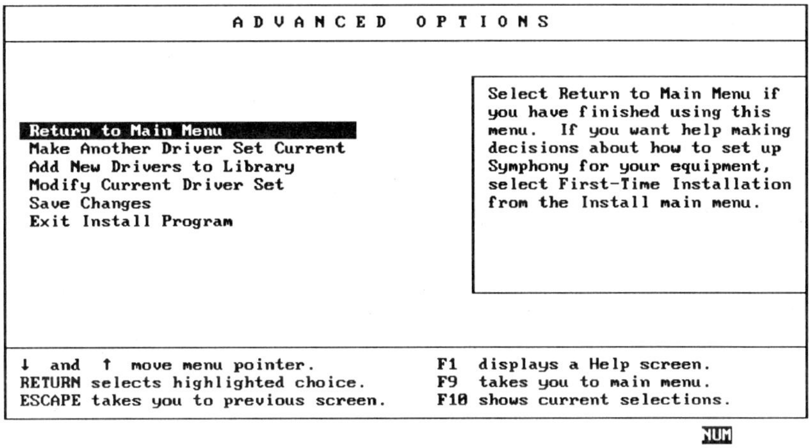

FIGURE A-11 Advanced options

current SET. How do you specify a SET before loading Install? By loading Install through the Symphony Access System, which you will have first loaded with a specific SET, as in **ACCESS MY.SET**. This command would mean that when you choose Install from the Symphony Access menu, the current SET is MY.SET.

If you want to find out which SET is current or want to make changes to a SET other than the one with which you loaded Install, choose the Make Another Driver Set Current option from the Advanced Options menu. When you pick this command, it shows you the name of the current SET. You type in the name of the SET that you want to alter and press (ENTER). To confirm the current SET, you just press (ENTER). Alternatively, if you want to create a new SET or save changes to a SET other than the one you know is current, the Saves Changes option gives you a chance to type in the name of the SET that will store your changes. You can either type in the name of an existing file or type a new file name and have Install create the file for you.

```
To change a driver, highlight the driver type and press RETURN.  If you
don't know how to combine Text Display and Graph Display, use Change
Selected Equipment, Screen Display. To exit, select Return to menu or
press ESC.

Return to menu          Leave driver list
Text Display            Universal Text Display - Separate·
Graph Display           Hercules Card (80 x 25) - Separate·
Keyboard                IBM Keyboard·
Port Intrface           IBM Port Interface·
Comm Port               IBM COM1/COM2 Asynchronous·
Modem                   Hayes and Compatible Modems·
Comm Protocol            XMODEM/B Protocol·
Math Unit               Coprocessor Floating Point Driver·
                        Software Floating Point Driver·
Collating Seq           Numbers first·
Text Printer            HP·2686 LaserJet Series·
Graph Printer           HP·LaserJet+ or LaserJet II

                                                              NUM
```

FIGURE A-12 The current settings

When you have established the SET you want to modify, you can choose Modify Current Driver Set. This produces a list of the current settings, arranged in two columns, as shown in Figure A-12. The items and categories on the left can all be selected by highlighting and pressing (ENTER). You will find that a wider range of options are available from this menu than from the original installation options. The Text and Graph Display options show the term "Separate" indicating that the current setting is not to show graph and text together. When you select Text Display or Graph Display, you will see an extended list of monitors and a choice between Separate and Combined, the latter choice meaning that you will be able to see graphs and text together. Table A-2 lists the extended range of displays.

The Keyboard option is normally set to IBM, but users of the LINK keyboard can specify their special keyboard here. Users of specialized input/output ports can use the Port Interface and Comm Port options to select special port drivers. The Modem option

AT&T Hi-Res B&W	Combined
AT&T Hi-Res B&W	Separate
Alternate Enhanced Graphics	Combined
COMPAQ Portable III	Combined
COMPAQ Portable III	Separate
GRiDCase Series	Combined
GRiDCase Series	Separate
Hercules Card (80 x 25)	Combined
Hercules Card (80 x 25)	Separate
Hercules Card (90 x 38)	Combined
IBM 3270-PC Hi-Res	Separate
IBM 3270-PC Med-Res	Separate
IBM 3270-PC/GX Hi-Res	Combined
IBM 3270-PC/GX Hi-Res	Separate
IBM 3270-PC/GX Med-Res	Separate
IBM 8514 Adapter (128 x 54)	Combined
IBM 8514 Adapter (146 x 51)	Combined
IBM 8514 Adapter (85 x 38)	Combined
IBM 8514 Adapter	Separate
IBM Color Card Med-Res	Separate
IBM Enhanced Graphics	Dual
IBM MCGA	Combined
IBM MCGA	Separate
IBM VGA	Combined
IBM VGA	Dual
IBM VGA	Separate
IBM or COMPAQ Hi-Res	Combined
IBM or COMPAQ Hi-Res	Dual
IBM or COMPAQ Hi-Res	Separate
IBM or COMPAQ Med-Res	Dual
IBM or COMPAQ Med-Res	Separate
IBM\COMPAQ Enhanced Graphics	Combined
IBM\COMPAQ Enhanced Graphics	Separate
Plantronics ColorPlus Hi-Res	Combined
Plantronics ColorPlus Hi-Res	Separate
Plantronics ColorPlus Med-Res	Separate
Tecmar GM card	Dual
Tecmar GM card	Separate

TABLE A-2 Extended Graphics Display List*

Toshiba T1100 Plus	Combined
Toshiba T1100 Plus	Separate
Toshiba T3100	Combined
Toshiba T3100	Separate

*"Separate" indicates Text or Graph; "Combined" indicates Text and Graph. The term "Dual" indicates the use of two different monitors, one for graphs and the other for text.

TABLE A-2 Extended Graphics Display List (*continued*)

allows you to alter your choice of modem. The Comm Protocol option allows your choice of communications protocol to be changed. The Math Unit option allows you to choose between two ways of supporting floating-point math (math involving decimals). The choices are Coprocessor Floating Point Driver and Software Floating Point Driver. As you can see from Figure A-12, both can be selected, and Symphony selects both by default. If you have a math coprocessor installed in your system—that is, an extra chip like the 8087 or 80287—Symphony automatically uses the first option; otherwise, the second option is used. Following the instructions provided on-screen, you can safely delete the driver that is not needed, although this seems to have little effect on performance and does not increase available memory.

Continuing down the list of options in Figure A-12, the Collating Sequence Option deserves special attention. The Text Printer and Graph Printer options simply list the same choices you have during initial installation, but the Collating Sequence option is not presented during initial installation. This option allows you to alter the collating sequence, the way in which Symphony sorts information with the Sort command. There are three choices: ASCII, Numbers First, and Numbers Last.

The default setting is Numbers First. This means that when you are using the Sort command on a key column or field that contains both numbers and labels, all of the numbers will come before the labels, and upper- and lowercase letters will have equal priority. This can be illustrated by a sort of addresses in Ascending order:

10 Downing Street
11 Downing Street
One Whitehall
Picadilly Circus
Ten Downing Street

The Numbers Last option would present an Ascending sort of the same addresses like this:

One Whitehall
Picadilly Circus
Ten Downing Street
10 Downing Street
11 Downing Street

The ASCII option refers to the American Standard for Commu nication Information Interchange, an agreed set of numbered codes that represent the main characters and numbers of English and several other languages. Since ASCII codes for lowercase come after those for uppercase, they have higher numbers. The assignment of priority to uppercase characters in an Ascending sort is referred to as *ASCII order*. This means when you perform an Ascending order sort, "AUNT" comes before "Aunt" and even before "Ant". ASCII order also puts numbers after words in an Ascending sort.

Having made your selections from the Current Driver Set list, you can select Return to menu. Choose Save Changes to record your new selections, and then choose Exit the Install Program.

```
Copyright 1986, 1990 Lotus Development Corp.  All Rights Reserved.  V2.2   MENU
Select graphs for printing
Image-Select  Settings  Go  Align  Page  Exit

 GRAPH        IMAGE OPTIONS                          HARDWARE SETUP
 IMAGES        Size                Range Colors        Graphs Directory:
 SELECTED       Top         .395   X                     A:\
                Left        .750   A                   Fonts Directory:
                Width      6.500   B                     A:\
                Height     4.691   C                   Interface:
                Rotate      .000   D                     Parallel 1
                                   E                   Printer Type:
               Font                F
                1  BLOCK1                              Paper Size
                2  BLOCK1                                Width       8.500
                                                         Length     11.000

                                                     ACTION OPTIONS
                                                       Pause: No   Eject: No


                                                  NUM
```

FIGURE A-13 The PrintGraph menu

```
Copyright 1986, 1990 Lotus Development Corp.  All Rights Reserved.  V2.2   ERROR


 GRAPH        IMAGE OPTIONS                          HARDWARE SETUP
 IMAGES        Size                Range Colors        Graphs Directory:
 SELECTE
            Disk drive not ready.  Insert Disk and

                  Press [ESCAPE] or [RETURN]
                         to continue.

               Font                F
                1  BLOCK1                              Paper Size
                2  BLOCK1                                Width       8.500
                                                         Length     11.000

                                                     ACTION OPTIONS
                                                       Pause: No   Eject: No


                                                  NUM
```

FIGURE A-14 PrintGraph error message

The PrintGraph Font Directory Problem

Symphony 2.2, which is designed to be installed on a hard disk, contains a rather frustrating throwback from the days of floppy-disk drives. As you can see from Figure A-13, the first time you load PrintGraph it will expect your graph files (those created with Image-Save, having the PIC extension) and your font files (those used to print text in the graph, having the FNT extension) to be stored on a floppy disk in drive A. It is unlikely that you will want to store your PIC and FNT files on a floppy disk. Typically, you will have the FNT files stored in the Symphony program directory, normally called C:\SYM22, and PIC files will be stored in a data directory such as C:\SYM22\DATA.

To inform PrintGraph of the correct location of the files it needs, you must change the Graphs Directory and Fonts Directory settings, using the Settings Hardware command. When you have done this, you should choose Quit from the Hardware menu and then select Save from the Settings menu to record your choices for future sessions. The problem with Symphony's default setting of A:\ is that while this setting is still in effect, choosing Image-Select from the main PrintGraph menu causes Symphony to look for a disk in drive A, resulting in the message shown in Figure A-14. You will get the same message if you select Settings Image Font. This message can be disconcerting to a new user, so it is important that PrintGraph be configured with the correct settings before users attempt to print a graph.

B

SYMPHONY AND @BASE FUNCTIONS

As you saw in Chapter 3, and again in Chapter 9, Symphony provides a powerful set of functions that can be used in the SHEET environment. Known as the @functions, because when they are entered into formulas they are preceded by the @ sign, the @functions can be classified into nine groups: aggregate and statistical; arithmetic; database; financial; logical; string; trigonometrical; string; and @cell and other special functions.

This appendix presents the functions, by group, together with the required arguments. Also covered are the functions supported by the @BASE add-in, discussed in Chapter 10, and known as the @DB functions. The appendix ends with a brief review of the Lotus International Character Set, which is used to deal with foreign characters.

AGGREGATE AND STATISTICAL FUNCTIONS

Aggregate functions perform some of the most commonly used calculations in spreadsheet work. This group includes functions that aggregate a range of cells, count the contents and average the range, find the largest and smallest numbers in the range, and determine degree of variance. Some of these functions also work with several different ranges at once or with numerous individual cells.

@SUM The @SUM function is one of the most frequently used functions. You can use @SUM to total value entries in columns, rows, and ranges that include both columns and rows. All that @SUM needs to know is the coordinates of the range to be summed. The syntax is

@SUM(Range)

The range does not need to have values in every cell; the empty cells will be ignored. The @SUM function works well with range names, so that @SUM(TOTAL) will give the total of values in the range of cells named TOTAL. You can sum several different ranges at once if you separate the ranges by a comma, as in

@SUM(TOTAL1,TOTAL2), which sums two ranges, one named TOTAL1 and the other named TOTAL2.

There are advantages to using @SUM to add up cells, rather than a "cell+cell+cell" formula. Rows or columns inserted within a summed range are automatically included in the range. Inserting new rows within the summed range expands the range to include the new cells, whereas the new cells are not automatically added to formulas constructed with "+cell" references. As a rule, if you insert a row while selecting the second cell of a summed column, or the last cell, or any cell in between, the cell is automatically added to the summed column.

Since it is quite natural to add numbers to the bottom of a list, you might want to include the row below the last number when you create an @SUM formula. When Symphony calculates the @SUM function, blank cells and label entries in the range have a value of 0 and so do not affect the answer. If you delete the first or last row or column referenced in a vertical or horizontal @SUM formula, the formula is corrupted and the cell range in the formula is replaced by ERR.

@COUNT The @COUNT function counts the number of items or non-empty cells in a range of cells. This function is useful for such projects as inventory tracking, since @COUNT can tell you how many entries there are in a column and thus how many inventory items there are in a list. You simply need to tell the function where the cells to be counted are. The syntax is

@COUNT(Range)

Note that Symphony includes labels when calculating @COUNT. Thus, the count for a summed range that includes a line of labels might be greater than you expect. For example, the following arrangement results in an answer of 6 when summed, an answer of 4 when counted:

B1:	2	B1:	2
B2:	2	B2:	2
B3:	2	B3:	2
B4:	====	B4:	====
B5:	@SUM(B1..B4)	B5:	@COUNT(B1..B4)

If cell B4 was empty, the count would be 3.

@AVG To get the average of values in a range of cells, you use @AVG. The syntax of the function is

@AVG(Range)

Like @SUM, the @AVG function works well with columns, rows, and larger ranges, particularly if you use a range name. However, label cells are used in calculating the average. Essentially, the @AVG function combines @SUM with @COUNT. You could say that @AVG=@SUM/@COUNT. Since @COUNT gives a value of 1 to a label, the arrangement shown here would produce 6 when summed, but 1.5 when averaged:

B1:	2	B1:	2
B2:	2	B2:	2
B3:	2	B3:	2
B4:	====	B4:	====
B5:	@SUM(B1..B4)	B5:	@AVG(B1..B4)

Only if cell B4 were empty or contained a value would the average of the values be correctly determined by @AVG.

@MAX To find the largest value in a specified range or collection of values, use @MAX. The syntax is

@MAX(Range)

Like the @SUM function, @MAX works well with range names. The @MAX function is useful when evaluating projections, since it can tell you the largest number that results from a change in assumptions.

You can also use @MAX with single cells if you separate them with commas. Thus, @MAX(B5,G3,K7) will tell you the largest amount in those three cells. This is handy when you want to perform a tax-form calculation and need to enter the larger of the numbers from two rows. You can also use @MAX to compare a cell to a number. Thus, @MAX(G5,10) will return the value in G5 if it is greater than 10; otherwise, you will get the value 10. Again, this is useful for tax calculations, when a subtraction results in a negative number, but you must enter 0 instead of the negative number. The formula @MAX(G5,0) will return either the value in G5 or 0, whichever is greater. If G5 is negative, the result is 0.

@MIN Corollary to the @MAX function, the @MIN function returns the smallest value in a range of cells with this syntax:

@MIN(Range)

This function can be used to identify low levels in projections and inventory lists. You can also use @MIN and @MAX to determine the highest and lowest balances for a customer's credit or checking account.

@STD To determine the standard deviation for a given range of cells that represent a population of data, use @STD. The syntax is

@STD(Range)

The standard deviation of a set of values is a measure of how much variation there is from the average of the values. The standard deviation is the square root of the variance.

@VAR The @VAR function returns a measure of variance for a range of cells—that is, the amount of variation between individual values and the mean of the population. The syntax is

@VAR(Range)

The result of the @VAR function is the square of the standard deviation of the same set of values.

ARITHMETIC FUNCTIONS

These functions affect the way numbers are calculated. They are often used when the outcome of a formula needs to be modified; for example, if it should be rounded or if a negative number should be turned into a positive.

@ABS To arrive at the absolute value of a number, you use the @ABS formula. The syntax is

@ABS(Value)

The formula @ABS(B5) returns the absolute value of the value in B5. The absolute value of a number is its positive equivalent, so if B5 is -1.5, @ABS(B5) equals 1.5.

@INT At times, you need to drop the decimal places from a number, rather than rounding them up or down. This can be done with the @INT function. The syntax is

@INT(Value)

Thus, when B5 contains 2.75, the formula @INT(B5) = 2. The value is stripped of digits following the decimal place, not rounded up to 3.

@MOD You use the modulus function when you need the number that is left after two other numbers are divided. It returns the remainder of X divided by Y. The syntax is

@MOD(X,Y)

Thus, the formula @MOD(B5,5) = 1 when B5 contains the value 36. This function is very useful when you need to figure shipping factors. You could use, for example,

@MOD(Cases_In_Order,Cases_Per_Truck)

to determine how many cases will be left after a large order has been put on the trucks. Note that using zero as the value for Y is not valid, since you cannot divide by zero. Doing so produces an ERR message in the formula cell. Also note that although the formula divides X by Y, the comma argument separator is used between values X and Y and not the division sign.

@RAND When you need a random number in a cell, you can use @RAND. This function takes no argument. The syntax is

@RAND

@RAND produces a uniformly distributed random number greater than or equal to 0 and less than 1. You may want to combine @RAND with a formula to produce a random number within a certain range. You do this by putting the high end of the range and the low end, separated by a minus sign, in a pair of parentheses and then multiplying that by the @RAND function added to the low-end number. Thus, a random number from 3 to 12 would be produced by

```
(12-3)*@RAND+3
```

If you need to get a whole number from the @RAND function, you will need to use @INT or @ROUND.

Although random numbers might not seem to be very useful in a program that is designed to help you organize and accurately analyze information, they can be essential when you want to fill cells with numbers to test a spreadsheet design. Several of the models in this book were created from random numbers.

The result of an @RAND function changes each time the worksheet is recalculated or a new entry is made. This can cause problems if you are trying to use the function to create values used elsewhere in the worksheet. You may want to use the Range Values command to fix data generated by @RAND; that is, change the formula to a value. This step is also used to hide the fact that the numbers you have created with @RAND are just random numbers. You can also change the result of a formula containing @RAND by using the EDIT key (F2). Highlight the cell containing the formula, and press EDIT. When you press ENTER to place the formula back in the cell, you will see that the @RAND function has picked a new number. If you press CALC (F8) before pressing ENTER, you will convert the function to a fixed number.

@ROUND For some records, you may need to have the numbers displayed and printed to be rounded. As you know, Symphony retains up to 15 decimal places in calculations that result in fractions. When you use a display format that sets the number of decimal places to 0, these fractions are not displayed but are still active. This produces a visual problem when totaling fields of numbers accurate to fractions of an amount but formatted with no decimal places. As the fractions accumulate, the total appears incorrect.

Suppose cell A1 contains the value 10, representing dollars that must be divided between three people. If the following formulas in column B are displayed in Fixed format, 0 decimal places, the total would look wrong:

B1: +A1/3	Result is 3.3333r but appears as 3
B2: +A1/3	Result is 3.3333r but appears as 3
B3: +A1/3	Result is 3.3333r but appears as 3
B4: @SUM(B1..B3)	Result is 9.9999r but appears as 10

To solve this problem, the numbers being totaled need to be rounded with @ROUND. The syntax of the function is

@ROUND(X,Y)

The function rounds off the value of X, using Y as the number of decimal places to round to. The value of Y should be between -15 and +15 and should be a whole number. Symphony will round X to a whole number. The effect on this example is shown here:

```
B1: @ROUND(A1/3,0) = 3
B2: @ROUND(A1/3,0) = 3
B3: @ROUND(A1/3,0) = 3
B4: @SUM(B1..B3) = 9
```

Note that this solves the problem of appearances but not the problem of what to do with the dollar left over in a three-way split.

You can combine @ROUND with @RAND to produce a whole number within a specified range, as in the following formula:

```
@ROUND(((48-18)*@RAND+18),0)
```

This produces a number from 18 to 48 with no decimal places.

@EXP The exponent function returns the value of e (a constant, approximately 2.718) raised to the power of X. The syntax is

@EXP(X)

where X is a numeric value less than 709. Thus, if X is 2, then e has been squared. This function is the inverse of a natural logarithm, @LN. If the value of X is greater than 709, the @EXP function returns ERR because the result exceeds the maximum number that Symphony can handle.

@SQRT You can find the square root of a number or formula in Symphony with the @SQRT function. The syntax is

@SQRT(Value)

Thus, @SQRT(B5) returns the square root of the value in B5. Square roots of negative numbers produce the response ERR. Use the negation operator or the @ABS function to make the value a positive number. One typical use of @SQRT is in the calculation of the hypotenuse, or slope, of a triangle. An example is

```
@SQRT(Base*Base+Height*Height)
```

@LN AND @LOG The @LN(X) and @LOG(X) functions return the log base e of X and the log base 10 of X, respectively. Thus, @LN(100) = 4.60517 and @LOG(100) = 2. If the value of X is less than or equal to 0, these functions return the ERR message in the cell in which they were applied.

DATABASE FUNCTIONS

When you want to find the total of a column of numbers, you normally use the aggregate function @SUM. You can use @SUM to total a column of numbers that constitutes a field in a Symphony database—for example, the Salary field in a personnel database. If you want to sum selected records within a database, such as the Salary values for employees in the Accounting Department, you would turn to the Symphony database functions. (These are different from the @BASE functions, discussed later in this appendix.)

The basic operation of a database function is to provide Symphony with three pieces of information:

- Which range of cells to look at: This is the database_range argument.
- Which column of the range you want the function applied to: This is the column_number argument.
- Which records to include: This is the criterion_range argument.

You must structure database_range and criterion_range like the database and criterion ranges you used in Chapter 5 with the Query Settings Basic command, although the ranges you use with database functions need not be those specified on the Query settings sheet. The database_range is made up of consecutive columns with field names as column headings, plus consecutive rows of entries within the column, each row constituting a record, as in

A1: Name	B1: Department	C1: Salary
A2: Adams, Fred	B2: Marketing	C2: 3455
A3: Doe, John	B3: Accounting	C3: 2545
A4: Smith, Tim	B4: Accounting	C4: 2875

where A1..C4 constitutes a database_range.

The criterion_range argument is a range of cells in which you have entered the criterion value you want to match beneath the name of the field you want to match in. For example, the criterion "Accounting" entered in the worksheet under the heading "Department" can be used to tell Symphony to select records that have the label "Accounting" in the Department field, as in

```
B21: Department
B22: Accounting
```

where B21..B22 constitutes a criterion_range.

The database function matches records from the database_range based on the entry in the criterion_range and then performs a statistical analysis on one field of the matching records, the field being specified by the column_number argument. Each column in the database range is numbered, starting with 0 for the first column on the left. In the previous example, Name is column 0, Department is column 1, and Salary is column 2. To sum salaries in the database for all records that have "Accounting" in the Department field, you would use this formula:

```
@DSUM(A1..C4,2,B21..B22)
```

The answer would be 5420.

The rest of the database functions are as follows:

@DAVG(database_range,column_number,criterion_range)
This function returns the average of matched values, so that

@DAVG(A1..C4,2,B21..B22) = 2710

@DCOUNT(database_range,column_number,criterion_range)
This function returns the number of matched values, so that

@DCOUNT(A1..C4,0,B21..B22) = 2
@DCOUNT(A1..C4,1,B21..B22) = 2
@DCOUNT(A1..C4,2,B21..B22) = 2

@DMAX(database_range,column_number,criterion_range)
The @DMAX function returns the maximum of matched values, so that

@DMAX(A1..C4,2,B21..B22) = 2875

@DMIN(database_range,column_number,criterion_range)
This function returns the minimum of matched values, so that

@DMIN(A1..C4,2,B21..B22) = 2545

@DSTD(database_range,column_number,criterion_range)
The @DSTD function returns the standard deviation of matched values.

@DVAR(database_range,column_number,criterion_range)
This function returns the variance of matched values.

FINANCIAL FUNCTIONS

The functions provided for financial calculations in Symphony are extensive. You can calculate annuities, mortgage payments, present values, and numerous other figures that would otherwise require a lengthy formula to be composed.

@PMT As you saw in Chapter 1, it is easy to use the @PMT function to calculate the amount required to pay back a loan in equal payments based on a given principal or amount borrowed, a rate of interest, and a loan term. The syntax of the function is

@PMT(Principal,Interest_per_period,Term_periods)

The definition of the function is the fully amortized mortgage payment of borrowing Principal amount, at the rate specified by Interest_per_period, over the amount of time specified in Term_periods. Each of the three arguments can be a numeric constant, a numeric field, or a formula that results in a number. Note that Interest_per_period must be greater than −1, and Term_periods cannot be 0.

Since the interest needs to be stated as a rate per period but is normally quoted as an annual percentage rate (APR), the loan payment formula often divides an annual percentage by 12, as in

```
@PMT(Principal,APR/12,Term_periods)
```

Likewise, the term of a long loan is often stated in years, so it then needs to be multiplied by the number of payments per year—say 12 for monthly payments—as in

```
@PMT(Principal,APR/12,YEARS*12)
```

@PV When you are evaluating a potential investment, it helps to know the "present value" of the investment. Suppose you have been offered an investment opportunity that promises to pay you $1050 after one year if you invest $1000 now. To evaluate this proposition, compare it with simply putting the $1000 in a risk-free savings account at 6% interest. This will turn the $1000 into $1060 within a year, so the proposed investment does not seem worthwhile. To put it another way, the investment promises a 5% yield, whereas you can get 6% elsewhere.

Another way of making this comparison between the promised yield of an investment and your estimate of realistic alternative yields is to *discount* the payment from the investment. If the discounted value is greater than the amount you are considering investing, then the investment is not a good one. In the case of the $1050 venture, you would take the $1050 and divide it by the number of payments plus the rate of return on the alternative investment, in this case, 6%. The formula is thus 1050/(1+.06) and the answer, the present value of $1050 received a year from now discounted at a rate of 6%, is $989. Since the present value is less than the price of the investment, $1000, the investment is apparently not a good one. If the promised returned was 1070, then the result of the discount calculation would be 1014.15, indicating that the proposal offered a higher return that the 6% you would get from a risk-free investment in a savings account. Of course, promised returns are not everything, and you would have to weigh the level of risk in the proposal.

To use Symphony for this kind of analysis, you use the @PV function, which can handle investments promising more than one annual payback amount. To calculate the present value of a simple annuity, a regular series of equal payments, use the @PV function, which takes the form

```
@PV(Payment,Interest,Term)
```

The full definition of @PV is that it returns the present value of the annuity, where Payment is received for Term periods and is discounted by the rate of Interest per period. Each of the arguments can be a numeric constant, a numeric cell, or a formula that results in a number. Interest must be greater than −1.

Consider the promise of five annual payments of $30,000 in return for an initial investment of $100,000. You can enter the payments, a discount rate of 12%, and the term into the @PV function like this:

```
A1:  30000
A2:   0.12
A3:      5
A4: @PV(A1,A2,A3)
```

You get a result, rounded to two decimal places, of $108,143.29. This is the most you should consider investing to get the promised return. The @PV function allows you to take the time value of money into account when comparing investment opportunities.

@NPV A function closely related to @PV is @NPV, which calculates the *net present value*. This handles unequal amounts returned from the investment, using this syntax:

@NPV(Interest,Range)

The Range argument is a column of cells containing the expected cash flows of the investment, such as the initial negative outflow to make the investment followed by one or more positive returns. The cash flow amounts and interest can each be numeric constants, numeric cells, or formulas that result in a number. Interest must be greater than –1. Here, you can see the proposed cash flow for an initial investment of $30,000, returning a payment of $14,000 one year and $22,000 the next, together with the net present value calculation used to analyze it:

```
A1:  -30000
A2:   14000
A3:   22000
A4: @NPV(0.12,A1..A3)
```

The result, rounded to two decimal places, is 34.17. A net present value greater than 0 means that the investment is an attractive one. A negative NPV would indicate a poor investment.

@IRR When you want to compare the payback you will receive from different investments, you can use the @IRR function to calculate their internal rate of return. The syntax is

@IRR(Guess,Range)

The Guess is your estimate of what the rate of return will be, expressed as a percentage. The Range is the group of cells containing the payments you will receive from the investment. This function can be seen here:

```
A1:      .12
A2:   -10000
A3:     5000
A4:     7000
A5:   @IRR(A1,A2..A4) = .1232 or 12.32%
```

The @IRR function actually calculates the NPV of an investment based on your guess of the rate of return. If the NPV is less than 0, then the calculation is repeated with a higher rate until the NPV is 0. Each recalculation is called an iteration. If Symphony cannot reach an NPV of 0 in 20 iterations, you get the ERR response, which indicates you should try a different guess (although this rarely happens).

@FV To see what a series of payments will be worth over time, given that they earn interest, you use the @FV function. The @FV function has the following syntax:

@FV(Payment,Interest,Term)

Payment is a numeric value representing the amount of equal payments to be made. Interest is a numeric value greater than 0, representing periodic interest rate. Term is a numeric value representing the number of periods in the investment. The @FV function calculates the future value of an investment, where Payment is invested for Term periods at the rate of Interest per period.

You can use @FV to see the effects of regular savings plans and evaluate such investments against alternative uses of funds. This can be seen here, where the @FV function returns the future value of the annual retirement fund investment of $10,000 per year, earning 15% per year, over a 20-year term:

```
@FV(10000,0.15,20)
```

The result is over $1 million.

@TERM If you have a target figure or goal in mind for your investments, you can determine how long it will take to reach that goal by using the @TERM function. It calculates how long it will take a series of equal, evenly spaced investments to accumulate to a target amount, based on a steady rate of interest. The syntax of the @TERM function is

@TERM(Payment,Interest,Future_Value)

You can see this function being used here to determine how long it will take annual deposits or payments of $10,000 to create $1,000,000 given that they earn interest of 15%:

```
@TERM(10000,0.15,1000000)
```

The answer is almost 20 years.

@CTERM This function is used to compute what an invested amount will be worth over a period of time. @CTERM has the following syntax:

@CTERM(Interest,Future_Value,Present_Value)

Interest is a numeric value representing the fixed interest rate per compounding period. Future_Value is a numeric value representing the value the investment will reach at some point. Present_Value is a numeric value representing the present value of the investment. The @CTERM function calculates the number of time periods required for an investment of Present_Value to reach a value of Future_Value, while earning interest of Interest per compounding period. You would calculate the goal of growing $1 million from an initial investment of $10,000, earning 15% per year, like this:

```
@CTERM(0.15,1000000,10000)
```

The answer is that it will take 33 years.

@RATE If you have a starting amount of $1000 and want to invest it in order to accumulate a target figure of $10,000, and you were prepared to spend 10 years doing this, what rate of interest would you have to get on your initial investment to reach your goal? The answer is 26%. This is the kind of question answered by the @RATE function, which uses the following syntax:

@RATE(Target_Value,Present_Value,Term)

The example would be expressed

```
@RATE(10000,1000,10)
```

and the exact answer would be .2589 if you limit it to four decimal places, or 25.89% if you display it as a percentage with two decimal places. The @RATE function returns the rate of interest required to grow a present value sum into a specified target value over a stated term.

TIME FACTORS You must exercise care when using Symphony financial functions that require a rate of interest or life/term argument, as in such functions as the @PMT, @NPV, and @FV functions. You must be consistent in expressing the rate and term based on the same time period. Thus, if the term is years, the rate of interest should be in years. Quarterly or monthly calculations require an appropriate change in both the rate and term arguments.

Functions such as @NPV and @PV assume that the cash flows occur at the end of the period; that is, that you make your investment and receive your return at the end of the year, rather than the beginning. This is often not the case. You may well want to calculate the effect of investing now, and then again a year from now, and so on. This is easy enough to account for in Symphony. For the @PV calculation, simply add the first-year payment to the result of the formula and subtract 1 from the term. You can see this in the example here:

```
A1:     30000                A1:     30000
A2:       0.12               A2:       0.12
A3:          5               A3:          5
A4:   @PV(A1,A2,A3)          A4:   @PV(A1,A2,A3-1)+A1
      = 108,143,20                 = 121,120.48
```

The difference in results is noticeable. With @NPV, the formula is adjusted to calculate the second through last flows and add the initial flow to the result.

The same factor of timing affects the @FV and @TERM functions. To adjust the @FV calculation to reflect investment payments beginning at the time of the calculation rather than in 1 year's time, you use

@FV(Payment,Rate,Term −1)+Payment

You adjust the @TERM function by using

@TERM(Payment,Rate,Goal)/(1+Rate)

By bearing in mind these timing considerations, you will make more accurate use of these powerful functions.

@SLN Symphony offers three different methods for calculating depreciation. These are used to account for the fact that most goods decrease in value over time, and business income tax laws sometimes allow businesses to deduct a portion of this loss from profits. The straight-line method results in equal amounts of depreciation per period. The syntax is

@SLN(Cost,Salvage,Life)

This is the simplest form of depreciation. The Cost argument is the original cost of the goods. The Salvage argument is what the goods are worth at the end of the period. The Life argument is the length of time that the goods have been in service.

@SYD The @SYD function uses a method called the sum of the years to vary the rate at which depreciation is taken, and thus needs to know the year for each calculation. The syntax is

@SYD(Cost,Salvage,Life,Period)

An interesting application of the @SYD function is in the computation of a loan payout based on the "rule of 78," which results in a larger payoff for loans than the simple interest calculation.

@DDB The @DDB function calculates depreciation based on the double declining balance method, using the following elements:

@DDB(Cost,Salvage,Life,Period)

As in all of the depreciation functions, Cost is a numeric value representing the amount paid for an asset. Salvage is a numeric value representing the worth of an asset at the end of its useful life. Life is a numeric value representing the expected useful life of an asset. Period is a numeric value representing the time period for which you want to determine the depreciation expense. The @DDB function determines accelerated depreciation values for an asset, given the initial cost, life expectancy, end value, and depreciation period.

LOGICAL FUNCTIONS

Symphony provides a variety of functions that can be very useful for situations in which logical arguments need to be entered into formulas.

@IF The @IF function instructs Symphony to choose between two actions or results, based on a condition being either true or false. The condition is stated as a true/false formula, as in

```
A1>100
```

The result is true if the value in A1 is greater than 100, but false if the value in A1 is less than 100. If you enter the formula just shown in a cell, Symphony represents the answer true as 1 and false as 0.

The @IF function uses conditional formulas like

```
@IF(A1>100,"Yes","No")
```

so that the result is a label reading "Yes" if A1 is greater than 100, and a label reading "No" if A1 is less than 100.

The format of the @IF function is

@IF(Conditional_formula,Then,Else)

This syntax means that if Conditional_formula is true, the Then argument is executed;. otherwise, the result is that in the Else argument. The Then and Else arguments can be formulas resulting in values or labels, cells references, or constants.

Suppose that you are budgeting revenue and expenditures for a computer store. You have attained good results from spending 5% of each month's revenue on advertising. Thus, advertising is normally Revenue * 0.05. However, you know that money spent on advertising beyond a certain dollar amount is not effective (say, $110). What you want to do is budget your advertising expenditures at 5% of revenue with a ceiling of 110. You want a formula that says this:

> If Revenue * .05 is less than 110, then Advertising = Revenue * 0.05, otherwise Advertising = 110

This is done by using the @IF function. If the Revenue figure is in B11, the formula is as follows:

```
@IF(0.05*B11<100,0.05*B11,110)
```

When you want to apply several conditions to a calculation, you can nest @IF statements. An example of nesting @IF statements can be seen in the formula used to calculate commissions based on a percentage (4%-6%) of sales.

```
@IF(C5<40000,0.04*C5,@IF(C5<5000,0.05*C5,C5*0.06))
```

This formula says that if the sales in C5 are less than $40,000, the commission will be 4% (0.04) of sales; otherwise, if sales are greater than $40,000 but less than $50,000, the commission will be 5%. If sales are greater than $50,000, the commission will be 6%. The nesting of @IF statements takes a little planning, but if you write out the statement first, you can usually frame the actual formula to fit most conditional situations.

@VLOOKUP When you want to make a formula dependent on a range of conditions, you have an alternative to nesting @IF functions. You can have Symphony refer to a table of conditions, called a *lookup table*. This is a vertical or horizontal list of numbers with related values. A lookup table offers a simple way to determine the commission rate based on a broader range of sales levels.

This vertical list of sales levels in column A and related commission rates in column B shows the rate applicable to any given level of sales:

A1:	0	B1:	.04
A2:	30000	B2:	.05
A3:	40000	B3:	.06
A4:	50000	B4:	.07

Any sales amount below $30,000 earns a commission of 4%. Sales from $30,000 to $39,999 earn 5%, and so on. The bottom of the table shows that sales of $50,000 and up earn 7%. This table of numbers, cells A1..B4, can be named TABLE with the Range Name Create command.

If you have a sales figure entered in C5, you can then use a formula like this to determine commission:

```
@VLOOKUP(C5,TABLE,1)*C5
```

This means the vertical lookup function is invoked to look up the value of cell C5 in the range of cells named TABLE and read the corresponding value from column 1. The value that is found in the table is then multiplied by cell C5 to calculate the commission amount. The syntax of the vertical lookup function is thus

@VLOOKUP(Index,Table,Column)

The Index is the cell containing the value you are looking up in the table. The Table argument should be consecutive columns of values. The Column argument is the column in the table that the formula should look to for its result. The column numbering is 0 for the first column, 1 for the next column to the right, and so on. In the example, the contents of C5 and of column 0 of the lookup table must be values. The column 0 values must be a consecutive range of values. However, the contents of columns 1 and of any additional columns in the table can be labels.

@HLOOKUP A lookup table can be laid out horizontally. For example, the table just shown can be rearranged like this:

A1:	0	B1:	30000	C1:	40000	D1:	50000
A2:	.04	B2:	.05	C2:	.06	D2:	.07

The syntax of the @HLOOKUP function is

@HLOOKUP(Index,Table,Row Number)

If you entered a sales figure in C5, you could use this formula to calculate commission:

```
@HLOOKUP(C5,A1..D2,1)*C5
```

Row 0 of the table must be a series of values. Successive rows can be values or labels.

Note that you do not have to use a range name for the lookup table reference in the formula. However, a range name makes it easier to refer to the cells of the table than when typing coordinates, particularly if you want to copy the formula containing the reference table and thus need to make the cell references absolute. A reference to a range named TABLE can be made absolute by preceding it with a dollar sign, as in

```
@VLOOKUP(C5,$TABLE,1)*C5
```

@CHOOSE A function comparable to a lookup table is @CHOOSE, which selects its responses based on a number. For example, if you had four salespersons, each of whom had a number, you could enter the number in a cell and have @CHOOSE automatically enter the corresponding name in another cell. If the salesperson's number was entered in A1, this formula could be used in A2 to return the name:

```
@CHOOSE(A1,"Smith, H.","Gore, B.","Sloan, R.","James, E.")
```

The number 2 entered in cell A1 would thus result in the response "Gore, B" in A2.

The syntax of the @CHOOSE function is

@CHOOSE(X, Case0, Case1,...,Case*n*)

If X = 1, then Case1 is used. If X = 2, Case2 is used, and so on. The value of X must be a number between 1 and the total number of cases in the argument. Values of X outside that range will cause an error. If X includes a decimal, Symphony rounds off the value. The value X can be a numeric constant, a cell, or a formula, as in the previous example, where you see that this function is a compact way of handling small lists of results. The results can be constants or formulas of any data type. However, all results must have the same data type.

@ERR When you want a cell to reflect an error, you can use the @ERR function. This function takes no argument. @ERR returns the value ERR in the current cell and, in most cases, also creates the ERR message in any other cells that reference the cell in which you created the ERR condition. The exceptions to this are @COUNT, @ISERR, @ISNA, @ISNUMBER, @ISSTRING, @CELL, and @CELLPOINTER formulas. These formulas do not result in ERR if they reference a cell that contains ERR. The ERR value resulting from this function is the same as the ERR value produced by Symphony when it encounters an error.

@NA The @NA function works the same as @ERR except that it returns the value NA, which distinguishes it from the ERR message that Symphony uses when a formula is typed incorrectly. The term "NA" stands for "Not Available."

@INDEX The @INDEX function is related to the vertical and horizontal lookup tables. You can use @INDEX to select a value from a block of values. You provide the column number and row number, and @INDEX returns the contents of the cell that matches that column and row. Columns and rows are numbered from zero. For example, consider this block of price figures:

```
D3:   45    E3:   48    F3:    54
D4:   47    E4:   55    F4     63
D5:   49    E5:   62    F5:  Out of Stock
```

As far as the @INDEX function is concerned, column D is column 0 and row 3 is row 0. The formula

```
@INDEX(D3..F5,2,1)
```

returns 63 because this is the entry in column 2, row 1(of the block, not the worksheet).

The function has the syntax

@INDEX(Range,Column,Row)

The entries in the Range argument can be numbers or labels. The Column and Row arguments can be cell references or formulas. Bear in mind that these arguments refer to the number of the column and row within the table. Suppose that the above table refers to prices for shoes. The columns represent width fittings A, B, and C. The rows represent sizes 8, 9, and 10. Thus, a 9B would cost 55. You could enter width in A1 and size in A2. You might be tempted to try the formula

```
@INDEX(D3..F5,A1,A2)
```

but this would not work, since the entries in A1 and A2 do not reflect the columns and rows of the table. The size number in A2 needs to be reduced to a base of 0, and the width letter in A1 needs to be converted to a number, also with a base of 0. This formula does work:

```
@INDEX(D3..F5,@CODE(A1)-65,A2-8)
```

If you enter **9** in A2, then it is converted to 1, the correct row number. The @CODE function, described later under "String Functions," gives a numeric code to a letter, so that A=65, B=66, and so on. If you enter the letter **B** in A1, it is converted to 1, the correct column number. Thus, a 9B costs 55. Note that entering **C** in A1 and **10** in A2 would result in the label "Out of Stock." Column and Row arguments beyond the range of the table result in ERR, and Symphony rounds all index numbers down to the nearest whole number.

@TRUE AND @FALSE Two apparently redundant functions are @TRUE and @FALSE. These functions take no argument and provide the values 1 and 0, respectively. For example, entering **@TRUE** in a cell results in 1.

You will probably not use these functions unless you want to make a formula more explicit. Consider the formula +A1>99. This results in 1 if A1 contains any number larger than 99, or 0 if A1 contains a number less than 99 or a label (labels have a 0 value). However, to make the formula more explicit, it could be replaced by this formula:

```
@IF(A1>99,@TRUE,@FALSE)
```

TRIGONOMETRICAL FUNCTIONS

If you work with geometry and trigonometry, Symphony offers many useful functions. These are mainly used in engineering and scientific applications, but they can be very handy in many different situations.

@PI The @PI function provides the value of pi (π) to ten decimal places and can be used in calculations that require the value of pi. The @PI function takes no argument; it simply returns the value 3.1415926536. The formula to calculate the circumference of a circle, the radius of which is stored in A1, is thus 2@PI*A1. The area of a circle can be calculated by combining @PI and the exponent function, as in @PI*A1^2.

DEGREES AND RADIANS Another application of @PI is to convert radians to degrees. In Symphony, the trigonometric func-

functions like @SIN and @COS produce answers in radians. You can use pi to express angles measured in radians as degrees and convert degrees to radians, using the following formulas:

1 Radian = $360^{\circ}/(\text{pi} \times 2)$	or 180/pi
1 Degree = $(\text{pi} \times 2 \times \text{radian})/360^{\circ}$	or pi/180

Users of trigonometric functions in Symphony thus employ the expressions 180/@PI and @PI/180 to make the necessary conversions from radians to degrees and vice versa. One shortcut is to enter these expressions in cells to which you have assigned appropriate range names, and then use the range names in formulas. For example, consider a right-angled triangle with a base (X) of 4 feet, a height (Y) of 3 feet, and a slope (Z) of 5 feet. Suppose you want to compute the angle between the height and the slope. You would do this with the formula

Angle = @ASIN(Base/Slope) or @ASIN(X/Z)

If you enter the value of (X) in B1 and the value of (Z) in B2, you can compute the angle between the height and the slope in B3:

```
B3 = @ASIN(B1/B2)
```

The result, expressed to six decimal places, is .927295. This is the angle measured in radians, not degrees. To convert from radians to degrees, you could use this formula:

```
B3 = @ASIN(B1/B2)*180/@PI
```

The result, expressed to four decimal places, will be 53.1301. Alternatively, you could use the formula

```
B3 = @ASIN(B1/B2)*RAD2DEG
```

where RAD2DEG is the range name given to a cell containing the formula 180/@PI.

@SIN, @COS, AND @TAN These three functions, expressed as @SIN(X), @COS(X), and @TAN(X), return the trigonometric sine, cosine, and tangent of X, an angle measured in radians. You convert an angle measured in degrees to one expressed in radians by multiplying the angle by @PI/180. Thus, @SIN(60*@PI/180) returns the sine of a 60-degree angle.

@ASIN, @ACOS, AND @ATAN The inverse trigonometric functions, which are expressed as @ASIN(X), @ACOS(X), and @ATAN(X), are created by Symphony, saving you from having to create them from the @COS, @SIN, and @TAN functions. They return an angle, measured in radians, given its sine, cosine, or tangent. The @ATAN2(X,Y) function calculates a four-quadrant arc tangent from the X and Y coordinates of a point.

STRING FUNCTIONS

A particularly powerful group of Symphony functions are those that help you manipulate strings. To Symphony, a string is a sequence of characters with no numerical value. This can be a word like **Symphony** or a group of characters like **'123**, since they are preceded by a label prefix.

String Math

Say the labels **John** and **Doe** are entered into B1 and B2. Separate cells can be added together by this formula:

```
+B2&B1
```

The result is "DoeJohn." If you want to place a comma and a space between the entries, you would use the formula

```
+B2&", "&B1
```

which results in "Doe, John." This use of the ampersand (&) to add or concatenate label entries and strings of text supplied in quotes is very handy. In this case, the text added to the cell entries is a comma and a space (", "). Text supplied in quotes is referred to as a text constant.

Consider a database of sales figures, the first two rows of which appear like this:

A1:	First	B1:	Last	C1:	Sales
A2:	John	B2:	Doe	C2:	34000

Suppose you have sorted the list in Descending order by sales, and John Doe has come out on top. You could reflect this in the following formula:

```
+"The top salesperson is "&A2&" "&B2&"."
```

The result would be "The top salesperson is John Doe." This concatenates the label entries in A2 and B2 with string constants in quotes.

Suppose you were to update the sales figures, sort the list again, and someone else was top of the list, as shown here:

A1:	First	B1:	Last	C1:	Sales
A2:	Fred	B2:	Smith	C2:	34500

The same formula would produce "The top salesperson is Fred Smith." You might like to go further, as in this formula:

```
+"The top salesperson is "&A2&" "&B2&" with sales of "&C2&"."
```

The desired result would be "The top salesperson is Fred Smith with sales of 34500." However, this is not the result, since you cannot directly concatenate numeric entries. You must use the @STRING function, as shown here:

```
@STRING(C2,0)
```

Used in place of the reference to C2, this turns the numeric entry in C2 into a label with zero decimal places.

The @STRING function is just one of a group of functions referred to as "String functions," which can be used to create text from SHEET entries and alter text. The string functions can convert numbers to strings and vice versa. They are particularly valuable when you are working with data imported from other programs in the form of text files. They can also be used effectively with some macro commands.

@CHAR Many computer programs store, display, and print information by using ASCII characters. This is a standard set of characters, numbers, and symbols, each of which has a code number defined by the American Standard Code for Information Interchange. There are 256 ASCII characters, numbered from 0 to 255. Many of them are symbols not found on the keyboard, such as the yen sign (¥). The @CHAR function can display some of these codes in Symphony. @CHAR returns the character corresponding to a given code number. Its syntax is

@CHAR(Code)

where Code is a numeric value between 0 and 255. In fact, Symphony does not use the standard ASCII code numbering system, but instead uses a system known as LICS, for Lotus International Character Set. Both the LICS character set and the normal ASCII set are listed in tables near the end of this appendix.

Symphony uses the LICS system rather than normal ASCII for several reasons. First of all, not all printers can print all of the ASCII characters, whereas LICS, together with the COMPOSE function key, allows Symphony users to print more characters than their printers actually support. Also, LICS handles a wider variety of international characters and enables foreign character conversion. For example, in the COMM environment Symphony allows you to use the Settings Terminal Translation command to specify translation of your characters to those used in another country, and vice versa. You can also create a custom translation file (CTF) that lists characters by their code numbers in two columns, indicating which codes should be translated to other codes.

@REPEAT The @REPEAT function repeats a string of characters a specified number of times. Its syntax is

@REPEAT(String,Number)

where String is a string value in quotes and Number is a numeric value greater than or equal to 0. @REPEAT returns as many copies of the string as you specify with Number. The result is a label.

This function is somewhat similar to the repeating label prefix (\) used to produce dashed lines in a cell. The main difference is that with @REPEAT, you can specify exactly how many times you want the string to be repeated. Also, the label prefix adjusts the number of repeated characters to fit the column, even when the width is changed. The @REPEAT function can display a fixed number of characters that does not change. When you specify a text string with @REPEAT, it must be surrounded by double quotes (").

The Number argument in the @REPEAT statement can be a constant, a formula, or a cell reference. This argument can be used to repeat a character or characters according to a variable factor. An application of this ability is seen in the formula used to produce a dashed line that is one character shorter than the width of the column. For example, when you have a column that is 7 characters wide, you can obtain this effect:

```
May-88  Jun-88  Jul-88
======  ======  ======
```

In contrast, using the cell fill command (in this case, \ ) produces a continuous row of equal signs, as in this:

```
May-88   Jun-88   Jul-88
=====================
```

The formula that creates the short line uses the @CELL function to measure the width of the current column, as in

```
@REPEAT("=",@CELL("width",X)-1)
```

where X is the cell above the one in which the formula is placed. Note that although the @CELL function will read the current column width when you enter the formula, it does not respond to changes as quickly as the cell fill (\) command.

If you alter the column width after entering the @CELL formula, you will need to press the CALC key, (F8), to update the @CELL reading. One important difference between using \ and the @REPEAT function is that @REPEAT can be used with the @CHAR function. In this way you can repeat any of the LICS/ASCII characters.

@CODE A reverse of the @CHAR function, the @CODE function tells you the LICS/ASCII code of a special character. Sometimes, data that you import from another program is corrupted by odd characters. Identifying them with the @CODE function could help you determine their origin. Its syntax is

@CODE(String)

where String is a string value, and the first letter is evaluated by @CODE to return the LICS/ASCII code.

As you have seen, using the results of the @CHAR function allows you to produce odd characters yourself in a Symphony spreadsheet. You can determine the character's LICS/ASCII number by applying the @CODE function to it. Another way of producing some special characters in Symphony is to hold down (ALT) and type the true ASCII code of the character from the numeric keypad, then release the (ALT) key. This results in the character corresponding to the code number you typed. For example, (ALT-156) returns the pound sterling symbol.

@FIND The @FIND function uses three arguments to find characters within a string. Its syntax is

@FIND(SubString,String,StartNumber)

where SubString is a string value representing the target pattern to search for, String is a valid string value representing the source value to search within, and StartNumber is a numeric value of 0 or greater representing the character position to begin searching with. The @FIND function returns the character position at which the first occurrence of the target was found.

The number 0 represents the first character in the string, the second is 1, and so on. Thus, @FIND("t",A1,0) returns the value 2 if A1 contains the label "Lotus," because the letter "t" first occurs at position 2. Note that the StartNumber value tells Symphony to begin the search at that number of characters in the string. You will receive an error message if the value of StartNumber is more than the number of characters in String minus 1. You also get an error message if @FIND fails to find any occurrences of the SubString.

Suppose that someone has entered information about employees in the following format:

A2: John Doe, $1,200.00 Accounting
A3: Al Smith, $1,500.00 Marketing

The user who created this list is new to spreadsheets and entered the data as one long label, rather than as separate facts in separate cells. You need to convert the data to a more normal format. This example will be used several times in the following sections to demonstrate string functions. Note that the names of employees are exactly the same length, and both of the labels have a dollar sign ($) in them. The dollar sign might help break the labels into their separate parts.

The @FIND function can be used to measure the position of the dollar sign, as in @FIND("$",A2,0), which returns 10. Although this might not seem like vital data, it shows how the function can be used to compare labels. The @FIND function proves useful in combination with other string functions.

@EXACT Another way to compare labels is to use the @EXACT function. This function has the syntax

@EXACT(String1,String2)

where String1 is a string value or cell containing the label, and String2 is a second string value or cell containing a string value.

The @EXACT function compares the values of String1 and String2. If the values are exactly identical, including capitalization, it returns a value of 1. If there are any differences, it returns a 0 value. The arguments can be cell references or string constants. String constants must be surrounded by double quotes, as in

@EXACT(A1,"Name")

which returns 1 if A1 contains the label "Name."

If you attempt to compare one or more numbers or empty cells with @EXACT, the result is ERR. Label prefixes are ignored in @EXACT comparisons. Remember that the syntax uses an argument separator between the compared items, not an equal sign.

To compare strings or cell contents without regard to capitalization, you can use the @IF function. The @IF function is not case-sensitive. For example, @IF(A1=A2,1,0) will return a value of 1, meaning true, if the contents of the cells are the same but capitalized differently (for example, if A1 contained "YES" and A2 contained "Yes"). Another formula that you can use to check for a spelling match that disregards capitalization in a string is simply +A1="Yes", which also lacks case sensitivity. However, this formula returns ERR if the comparison cell is empty.

@REPLACE With four arguments, the @REPLACE function can be used to replace a string of characters within a label. Its syntax is

@REPLACE(String,StartNumber,Num,NewString)

where String is a string value, the label to be worked on; StartNumber is the character position to begin with; Num is the number of characters to delete; and NewString is a string value, the characters to insert at the position marked by StartNumber. You can use this function to change one label into another. For example,

```
@REPLACE(A2,10,1,"earns $")
```

changes the label shown earlier in A2 into

```
John Doe, earns $1,200.00 Accounting
```

Another use of @REPLACE is to add one string to the end of another. You do so by specifying as StartNumber a number that is one greater than the number of characters in String. To delete part or all of a string, specify " " as NewString.

@LEFT AND @RIGHT The @LEFT and @RIGHT functions are used to find strings of characters within labels, based on the position of those characters. The functions follow the same basic syntax:

@LEFT(String,Number)

where String is a string value and Number is a numeric value of 0 or greater.

The @LEFT function returns the leftmost characters of String, the number of characters returned being that specified by the Number argument. The formula @LEFT(A2,8) returns "John Doe" from cell A2, since those are the eight leftmost characters. This function could be used to extract the employees names, except that varying name lengths would cause a problem. This can be solved by using the @FIND function. You use it to specify how far the reading of the leftmost characters must go—in this case, as far as the first comma. The combined formula would be

```
@LEFT(A2,@FIND(",",A2,0))
```

The @RIGHT function is sometimes easier to apply; it takes the last X number of characters out of a label. An example of @FIND would be @RIGHT(A2,10), which returns "Accounting." Another example will be given in a moment.

@MID When you want to extract characters from the middle of a string, use the @MID function. The function has the following syntax:

@MID(String,StartNumber,LengthNumber)

The function extracts the number of characters specified by the LengthNumber argument, from the text identified as String, beginning with the character in StartNumber position. The first character of a string is numbered 0, the second is numbered 1, and so on.

@TRIM AND @LENGTH The @TRIM function removes any extra spaces from a piece of text string and has the syntax

@TRIM(String)

where String is the text to be acted upon. The extra spaces that @TRIM removes include the trailing spaces following the last non-space character, spaces preceding the first non- space character, plus duplicate spaces between words. If the cell in the String argument is empty or contains a numeric value, the @TRIM function returns ERR. This function is particularly useful when you are working with data from other programs that pad some data to equal lengths by using trailing spaces.

The @LENGTH function is used to measure the length of a label. It uses the syntax

@LENGTH(String)

Thus, @LENGTH(A2) returns 32. Likewise, @LENGTH(A1) returns 4 if A1 contains the word "Name." This function is sometimes combined with other string functions to locate text within a string.

@LOWER, @UPPER, AND @PROPER These three functions change the case of a string of text, turning into all lowercase, all uppercase, or mixed cases. The syntax for these functions is:

@LOWER(String)
@UPPER(String)
@PROPER(String)

You can use @LOWER to turn a string into all lowercase characters. The @UPPER function returns all uppercase characters; that is, it capitalizes the string. A typical use of these three functions is to change the capitalization of an entire range of labels, which can save you from doing extensive editing.

The @PROPER function converts the first letter of every word in the string to uppercase and the rest of the characters to lowercase. In Symphony, a word is defined as an unbroken string of alphabetic characters. The @PROPER function considers any blank spaces, punctuation symbols, or numbers as marking the end of a word. Thus, the formula

```
@PROPER("LOTUS DEVELOPMENT")
```

returns the label

```
Lotus Development
```

as does the formula @PROPER(A1) if A1 contains the text LOTUS DEVELOPMENT. In all three functions, numbers and symbols within the string are unaffected by the function. If the cell is blank or is a numeric or date value, the result is ERR.

@STRING Used to convert numbers to labels, the @STRING function has the syntax

@STRING(X,DecPlaces)

where X is a numeric value and DecPlaces is a numeric value between 0 and 15, representing the number of decimal places to the right of the decimal point. Suppose that cell A1 contains the value 20.01. The statement @STRING(A1,0) converts 20.01 to a label, 20, rounding it to the decimal precision indicated by the second argument (0).

You can use @STRING when combining numbers with other pieces of text. An example is to convert a ZIP code entered as a number into a piece of text that can be concatenated with the rest of the address: @STRING(D5,0) returns the label 94109 if cell D5 contains the value 94109.

Earlier, you saw how the @STRING function is needed in a concatenation formula that refers to a numeric cell entry. Given the cell entries

```
A1:   First     B1:   Last      C1:   Sales
A2:   Fred      B2:   Smith     C2:   34500
```

the formula

```
+"Top salesperson is "&A2&" "&B2&"."
```

produces this result:

```
Top salesperson is Fred Smith.
```

The formula

```
+"Top salesperson is "&A2&" "&B2&" with $"&@STRING(C2,0)&"."
```

produces this result:

```
Top salesperson is Fred Smith with $34500.
```

@VALUE The @VALUE function converts a label that looks like a number to a true numeric value. The syntax is

@VALUE(String)

where String is a string value that can contain any of the arithmetic operators but must not contain dollar signs, commas, or embedded spaces. One period, interpreted as the decimal place, is permitted, and leading and trailing spaces are ignored. For example, when you extract a series of numbers from a label using the @LEFT or @RIGHT function, these numbers cannot be used as values right away; they must be converted to values with @VALUE. You can see this function at work, creating a value from the label in A2 in the earlier example of an employee list:

```
@VALUE(@MID(A2,@FIND("$",A2,0)+1,6))
```

The result is the number 1200. This formula uses the @MID function described earlier.

@DATEVALUE AND @TIMEVALUE These functions, together with the @VALUE function, are very useful for converting to numbers data that was imported as text with the File Import command but was not converted automatically into values. You can also use this function to return values for numbers that have been turned into labels. The @DATEVALUE function creates a date serial number out of a label that looks like a date. The label can be in any of the following formats:

4/1/91 1-Apr-91 4/1 01-Apr Apr-91

Thus, @DATEVALUE(A1) results in 33329, the date serial number for April 1, 1991, if A1 contains any of these labels. When the year is missing, as in the third format, the current year is assumed. When the day of the month is missing, the first is assumed.

The @TIMEVALUE function reads a time from a label, as in @TIMEVALUE(A1), which returns .458333 when A1 contains any of these labels:

11:00 11:00:00 AM 11:00:00 11:00 AM

@CELL AND OTHER SPECIAL FUNCTIONS

The @CELLPOINTER and @CELL functions return information about a cell. The type of information produced by the function depends on the code specified in the function statement. The cell about which information is returned is, in the case of @CELLPOINTER, the cell that the pointer currently occupies. In the case of @CELL, the cell is the one referred to by a cell reference or the one in the top left corner of a named block referred to by name in the function statement. The syntax is as follows:

@CELLPOINTER(Code)
@CELL(Code,Cell)

The Code argument is a string that determines the information about the cell that the function references. There are nine of these codes, and they are shown in Table B-1. With careful use of these codes, particularly when combined with the macro keyword {IF} or the @IF function, you can extract valuable information about cells of the worksheet for use in macros and formulas. Remember that if you use a range name to refer to the cell required in the @CELL function, the cell addressed will be the one in the top left corner of the block.

Since the cell used by the @CELLPOINTER function is the current cell, this function is useful for controlling looping macros, such as the following one, called CENTER, which turns a column of numbers into centered values:

```
CENTER    {EDIT}{HOME}^~{DOWN}
          {IF @CELLPOINTER("TYPE")="B"{QUIT}
          {BRANCH CENTER}
```

Argument	Result
address	Absolute address of the cell (for example, $C$4).
row	Row number. The possible results are 1 to 8192.
col	Column number. The possible results are 1 to 256.
contents	The cell entry as either a string or numeric value.
type	Type of value stored in the cell. The possible results are b cell is blank, has no cell entry. v cell contains a number, numeric formula, or string formula. l cell contains a label.
prefix	Label-prefix. The possible results are: ' cell contains a left-aligned label " cell contains a right-aligned label ^ cell contains a centered label | cell contains a special label, such as a DOC format line.
protect	Displays the current protection status of the range specified in the argument. Displays 1 if the range has a "Prevent-Changes" status, 0 if the range has an "Allow-Changes" status, set by the MENU Range Protect command.
width	Column width. The possible results are numbers from 0 to 240. The column width of a hidden column is 0. The column width belongs to the window, not to the cell. This function may yield different results for the same cell viewed in different windows. There is no way to tell if column width is assigned to the individual column or is the default column width.
format	Numeric display format. The possible values are the letter-number codes displayed in the control panel to indicate the cell's numeric format. These are G General F0 to F15 Fixed, 0 to 15 decimal places P0 to P15 Punctuated, 0 to 15 decimal places C0 to C15 Currency, 0 to 15 decimal places S0 to S15 Scientific, 0 to 15 decimal places

TABLE B-1 Arguments and Results for @CELL Function

%0 to %15	Percent, 0 to 15 decimal places
D1 to D5	Date formats 1 through 5
T1 to T4	Time formats 1 through 4
L	Literal format (formula text displayed)
H	Hidden format

Note: @CELL does not recalculate automatically when you change the width of a column or format of the range. Press CALC to update the cell attributes.

TABLE B-1 Arguments and Results for @CELL Function (*continued*)

The first line of the macro edits a cell, places a center label indicator in front of the contents, and then moves down to the next cell. The second line of this macro checks if the next cell is blank and quits if it is. If the current cell is not blank, the macro loops to the beginning. Note that the response to the function as well as the @CELLPOINTER code must be identified with quotes.

@@ FUNCTION Another function that responds with information about cells is the @@ function. The @@ function has the syntax

@@("Cell")

and returns the contents of the cell specified in the function argument. Thus, @@("A1") returns the contents of A1.

@COLS AND @ROWS When you need to know how many columns or rows there are in a block of cells, you use the @COLS and @ROWS functions. Thus, @COLS(DATA) returns the response 3 if DATA is the name given to cells A1..C10. The response to @ROWS(DATA) would be 10.

@IS FUNCTIONS @ISERR and @ISNA are true/false functions that give you the means to check whether a formula or cell entry results in either the ERR or NA response, respectively. These functions take the form

@ISERR(Value)
@ISNA(Value)

where Value is a cell reference or a formula.

The @ISERR function returns the response 1, meaning true, if Value results in ERR, as is the case with @ISERR(1/0) or @ISERR(A1/A2), where A2 contains the value 0. A typical application of the @ISERR function is to avoid the problem of dividing one column of numbers by another when some of the cells in the columns might be empty or contain zeroes. Thus, the division of a total sales figure by the number of salespersons would result in an ERR message if the number of salespersons was 0 or the cell was empty.

You can combine the @IF function with @ISERR to turn the ERR result into the string of text "Not Available." For example, with sales in column C and the number of salespersons in column D, you might use a formula like this:

```
@IF(@ISERR(C2/D2),"Not Available",C2/D2)
```

The @ISNA function is used in the same manner as @ISERR. However, @ISNA is used less frequently. The value NA is less common than ERR, since formulas do not give this result unless you design them that way.

@ISNUMBER(Value) and @ISSTRING(Value) are used in Symphony to test whether the referenced value is a number or a string. @ISNUMBER produces 0 when it is applied to a cell containing a label; @ISSTRING produces 0 when it is applied to a cell containing a number.

THE @BASE FUNCTIONS

When you attach the @BASE.APP and @BASEFUNC.APP applications to Symphony, and open one or more DBF files, as described in Chapter 10, you can use a special set of functions to manipulate data. These are referred to as the *@DB functions* because they all begin with "@DB."

Using @DB Functions

You use @DB functions to manipulate @BASE database files from within a Symphony worksheet. However, you must first attach the BASEFUNC.APP add-in. You can then enter @DB functions directly in cells as worksheet formulas, or you can include @DB functions in {LET} statements for Symphony macros. The three types of @DB functions are

- Statistical functions, which perform statistical calculations and queries on database records and return the resulting value
- Logical functions, which perform true-false tests on database records and return 1 for true or 0 for false
- File manipulation functions, which perform many of the activities that @BASE commands perform and return a value resulting from the activity

All @DB functions have the following syntax, where arguments are separated by commas or by whatever argument delimiter you have set:

@DBFUNCTION(Argument1,Argument2,...,Argument*n*)

When the argument is Alias, this refers to the alias name you have given to a database file (typically the first part of the file name, as in SALES for SALES.DBF). When the argument is Field_name, this is the name of a field within the database. Alias and Field_Name arguments must be entered in quotes.

The argument Record_number refers to a record number that has been assigned to each record in a database file. The argument Criteria, which is often optional in @DB functions, refers to a criteria formula, as in +SALES>2000 or REGION='West'. You can also use a cell reference to specify criteria entered in another worksheet cell. Including criteria limits the function to records that match the criteria; for example, all records where the entry in the SALES field is greater than 2000.

Statistical @DB Functions

The first set of @DB functions to consider are those that perform statistical calculations. They allow you to count the number of records in a database and determine averages and totals.

@DBAVG @DBAVG calculates the average value for a numeric or date field. The syntax is

@DBAVG(Alias,Field_name[,Criteria])

For example, when SALES is the alias for a sales database, the formula

@DBAVG("SALES","TOTAL","REGION='West'")

returns the average of the figures in the TOTAL field for all records in which the REGION field contains West.

@DBCNT This function reports the total number of active records in a database. The syntax is

@DBCNT(Alias[,Criteria])

@DBMAX @DBMAX reports the largest value in a numeric or date field. The syntax is

@DBMAX(Alias,Field_name[,Criteria])

@DBMIN @DBMIN reports the smallest value in a numeric or date field. The syntax is

@DBMIN(Alias,Field_name[,Criteria])

@DBRECS This function reports the total number of records in a database. The syntax is

@DBRECS(Alias)

@DBSUM @DBSUM calculates the sum of the values in a numeric or date field. The syntax is

@DBSUM(Alias,Field_name[,Criteria])

Logical @DB Functions

There are three functions which allow you to obtain special information about records in a database. The logical @DB function can test whether records are deleted or active.

@DBISACT This function tests whether a record is active or inactive. The syntax is

@DBISACT(Alias,Record_Number[,Criteria])

The result is 0 for No, 1 for Yes.

@DBISDEL @DBISDEL tests whether a record is marked for deletion. The syntax is

@DBISDEL(Alias,Record_Number)

@DBISNA @DBISNA tests whether a record includes an entry for a specified field. The syntax is

@DBISNA(Alias,Field_name,Record_Number)

File Manipulation @DB Functions

To add records to a database, you can use the file manipulation functions. These also allow you to open and close @BASE files.

@DBOPEN This function opens an @BASE database file. The syntax is

@DBOPEN(Database[,Alias,Criteria,Access-type,Codepage])

where Database is the full DOS name for the files.

@DBAPP @DBAPP appends a new record to a database. The syntax is

@DBAPP(Alias[,
Field_name1,value1,...,Field_name*n*,value*n*])

Whenever this function is entered, a new record is added to the end of the database and the cell containing the function returns the record number of the added record.

@DBCLOSE This function closes an open database file. The syntax is

@DBCLOSE(Alias)

@DBDEL @DBDEL marks or unmarks a database record for deletion. The syntax is

@DBDEL(Alias,Record_Number,Del_flag)

where Del_Flag is the delete marker.

@DBFLD For a specified record, this function returns the contents of a specified field. The syntax is

@DBFLD(Alias,Field_name,Record_Number)

@DBFIRST This function searches for the first record in a database that matches the current criteria. The syntax is

@DBFIRST(Alias[,Criteria])

@DBLAST @DBLAST searches for the last record in a database that matches the current criteria. The syntax is

@DBLAST(Alias[,Criteria])

@DBNEXT Starting from the current position in the database, this function searches forward for the first record that matches the current criteria. The syntax is

@DBNEXT(Alias,[,Criteria,Next_Flag])

@DBPREV Starting from the current position in the database, this function searches backward for the nearest record that matches the current criteria. The syntax is

@DBPREV(Alias[,Criteria,Prev_Flag])

@DBUPD For a specified record, @DBUPD changes contents of a specified field. The syntax is

@DBUPD(Alias,Field_name,Record_Number,Value)

@DBMAIN @DBMAIN reports whether @BASE is currently displaying a command menu. The syntax is

@DBMAIN(0)

To Enter:	Press (ALT-F1) then:
¶	!p
§	so
¢	c\
£	l=
¥	y=
f	ff
±	=–
≥	>=
≤	<=
÷	:-
π	pi
½	12
¼	14
©	co
™	tm

TABLE B-2 Commonly Used COMPOSE Sequences

Working with @DB Functions

You enter @DB functions in the SHEET environment. To copy an @DB function that contains relative cell references in its Criteria argument from one cell to another in a Symphony worksheet, you do not use the SHEET Copy command. Instead, you use the @BASE Utility Criteria-Copy command, since it automatically adjusts the relative cell references as it copies the @DB function but preserves absolute references (those in which a dollar sign precedes the address or range name).

COMPOSE SEQUENCES AND LICS/ASCII CODES

A *compose sequence* is a series of keystrokes you use to enter a character that is not on your keyboard. To enter such a character, press COMPOSE ((ALT-FI)) and the appropriate compose sequence. For example, to enter a British pound sign, you press COMPOSE and type **L** =. For some composed characters, more than one compose sequence is valid. To produce @, the compose sequence is either **aa** or **AA**. Commonly used compose sequences are provided in Table B-2. Those marked with an asterisk (*) must appear in the order shown; otherwise, the order does not matter (do not type the asterisk as part of the compose sequence). The compose sequences are made possible by the Lotus International Character set (LICS). This attaches a three digit code to a variety of special characters, much the same way as the American Standard Code for Information Interchange (ASCII). LICS codes differ from the ASCII codes. Commonly used LICS codes are listed in Table B-3, followed by the standard ASCII codes in Table B-4.

LICS Code	Character	Compose Sequence
0	Control @	
1	Control A	
2	Control B	
3	Control C	
4	Control D	
5	Control E	
6	Control F	
7	Control G	
8	Control H	
9	Control I	
10	Control J	
11	Control K	
12	Control L	
13	Control M	
14	Control N	
15	Control O	
16	Control P	
17	Control Q	
18	Control R	
19	Control S	
20	Control T	
21	Control U	
22	Control V	
23	Control W	
24	Control X	
25	Control Y	
26	Control Z	
27	[ESC]	
28	FS	
29	GS	
30	RS	
31	US	
32	(Space)	
33	!	
34	"	
35	#	+ +
36	$	
37	%	
38	&	
39	'	
40	(	
41	)	
42	*	
43	+	
44	,	
45	–	
46	.	
47	/	
48	0	
49	1	
50	2	
51	3	
52	4	
53	5	
54	6	
55	7	
56	8	
57	9	
58	:	
59	;	
60	<	
61	=	
62	>	
63	?	
64	@	a a or A A
65	A	
66	B	
67	C	
68	D	
69	E	
70	F	
71	G	
72	H	
73	I	
74	J	
75	K	
76	L	
77	M	
78	N	
79	O	
80	P	
81	Q	
82	R	
83	S	
84	T	
85	U	
86	V	
87	W	
88	X	
89	Y	
90	Z	
91	[	((
92	\	/ /
93	]	))
94	^	v v
95	_	
96	`	
97	a	
98	b	
99	c	
100	d	
101	e	
102	f	
103	g	
104	h	
105	i	
106	j	
107	k	
108	l	
109	m	
110	d	
111	o	
112	p	
113	q	
114	r	
115	s	
116	t	
117	u	
118	v	
119	w	
120	x	
121	y	
122	z	
123	{	(–
124	|	^ /
125	}	) –
126	~	– –
127	DEL	

TABLE B-3 The Lotus International Character Set

LICS Code	Character	Compose Sequence	LICS Code	Character	Compose Sequence
128	‘	* ‘ Spacebar	192	À	A‘
129	’	* ’ Spacebar	193	Á	A’
130	ˆ	* ˆ Spacebar	194	Â	Aˆ
131	″	* ″ Spacebar	195	Ã	A~
132	~	* ~ Spacebar	196	Ä	A″
133			197	Å	A*
134			198	Æ	* AE
135			199	Ç	C,
136			200	È	E‘
137			201	É	E’
138			202	Ê	Eˆ
139			203	Ë	E″
140			204	Ì	I‘
141			205	Í	I’
142			206	Î	Iˆ
143			207	Ï	I″
144	‘	* Spacebar ‘	208	D̲	D_
145	’	* Spacebar ’	209	Ñ	N~
146	ˆ	* Spacebar ˆ	210	Ò	O‘
147	″	* Spacebar ″	211	Ó	O’
148	~	* Spacebar ~	212	Ô	Oˆ
149	ı	i Spacebar	213	Õ	O~
150	_	_ Spacebar	214	Ö	O″
151	▲	ba	215	Œ	* OE
152	▼	ea	216	Ø	O/
153	■		217	Ù	U‘
154	(Hard space)	Spacebar Spacebar	218	Ú	U’
155	←	mg	219	Û	Uˆ
156			220	Ü	U″
157			221	Ÿ	Y″
158			222		P_
159			223	ß	ss
160	ƒ	ff	224	à	a‘
161	¡	!!	225	á	a’
162	¢	c| C| c/ or C/	226	â	aˆ
163	£	L= l= L– or l–	227	ã	a~
164	„	″ ˆ	228	ä	a″
165	¥	Y= y= Y– or y–	229	å	a*
166	Pt	* PT pt or Pt	230	æ	ae
167	§	SO so So or sO	231	ç	c,
168	¤	XO xo Xo or xO	232	è	e‘
169	©	CO co Co or cO	233	é	e’
170	ª	a_ or A_	234	ê	eˆ
171	«	<<	235	ë	e″
172	∆	dd pr DD	236	ì	i‘
173	π	* PI pi or Pi	237	í	i’
174	≥	* >=	238	î	iˆ
175	÷	: –	239	ï	i″
176	°	ˆ)	240	d̲	d_
177	±	+ –	241	ñ	n~
178	²	ˆ 2	242	ò	o‘
179	³	ˆ 3	243	ó	o’
180	″	″ v	244	ô	oˆ
181	µ	* / u	245	õ	o~
182	¶	!P or !p	246	ö	o″
183	·	ˆ .	247	œ	* oe
184	™	* TM Tm or tm	248	ø	o/
185	¹	ˆ 1	249	ù	u‘
186	º	o_ O_	250	ú	u’
187	»	>>	251	û	uˆ
188	¼	* 14	252	ü	u″
189	½	* 12	253	ÿ	y″
190	≤	* =<	254		p_
191	¿	??	255		

** Indicates that you must enter the compose sequence in the order shown. Do not type the asterisk (*).*

TABLE B-3 The Lotus International Character Set (*continued*)

DEC	OCTAL	HEX	ASCII	DEC	OCTAL	HEX	ASCII
0	000	00	NUL	40	050	28	(
1	001	01	SOH	41	051	29	)
2	002	02	STX	42	052	2A	*
3	003	03	ETX	43	053	2B	+
4	004	04	EOT	44	054	2C	,
5	005	05	ENQ	45	055	2D	—
6	006	06	ACK	46	056	2E	.
7	007	07	BEL	47	057	2F	/
8	010	08	BS	48	060	30	0
9	011	09	HT	49	061	31	1
10	012	0A	LF	50	062	32	2
11	013	0B	VT	51	063	33	3
12	014	0C	FF	52	064	34	4
13	015	0D	CR	53	065	35	5
14	016	0E	SO	54	066	36	6
15	017	0F	SI	55	067	37	7
16	020	10	DLE	56	070	38	8
17	021	11	DC1	57	071	39	9
18	022	12	DC2	58	072	3A	:
19	023	13	DC3	59	073	3B	;
20	024	14	DC4	60	074	3C	<
21	025	15	NAK	61	075	3D	=
22	026	16	SYN	62	076	3E	>
23	027	17	ETB	63	077	3F	?
24	030	18	CAN	64	100	40	@
25	031	19	EM	65	101	41	A
26	032	1A	SUB	66	102	42	B
27	033	1B	ESC	67	103	43	C
28	034	1C	FS	68	104	44	D
29	035	1D	GS	69	105	45	E
30	036	1E	RS	70	106	46	F
31	037	1F	US	71	107	47	G
32	040	20	SPACE	72	110	48	H
33	041	21	!	73	111	49	I
34	042	22	"	74	112	4A	J
35	043	23	#	75	113	4B	K
36	044	24	$	76	114	4C	L
37	045	25	%	77	115	4D	M
38	046	26	&	78	116	4E	N
39	047	27	'	79	117	4F	O

TABLE B-4 ASCII Character Codes

DEC	OCTAL	HEX	ASCII	DEC	OCTAL	HEX	ASCII
80	120	50	P	115	163	73	s
81	121	51	Q	116	164	74	t
82	122	52	R	117	165	75	u
83	123	53	S	118	166	76	v
84	124	54	T	119	167	77	w
85	125	55	U	120	170	78	x
86	126	56	V	121	171	79	y
87	127	57	W	122	172	7A	z
88	130	58	X	123	173	7B	{
89	131	59	Y	124	174	7C	|
90	132	5A	Z	125	175	7D	}
91	133	5B	[	126	176	7E	~
92	134	5C	\	127	177	7F	DEL
93	135	5D	]				
94	136	5E	^				
95	137	5F	—				
96	140	60	‘				
97	141	61	a				
98	142	62	b				
99	143	63	c				
100	144	64	d				
101	145	65	e				
102	146	66	f				
103	147	67	g				
104	150	68	h				
105	151	69	i				
106	152	6A	j				
107	153	6B	k				
108	154	6C	l				
109	155	6D	m				
110	156	6E	n				
111	157	6F	o				
112	160	70	p				
113	161	71	q				
114	162	72	r				

TABLE B-4 ASCII Character Codes (*continued*)

C

COMMAND LANGUAGE KEYWORDS

As you saw in Chapter 9, Symphony's macro feature is supplemented by a command language made up of keywords, several of which were described in Chapter 9. Using keywords, you can build statements that tell Symphony to perform actions that are not available as menu commands or that provide shortcuts to menu commands. This appendix lists all of the keywords.

COMMAND KEYWORD SYNTAX

Like some @functions, some keywords require arguments and others use optional arguments. The following descriptions of the keywords show the arguments that the keywords take and present command language syntax in this format

{KEYWORD}

or

{KEYWORD Argument1,Argument2,...Argument*n*}

When entering keywords in your macros, you always separate the keyword from the first argument by a space. The arguments are separated from one another by commas (or the argument separator you have defined on the International settings sheet). Square brackets are used here to indicate that an argument is optional, as in

{BEEP [Number]}

where the [Number] argument is an optional one used to modify the sound made by the {BEEP} keyword. Although Symphony does not distinguish between uppercase and lowercase when reading keywords in macro statements, capitals have been used for keywords in the following listings to make them easier to identify, and arguments are presented with initial capitals.

There are three types of argument that can be used with keywords, with each keyword assuming one type as the default. The types are as follows:

NUMBER	A number or expression resulting in a numeric value
STRING	Any string of characters. To include an argument separator, normally the comma, in a string, you must enclose the string in quotes (",")
LOCATION	A cell address, range address, or range name (if the range includes any argument separators, enclose the range in quotes (",")

To specifically declare a type, follow the argument by a colon and the type. For example, the keyword {LET} is used to place a value in a cell, so {LET A1,99} places 99 in cell A1. This keyword assumes that 99 is a number, so to enter 99 in A1 as a label you would use {LET A1,99:STRING}. If you omit the type, Symphony assumes the default type for the keyword.

WORKING WITH SUBROUTINES

One keyword deserves special attention, since it shows the potential of the Symphony command language to emulate a programming language. The {*subroutine*} keyword is a powerful part of advanced macro code, but it is also easy to use. The actual text used within the braces varies according to the macro code being used.

For example, suppose that you have a macro like this:

```
G1: {EDIT}
G2: {CALC}~
```

This macro turns a formula entry into a result. Suppose you name cell G1 as CALCULATE. Whenever you need this bit of macro code, you *call* it as a subroutine, like this:

```
B1: @NOW~
B2: {CALCULATE}
B3: {MENU}WS12~
```

This code enters the @NOW function, turns it into a date/time serial number, and widens the column. The flow of the macro goes from B1 to G1, the cell named CALCULATE. From there the flow goes down the column to G2. Finding no macro code in G3, flow returns to the main macro, the one that called the subroutine. In this way you can build code in sections and fit the sections together as needed.

If there was further macro code below G2, the flow would continue down the column until it encountered a blank cell, a value entry, or a branching keyword such as {BRANCH} or {RETURN}. If the subroutine code ends in {QUIT}, then both the subroutine and the main or calling macro ends.

THE KEYWORDS

This section lists all of the keywords except for those used to control reading from and writing to disk files. The file control keywords are listed at the end of this appendix.

{BEEP} The {BEEP} keyword uses the following syntax:

{BEEP [Number]}

The {BEEP} keyword sounds the bell or tone in your computer. The Number argument specifies the tone (normally 1 for low and 4 for high, but the results may vary according to your computer).

A useful keyword for testing the flow of macros, it can be temporarily substituted for a more complex action.

{BLANK} The {BLANK} keyword has the following syntax:

{BLANK Location}

The {BLANK} keyword erases the cell specified by the Location argument. Thus,

```
{BLANK A1}
```

erases A1, and

```
{BLANK TOTAL}
```

erases the range of cells named TOTAL. This keyword is often used at the end of a macro to clear entries made during the macro, ready for the next time the macro is used.

{BRANCH} The {BRANCH} keyword has the following syntax:

{BRANCH Location}

The {BRANCH} keyword is a "flow-control" keyword, directing macro flow to the cell specified in the Location argument. If the Location argument is a range name, the upper-left cell of the range is used.

When Symphony is executing a macro, it begins reading instructions from the first cell in the range that bears the macro name, and then from the cell immediately below that. Macro flow is down a column of cells until an empty cell is reached or a flow-control keyword is encountered. Other flow-control keywords include {DISPATCH}, {MENUBRANCH}, {MENUCALL} and {*subroutine*}.

When macro flow is redirected by {BRANCH} and the commands at the branch location have been executed, the flow does not return to the cell after the {BRANCH} statement unless a further {BRANCH} statement is used. To execute code at a different location and then return flow to the original location, use the {*subroutine*} keyword.

{BREAKOFF} The {BREAKOFF} keyword uses the following syntax:

{BREAKOFF}

It disables the use of the BREAK key (**CTRL-BREAK**) to interrupt macro execution. Normally, you can use **CTRL-BREAK** to interrupt a macro, but you can prevent this with {BREAKOFF}. Only include this command in a macro when you have thoroughly tested the rest of the macro. You might use this key to prevent a user from interrupting an important operation.

{BREAKON} The {BREAKON} keyword has the following syntax:

{BREAKON}

This keyword enables the use of the BREAK key (**CTRL-BREAK**) to interrupt macro execution. This keyword is used to restore normal operation after using {BREAKOFF} to suspend the use of the BREAK key.

{CONTENTS} The {CONTENTS} keyword has the following syntax:

{CONTENTS Destination_location,Source_location, [Width_number], [Format_number]}

The {CONTENTS} keyword places the contents of the cell specified as Source_location into the cell specified as Destination_location, as a label. Optionally, you can use the specified Width_number and Format_number arguments to adjust the cell. Allowable formats are shown in Table C-1. For example, the statement

```
{CONTENTS ANSWER,REPLY,10,34}
```

places the contents of the cell named REPLY in the cell named ANSWER, setting the width of the ANSWER cell to 10 and formatting the contents with the Currency format, 2 decimal places.

{DEFINE} The {DEFINE} keyword has the following syntax:

{DEFINE Cell1:Type1,Cell2:Type2...Cell*n*:Type*n*}

This keyword specifies cells that will store arguments used in a call to a subroutine. If you want to use {DEFINE}, it must be the

Number	Format
0..15	Fixed, 0-15 places
16..31	Scientific, 0-15 places
32..47	Currency, 0-15 places
48..63	Percent, 0-15 places
64..79	Comma, 0-15 places
112	+/-
113	General
114	DD-MMM-YY (D1)
115	DD-MMM (D2)
116	MMM-YY (D3)
117	Literal
118	Hidden
119	HH:MM:SS AM/PM (T1)
120	HH:MM AM/PM (T2)
121	Full International Date (D4)
122	Partial International Date (D5)
123	Full International Time (T3)
124	Partial International Time (T4)
125	General

TABLE C-1 Width and Format Number Arguments for {CONTENTS}

first command in the subroutine. Type can be NUMBER or STRING; if you do not specify the type, Symphony assumes STRING.

{DISPATCH} The {DISPATCH} keyword has the following syntax:

{DISPATCH Location}

This keyword branches macro flow to the destination specified in Location. It is similar to {BRANCH} but is typically used with a single cell reference rather than a range reference.

{FOR} The {FOR} keyword, used to set up repeating macros, has the following syntax:

{FOR Counter_location,Start_number,Stop_number,
Step_number, Subroutine_location}

You use {FOR} when you want to have a macro command or group of commands repeated a set number of times. The {FOR} keyword executes the commands at Subroutine_location the number of times defined by Start_number and Stop_number plus the Step_number, which represents the increment. The number of times the commands have been carried out—as it were, the cycle count—appears in the cell specified as Counter_location. When the {FOR} command is executed, the Counter_location cell is initialized with the value specified as Start_number.

Consider this example, which allows you to control the number of copies of a report that are printed:

```
MAC        {GETNUMBER "Number of copies to print: ",TOTAL}
           {FOR COUNTER,1,TOTAL,1,ACT}

ACT        {SERVICES}PAG
           {RETURN}

COUNTER    1
TOTAL      5
```

The macro begins by asking the user for the number of copies to be printed. A number is typed, and this is placed in a cell called

TOTAL (in this example, the user entered 5). When Symphony reaches the second line of the macro, the cell called COUNTER is set to 1. The macro code called ACT is executed once, and then the counter is incremented by 1, and this is repeated until the counter reaches 5. The ACT macro sends Symphony the Print Align and Print Go commands.

{FORBREAK} The {FORBREAK} keyword has the following syntax:

{FORBREAK}

This keyword terminates a {FOR} statement immediately; macro execution continues just after the {FOR} statement.

{GET} The {GET} keyword has the following syntax:

{GET Location}

This keyword makes Symphony wait for the user to type a single character and then places it in the cell specified by the Location argument.

{GETLABEL} The {GETLABEL} keyword has the following syntax:

{GETLABEL Prompt_string,Location}

This keyword displays Prompt_string, which asks the user to type a response. When the user presses **ENTER**, {GETLABEL} places the user's response in the cell specified by the Location argument as a label.

{GETNUMBER} The {GETNUMBER} keyword is another user input keyword. It has the following syntax:

{GETNUMBER Prompt_string,Location}

This keyword displays Prompt_string, which asks the user to type a response. The user then presses **ENTER**. The keyword then places the user's response in the cell specified by the Location argument as a value. If the user types a response that is not a value, an error message results.

{HANDSHAKE} This keyword is used when automating communications with Symphony macros. The syntax is

{HANDSHAKE Send_string,Receive_string,Timeout_value,
[Capture_location]}

This keyword automates dialog with a remote computer by issuing Send_string and waiting for Receive_string, during a length of time specified by Timeout_value. Optionally, the command places a line containing Receive_string in the cell specified by the Capture_location argument.

{IF} The {IF} keyword is a macro flow-control keyword that has the following syntax:

{IF Logical_expression}

The {IF} keyword conditionally executes the commands that follow the {IF} statement in the same cell. If the Logical_expression argument is not true, the macro flow continues at the cell below the {IF} keyword.

{INDICATE} The {INDICATE} keyword has the following syntax:

{INDICATE [String]}

Used without an argument, {INDICATE} resets the control panel mode indicator after a macro has changed it. Used with an argument, this keyword allows you to alter the mode indicator wording while macro code is executing. As the String argument, you enter the text you want in the mode indicator, up to 7 characters in length.

{LET} The {LET} keyword has the following syntax:

{LET Location,String}

This keyword places a string in the cell specified by the Location argument.

{LET} The {LET} keyword has the following syntax:

{LET Location,Value}

It places the value of an expression in the cell specified by the Location argument.

{LOOK} The {LOOK} keyword has the following syntax:

{LOOK Location}

This keyword looks in Symphony's type-ahead buffer and continues macro execution. If it finds a character in the buffer, it places it in the cell specified by the Location argument; otherwise, it inserts a blank label.

{MENUBRANCH} The {MENUBRANCH} keyword has the following syntax:

{MENUBRANCH Location}

This keyword prompts the user with a menu found at the cell specified by the Location argument. A menu is a range of cells consisting of at least two rows and up to eight columns. The first row contains commands, such as Report or Widen. The second line contains prompts, such as "Prints a report" or "Makes column wider." Cells under the prompts contain the macro instructions which Symphony executes according to the user's choice.

{MENUCALL} The {MENUCALL} keyword has the following syntax:

{MENUCALL Location}

This works like {MENUBRANCH}, but after executing the instructions under the line of prompts, Symphony continues macro execution in the cell after the {MENUCALL} statement.

{ONERROR} The {ONERROR} keyword has the following syntax:

{ONERROR Branch_location,[Msg_location]}

It traps errors that occur during macros, passing control to the cell specified by the Branch_location argument and optionally capturing the error message in the cell specified by the Msg_location argument.

{PANELOFF} The {PANELOFF} keyword has the following syntax:

{PANELOFF}

This keyword suppresses the display of the control panel during macro execution, which improves the speed of macro execution and can make macros less confusing for the user.

{PANELON} The {PANELON} keyword has the following syntax:

{PANELON}

It restores normal control-panel operation.

{PHONE} The {PHONE} keyword has the following syntax:

{PHONE Number_string}

This keyword calls over the modem, using Number_string (in the form required by the Phone Call command). The Number_string argument can be a string formula.

{PUT} The {PUT} keyword has the following syntax:

{PUT Location,Col_num,Row_num,String}

The {PUT} keyword stores a string at the specified location, defined by the Col_num and Row_num arguments within a range. These arguments are stated in offset form: the first column is 0, the second is 1, and so on.

{PUT} The {PUT} keyword has the following syntax:

{PUT Location,Col_num,Row_num,Value}

It stores a number at a specified location, defined by the Col_num and Row_num (offset) arguments within a range.

{QUIT} The {QUIT} keyword takes no arguments; it simply ends macro execution. This keyword is useful to mark the end of a macro clearly, as opposed to just using an empty cell.

{RECALC} The {RECALC} keyword has the following syntax:

{RECALC Range}

This keyword causes Symphony to recalculate formulas within the cells specified in the Range argument, going row-by-row.

{RECALCCOL} The {RECALCCOL} keyword has the following syntax:

{RECALCCOL Range}

This keyword causes the recalculation of the formulas in Range, going column-by-column.

{RESTART} The {RESTART} keyword has the following syntax:

{RESTART}

It continues macro execution after clearing the subroutine stack.

{RETURN} The {RETURN} keyword has the following syntax:

{RETURN}

It causes macro flow to return to the main macro from a macro subroutine.

{WAIT} The {WAIT} keyword has the following syntax:

{WAIT Time_serial_num}

This keyword waits until the time specified by a time serial number. Note that the Time_serial_num argument must be greater than 1.

{WINDOWSOFF} The {WINDOWSOFF} keyword has the following syntax:

{WINDOWSOFF}

It suppresses the redrawing of the current window whenever Symphony recalculates data in the worksheet. This function is useful at the beginning of a macro to stop constant screen changes and speed up macro execution.

{WINDOWSON} The {WINDOWSON} keyword has the following syntax:

{WINDOWSON}

It restores the normal updating of the display screen, thus reversing a {WINDOWSOFF} statement.

{?} The {?} keyword has the following syntax:

{?}

It halts macro execution temporarily, allowing the user to type and move the cell pointer around. The macro continues when the user presses **ENTER**.

THE FILE CONTROL KEYWORDS

A special set of keywords is provided by Symphony to control reading from, and writing to, disk files. This is a fairly advanced activity, and one which has the potential to corrupt valuable data files if not handled correctly, so the file control keywords are grouped in this special section.

The commands work with ASCII or text files. These are files like the ones created by the Symphony Print command when the destination is a file. Such files are sometimes used for exchanging information between programs that cannot read more sophisticated file formats, such as WR1 or DBF.

A typical application of these keywords would be when you want to write information, one line at a time, to a text file. The following macro code writes the contents of cell A21 to a file called INFO.DAT:

```
{OPEN "INFO.DAT","M"}
{FILESIZE SIZE}
{SETPOS SIZE}
{WRITELN A21}
{CLOSE}
```

The macro opens the file to be modified, reads the size of the file in bytes into a cell called SIZE, and then positions the byte pointer at the end of the file. The byte pointer is like an invisible cursor within the disk file you open. When a file is first opened, the byte pointer is located at the first character of the file. Any reading from or writing to the file occurs at the location of the byte pointer. You can position the byte pointer with {SETPOS}. The rest of the file manipulation keywords are described here.

{CLOSE} The {CLOSE} keyword takes no arguments. It closes a file that was opened with the {OPEN} macro keyword. This is one of several keywords that enable macros to read from files on disk and write information to disk files.

{FILESIZE} The {FILESIZE} keyword has the following syntax:

{FILESIZE Location}

It records the size of an open file, stated as a number of bytes, in the cell specified as Location, which can be a cell or range name.

{GETPOS} The {GETPOS} keyword has the following syntax:

{GETPOS Location}

It records (in the cell specified by the Location argument) the byte pointer's current position. The position is read as an offset number; the first character of a file is 0, the second is 1, and so on.

{OPEN} The {OPEN} keyword has the following syntax:

{OPEN FileName,Access_mode}

The {OPEN} keyword opens a file for reading, writing, or both. The Access_mode argument is one of three characters:

W Opens a new disk file to which you can write information. This is potentially dangerous, since there is nothing to stop you from overwriting an existing file. Be sure that the FileName argument does not refer to a file that you want to preserve.

M Opens an existing file so that you can modify it. This allows you to use the read and write commands. It, too, is dangerous; what you write to a file will overwrite existing data if the byte pointer is not positioned at the end of the file.

R Opens a file so that you can read information from it. This is the safest form of file access, since it prevents writing to the file.

{READ} The {READ} keyword has the following syntax:

{READ Byte_count,Location}

The {READ} keyword copies the number of characters, specified by the Byte_count argument, from the file to the cell specified by the Location argument. The command starts reading at the current position of the byte pointer.

{READLN} The {READLN} keyword has the following syntax:

{READLN Location}

This keyword copies a line of data from the file to the cell specified by the Location argument. The command starts reading at the current position of the byte pointer and stops at the end of the current line.

{SETPOS} The {SETPOS} keyword has the following syntax:

{SETPOS File_position}

This keyword sets a new position for the byte pointer in the currently open file. If you read the file size and use this as the File_position argument, you will locate the end of the file and be able to add data to it.

{WRITE} The {WRITE} keyword has the following syntax:

{WRITE String}

It copies characters into an open file at the byte pointer's current location. The String argument can be a single cell or a named single-cell range. The command does not add a line feed at the end of what is written.

{WRITELN} The {WRITELN} keyword has the following syntax:

{WRITELN String}

The {WRITELN} keyword copies characters into an open file. The String argument can be a single cell or a named single-cell range. The command adds a line feed sequence at the end of the string of characters as it writes the string to the file. Thus, you can use a series of {WRITELN} statements to add successive lines of data to a file.

AN @BASE MACRO EXAMPLE

The following steps show you how to set up an @BASE database, a form letter that contains spreadsheet formulas, and a macro that carries out the merging of data from an @BASE file into the form letter. You begin by defining the @BASE file.

1. Attach both BASE.APP and BASEFUNC.APP, using SERVICES Application Attach. Quit back to SHEET mode.

2. Press TYPE and select BASE. When in BASE mode, press MENU and select File Define. When prompted for a file name, type **STAFF1** and press ENTER.

3. When prompted for a field name type **LAST** and press ENTER. The field type will be Character, so press ENTER to accept this type.

4. The field length you need is 10, so type **10** and press ENTER.

5. Define the second field by typing **FIRST** as the name and then pressing (ENTER). To select Character as the type, press (ENTER). For the field length, type **10** and press (ENTER).

6. Define the third field by typing **DEPT** as the name and then pressing (ENTER). To select Character as the type, press (ENTER). For the field length, accept **8** by pressing (ENTER).

7. Define the fourth field by typing **SALARY** and pressing (ENTER). Select Numeric as the type. To accept a field length of 8, press (ENTER), and to accept 2 decimal places, press (ENTER).

8. To complete the file creation process, press (ESC) twice and then select Save. When prompted for an alias, press (ENTER) to accept STAFF1.

You will be returned to the main menu. The file is now created and ready for data. To enter records,

1. From the main menu, select Data and then Form. Choose STAFF1 as the file to use.

2. In the FIRST field of the first record, type **Smith** and press (ENTER). In the second field—that is, LAST—type **Fred** and press (ENTER). In the DEPT field, type **Acc** and press (ENTER). In the SALARY field, type **2300** and press (ENTER).

3. To add this record and create a new blank entry form, press (INS). You should see a form like the one completed here:

```
                                                                   FORM
File STAFF1
Record  1             of 4

Name          Value
        LAST  Smith
       FIRST  Fred
        DEPT  Acc
      SALARY    2300.00
```

4. Complete the next three records with this information:

   Doe, Joe, Acc, 2500
   Plane, Jane, Sales, 1800
   Rice, Don, Sales, 1750

   Remember to press (INS) after entering each record, including the last one.

5. Now press (ESC) to complete the data entry and return to the main menu.

You have created four records to use in this test database. You are now ready to compose the letter, following these steps:

1. Press (ESC) to clear the @BASE menu, and press TYPE. Select DOC. At line 1, character 1, type **April 1, 1991** and press (ENTER).

2. At line 10, character 1, type the following text, allowing Symphony to wrap the lines according to the current DOC format line:

   As a valued employee of Ohmobile you have helped us become Number One in electric car sales in North America! To celebrate this accomplishment, and to reward your efforts over the last twelve months, we have awarded you a bonus. Your bonus, which will be included in your next pay-check, is:

3. At line 21, character 1, type the following text:

   We trust that you will enjoy this bonus and see it as part of the caring approach to employee relations here at Ohmobile.

4. At line 24, character 1, type **Yours sincerely,** and press (ENTER) twice. Type **Ohmobile, Inc.** and press (ENTER).

5. Press MENU and select Page to insert a page break. The end of the letter will appear as shown here:

```
Line 27    Char 1    Page 1,32          *          Left, Single          DOC

We trust that you will enjoy this bonus and see it as part of
the caring approach to employee relations here at Ohmobile.

Yours sincerely,

Ohmobile, Inc.
::
```

You are now ready to create the macro code and range names that will be used to merge the @BASE file and the letter:

1. Press TYPE and select SHEET. Press MENU, select Settings, and select Width. Set the width to **12**.

2. Move to cell M1 and enter the right-aligned labels you see in column M of Figure C-1.

```
N3: 'Dept="SALES"                                                    SHEET
            M           N           O           P           Q           R
1         TEMP           1
2      COUNTER           3
3     CRITERIA Dept="SALES"
4          REC           0
5
6           \M {WINDOWSOFF}{PANELOFF}
7              {LET TEMP,@DBOPEN("C:\SYM22\DATA\STAFF1.DBF","STAFF1")}
8              {S}PA
9              {LET REC,@DBFIRST("STAFF1",CRITERIA)}
10             {FOR COUNTER,1,@DBCNT("STAFF1",CRITERIA),1,PRINTER}
11             Q
12             {LET TEMP,@DBCLOSE("STAFF1")}
13             {PANELON}{WINDOWSON}{QUIT}
14
15     PRINTER {RECALC DOCUMENT}G
16             {LET REC,@DBNEXT("STAFF1",CRITERIA)}
17
18
19
20                                                                   MAIN
04-Apr-91  03:12 PM                                               Num
```

FIGURE C-1 Macro code for merging

3. Enter the numbers and macro code that you see in column N of Figure C-1. Note the entry in N3, which sets the criteria to be used by the macro when selecting records from the database.

4. Place the cell pointer in M1 and press MENU. Select Range Name Labels Right. Press (DOWN ARROW) to include cells M1..M15, and press (ENTER). Now press (HOME).

The letter is now ready for the spreadsheet formulas it needs to produce the final mail-merge document. You will use the @DB function @DBFLD, so the @BASEFUNC.APP add-in must be attached.

1. Enter the following formula in A4. This will insert the name of the person to whom the letter is addressed.

   ```
   @TRIM(@DBFLD("STAFF1","FIRST",REC))&"
   "&@TRIM(@DBFLD("STAFF1","LAST",REC))
   ```

   The cell will appear blank when the formula is entered, because the @DBFLD formula is not calculated yet.

2. Enter this formula, which inserts the name of the department, in cell A5:

   ```
   @TRIM(dbfld("STAFF1","DEPT",REC))&" Department"
   ```

   The result in the cell will appear as "Department" until the macro is run.

3. Enter this formula in A8. It will insert the first name of the person to whom the letter is addressed.

   ```
   +"Dear "&@TRIM(@DBFLD("STAFF1","FIRST",REC))&":"
   ```

   The result in the cell appears as "Dear :" until the macro is run.

4. In cell B16, enter the label **Base salary**. In cell B17, enter the label **Bonus rate**. In cell B19, enter the label **Bonus.**

5. Format cell C16 to Currency, 0 decimal places, and enter this formula:

   @dbfld("STAFF1","SALARY",REC)

   The cell will appear blank until the macro has been run.

6. In cell C17, enter **0.1** and format the cell to Percentage, 1 decimal place. In cell C18, enter the label \-.

7. Use the Range Name Create command to name C16 SALARY and C17 RATE.

8. Format cell C19 to Currency, 0 decimal places, and enter this formula:

   +SALARY*RATE

```
C16: (C0) @dbfld("STAFF1","SALARY",REC)                                SHEET
     A           B           C           D           E           F
1   April 1, 1991
2
3
4
5    Department
6
7
8   Dear :
9
10  As a valued employee of Ohmobile you have helped us become
11  Number One in electric car sales in North America!  To celebrate
12  this accomplishment, and to reward your efforts over the last twelve
13  months, we have awarded you a bonus.  Your bonus, which will be
14  included in your next pay-check, is:
15
16                Base salary
17                Bonus rate        10.0%
18                            ----------
19                Bonus             ERR
20
                                                                        MAIN
04-Apr-91  03:13 PM                                                 Num
```

FIGURE C-2 Completed letter in SHEET environment

The result will be ERR because the entry in cell C16, the cell called RATE, is not calculated yet.

9. Finally, use the Range Name Create command to name the cells that make up the letter as **DOCUMENT**. The range is A1..F27. This will be used as the print range by the macro.

The letter will now appear as in Figure C-2. You now need to prepare for printing the merged letters by using the macro.

1. First check the print range. Use the SERVICES Print Settings Source Range command to specify the range called DOCUMENT; that is, A1..F27.
2. Select Destination and make sure it is Printer.
3. Quit from the menu, and press (HOME).
4. Make sure that your printer is on and has four sheets of paper loaded.
5. Press (ALT-M). This will run the \M macro, which prints one letter for each record that meets the criteria.

The \M macro actually opens the STAFF1 database if it is not already open, uses the criteria in N3, counts the number of records meeting the criteria, and then prints the letter once for each record. The PRINTER macro updates the letter for each new record printed. The \M macro closes the database when it has printed all of the letters.

INDEX

B

C

D

E

F

G

M

N

O

P

Q

R

S

T

U

V

W

X

Y

Z